CONTENTS

The EVOLUTION
of AMERICAN
URBAN DESIGN

A Chronological Anthology

David Gosling
with
Maria Cristina Gosling

⊛WILEY-ACADEMY

Published in Great Britain in 2003 by
WILEY-ACADEMY,
a division of
JOHN WILEY & SONS Ltd

ISBN 0471983454

Copyright © 2003   John Wiley & Sons Ltd, The Atrium,
Southern Gate, Chichester,
West Sussex PO19 8SQ, England
Telephone (+44) 1243 779777

Email (for orders and customer service enquiries): cs-books@wiley.co.uk
Visit our Home Page on www.wileyeurope.com or www.wiley.com

Other Wiley Editorial Offices

John Wiley & Sons Inc., 111 River Street, Hoboken, NJ 07030, USA

Jossey-Bass, 989 Market Street, San Francisco, CA 94103-1741, USA

Wiley-VCH Verlag GmbH, Boschstr. 12, D-69469 Weinheim, Germany

John Wiley & Sons Australia Ltd, 33 Park Road, Milton, Queensland 4064, Australia

John Wiley & Sons (Asia) Pte Ltd, 2 Clementi Loop #02-01, Jin Xing Distripark, Singapore 129809

John Wiley & Sons Canada Ltd, 22 Worcester Road, Etobicoke, Ontario, Canada M9W 1L1

Designed and typeset in Times by Florence Production Ltd, Stoodleigh, Devon EX16 9PN
Printed and bound in Great Britain by T.J. International Ltd
This book is printed on acid-free paper responsibly manufactured from sustainable forestry in which at least two trees are planted for each one
used for paper production.

INTRODUCTION

The idea for this book emerged several years ago with the decision, with my friend and colleague Michael Wilford, to write a study of urban design, tentatively called 'A Philosophy of Urban Design'. The study was to draw upon our teaching and experience in the US and UK. However, this was not to be. The untimely death of Sir James Stirling meant that sole responsibility for the practice fell into the hands of Michael Wilford. In addition, a number of commentators, including my own students, suggested this would have been a divisive study since urban design is a worldwide phenomenon and not confined either to the US or the UK.

Critics of an earlier book, *Concepts of Urban Design*,[1] suggested that the work attempted to be too encyclopedic in covering twentieth-century urban design on a worldwide basis. The definitions of 'urban design' are covered in the first chapter of this book. It seems that urban design was indeed recognised as a distinct discipline both in the UK in the 1950s, as illustrated by Gordon Cullen's emerging theories at the time, *Townscape*,[2] in the pages of the *Architectural Review*, and in the US where Kevin Lynch dealt with cognitive aspects of the city.[3]

The wealth of available literature and case studies on urban design over the last half-century presented the danger of repeating the problems of *Concepts of Urban Design*. The subtitle of this book is therefore 'A Chronological Anthology'. It should be noted that the book reflects a personal overview of the major influences in urban design literature, and inevitably omissions will occur.

My mentor has been Gordon Cullen in the UK, a close friend and colleague for more than twenty years until his death in 1994. In the US I studied at the Massachusetts Institute of Technology (MIT) and Yale University between 1957 and 1960, under such notable architectural teachers as Kevin Lynch, Lewis Mumford and Gyorgy Kepes at MIT, and Christopher Tunnard at Yale. All contributed substantially in establishing the idea of urban design as a discipline in the US, followed much later by major theorists and designers across the world.

Anne Vernez-Moudon in her paper 'A catholic approach to organising what urban designers should know'[4] suggests there is a distinction between normative and prescriptive information and substantive and critically descriptive knowledge. She also notes that the majority of the research on urban design looks not only for explanations of the city but uses evaluation techniques and recommendations for future designs. Whereas Vernez-Moudon concentrates on substantive research and theories, this present work focuses on prescriptive material. There is an important reason for this.

Urban design appears to be a generic term for many different things, but if it does not result in tangible, 'good' built form, then why bother with it at all? As this study will reveal, often the most imaginative of urban design proposals are never built. Many major US cities demonstrate a woeful lack of any coherent urban design policy except, predictably, in historic districts and neighbourhoods. Rather, it seems, both the public and private sectors employ urban designers for reasons of political expediency or public relations. Unless urban designers are also the architects of the ultimate built form, it is unlikely that their plans will be implemented.

A problem may be that the American constitution is unique in emphasising the freedom of the individual. It is astonishing to a European to hear strong opposition from an articulate audience to the designation of a particular area as a historic district on the basis that such restrictions would diminish property values. The opposite is true in European cities. Similarly, 'wirescape' is an unsightly feature in many US neighbourhoods, yet in most European cities power and telecommunications lines have for many decades been constructed underground.

There are notable exceptions of course. Strong urban design policies have had good results in major US cities such as Boston and Baltimore on the East Coast, Portland and San Francisco on the West Coast, and San Antonio in the south.

According to Anne Vernez-Moudon: 'It is unlikely that the field of urban design will ever become a discipline with its own teachings, separate from the established architecture, landscape and planning professions'.[5] This is a slightly pessimistic view because without the establishment of urban design as a distinct discipline, the surrounding rhetoric to some extent becomes meaningless.

For all our investment in the complexity of individual buildings, on the one hand, and in elaborate engineering infrastructures on the other, we have failed to achieve a physically humane setting for a social existence at a time when the abstract setting of life is increasingly bureaucratised and constrained. Frank Lloyd Wright's iconic architecture in America in the earlier part of the twentieth century, and the iconoclastic architecture of Frank Gehry and Peter Eisenman in the later part of the century are often not connected with comprehensive urban form, although the unbuilt design projects of Peter Eisenman in Germany do address urban issues on a major scale.

Urban design is, or should be an integral part of the process of city and regional planning. Although it is essentially three-dimensional design, it must also deal with the non-visual aspects of the environment, concentrating on the external space and the relationships of the elements within it, as distinct from the internal space. Urban design is concerned with the effects of new development on the existing city form, to the extent that social, political and economic demands and available resources will allow. In addition, it needs to consider the different forms of movement within urban development.

As well as a lack of clarity as to the function and status of the term 'urban design', the boundaries of architecture and urban planning also remain uncertain. A recent resurgence of speculation in the field was exemplified by a spate of projects and competitions, the most notable of which was perhaps the 'Progressive Architecture' awards in the US. This renewal of interest from designers with a much wider range of sympathies than hitherto is a response to the state of uncertainty within which the two disciplines find themselves.

US urban planning legislation hardly addresses these issues. During my time as a regional planning commissioner in Ohio, I noticed a remarkable gap. All planning applications are considered within the framework of land-use plans and rigid zoning codes. Little consideration is given to aesthetics and particularly the three-dimensional aspects of design or, more essentially, contextual design. Indeed, in some schools of architecture and urban planning across the country, a lack of regard for urban context is all too common. The iconographic images produced could be sited anywhere on the planet. Apart from city and regional planning commissions, the only other urban design mechanisms are design review panels of architects that help to ensure a modicum of satisfactory three-dimensional visual design. However, the reviews tend to be on a site-by-site basis rather than within the contextual whole.

In Europe, the legislative system is little better. The UK, for example, subscribes to a negative system of development control in which planning applications are reviewed by junior staff, often lacking or with no visual training. The planning profession perceives that work in strategic and economic planning is more prestigious. In both countries, though urban design guidelines are available, they are largely ignored by both public and private sector developers.

As mentioned above, this study is inevitably selective, with an emphasis on projects of the latter decades of the twentieth century. In an attempt to identify American urban design, the book examines theories, ideas and projects (both built and unbuilt) in America from 1950 to the end of the century. Projects outside, but originating from America are also discussed. In summary, this anthology is about the impact of the origins and evolution of American urban design on the rest of the world.

Notes

1 Gosling, D. and B. Maitland (1985) *Concepts of Urban Design.* New York: St. Martin's Press. First edition 1984. London: Academy Editions.
2 Cullen, G. (1961) *Townscape.* London: Architectural Press.
3 Lynch, K. (1960) *The Image of the City.* Cambridge, MA: MIT Press and Harvard University.
4 Vernez-Moudon, A. (1992) 'A catholic approach to organizing what urban designers should know', *Journal of Planning Literature*, pp. 331–49.
5 Ibid., p. 337.

Chapter One

DEFINITIONS OF URBAN DESIGN[1]

INTERNATIONAL PRECEDENTS

Urban design, as opposed to urban design theories, is as old as civilisation itself. According to Arthur Gallion,[2] the city of Kahun in Egypt, dated around 3,000 BC, was built for slaves and artisans working on the construction of the Illahun pyramid. It was constructed on a rectilinear cluster system with an assembly of cells arranged in rectangular blocks, and access from narrow alleys. In Greece, the architect Hippodamus not only planned his own city of Miletus in the latter part of the fifth century BC, but also the city of Olynthus. Hippodamus has been credited with the origination of the gridiron street system, though, as Gallion points out, similar systems also existed in Egypt, Mesopotamia and the Indus valley. The application of the Hippodamian gridiron system in Greece, however, was curious in that the sites were often in areas with steep topography.[3]

Urban design guidelines, too, are not new. In Italy one of the earliest recorded building laws is a statute of 1262 regulating the form of houses fronting the Piazza del Campo in Siena. A further regulation enforcing compatibility of window design with that of the Palazzo Pubblico was adopted during the following century. Unlike the Piazza Ducale in Venice, which was designed and constructed as a single development, and the Piazza di SS Annunziata in Florence (each side of which formed one project, related by its architect to what had gone before, as part of the next phase of a 200-year programme), the Piazza del Campo was largely formed by the imposition of a public idea upon a large number of private actions.

In the early Renaissance, Filippo Brunelleschi's first building, Ospedale degli Innocenti (the Foundling Hospital) in Florence (1419), embodied rational and systematic principles of design.[4] The colonnade, or more accurately the loggia, is based on repeated modular elements. The grand plan of the hospital,

Piazza del Campo, Siena, Italy.

with two cloisters, a church and dormitories, is governed by modular and mathematical proportions without necessarily being symmetrical. Nevertheless, it provided an impressive unifying element across the public space of the piazza and provides weather protection both in summer and winter. Indeed, Florence is interlaced with such colonnades and arcades that followed over several centuries Brunelleschi's proportional systems of creating a visually coherent whole and strong urban design imagery. The Piazza of St. Peter's in Rome (1656) provides a grand forecourt matching the impressive architecture of the Basilica itself. Bernini designed a vast oval piazza surrounded by Doric colonnades. In the seventeenth century Bernini's piazza was reached from the narrow streets of the Borgo, and the contrast between confinement and open space provided much of the drama and surprise so important in urban design.

AMERICAN PRECEDENTS

Planned cities in the US date back to colonial times. For example, in 1682 the surveyor Thomas Holme was commissioned by William Penn to produce a master plan for Philadelphia using a rigid gridiron system. A public square was positioned in the geographical centre of the plan, with a square park in each of the four quadrants. In 1733, James Oglethorpe produced an imaginative plan for Savannah, Georgia, also using a gridiron system. Oglethorpe's plan could be considered more imaginative than that of William Penn for Philadelphia. It was symmetrically designed with an avenue on the axis of the main city park, leading to the edge of the Savannah River. The neighbourhoods boasted many more local parks or gardens, alternating with circular and rectilinear squares. The linking of the streets and parks made an attractive series of spatial sequences, though many of these have now disappeared.

The most ambitious proposal was that for Washington, DC, on the banks of the Potomac River. French architect Pierre L'Enfant's plan for a new capital was adopted by both George Washington and Thomas Jefferson in 1791. It utilised diagonal and radial streets superimposed upon a traditional gridiron system.

A more lyrical example of the application of urban design principles through the use of continuous colonnades can be found at the University of Virginia, Charlottesville, designed by Thomas Jefferson between 1817 and 1826. The plan consists of a wide, rectangular, tree-lined open space on each of its longer sides. On these are ranged five double-storey pavilions, housing teaching staff and lecture rooms, with classical porticoes and linked to one another by low, single-storey colonnades. Jefferson had established a pattern for campus planning that would be used in later American universities.

In the nineteenth century, the Chicago World Fair was the catalyst for the City Beautiful movement. Daniel Burnham was the chief architect for the fair, called the Columbian Exposition (1893), and was also commissioned to prepare a plan for San Francisco after the earthquake and fire of 1906. It is suggested by Gallion[5] that the École des Beaux Arts in Paris was

the fountainhead for the designers of this period and 'civic centres' were to be the focus of such plans. Gallion also notes that the seeds of city planning had been planted, citing examples such as the establishment of a Town Planning Board in Hartford, Connecticut, in 1907, the first National Conference on City Planning held in 1909, and the founding of the National Housing Association in 1911. Burnham's plan for Chicago depended upon neoclassical systems of city planning similar to that of Washington, DC, with symmetrical patterns and radial streets superimposed upon a gridiron street system.

The garden city movement emanated from the UK with the writings of Ebenezer Howard, and his most influential work, *Tomorrow*.[6] Before his death in 1928, Howard saw his idea become a reality. The Garden City Association was founded in 1899. In 1903, the first Garden City Limited bought 1,820 hectares (4,500 acres) of land, 55 kilometres (34 miles) north of London, and began the construction of the garden city of Letchworth, designed for a maximum population of 35,000 with an agricultural belt of 1,215 hectares (3,000 acres).

One of the first large-scale residential subdivisions in the US was a 650-hectare (1,600-acre) site known as Riverside, in Chicago, designed by Frederick Law Olmstead and Calvert Vaux in 1869. Garden City, Long Island, was a similar development. Olmstead was perhaps better known as a landscape architect who designed open spaces for the enjoyment of the urban population, rather than the overbearing neoclassical spaces that followed the École des Beaux Arts ideal. His design for Central Park in New York City is the epitome of such an aim.

Howard's garden city ideals were later embodied in communities in the US. For example, in 1921 New York architect John Nolan designed Mariemont, a garden city in Ohio, near Cincinnati. Mary Emery, the daughter of an Ohio industrialist, had visited Letchworth and Welwyn Garden City in England and went on to create a community for factory workers in an Arcadian setting. This comprised mainly single-family homes with a density of six to seven houses per acre, and embodied many of the ideals of the garden city movement. In visual imagery it reflected the nostalgia for Tudor and Elizabethan architecture, and though it has long since ceased to be a community for factory workers, because of the increased value of the property, it remains a vibrant community today.

Other important towns were planned around the same time. River Oaks, Texas, covers an area of over 400 hectares (1,000 acres), but perhaps the most important was the Palos Verdes development, south of Los Angeles and overlooking the Pacific Ocean. This was a major development on 1,215 hectares (3,000 acres) of low density, with housing lots ranging from 0.2 to 12 hectares (0.5 to 30 acres), and included schools, parks, libraries, churches, shopping, and recreational as well as landscaped parkways.

In 1926, Henry Wright and Clarence Stein designed Sunnyside Gardens, Long Island. Their 'garden apartments' were composed of perimeter blocks surrounding an internal garden. The design introduced the concept of row housing and two-storey apartments with separate, private entrances.

University of Virginia Campus, Charlottesville (1817–26),
Thomas Jefferson.

More important in developing the garden city idea was the City Housing Corporation, responsible for Sunnyside Gardens and Long Island, and now the development of Radburn on a site in New Jersey. Radburn was to be a revolutionary idea in urban design. Wright and Stein planned the new community based upon a 'superblock' concept.[7] Superblocks ranging from 12 to 20 hectares (30 to 50 acres) in size eliminated through vehicular traffic. Roads were enclosed within rather than traversing the areas, and single family houses were grouped around cul-de-sacs. Houses were oriented in the reverse of conventional siting. Kitchens and garages faced the road and living rooms turned towards the garden. This was not dissimilar to Frank Lloyd Wright's later usonian houses. Pedestrian paths gave access to a continuous linear parkway, which connected with communal open spaces within the superblock. Pedestrians and traffic were segregated with underpasses beneath highways, to allow continuity in the pedestrian system. Radburn's new towns construction programme was to have an international impact after the Second World War, particularly in Europe. In the UK, this was demonstrated, for example, by Harlow New Town in the phase I period, Cumbernauld New Town in the phase II period, and Runcorn New Town in the phase III period. At the same time, construction of new towns such as Vallingby in Sweden began to emerge throughout Scandinavia.[8]

The Greenbelt New Towns in the US were part of the Federal Government's quest for new city planning solutions. The responsibility of the Resettlement Administration, the programme commenced in 1935 with the objective to create satellite communities near large cities, all based, like Mariemont, Ohio, on Howard's garden city idea. Unlike the later British New Towns, these were not self-sufficient in terms of employment, but rather commuter villages with industrial bases in nearby cities. The four Greenbelt New Towns built by the Resettlement Administration were named as such because each was surrounded by permanent open space for farming or gardens. Greenbelt, Maryland, was on an 850-hectare (2,100-acre) site, half an hour by car from Washington, DC. Around a thousand dwellings (including both houses and apartments), occupied about 25 per cent of the site. Greenbelt was one of the first communities in the US to have a completely separate pedestrian system using underpasses beneath the road system. The commercial and recreation area was located in the geographical centre of the community, which meant minimum walking distances. The new town of Greenhills, Ohio, served Cincinnati. Its density was somewhat higher than Greenbelt, Maryland, with 3,000 dwellings on less than 2,430 hectares (6,000 acres). The permanent open space was 280 hectares (695 acres). The two other Greenbelt towns were Greendale, Wisconsin (near

Milwaukee), and Greenbelt, New Jersey (approximately halfway between New York and Philadelphia).

The period also saw the visionary planning of new cities (though many were never built), the most notable of which was Broadacre City by Frank Lloyd Wright. In the late 1920s and early 1930s, Wright had been forced into voluntary obscurity by lack of commissions until Edgar J. Kaufmann's 1935 commissioning of Falling Water in Pennsylvania, which once again brought Wright to international prominence.[9] By this time, Wright had abandoned his earlier enthusiasm for the Chicago 'machine city' and sought to overcome its problems with the reduction of its density to an incredible one acre per person – to the point where urban form and urban economics were disintegrated. Although he believed that new technology, in particular the motor car and telephone, favoured such a development, it was the social implications of Broadacre City that were to be paramount. According to Wright, through this decentralisation society would be freed from the insidious controls and exploitation that urban life imposed upon it, above all in the exaction of 'rent':

> The city itself has become a form of anxious rent, the citizen's own life rented, he and his family evicted if he is in arrears or the system goes to smash. Should this anxious lockstep of his fall out with the landlord, the money lord, or the machine lord, he is a total loss.[10]

In contrast, however:

> When every man, woman and child may be born to put his feet on his own acres, then democracy will have been realized.[11]

Wright envisaged that some sort of central control would be necessary to maintain this usonian ideal, which would depend on the initial expropriation of land-holding larger than a single family would require, a step with which the 'Drop Communards' of the 1960s – who were continually troubled by the American laws of trespass – would no doubt have had some sympathy.[12] In addition, something of Wright's own autocratic personality may be glimpsed in the figure of The County Architect, the most important official in Broadacre City, responsible for both the design and maintenance of the public infrastructure and for a measure of building control over each individual homestead to ensure it was subject to his sense of the whole as organic architecture. Despite this element of enlightened control, Wright's utopia formed an important reference for those troubled by the increasing authoritarian stance of centralised planning. For most European urbanists, however, the essential premise of Wright's solution – very low-density development – was seen as unattainable.[13]

Uncannily, some of Wright's utopian[14] vision for the future was fulfilled in suburbia across the US, though often in a somewhat negative way. His eloquent drawings portrayed aerial scenes of freeways with multilevel intersections, very low-density housing, shopping malls, business parks and so forth.

These prophecies can be found in Joel Garreau's book, *Edge City*:[15] 'The suburbs/commuting to the city is getting old and the American people once again are on the edge of developing a new type of community'. There are a number of historical reasons for this.

The interstate highway (or freeway) system was constructed during President Eisenhower's administration in the 1950s. This was at the height of the Cold War when military defence considerations were paramount, and the system was designed chiefly to enable the rapid movement of troops across the US.[16] In the event, the road system was never used for this purpose; however, it did provide a new freedom of mobility for American citizens. Though Wright's low-density Broadacre City was impossible in Europe because of high land-acquisition costs, the available land mass in the US, albeit with a large population, was relatively inexpensive to acquire, inevitably leading to the creation of the suburbs on former farmland.

In addition to the above, the 1950s and 1960s heralded an unprecedented period of prosperity. The single family motor car disappeared to be gradually replaced by cars for each member of the household except for low-income groups. The degeneration of the central city was almost inevitable; social tensions and economic pressures such as rising taxes drove commerce and retailing out of the city, and a declining tax base caused the more affluent members of the community to flee to the new suburbs. Another result of this was the decline in public transport.

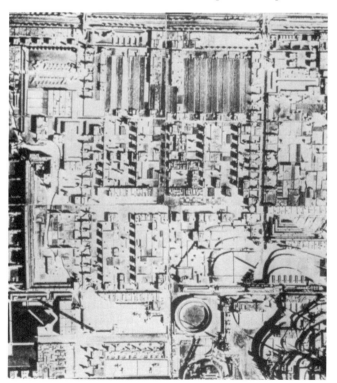

Broadacre City (mid-1930s), Frank Lloyd Wright.

DEFINING URBAN DESIGN

How then can urban design be defined? In *Concepts of Urban Design*,[17] it was noted that

There is a widely held view that planning methods over the latter half of this century have often failed to produce a satisfactory physical environment. These methods have resulted in a proliferation of land use plans, traffic studies, zoning codes and economic and demographic surveys, while, more recently, within the last decade, sophisticated Geographical Information Systems (GIS) and advanced three-dimensional computer modeling techniques have been used to optimize the land use matrix. But all of this has little to do with the way in which the ordinary citizen actually perceives, uses and enjoys his or her environment. It has become apparent in recent years that the physical development of world cities has been going wrong if one examines such disparate cities as São Paulo, Brazil, Calcutta, India or even large sectors of Tokyo, and there seems to be uncertainty as to what the logical priorities should be.

At the beginning of the 1960s, an article by Morton Hoppenfeld appeared in the *American Institute of Architects Journal*.[18] Interestingly, Hoppenfeld held a position as civic designer for the National Planning Commission in Washington and taught architectural design at Harvard University. He was formerly chief of the special area planning section for the Philadelphia City Planning Commission. While there is little reference in his article to US cities (he prefers to cite examples such as the Agora of Athens or the Piazza San Marco in Venice), he does pay homage indirectly to Kevin Lynch, though not mentioning him by name, but rather by implying the need for 'establishing the image of a city'. Civic design embraced the concept of the master plan and was concerned generally with major civic buildings. Hoppenfeld suggests that 'the image of the city in the mind of the beholder depends largely on the paths he treads as he moves about in it over the course of time; but for most people, in most cities their image lacks clarity, interest and wholeness'. He later notes that in creating and reconstructing cities a new urban scale must be achieved, and new kinds of spaces must be created.[19] On the other hand, he writes that while it is desirable that design becomes more clearly recognised as a vital part of the planning process, there is the danger of misuse in producing a master plan of the entire city. This plan often obscures the key ideas and fails to serve as an adequate guide to development. The proper and most effective role of the planner's design should be to erect a basic design framework.[20]

It was in the 1960s that two developments brought a new urgency to this general background of concern with the form of the modern city. The first related to changes in the education of the designers concerned, and threatened to aggravate the difficulties of achieving coherent solutions; for if earlier design attitudes had seemed crude and mechanistic, the possibility now arose that the design would be further fragmented by selections and training in two mutually uncomprehending groups. Adopting policies that were also taken up in many other countries, both architectural and city planning professional institutes in the US opted for separate courses for educating students. However, this dissociation of the two professions existed to a lesser extent in the US than in other countries, especially the UK. In the middle of the century, urban design was beginning to be taught at major schools in the US, such as the University of California, Berkeley, the University of Pennsylvania, Harvard University and MIT. MIT was a particularly interesting example. The graduate division of the school of architecture was largely studio based and taught rigid adherence to the principles of the modern movement/international style, demanding iconic architectural design on vaguely determined sites. With the exception of Gyorgy Kepes in the school of architecture, it was the school of planning that taught urban design under the guidance of Kevin Lynch. However, architectural students were able to take elective studios with Lynch.[21]

As mentioned in the introduction to this book, urban design is (or should be) an integral part of the process of city and regional planning. It is primarily and essentially three-dimensional, but must also deal with non-visual aspects of the environment such as noise, water, air pollution and traffic safety, which contribute significantly to the character of an area. Its major characteristic is the arrangement of the physical objects and human activities that make up the environment; this space and the relationship of elements within it is essentially external, as distinct from internal design, and embraces the discipline of landscape architecture. Urban design includes concern for the relationship between new development and existing city form (context), as much as the social, political and economic demands and available resources. It is equally concerned with the relationship of different forms of movement within urban development.

Reyner Banham, in his book *Megastructure*,[22] notes the growing recognition during the 1960s of an interdisciplinary gap between architecture and planning, suggesting that the intermediate field of urban design was concerned with urban situations about half a mile square. Banham's book also draws attention to another factor which at the same time gave particular urgency to the need to find appropriate techniques and models of urban design: the unprecedented scale of urban redevelopment programmes, a process being repeated throughout the present decade. Such redevelopment too often appears to undermine the terms and patterns in which urban forms were conventionally understood.

A new scale of development agency in both private and public sectors has made it possible to consider urban *quartiers* (districts or neighbourhoods), as single design problems undertaken by one developer, one design team and one contractor. Such an example from the late 1980s is Battery Park City in New York, master-planned by Skidmore, Owings and Merrill for developer Olympia-York. Though more successful in its visual imagery and composition than the same company's Canary Wharf development in London, it is nevertheless of gargantuan scale. The conventional distinction between the building and the city is called into question, along with assumptions about the ways in which change and growth are accommodated in the city fabric. Whether for economic or administrative reasons, the new mechanisms of development tend to exaggerate the tendency of city areas towards functional specialisation, and a picture has thus emerged of large, single-use increments of development, of radically different form from the surrounding fabric that has been blighted by the expectation of future extensions of the new pattern (usually in the form of surface parking lots). The status of public areas within the new precincts (whether retail, office or residential) is ambiguous, often being closed off at night and patrolled by private security organisations.

It is possible to envisage the regeneration of city planning through a new concern for its physical manifestations at the scale of the *quartier*. Similarly, for architecture, it is believed that the modern movement proposition, that the internal logic of the programme is the primary source of building form, might be modified by a complementary proposition regarding the integrity of its counter form, public space, and that this new dialectic might supply a significant element in a revitalised contemporary architecture.

VISUAL DESIGN ANTECEDENTS AND URBAN DESIGN: SEMIOTICS

It is associations of quantifiable elements that form the city, and we can therefore borrow methods from 'set theory' in the field of pure mathematics to help us manipulate these. Again, since the city is a cultural invention, imbued with meaning for its inhabitants, it can be likened to a language, and insights sought from the discipline of linguistics, either in terms of syntactic structure or through the study of the meaning of signs, in semiotics.[23] This was the subject of a major study by Geoffrey Broadbent, Charles Jencks and others,[24] and was described by British theorist Gordon Cullen as the 'language of gestures':

> Communication between people and the towns they live in is primarily affected by signalization . . . Rapport between ourselves and the environment brings continuing interest. Obviously this can only be achieved by signals and gestures that bring home to us the identity latent in environmental problems; hence, the need for a comprehensive language of gestures. [25]

Cullen proposed that if a theory of navigation could be applied to the urban design process, then a coherent urban structure might be a future possibility. He added that: 'In viewing the physical environment with its highways, bridges, buildings, vegetation and so on, there are two ways of looking . . . the associational and the objective. That is to say one's front door may be "home" or a rectangle of color. As far as the urban scene goes it is nearly always the former, hardly ever the latter and no terminology exists to isolate and communicate our feelings'.[26]

This language of gestures can be seen as either the invention of a carefully structured system by the urban designer, or a successful accident. In the accompanying illustrations an anonymously designed letter box and doorbell in Venice, for example, has similar impact and meaning in terms of imageability as the piece of sculpture laid carefully in the ground at the Louisiana Museum in Denmark.

Anthropology and psychology are also relevant here since

Letterbox and doorbell,
Central Venice, Italy.

Sculpture of face
carved from rock,
Louisiana Museum,
Denmark.

their focus is humankind and they have been keenly studied for directly 'applicable' results. In the case of the former, the concept of 'territoriality' seems important in the sense that the city could be regarded as the physical operation of such a principle. 'Territoriality' has been studied in both animals and humans, with some remarkable results. The scientist J. B. Calhoun, for example, has described the effects of increasing density and space restrictions upon laboratory populations of mice, tracing changes in fertility, physique, behaviour and susceptibility to disease, extrapolating the results for human groupings.[27]

If our instinctive appreciation of 'ownership' and occupation of territory in the city is crucial to its success, the question of how we actually perceive and understand its complex spatial variation is therefore important, and has been one of the most active areas of interest for urban design theorists, bringing them into contact with a number of developments in the arts and sciences. The work of the Gestalt psychologists in the early part of the twentieth century was one of the first such developments which seemed to offer a firmer and more rational basis for the discussion of perception. Its essential message that 'vision is not a mechanical recording of elements but the grasping of significant structural patterns'[28] accorded with the feelings of many engaged in visual design, and provided a description of the way in which such patterns are recognised.

Six conditions were identified as playing an important, if not exclusive role in producing visual forms: the law of proximity, by which objects close to one another tend to form groups; the law of similarity, where like objects are read as groups; the law of closed forms, whereby lines enclosing a surface tend to be seen as a unit; the law of 'good' contour or common destiny, by which continuity of form is implied across interruptions; the law of common movement, describing the ability of the eye to group elements that move simultaneously and in a similar manner; and the law of experience, which acknowledges the partial dependence of the comprehension of symbolic forms upon the circumstances under which they were learned.[29] These laws are reinforced by a fundamental law, described by Freidrich Wulf in 1922 as 'the law of *Prägnanz* (conciseness), according to which every Gestalt becomes as good as possible . . . it is for this reason that memorable Gestalten tend toward unique forms . . . well-known forms (structures) are themselves already stable'.[30]

This visual bias in favour of simple regular forms seemed an especially challenging discovery, as was the Gestalt discovery of figure-ground. The latter was of particular interest to those concerned with the urban environment, since the inhabitants of cities must as a matter of course continually identify key signals against chaotic backgrounds. Again, the whole concept of urban design is based upon a classic figure-ground reversal, in which what is normally regarded as figure (buildings) must be read as ground, and what is normally seen as ground (the surrounding spaces) becomes figure, a flip vividly demonstrated by the graphic technique employed by Giambattista Nolli in drawing his 1748 plan of Rome (*see overleaf*). Figure-ground applica-

Gestalt figure-ground images (1930s).

tions are to be seen at their best in the urban design studios held by Colin Rowe, Matthew Bell and others at Cornell University throughout the 1980s.[31]

Though subsequently superseded by the work of the Swiss children's psychologist Jean Piaget and the concept of 'schemata' or stereotyped responses to situations,[32] the theories of the Gestalt school of psychology were accepted into the thinking of many theorists in designs of the interwar years, and embraced in Bauhaus teaching with a second body of ideas on the question of perception, stemming this time from the arts. Concerned in particular with a redefinition of the notion of space, the set of ideas propounded by Siegfried Giedion[33] is worth recalling in this regard. Paul Klee's work was also notable, not only for the numerous drawings and paintings of imaginary city forms he made during the 1920s, but also for the attention he drew to the relationship between the techniques of drawing and the sequential recording of experiences. Another direction, taken from DeStijl painting and the architecture of Frank Lloyd Wright, was the concept of space as a natural continuum, with no distinction between internal and external spaces. This was lucidly expressed by Mies van der Rohe's 1940 master plan for the Illinois Institute of Technology (IIT) Campus in Chicago, in which the structure of the buildings seemed simply a manifestation of an implicit Cartesian grid pervading the whole area.

The second important concept was that of a freely moving observer, which introduced the possibility of simultaneous, fragmented and multiple vision, first postulated by the cubist and futurist painters and sculptors. The two ideas were invoked by Giedion in the term 'space-time', which though misleadingly seeming to imply some connection with Einstein's theory of relativity, indicated the knowledge of perception involved. Whether, as Giedion argued, a moving observer's experience of the Rockefeller Center is different in kind from that of the Tower of Bologna,[34] the emphasis upon motion and a variable point of observation had obvious relevance to questions of perception of urban phenomena, the implications of which, as with so many

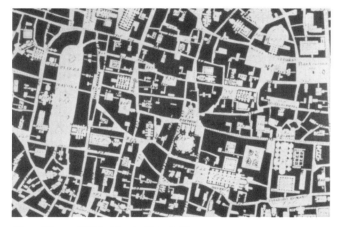
Plan of Rome (1748), Giambattista Nolli.

novelties of the modern movement, were first explored by painters.

In his 1920 essay 'Creative confession', Klee asks the reader to accompany him on a walk, a short excursion into the country: 'We shall see how the phenomena of nature are represented by the graphic elements and their combinations. We start off from a point: that gives a line. We stop once or twice; the line has been broken or articulated. We cross a river by boat (an undulatory movement). A ploughed field (a surface scored by lines). Mist in a valley (a spatial element). We meet people. Basket makers coming home with their cart (a wheel). They have a child with them with funny curls (a corkscrew motion). Later the weather becomes sultry and lowering (spatial element). A flash of lightning on the horizon (a zigzag line). There are still stars overhead (scattered dots).' To sum up, he writes: 'All different kinds of different lines. Blobs of color. Stippling. Stippled and striped surfaces. Undulatory movement. Broken, articulated movement. Countermovement. Objects interlaced and interwoven. Masonry, peeling stone. Harmony with one voice. With several voices. Line losing itself (gaining strength) (dynamic)'.[35]

The description of a shorthand graphic technique for recording a series of experiences foreshadowed a recurring preoccupation of later theorists, where desire to treat perception as objectively as possible led them to the need for a precise notation flexible enough to describe the great variety of events encountered in a city. Laszlo Moholy-Nagy, also a Bauhaus artist, was similarly concerned with finding techniques to record and communicate complex events, particularly through the use of new media. Following his notorious 'telephone paintings' (made by workmen in an enamelling workshop to instructions dictated over the telephone), he encouraged experimentation at the Bauhaus in new techniques, particularly in the use of film and collaged photography of the city. As with artists like Duchamp and Klee, Moholy-Nagy's prewar work culminated in his own version of the machine, in the form of a kinetic light sculpture, the Light-Space Modulator, the variable lighting effects of which could be recorded on negative film. After he emigrated to the US, Moholy-Nagy recorded these interests in his book *Vision in Motion*,[36] a mixture of theory, Bauhaus Vorkurs exercises and demonstrations of experimental photographic and film techniques. These included his interpretation of the history of developing spatial concepts and a discussion of the problems of 'rendering motion (space-time) on the static plane', with an emphasis on the relevance of developments in the fields of cinema, theatre and dance.

THE BAUHAUS AS GENERATOR

What was the relevance of the German Bauhaus to the development of design theory in the US (particularly in the emerging field of urban design)?

The Bauhaus was not an institution with a clear program, it was an idea, and Gropius formulated this idea with great precision . . . the fact that it was an idea may be the cause of the enormous influence the Bauhaus had on every progressive school around the globe. You cannot do that with organization, you cannot do that with propaganda.[37]

IIT Campus, Chicago (1940), Mies van der Rohe.

The Bauhaus was the first multidisciplinary professional school of the twentieth century. It was founded by Walter Gropius and others in Weimar, Germany, in 1919 after the formation of the Weimar Republic following Germany's defeat in the First World War. It remained in Weimar from 1919 to 1925, to be re-established in Dessau between 1925 and 1932, and for a brief period in Berlin between 1932 and 1933. Following intense Nazi persecution it was closed, and many of its faculty and students left for the US, UK and Switzerland: 'Institutionally, the Bauhaus was an institute for art, which emerged as the successor to an academy and a school of arts and crafts through their mutual integration . . . How and where is the achievement of the Bauhaus to be concretely grasped . . . Does it lie, first and foremost, in the powerful impulse given to the "New Architecture" by the Bauhaus architects, especially Walter Gropius and Ludwig Mies van der Rohe? Is it in the contribution that the Bauhaus made to the revolutions in the field of home environment and industrial design? Or should it be seen primarily in the creative contributions of the Bauhaus painters to the history of art, in that they more than others influenced the development of Modern art in the twentieth century? The fundamental teaching methods of the Bauhaus have transformed art-teaching methods throughout the world'.[38]

The relevance of the Bauhaus teachers to the start of true urban design theory in the US may be summarised in a statement by Kevin Lynch in his preface to *The Image of the City*.[39] According to Lynch: 'The work that lies behind this study was done under the direction of Professor Gyorgy Kepes and myself at the Center for Urban and Regional Studies of the Massachusetts Institute of Technology'. Kepes was one of the most prominent of the Bauhaus teachers who, together with Walter Gropius, Mies van der Rohe, Josef Albers and Laszlo and Sybil Moholy-Nagy came to the US before the Second World War to set up design schools in Chicago and later at Harvard University, Yale University and elsewhere. It was Kepes especially who had a profound influence on his colleagues and students in understanding the perception of the city that led to the foundation of theories of urban design. The abbreviated biographies of the most significant teachers are given in the box below.

The Bauhaus then, through the immigration of its teachers to the US in the late 1930s, was to have a profound influence on the direction of the teaching of architecture and urban planning, and subsequently urban design in that country.[40] Regarding the influence of these Bauhaus designers and artists upon architectural education in the US, Paul Klee's essay 'Creative confessions' was to have a major impact. His description of a shorthand graphic technique for recording a series of experiences foreshadowed a recurring preoccupation of later theorists whose desire to treat perception as objectively as possible led them to the need for a precise notation, flexible enough to describe the great variety of events encountered in a city.

Both Giedion's 'space-time' and Moholy-Nagy's *Vision in Motion* drew attention to a more dynamic approach to visual understanding that seemed to offer new insights into the processes of describing and analysing urban environments. The distinction between this appreciation, based upon a mobile observer, and the former perception from static, frontal viewpoints, was subsequently developed by other commentators, including Roger Hinks: 'In all acts of human observation, time is accommodated to space, or space to time. When the viewpoint is fixed, time yields to space. When the viewpoint is

Seagram Building skyscraper, New York (1959), Mies van der Rohe.

Walter Gropius established the Bauhaus teaching regulations in January 1921 by saying that: 'The Bauhaus endeavors to educate artistically gifted men and women to become creatively designing craftsmen, sculptors, painters or architects. Thorough training of all students in the crafts provides the unifying foundations'.[41] In short, there was to be the cross-fertilisation, not compartmentalisation of ideas and theories, an ideal that is seldom apparent today in university education. Gropius said that members of the Bauhaus were to be masters, junior masters, journeymen and apprentices. Of the Bauhaus teachers who came to the US, Gropius, along with Mies van der Rohe and Gyorgy Kepes, was perhaps one of the most significant as far as the future of urban design was concerned. Gropius was born in Berlin in 1883. He studied architecture at the Institutes of Technology in Berlin and Munich from 1903 to 1907. At first an assistant to Peter Behrens in Berlin, he opened his own office in 1910 and was invited to Weimar in 1919 to found the Bauhaus. In 1928 he resigned his directorship. In 1934 he emigrated to England and worked in partnership with British architect Maxwell Fry until 1937 when he was appointed to the Graduate School of Design at Harvard University. From 1938 to 1952 he was chairman of the Architecture Department at Harvard, and in 1946 founded the Architects' Collaborative, working on major architectural and urban design projects. He died in 1969.

Paul Klee was born near Bern, Switzerland, in 1879. From 1920 to 1931 he was a Master at the Bauhaus. In Weimar he was responsible for the stained glass workshop. However his greater influence was in the educational field of the preliminary course. As political developments worsened in Germany, he returned to his native Switzerland in 1933.

Wassilly Kandinsky was born in Moscow in 1866. Disillusioned after a period as director of the New State Museum in Moscow, he resigned and went to Germany where he took up a position at the Bauhaus, until its final dissolution in 1933. During the Weimar period he led the wall-painting workshop. Of outstanding importance were his investigations into visual problems. In 1933 he emigrated to France where he died in 1944.

Laszlo Moholy-Nagy was born in Hungary in 1895. He followed the work of the German expressionists and the Russian avant-garde. In 1919 he founded the group Ma (Today), and founded an art journal. From 1921 to 1923 he lived in Berlin and first started exhibiting his work in his own gallery, Sturm. In 1923 he was appointed to the Bauhaus as head of the metal workshops where he made important contributions to the courses in preliminary instruction. He was also co-editor of the Bauhaus publications. In 1928 he moved back to Berlin

and experimented with film and stage design. He emigrated to England in 1934, working on animated and documentary films, and three years later took over the direction of the New Bauhaus, which had been founded by the Association of Arts and Industries in Chicago. Following its closure, in 1938 he opened his own school in Chicago, the Institute of Design, which he directed until his death in 1946. Moholy-Nagy was the initiator of photographs without a camera (photogram) and was one of the first to become aware of the artistic and psychological advertising possibilities of composition.[42]

Josef Albers was born in Westphalia in 1888. He studied at the Royal Art School in Berlin from 1913 to 1915. After further studies he attended the Weimar Bauhaus from 1920 to 1923. He became technical director of the glass workshop and taught the preliminary workshop course. In 1925 he was given the junior master's position in the Dessau Bauhaus, and remained in that position after the resignation of Moholy-Nagy in 1928. Albers took over Marcel Breuer's position as head of the furniture workshop in 1928. He remained a member of the Bauhaus until the Nazis permanently closed it in Berlin in 1933, at which point he emigrated to the US where he taught at Black Mountain College in Colorado until 1949. He also taught courses at Harvard, as well as acting as guest lecturer at the Cincinnati Art Academy. In 1950 he was appointed a professor at Yale University and became chairman of the Department of Design. Next to Gropius, Albers contributed decisively to the dissemination of Bauhaus ideas. He died in 1976.

Marcel Breuer was born in Hungary in 1902. In 1920 he studied at the Bauhaus, training mainly in the cabinet-making workshop. As early as 1921 he attracted attention with his unconventional design for chairs and tables. He was put in charge of the cabinet-making workshop (furniture) at Bauhaus Dessau in 1923, producing the world's first tubular steel chair. Between 1928 and 1931 he worked for Walter Gropius in Berlin, moved to England in 1935 and to the US in 1937, where he accepted a professorship at Harvard. In 1946 he opened his own architectural practice in New York and became renowned as an architectural and furniture designer.

Ludwig Hilbersheimer, a key figure in influencing urban design concepts in the US, was born in Germany in 1885. He was put in charge of the architecture department at the Bauhaus in 1929, and remained with the Bauhaus until its closure in 1933. He was forced to emigrate in 1938 and, like his colleague Ludwig Mies van der Rohe, went to the US where he became a professor of city planning in the Architecture Department of IIT in Chicago. He remained in Chicago after being named Professor Emeritus and continued his writings on the subject of 'the city' until his death in 1967. While his

proposals for a skyscraper city, prepared during his tenure at the Bauhaus in 1927, had similarities to Le Corbusier's equally visionary 1922 proposal for a city for three million inhabitants, Hilbersheimer's vision was even more austere and doctrinaire. His aim was to find a way out of the chaotic absence of order and the paralysing effect of the vastness of the city on the individual. He wanted to reduce the area covered by building in favour of green acres. With the separation of pedestrian and road traffic, living units in Hilbersheimer's ideal project were separated by a vertical separation of levels. It produced, nevertheless, a bleak vision of the city of the future where the individual, far from being given enhanced freedom, was subjugated by the city as machine. Many of the public housing 'projects' in the US owed much to this vision with its attendant social problems, including crime and isolation.[43]

Ludwig Mies van der Rohe, with Walter Gropius, was probably one of the most important Bauhaus émigrés to the US. Ranking alongside Frank Lloyd Wright as one of the most significant American architects of the twentieth century, his approach to design was almost the opposite, showing an ascetic, rarefied set of rigid design principles of man in opposition to nature. Born in Aachen in 1886, he worked as an apprentice in the office of Bruno Paul until 1907, and from 1908 to 1911 as an assistant to Peter Behrens. He arrived at his own independent concept in refining engineering architecture and produced some of the boldest steel and glass building designs (though alas these were never built), such as his 1921 model of a glass skyscraper. In 1926 he was appointed vice-chairman of the German Werkbund and was in charge of the design and construction of the 1927 Weissenhof housing development in Stuttgart, employing other architects such as Le Corbusier and Gropius. During his period at the Bauhaus, his 1929 design for the Barcelona Pavilion at the Barcelona World's Fair was probably the pinnacle of the modern movement and became the prototype of the modern exhibition building. In 1938 van der Rohe emigrated to the US and settled in Chicago, becoming head of the architecture department at the Armour Institute, after 1940 renamed the Illinois Institute of Technology (IIT). His most famous achievements were the complete planning and design of the IIT.[44] Of his individual buildings, apart from the Barcelona Pavilion his best is most likely the Seagram skyscraper on Park Avenue in New York City, designed in collaboration with Philip Johnson, at the time an ardent admirer of van der Rohe's design theories. Completed in 1959, the skyscraper contributed much to a new concept of urban design – that of associating commercial structures with public open plazas. It was preceded earlier in the 1950s by Skidmore, Owings and Merrill's smaller Lever building, designed by Gordon Bunschaft and also on Park Avenue.

Lever Building from Seagram Building, New York (1959).

MIT with Lynch, Mumford and Appleyard. His book, *The New Landscape,*[47] emphasised the importance of photography as a technique for enlarging the scope of normal vision as in the use of microphotography, telephotography and recorded effects on photosensitive film. In particular he drew attention to the fifth Gestalt condition, regarding the perception of movement, in the way in which very extended, or very compressed sequences could be made legible and continuous by the use of accelerated or decelerated films.

FURTHER DEFINITIONS OF URBAN DESIGN

Addressing some of the problems in defining urban design, Anne Vernez-Moudon[48] describes concentrations of inquiry in this field, including urban history studies, picturesque studies, image studies, studies of environmental behaviour, place, material culture, topology-morphology and nature ecology, and provides a useful list of major contributors in each area. However, she points out that these distinctions are not well articulated in the planning and design fields.[49] As an example, Vernez-Moudon writes that the Anglo-Saxon term 'urban design' is coveted by Latin-language speakers who have to contend with *urbanisme* or *urbanismo* – terms that 'are clearly more reflective, less action-oriented than "urban design". Only in Italy can one find "urban science" and "urbanism" used commonly to define the spectrum of description versus prescription, research versus urban design'.[50]

Even in English-speaking countries the use of the word 'urbanism' as opposed to 'urban design' is misleading.[51] When one of the authors of this present work was a visiting professor at the University of Brasilia between 1975 and 1976, his task was to introduce a new course in urban design in the post-graduate curriculum in city planning. There was no Portuguese expression to define it and the literal translation of *desenho urbano* was 'urban drawing'. In Brazil nowadays *desenho urbano* is an accepted description, but at the time the students, more preoccupied with political and social injustices, fought against the relevance of urban design despite visits by North American urban designers such as Allen Jacobs from San Francisco in 1976.

One of the foremost teachers at the University of Brasilia in the field of urban design was Maria Elaine Kohlsdorf who drew as much from Gestalt theory as from North American theory.[52] In other writings she indicates that Gestalt is the German word for configuration, adopted for a school of psychology by such writers as Wertheimer, Kohler and Koffka, who came into prominence in the earlier part of the twentieth century. Gestalt psychology devoted much attention to the artistic aspects of experience and form perception.[53] In urban Gestalt and sequential form, Kohlsdorf developed analytical techniques stemming from Moholy-Nagy and other Bauhaus teachers. In her monograph on urban spatial sequences,[54] she investigates the relationship of people with their environment and suggests that the environment is capable of provoking, through a com-

movable, space yields to time. Brunelleschian perspective presupposes one eye, not two; in a rigid head, not a movable one, set on a rigid body. The eye gazes fixedly at a vanishing point; and the lines that flow from that point are called orthogonal. In the perspective of experience, we must allow for two eyes and a movable head, on a movable body. The eye roves, rather the eyes rove, from one vanishing point to another in endless sequence; planes become curved surfaces; and straight lines become parabolas.'[45]

Similarly, the Japanese architect Arata Isozaki maintained that the Japanese do not recognise the Western serial concept of space and time.[46] Both are conceived in terms of intervals as reflected in the use of the term 'Ma' in architecture, landscape design, music and drama, a concept that can signify the 'natural distance between two or more things existing in continuity' or space delineated by posts and screens.

THE BAUHAUS AND GESTALT PRINCIPLES

The influence of the Bauhaus tradition upon American postwar urban designers was reinforced by Gyorgy Kepes, a teacher at plex of physical-sensorial elements, differing stimulations and impressions. The inhabitant needs elements that are known, constant and traditional. The environment is perceived and used by these inhabitants, yet planned by 'specialists'. In terms of Urban Gestalt, it can be expressed thus: The whole process of urban creation must follow an analysis of consumption or use, based upon the classification of outputs and the manipulation of inputs. That is to say, given any urban system, the functions are not considered as much as the relationship between the variable inputs and the resultant outputs. Keifer defines form as the exterior, the appearance of the superficial and quantifiable dimension of the perceived object.[55] Gestalt is the internal relationship of a composition (or organisation or formation) and is understood as the perceived structure of permanent objects in all possible transformations and transpositions.

Gestalt concepts are characterised by the effect they produce, independent of the effect produced by other spaces. Each spatial effect is a state, a moment which may vary according to the viewpoint of the observer, but which does not depend on transmitting its effect on continuous movement within the space. Dynamic Gestalt concepts, however, exist only from a temporary combination of static Gestalt concepts. It is a phenomenon of movement and each static effect is called a station or moment, and its combination is a sequence. A group of static Gestalt concepts might be listed as follows:

1 *Involvement* The effect of being involved is provoked by limited space, sufficiently noticeable physical elements on all sides, and in which the exterior of the space is visible from the interior. The effect has varying degrees of intensity.
2 *Impediment* The effect of visual interruption from certain observation points, resulting from a collection of various types of visual barriers.
3 *Accentuation* The effect of accentuation is to draw to the observer's attention a predetermined physical-spatial element, achieved by colour, light, material and form.
4 *Narrowing of enclosure* An effect achieved by physical-spatial elements creating linear space or the effect of enclosure.
5 *Exposure* The opposite of narrowing, where the physical elements allow exposure of the observer outside the immediate space of the viewpoint.
6 *Privileged space* Privileged space is one which has a particular quality compared with others. A sensation, in Gestalt terms, signifies a predetermined space and has good visual characteristics compared with adjacent spaces.

The study of an urban sequence starts in principle with the environment and is experienced as much in repose as in movement. It is the product of a continuous succession of psychological effects. As a dynamic system, the sequence can be interpreted as a system of channels[56] in which the individual moves from origin to destination, and is a communication system that provides the observer with a series of information. It is the relationship between repetitive elements and elements of surprise, and it characterises the type of sequence with the objective of establishing equilibrium between monotony and chaos. In the final analysis it is intended to obtain the best Gestalt qualities. The base of continuity could tend towards monotony, while the elements of surprise may be responsible, on occasion, for chaotic sequences.

Each sequential element may be characterised according to its impact. The involvement may be of different intensities according to the height of the elements. The canyon-like streets in the Wall Street district of New York City provide a good example. Each sequential element can have different temporal durations and sizes, for example the garden courtyard or the civic square. Each sequential element is composed of different elements from the environmental repertoire – the height of the space, vegetation or building all create differing effects. The idea of sequential space is discussed in the following two chapters with references to the work of Donald Appleyard and the influence of British theorist Gordon Cullen.

DEFINITIONS OF URBAN DESIGN WITHIN PLANNING AND ARCHITECTURE

The attitudes of urban designers towards their subject are as varied as those of the architects and planners to their respective fields. An appraisal of the main lines upon which these attitudes are based has been undertaken by Javier Cenicacelaya Marijuan.[57] He defines a series of approaches to urban design, classified in three broad groups:

A. *Dependent on a particular politico-cultural system*
    1 Marxist[58]
    2 utopian
    3 capitalist

B. *Related to a variable politico-cultural system*
    1 mathematical
    2 descriptive, functionalist
    3 morphological:
       a analysis of human geography
       b morphology of the plan
       c network analysis
    4 historical

C. *Not dependent on any politico-cultural system*
    1 perceptual
    2 the city as an image
    3 the city as sequences
    4 the city as underrated architecture

Following is a brief description of what is meant by each of these categories.

Marxist theory predicated an attitude towards the city as well as towards society in general. According to such an analysis, the city is seen as representing the state of the class struggle within it, and the ultimate objective of the urban designer is to eliminate inequalities in the benefits the city offers its citizens. The central problem for Marxist commentators dates back to the ninth of Marx's ten measures in the 1848 Manifesto of the Communist Party, the necessity for the establishment of a communist society, which required the 'combination of agriculture with manufacturing industries and gradual abolition of the distinction between town and country by a more equable distribution of the population over the country'.[59]

Historically, the difficulties inherent in trying to formulate a planning policy have been set out in a fascinating account by Kenneth Frampton[60] as they surfaced after the Revolution in Russia when two rival schools of Marxian urbanism were competing for official recognition. For Sabsovitch and the 'urbanists', the appropriate strategy lay in the dismemberment of existing large towns (being an expression of the capitalist regime) and their reassembly in 'agglomerations', each of about 50,000 inhabitants and set in open country – not dissimilar to the British New Towns programme between 1950 and 1990, or the privately financed American New Towns programme including Reston, Virginia, or Irvine, California, or even Seaside in Florida from 1970 onwards. On the other hand, Miliutin, who led the 'disurbanists', proposed a Marxian development of the linear city concept proposed in 1882 by Soria y Mata for the Cuidad Lineal, Madrid, comprising six continuous parallel linear zones for communications, industry, open space, dwellings, public buildings and agriculture, extending to form a city of 100,000 to 200,000 inhabitants.

Seductive as the second theoretical proposal was, both Miliutin and Ernst May, who was recruited with other German planners in 1930 to assist the Russian effort in planning the new town of Magnitogorsk, were unable to apply the ideal structure to a real topography with the rigour demanded by its inventor. Instead, agglomerations became the official policy until, in 1931, the central committee renounced all *utopian* proposals, whether urbanist or disurbanist, and all foreign planning theories including Wright's Broadacre City. It is ironic that the Stalinist regime subsequently adopted a brutal version of the neoclassical city, which in itself was a contradiction of egalitarian society.[61]

An even bleaker view of rejecting utopian ideals could be seen in the extraordinary action of Pol Pot's Khmer Rouge army on 15 April 1975 in disurbanising Cambodia, forcibly evacuating two million inhabitants of Phnom-Penh overnight, and leaving the city deserted after conducting massacres of massive numbers of the intelligentsia as well as enforcing the return to a total agrarian society.

Marijuan[62] suggests that the utopian concept refers to Plato's proposal that a perfect environment is the result of a perfect society. Thus, utopian planning proposals historically have been based upon particular concepts of society, and have assumed the creation of a new mentality in mankind. Most such proposals have adopted rigid geometrical forms.

The *capitalist* view of the city is held to be that of a field in which forces struggle for predominance in urban life. The forces, historically, have been related to particular power structures, such as the government, church, multinational economies and, more recently, the pursuit of market economics and global economics, especially in the US. The city, thus, reflects an equilibrium of power, whether relative or absolute. The emphasis in the city structure may variously be on protection (of the natural environment or historic conservation), beauty, identity, or other general ideas. The combination of market economics in a democracy defined by the American Constitution militates against prescriptive planning such as urban design.

In a variable politico-cultural system, the term mathematical-economic does not necessarily imply a geometric proposal for the city and its growth. Rather it refers to a consideration of the city as a field of complex needs which are to be satisfied. The city is analysed within the framework of an interchange of goods and services. The main objective is to achieve an adequate infrastructure for the city and its hinterland based upon a highly detailed analysis of networks and interrelationships. *Mathematical* models for retail distribution may be considered an example of network theory. The work of the Cambridge School in England[63] has been developed from related concepts of architectural geometry. Architectural form is reduced to geometric conditions and architectural space becomes pure space. Urban structure is seen as a mathematical relationship between different activities.

The *functionalist* view arose out of a reassessment of the major European industrial cities at the beginning of the twentieth century. Building on the work of Tony Garnier, Le Corbusier proposed such a view in which the functions of the city (living, working, leisure and transport) were identified as discrete systems both for analytical purposes and as criteria for future proposals.

The term *morphological* is intended to cover those approaches that concentrate upon classification and study of the form of cities. The morphology of the plan produces a classification of city plans in terms such as reticular, radial, linear, concentric and polycentric, and aims to establish underlying principles of formation. In the context of morphological approaches, network analysis takes as its point of departure the hypothesis that the city or its hinterland is structured by networks, and is then analysed through the observation of the elemental categories in different areas and the combination of categories.

The study of human geography emphasises the importance of topographic factors in the determination of its form. Cities may be classified as those sited on hillsides, river crossings, coastal sites and so on. Such analysis tends to be more descriptive than explanatory.

The *historical* approach stems from the study of classical cultural periods of urban history and is epitomised in the works of Lewis Mumford and Patrick Geddes among others.

Architecture is considered the main element in the construction of the city throughout history, and with it comes the sense of permanence, locus, individuality and memory.

The study of *perception* and interpretation of the environment attaches great importance to the attitude of the individual and to his or her relationship with the city and the surrounding world. It is based upon the preoccupations of psychologists and sociologists, though it has been pioneered as much by architects and urban designers, such as the Bauhaus teachers.

The city as an image, mainly developed by Kevin Lynch, is analysed through five main constituent elements – paths, edges, nodes, landmarks and districts – with the interrelationship between the elements.

The city as sequences refers to the type of study developed by Gordon Cullen. Based upon architecture and the spaces generated, the city is seen as a succession of sequences and a chain of different events.

The city as underrated architecture relates to a range of recent attitudes – from a total rejection of conscious design to a renewed interest in vernacular models – which share two underlying assumptions: first, that architecture is a particularly truthful record of its period and, second, that any previous period is better than today. It could be said that the new urbanism movement of the 1990s in the US is a reflection of this.[64] According to this view, the accumulation of past forms within the city is not only justified, but highly desirable, and as it manifests itself variously in picturesque and vernacular design, it regards the city as theatre.[65]

AN ALTERNATIVE DEFINITION OF URBAN DESIGN

An urban design plan can be seen as the amalgam of two sectors – 'the public realm and the private realm'. The public realm is concerned with public spaces formed by new and existing buildings, natural landscape, streets, plazas, pedestrian networks, movement systems, squares, arcades, colonnades, open spaces and parks, all at the level of the *quartier*, which form the urban morphology or physical shape of the urban design plan. The private realm is the design of individual buildings or groups of buildings. In urban design, visual and social success is seen as possible only if the development is within a public framework that has sufficient coherence and identity. This is the essential purpose of an urban design plan as opposed to urban design guidelines, which usually set down rules about detailed architectural design and the use of materials.

The public realm is, then, the three-dimensional skeletal structure of the city, but this does not necessarily imply that it is based entirely upon public-sector investment. Given a public realm plan as part of the urban design process, which is sufficiently strong and functional as well as visually memorable, and a system which is easy to navigate and enjoy, then the private realm of buildings created within this framework can have greater rather than less freedom of architectural expression. Without a strong public realm design, visual anarchy prevails

and the very fabric of the city is destroyed. A public realm plan must have flexibility of growth as well as change. In planning legislation, through land use control, zoning, building densities, plot ratios and traffic systems are catered for at one end of the spectrum and development control, including aesthetic guidance through design review or design guidelines, at the other end of the spectrum. There is still no real statutory provision for the urban design plan or the public realm plan in the US.

The hypothesis is that if the public realm is sufficiently well ordered and has strength in terms of image, memory and navigation, then this could eliminate the need for negative and repressive planning controls.

Using historical references, one of the components of an urban design plan might be the use of the colonnade throughout the *quartier*. In the early Renaissance, Filippo Brunelleschi's first building, Ospedale degli Innocenti, of 1419, embodied rational and systematic principles of design. As mentioned earlier, it provides an impressive unifying element across the public space of the piazza, and weather protection both in summer and winter. Given the climatic extremes of the US, particularly in the Midwest, such a system applied uniformly to individual buildings or groups of buildings in a downtown area would have a utilitarian function as well as supporting aesthetic unity. A contemporary example may be found in Peter Eisenman's design for the Wexner Center for the Visual Arts (1990) at Ohio State University in Columbus, which uses a combined colonnade/arcade/loggia to unite disparate pieces of architecture spanning over a century.

The colonnade is just one example of how an urban design plan might incorporate elements to unify the city. It is important in the context of another important aspect of the urban design plan. 'Serial vision', first identified by British theorist Gordon Cullen,[66] suggested that the perception of the town as a piece of moving scenery rarely enters the head of the man in the street, yet this is what the town is – a moving set. Cullen illustrated this in a remarkably evocative way, showing an uninterrupted sequence of views, which would unfold themselves like stills from a film.[67] In *Townscape*, Cullen notes: 'To walk from one end of the plan to another, at a uniform pace, will provide a series of revelations which are suggested in serial drawings, reading from left to right. Each arrow on the plan represents a drawing. The even progress of travel is illuminated by a series of sudden contrasts and so an impact is made on the eye, bringing the plan to life (like nudging a person who is going to sleep in church). My drawings bear no relation to the place itself; I chose it because it seemed an evocative plan. Note that the slightest deviation in alignment and quite small variations in projections or setbacks on plan have a disproportionally powerful effect in the third dimension'.[68] Thus, an agreed colonnade or other system applied in a city could provide an enhanced experience of sequential experiences for the pedestrian or even the driver of a motor car.

It can also be argued that public response to the environment is an essential part of the design process. Citizen participation and advocacy planning cannot work in isolation. Had computer-based data and analysis been available, Lynch's comparatively small statistical samples could have been greatly enlarged to test responses across a much wider cross-section of the population. The development of expert or intelligent systems would allow an evaluation of citizen response to the urban environment, which in turn could be linked to a variety of urban design proposals to be tested. There might be four control groups: the inhabitants of the city selected in random fashion, the visitors to the city, the professional designers (landscape architects, architects, planners, engineers and urban designers) and the city officials and elected politicians. Public response and testing using animated three-dimensional computer graphics of potentially infinite variety would allow public integration into the planning process.

NOTES

1. Gosling, D. and B. Maitland (1984) *Concepts of Urban Design*. New York: Academy Editions London and St. Martin's Press, p. 109. This chapter includes a number of extracts from *Concepts*, since the development of research for the basis of urban design theories had already been carried out.
2. Gallion, A. B and Eisner, S (1950) *The Urban Pattern*. New York: Van Nostrand Reinhold, p. 7.
3. Ibid., pp. 15–16, 20.
4. Sir Bannister Fletcher, *A History of Architecture on the Comparative Method*. London: Batsford, revised 1948.
5. Gallion and Eisner, op. cit., p. 81.
6. Howard, E. (1902) *Garden Cities of Tomorrow*. London. First edition, *Tomorrow*, London, 1898.
7. The idea of the superblock was to be developed in its ultimate form in Brasilia, the new capital city of Brazil, inaugurated in 1961, and planned by Lucio Costa. The *superquadra*, or superblock, reflected many of the ideas of Wright and Stein. The plan was based upon a national competition for the new capital, won by Costa in 1957. The intention was to build a 'social' city of mixed socioeconomic groups. Costa hoped that low-income workers would live in *superquadras* of the *plano-piloto* (central zone) in the same way that other *superquadras* would house higher-paid civil servants.
8. Gallion and Eisner, S, op. cit., pp. 144–46.
9. See Wright, F. L. (1932) *The Disappearing City*. New York: Publisher unknown. Also, R. Fishman (1977) *Urban Utopias of the Twentieth Century*. New York: Basic Books.
10. Wright, op. cit, cited by Fishman, op. cit., p. 125.
11. Wright, F. L. (1958) *The Living City*. New York: Publisher unknown, p. 119.
12. The Drop Communards of the 1960s were established in the western and southwestern states as intellectuals from different walks of life literally dropped out of conventional society to form closely integrated small communities committed to ecological issues and antiwar demonstrations. Legal squatting rights did not really exist in the US, but were present in Western Europe, particularly in the UK and the Netherlands.
13. Gosling and Maitland, op. cit., p. 37.
14. The term 'utopia' itself means both a place and a state of things, and it is often difficult to separate the two. Language and literature contain many references to this identification of the idealised society with the city, as in the New Jerusalem and the Heavenly City, and indeed the circumstances of the design method itself are often uncannily close. T. E. Lawrence described the established pattern for the lives of social reformers and prophets of the Middle East: 'Their birth set them in crowded places. An unintelligible passionate yearning drove them out into the desert. There they lived a greater or lesser time in meditation or physical abandonment and thence they returned with their imagined message articulate, to preach it to their old and now doubting associates'. T. E. Lawrence (1964) *The Seven Pillars of Wisdom*. Harmondsworth: Penguin Books, p. 37.
Campanella, Bacon, Fourier, Howard, Le Corbusier and Wright all devised their utopian models during periods of either enforced or voluntary obscurity and isolation. Moreover, the relationship between the ideal society and its ideal city has not been a simple one of programme and its delineation. As Fishman has pointed out, the idea of the planner may precede even a statement of the problem let alone the formulation of the plan, as in the case of Wright's early assertion that 'The creative artist . . . must dominate and transform this greatest of machines, the city, and give it a SOUL' (Fishman, op. cit., p. 109).
15. Garreau, J. (1991) *Edge City: Life on the New Frontier*. New York: Doubleday.
16. There were other historical precedents for the construction of freeways. The autobahn system in Germany was built under the Nazi regime during the 1930s for military strategic purposes.
17. Gosling and Maitland, op. cit., p. 7.
18. Hoppenfeld, M. (1961) 'The role of design in city planning', *AIA Journal,* vol. XXXV, no. 5 (May), pp. 40–44.
19. Ibid., p. 43.
20. Ibid., p. 44.
21. Gosling and Maitland, op. cit., p. 7.
22. Banham, R. (1976) *Megastructure: Urban Futures of the Recent Past*. London: Thames and Hudson, p. 130.
23. And later the development of further linguistic theories such as postmodernism and deconstruction.
24. Broadbent, G., R. Bunt and C. Jencks (eds) (1980) *Signs, Symbols and Architecture*. New York: John Wiley.
25. *Domus* (1975), vol 543, Feb, pp. 1–7. Italy.
26. Kevin Lynch was also to express this sentiment during his preparation of *The Image of the City*. Lynch, Kevin (1960) *The Image of the City*. Cambridge, MA: The Technology Press and Harvard University Press.
27. Calhoun, J. B. and A. H. Esser (eds) (1971) 'Space and the strategy of life', in *Behavior and Environment*. New York: Plenum Press.
28. Arnheim, R. (1956) *Art and Visual Perception: A Psychology of the Creative Eye*. London: Faber and Faber, p. viii.
29. Katz, D. and R. Tyson (trans.) (1951) *Gestalt Psychology*. London: Methuen & Co., pp. 24–29.
30. Wulf, F. (1922) '*Uber die Veränderung von Verstellungen (Gedächtnis und Gestalt)*', in Ellis, W. D. (1938) *A Source of Gestalt Psychology*. London: Routledge & Kegan Paul, p. 148.
31. Ahmed, I. and M. Bucholz (eds) (1991) *The Cornell Journal of Architecture,* no. 4, pp. 178–205.
32. Piaget, J. and B. Inhelder (1956) *The Child's Conception of Space*. London: Publisher unknown.
33. Giedion, S. (1959) *Space, Time and Architecture: the Growth of a New Tradition*. Cambridge, MA: Harvard University Press. First edition, 1941.
34. Ibid., p. 753.
35. Lazzaro, G. di San and S. Hood (trans.) (1957) *Klee*. London: Thames and Hudson, p. 107.
36. Moholy-Nagy, L. (1956) *Vision in Motion*. Chicago, IL: Paul Theobald.
37. This was a statement by Ludwig Mies van der Rohe and is quoted from Siegfried Giedion (1954) *Walter Gropius*. New York: Reinhold Publishing Corporation.
38. The monumental and most definitive work on the Bauhaus is Hans Wingler (1978) *The Bauhaus – Weimar, Dessau, Berlin, Chicago*. Cambridge, MA: MIT Press. This was originally published in German in 1962 under the name *Das Bauhaus* (Cologne, Germany: Verlag Gebr. Rasch and Co., Bramsche and M. Dumont Schauberg). The MIT Press version was translated by Wolfgang Jabs and Basil Gilbert, and edited by Joseph Stein.
39. Lynch, Kevin (1960) *The Image of the City*. Cambridge, MA: The Technology Press and Harvard University Press, p. v.

40. On 20 July1933 Mies van der Rohe sent this chilling note to the Gestapo in Berlin at the office of the State Secret Police:

> Dear Sir, I beg to inform you that the faculty of the Bauhaus at a meeting yesterday saw itself compelled, in view of economic difficulties which have arisen from the shutdown of the Institute, to dissolve the Bauhaus Berlin.

This was followed by a second letter (21 July 1933) from the State Secret Police to Mies van der Rohe, stating:

> 'In agreement with the Prussian Minister for Science, Art and Education, the reopening of the Bauhaus Berlin is made dependent upon the removal of some objections. Ludwig Hilbersheimer and Vassily Kandinsky are no longer permitted to teach . . . Their places have been taken by individuals who guarantee to support the principles of National Socialist ideology'. (Wingler, op. cit., pp. 188–89).

The extremists in the National Socialist Party hated the Bauhaus for its liberal attitudes and deemed it erroneously a nest of Bolshevist thought. The conflagration of the Reichstag building on 28 February 1933 was no coincidence. Though Walter Gropius and others had sought refuge in England in 1933, where they worked with the British modern movement architects such as Maxwell Fry, inevitably many of them left the UK to settle in the US, where there was greater artistic freedom and more opportunities. Gropius became professor of architecture at Harvard University, as did Serge Chermayeff some years later. Mies van der Rohe directed the school of architecture at the IIT in Chicago and was joined by Hilbersheimer as professor of city planning. Laszlo Moholy-Nagy established the Institute of Design in Chicago and Gyorgy Kepes became professor of visual design at the MIT. Josef Albers ultimately took up a position at Yale University and Eric Mendelsohn (not a member of the Bauhaus) settled in California. At the same time there were, of course, many artists, writers and musicians from Germany and Hungary, like the composer Béla Bartók, who fled to the US, though his genius, unlike that of the architects, was never fully recognised there until just before his death in 1945.

41. Wingler, op. cit., p. 44.

42. For full biographies see Wingler, op. cit., pp. 237–76, also pp. 422, 424, 496 and 533.

43. A gentler version of both Le Corbusier's and Hilbersheimer's visions may be found in built form in Brasilia, the new capital of Brazil (see note 7). Based upon the notions of both Le Corbusier and Hilbersheimer, with superblocks for the apartment buildings and governmental buildings designed by Oscar Neimeyer, it was built rapidly and had already exceeded its target population of 500,000 for the *plano-piloto* within ten years. Its metropolitan area now has a population greater than two million. The purity and clarity of the initial plan have been degraded to an extent; although initially there was vociferous opposition and unpopularity among the families of civil servants, it is now a popular city in which to live. This is partly due to the mature landscaping and partly to do with a more human scale of the superblocks, as opposed to Hilbersheimer's more gargantuan scale.

44. In 1997 there were moves to build the first new academic building on the campus not in accordance with the 'Mies Aesthetic'. A limited competition was held among some of the most distinguished designers of both the postmodernist and deconstructivist movements. Whether such a decision by the university administrators was wise is, to say the least, debatable.

45. Hinks, R. (1955) 'Peep show and the roving eye', *The Architectural Review*, vol. 118, no.263 (August).

46. See *Japan Architect* (February 1979).

47. Kepes, G. (1956) *The New Landscape*. Chicago, IL: Paul Theobald and Co.

48. Vernez-Moudon, A. (1992) 'A catholic approach to what urban designers should know', *Journal of Planning Literature*, vol. 6, no. 4 (May), pp. 331–49.

49. Ibid., p. 334.

50. Ibid.

51. One of the authors of this present work edited a special issue of *Architectural Design* magazine entitled 'Urbanism' (*AD* profile 51, *Architectural Design*, vol. 54. (1984), pp. 4–88.) The title was chosen by the former editor, Andreas Papadakis. In reality the analysis of projects selected was concerned with urban design, not the much broader realm of urbanism as it relates to city planning.

52. Kohlsdorf, M. E. (1996) *A Apreensão da Forma da Cidade*. Brasilia, Brazil: Editora Universidade de Brasilia. Her bibliographic references draw upon the work of many pioneer theorists in the US, including Appleyard, Bacon, Halprin, Kepes, Mumford and Venturi. Vicente del Rio, professor of urban design at the Federal University of Rio de Janeiro is another Brazilian author using the term *desenho urbano* in his definitive works.

53. Osborne, H. (1970) *Oxford Companion of Art*. Oxford: Clarendon Press, p. 473.

54. Kohlsdorf, M. E. (1976) *Sequencias espaciais urbanas*, Monograph (February).

55. Keifer, G. (1971) 'Wahrnehmungst Theorie', *Kommunikation und Morphologie*.

56. Such analogies were used in Louis Kahn's plan for Philadelphia (1952–53), which will be discussed in the following chapter.

57. Cenicacelaya Marijuan, J. (1978) 'Towns in expansion: historicist approach or perceptual approach?', MA Dissertation in Urban Design (unpublished), Oxford Polytechnic (now Oxford Brookes University), England. Marijuan, originally from Spain, now teaches in the US.

58. This study was, of course, written over a decade before the collapse of the Soviet Union in Russia. Indeed, the totalitarian Stalinist government and its successors could hardly be regarded as following the socialist ideals of Marx, Engels, Trotsky or even Lenin. Major communist societies still exist, the most significant of which is the People's Republic of China, but even here there are evident moves towards a capitalist society as the vast nation moves towards a form of market economy. A more democratic form of socialism may be seen in recently elected governments in Western Europe, such as the Labour Party victory in the UK in 1997, however this party now espouses a very diluted form of the Welfare State in contrast to the post-Second World War Labour government in 1945.

59. Marx, K. and D. Fernbach (eds) (1978) *The Revolution of 1848: Political Writings, Volume 1*. Harmondsworth: Penguin Books, p. 87. It is ironic, however, that this proposition is exactly what has been achieved in a democratic capitalist society. A view of any major American metropolis, such as the cities of Cincinnati, Cleveland or Columbus in Ohio, shows that the lateral spread of these cities, commencing in the 1950s, reveals this curious mixture of widening, radial and alternating bands of industry and residential areas in a juxtaposition with farmland, making this a major manufacturing/agricultural system.

60. Frampton, K. (1968) 'Notes on soviet urbanism, 1917–1932', *Architects' Year Book XII*. London: Elek Books, pp. 238–52.

61. Ibid., p. 252.

62. Marijuan, op. cit.

63. The Centre for Land Use and Built Form was established by Sir Leslie Martin and Professor Lionel March at Cambridge University in the late 1960s.

64. See Katz, P. (1994) *The New Urbanism: Toward an Architecture of Community*. New York: McGraw-Hill.

65. As in Robert Venturi's seminal study: Venturi, R., D. Scott-Brown and S. Izenour (1972) *Learning from Las Vegas*. Cambridge, MA: MIT/Harvard University Press.

66. Cullen, G. (1961) *Townscape*. London: Architectural Press, p. 17.

67. See Gosling, D. (1996) *Gordon Cullen: Visions of Urban Design*. London: Academy Editions, p. 24.

68. Cullen, op. cit., p. 17.

Chapter Two

1950–1960

THE FIRST DECADE

After the Second World War, a revolutionary new culture of popular and classical music, painting, sculpture, literature, industrial and furniture design, as well as architecture, swept across the US and then the rest of the world. Yet urban design, together with the linguistic theory of postmodernism, did not follow until almost a decade later. This chapter looks at the background to the emergence of urban design.

THE NEW CULTURAL BACKGROUND

One of classical music's most outstanding composers in the 1940s was Aaron Copeland. In recording notes in 1960, William Flanagan[1] says Copeland's celebrated suite for the Martha Graham ballet, 'Appalachian Spring', is one of the finest lyrical compositions of the twentieth century. Copeland's collaboration with Martha Graham, the renowned American dancer and choreographer, was the result of a commission by Elizabeth Sprague Coolidge. The premiere of this ballet, a pioneer celebration of spring,[2] was performed in October 1944. In 1945 it won the Pulitzer Prize for Music and the New York Music Critics' Circle Award. Flanagan notes that it was 'an achievement in the pan-diatonic tonal techniques which were so much a part of American Composition during the 1940s'.[3]

Copeland's next major commission, 'The Tender Land' opera in the 1950s, was the result of a Rodgers and Hammerstein commission. The New York City Opera Company premiered it on 1 April 1954. Like 'Appalachian Spring' it centred upon a lower-middle-class farm in the Midwest, though the former composition was specifically based on the Appalachian Mountains in Pennsylvania.

Chapter 1 noted the importance of European influences in the development of the modern movement of architecture in the US. While this was due to the fleeing from persecution in Europe of many artists, Copeland, paradoxically, born in 1900, went to France in 1920 to seek out the influence of European, primarily French, composers, and did not return to the US until 1924.[4]

In contrast with the harmonic compositions of Copeland during this period were the revolutionary atonal compositions of Henry Cowell and John Cage, using a 'prepared piano', one with non-musical objects attached to or between strings. The effect, in many of Cage's works (such as his sonatas and interludes), is not dissimilar to Indonesian gamelan music. Cage wrote many aleatory pieces, that is, works in which an element of chance is involved. But such an approach was quite different from contemporary or progressive improvisational jazz of the period. In his 'Theater Piece', the performers randomly selected words from a dictionary and developed different ways of using words and/or music.

John Cage was born in Los Angeles in 1912 and studied music, art and architecture in Paris, Berlin and Madrid from 1930 onwards. He returned to California and studied with Weiss, Cowell and Schoenberg. In 1951 he wrote a concerto for prepared piano and orchestra, followed in 1954 by '34'46,776' for a prepared piano and, in 1957, 'Winter Music' for one to twenty pianists. 'Fontana Mix', in 1958, was a score for the production of one or more prerecorded tape tracks to be performed in any way.

Henry Cowell, a contemporary of Cage, studied at the University of California and was prolific in his compositional output until his death in 1965. His works included 'Symphony no. 12' (1955–56), and a septet for five wordless voices, clarinet and keyboard, as well as antiphony for a divided orchestra in 1958.

It is interesting to note that Cowell's use of the tone-cluster, which he invented, impressed the Hungarian composer Béla Bartók so much that he sought permission from Cowell to use it himself.

A collaborator was Louis Theremin, who had also created an eponymous instrument that produced the high-pitched warbling sounds heard on the Beach Boys' recordings, such as 'Good Vibrations', in the 1960s. The use of the 'Theremin' has reappeared at the beginning of the twenty-first century and was heard at a recital of 'A Celebration of the Theremin' in the Electronic Evolutions series at the Lincoln Center Festival 2000 in New York. Performed by Lydia Kavina, a distant relative of Theremin, with Stephen Gosling as pianist, the performance of the Ensemble Sospeso was reviewed by Allan Kozinn of the *New York Times* in July 2000. Though Robert Moog's keyboard-based synthesizer was to replace it in electronic music in the 1960s, the Theremin was among the first electronic instruments.

Another major composer during this period was George Crumb, who presented an entirely new way of handling sonority and timbre, as demonstrated in 'Variazioni for Orchestra'

Popular music in the twentieth-century US was ba something that was also uniquely American. Arising African-American culture, jazz was to have a great in popular culture to the present day. Early jazz evolved in Louisiana in the city of New Orleans, and somewhat later in Chicago and Kansas City. Most jazz was based upon improvised, syncopated music performed mainly by African-American musicians. Its influence has been global throughout the twentieth century and led in turn to the evolution of rock 'n' roll. In the 1920s the pianist Meade Lux Lewis created a new type of music of which 'Honky Tonk Train Blues' was his finest work (written and performed by him between 1939 and 1954). Born in 1905 in Louisville, Kentucky, Lewis was part of a triumvirate of Boogie-musicians with Albert Ammons and Pete Johnson.[5]

However, the late 1940s saw the emergence of a new, revolutionary type of jazz, based in New York City. The New Orleans-based music was superseded by a completely new sound – 'traditional jazz'.

Charlie Parker, another African-American musician, was born in Kansas City in 1920. Between 1944 and 1948 he created what was later to become known as 'bebop'. Atonal and highly improvisational in style, it transformed the world of jazz. Parker, a baritone saxophone player, joined forces with the trumpeter Miles Davis and drummer Max Roach for a highly original recording.[6] In 1949 and 1950 Miles Davis was joined by Gerry Mulligan and Lee Konitz, respectively. Other musicians in the 1950 New York City recording[7] included trombonists Kai Winding and JJ Johnson, as well as pianist John Lewis. In 1951, four African-American ex-members of the Dizzy Gillespie band – John Lewis (who took advanced studies at the Manhattan School of Music), along with vibraphonist Milt Jackson, bassist Percy Heath and drummer Connie Kay – formed the Modern Jazz Quartet, a true chamber music group. Jackson was the first to adapt bebop to the electric vibraharp and vibraphone and ushered in electronic music.[8]

Around the same time, a white musicians' chamber quartet including Gerry Mulligan, Bob Brookmeyer (trombonist), Red Mitchell (bassist) and Frank Isola (drums), took Afro-American bebop a step further.[9] In 1957, Mulligan experimented with a new group including the revolutionary African-American pianist and composer Thelonius Monk, bassist Wilbur Ware and drummer Shadow Wilson,[10] with compositions by both Monk and Mulligan. In January 2001, legendary filmmaker Ken Burns produced a ten-part PBS series on jazz, reviewing this particular music as a uniquely American art form.

The powerful influence of rhythm and blues experienced rising popularity in the 1950s, and was to develop into rock 'n' roll. Rhythm and blues, which was mostly instrumental, had its roots in remote rural areas such as Appalachia. Among the seminal, short compositions were the performances of Paul Williams ('The Hucklebuck'), Milton Buckner ('Lights Out') and Jay McNeeley ('The Deacon's Hop'), all recorded for the Savoy Record Company of Newark, New Jersey. That this clearly influenced the music of Elvis Presley in the 1950s was reflected in notable films about teenage disaffection, such as *The Blackboard Jungle* in 1955, in which Glenn Ford portrayed a schoolteacher in an innercity New York neighbourhood. The film was followed in 1956 by *Rock Around the Clock*, a mediocre film directed by Sam Katzman in which Bill Haley led a rock

'n' roll band. The impact on a new generation of teenagers was electric. During the latter part of the 1950s, musicians like Little Richard, Fats Domino and Chuck Berry shot to stardom.

But the real revolution in popular music was to come in 1960 when four British musicians – Paul McCartney, John Lennon, George Harrison and Ringo Starr – formed The Beatles. They acknowledged their influences as being primarily based in African-American rock 'n' roll music, especially that of Chuck Berry. Previously, there had been a separation of white and African-American musicians, but the immense popularity of The Beatles' highly original compositions during the following decade was to change the landscape of popular music across the world. The group's first tour of the US in 1964, with a totally new form of music based upon American black, not white, music was to be a landmark in cultural history.

The US also introduced revolutionary ideas in fine art. During the 1920s and 1930s, modern art was Eurocentric, based mainly in France.[11] Apart from the leading immigrant artists such as Moholy-Nagy, Gyorgy Kepes and Josef Albers from the Bauhaus,[12] the American sculptor Alexander Calder introduced kinetics and invented the mobile, for example the 'yellow bottle mobile' (1945) where currents of air constantly moved coloured disks interlinked with black metal struts.[13] Two leading sculptors in the abstract expressionist movement were Seymour Lipton and David Smith. Lipton (born in 1903), began with figurative work in wood but became an abstract artist in 1950 when he began using sheet metal. Smith's powerful works were welded metal sculpture.[14] Naum Gabo, a Russian born in 1890, emigrated from Russia in 1922, spending some years in Germany and England before leaving for the US in 1946. Here he started to apply the principles of pre-Stalinist Russian constructivism, using aluminium, bronze, precious metal wire and transparent materials such as Perspex. A good example is his 'Translucent Variation on a Spheric Theme' (1951).[15]

Abstract expressionism in painting was developed in New York in the 1940s. Unconcerned with the painting of illusions, it aimed to transmit inner emotion[16] and was influenced to some extent by surrealistic painters such as Max Ernst and Marcel Duchamp. Another influence may have been the philosophy of Zen Buddhism, as exemplified in a 1952 painting by Franz Kline showing a dramatic monochromatic tension between black and white strokes. One of the most notable American abstract expressionists was Jackson Pollock, whose 1952 painting 'Convergence' was perhaps his finest work.[17] Willem de Koonig came from Holland in 1926 and entered the movement in 1948. 'Woman and Bicycle', painted between 1952 and 1953, is one of his better known works. Clifford Still taught in California and helped to develop the Pacific (or West Coast) school.

It was towards the end of the 1950s that a figurative movement known as pop art came to the fore. Its leading exponents were Robert Rauschenberg, Jasper Johns, Larry Rivers, Roy Lichtenstein and, especially, Andy Warhol.[18] Jasper Johns' 1959 painting 'Numbers in Color' is a good example of this movement.[19] In contrast, in the same year German artist Josef Albers, teaching at Yale University, explored the effects of colour and line on the canvas in such works as his 1959 'Homage to the Square: Apparition'.[20]

One of the earliest examples of pop art is Richard Hamilton's 1956 painting 'Just What Is It That Makes Today's Homes So Different?'. This astonishing work, which might be considered as deliberately erotic, depicts a male bodybuilder, shielding his bikini-clad thighs with a tennis racket cover with the logo 'Pop', and a blonde bikini-clad woman, with a television in the background and a reel-to-reel tape recorder in the foreground. It is a montage of contemporary domestic appliances, comic strips, pinups, canned food and advertising, all of which were to become hallmarks of the modern movement. Hamilton was really a commercial artist, and his paintings, including the 1957 'Homage à Chrysler Corp.', employed techniques of advertising art. Photographic techniques were also used by the artist Peter Blake, combining trompe l'oeil photographs with printed matter in a three-dimensional precursor of the later art of photo-realism.[21]

By the end of the 1950s, Andy Warhol was already a successful commercial artist. When he entered the world of fine art at the end of the decade he used comic strips such as 'Dick Tracy' as the subject for his initial paintings.[22] His supermarket grocery models such as Campbell's Soup and Coca-Cola, became iconic images of the time, mechanically repeated through silk-screen printing techniques, implying the boredom of a society based upon mass production. Warhol was even more controversial as a filmmaker, demonstrated in his later 1965 work *The Kiss*, and equally so in his paintings including the terrifying 'The Electric Chair' (1964).

In the mid-1950s Jasper Johns also took images and objects from the supermarket, but the assembly of the images set them apart from the photo-realism of other pop artists. Johns also took stereotypes such as the American flag, targets and beer cans, and translated them on canvas or bronze. Unlike other pop artists of the time, Johns questioned the processes and sources of art.[23]

Of all these innovative artists, perhaps Roy Lichtenstein was most unique. Lichtenstein, who died in October 1997, was described in an obituary in *The New Yorker* as an artist with 'the quiet undercurrent of emotion, the genuine charm of ingeniousness and a lack of competitive excitement, a kind of comic book-Zen detachment from the usual overheated art world fretfulness'.[24] He converted modern screen-printing techniques into high art, using original comics, the Ben Day dots, a technique used in the printing of American comics, which were invisible in screen-printing. Lichtenstein examined romance and war comics for his inspiration and above all 'remained true to the inheritance of modernism'.

In the world of literature, America also introduced important writers during the 1950s. Among the more revolutionary were the works of playwright Samuel Beckett and poet Alan Ginsburg, but it was author Jack Kerouac who had the greatest impact with his novel *On the Road*[25] – the bible of the 'beat generation' of West Coast authors and poets that was to influence the way in which sequential experiences of American urban scenery could be viewed. Many sections of the novel were published in erudite literary magazines of the time, such as *The Paris Review*, *New World Writing* and *New Directions*.

On the Road was a required reading text in Christopher Tunnard's city planning programme at Yale University. The book describes the odyssey from New York to San Francisco of two young men refusing to conform to a society they could not accept. Towards the end of the first part of the journey, the description of the approach to San Francisco is lyrical: 'It seemed like a matter of minutes when we began rolling in the foothills before Oakland and suddenly reached a height and saw stretched out ahead of us the fabulous white city of San Francisco on her eleven mystic hills with the blue Pacific and its advancing wall of potato-patch fog beyond, and smoke and goldenness in the late afternoon of time'.[26]

In the cinema, the writings of Kerouac could be paralleled by the works of the actors James Dean and Marlon Brando. James Dean died a tragic death in September 1955 shortly after the release of *Rebel Without a Cause*, his second film, and became the icon of an angst-ridden young generation. The story was less relevant than the imagery, implying emotional hope. Dean himself had a pessimistic vision of the world both on-stage and off, and led a lonely life. *Rebel Without a Cause*, directed by Nicholas Ray, was a masterpiece of a new type of acting, although his first film, *East of Eden*, directed by Elia Kazan and also released in 1955, and his last film, *Giant*, released in 1956, were also notable.[27]

Marlon Brando was to have a much longer career. His revolutionary acting technique was based upon the methods of the Russian drama theorist Constantine Stanislavsky who had established 'The First Studio' in Moscow in 1912. Referred to as 'method acting' it produced a new realism in the narrative cinema. Stanislavsky's system was elaborate, involving study of the psychology of character, and was paralleled by the growth of realism in the plays of Anton Chekhov and Maxim Gorky. Prior to 1945, Hollywood had ignored Stanislavsky's techniques, but in 1947 Elia Kazan founded the Actor's Studio in New York, an advanced study centre for experienced actors, stressing the techniques of improvisation. After a brief period with the Actors Studio, Marlon Brando performed as the brutal Stanley Kowalski in Elia Kazan's 1951 film of Tennessee Williams' play *A Streetcar Named Desire*. The rebellious nature of Brando's character was reflected in his role as a biker in *Wild One* (1953) and a dockworker in *On the Waterfront* (1956).[28]

The director Alfred Hitchcock, born in England, spent most of his career in the US and became one of Hollywood's most famous innovators. *Rear Window* placed James Stewart, as a homespun philosophic photographer, in an unusually violent urban context, with nearly all the action taking place in a single room. Other notable Hitchcock films were *Dial M for Murder* (1954) and *Vertigo* (1958), but it was *Psycho*, filmed at the end of the decade and released in 1960, which is his most famous work. Hitchcock's direction included innovative musical scores and the elimination of one of the main characters, played by Janet Leigh, midway through the film in what was one of the most shattering murder scenes ever to appear on film.[29]

While the links between the writings of the poets and novelists of San Francisco could be seen to parallel an equally radical movement in the cinema, other more astonishing novels appeared around the same time, reflecting a major change in cultural direction. Of these, the novels of the African-American writer James Baldwin were notable: *Giovanni's Room* was one of the first literary works of the twentieth century to confront homosexual and bisexual issues as well as racism.[30] In the urban setting of Paris, it describes the involvement of a young American expatriate with both a female lover and a male lover. Better known perhaps is *Another Country*.[31] Although Baldwin spent ten years in self-imposed exile in Europe, *Another Country* is set in New York, and combined with references to the revolution in contemporary American jazz. It is a tumultuous and violent story that demolishes the barriers of sex, colour and contemporary conventions and identifies Greenwich Village as the epicentre of this cultural shift.

Two other novels, even more radical than those of Baldwin, were published at this time. *Last Exit to Brooklyn*[32] by less well-known author Hubert Selby Junior, describes the violent behaviour of union strikers in the Brooklyn dockyards. It presents social horrors out of reformist zeal, not out of a desire to titillate or corrupt. The book was constructed as a series of linked short stories with an emphasis on sexual inversion, while maintaining a remarkable balance between clinical curiosity and disgust at human degradation. The story of 'Tralala' ends with a horrifying image summarising not just the depravity of the lawless streets on Brooklyn, but the evil of the world in the description of a multiple rape. It is within that description of social chaos that the novel provides a new view of the physical urban setting of a slum. *Naked Lunch*, by William Burroughs, has a quite different focus, a surreal and horrifying story described by Burroughs as a self-confessed drug addict. It was considered by many distinguished literary figures of the time as the major American novel of the decade. Burroughs' hallucinatory visions, described in *The British Journal of Addiction*,[33] deal with the use of opium derivatives such as morphine and heroin within the context of violent homosexual behaviour, and a vivid description of urban settings: 'Chicago: invisible hierarchy of decorticated wops, smell of atrophied gangsters, earthbound ghost hits you at North and Halstead, Cicero and Lincoln Park, panhandler of dreams, past invading present, rancid magic of slot machines . . . into the Interior: a vast subdivision, antennae of television to the meaningless sky. In life proof houses they hover over the young, sop up a little of what they shut out. Only the young bring anything in and they are not young very long. (Through the bars of East St. Louis lies the dead frontier, the river boat days, Illinois and Missouri, miasma of mound building peoples, groveling worship of the Food Source, cruel and ugly festivals . . .)'[34]

In the academic world, the architectural historian Lewis Mumford took *The Culture of Cities*, his renowned 1930s work, as the base for *The City in History*,[35] published in 1961. Mumford, like Kevin Lynch, used his preparation of the text for his postgraduate courses held at MIT during the late 1950s. In tracing the evolution of cities from the burial tombs of Palaeolithic man, he turned his attention during this decade to the impending problems of the new American metropolis, mentioning the Radburn Plan as the significant twentieth-century departure in city planning, described in Clarence Stein's *New Towns for America*. He suggested that the motor car had done more than just remove the limits of suburban sprawl and destroy pedestrian scale; it doubled the number of cars needed in each family and turned the suburban woman (before the advent of two-income families) into a full-time chauffeur. It was also responsible for the dismantling of the electric rail transport system. He says: 'Far from supplementing public rail transportation, the private motor car became largely a clumsy substitute for it'.[36] And goes on: 'Whilst the suburb served only a favored minority, it neither spoiled the countryside nor threatened the city. But now that the drift to the outer ring has become a mass movement, it tends to destroy the value of both environments without producing anything but a dreary substitute for it . . . By allowing mass transportation to deteriorate and by building expressways out of the city and parking garages within, in order to encourage the maximum use of the private car, our highway engineers and city planners have helped to destroy the living tissue of the city and to limit the possibilities of creating a larger urban organism on a regional scale'.[37]

In his penultimate chapter, 'The Myth of Megalopolis', Mumford claims that 'though the great city is the best organ of memory man has yet created, it is also – until it becomes too cluttered and disorganized – the best agent for discrimination and evaluation, not merely because it spreads out so many goods for choosing, but because it likewise creates minds of large range capable of coping with them'.[38] Though Mumford lived long enough to see the amazing growth of the use of personal computers within a new age of information technology, at the time he acted as a prophet, since in the 1950s computers existed only in universities as cumbersome mainframe systems.

In industrial design, the 1950s heralded innovations not born in Europe, as in the Mies van der Rohe Barcelona Chair (1929) or Marcel Breuer's tubular stainless steel and leather club chair (1925), but, later, in works by American architects and urban designers such as Charles and Ray Eames and George Nelson.[39] Charles Eames and his wife, Ray, were a brilliantly creative couple. Their home in California was an innovative example of industrial architecture. Two distinct buildings of residence and studio were, perhaps, a more elegant, lighthearted version of Mies van der Rohe's Chicago aesthetic. Constructed with an exposed light steel frame, comprising standard sections from a manufacturer's catalogue, infillings were plate glass, wire glass, asbestos, plywood and plaster in various colours, unlike the monochromatic architecture of van der Rohe. The pair were also toy designers and advanced filmmakers using new animation techniques.

Charles Eames' most famous design was his lounge chair and matching ottoman (1955–56). The Rizzoli catalogue states that as 'a status symbol it ranks with the chair of Mies van der Rohe for the Barcelona Pavilion and Le Corbusier's Chaise Longue'. It is one of the most luxurious and comfortable of all modern chairs. It has a five pronged base of black aluminium with a moulded rosewood plywood hard-finished shell, hand-finished in beeswax. The leather upholstery was in black or brown. It represented a notable contribution in a mid-century trend away from the austere geometrical forms of modern design.[40]

Isamu Noguchi, a Japanese American interned during the First World War, began to produce furniture designs in 1944. One of his most famous designs, his 1954 table made from a

Charles Eames' house, Santa Barbara, California.

black lacquered cast-iron base, mirror-polished and chrome-plated steel wire supports in the form of a helix and a marine plywood top covered in high-pressure plastic laminate, was put into production by Knoll Associates that year.[41]

George Nelson, another American furniture designer, was also editor of the influential *The Architectural Forum* magazine. From 1945 until 1962 he was design director of Hermann Miller Inc. The double bed he designed for that company in 1952 was part of a residential storage system of cabinets mounted on aluminium poles. It is suggested by Palazzeti[42] that its graceful appearance was derived from Scandinavian design. The bed remained in production until the 1960s.

Italian-born sculptor Harry Bertoia was a faculty member of the Cranbrook Academy in Michigan when Charles Eames was the head of the department of Experimental Design. Bertoia's chair and armchair, designed in 1952, emulated Eames' 1951 design and yet was distinct in its use of polished, welded steel wire and chrome plate, with a foam cushion covered in fabric or leather.[43]

The architect Eero Saarinen, famed for his airport terminal designs in Washington, DC and New York, as well as the Yale Ice Hockey arena, was another follower of this trend. Using hyperbolic parabaloid designs, he produced a classical pedestal

table in 1956[44] with base and stem of cast aluminium, lacquered in black or white, and a top made from white Calacatta marble.

Motor car design was also revolutionised during the decade. Ford, General Motors and particularly the Chrysler Corporation produced exuberant designs with gigantic tail fins. Yet in 1953, the industrial designer Raymond Loewy produced a very elegant coupé (Champion and Commander) for Studebaker. Sadly, it was not popular. It had little chrome plating and was low slung, but remains to this day one of the finest motor car designs, matched only by Ferrari and Maserati in Italy and Porsche of Germany.

THE RISE OF USONIAN ARCHITECTURE

In architecture, however, revolutionary ideas had evolved throughout the twentieth century. The leading figure was Frank Lloyd Wright. Whereas Wright had built his iconic masterpieces such as Falling Water in Bear Run, Pennsylvania, between 1935 and 1938 for the Kaufmann family having previously produced his manifesto for Broadacre City, his real contribution to urban design came relatively late in his career. Based upon the term 'usonia' (United States of North America with an 'I' inserted to

Studebaker motor car design (1953), Raymond Loewy.

Falling Water, Bear Run, Pennsylvania (1938),
Frank Lloyd Wright.

make the word euphonious), attributed to Samuel Butler, this concept was, according to Storrer,[45] 'an ideal to Wright; affordable, beautiful housing for a democratic America ... The Usonian concept was spatial "the space to be lived in" not structural. Spatially, the masonry core was important. This work space – kitchen, laundry, utilities and the like – places the housewife at the heart of domestic activities'. Yet the space allocated to these activities was minuscule. In this, Wright misjudged future American society. He did not imagine, for example, a situation where both partners in a marriage would work and that far from merely cooking breakfast, eating out in restaurants or using caterers as he implied, the family would make the kitchen the central focus of its activities. Though the usonian houses were said to begin with the Jacob residence in Madison, Wisconsin, in 1936, the majority were built in the 1950s, with the cantilever based on an L-plan design.[46]

Wright also used natural clerestory lighting during the usonian era. The private side of the house was angled to take advantage of the sun and the view, but used major roof overhangs to shield interior spaces from the heat and light of direct sunlight. In roof types he used a mixture of flat roofs, butterfly roofs, hipped roofs and end-gabled roofs, often applied to a T-plan. His extensive use of flat roofs, particularly in the Midwest

where there are great extremes of climate in summer and winter, was to prove disastrous.

The 1951 Benjamin Adelman Residence in Phoenix, Arizona, was an early example of the usonian 'automatic' house, using concrete blocks and a waffle-iron concrete ceiling. However, Storrer suggests that the Peiper residence, built in California in 1952, is actually the first constructed example of Wright's ideal of self-help, self-build construction.[47]

Arthur Peiper, a Taliesin West student whose wife made moulds for 7.5-centimetre (3-inch) thick concrete blocks, poured the concrete and knitted together the blocks with reinforcing steel rods and grouting. The use of such reinforced, prefabricated concrete techniques during this period was unique.

Other examples of usonian houses of the time include the Gerald B. Tonkens residence built in 1954 in Amberley Village, Ohio.[48] The plan is Type 'G' of seven usonian automatic designs dating from 1936 and based on an L-shaped plan, utilising reinforced concrete block construction and a reinforced concrete coffered ceiling and roof. Also constructed in Ohio in 1954 is the Cedric Boulter Residence in Cincinnati; steel-reinforced concrete block construction and Douglas fir were used for the structural system, and the design also incorporated the use of plate glass.[49]

Boulter House, Cincinnati, Ohio (1954),
Frank Lloyd Wright.

Although at the dawn of the 1950s it was generally considered that the battle of stylistic revivals had been won in favour of modernism, there was still confusion in seeking a human as well as a scientific ideal.[50] In the 1980s the postmodern movement was to raise similar questions. According to J. M. Richards, editor of *The Architectural Review*: 'The time, in fact, is already coming when the functional style will have become a formalism of its own, with a brutalizing effect on the art of architecture because the organism will have become fossilized before being given a chance to mature'.[51]

Richards identifies key stylistic approaches away from pure functionalism, such as in Pietro Belluschi's office building in Portland, Oregon, in 1948, calling it 'diagrammatic', in the sense that a new type of architecture was to be found as a result of mechanisation, including air-conditioning. This mechanisation takes the building to its logical conclusion, and the building becomes *purely* diagrammatic as a framework for art, rather than a means of expression in its own right. This was preceded by 'machine aesthetic', the greatest exponent of which was Mies van der Rohe with his designs for the Chicago Institute of Technology in 1947 (later to become the Illinois Institute of Technology). Yet Richards refers to a separate stylistic direction which he terms 'regional organic', an example of which, paradoxically, is the 1948 Menefee House by Pietro Belluschi in Yamhill, Oregon. Analogous to the organic architecture of Frank Lloyd Wright, Belluschi's design for the Menefee House evolved into the 'bay region' style of the Pacific Coast,

exemplified by the houses designed by Albert Henry Hill in the San Francisco Bay area. At the forefront of all of this was Frank Lloyd Wright himself, who was vehemently opposed to functionalist or mechanistic architecture. His headquarters in Taliesin West, near Phoenix, Arizona, completed in 1948, was to have a profound influence on the relationship between the natural landscape and architecture. This was described by Siegfried Giedion of Harvard in a previous article on the Finnish architect Alvar Aalto as the need to 'dare to leap from the rational-functional to the irrational organic' and to 'discover an emotional equivalent that may rescue us from drowning in the flow of technical processes that is being poured over us'.[52]

Frank Lloyd Wright's practical excursion into urban design, as opposed to his theoretical proposals for Broadacre City, was evident in his layout for usonian homes in Pleasantville, New York, from 1947. Occupying 97 acres within commuting distance of New York, the plan had 55 circular plots, each house occupying one acre with an additional acre for community use. The circles were eventually adjusted to polygons to satisfy the demands of the local Board of Assessors (it was not unusual for Wright to battle over building codes, zoning or local planning restrictions in general). Usonia Homes Inc. was a cooperative, Wright designed only three of the houses himself and the community centre was never built. The last house to be constructed was the Reisley Residence in 1951, with an addition in 1956.[53]

Taliesin West, Phoenix, Arizona (1948), Frank Lloyd Wright.

Bay region house, California (1954), Albert Henry Hill.

The Emergence of Urban Design

Within this cultural context in the middle of the twentieth century, what were the causative factors in the emergence of urban design as a distinct discipline?

Though it is still difficult to establish the origin of the expression 'urban design', it seems to have first appeared in 1956 at the first conference on urban design, sponsored by the Faculty and the Alumni Association of the Graduate School of Design at Harvard University.[54] Walter Gropius, Senior Professor of Architecture at Harvard in 1937 and designer of the Harvard University Graduate Center between 1949 and 1950, had already retired from the University in June 1953 and returned to practise with the Architects' Collaborative, which he had founded in 1945. The new Dean of the Graduate School of Design was José Luis Sert, a well-known city planner who, together with Le Corbusier, had produced major master plans in South America.

The meeting was an invitation conference with some notable speakers, but was distinguished by the absence of the key figures who were to emerge in the field of urban design.[55] These included Kevin Lynch, who had commenced teaching at MIT in 1948,[56] and Louis Kahn in Philadelphia. There is no record of whether or not they had been invited.

The programme notes of the conference began: 'This Invitation Conference is intended to be exploratory, not didactic, and to try and find a common basis for the joint work of the Architect, the Landscape Architect and the City Planner in the field of Urban Design'.[57] The introduction correctly suggested that (in the minds of its sponsors) urban design is wider than the scope of the above professions, that others share their concern with the frequent absence of beauty and delight in the contemporary city, and that there was 'in much current development, mainly occupied with a quick return on investment, too little attention paid to these public needs'. The sponsors avoided the term 'civic design' (in common usage at the time) as having a specialised or grandiose connotation. A better knowledge of the coming physical form of the city would assist the framing of the necessary legislative and financial measures that can transform vision into reality.

Sert, in his introductory speech, said that city planning had developed as a new science and that city planners of 'today' were concerned with the structure of the city. He noted that city planners addressed the geographic, social, political and economic factors that shape the city, with an emphasis on scientific rather than artistic knowledge. On the other hand, he attacked The City Beautiful movement epitomised earlier in the century by Daniel Burnham's work in Chicago and elsewhere. Yet Burnham's proposals, for all they were based on neoclassicism, were what urban design was all about. Urban design, Sert asserted, was that part of city planning which deals with the physical form of the city. He added that with a new approach to architecture, landscape architecture, road engineering and city planning, it could establish a new set of principles and a new language of forms. But alas, 50 years later, with the exception of interstate highway design, this does not seem to have been the case.

Much of Sert's speech was rich in rhetoric but thin in positive ideas. He said the necessary process was not one of decentralisation but recentralisation, and that there would be a reversal of these trends. The following decade was to prove just how wrong he was.

Tremaine House, Santa Barbara, California, Richard Neutra.

A key speaker at the conference was the architect Richard Neutra, famed for his elegant residential designs in California. Born in Vienna in 1892, Neutra emigrated to the US in 1923 and for a time worked with Frank Lloyd Wright. Wright's influence was evident in his most famous works such as the Kaufman Desert House in Palm Springs, completed in 1947. But the reinforced concrete Tremaine House in the forests around Santa Barbara had a particular elegance, quite separate from the imagery of Wright. However, at the time there was no evidence in Neutra's career of any interest in city planning, let alone urban design. His architecture was composed of unique iconic designs in isolated settings. At the conference he spoke broadly about ecological issues and predicted that Los Angeles was on the way to eliminating airborne pollution![58] Renowned landscape architect Garrett Eckbo said that the urban landscape had no boundaries and that the professions would have to learn to work in terms of continuity of design, with an enriching in detail and a breaking down of scale.

Lloyd Rodwin, a professor of city planning at MIT, warned that conference delegates should be disturbed by the failures in urban design and 'the frequent absence of beauty and delight in the contemporary city'.[59] Again, like so many speakers, his presentation tended to be a litany of generalities rather than specific suggestions, though his MIT colleague, Charles Abrams, did identify forthcoming problems. He noted that overcrowding among ethnic minorities was six times as great as among the majority Caucasian population. The new suburbs, he said, were 'circumscribing the teeming, heaving cities and now proclaimed the no trespass sign'.[60]

Secure in their new autonomy, they ban the new migrant as an outlander . . . The four-room slum becomes the three-room slum. The two-room efficiency becomes the one-room dormitory. Simultaneously, the one-story slum becomes the ten-family furnished house, which in turn soon gives way to the 400-family housing project. Tossed into this world of grim reality, comes the architectural graduate with six years of irrelevant information on cities and the city planner with two.[61]

Abrams rightly stated that obsolete codes, absolute financing restrictions and resolute zoning laws were the real arbiters of the destiny of the city. Legislative architecture, financial tyrannies and social and political taboos designed houses, located industries and hardened traffic arteries. Abrams said that the more developed a country, the worse is its housing problem, an odd observation given the *barriadas* and *favelas* of Latin America or the shanty towns of South Africa. Perhaps he ought to have said, the larger the city, the worse its housing problems.

Gyorgy Kepes also contributed to the conference. He indicated that the last phase in the visual arts of the previous one hundred years was a frantic search to find new meaning to structure, a new aspect of order. He said that one of the more important aspects in creating a better environment was 'to open the eyes of man who is involved in design to these values which have gradually and in a very stuttering way developed in the work of the painters, the sculptors, and those other people who

have been perhaps more frustrated, perhaps more sensitive in responding to the difficulties of the surroundings'.[62]

The landscape architect Hideo Sasaki was behind the most telling remark at the conference:

I should like to dwell on one significant force instrumental in shaping the city, which I think needs mentioning; and this is the force of the *designers*. The visual aspect of the city is only that which is created. The chief faults of design were Eclecticism without meaning, used under the guise of architectural harmony, stylistic conformity of present periods as well as the past, as well as monumentality without scale and a lack of relationship with surroundings and an emphasis on the spectacular.[63]

Jane Jacobs, then associate editor of *The Architectural Forum*, suggested that neighbourhood stores were social centres and served this important function as much as the supply of goods and services. When these disappear, they are replaced by an unplanned, chaotic, prosperous belt of chain stores. Lewis Mumford, in agreeing with Jacobs' comments, said that it was absolute folly to create a physical structure at the price of destroying the intimate social structure of the life of the community.

Practising urban designers who attended the conference included Francis Violich, then teaching at the University of California at Berkeley, who criticised a project for the construction of the downtown elevated freeway project in San Francisco. The freeway was placed in front of the pre-earthquake Ferry building. According to Violich, it should have been curved nearer to the shoreline, allowing a plaza and park to be built in front of the building, and he criticised the American Institute of Architects and the American Institute of Planners for not taking a stand on this issue.[64]

Another practitioner was Edmond Bacon, executive director of the Philadelphia City Planning Commission. Congress had recently appropriated one billion dollars (an enormous figure at the time) for creating a new urban environment. Bacon's department had already produced a plan for downtown Philadelphia. The 'Old City Redevelopment Area Plan' included a proposal for green ways connecting historic buildings such as Independence Hall, Carpenters Hall and the First Bank of the US. These connecting garden walks in the centres of street blocks made possible a sequential experience.[65] Bacon said that they had rediscovered the underlying principles of urban aesthetics which were: 'The quality of space; the articulation of space for its experiencing by people and the continuity of space experience, the realization that we are dealing not with one single sensation but a series of sensations in sequence'. Architecture in urban design, Bacon went on, 'is the articulation of space so as to produce within the participator a definite space experience in relation to previous and anticipated future space experience'.[66]

In early plans for the redevelopment of Philadelphia, the only justifiable purpose for the investment of money was the elimination of blight. Neighbourhoods were regarded as dynamic organisms which have the seeds of self-regeneration. Bacon credited much of their inspiration to Louis Kahn, in his housing project for the Mill Creek area. Bacon's contribution to the conference was significant in that it translated urban design rhetoric into tangible ideas.

A similar contribution was from architect Victor Gruen, who described his proposals for Fort Worth in Texas. At that time it was a city of 350,000 inhabitants with a metropolitan population of around one million people. The intention of the plan was to make the downtown business core as compact as possible. Gruen introduced the concept of a fully pedestrianised city with six major parking structures on the periphery of downtown, built so that they were directly accessible from the loop freeway, all within two minutes from the centre of the city. He proposed that the parking structures would be attached to moving sidewalks. Delivery trucks would be underground, feeding basement docking areas. The underground system would be a loop and a number of short service roads with turnarounds on the ends. Gruen also maintained that his proposals would avoid demolishing all existing structures more than three storeys in height. He contended that the plan would work because people would be willing to walk such a short distance: 'Automobiles have disappeared and city streets have gone. Instead of long bands bordered by parallel buildings, the streets become a series of different kinds of spatial rooms. Some narrow, some wide, sometimes widened out into plazas, some reduced to a much greater narrowness . . . in some cases streets have been covered, in other cases low buildings have been demolished or existing (surface) parking areas taken over as public spaces. Thus, moving around the new pedestrian city, we will experience a steady surprise of new features – of new space experiences. A new kind of urban environment is created . . . I believe one of the reasons for our great complaint about the dullness of Modern architecture is to be found in the fact that nobody walks to see it, and I believe that the pedestrian city will offer new possibilities for architectural expression and art'.[67]

However, Gruen's plan was never implemented and the US moved onward with an automotive culture. (Nevertheless, his concept of covered suburban shopping malls such as Randhurst at Mount Prospect, Illinois, and Yorktown shopping centre, Illinois were successful, and his ideas were followed by European countries about a decade later.) In fact, one of the earliest and most successful pedestrianisation schemes was for the centre of Copenhagen, completed in the 1960s. It was based upon the main shopping street, the Stroget, in which a series of five successive shopping streets, running from Rådhusplasan by Tivoli Gardens to the Royal Theatre on Kongens Nytorv, were closed to traffic and planted or paved. Other European countries such as Germany, the Netherlands and in particular the UK, quickly followed.[68]

José Luis Sert concluded the conference by saying: 'I think we should in our next conference plunge deeply into these dangerous waters of the design phase of planning – or the urban design phase of architecture – for I believe it is only by throwing ourselves into these waters that we shall learn to swim'.[69] Though the conference established the identity of urban design as a distinct discipline in 1956, American urban design, as such, had been seen in built and unbuilt projects at the beginning of the decade.

URBAN DESIGN EDUCATION

The first urban design programme appears to have commenced at Harvard in the Graduate School of Design in 1953, as reported by Lawrence Cutler,[70] at a Washington University, St. Louis, conference on urban design education, though few details of the curriculum are available. Later, in 1966, the University of Pennsylvania introduced an urban design course under the direction of Holmes Perkins.

Another course, at the University of California, Berkeley,[71] was introduced in spring 1959. The curriculum begins with the statement that the process of urban design in the US had yet to be clarified and that there was no clear idea of how cities should be designed. Nor was there any concept of design quality in many buildings. The aim of the course, therefore, was to explore the potential methods of consciously guiding the design of functional, visual units in the urban realm. The method was examining the five case study areas chosen by the class. The sites were located in Berkeley and San Francisco.

The first phase of the class studied the current situation, such as existing land use and structures, visual qualities and aesthetic character, social and economic life, and the specific forces that shaped the area, concluding with specific recommendations for improvement.

A second phase focused on concepts for redesign related to the principles, standards and processes necessary for the accomplishment of visual quality. For each area a policy was formulated that could be adopted by a city within its urban planning process. The class then attempted to demonstrate how such a policy could be expressed in physical terms while being supported by administration and development regulations.

Such a study reflected the growing inclusion of urban design in the planning profession. Planners were beginning to believe that the best means of achieving design quality was through the incorporation of urban design guidelines within legislation.

Notable among the researchers in urban design was Philip Thiel at the University of California, Berkeley. In the introduction to his recently published life's work[72] he said that his work began in 1951 at MIT. As a student there his urban design thesis was concerned with the visual redevelopment of a sector of the city of Boston. He attributes this project to Professor Lawrence Anderson.[73]

Thiel's project was a proposal to heighten visitors' experiences of the large number of historically important buildings and sites in the area of Boston, extending from Beacon Hill northeastward to the waterfront, by organising their viewing sequence along a pedestrian pathway. In 1956, he acknowledges the influences of Gyorgy Kepes and Kevin Lynch at MIT. His transfer to the University of California at Berkeley, with financial aid from the research committee of the College of Architecture, started the germination of Thiel's ideas. In an unpublished paper at the time he emphasised the use of the 'Study of the visual representation of architectural and urban space', in which space-time sequences were notable.[74]

Acknowledging the work of James Gibson[75] in classifying methods of representing space as viewed from a fixed point,

Thiel suggested five techniques for extending these to indicate the experience of a moving observer:

1   Modification of linear perspective by the use of multiple vanishing points and horizon lines in which a plurality of observation points is equivalent to movement in space. Saul Steinberg's drawings provide examples of this technique, as do scroll paintings and some of the work of Leonardo da Vinci.
2   Transparency of overlapping forms to provide simultaneous representation or more than one point of view; examples can be drawn from x-rays, multiple exposure photography and primitive paintings.[76]
3   Reflections and mirroring, alone or in conjunction with transparency. Thiel himself experimented with this device, shooting a film in a bay area rapid transit train at a point where window reflections in an articulated two-car unit produced a multiple image of the views forward and to the left and right. The Gestalt fifth condition operated to enable each to be read independently, and Thiel proposed extending the technique with the use of spherical and half-silvered mirrors.
4   Rotations of orthographic projections, used by geometers, primitives and cubists. An early example of this technique for a purpose analogous to that of the urban designer is a book of maps, published by the British surveyor to King Charles II, John Ogilby, to make a survey of the main roads through England and Wales in 1698.[77] John Senex, who produced a pocket-sized version in scroll format of Ogilby's maps in 1757 as a more useful device for the traveller on horseback, made simultaneous presentation of separate representations of successive events, commonly used in medieval paintings and twentieth-century comic strips.[78] Thiel also used the analyses of the early Soviet director, Sergei Eisenstein, described in the film *Sense*,[79] implementing correlated strip sequences to show: film frames (stills), phrases, musical score, length (through measurement), diagrams of pictorial composition and linear diagrams of movement. From these explorations he then proposed a corresponding system of annotating urban sequences in a rolled or paged scroll form.

These effects can also be reproduced by aircraft vapour trails, time exposure photography of car headlights or stop frame video and cinematography.

THE FIRST URBAN DESIGN PROJECTS

Progressive Architecture was also notable for the introduction of its first Design Awards Programme in 1954. Over 600 entries were received and the awards were selected by a distinguished jury of Victor Gruen, Eero Saarinen, George Howe and Fred Severud. Most of the award-winning entries were individual pieces of architecture, with the Architects' Collaborative, Skidmore Owings and Merrill, Marcel Breuer, I. M. Pei and Paul Rudolph among those receiving prizes, and all designs were still clearly rooted in the modern movement.[80]

At the time there were no separate divisions for urban design or research; this was to follow later. However, the top award went to a scheme that could truly be termed urban design. This was a proposed redevelopment of a major part of the historic Back Bay development in Boston. Designed by Pietro Belluschi (then Dean of Architecture at MIT), Walter Bogner, Carl Koch, Hugh Stubbins and the Architects' Collaborative, it was described in the magazine as follows: 'This stunning complex rose above every other entry in the Design Awards Program to receive from the Jury the overall First Design Award. It was also given the top Design Award in the Commercial category . . . the proposed Back Bay Center is an extraordinarily impressive scheme – particularly so to anyone who knows Boston. For, though that proper city has a distinguished architectural past and there are numerous excellent, smaller contemporary structures and residences in the environs, it was by no means notable for its commercial structures built in the twentieth century. Now all of a sudden, the proposal is to construct as lively a group of buildings as any city anywhere can boast – a shining new core for the old metropolis'.[81] And yet, with hindsight, this is precisely what was wrong with the proposal. The editorial comment continued: 'And this, right in the heart of the present city, within two blocks of H. H. Richardson's Trinity Church, McKim, Meade and White's Boston Public Library, and the huge dome of the extension to the mother church of the First Church of Christ Scientist (Charles Brigham, Chief Architect). Most fortuitously the design is in the hands of a group of some of the most progressive architects in this country'. Though this was true, did it really reflect the sensitivity of Pietro Belluschi's earlier architecture in the Pacific Northwest, particularly in Oregon, or the Architects' Collaborative architecture in the suburbs of Boston? Contextualism was certainly not their concern here, given the parallel streets of Commonwealth Avenue and Beacon Street's fine four- and five-storey nineteenth-century brownstone row houses; nevertheless, taken out of context, it was an elegant design.

In fact the scheme was never built. In its place was constructed, some years later, an even more gargantuan scheme designed by I. M. Pei. Its 12-hectare (30-acre) site had been used as marshalling yards for the Boston and Albany railroad. The removal of all tracks, except for a 25-metre-wide (82-foot-wide) corridor for the main diagonal line, made the site free for development. The design proposals included a splay-sided 40-storey office building, at right angles to which was a rectangular structure with a low U-shaped wing enclosing a courtyard, resulting in a 750-room combined hotel/motel, the rooms of which would be accessed by a switchback automobile ramp from the adjacent Boylston Street. It also included a huge department store and an air-conditioned enclosed shopping promenade with a glass roof. Adjacent to the commercial development was a circular convention hall. *Progressive Architecture* claimed that 'one of the most agreeable things about the entire development is that, throughout, the man once again comes into his own. Yet their automobiles – 6,000 of them, to be exact – can be accommodated on underground parking levels', presumably assuming all shoppers were men, possibly accompanied by spouses and children.

What the plan achieved was precisely the opposite of what Thiel was suggesting in his earlier MIT thesis. No thought was given to pedestrian continuity between the development and the residents of Back Bay. It was also a private initiative financed by the Stevens Development Corporation which then owned the Empire State Building in New York. There was little input from the city of Boston. An urban design proposal with possibly greater merit, though also never built, was Louis Kahn's earlier 1953 Center City Plan for Philadelphia. In this proposal Kahn accepted traffic as the generator of his design, but in a way that made the pedestrian of paramount importance. At the time this plan was not referred to as urban design, but Kahn truly considered the three-dimensional structure of the city as well as sequential space.

By the 1950s in North America, and in the 1960s in Western Europe, the honeymoon period had come to an end as car ownership had increased beyond the point (about one car per ten people) where serious and unexpected side-effects were becoming apparent. These included, in particular, the congestion of the downtown area, coupled with the dispersal of some of its key elements to out-of-town sites made accessible by new regional highway systems such as the Interstate programme in the US.

Louis Kahn, in his plan, suggested it might be more than mechanical necessity. His analogy between the flow of traffic and the flow of rivers provided a novel analysis of the movement patterns of a large metropolitan area in almost Venetian terms, by which the city would not only function, but would also become legible:

Expressways are like RIVERS
    These Rivers frame the area to be served.
    RIVERS have Harbours
        HARBORS are the municipal parking towers
From the HARBORS branch a system of CANALS that
    serve the interim.

    The CANALS are the go streets.
From the CANALS branch cul-de-sac DOCKS.
        the DOCKS
serve as the entrance hall to the buildings.

This poetic analogy, offering a new and symbolic urban design function to the banal structures serving traffic, was subsequently developed by Kahn in his designs for the elements. First there were the parking garage 'harbours', each accommodating 1,500 cars off the expressway and illuminated in different colours at night to identify the city sectors they served. Later, in his project for Market Street East, came a full repertoire of 'gateways', 'viaducts' and 'reservoirs'. Kahn also said that the tower entrances and parking terminals would provide a new stimulus for unity in urban design, which would find expression from the new order of movement. At night the towers would be recognised by coloured illumination– yellow, red, green, blue or white – informing the motorist which sector of the city he or she was entering. Along the approach, light would be used to regulate speed.

Born in Estonia in 1901, Kahn studied in the US within a beaux-arts system of architectural education at the University of Pennsylvania, graduating in 1924. However, it was not until the 1950s that he really began building. In 1947 he was hired as Visiting Critic at Yale University, and in 1950 spent time at the American Academy in Rome. When he returned to Yale in 1951, the chairman of the department of architecture was George Howe (until 1954 when he was succeeded by Paul Schweiker). At the time Kahn was in close contact with Philip Johnson for, according to Vincent Scully, the 'debilitating hostility between architect and historian which had characterized some of the pedagogy of the Modern Movement was on the wane at Yale'.[82] Apart from his Yale University Art Gallery and Design Center, which heralded the 'new brutalism' movement in architecture,[83] Kahn had little work.

Kahn's departure in 1957 from Yale to the University of Pennsylvania in Philadelphia represented a metamorphosis in his career. His 1952/53 urban design proposals for the city were to have a revolutionary impact, and his designs for the Medical Laboratories at the University of Pennsylvania, incorporating his concept of 'served and servant spaces' (see below), changed the theories of architecture.

In his 1953 plan for Center City, Philadelphia, Kahn remarked that: 'Architecture is also the street. There is no order to movement on streets. Streets look alike, reflecting little of the activities they serve – Carcassone without walls, cities without entrances, indiscriminate movement without places to stop. The design of the street is the design for movement'.[84] The drawings were an attempt to redefine the use of streets and separate one type of movement from another so that cars, buses, trams, lorries and pedestrians could move and stop more freely. The system utilised existing streets. Kahn went on to say that his proposal was not designed for speed, but for order and convenience. The existing mixture of staccato, through and stop-and-go traffic made all the streets equally ineffectual. The orderly discrimination of traffic of varying intention tended to facilitate flow and thereby encourage rather than discourage entrance of private cars into the centre of town. He proposed Chestnut Street as a pedestrian way with a single tram-line track.[85] By designating specific city streets for the staccato movement of buses and trams, specific streets for 'go' traffic, and others as terminal streets for stopping, the efficiency of street movement would be considerably increased. Zoning would grow naturally out of the movement on a street. Kahn further proposed that a transportation gateway should be built over part of the railway yards of the 30th Street Station of Philadelphia, tying together two levels of passenger tracks, a high-level freight line, a trucking level and a helicopter air connection as a transportation and freight centre.

The tower entrances to the city and interchanges and parking terminals represented a new stimulus to unity in urban architecture that would find expression from the order of movement. Shopping would have no 'go' traffic. Promenades would induce new and revive old merchandising ideas. He proposed an inter-weaving of people, glass, escalators, trees, gardens and exhibits. 'Shopping', he said, 'is walking. Walking is also resting – in shade, at the sidewalk café . . . shopping promenades lead to a

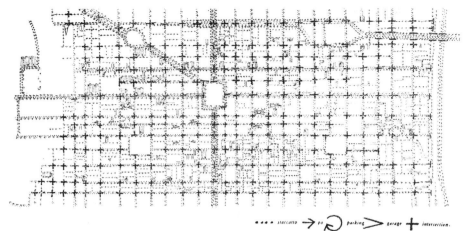

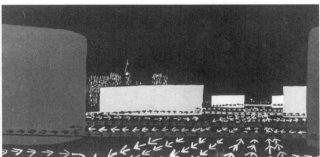

Louis Kahn's Plan for Philadelphia (1953): traffic circulation plan.

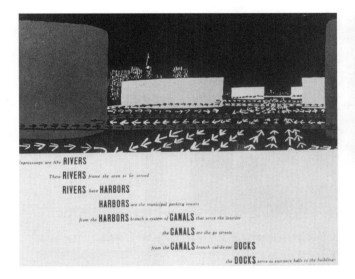

Louis Kahn's Plan for Philadelphia (1953): imagery of parking towers

larger area – the site for theatres, dance halls, bowling alleys, concert hall, places for food and refreshment'.

Louis Kahn believed that the motor car had completely upset the form of the city and that the time had come to make a distinction between the viaduct architecture of the car and the architecture of man's activities.

Revolutionary as Kahn's proposals for Philadelphia were, it was a more pragmatic plan for Philadelphia that was eventually implemented. Edmond Bacon had taken over the leadership of the City Planning Commission in 1947 and was its Executive Director. Between 1947 and 1955 the emphasis had changed from research to major redevelopment projects in different parts of Philadelphia. In 1952 a comprehensive development plan was prepared, to be published in 1960. Though not a statutory document, it included statutory powers such as zoning requirements and a six-year capital building programme. Bacon realised that three-dimensional concepts had to be built quickly enough to ride with the enthusiasm for political reform. He chose powerful design ideas which, even when compromised, were strong

enough to create a new sense of urban environment. Kahn's 'green way concept' first appeared in his proposals for the South West Temple Redevelopment Area. Green ways, under Bacon's guidance, formed the spine of all residential projects in Center City. Without Bacon, Kahn's ideas would have been lost. Market East represented the first American use of multilevel design with an upper-level pedestrian walk.[86] The Planning Commission in Philadelphia at the time was chaired by the architect-planner G. Holmes Perkins, Dean of the University of Pennsylvania's School of Fine Arts, where he introduced the concept of urban design education.

In 1956, the Washington Square redevelopment plan was published for the Society Hill neighbourhood. In the first proposed plan, the main emphasis lay in rehabilitating the historic dwellings and relating new development to both historic dwellings and institutional landmarks. The central design concept was based on a major east–west green way axis with subsidiary green ways, linking together the major historic landmarks of Independence Hall, the Customs House, the Historic

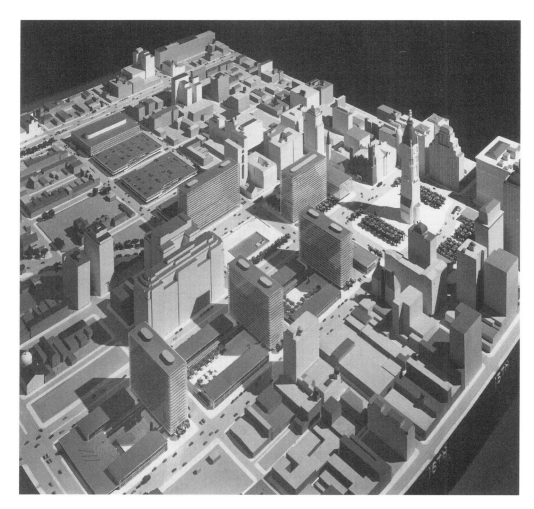

Edmond Bacon's Plan for Philadelphia (1952).

Parks and both old and new development. Locust Street, as the east–west axis, was to be conserved as a tree-lined residential street linking William Penn's Rittenhouse and Washington Square.

Though Louis Kahn's urban design ideas based on traffic movement were not implemented, he did design and build the Mill Creek public housing project with Christopher Tunnard as consultant landscape architect. The scheme was completed in 1955, and Kahn brought back the principle of pedestrian way or green way, using a central, lushly planted promenade. The pivot point of the promenade was a 13-storey point block with its own plaza.

The Center City Plan for Philadelphia was developed between 1952 and 1962, at which time the city was the regional capital of an eight-county administrative area with a population of around four million. Kahn's green way system was implemented to some extent by Bacon and his head of the urban design section, Willo Von Moltke.

Penn Center was the first section of the Center City Plan to be developed in 1952. The Transportation Center, designed by Vincent Kling, was the focus of the development and established the precedent of vertical segregation of traffic and pedestrians in commercial development. The City Hall west plaza incorporated the Municipal Services building, completed in 1962; this included the idea of a public ice-skating rink not dissimilar from Rockefeller Plaza, New York, which was built in the 1930s. Louis Kahn had also proposed a prototypical city tower, exhibited in a 1957 study for 'Tomorrow's City Hall', funded by the Universal Atlas Cement Company, and using a triangulated structure of concrete elements, bracing itself diagonally as a vertical truss against the wind.[87]

Louis Kahn's Richards Medical Research building at the University of Pennsylvania, designed in 1957 and completed in 1961, was in itself a contribution to a new view of urban design. Conceived not as a single monolithic building but as a series of buildings and connecting towers, his was a revolutionary concept in addressing the problems of a highly complex programme. Kahn referred to the main laboratory floors, which had clear spans allowing future flexibility, as 'served spaces', and the towers that provided vertical access as well as service ducts as 'servant spaces'. Vincent Scully suggested that the towers were 'reminiscent surely of San Gimignano and Siena, but hardly arrived at through any simple Picturesque-Eclectic process'.[88] Indeed, Kahn's early visits to Europe (as far back as 1928) seem to have inspired much of his later architecture through the imagery of North Italian hill towns and fortified medieval French cities. He said that 'Carcassone was designed for an order of defense. A modern city will renew itself from its order concept of movement which is against the destruction by the automobile'.[89] This emphasis on the renewal of an existing

San Gimignano, Tuscany, Italy.

Rockefeller Plaza, New York (mid-1930s).

city by its assimilation of a new circulation infrastructure, just as a medieval town might have been renewed by the construction of a new set of defensive works in response to development in the technology of warfare, distinguished Kahn's proposals of the 1950s and 1960s.

A bleaker view of Kahn's innovative ideas was expressed in an extract from Andrew Saint's book *The Image of the Architect*.[90] In a book written by Kahn's engineer, August Kommerdant, the author claims that 'it was typical of Kahn not to give credit to any one of his associates, regardless of how great or extensive their contribution to a project was ... only very secure persons, with ability and progressive views, teach and develop their successors to one day carry on their ideas and work ... Kahn never discussed economy in his class; it was a dirty word for him'.[91] Certainly Kahn's own drawing ability never matched the intricate perspectives of his successor at Yale, Paul Rudolph.

URBAN DESIGN CONTRIBUTIONS TO URBAN COMMERCIAL ARCHITECTURE

In February 1952, Winston Weisman, a professor of architecture at the University of Texas, in an article entitled 'Slab buildings' for the British periodical *The Architectural Review*,[92] describes how the term 'slab structure' was coined in the 1930s to describe the RCA Building at the Rockefeller Center in New York City. After the Second World War the United Nations Secretariat Building was the first example of a new type of slab building.

Unlike the Rockefeller Center it did not have numerous setbacks caused by complex New York building codes, though John Todd, president of Todd, Robertson and Todd, managers of the Rockefeller Center, said experience had taught him that deep space (such as the Empire State Building) was as costly to construct as shallow space, but could not command the price or market. Yet setback construction was relatively expensive and provided little rentable space. The United Nations Secretariat Building, designed in 1947 by an international team headed by Wallace Harrison and Le Corbusier, had a strong input from the Brazilian architect Oscar Niemeyer, the emerging leader of the 'heroic period' of the modern movement in Brazil. The building avoided setbacks in favour of simple straight profiles and the initial use of a form of curtain walling. The building stood alone as a piece of iconic architecture, together with the auditorium building and plaza.

However, it was the firm of Skidmore, Owings and Merrill that created a new building type with the 1952 design for Lever House on Park Avenue in New York.[93] Clearly influenced by the Chicago architecture of Mies van der Rohe, the 24-storey building was unique in a number of ways. It became the model prototype of the multistorey office block in which the load-bearing frame, instead of being clad in masonry as was the earlier Rockefeller Center, was concealed, and the fully glazed outer skin formed a curtain wall. Verticals and horizontals are equally distributed in the treatment of the glass facade. The division by storeys is displayed clearly with the structural frame clearly discernible through the transparent glass. Lever House was also notable in that, on an expensive site on one of the most fashionable streets in New York, its clients and their architects decided not to cover the plot with one building but instead to build a two-storey podium on columns, with a central courtyard, open to the public as a landscaped plaza, expanding the street itself into a sequential space.

This was followed later by the construction of the Seagram Building, also on Park Avenue on the opposite side of the street, slightly south of Lever House. Designed by Mies van der Rohe and completed in 1958, it drew heavily upon van der Rohe's earlier 1921 hypothetical project for a glass skyscraper. The Seagram Building is a larger and more sombre structure than Lever House, and twice the height. It appears as 'a dense, dark cliff behind the absolute void of its extreme plaza. The axis of the plaza culminates in the formal grandeur of the entrance with its two-storey stilts each backed by the pylons of the elevator shafts . . . the reconciliation of tension in a formal climax'.[94] The two plazas in Park Avenue, almost diagonally opposite one another, were a major breakthrough in American urban design.

CRITIQUES OF THE EXISTING AMERICAN URBAN SCENE

At the beginning of the decade, Christopher Tunnard, professor of city planning at Yale University, was invited to be the key author of a special issue of British magazine *The Architectural Review*.[95] In the introductory editorial of the 'Man-Made America' issue it was said that: 'Briefly the theory is that the landscape, regarded as the full complement of townships, roads, railways, electricity grids, clearings, afforestation schemes, backyards, real estate ventures, wastes, wilds, ornamental parkways, ribbon development – the landscape whether created consciously or unconsciously, by acts of commission or omission by a given society, is in the nature of things a realization in three dimensions of that society's *form-will*'.[96]

The editorial continued that there were five characteristic physical features of the American man-made landscape which stand out. The first was the gridiron plan, which (from a European point of view) was universal, with just a few exceptions, across the US. It suggested that this resulted in tree-embowered, community-gardened suburbs, which 'in their straight street, magnificent trees, absence of fences and multiplicity of individual buildings, provide an object-lesson for the world in the right relationship of unity to anarchy'.[97] The third and fourth features are really two aspects of the same thing, namely town centres. Here, the editorial went on, was 'another kind of visual unity . . . imposed on another kind of anarchy. A fantastic agglomeration of objects – advertisements, water tanks, sidewalls, back walls and "architectural" front walls, two-storey buildings next to twenty-storey buildings, thanks, in spite of its faults, to the gridiron which lines them up at right angles to one another, combine and recombine as the spectator moves through them into Cubist compositions, often of unearthly beauty'. The fourth characteristic was particular to the US – the strange pyramidal effect seen in cities such as Cincinnati, Philadelphia and Pittsburgh, or sometimes a cliff-like effect such as Lake Shore, Chicago, or New York, seen from Staten Island as pyramidal.[98] The fifth outstanding contribution of the American scene to the art of urban landscape were vast projects, such as the Rockefeller Center in New York, or, in the rural landscape, the works of the Tennessee Valley Authority (TVA). The latter, by controlling or excluding the vagaries of nature, created an artificial environment on a hitherto unknown scale. Cape Canaveral, Florida, site of US rocket launches, was to do the same a decade later.

In the following part of the special issue, Christopher Tunnard suggested that the American city was unique. The American community was not a standardised product like the American automobile. It may have its tallest buildings in the centre and its smallest houses on the perimeter – easily recognisable and recurring phenomena; it may use standardised building materials and motifs on banks and shop-fronts so that 'Main Street in an Ohio town becomes a model in Massachusetts';[99] it may employ standardised fixtures supplied by General Electric; national advertising spells out Pepsi-Cola on billboards from coast-to-coast – mobile America looks the same everywhere. Even dress is almost standardised. For every significant view, Tunnard went on, are miles and miles of insignificant building, until the eye is arrested by a Brooklyn Bridge or a lively street market. A collection of urban scenes such as those by Hopper, Shahn, Stella and Gugliemi gives rise to melancholy feelings. This was due, Tunnard thought, to the artists' special preoccupations; the American city itself was seldom melancholy, despite slums, smoke and paper blown urban wastes. Convenient the city was not, in the planning sense. The separation of vehicular and pedestrian traffic would take years to accomplish (and has still not been accomplished half a century later). Unless metropolitan as opposed to city planning made more headway, there would be no means of coordinating suburban and central district planning. Indeed, that is still the situation at the start of the twenty-first century where city planning commissions often act without reference to their regional planning counterparts. In the 1949 Act of Congress, Title One of the Housing Act would for the first time allow for federal financial assistance for the rebuilding of blighted urban areas, and urban redevelopment authorities were established.

Tunnard claimed that 'there were far too many people in high places who were unable or unwilling to recognize chaos when they saw it'.[100] It was up to American planners to convince these people that overall planning of metropolitan areas was an immediate necessity and to persuade the American public that the speculative builder could satisfy the demand for a good life in a usonian landscape. Given the philosophy of a free market economy, sweeping the world since the early 1980s, that goal seems ever more difficult to achieve.

Tunnard completed his contribution with a survey of his own city of New Haven, Connecticut (the location of Yale University). Starting with an examination of exurban highways (interstates had not yet been constructed in that part of Connecticut), uncontrolled petrol stations, approaches or entrances to the urban environment, including suburban outskirts, old and new residential areas and weekend traffic problems at the seaside, it all made dire reading. It was followed by some evocative cartoons of New York City by Saul Steinberg, as well as a more optimistic view of contemporary America including work by William Wurster on the West Coast, Frank Lloyd Wright's plan for Florida Southern University, shopping centres by Victor Gruen, designs by Charles Eames and Buckminster Fuller, and enormous space-frame structures by the architect Konrad Waschmann and engineer Paul Weidlinger.

Despite this, the special issue of *The Architectural Review* provoked a violent reaction among American architects. *The Magazine of Building*, published in the US, responded with a form of counterattack to which *The Architectural Review* retaliated in its October issue.[101] Visual analysis of the environment, the editors suggested, required an eye trained in a field much wider than that of architecture.

Rarely, according to *The Magazine of Building*, had a cultural publication, published in a friendly country, issued so wholesale a condemnation of American civilization.[102] It attacked the statement that 'never before in ten thousand years has Western man . . . created the kind of squalor we are talking about here'. *The Architectural Review* responded by saying that the 'disease is widespread in *every* industrialized society'. It also pointed out that the reaction of *The Magazine of Building* (a professional journal) and the news magazine *Time* was very different from what it had intended. Yet *The Magazine of Building* went on: 'Thoughtful Americans were unreservedly thankful for the sharp reminder from an outside source, that some of the "mess" is really there',[103] and quoted an American author in *The American Institute of Architects Journal* as saying 'we are building a tin can civilization'. *The Magazine of Building* accused *The Architectural Review* of 'Europe-rooted authors,' yet this could hardly be true given that the contributors, such as Tunnard and Henry Russell Hitchcock (who quoted younger historians such as Vincent Scully), or the artist Saul Steinberg, were all Americans. The kernel of the argument of *The Magazine of Building* was that North America was a continent with a 'persistent high velocity of change' and 'the certainty that the future is uncertain'. But there was, and is, little evidence of a movement to clear up the urban mess in the US.

Three later publications in this decade reinforced the latter views. *Planning and Community Appearance*[104] appears to be the first formal attempt to produce urban design guidelines. However, it was important not so much for its proposed methods and techniques but for forcefully expressing opinions about the critical issues of the contemporary city. The book's introduction asks the question, 'Why are our cities so ugly? How can communities be more beautiful . . . since our past is rich in lovely towns and villages and even cities . . . This occurred long before there was any thought of design control by Master Plans (and) zoning ordinances . . . Today growth often brings only ugliness. Countryside disappears before the advance of suburbia'.[105]

The authors considered that public action towards improving the appearance of communities was necessary. There was a need to introduce aesthetic considerations alongside other factors in the major decisions that determine the land development patterns of the master plan. It was also essential that overall neighbourhood context for the ultimate designers of the individual structures be provided by creating and adopting three-dimensional district plans as integral parts of the municipal master plan.[106] The authors further proposed that all things seen from public spaces should be considered, not just building facades and signs, but the three-dimensional interrelationships of structures and their surroundings. The book was produced by a joint committee of planners and architects who met from 1953 to 1957 to review methods by which communities in various parts of the country, as well as overseas, were attempting to prevent ugliness and achieve visual harmony. Six approaches were examined:

1. Look-alike regulations, enforcing uniformity.
2. No look-alike regulations, compelling variety.
3. Regulations to maintain open space, vistas and views.
4. Regulations for the preservation of historic buildings.
5. Architectural design review boards, to which the designs of new structures are referred.
6. Regulations promoting a positive search for aesthetic appropriateness in relation to a comprehensive development plan.

The suggestion by the planner Sydney Williams, that the visual survey examining the three-dimensional aspects of the total city could be recorded and analysed using traditional map and notebook form,[107] seems naive.[108]

American Skyline by Christopher Tunnard[109] also examined these issues. Tunnard's book was really a concise history of American cities from 1607 onwards. In his concluding chapter, 'The Regional City 1933', he stated that 'if modern urban development, housing and even commercial structures seem lacking in character and design by comparison with earlier American architecture and planning, the reason is not too hard to seek'.[110] He said that the bare slabs and blocks that pass for architecture are the result not of economy but of taste, and indicated that the philosopher Thorstein Veblen's harsh condemnation of ornament, during the 1930s economic depression, was a convenient artistic philosophy. Also to blame, Tunnard thought, was the importation of 'functional architecture' from Europe by leaders of the modern movement, such as Walter Gropius.

Apart from taste, it was also obvious that there were other causative factors, and the most important of these was traffic. Detroit at that time had planned a $195 million budget for future expressways. The great highways, Tunnard predicted, would cause as many problems as they would solve: 'Granted that the new suburbs must have access to the central city, we must be careful to see that we are not creating pythons to strangle the suburbs as they are already strangling the city'.[111] In another prophecy he suggested that in addition to the problems of the highways, the worst blot on the American urban scene since the coming of railway yards was the open-air car-park: 'The city can no longer smile, because so many of the teeth are missing'.[112] Tunnard went on to say that if cities were properly planned, we could ensure that 'traffic ran in its proper groove, separated from pedestrian movement and child play. We should ensure that fast-moving and slow-moving traffic is kept separate, so that high-speed routes did not run through residential neighborhoods. We could build more underground garages for cars, right beneath the buildings where the owners wanted to go, as San Francisco has done under Union Square'.[113] He proposed reviving the idea of rapid transit as a public service. There was reference to atmospheric pollution, particularly caused by the motor car, and to the newly invented catalytic converter as a device for partially solving this problem.[114] The regional city,

Union Square,
San Francisco
(1958),
Gordon Cullen.

Sequential views, Louisville,
Kentucky (1960),
Gordon Cullen.

San Antonio riverwalk (1960),
Gordon Cullen.

Above: The floor of the city can be expressive. Here, in Louisburg Square in Boston, are cobbles in the square (no through traffic); asphalt to the rear for automobiles, stone slabs for the pedestrians crossing the square.

Louisburg Square, Boston, Gordon Cullen.

Tunnard concluded, should be different enough from the existing city to capture the imagination.

Probably the most significant book published towards the end of the decade was *The Exploding Metropolis* (1957).[115] Following the publication of a special issue of *Fortune Magazine*, this book was an incisive critique of the American mid-twentieth-century city. Though *The Exploding Metropolis* was criticised at the time of its publication by planners and architects for its journalistic approach, it seems apt that a national business periodical, read by many of the most influential people in American society, should address urban problems in a virile and aggressive way.

Contributions were invited from young writers such as William Whyte and Jane Jacobs. The introduction, by William Whyte, stated that this was a book about people who *like* cities. Its chapters (by different contributors) included the decline of mass transit and whether the new highway network would accelerate the centrifugal movement away from downtown; the question of urban residential development for a revival of city living; the function of city government; the growth of slums and especially the decline in the qualities of downtown. The first chapter asked, 'Are cities un-American?' – a strange question given the archetypal and unique American city. It suggests that the growth of the metropolis and the growth of the city are not necessarily

complementary, in fact, quite the opposite. There seemed to be a growing alienation between the city and what most people conceived as the American way of life. The city was becoming a place of extremes – a place for the very poor (such as Harlem) or a place for the very rich (Upper East Side), both in New York's Manhattan district. From 1945 onwards there were more Americans who were homeowners than renters, an increase that took place in the new subdivisions of suburbia.

The final chapter of *The Exploding Metropolis* was the most telling. In 'Downtown is for people' Jane Jacobs gave a preview to her later book, *The Death and Life of Great American Cities*.[116] Jacobs noted that 'from city to city the architects' sketches conjure up the same dreary scene; there is no hint of individuality or whim or surprise, no hint that there is a city with a tradition and flavor of its own'. Illustrating this was a sketch of a hypothetical project credited to the British urban design theorist Gordon Cullen and the American architectural illustrator Helmut Jacoby, followed by a series of drawings by Cullen entitled 'The scale of the city'. In her introduction to the drawings Jacobs remarked that 'Human scale, something all designers of downtown projects praise in theory and most obliterate in projects, is the quality the city so desperately needs.

> Few men have so perceptive an eye as Gordon Cullen and Ian Nairn of *The Architectural Review*.[117] Together they produced two critiques on the English landscape and townscape, "Outrage"[118] and "Counter-Attack", that provoked much attention – and second thoughts – from architects, planners and citizens that a "Counter Attack" bureau has been set up to handle the flood of inquiries. The editors (of *Fortune*) asked Mr. Nairn and Mr. Cullen to look at the townscape of our own cities, to sketch not the horrors known so well, but the strengths so easily overlooked. Mr. Cullen, who likes to draw cities the way people actually see them, from eye level, has done the drawings. Mr. Nairn, who did the walking, has written the captions'.[119]

Nairn and Cullen chose a number of renowned public spaces across the length and breadth of the US. An obvious choice was Rockefeller Plaza, with its sunken public ice-skating rink and cafés, which created an oasis among the chasms formed by the skyscrapers. However there were also lesser known examples, such as the arcades recently cut into Louis Sullivan's Chicago Auditorium, the metal framework of the overhead railway, the Loop, framing the end of the vista. San Francisco's Union Square was, they thought, the city at its best with all the requisite bustle and activity, but with the traffic confined to a subterranean car-park leaving the square itself free from unwanted intrusions. The city square in Louisville, Kentucky, was another example. But of all the drawings by Cullen, the most atmospheric was a sketch of the riverwalk in San Antonio, Texas. Here, a meander in the downtown river has been transformed, through an imaginative public works programme during the Great Depression, from a storm water channel into a linear park with cafés, restaurants, bars and theatres along its tree-lined grass banks. It was, Nairn wrote: 'The pedestrian's world complete: water, changes of level, constantly changing vistas, a café just around the corner, the bustle of the city above'. Forty years later the San Antonio riverside, though greatly extended and commercialised, is still a model example of what downtown should be all about.

THE CLOSE OF THE DECADE

Though major contributions to urban design, in the form of individual buildings such as Lever House and the Seagram Building in New York City, had changed attitudes towards what architecture could contribute to urban design, there was little consensus in the discipline of city planning as to the way forward. Certainly this mid-century decade had seen an explosive change in culture at all levels. The crossover between this decade and that which followed saw the emergence of key figures who were to establish urban design as a distinct discipline.

The critiques of the American urban scene described at the end of this chapter were to act as catalysts for a new generation of theorists. The influence of the former Bauhaus teachers had been paramount in providing new ideas of visual perception and analysis of the three-dimensional form of the city. If any planning proposal could be seen as the first radical urban design plan, it was that of Louis Kahn in his 1952/53 proposals for Central Philadelphia.

NOTES

1. Copeland, Aaron, 'Appalachian Spring'. *The Tender Land Suite, Fall River Legend.* (CD) RCA Victor 09026–61505–2, Aaron Copeland, conductor, Boston Symphony Orchestra, recorded 23 April 1959. Program Notes pp. 4–8.
2. Though quite different from Igor Stravinsky's earlier, but much darker 'The Rites of Spring', which was also a composition for ballet.
3. Copeland, Aaron and William Flanagan (notes), op. cit., 1960, p. 4. See also Cage, John D. and Eric Gilder (1985) *The Dictionary of Composers.* New Pomfret, Vermont: David E. Charles, pp. 78–79.
4. Copeland had a deep interest in the music of Debussy, Ravel, Scriabin, Mussorgsky, Milhaud, Poulenc and others in Paris during that period. (Much of this material has been drawn from a doctoral dissertation by Stephen Gosling, pianist, at the Julliard School of Music in New York City. The degree was awarded in May 2000 and the Ensemble Sorpeso, of which Stephen Gosling is a member, performed an entire programme of Theremin's music in July 2000.)
5. Meade Lux Lewis, 1939–56. (CD) 'Story of Blues' 3506–2. First recorded on Storyville Records SLP 155, SLP 273 and SL 229. Most were performed during this period in New York City and San Francisco.
6. 'Charlie Parker Memorial', vol. 2. Savoy Records MG-12009.
7. 'Birth of the Cool', Capitol Records T-762, 1949–50. This recording startled jazz listeners since, according to the recording programme notes, it could be regarded as 'the beginnings of modern chamber voicings in jazz'.
8. 'Pyramid', The Modern Jazz Quartet. Atlantic Records/London Records LTZ-K 15193. The Quartet was first heard in New York in 1952 and was critically acclaimed.
9. 'Gerry Mulligan Quartet – Paris Concert', Pacific Jazz PJ-1210, 1954. All the pieces were written compositions, the most famous of which was 'Walkin' Shoes' by Mulligan. This was probably the first jazz piece to become no. 1 in the popular music charts in the US and Europe.
10. 'Mulligan Meets Monk', Riverside Records RLP 1106, 1957. Whereas modern jazz had been based in New York City, in the late 1950s a new movement in modern jazz began to emerge on the West Coast of the US, mainly in California, to become known as West Coast Jazz.
11. The cubist movement in France was the most dominant, led by artists such as Picasso and Braque, but also of importance was the DeStijl movement in the Netherlands, of which Piet Mondrian and Van Doesburg were the leading painters.
12. See notes on these artists in Chapter 1.
13. Huyghe, R. (ed.) (1961) *The Larousse Encyclopedia of Modern Art.* Paris: Librarie Larousse, p. 305. Fine examples are to be found on permanent display in the Guggenheim Museum, designed by Frank Lloyd Wright, in New York City.
14. Ibid., p. 411.
15. Ibid., p. 412. Also on display in the Guggenheim Museum.
16. Ibid., p. 418.
17. Pollock's painting can be seen at the Albright-Knox Museum in Buffalo.
18. Huyghe, op. cit., p. 419.
19. Ibid.
20. Albers' painting can be seen at the Guggenheim Museum, New York.
21. Huyghe, op. cit., p. 428.
22. Ibid.
23. Ibid., p. 430.
24. Gopnik, A. (1997) *The New Yorker,* 13 October, p. 72.
25. Kerouac, Jack (1955) *On the Road.* New York: Viking Press.
26. Ibid., p. 141.
27. Thomson, D. and Ann Lloyd (eds) (1982) 'James Dean, the grace of loneliness', *Movies of the Fifties.* London: Orbis Publishing, pp. 78–83.
28. Herman, G. (1982) 'Method in their acting', in Thomson and Lloyd, op. cit., pp. 131–33.
29. Taylor, J. (1982) 'To catch a star', in Thomson and Lloyd, op. cit., pp. 172–75.
30. Baldwin, J. (1957) *Giovanni's Room.* London: Michael Joseph Ltd.
31. Baldwin, J. (1960) *Another Country.* New York: Dell Publishing.
32. Selby, Hugh Jr (1957) *Last Exit to Brooklyn.* Hardcover unexpurgated edition. London: Calder and Boyers, 1966. Like the Supreme Court challenge during the early part of the decade concerning D. H. Lawrence's *Lady Chatterley's Lover, Last Exit to Brooklyn* was challenged in the British courts by the Director of Public Prosecutions under the Obscene Publications Act as criminal pornography.
33. Burroughs, W. (1964) *The Naked Lunch.* London: John Calder, Ltd. Originally published in Paris by Olympia Press, 1959. *British Journal of Addiction* (1956), vol. 53, no. 2.
34. Burroughs, op. cit., p. 29.
35. Mumford, L. (1961) *The City in History.* New York: Penguin Books.
36. Ibid., p. 576.
37. Ibid., p. 580.
38. Ibid., p. 640.
39. An excellent catalogue of furniture designs describing all of these works is Palazzeti, Sergio (1984) *I Classici del Mobile Moderno: the Classics of Modern Furniture.* First edition. New York: Palazzeti. Alivar made this edition available to the American public and research was carried out by Vincent Masucci.
40. Ibid., pp. 355–56.
41. Ibid., pp. 365–66.
42. Ibid., pp. 372–73.
43. Ibid., pp. 379–80.
44. Ibid., pp. 384–85.
45. Storrer, W. A. (1993) *The Frank Lloyd Wright Companion.* Chicago: University of Chicago Press, p. 241. This study by Storrer is surely one of the most comprehensive, literate works produced on the extant structures designed by Wright.
46. Ibid., p. 339. In his diagrams Storrer shows L-plan cantilevers based on a three-bedroom plan with a back gallery. A cantilevered car port ensures privacy of entry, but assumes one, or at most two cars for the American family – a prediction that was to be proved wrong.
47. Ibid., p. 370.

48. Ibid., p. 414.
49. Ibid., p. 407.
50. Storrer, op. cit., pp. 330–33. One of the editors of *The Architectural Review* at the time was J. M. (later Sir J. M.) Richards, who had long been an ardent supporter of the modern movement and functionalism espoused by Le Corbusier, Walter Gropius and Mies van der Rohe. See *The Architectural Review* (1950), vol. 107, no. 639 (March), pp. 165–81.
51. Ibid., p. 167.
52. Giedion, S. (1950) 'Alvar Aalto', *The Architectural Review* (February), pp. 77–84.
53. *The Architectural Review* (1950), vol. 107, no. 639 (March), pp. 174–75.
54. *Progressive Architecture* (1956), vol. XXXVII, no. 8 (August): pp. 97–112.
55. Ibid.
56. Banerjee, T. and M. Southworth (eds) (1990) *City Sense and City Design: Writings and Projects of Kevin Lynch*. Cambridge, MA: MIT Press, p. 19.
57. *Progressive Architecture*, op. cit., p. 97. The use of capitals to designate the different professions is a little curious in that it suggests singular persons, not professionals as a whole, in the way in which Frank Lloyd Wright designated The County Architect in his Broadacre City manifesto.
58. Ibid., p. 98.
59. Ibid., p. 99.
60. Ibid., p. 100.
61. Ibid., These were brave words in a political world of anti-communism and the existence at the beginning of the decade of the House Un-American Activities Committee of Congress.
62. Ibid., p. 101. It was about this time that Kepes and Kevin Lynch commenced courses in visual perception in the planning and architectural schools at MIT.
63. Ibid., In the 1970s the rise of postmodernism heralded in such a movement. The most vapid examples are to be seen in the architecture of commerce.
64. The freeway known as the Embarcadero Freeway was in fact demolished in the mid-1990s.
65. *Progressive Architecture*, op. cit., p. 108. The idea was not dissimilar from that of British urban design theorist Gordon Cullen's outline in 1947 of 'serial vision'. See Gosling, D. (1996) *Gordon Cullen: Visions of Urban Design*. London: Academy Editions, pp. 22–24.
66. Ibid., p. 108.
67. Ibid., p. 111.
68. See Gosling, D. and B. Maitland (1984) *The Design and Planning of Retail Systems*. London: Architectural Press. First edition 1976.
69. *Progressive Architecture*, op. cit., p. 112.
70. Cutler, L. and S. (1976) *Recycling Cities*. Boston: CBI Publishing.
71. University of California, Berkeley. Curriculum for CP 258, Urban Design, Department of City Planning (Spring 1959).
72. Thiel, P. (1997) *People, Paths and Purposes: Notations for a Participatory Envirotecture*. Seattle, WA: University of Washington Press.
73. Anderson's encouragement, although he does not acknowledge it, may have been inspired by Gordon Cullen's serial vision theories, published in *The Architectural Review* in 1947. See *The Architectural Review* (1947), vol. CII, no. 611 (November), pp. 159–70. It is strange, however, that when the author of this present volume, as a postgraduate student at MIT, wanted to emulate Thiel's precedent, at Kevin Lynch's suggestion, Anderson was strongly opposed to it.
74. Thiel, P. (1958) 'A study of the visual representation of architectural and urban space-time sequences'. Unpublished paper, University of California, Berkeley. The paper was given to David Gosling by Kevin Lynch that year as encouragement to pursue this path despite the opposition described above.
75. Gibson, J. (1950) *The Perception of the Visual World*. Boston: Houghton-Mifflin.
76. Such techniques were exemplified in the works of Laszlo Moholy-Nagy and his former colleague Gyorgy Kepes.
77. John Ogilby's maps were produced on a hundred large folio copper plates. But in 1757, John Bowles and Sons, London, produced pocket-sized scroll maps, by the geographer John Senex.
78. The American Automobile Association still provides such a device for its members in providing 'triptik' routes between cities. The art of the comic strip was an American invention, epitomised in the 'Superman' comics of the late 1930s and 1940s.
79. Eisenstein, S. (1957) *The Film Sense*. New York: Meridian Books.
80. *Progressive Architecture* (1954), vol. XXXV, no. 1 (January), pp. 67–68 and 73–135.
81. Ibid., p. 74.
82. Scully, V. Jr (1962) *Louis I. Kahn: Makers of Contemporary Architecture*. New York: George Braziller, p. 19.
83. 'New brutalism' or *'beton brut'* of Le Corbusier's latest phase of design during this period, or that of the British architects Alison and Peter Smithson with their Hunstanton School in Norfolk, England (1951–53) heralded a new architectural imagery later epitomised in Paul Rudolph's Art and Architecture building, with the use of shutter-marked reinforced concrete construction or exposed steel structures.
84. Kahn, L. I. (1962) 'Prospects', *Architectural Design*, vol. XXXII, no. 8 (August), p. 383.
85. Such a proposal was enacted successfully towards the end of the century in downtown Portland, Oregon.
86. This was implemented somewhat later on a large scale in Cincinnati and particularly in Minneapolis. In the latter city, the skywalks were especially successful due to the extreme winter climate.
87. Kahn, L.I. (1957) 'Perspecta 4', *Yale University Architectural Journal*, pp. 58–65.
88. Scully, V. Jr, op. cit., p. 28.
89. Kahn, L. I. (1952/53) 'Planning proposals for Central Philadelphia'.
90. Saint, A. (1983) *The Image of the Architect*. New Haven, Connecticut: Yale University Press, p. 155.
91. Kommerdant, A. (1975) *18 Years with Architect Louis I. Kahn*. Publisher unknown, pp. 130–31 and 185.
92. Weisman, W. (1952) 'Slab buildings', *The Architectural Review*, vol. III, no. 662 (February), pp. 119–23.
93. A key figure in the firm at the time was one of the design partners, Gordon Bunschaft, who virtually created a house style which lasted many years.
94. Jordy, W. H. (1963) 'Mies van der Rohe', *Encyclopedia of Modern Architecture*. London: Thames and Hudson, p. 198.
95. Tunnard, C. (1950) 'Man-Made America', *The Architectural Review*, vol. 108, no. 648 (November). Christopher Tunnard, a Canadian, lived in England for 12 years, working with architects such as Serge Chermayeff. He became a US citizen in 1949, and Director of Planning Studies at Yale. About this time he initiated a new course to coordinate the visual arts in city planning. His research for this issue was subsequently to become the basis of his seminal book, *Man-Made America: Chaos or Control?*, published by Yale University Press in 1963.
96. *The Architectural Review* (1950), vol. 108, no. 648 (November), p. 341.
97. Ibid., p. 342.
98. Subsequently many world cities such as São Paulo, Brazil and Sydney, Australia, were to adopt this pyramidal morphology.
99. *The Architectural Review* (1950), vol. 108, no. 648 (November), p. 346.
100. Ibid., p. 359.
101. *The Architectural Review* (1951), vol. 110, no. 658 (October), pp. 217–20.
102. This comment was strange, since the criticism was not written by the British editors of *The Architectural Review*, but by a US citizen, Christopher Tunnard, professor of city planning at Yale University.
103. Ibid., p. 218.

104. Fagin, H. and R. Weinberg (eds) (1968) 'Planning and community appearance: a report of the Joint Committee on Design Control of the New York Chapter of The American Institute of Architects', Regional Plan Association (May).

105. Ibid., p. 1.

106. Despite this 40-year-old suggestion there is little evidence of *statutory* three-dimensional plans being imposed on or agreed with developers.

107. Williams, S. (1953) *Urban Aesthetics in Planning.* Chicago: American Society of Planning Officials.

108. Today this can be achieved using computer-generated three-dimensional mapping techniques, but these were not available during the 1950s.

109. Tunnard, C. (1956) 'And Henry Hope Reed', *American Skyline.* New York: The New American Library.

110. Ibid., p. 185.

111. Ibid., p. 186.

112. Ibid., p. 187.

113. Ibid., p. 188.

114. It is interesting to note that many of these prophecies came to be true, particularly the existing urban problems of surface car-parking; however, there seems to be little attempt to solve them except perhaps in a few large cities.

115. *Fortune* Editorial Staff (1958) *The Exploding Metropolis.* Garden City, New York: Doubleday.

116. Jacobs, J. (1958) 'Downtown is for people', *The Exploding Metropolis*, op. cit., pp. 157–84.

117. See Gosling, op. cit., pp. 63–65.

118. Cullen, G. and I. Nairn (1955) 'Outrage', *The Architectural Review*, vol. 117, no. 702 (June), pp. 363–454.

119. Jacobs, op. cit., pp. 158.

Chapter Three

1960–1970

THE SECOND DECADE

While the preceding decade established urban design as a discipline within the context of a major cultural and artistic revolution in the US, key figures were to emerge mid-century to establish a new set of urban design theories. These were authorities such as Kevin Lynch, Philip Thiel, Donald Appleyard, Christopher Alexander and Jane Jacobs. Lynch, Thiel and Appleyard, in particular, were to examine the 'recognisability' of the city from the perception, not of the architect or city planner, but of the lay person, in relation to structural form and meaning.

THE COGNITIVE CITY

Two research projects, at MIT and Yale University, were to lead this new change in direction. Kevin Lynch, who had received his initial architectural education at Yale from 1935, became dissatisfied with the traditional beaux-arts education there and, during his sophomore year, seeking to join the Taliesin Fellowship, began correspondence with Frank Lloyd Wright.[1] Lynch enjoyed the hands-on approach of Wright's architectural education and studied with him for 18 months between 1937 and 1938, the period when Wright established Taliesin West in Arizona. Though he did not agree with Wright's social philosophy, having been an adolescent during the Great Depression and also deeply moved by the Spanish Civil War, he respected Wright's genius for form and design. Feeling uneasy with Wright's unreasonable treatment of his young designers, Lynch, described by Banerjee and Southworth as 'a gentle, fair and kind teacher',[2] eventually left Taliesin. Wright apparently did not take kindly to his departure.

Though he briefly enrolled at Rensselaer Polytechnic to study civil engineering, Lynch was drafted into the army during the Second World War in 1944 and eventually returned to the US to study city planning at MIT. This was significant in the sense that, although as an Irish-American he had a relatively affluent background, his mother, an Irish Catholic, was a freethinker, sending him to the Francis Parker School in Chicago, which followed educator John Dewey's philosophy of 'learning by doing'. He also married Anne Borden at Chicago Commons, a settlement house where Anne's parents had been social workers.

Lynch chose MIT because he had been greatly influenced by Lewis Mumford's *The Culture of Cities,* and his 1947 thesis impressed MIT faculty members Lloyd Rodwin, Burnham Kelly and John Buchard. The thesis dealt with theories of change, decay and renewal,[3] which Lynch was to develop in later books such as *What Time is this Place* and *Wasting Away* (his last book).

Lynch did not have a higher degree beyond his bachelor's in city planning, yet at the age of 30 he was offered a faculty position at MIT. Here he taught until the early 1980s, though he formerly retired in 1978. He died in 1984 aged 66.

Banerjee and Southworth[4] write that although the idea of master-planning, for example Clarence Stein's 'superblock' concept, was generally regarded as the correct framework in city planning, from the late 1950s onwards this view was increasingly challenged by social scientists who openly questioned the physical determinism of design. They argued that the physical form of a city had little to do with the social form of environments. Lynch wrote a number of articles during this period, including 'A theory of urban form' with Lloyd Rodwin in 1958, and 'The city as environment' in 1965. Funded by the Rockefeller Foundation, he prepared a study of three American cities: Boston, Jersey City and Los Angeles, which eventually led to the publication of his book *The Image of the City.*[5]

In late 1957, Lynch offered a radically new course in the form of a cooperative studio involving graduate students in both city planning and architecture, based upon his current research for a book.[6] In his preamble on the 'Public image of Boston', Lynch was trying to establish a 'unanimous image':

> We can make a surprisingly consistent composite image of the city, its parts and their connections, from a detailed analysis of the field and office interviews. Certain concepts are unanimously held, while others seem to be the property of a great majority of the citizens.[7]

He went on to say that Boston was a city marked for having many distinctive, recognisable districts or regions, as well as crooked, winding and confusing paths. This was symbolised, he thought, by Boston Common, the Statehouse with its golden dome and views across the Charles River from the Cambridge side.

Among the graduate students participating in this project were David Gosling from architecture and Donald Appleyard from city planning. The research was carried out under direction of Lynch and Gyorgy Kepes of the Center for and Regional Studies at MIT.

Lynch suggested that the city had a 'gross' structure to go with the above description. The Charles River with its bridges made a strong clear edge to which the principal Back Bay streets, particularly Beacon Street and Commonwealth Avenue, are parallel. On the lower side of Boston Common are Tremont and Washington Streets, parallel to each other and interconnected by several smaller streets. In most people's minds, he said, Tremont Street goes as far as Scollay Square, and from this node Cambridge Street runs to another node at the Charles Street Rotary, thus tying into the river again. Farther away from the river appears another strong edge: Atlantic Avenue and the harbour front.

More vague and confusing images occurred elsewhere in the central Boston peninsula, such as the triangular area between Back Bay and the South End. South of North Station was perceived as a no-man's-land, and there existed a confusing pattern of paths in the financial district.

Lynch proposed that a much fuller image could be developed if one moved away from unanimous ideas to consider various shades of common or uncommon concepts. Substantial numbers of interviewees would add other characteristics about the Boston of that era: that it lacked open space and recreation space, was an 'individual', small- or medium-sized city (an image which is hardly true at the start of the twenty-first century), and that it had large areas of mixed use. In architectural terms the city was marked by bay windows, iron fences and brownstone fronts. However, it became evident that the majority thought in terms of elements such as use, density, space and traffic. This tendency was reversed only in considering regions or landmarks of unusual clarity, such as the Statehouse or Beacon Hill.

In addition, Lynch studied favourite city panoramas and particularly the role of water and space. He cited the perspective of Boston from its harbour, which was not dissimilar from the view of Lower Manhattan from the Statue of Liberty. Such views seem to be memorable and satisfying. The city lights at night, from near or far, were another favourite sight, casting upon the city the air of excitement it normally lacks. Other memorable architectural details of the Boston image were its cobblestone streets and purple or violet painted windows, frames and doors.

One of the more interesting points raised by Lynch was the question of spatial ambiguity. At the time the only true skyscraper in the city was the John Hancock Insurance Building, otherwise Boston still had the appearance of a European city. The Hancock building was an extremely important Boston landmark, visible for miles. However, as Lynch pointed out, it had 'a very vague positional relation to Copley Square or Back Bay, but for most people it "floats", recognizable from afar but with a base which cannot be pinned down to any specific location or relationship'.[8] Another visual phenomenon was Boston Common itself. According to Lynch: 'Next to the Back Bay is the twin element of the Public Garden – Boston Common, a landscaped open space in the heart of the city. This makes an extremely sharp image in everyone's mind, and along with the River, Commonwealth Avenue and Beacon Hill, is most often mentioned as a particularly vivid spot. Structurally for many people it is the core of their image of the city and often, in their real or mental trips, they will veer from the direct course to "touch base" here as they go by. The image of the two areas, formally separate, sometimes fused, sometimes kept apart. It is pictured as a green open space, bordered by one or two main shopping streets . . . for all, this is a favorite pleasant spot . . . on the other hand, this thematically clear area has an ambiguous chapter'. (More than two-thirds of Lynch's interviewees found this to be so). 'This is a four-sided figure,' he continued, 'which

Beacon Hill, Boston, Massachusetts.

implies the omission of one of the five bounding streets, and twists their relative angles. Usually Park Street is dropped out, sometimes Boylston . . . the urge to regularize what is in reality a figure with five right-angled corners is quite powerful. This suppression and twisting relates to difficulties that are propagated throughout the field of the city image. The Boylston-Tremont intersection is the hub of the problem. These two important paths, here locally intersecting at right angles, are in the larger structure only slightly divergent from a parallel alignment.'[9] Whereas Back Bay was built along a typical American gridiron system, Boston Common presented this strange anomaly and visual ambiguity in city structure and was to be the subject of investigation by many subsequent commentators.

Lynch describes the graphic interpretation of his survey in his preliminary research.[10] A composite set of drawings was prepared based upon his main sources of data: office interviews, maps and field trips of some twenty subjects.[11]

One map showed the variances in regional boundaries, given by different subjects, which demonstrated a high degree of agreement within regions like Beacon Hill, with less clear determinations in the South End. Another indicated all those major physical elements that were purely conceptual: the cross streets of the Back Bay, the longitudinal streets in the South End and landmarks in the downtown area. A third map showed the frequency and also the order with which elements were put down on drawn maps (in this case the sample came from thirty subjects). An alternative map showed the qualities of detail within each square of an arbitrary grid. These qualities were divided into a range of six classes and graphically symbolised. The visual 'heart' of the city was strikingly illustrated.

Lynch concludes the section with the following remarks: 'The principal point is that all but the poorest maps are topo-logically in variant, there are few or no tearings, the sequences remain the same in every direction. This would seem to be the criteria for a useful schema, and a topological inversion is almost always the sign of confusion and ignorance. This may have some meaning as to the relative importance of rigid geometry in the city plan'.[12]

To accompany his paper, Lynch provided the class with another, more detailed survey – 'Go take a walk around the block'. This was eventually published as a paper in 1959,[13] with Malcolm Rivkin as co-author, and is published in full in Banerjee's and Southworth's *City Sense and City Design*.[14]

In the studio paper,[15] Lynch's literary style was almost conversational: 'We are standing at the corner of Berkeley and Boylston Streets in Boston, with an ill assorted group of some 27 sightseers, old and young, male and female, some of them strangers and some who have gone past this corner for years. We have asked them just to walk along with us and to tell us what they see and hear and smell and to talk about these things as the spirit moves them'.[16] With the aid of a tape recorder the party expressed their spontaneous opinion as the walk progressed, for example: 'an interesting contrast coming up here . . . Bonwit Teller in the foreground and New England Mutual in the background. Bonwit Teller (that doesn't look like a store at all . . . I like it when a building recedes like this, leaving an open square in front . . . The first spot of greenery!)'.[17]

The second part of the paper[18] asked the question, 'What was the purpose of taking this brief if elaborate walk? We assume that perception is selective and organized, a two-way process between observer and object in which the qualities of the object itself play a significant role in the final perceptual result. We have the general purpose of learning how to manipulate the physical environment so that it will facilitate the perceptual

Copley Square, Boston (1958).

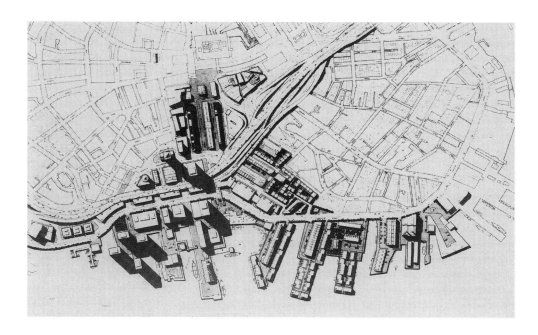

Waterfront development plan, Boston, Massachusetts (1959), Kevin Lynch, John R. Myer and Donald Appleyard.

process of the citizen, and heighten his pleasure in his city. What can be done to make his world more "visible" more "habitable" in a general sense of the words?'.

In Lynch's survey of thirty and subsequently twenty-seven subjects, he did not attempt to control anything but two variables: sex and familiarity with the area. The 'familiar' subjects either lived or worked in the blocks immediately surrounding the study block. The 'unfamiliar' subjects had either never visited the block before, or had passed by it only once or twice without being actively related to it. Three were foreign visitors. The sample was largely middle income and almost half were students or their spouses.

In a self-analysis, Lynch confessed to a number of objections to the study. First, the perceptual process was too rapid and too complex to be reduced to verbal symbols. Second, that certain perceptions were not verbalised because they were taken for granted, and third that there may be a whole level of perceptual interaction that was truly unconscious. He assembled the table shown below (left).

In summary, Lynch said that the fundamental impressions for nearly all observers were certain individual buildings and particular open spaces. There were strong emotional feelings associated with spatial characteristics – of freedom, confinement, confusion, delight, barrenness, darkness, light and so forth.[19] Less strong, but still a dominant impression is that of the city floor, or at least the sidewalk (pavement).[20] Shop fronts and their window displays were next in interest, followed by various signs. Class attitudes were also revealed as in the noted contrast between the seamstresses in alley basements, the well-dressed women on Newbury Street and the skaters in the Gardens. (There was a heightened attention, according to Lynch, toward 'high-heeled women', which implies an interplay, perhaps, of sexual psychology.)

Significant differences appeared between familiar and non-familiar observers as to the degree to which they cut up the environmental continuum, and to the extent to which parts seemed joined together. A recorded walk, Lynch concluded, tended to heighten the perception of the city. Combined with a discussion in the field of general interview results, along with the critique of the existing forms of the surround, it should prove 'an excellent means of awakening the citizen's interest in the form of the city'.[21]

THE POSTGRADUATE STUDIO ON THE BOSTON IMAGE

Given the framework of Lynch's papers, the studio held in the first semester of 1957/58 produced many different and often conflicting results with a clear distinction between the students of architecture and those of city planning.

Percent of subjects mentioning by class of element and when mentioned to nearest 5%				
Class of element	While walking	Spontaneous recall	After questioning	Composite index
Buildings	100	90	5	95
Spaces	100	85	5	95
Floor	95	65	20	85
Stores	95	65	15	85
Signs	95	5	60	75
Details	80	55	15	70
People	80	45	40	70
Traffic	65	45	45	65
Vegetation	80	25	15	55
Sounds	25	10	70	35
Smells	25	10	35	30
Weather	35	10	25	30

This was Lynch's first attempt at a visual survey and design plan for the downtown Boston peninsula. The visual survey can be examined from two different aspects. On the one hand, there is the method of dynamic analysis. This is where the observer is concerned not only with the spatial structure of the environment, but also with the temporal aspects, or the actual progression through spatial sequences. This is an important, and often ignored, aspect of urban planning. The other aspect of the survey may be termed static analysis. Here, the observer is looking at isolated objects, structures or settings, which together form the total environment. Though this latter aspect of cityscape had been realised for many years, comprehensive examination techniques had not been hitherto considered seriously.[22]

Visual representation may take a number of different directions. According to Kepes, these may be termed the conceptual, the representational and the emotional. The first is the synthesis of what one sees, and what one knows about the subject, the second merely represents optical characteristics, while the third expresses individual emotional responses. Lynch's studies were directed along the lines of the conceptual approach. During this decade, the motivating force behind these research projects in the US was the Rockefeller Foundation. The Foundation awarded large grants to a number of academic centres to enable inquiry into the state of visual chaos in modern cities. It made no stipulation as to the direction of the research, but required preliminary studies to be completed at the end of a three-year programme. The liberation from any dogma or need for justification allowed a fascinatingly wide angle of approach.

Objections can be made to the effect that the perceptual process is too rapid and too complex to be reduced to verbal symbols, and that certain perceptions are not verbalised because, being so common, they are 'taken for granted'. There may also be an important level of perceptual interaction that is truly unconscious or repressed. To this last objection there can be no answer. The major objection is an inherent difficulty in the verbal method that might be diminished by using techniques such as a photographic recognition test.

Prior to the studio, Lynch and Kepes, using video cameras, had already made a study of a main highway leading into Boston.[23] For the peninsula study Lynch drew up a short-list of salient structural elements of the city: nodes, paths, districts, barriers and landmarks. In an extract from the programme he said:

We will take as our subject the central peninsula of Boston, inwards from Massachusetts Avenue, with the object of analyzing its present visual form which will also be discussed. Results of current research into city imageability will be used as a springboard into the problem, employing both the theoretical speculations and also the detailed reconnaissance and interview data of the problem area. All other aspects of the urban problem (economic, social, technical and administrative) will be assumed to be non-limiting within the very elastic bounds of common sense. Plans must be extremely realistic, however, in regard to the existing visual form, as to how the city image is produced and affected, and to the meaning of the sensuous city to its inhabitants.[24]

The studio project achieved a modicum of success, one of the more interesting results being to indicate the structural growth of the city. The greatest value of Lynch's work seemed to lie in his analysis of the elements of the environment, which are the most meaningful to the inhabitant. Lynch himself was not very much concerned with graphic presentation or the finesse of his analytical elements.

The results presented a dichotomy between the postgraduate planning students and the postgraduate architectural students, a stronger graphic ability being displayed by the architectural students (a situation which prevails to the present day). Among the results produced in 1958 was a general consensus that the restructuring of the downtown area of Boston was to give it an identifiable image, instead of the confused character experienced by most citizens. The study highlighted, among other necessary physical changes, certain desirable design characteristics, such as re-establishing the strong 'urban grain' (Lynch's term) of Back Bay on the northern side of the peninsula.

One of the authors, David Gosling, proposed the introduction of a series of squares and pedestrian routes, utilising derelict land and buildings in the South Boston Roxbury ghetto area, in order to induce an increased sense of public security. Additionally, historical research shows that at the establishment of Boston in the early eighteenth century, the peninsula had been more of an island in which the proximity of the river and sea had been more clear, and the peninsula had been separated from the hinterland in the form of marshes, where the Fenway was subsequently constructed.

In the proposal, the sea and the river were drawn back into the city in the form of a new extended harbour, and other bays north and south of the peninsula with indicated sequential routes based upon Philip Thiel's earlier proposals.

Following Gordon Cullen's concept of 'serial vision' (a point not emphasised by Lynch), Gosling drew up sequential illustrations to show different routes to downtown (for pedestrians, cars and public transport). An outcome of this technique was a proposal to clarify the subway routes using coloured illuminations and paints indicating place and direction, an idea rediscovered by the Boston Mass Transit Authority some twenty years later in 1977.

'Boston Image' student project at MIT, David Gosling, directed by Kevin Lynch (1958).

This set of proposals was preceded by the earlier studies of David Gosling under the direction of Gyorgy Kepes at MIT. Kepes had provided a strong influence in evoking new techniques of spatial representation. The studies involved the recording of spatial sequences in an old environment (Beacon Hill, Boston) and a new environment (Shoppers' World, Framingham, in Greater Boston). The three-dimensional sketches were supplemented by graphs representing a musical score. The horizontal scale was the time-scale or actual measurement of progression through the sequence, and the vertical scale indicated the apparent expansion or contraction of space through the sequence. Both apparent space and intensity of space were recorded, similar to amplitude and frequency modulation in sound recording. A second analysis of the two sequences involved what Kepes termed the 'complexity factor'. This dealt with the psychological value of the visual character of the sequence. Both Gibson and Thiel had experimented in the field, but no really satisfactory graphic method had evolved at that point. Gosling's analysis was based on the relative dominance of experience character – confusion, bleakness, repose, intimacy, bustle and so on. Each of these elements was indicated on the graph in a different transparent colour. The size of the coloured area indicated the extent of that particular characteristic. However, the method was confusing since there was no agreement in people's minds as to the actual meaning of the terms used, and besides, the technique was highly subjective.

It is clear that the techniques described above have greater value if, as in the case of Thiel's experiments, they are carried out by a group, so that a comparative appraisal might be made. If the group is composed of lay persons rather than professional planners, a consensus view might be obtained, which could be translated by the planner in graphic analyses. The difficulty lies in establishing common terms that have the same meaning to all people in the group.

THE IMAGE OF THE CITY

The novelty of Lynch's approach lay in his consideration of the visual character of the American city through the study of the mental images of a city, held in the minds of its citizens. Asserting that 'legibility' was a crucially important characteristic of a city environment, enabling inhabitants to place themselves within the general structure and establish a framework for individual action, he argued that such legibility depended upon the ability of the environment to communicate a clear 'image' of itself. This image would undoubtedly vary from individual to individual, but nevertheless certain strong common features would emerge to constitute a 'group image'. Thus the legibility of the city may be enhanced or diminished as this group image is reinforced and weakened. Interviews with citizens, including trips through the city, meant that memorable features contributing to the overall imageability could be identified. This was demonstrated in *The Image of the City* in the cases of the central areas of three cities: Boston, Jersey City and Los Angeles. From these studies, Lynch concluded that, although a variety of features contributed to group images, they could be classified as belonging to one of the five types of urban element referred to above: nodes, paths, districts, barriers and landmarks. (The latter has itself proved to be one of the most imageable features of subsequent urban design theory.) In addition to the 'objective' method of approach, Lynch's study also owed its popularity to the fact that it provided, almost for the first time, an effective definition of precisely what it was that urban designers should be concerned with and the method they might adopt to achieve their goals (the reinforcement of the five elements).

The effectiveness of defining the task of the urban designer in terms of these essential distillations of the city's characteristics is attested by subsequent attempts to improve the menu, including Jane Jacobs' *Four Conditions* and Christopher Alexander's *253 Patterns*. Charles Moore provided his version in *Body, Memory and Architecture* (without referring to Lynch's work): 'The inhabited world within boundaries then, can be usefully ascribed a syntax of place, pattern and edge. Within each of these four, architectural ordering arrangements can be considered which are made to respond to the natural landscape as well as to human bodies and memories'.[25] Christian Norberg-Schulz (who does acknowledge Lynch) suggests: 'Place and Node; Path and Axis; Domain and District'.[26]

These classifications of essential concepts contrast markedly with that of another seminal work, *Townscape* (published in England in 1961, a year after *The Image of the City*) by British theorist Gordon Cullen.[27] Cullen's investigations of the desirable qualities of good urban environments differed considerably from the academic analyses of Lynch. Ironically, the personal vision and graphic fluency that Cullen brought to the explanation of his ideas were to some extent a handicap, arousing suspicion in the minds of those for whom a more 'objective' explanation was the purpose of the urban designer. Cullen reinforced the impression of an 'unscientific' approach by a similarly evocative and poetic use of language to accompany the visual images, in an attempt to communicate the great variety and subtlety of overlapping qualities of urban elements. Thus his list of essential concepts, as set out in the pages of *Townscape* (and in previous issues of *The Architectural Review* dating back as far as 1947) was a mixture of the architectural ('silhouette', 'division of space', 'looking out of enclosure'), the painterly ('distortion', 'texture'), the poetic ('the telltale', 'taming with tact') and the practical ('lettering', 'multiple use') that the urban designer should respect. Nevertheless, Cullen's method included, on occasions, a systematic framework for these sometimes-elusive qualities through the idea of serial vision. This paralleled the efforts at MIT to devise a way of handling the temporal in urban design, and, as in examples of Cullen's illustrated work, coupling a plan of a town with a series of photographs or drawings representing the sequence of key events on the route through it (for example as in the work of Philip Thiel).

While the architectural faculty at MIT during this period was totally disparaging about Cullen's artistic approach[ ] ing it as 'sheer romanticism', they were more s[ ] Lynch's 'scientific' approach. This is all the mor[ ] Gyorgy Kepes' own work contained many su[ ] terms. Lynch himself was less critical of Culle[ ] ledged Cullen's contribution to urban design th[ ]

Venice, Italy.

The Image of the City did establish a graphic system to relate to Lynch's structural system of nodes, paths, districts, barriers and landmarks, using 75 per cent or more frequency of observation, with graphs of 50–75 per cent, 25–50 per cent and 12–25 per cent frequencies.[29] Yet without the written description of the graphic symbols it was difficult for a lay person to determine what they stood for. In the main body of the text, the marginal sketches without verbal descriptions were occasionally more difficult to understand. Despite such criticisms concerning the shortcomings in the graphic skills of the illustrations, the work as a whole was a major and powerful piece of original thinking. It received many enthusiastic reviews, not only from the architectural and planning journals, but from journals in other professional fields as well as the press in general.[30]

In his book, Lynch suggests that there may be a definition of imageability: 'That quality in a physical object which gives it a high probability of evoking a strong image in any given observer. It is that shape, color, or arrangement which facilitates the making of vividly identified, powerfully structured, highly useful mental images of the environment. It might also be called legibility, or perhaps visibility in a heightened sense, where objects are not only able to be seen, but are presented sharply and intensely to observers'.[31]

Visual form of Boston, Massachusetts.

Lynch went on to say that the city of Venice, Italy, might be an example of such a highly imageable environment. In the US he indicated such cities as San Francisco, Boston, the Chicago lakefront and Manhattan.

Perhaps inevitably the Boston analysis was the most vivid of the three cities Lynch studied. The book draws heavily upon the studies described previously, but expands them in a more coherent way. An important map of the Boston peninsula highlights 'Problems of the Boston image'.[32] It includes directional ambiguity, characterless paths, lack of direction, weak or absent boundaries, points of confusion, isolation, bottomless tower, chaotic and/or characterless areas, shape ambiguity, discontinuity and a disconnected or hidden waterfront. It also included more ambiguous terms such as an incomplete broken path and lack of relation. In his introduction Lynch acknowledges the major influence of Gyorgy Kepes, and it certainly seems likely that many of these descriptions stem from that source.

In *The City and Its Elements,* Lynch describes his terminology in further detail.[33] Paths he describes as 'channels along which the observer customarily, occasionally or potentially moves. They may be streets, walkways, transit lines, canals, railroads'. Edges are 'the linear elements not used or considered as paths by the observer. They are the boundaries between two phases, linear breaks in continuity: shores, railroad cuts, edges of development, and walls. They are lateral references, rather than coordinate axes. Such edges may be barriers'. Districts are, he says, 'medium-to-large sections of the city, conceived as having a two-dimensional extent, which the observer mentally enters inside of and which are recognizable as having some common, identifying characters'. Nodes are 'the points, the strategic spots in a city into which an observer can enter and which are the intensive foci to and from which he is traveling'. Finally, Lynch defines landmarks thus: 'Landmarks are another type of point reference, but in this case the observer does not enter them, they are external. They are usually a defined physical object: building, sign, store or mountain'.[34]

In the Appendices, Lynch remarks that the role of form plays an important part in the cognitive city, but he also warns that there are disadvantages of imageability. He quotes archeological examples where a landscape with magical meanings may inhibit practical activities, as the ancestral grave mounds in China inhibit the use of needed arable land, or among the Maori in New Zealand where myth forbids the best sea landing berths. In this he refers to what he describes as 'the Chinese Pseudo Science of Semantics',[35] a complex lore of landscape influence, where winds of evil are controlled by hills, rocks or trees seeming visually to block dangerous gaps, and where good water spirits are attracted by ponds, courses and drains.

In his field surveys, a major discrepancy occurred between two sources, regarding connections and general organisation. Known connections persisted in the sketches, but others disappeared. Lynch acknowledged that the difficulties of drawing and fitting everything together simultaneously fragmented and distorted sketch maps, and they were therefore not a good index of the known connective sketches. He illustrated this with plans of the Boston image derived from verbal interviews, another derived from subjects' sketch maps resulting in another map of the distinctive elements of Boston, and finally with the visual form of Boston as seen in the field. Parallel maps were drawn for Jersey City and Los Angeles.

In his conclusions, Lynch acknowledges that 'City Perception is in essence a time phenomenon and it is directed toward an object of very large scale'. He goes on to say that in future it would be important to find ways of understanding such entities, including the handling of problems of sequence and unfolding patterns. In the last of the appendices, the book analyses two adjacent but very different local neighbourhoods – Beacon Hill (a historic, coherent, upper-income district) and Scollay Square (a confusing, run-down and tawdry commercial district).

The Image of the City, despite some interpretation difficulties in the graphics, was to become the most important and influential study of American urban design in the second half of the twentieth century.

THE YALE ROCKEFELLER RESEARCH PROJECT

Parallel with Lynch's work was a research project funded by the Rockefeller Foundation. Professor Christopher Tunnard, director of the City Planning Program at Yale (a two-year postgraduate course), invited David Gosling and James Skeritt to participate in the research. At the outset, a composite table was drawn up of the major visual structural elements of the city to be analysed and considered – an attempt to list the parts of the total image of the city.

The project was aimed at the development of a comprehensive analysis or visual map of an entire small city. New Haven, Connecticut, was selected as the base. The most significant part of the study – aside from consideration of the total envelope of the city and its structural form, the skyline hierarchies, approaches and gateways – was the series of district or neighbourhood analyses. The natural physical structure was also considered: natural land formations of rock outcrops (either revealing or obscuring), water, marshes, rivers, harbours, ponds and woodland all contributed toward the identity of the city. Also included in the physical structure were man-made elements, such as railway yards, garbage landfills, brickyards, quarries, power lines and billboards that together created the typical confusion of the urban scene.

In the second stage of the city analysis, the various districts were considered separately, but according to visual character rather than sociological, political or economic determinants. Within this category were the new subdivisions, the old residential districts (both high and low income), entertainment districts (theatre districts), wholesale districts (the warehouse and clothing districts of New York) and Chinatown (as in Boston, San Francisco and New York).

Another section of the visual survey were the 'lines'. These were not districts in themselves, nor were they described as structural features of districts. Examples included exclusive shopping districts like Newbury Street in Boston, Maiden Lane in San Francisco and Fifth Avenue in New York. However, this category did not only include streets. In certain instances barriers, either natural or man-made (terms used by Lynch) could also be termed as linear; for example a man-made barrier would be a railway cutting; a natural barrier would be a river.

Further down the scale were listed accents within the city. These could be short lengths of streets with symbolic significance, squares and parks such as Boston Common, New York Central Park and New Haven Green, old historic buildings such as the three churches on New Haven Green, or monuments and landmarks such as the Harkness Tower at Yale University. Finally, street furniture, including signs, lamps and paving surfaces, was included at the detailed end of the scale.

Using Gyorgy Kepes' terminology, a list of characteristics at the end of the table included solids and voids, light and shade, accent, surprise, contrast, harmony, monotony, historical significance, texture and colour, repetitive elements and scale relationships.

Before the studies commenced, a list of possible techniques was added to the preceding table. Under the first section it was proposed that a large-scale map of the features could be used in conjunction with a model, aerial photographs and high- and low-level perspectives. Cut-out models of elevations and sections of the city could be used to study skyline and silhouette effects. For the study of approaches and districts, several techniques included written reports and annotated sketches, with bulk and space studies used for the study of districts,

together with a map showing transition zones.

Gosling's studies emphasised the preparation of the visual survey and the urban design plan. One of the first undertaken was a broad graphic analysis of the entire city of New Haven, using Lynch's criteria of nodes, paths, barriers, districts and landmarks. The map was to serve as the basis of later analyses and hence the graphic representation was intended to stress the visual characteristics rather than topographical data, traffic patterns or zoning. Visual barriers were included and focal points were stressed. High land was portrayed graphically to show how it acted as a visual definition within the city. The exits and entrances to the city were inserted. The map was purely objective, and no attempt was made to suggest any proposals at that stage. The method used was a reproduction of the city map, mounted on a baseboard and using overlays to indicate high land, and coloured pins to indicate focal points.

A route sequence study was made of the Prospect Hill District of New Haven. This was linear in character with two main structural lines in the form of Whitney Avenue and Prospect Street. Various points were taken along the routes in chronological order. Three-dimensional sketches were made of these sections of the route, below which was inserted a spatial diagram of the street as it was actually perceived in the drawing.

Two districts or neighbourhoods were selected for analysis. The first district was the downtown area of New Haven, including parts of the adjacent Hill District and Prospect Street. A large aerial photograph was used as a basic tool, in prepara-

Churches, New Haven Green, Connecticut (1958).

tion of an aerial perspective, which was to serve as the base map. The technique differed from that used by Lynch, which, for the Boston peninsula, was entirely two-dimensional. A perspective has more impact, graphically, than a photograph, in that the artist is able to stress certain features and suppress others. The perspective included the city's future redevelopment proposals. Next, a transparent overlay was used for the analysis of the physical structure. This overlay depicted districts, nuclei (places where people tended to congregate, such as church/chapel streets and Broadway/The Yale Coop), paths (which were not necessarily main traffic routes but those that people found convenient), landmarks (generally buildings that people used to orient themselves) and barriers (in New Haven these were manmade barriers – the railway yards, the expressway embankment, the sunken expressway). In interviews with lay persons, this method of showing the visual structure of an area was found to be more useful than the two-dimensional map.

A second analysis of the district was made using the same overlay technique. The author again adapted a Gyorgy Kepes' 'complexity factor' technique. Here, an attempt was made to delineate areas of repose or calm, activity and excitement, bleakness and also confusion by means of various colours. Buildings of symbolic significance were also included. Again, the main drawback was the ambiguity of the terminology. However, if a consensus of agreement concerning the terminology could have been established, such an analysis would have been of value.

The second district selected was the Wooster Square area. Similar graphic techniques were used and it was possible, using the perspective technique, to stress the expressway, gas tanks, Chapel Street and Wooster Square.[36] Though the techniques were the same as those used in the previous study, the analyses were different: the main concern here was the analysis of the two major routes through the district (the expressway and interchange on the boundaries of the district and Chapel Street and Wooster Square as the main thoroughfare). The first analysis, using a transparency and colour overlay, was a contrasting space sequence study of both routes. The second analysis concerned the route characteristics of the district. Accents (structures such as the Wooster Square church, gas tanks and bridges), barriers (railway tracks and the river estuary), lines (workshop rows, a single railway track) and surprise (sections of the routes where the visual impact suddenly changed, giving a sense of drama and alteration in spatial conditions) were all symbolised.

In late 1959, David Gosling was appointed as a civic design consultant to the New Haven City Planning Commission.[37] At the time, New Haven had a dynamic city mayor, Richard C. Lee, who did much to introduce the new concept of urban renewal and rehabilitation, a radical alternative to complete slum clearance. The Oak Street 'connector' to the Connecticut Turnpike (the expressway described above) was the key to linking suburbanites to the downtown area of the city. Early in his 16-year term of office, Lee had appointed Edward Logue as his development planning administrator. Logue later left New Haven to take over Boston's redevelopment programme in 1961 and was responsible for the administration of the construction of Boston's Government Center with a master plan by I. M. Pei

and a new City Hall, designed by Kallman, McKinnel and Knowles, the result of a national architectural competition.

David Gosling was invited by Logue to take the Hill District of New Haven as a case study area. The reason for his choice was that this was a district almost completely lacking in any identifiable structure. It had, nevertheless, a composite character of its own; it was adjacent to the downtown area and it had fairly well defined barriers and boundaries. A minor section contained dilapidated slum housing and required clearance, but the majority of the district was reasonably well maintained. One of the main issues was to give it some degree of visual coherence without radical redevelopment. Christopher Tunnard and James Skerritt were also consultants to the City Planning Commission.

The first stage of the study was a detailed survey of the district. This was accomplished by multiple tours of the area using spot notes and sequential photographs. The three-dimensional base map for the visual analysis used transparent overlays, as in the previous Rockefeller studies. The analysis indicated, in abstract form, features such as tree-lined avenues, row houses, small gardens, the workshop district, derelict district, shops, visual barriers and paths. Again in abstract form, a subsequent plan showed how the visual characteristics of the proposal should take effect. This was followed by the urban design plan itself. The analysis revealed that there was no core to the district despite a boulevard traversing it. The Hill District, which was located on the east side of downtown and adjacent to the railway station, was something of a misnomer, since topographical changes were small. The proposals inserted a linear shopping and entertainment area with a line to a small interrelated square. An important feature was an obsolete railway cutting through the entire district. Inspired by the river walks in San Antonio, Texas, a small boating canal was proposed along its length. (It had been a feeder canal between the two sides of the harbour before the railway was constructed.) Cafés, shops and small garden apartments were to line both sides of the new canal. The new small square on Portsea Street, as the urban nucleus, would be linked with this linear park, forming a pedestrian network. Most houses were timber-framed houses on tree-lined avenues, with a proposed colour scheme so that each subdistrict could be identified. Various street junctions were realigned to provide a more defined flow to the street pattern and eliminate ambiguous junctions.

A proposed Church Street expressway connection across the eastern boundary created a new visual barrier where none existed previously. Howard Avenue was a natural visual boundary on the western side, and a new junior high school was proposed on the northeastern boundaries. The most radical proposal was the closing of Liberty Street, Portsea Street and Cedar Street to form a continuous pedestrian network at a time when pedestrianisation was unheard of. The existing square, a concrete playground surrounded by chain-link fences, would be brick paved and planted with trees; sitting spaces would be provided as well as a skating and wading pool for children. The pedestrian network was developed around this central core, and the backyards of each block were opened up into communal gardens or greens. Each block would become its own community, strengthening the existing social interaction.[38] Other

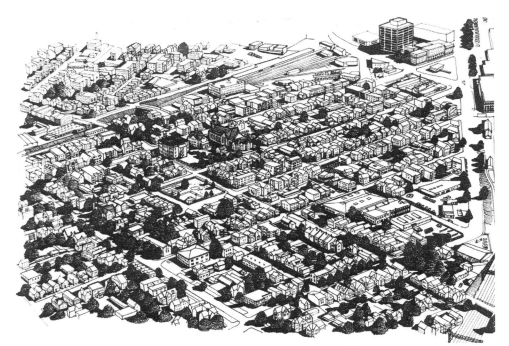

Hill District, New Haven, Connecticut.

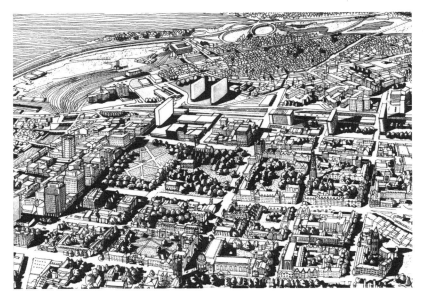

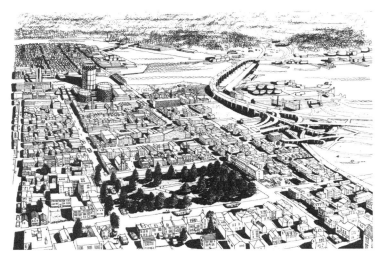

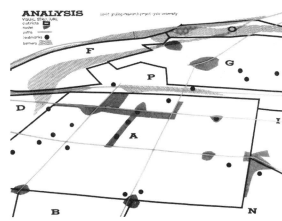

Berlin Turnpike,
Connecticut:
existing (1959).

studies carried out under Christopher Tunnard's direction included contrasting colour studies of Beacon Hill, Boston and Dixwell Avenue, New Haven, by examining colour applied to buildings, street furniture, textures, floor patterns and surfaces.

The final study carried out by David Gosling and American author Geoffrey Baker,[39] and inspired by Gordon Cullen's article in *The Architectural Review*,[40] was an investigation into the visual aspects of commercial highways between cities. This was about the time when the Eisenhower Administration introduced the Federal Government's Interstate Highway Program.[41] There was an analogy between the Gosling–Baker project and the Atlantic Region Study, in that the consideration of the macro-landscape and the micro-landscape was of prime importance. There had been a visual disintegration of the landscape as a result of ex-urban linear commercial developments, sometimes extending for hundreds of miles. This was most prevalent in the eastern seaboard states and in California. The major highways had become a series of continuous strips of supermarkets, motels, drive-in restaurants, drive-in cinemas (now defunct) and gas stations. There was no physical order or visual coherence.

A 6-kilometre (10-mile) length of one such highway, on the outskirts of Hartford, Connecticut, was selected for the study. This strip of the Berlin Turnpike was a section of the New York–New Haven–Hartford–Boston highway, and its 400-kilometre (250-mile) length was particularly bad from a visual point of view.

The main basis of the study was a linear map analysis of the turnpike, drawn to scale. It included three analyses. The first attempted to portray the spatial sequence along the highway; the expansion and contraction of space caused by buildings, hills

Berlin Turnpike,
Connecticut:
proposed (1959).

and banks of trees combined with important single vistas indicated by arrows. The second analysis depicted, symbolically, commercial development along the length of the turnpike. The third analysis was a longitudinal section of the 6-kilometre (10-mile) length; the turnpike traversed a continuous belt of rolling countryside, and significant visual features were the siting of billboards, traffic signs and signals on the hillsides. The object of the three analyses was to give a complete picture of the visual characteristics of the highway and highlight the problems. It was intended as a reference to be read in conjunction with the three-dimensional sketches of proposals and existing conditions.

The three-dimensional sketches were intended to represent a driver's view. Each illustration was to show one or more of the important points governing the design of highways, with particular emphasis on commercial facilities. With each illustration of existing conditions came an accompanying perspective of proposals to improve the visual design.

One such illustration was a group of gas stations and service stations at the beginning of the study section. The proposal was that, by means of a standardised coloured sign (e.g. orange), some form of coherence might be achieved by the reduction of the confusing array of signs.[42] At that time the presence of a motel, for example, was indicated by an untidy collection of roadside billboards and neon signs. The study suggested that an arrow of white on black as an integral part of the road surface, and a single, brightly coloured sign in the line of vision, would achieve a greater degree of visual coherence. A significant factor that had an impact on the Berlin Turnpike was its topography. The highway swept across valley after valley in a straight line. One proposal was to plant groups of tall evergreens on the brow of the hills on either side of the road, creating a rhythmical visual punctuation.

The surface of the highway did not appear to have been studied by its traffic engineers. The Turnpike had ragged and ill-defined edges with a narrow grass centre median. Immediately adjacent, the concrete paving of the highway itself was bordered variously by loose gravel, grass and bare earth or asphalt, with an abundance of chain link or wire fences. The use of horizontal white directional signage inserted into the surface of a black asphalt paving, with double boarded white fencing on black posts, could emphasise the linear qualities of the highway.

The Hill District Rehabilitation Area

Under the leadership of the Mayor, Richard C. Lee, the city of New Haven was the first in the US to introduce the concept of urban rehabilitation of depressed areas instead of just clearance and redevelopment. After the Yale urban analysis project was presented to the New Haven City Planning Commission in May 1959, James Skerritt was appointed to the permanent staff as visual designer.[43] The general methods of the Yale Rockefeller project were accepted, and David Gosling was engaged in a trial experiment to integrate the research methods into a rehabilitation district design. The design proposals were completed in 1961.

One of the major problems in the execution of rehabilitation design plans, not encountered in redevelopment projects, was the degree of inflexibility. The object was to preserve as many of the existing structures as possible, while at the same time

creating a fresh visual environment. This could not be achieved by merely repainting and repairing all the houses in the area. Districts selected for rehabilitation were not categorised as slums, but rather as areas that were beginning to lose definition, and adjacent areas in which the first signs of structural decay and social problems were beginning to appear.

The proposed creation of the Church Street expressway across the eastern boundary created an effective visual barrier where none existed previously. There was an obvious need to form natural visual boundaries (not barriers) on the outer edges of the area. A large junior high school had already been proposed on the northeastern edge.

A preliminary visual study of the Hill District indicated that, topographically, the highest point was a small square (playground) in the centre of the district adjacent to Portsea Street. The streets fell away rapidly on the east–west axis, but less so on the north–south axis. The steepest streets were on the east side of the square with views of downtown New Haven.

Survey techniques followed that of the Rockefeller Project with predetermined route sequences. Visual characteristics of outlying districts were observed, such as the open land and vistas across the railway yards to the harbour, and views along Columbus Avenue towards the towers in downtown New Haven. Many of Lynch's techniques were followed, including his list of major visual structural elements. The route sequence studied every street intersection from a pedestrian standpoint.

Problems included the provision for the new junior high school, the adequate integration of the 'civic nucleus' (church, elementary school and community centre) and the redevelopment of the obsolete railway cutting. The proposals were all presented as eye-level and aerial perspectives, sequential perspectives and transparent overlays of proposals on existing street plans.

MAN-MADE AMERICA

Reference has already been made to Christopher Tunnard's and Boris Pushkarev's book *Man-Made America*.[44] This work, which received a National Book Award in the US in 1964, was the result of cumulative research for the Yale Rockefeller Project. In their preface, the authors acknowledge previous publications,[45] including the special 'Man-Made America' issue of *The Architectural Review*, published in December 1950, many years earlier. Whereas this latter publication was a critique of American urban scenery and aroused a lot of antagonism towards it in North America, the book of the same title was a much more positive view of what urban America could be. Tunnard, in fact, mentioned in his preface that the same journal had responded in kind with its 'Outrage' issue – an attack on British urban scenery published in December 1956. Tunnard writes that 'more than its title alone, this special issue (in 1950) of *The Architectural Review* was a precursor of our book'.[46] He stated that his studies for the book had begun in 1957 with the financial aid from the Humanities division of the Rockefeller Foundation.

The book is clearly structured in its analysis of the (then) contemporary scene of America, which reflected Tunnard's professional background as a landscape architect. According to Tunnard: 'An undertaking such as the British Town and Country Planning Act, which requires a proposed physical use for every acre of land in Great Britain, would be unwelcome here because of our *illusions* of freedom to expand in any way we like'.[47] Tunnard had already discerned the decline of the central city and the growth of suburbia, but recognised the gifts of the American natural landscape and, in particular, the National Parks System.

In a prophetic way, *Man-Made America* foresaw the studies of Jarreau's *Edge City* some thirty years later. Morphology as an important aspect of urban design had not been discussed hitherto. It had been developed twenty years earlier in Europe in the work of Aldo Rossi in Italy and Leon and Robert Krier in Belgium. But whereas the latter focused their attention on the morphology of European historic cities of the eighteenth and nineteenth centuries, Tunnard's emphasis was on the contemporary city. In Part One, Section 5, 'The new settlement pattern', Tunnard examined 'the morphology of the urban fringe'.[48] Here he noted the gradual trend towards larger residential subdivisions, encouraged by the major developers (who had been growing in number) in order to realise a substantial profit on the land as well as on the houses.[49]

In critical reviews, *Man-Made America* was received with acclaim by many publications, from *The American Institute of Architects Journal* to *The New York Times,* and from *The Architectural Forum* to *New Society*. Many reviews mentioned the chapter on freeways. Part Three, 'The Paved Ribbon', which examined the development of freeway form was followed by detailed analyses of the 'internal harmony of the freeway' and 'the external harmony of the freeway'.[50] It included many drawings prepared by Philip Lin and Vladimir Pozharsky, who were among the many contributors to this major work. The drawings, though somewhat sterile graphically, provided a guide for the ideal highway geometries to eliminate driver boredom, and provided a major breakthrough in highway design where, hitherto, intercity highways had taken a straight line, as far as it was topographically possible. It also emphasised the importance of integrating new highways with the landscape, an idea that drew upon previous Rockefeller Foundation research.

This interest in the car driver's visual perception of the highway as a sequential experience was paralleled by another important study, *The View from the Road,* by Appleyard, Lynch and Myer (see below).

Part Six, 'Something for the Future: the Preservation of Visible History,[51] also drew upon previous research. At a time when there was wholesale demolition of historic neighbourhoods in American cities, the authors made the plea that there was much to be gained by reversing this trend. In Section 5, 'Preservation and urban renewal',[52] Tunnard describes David Gosling's Wooster Square proposal for New Haven, an early example of advocacy planning and citizen participation. The final chapter also indicates Tunnard's use of the term 'urban design'. This final section covered the relationship between private enterprise preservation and urban design, and included examples such as the urban revitalisation of the Hill in Providence, Rhode Island.

THE VIEW FROM THE ROAD

Man-Made America was identified with intercity highway design; *The View from the Road,[53]* published about the same time, was also concerned with the visual aspects of intercity highway design, but in a particularly graphic way.

Authors of the book Donald Appleyard, Kevin Lynch and John R. Myer were at the time Assistant Professors at MIT. The work was particularly notable for its emphasis on sequential space. Though Gordon Cullen's *Townscape,* published in 1961, was acknowledged in the bibliography, Cullen's theory of serial vision, espoused in 1947, was not mentioned as a reference.

The monograph dealt with the aesthetics of highways and the way they appeared to drivers and their passengers, in addition to the implications for design. Developing further the theories of Philip Thiel, the one (and quite recent) type of urban experience was the variables of speed and sequence in a closely controlled and almost metronomic sequence of visual 'stills'. This was a kind of visual adaptation of Ogilby[54] to the world of the freeway. By the use of picture sequences and linear diagrams indicating the pattern of events along the route, the experience of an existing highway, the North–East Expressway in Boston, was analysed in a manner which made it possible to envisage

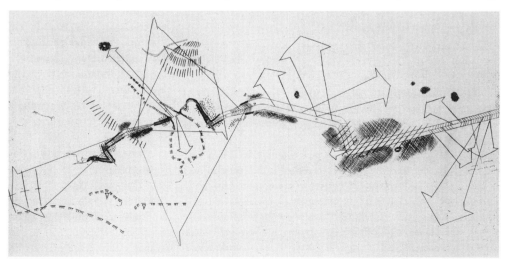

'View from the road' study (1964), Donald Appleyard.

the rigorous formulation and testing of a general 'highway aesthetic'. *The View from the Road* acknowledges that: 'For the most part, we have considered highways as single linear sequences. We have not dealt with a network of highways, or, more properly, with a system of movement in the city'.[55]

The authors suggested that pleasant visual episodes were possible on the highways into big cities such as New York, Chicago, Philadelphia and San Francisco. They added that 'in an affluent society, we may well choose to build roads in which motion, space and view are organized primarily for enjoyment. But even on highways whose primary function is the carriage of goods and people, visual form is of fundamental importance and can be shaped without interfering with traffic flow'.[56]

An introduction that contained sequential photographs of the Japanese shrine of Goshojinja, Kamakura also included the quintessential American roller coaster. While the graphic analyses were much clearer in symbolism than *The Image of the City*, and were also accompanied by three-dimensional sketch-perspectives, they remained abstruse to the lay reader. The use of tiny 'flick' perspectives in the right-hand and left-hand corners of every page (a technique hitherto used in studies in science and mathematics) was vivid in describing the journey along this particular highway, though the 68 sequential perspectives (on pages 58–62) accompanied by annotations were, perhaps, more useful. The most vivid of these sketches included the transfer from daylight to darkness (pages 39–43), describing the highway as it moved underground beneath the financial district.

Night scenes from highways were considered to be important, a recognition not really addressed in *Man-Made America*. This was described in lyrical fashion: 'At night new order reigns in the city. The chaotic skylines, jagged spaces, erratic forms and shapes disappear into the darkness, to be replaced by luminous dots, strips and diffused light. The path system becomes clearer . . . the more prominent intersections or nodal points gain extra emphasis with stop lights, directional signs or drugstores and certain areas, such as entertainment districts or shopping centers, become nocturnal landmarks'.[57]

Many of the interpretive diagrams clearly owed much to the theories of Gyorgy Kepes, for example those on page 51, indicating a graph of the driver's 'presumed attention'.

PROFESSIONAL RECOGNITION OF URBAN DESIGN

The First Annual Urban Design Conference was held in April 1956. However, the Twelfth Conference, which took place on 7 and 8 June 1968, was to be the last held at the Harvard Graduate School of Design for many years.

The conference was chaired, as was the first, by Dean José Luis Sert. It was described in the foreword to the proceedings as that of 'a giant critique'.[58] Unlike contemporary academic conferences, it seemed that throughout its 12 years of existence, no formal papers were submitted, let alone referred. Rather, the panels were composed of invited participants, among whom were Raymond Affleck, Adele Santos, Walter Isard, Kevin

Lynch, Donald Schon, Jerzy Soltan, Wilhelm von Moltke and Shadrach Woods. Notable among the students attending was Roger Trancick. Given such a distinguished list of participants, the proceedings, as published, were disappointingly vague in intent.

The keynote address was delivered by the distinguished American academic John Kenneth Galbraith. According to Galbraith, in reviewing the rise of the nineteenth-century industrial cities, 'the conception of the city was liberalized and decentralized. This was especially so of the Anglo Saxon world (of the industrial cities of Britain, the United States and the older countries of the British Commonwealth). Here the city ceased to be a reflection of individual, dynastic or collective personality: it became both the instrument, and the result, of industrial development'.[59] Galbraith went on to say that relatively uncontrolled land use was a manifestation of new attitudes toward efficiency. Land use was no longer subordinate to design, but rather that which served economic performance or resulted from economic development. It did not serve amenity or beauty but economic efficiency. If Galbraith presented an eloquent picture of the nineteenth-century industrial city – such as Chicago, Pittsburgh and Kansas City – he made little reference to the mid-twentieth-century city.

In addressing the issue of urban design, Galbraith said that 'those who argue for economic priority will invariably insist that popular taste is intransigently vulgar. Accordingly, it is arrogant and undemocratic for a minority to try to impose higher standards based on its pretense to better taste'.[60]

In the subsequent panel discussions, Adele Santos quoted Melvin Webber who, she believed, had described the emerging urban pattern in what he referred to as the non-urban role. She correctly predicted that strange urban patterns were occurring such as 'a sort of central city in the middle of a suburban area'. The growth of suburban shopping centres in the subsequent decade fulfilled her prophecies.

This first panel was concerned with the physical form of the city (the theme was 'The Environmental Implications of Compact Design'), while the following panel was about 'Regional Context and Economic Efficiency'. Walter Gronz proposed that a new town in the Boston metropolitan area could provide a 'superior environment, superior jobs and superior housing for lower income households, an alternative to the much more difficult job of attempting to bring employment into the ghetto'. He predicted that 'otherwise there may still be some 400,000 poverty households in the Boston region in 1990'.[61] Walter Isard argued that the advantages of compact communities were going to be those of scale economies with low transportation and infrastructure capital costs, suggesting an ideal population target would be 200,000 people.

During the discussion there was reference to the British New Towns programme by the chair of the panel, William Nash, who said that the 'Crown Corporation likes to maintain control so that it can recoup increases in land values which have resulted from urbanization'. This was erroneous, as was a remark from the floor stating that in England, subsidised housing was not available within the existing city.[62]

The next panel covered 'Community Process: the Interrelations of Social and Physical Factors'. There was much comment here regarding ethnic and racial prejudice, though many of the proposed solutions appeared to worsen the situation rather than improve it.

The panel of 'Implementation: Can the Compact Design Be Implemented?' included Kevin Lynch.[63] Lynch's contribution, as reported, was relatively minor. He said that he came from a town that was run by a town meeting. Lynch commented on the new town proposal presented to the conference participants as follows:

> even as an illustration [it] is completely laid out (down to a detailed site plan) for the whole with a program of development put forward from the start. If you are serious about user participation in any of these decisions, if you are serious about making an educational environment in which people can grow and have some control of their own, I am pretty sure this is the way you would *not* design a town. It would have mechanisms and an implementation process that allowed the people who will be in it to have a part in the growing of it, to shape it to their own desires.[64]

Morton Hoppenfeld reacted to Lynch's response in a hostile manner, claiming that the Harvard Graduate School of Design went to the US Government for a $90,000 grant to investigate something and learn something for the benefit of the people. This petulant reply hardly solved Lynch's questions concerning citizen participation. Later in the session Lynch was asked by William Doeble, the chair of the panel: 'What is the relation between density and urbanity, and how much should we pay for it assuming the cost figures are correct?'. To which Lynch replied tersely: 'The answer is simple. I don't know'.

The closing session was moderated by the young, aspiring politician Daniel Patrick Moynihan. He said that twenty years previously he had owned a house on Hilliard Street and that there was a similar concern with the issue of new towns and new cities. He stated that, during that period, the population of the US had grown by 50 million, increasing the populations of urban communities by 60 per cent, and that the level of prosperity and affluence had increased more than 100 per cent. Yet despite this achievement there were still the problems of segregation and poverty.

The conference was held within the framework of a growing awareness by some educators in the fields of architecture, and in particular city planning, that citizen participation in the planning process should be a necessity rather than an option. Yet design education persisted, as it does to this day, with the concept of the master plan imposed upon communities.

THE SOCIAL CITY: ADVOCACY PLANNING AND CITIZEN PARTICIPATION

Of equal importance to Lynch's and Appleyard's cognitive analyses were a number of studies that were not so much to do with the recognition of design aspects, but concerned with behavioural and territorial aspects of the city.

The city may be seen as a cultural invention, imbued with meaning for its inhabitants. It can be compared to a language and insights sought either in terms of syntactic structure, or else, through study of the meaning of signs, in semiotics.[65] This field, which was the subject of a major study by Geoffrey Broadbent and others, has been expressed by Gordon Cullen as the 'language of gestures'. According to Cullen: 'Communication, between people and the towns they live in is primarily affected by signalization . . . Rapport between ourselves and the environment, like conversation, brings continuing interest. Obviously this can only be achieved by signals or gestures that bring home to us the identity latent in environmental problems. Hence the need for a comprehensive language of gestures'.[66]

Two other fields, anthropology and psychology, seemed particularly promising, since their subjects are man and woman, and they have been keenly studied for directly applicable 'results'. In the case of the former, the concept of territoriality 'seemed particularly relevant since the whole city could be regarded as a physical representation of the operation of such a principle'. 'Territoriality' has been studied in both animals and man, with some remarkable results. The scientist J. B. Calhoun, for example, has described the effects of increasing density and space restrictions upon laboratory populations of mice, tracing changes in fertility, physique, behaviour and susceptibility to disease, and extrapolating the theoretical results for human groupings.[67]

Suggestive as such results may be, the urban designer had another, more immediate source of examples of territorial behaviour, most notably explored by Jane Jacobs.[68] Published the same year as Lynch's *The Image of the City*, Jacobs' seminal work was to have a profound influence in another direction. As Broadbent remarks: 'It was Greenwich Village (in New York City) that was drawn to the world's attention as one kind of ideal environment for urban living. Jane Jacobs lived on Hudson Street, not far from the river . . . When it was first published, in 1961, it infuriated those whose lives had been devoted to the design, planning and building of brave new worlds based on Le Corbusier's vision of the Radiant City. For Jane Jacobs, indeed, the streets and squares of the village were the very stuff of which real urban fabrics are made. For as she says (p. 39), "Think of a city and what comes to mind? It's streets. If the city's streets look uninteresting; if they look dull, the city looks dull".'[69]

Jacobs goes on to say:

> Cities are an immense laboratory of trial and error, failure and success, in city building and city design. This is the laboratory in which city planning should have been learning and forming and testing its theories. Instead the teachers of this discipline (if such it can be called) have ignored the study of success and failure in real life, have been incurious about the reasons of unexpected success, and are guided instead by principles derived from the behavior and appearances of towns, suburbs, tuberculosis sanitaria, fairs, imaginary dream cities – from anything but the cities themselves.

By observing the way in which cities were actually used, Jacobs was led to question accepted prescriptions for the improvement of city environments: 'In orthodox city planning, neighborhood open spaces are venerated in an amazingly uncritical fashion, much as savages venerate magical fetishes . . . Walk with a planner through a dispirited neighborhood and though it will be already scabby with deserted parks and tired landscaping festooned with old Kleenex, he will envision a future of More Open Space. More Open Space for what? For muggings? For bleak vacuums between buildings?'.[70] In place of this, Jacobs suggested four conditions which she believed to be essential for a successful district and which read like prototypes for Christopher Alexander's later book, *A Pattern Language*.

Her purpose seemed to be to attack current city-planning methodology and redevelopment proposals, particularly criticising housing projects for low-income groups. Citing the North End of Boston in the early 1960s, she argued that the neighbourhood was popular and vibrant with a good street atmosphere, low crime rates, low rents and low mortality rates. People from elsewhere in the city liked to visit the neighbourhood. In traditional streets there was a clear demarcation between public and private property. In the new public low-income high-rise housing projects, corridors and lifts became 'blind streets'. Zoning, she said, reduced diversity. Traditional neighbourhoods had small, specialised businesses, but in suburban areas businesses mainly comprised large chain stores. Primary functions should be placed near to complementary functions, for example theatres near restaurants. Concentration resulted in more specialties in a smaller area.

Central to Jacobs' thesis was the need for mixed primary uses.[71] Of the four conditions mentioned, the first was the need for primary uses. 'The district, and indeed as many of its internal parts as possible, must serve more than one primary function; preferably more than two. These must insure the presence of people who go outdoors on different schedules and are in the place for different purposes, but who are able to use many facilities in common'.[72] She cites Cincinnati as an unsuccessful example where downtown was dead by evening and moribund by day. Yet by mid-century, Cincinnatians made half a million visits a year to the generally expensive nightlife, including riverboat restaurants, bordellos and strip clubs across the Ohio River in the much smaller town of Covington, Kentucky. Such a situation still exists half a century later, though during the last decade there have been attempts to change the situation.

The second condition, according to Jacobs, was the need for small street blocks. Streets with frequent opportunities to turn corners were necessary. She cites the example of mid Manhattan, New York, as an example of huge street blocks, while further south, in Greenwich Village, the small street blocks created an intense community life. The sub-extension of this into TriBeCa, the triangle below Canal Street, as SoHo and Greenwich Village, became more fashionable and, therefore, more expensive, confirming Jacobs' views.

The third condition was the need for old buildings: 'Districts must mingle buildings that vary in age and condition, including a good proportion of old ones'. The wholesale destruction of old neighbourhoods in cities throughout the world in the name of modern redevelopment resulted in the loss of the very essence of what made cities a social success. Notable examples where this imminent destruction was recognised in time, include the historic district of Charleston, South Carolina.

Jacobs' final condition was the need for concentration. She stated that: 'The district must have a sufficiently dense concentration of people, for whatever purpose they may be there. This includes people there because of residence'. In Brooklyn, New York, the most generally admired popular and upgraded neighbourhood was Brooklyn Heights, with the highest density of dwellings in the area. In San Francisco, the district with the highest dwelling densities and highest coverage of residential land with buildings, too, was North Beach and Telegraph Hill – a slum before the Second World War.

Yet an examination of the work of many regional planning commissions across the US reveals that these lessons have gone unheeded. There is still strict adherence to zoning codes and land use plans which militate *against* successful mixed use and encourage ever lower residential development densities during the transformation from the American central city to the polycentric city of suburbia.

Jacobs' ideas also seemed to echo in one of Christopher Alexander's first important essays: 'A city is not a tree'.[73] In arguing against the imposition of city design, Alexander said that such attempts were based upon a mistaken appreciation of the structural relationship of the city's elements, which typically take the form of semi-lattices. The tree-like structure of most modern plans, such as Clarence Stein's Greenbelt, Maryland, represented 'a trivially simple' case of the semi-lattice structure and one in which 'life will be cut to pieces'.

At a time when Appleyard was beginning to develop his Environmental Simulation Laboratory at the University of California, Berkeley, Alexander was discussing similar investigations of design methods. His *Notes on the Synthesis of Form*[74] described a process for the design of an Indian village that attempted to reconcile all the functional requirements of the problem by the meticulous breakdown of its most basic statements and their subsequent recomposition according to rational methods.

However, Alexander's first major work was in collaboration with Serge Chermayeff, one of the original Bauhaus teachers at Harvard (see Chapter 1). *Community and Privacy,* by Alexander and Chermayeff, was subtitled: 'Towards a New Architecture of Humanism'.[75] The structure of the book was divided simply into two parts: the first dealing with the current problems of the human environment and the second proposing solutions to these problems. The authors outlined the issues brought about by massive increases in population, which caused the decay of cities. In a sense they contradict Jacobs' premise that a high-density environment is a positive asset in residential areas. Alexander points to the disappearance of natural areas, particularly regions of wilderness. Whereas older cities had physical clarity, purpose, order and plans, modern cities lack these positive attributes. With the growth of suburbia came the increase in the use of motor cars, strip development and decentralisation. With the modern city came increases in crime and a growing

Simulation Laboratory,
University of California,
Berkeley (1966),
Donald Appleyard.

Figure 4. Typical views from the Jerra Linda model recorded by a camera attached to the optical probe in the simulator. The scale of the model is 30 feet to the inch. Note the wealth of detail. Color motion pictures further enhance the effect of realism.

Model and images, Simulation Laboratory, University of California,
Berkeley, Donald Appleyard.

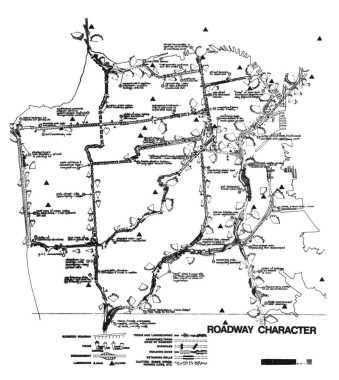

ROADWAY CHARACTER

Two-dimensional map using symbols
to interpret roadway character,
University of California, Berkeley,
Donald Appleyard.

lack of privacy. The modern pressures, according to Alexander, were excessive mobility, noise (man having lost the capacity to distinguish between noise and sound) and lack of peace.

In addressing his solutions to these problems, Alexander says that there are six domains of urbanity that could not be contained in private houses: urban public, urban semipublic, group public, group private, family private and individual private. In examining existing housing stereotypes, including suburban subdivisions and garden cities, Chermayeff and Alexander decided that courtyard housing provided the best solution to housing design within the urban context. Mainly for climatic reasons, as well as privacy, courtyard houses have been built throughout Latin America as well as Europe, particularly in Spain and Portugal, though these precedents are not fully discussed by the authors. The separation of people from vehicles, they thought, was of utmost importance. An outer room in the courtyard house, in contact with nature, would enhance the housing. The other main necessities were the family room, private bedrooms, service cores and climate control.

The following year Alexander published *Notes on the Synthesis of Form*,[76] and was to become one of the most prolific and authoritative writers in the field of urban design. It was to expound Alexander's analysis of the process of urban design. He suggested that in this process, context and form are complementary. Traditional design was not self-conscious. The design process was learned informally, knowledge slowly acquired and mistakes were altered gradually over time. The opposite was true, he believed, of contemporary design. Like *Community and Privacy*, this book was divided into two distinct sections. The second part was a programme for a system of design.[77] Alexander thought that designers needed to realise the problems they were trying to solve. The problem should be defined in broad terms, each variable must be solved, and when the problem was grasped, the solution would occur. Alexander provided graphs and flow charts to track the problem-solving process. He concluded that an important underlying structural correspondence existed between the patterns of a problem and the process of designing a physical form that answered that problem. Such a system produced the now vilified architecture of that decade and is certainly belied by the iconic and lyrical architecture of Frank Lloyd Wright, who generally ignored the requirements of his clients, including the Kaufmann family, and his clients for Falling Water in Pennsylvania.

Alexander became a faculty member of the University of California at Berkeley. In a paper published in 1966,[78] he examined the issue of the increasing loneliness of city dwellers in an environment that ought to act as a collection of meeting places. He differentiated between social contact and intimate contact. He termed the lack of intimate contact as 'autonomy-withdrawal syndrome', characterised by the growth of individualism, seen in its most extreme form as schizophrenia and caused by the breakdown of the nuclear family. His solutions bordered on social engineering in that people should 'work in small groups and adopt different types of housing, including a transparent communal room adjacent to the street'. However, this seems to contradict his recommendations, along with Chermayeff, in *Community and Privacy*.

An emerging problem in the inner cities during this period was the separation of socioeconomic groups. P. M. Hanser suggested, describing the characteristics of the inner city, that

this is the area characterized by 'blight' – the locus of the slums and the disproportionate shares of the institutional and personal pathology of the metropolis. Physically, this is the oldest residential area of the city, still available for residential use because the central business district, as it expanded with the growth of the city, absorbed that which may have been older. It became an area of decay, and this partly because of the anticipated expansion of the central business district, evidenced by its anomalous, relatively high land values and low rents. The land is, in the main, half designated for speculative purposes and frequently under circumstances which do not, on economic grounds, justify further improvement or even reasonable improvement or even reasonable maintenance of the residential housing.[79]

The availability of work in the central business district (CBD) drew new immigrants to this area, where the competition of high-rental, central-area uses forced them to live at high densities. This traditional function of the innercity slums as the reception area for newcomers was set out by Richard Sennett in his description of 'the city of necessity', which, he wrote, 'broke apart the self-contained qualities of the various ethnic groups. The groups were not like little villages massed together in one spot on the map; rather they penetrated into each other, so that the daily life of an individual was a journey between various kinds of group life. Each one different in its function and character from the others'.[80] Since the period of the great European migrations to American cities, however, the outward movement of Wolf's 'tidal wave' has undermined the employment basis at the centre. David Harvey outlines the result:

The urban system seems to have reacted very sluggishly indeed to the demand for low-income housing in suburban areas. The difficulty of expanding the supply in the inner city (partly due to institutional constraints such as zoning regulations) is that poor-quality, low-income housing is relatively high-priced and frequently more profitable for property owners than we would expect under true equilibrium conditions. Low-income families, therefore, have little option but to locate in the relatively high-priced inner city. In most American cities, of course, this condition has been exacerbated by the lack of an open housing market for the black population which, of course, just happens to constitute a large section of the poor. Meanwhile, most of the growth in new employment has been in the suburban ring and hence the low-income groups have been cut off from the new sources of employment.[81]

Writing in 1969, in the wake of widespread rioting and violence in American cities, P. Lupsha revived the great variety of explanations of root causes of urban violence from Plutarch onwards.[82] He concluded that, in the case of the American race riots, at any rate, the suggestion that violence was the result of 'the irrational rage of frustration' was quite wrong. On the contrary, 'It is an anger arising from a rational evaluation of the situation. It is an anger directed at the inability and inadequacy of the political system and its institution to live up to their promise. It is an anger directed at the inadequacy of the political system to process demands, and to make allocations in a responsive and responsible manner. It is the gap between the theory and the practice of government in the United States that is one of the root causes of urban violence'.

Harvey, however, would counter this with the suggestion that, 'We really do not have the kind of understanding of the total city system to be able to make wise policy decisions, even when motivated by the highest social objectives'.[83] This disturbing conclusion is based on Harvey's understanding of both social and ecological problems of the city, and it is towards the latter, he says, 'rolling out the carpet of opportunities in front of us while rolling it up even faster behind us, that we now turn'.[84]

The urban riots in 1967, 1968 and 1969, fomented in the main part by disenfranchised and disadvantaged African-American communities, particularly in such cities as Detroit and Pontiac, Michigan, led to the new movement of 'advocacy planning'. Poverty, social and economic deprivation and segregation were seen as the root causes of the riots in many of the major cities. Two organisations were set up in an effort to combat the decline of the cities.

The Council on Urban Design was set up by Mayor John Lindsay in New York City, with community design centres across the country benefiting from the services of volunteer architects, teachers and students. The R/UDAT (Rural and Urban Design Assistance Team)[85] started with a study of Rapid City, South Dakota in 1967. Four volunteer teams were established to work with all members of specific communities who requested aid. The professional services were free and the communities were called upon only to bear the expenses of the visits. Each team usually included four members from a variety of professions, depending on the requirements of the particular study. Architects were invariably represented in the R/UDAT teams, along with economists, planners, sociologists and geologists. Each visit occupied an intensive four-day study involving a physical inspection of the area by foot, bus and helicopter on the first day, as well as talks with the mayor, council, planning board, chamber of commerce and banking community. A town meeting open to all interested citizens including non-establishment groups (neighbourhood organisations, block groups, ethnic and minority representatives), who were usually called back for further discussions, was held on the second day. This was followed by a teamwork session to synthesise expenses. The third day of the visit consisted of a 24-hour session of production work on the report, providing a comprehensive framework for recommendations, with a final report (some 60–100 pages long) printed during the visit. Organising a visit from the American Institute of Architects took up to 12 months of pre-planning, and there was a highly organised follow-up programme. In its own document, published in 1983, R/UDAT says:

'The extent of the R/UDAT exercise is unequaled to any other urban design activity over the past decade. No consultant organization worked so closely with so many communities or government agency with such a variety of issues'.[86]

Another conclusion was that for urban design to be successful, the effort is as important as the product. The study must examine all elements of the community, be interdisciplinary and not the work of a single profession. Above all, there must be *citizen participation*. In addition, sponsorship from a particular community must come from a variety of sources and *not* reflect the pressures of one particular interest group. Successful media coverage was seen as essential. The urban design group felt that if public/private partnership in urban design was to work, government and community must mutually understand the development process and how to operate it in the best public interest. They must minimise the conflict of goals, improve quality, remove obstacles and misunderstandings and maximise public gain.

Among the communities studied were Springfield (where the main issue was conservation), Lansing (the problems of downtown), Kansas City (growth), Denver (transportation), Trenton (neighbourhoods), South End, Boston (social issues), New Orleans and Vancouver (parks, open spaces) and Louisville (process/directions).

LANDSCAPE AND URBAN DESIGN

Philip Thiel further developed the cognitive city theories of both Lynch and Appleyard in his previous MIT thesis, but his emphasis, particularly after his research in Japan, concerned the connection between designed and undesigned landscape and urban form and movement.

As early as 1961, Thiel had published an article in *The Town Planning Review*,[87] in which, acknowledging the influences of Kevin Lynch and Gyorgy Kepes at MIT as well as Kiyosi Seike of the Tokyo Institute of Technology, he started to relate the understanding of spatial sequences with spatial sequences in landscape design, particularly drawing from traditional Japanese landscape art. Thiel indicated that the only way to illustrate this graphically was a notational system similar to that used in choreography. Referring to a garden at Sakai in Japan, he says that the open view of the sea was obstructed by 'planting a grove of trees in such a way that only when the guest stooped at the stone water basin to wash his hands and rinse his mouth preparatory to entering the tea-house, he caught an unexpected glimpse of the shimmering sea through the trees – a glimpse of infinity'.[88] Thiel went on to say that there was no such thing as a purely plastic experience in architectural and urban space, and all spatial experience combines the plastic, visual experience with various levels of meaning-experience. In his diagrams, he includes the duration line, used to indicate both the size of the space and the period of temporal experience of the space. Size is indicated by the space zone in which the duration line is drawn, and the period of experience of the space by the location and length of the duration line with reference to the movement line.

In his paper 'Movement in Japanese environmental representation',[89] Thiel explores these theories further. Like Ogilby's maps of England in 1698, Thiel explores the maps of Kamakura Ezu, woodblock prints of the Edo Period. He states that the representation combines a map showing the positional relationships of roads, water courses, hills and mountains, monuments and buildings, with a pictorial representation of the latter, wherein each is shown from a different angle, selected to best reveal its specific and particular characteristics. He suggests that these 'achieve an almost kinesthetic effect as one "reads" between these local events; analogous to the experience of moving from one to the other. And this effect is continuous, not cumulative, over the entire picture plane'. Hishikawa Kichibei's 1690 illustrations for Tokaido Bunken no Ezu[90] shows a sequence of three facing pages from a type of guidebook in common use at the time. In these books, the roadway was delineated to run horizontally across the pages with only occasional indications of compass orientation. The author also mentions the publications of the Japanese National Railways during the 1960s – a folded strip of paper 10 centimetres (4 inches) wide by 145 centimetres (57 inches) long distributed for overseas tourists travelling on the Tokaido line and showing the equivalent of views on the left side or right side windows of the train.

Thiel's other work during this period included an article in *The Architectural Review* in 1962,[91] which expanded on his experience in Japan. The illustrations of the Jiko-in experience are the monuments by the Rinzai Zen Sect to Lord Sadamasi Kitagan in 1663, erected by Gyokushi, the 185th patriarch of the Daitoku-ji temple in Kyoto. Thiel suggests that the visitor experiences an excellent small-scale example of the quiet orchestration of spatial sequences. 'Arriving on foot,' he says, 'the visitor has been subtly processed and prepared for his moment of arrival in the course of his transit of the path that ascends from the plain toward the summit of the low hill on which the building stands.'

Thiel also reiterates the relevance of the notational systems of the temporal art of the dance with its own system of notation. However, he goes on to say that architectural and, particularly, urban design, are also temporal arts, but in an inverted sense, unlike the case of dance and music (and cinema). The members here are not passive, but free to determine the order and rate of the sequence of experiences at will . . . the perceived pattern of spaces and associated meanings is not ephemeral.

One of the most formidable talents in the realm of urban/landscape design was that of Garrett Eckbo. Eckbo was renowned in the 1950s as the landscape designer in the Bay Region architecture of San Francisco, epitomised in the houses of Albert Henry Hill in which his organic architecture had connections with the philosophies of Frank Lloyd Wright.

In 1964 Eckbo published a book on urban landscape design,[92] in which he considers the physical landscape as experienced by humans. He discusses the elements of spatial organisation using language, possibly derived from the work of Philip Thiel. Eckbo suggests that the landscape is continuous as far as we can see from wherever we are.[93] Human development, he goes on, had become disconnected from this continuity,

resulting in visual anarchy and, paradoxically, monotony. Like Thiel, Eckbo recognised that the perception of the landscape consists of sequences that are continuous throughout human lives. Detailed spaces consist of private gardens, public and private squares, colour, texture and details. Continuity and accents are important in design, and Eckbo cites the example of Manhattan as the most concentrated and exaggerated collection of architectural accents and structural emphasis, yet, in his opinion, successful in visual terms due to the right balance of accents and continuity.

Eckbo's formula was that design should be followed in a certain order:

1 detailed space organisation within buildings
2 detailed relationships between interior spaces and the outdoor spaces surrounding them
3 detailed space organisation between building units and neighbouring buildings
4 detailed space organisation between groups of buildings and the streets
5 organisation of relationships between buildings, open spaces, streets, the community and the region.

Without this hierarchy of design, Eckbo claimed, the resulting built environments were often poor. Yet it is hard to see, given the planning legislation in the US at the time, how such a process could have been achieved. In dealing with parks and playgrounds, he argued that they must have a separate approach in design, pointing out that playgrounds require more attention to construction details, whereas parks have 'limited' use and a flexible form. He differentiated between the two structural forms of the American city: the European type found on the East Coast and the grid system of the West. Neighbourhoods were typically a quarter to half a mile radius and he stressed the need for sequences[94] and continuity, spatial and sensory experiences as well as unity and variety. He suggested that all of this could be achieved with adequate urban design guidelines.

Another notable landscape architect of the time was Lawrence Halprin. His book *Cities* (1963) was the closest in its messages to Gordon Cullen's *Townscape*.[95] It dealt, by and large, with the micro urban landscape and is a richly illustrated study of the components that make up a successful city centre. Again, like Thiel and Eckbo, Halprin emphasises the importance of movement notation.

Halprin is probably best known for his work in Portland, Oregon, though in an applaudable way, but nevertheless frustrating, he rarely identifies his own designs in his book. The Portland fountains were designed as waterfalls echoing the cascades of the Columbia River in the High Sierra. Portland's open-space network is an eight-block-long linear sequence of parks, plazas, fountains, waterfalls, malls, promenades, vehicular ways and resting places. It acted, he said, 'as a connective tissue between downtown Portland and through a new large-scale redevelopment of the time, the Portland Center. Lovejoy Plaza is the crowning achievement of this urban design plan where the waterfalls and fountains were not merely intended as decorative elements. It opened in 1966 and has always attracted young and old residents as well as visitors and tourists. People may watch, move in, or splash in the water'.[96]

The auditorium forecourt is quite different, with the fountain beginning as a series of 'serene streams at the top of the block square plaza; then gaining in scale and intensity as it moves across the plaza, the water finally bursts from atop 80 foot wide cliffs to plummet 18 feet [5.5 metres] down to the pool below. Within the pool, plaza and cliff complex are many ways for people to become involved in the spectacle of the fountain: water stairs to be ascended or descended; caves to enter behind the waterfall; pools and wading courses at both the top of the falls and down below; wide concrete stepping stones for walking across the water without getting wet; places for sitting and reclining to watch the water and the activity of other people. The lower plaza facing the falls can become an amphitheater for outdoor performances, particularly when the falls are diminished or turned off. Night (flood) lighting is impressive for visitors to the park or to the cultural center across the way, and the acoustics of this space have been enthusiastically acclaimed'. Ada Louise Huxtable of *The New York Times*, on experiencing this moving culmination of the Portland open-space sequence, wrote that it 'may be one of the most important urban spaces since the Renaissance'.[97]

It is, in short, an urban design masterpiece and an appropriate epilogue to Halprin's book. The rest of the book considers, in separate sections, urban spaces (including stores, shopping streets, minor plazas, major plazas, neighbourhood parks, central parks, and waterfronts); gardens between walls (common gardens, private gardens); furnishing the street (light, benches, pots, signs and symbols, kiosks, bicycles, doors and entrances, drinking fountains, clocks, sculpture, children's sculpture); the floor of the city (granite sets, pebbles, cobbles, cut stones, brick, concrete, grids, precast pavers, asphalt); the third dimension (steps, ramps, bollards, fences, walls); water in the square (quiet water, gushing water, recreation, qualities of water, running water, waterfalls, edges, jets, bowls, pool bottoms, sculpture with walls, programming); trees for all seasons (design, pruning, planting, trees for use in the city); the view from the roof (public, garage tops); and choreography (pedestrians, cars and freeways, movement rotation, change, skyline). *Cities* was an important handbook on urban landscape design in the latter part of the twentieth century and is, in some ways, akin to the 'pattern books' of the eighteenth-century European architects.

Halprin also wrote a study of New York,[98] an investigation of open spaces in the city's housing and urban renewal areas. Commissioned by New York City, his practice was asked to make recommendations for improvement, and were innovative in the sense that they examined the relationship between urban dwellers, their surrounding space and the effect that space had on its users. Housing had always been a problem in New York. The major public housing projects of the 1960s were a response to demands created by increased immigration. Though there was the parallel dimension of the traditional slums in areas such as Harlem, the inhabitants of the new housing projects disliked them intensely. They lacked neighbourhood qualities with poor public spaces and few amenities. As an example,

Halprin cited the Westside. Located between Central Park West and Columbus Avenue, this was a neighbourhood of brownstone row houses and tenements, now replaced by tall apartment blocks. He suggested that the area could be improved by tree planting along all the streets, widening the sidewalks, adding common gardens, pedestrian bridges and a community centre, as well as a central plaza.

Halprin's goal in determining the factors affecting open space was to discover what people wanted. A good environment, he believed, produced less stress and an improved sense of territoriality. A successful housing project cannot be anonymous and must be seen to be part of the neighbourhood. He criticised current zoning regulations as being too restrictive in urban design, especially the design of open spaces, and proposed a multidimensional urban system that would allow the vertical expansion of the open space system. He concluded, like Jacobs, that cities needed more complexity to retain their vitality.

Another contributor to the theory of the integration of landscape design with urban design was Bernard Rudofsky,[99] who became renowned as the author of *Architecture Without Architects*, based on an exhibition held at the Museum of Modern Art, New York, between November 1964 and February 1965. The urban settlements illustrated ranged from the iconic towers of Bologna, Italy, fortified settlements of southern Morocco, cave dwellings of the Anchorite community in the Anatolia Valley of Goreme to the fortified tower villages of the western Caucasus. Unaccountably, Rudofsky omitted all mention of the Mesa cliff dwellings in the southwest US. The wide sample of folk structures, from China to Sweden and from Zanzibar to New Guinea, showed an arbitrariness that seemed to imply that all cultures possess such models of unselfconscious town building, in which, unlike twentieth-century cities, the natural landscape always abuts the hard edge of the settlement itself. Decrying the conventional concern only with 'formal' architecture of 'a few select cultures', Rudofsky made a point similar to that developed in modern linguistics which recognises no fundamental differences of relevance, structure or complexity between so-called 'civilized' and 'primitive' languages. The appeal of his argument was strengthened by the fact that his examples of communal structures were able to generate, from the most modest of individual parts, the most spectacular of results. The solutions he identified evolved through a close adaptation to a narrow range of circumstances.

In 1969, Rudofsky published *Streets are for People*,[100] a study of the pedestrian street. He believed that Americans did not care about streets but rather viewed them as the entrails of the city. In the nineteenth century, he suggested, many of the older parts of the city were destroyed and a gridiron street system overlaid, regardless of topography. The resultant chaos received public approval because it was seen to reflect wealth and vitality. Rudofsky's thesis seems somewhat dubious, given the nineteenth-century extremes of poverty in the central city in places like Chicago and New York. He adopted a romantic viewpoint in drawing comparisons between American streets and those in Italy, France, England and Spain, correctly stating that in these countries (especially Italy) canopies were built to protect pedestrians from the weather. He also pointed to the 'endless' variety of street activities in Europe. The problem, he said, was that Americans did not like to walk. A variation of the canopied street is the temporary market; however, permanent-covered markets do exist in the US, for example Faneuil Hall in Boston. Rudofsky's romanticism went further with his belief that the twisting streets found in Italy and Greece should be constructed in the US.

In *The Pedestrian in the City*,[101] David Lewis, who was to develop a national reputation as one of the founders of the R/UDAT (subsequently sponsored by the American Institute of Architects), took a somewhat different standpoint from that of Rudofsky. The publication was less theoretical but included major built projects to illustrate the central theme. While these projects were successful, Lewis saw them as 'fragments in a general sea of indifference'. He defined the changes of the age as population growth, urban sprawl, rural-urban migration, conurbation and circulation problems. The new city, he suggested, emerged as a result of a huge radius, especially in the US.

A contributor to the book, Peter Carter, examined the urban design solutions of Mies van der Rohe, including in 1951 the one for Lake Shore Drive, Chicago, the Illinois Institute of Technology Campus Plan, begun in 1940, and the Seagram Building in New York City in 1959.

Eleanor Smith Morris contributed to the 'New urban design', which examined the new concepts of green ways and movement structures in the Philadelphia Plan. The first new form was the green way system, a public open space consisting of landscaped pedestrian ways linking important local institutions and landmarks. The first built green ways were from Southwest Temple Street, at that time the main street in Philadelphia. Other green ways were built in the university area and smaller community projects in residential areas. Chestnut Street, one of the city's main shopping streets, was pedestrianised.[102] Most of these ideas were derived from the works of Patrick Geddes.

THEORIES OF URBAN GROWTH

Three generations were identified in the postwar development of the international style.[103] Kenneth Frampton calls the first the emigré masters (Walter Gropius, Marcel Breuer, José Luis Sert); the second generation was at the Harvard Graduate School of Design (Ulrich Franzen, Henry Cobb, I. M. Pei, Paul Rudolph, Ben Thompson and the Architects' Collaborative group); and a third generation produced 'White Architecture'. The most influential groups included Peter Eisenman, Michael Graves, Meier and, joining them later, John Hedjuk and Charles Gwathmey, who were later to become known as the New York Five. Meier's house designs were complex studies in the interpenetrations of external and internal volumes, epitomised in his 1965–67 design for the Smith House at Darien, Connecticut.[104]

However, less is known about Meier as an urban theorist. His book on urban growth, first published in 1962, is a study that defines the city as an open system dependent on information.[105] He states that most analytical methods view the city from a human scale by analysing architecture, open spaces and economic issues. One of the more important issues Meier raises is people's preference to congregate in large urban centres, implying that this is because they like face-to-face communication. However, he goes on to point out that such large, complex urban systems are frequently overloaded, causing a breakdown of communications industries. He also recognises the emerging American concept of the megalopolis.[106] While Meier's text mentions only design issues, it exemplifies the change in direction of urban theory in the early 1960s, and over-optimistically suggests that a total understanding of urban systems was possible, that many urban problems could be solved through 'better' design.

A later book by Richard Meier was *Megalopolis Formation in the Midwest*,[107] where he accurately describes the megalopolis as a 'multinucleated' region of overlapping interdependence of cities, suburban and agricultural areas. This, he remarks, was a new urban pattern, and he cites examples such as the corridors from Boston to Washington, DC, and the San Francisco Bay Area to Los Angeles.

Given what appears to be the terminal decline of inner cities some thirty years later, Meier's suggestion that the megalopolis has 'a functional role in providing good transportation, communication, finance, medical services, high culture, higher education and mass media' seems, in retrospect, hopelessly optimistic. However, it included an acknowledgment that the megalopolis had no overall government and relied on cooperation between separate city governments.[108] Cooperation over this period was relatively spasmodic.

Victor Gruen, who later became known as the pioneer designer of the suburban shopping mall, also addressed the theories of urban growth. In *The Heart of Our Cities*,[109] he also examined the existing urban crisis of the time and the much repeated observations of Meier concerning traffic congestion, pollution (both atmospheric and waterborne) and crime. He maintained that the city was ugly and amorphous – there was little difference between the 'city scape and landscape'. Gruen identified the contemporary American city as a series of concentric rings. The nucleus was the CBD. The secondary core consisted of urban elements not contained within the CBD. The core frame was intensive development with secondary functions and a high residential density. The core fringe had facilities serving other cores, but was less dense; this was surrounded by an urbanised area within city boundaries and an urbanised area outside city boundaries. Beyond that was the metropolitan region with half of all urban activity, covering a vast land area. Gruen cited Los Angeles as among the worst examples.

Sprawl was a reflection of the wealth and power within the US. Car and air travel were popular because of relatively low costs, which in turn caused the decline of local public transport and intercity rail travel. Urban areas were neglected as people sought a pastoral life in the suburbs. Examples of a declining urban core included Detroit, Milwaukee and Boston. Gruen suggested that 'architects, urban planners and administrators were really anti-urbanists'.[110] Social and ethnic segregation was created by land use zoning which, by separating function, destroyed the 'urbanity' of the city.[111] Manufacturing was seen by Gruen to be detrimental to urban structure.[112]

The final chapters of Gruen's book were devoted to specific recommendations for designing good cities. Reference was made to the writings of Le Corbusier and Frank Lloyd Wright who, in different ways, with La Ville Radiuse and Broadacre City, proposed the 'anti-city'. Reference was also made to the ideas of Geoffrey Jellicoes' 'Motopia' in the UK and the ideas of Doxiadis in Greece and elsewhere.

Perhaps it was self-serving as subsequent events will show, but Gruen believed that regional shopping centres could create order out of chaos through decentralisation. Such centres would separate cars and pedestrians. Controlling car traffic could improve the core of a city, he said, and should be combined with better public transport. He added that traffic engineers should not dictate the form of American cities. As an example Gruen used his own plan for Fort Worth in Texas, shutting down some areas to car traffic and providing free car-parking on the outskirts of the CBD.[113] He argued that public transport could take the form of a mixture of 'pod carriers', 'moving people belts', rapid transit and transregional buses, as well as monorails.

Finally, Gruen proposed a schematic plan for cellular metropolises based upon Ebenezer Howard's garden city ideals at the beginning of the twentieth century. Metropolitan areas would have an overall population of 3.3 million spread across 10 cities with a population of 280,000 each. The central city would have a population of 500,000. Each town would be divided into communities and each community into neighbourhoods.[114]

Another urban design plan of the time was one for Manhattan, as part of the Second Regional Plan for New York. Its author, Rai Okamoto, suggested principles to guide the growth of a high-density central business district.[115] Given that the street grid for Manhattan was established as early as 1811, plus the current high population density and high average income, according to Okamoto the outlook was one of chaos (though thirty years later this prediction has proved, in part, to be false).

Okamoto's urban design principles included:

1   Tallest buildings to be clustered around points of high accessibility in order to minimise walking distance from train doors to elevators.
2   Local open spaces to be established for each tall building, pooled in one place at the point of transit access.
3   Public spaces to be provided below street level to separate pedestrians and cars, to bring building entrances closer to trains and to break through the street membranes, providing sunlight to the underground.
4   Access to nature to be provided by building parks on waterfront areas.
5   Clear articulation of surface movement through the provision of more pedestrian spaces, a different location of street traffic and separate truck loading spaces.
6   Street furniture and signages to be redesigned.

Okamoto conceded that a positive public policy would be required. Too many agencies already existed at that time. Detailed business district plans and a permanent urban design staff were also recommended, as well as a development coordinator for each business district, together with citizen participation and incentive zoning.

Idealistic as Okamoto's proposals were, they were not workable within the Manhattan context. Radical proposals, such as that for Times Square, also included the closing off of 59th Street to 23rd Street to car traffic.[116] Another criticism is that the report makes relatively cursory mention of the need for historic preservation.

The final pages of the plan included ideas for the implementation of urban design for the future. Okamoto states that:

Urban design is a relatively new term to express a concept which is as old as city building itself. Essentially it is the relating of installations to each other in the urban setting which surrounds them.[117]

In his opinion, good existing urban design examples in Manhattan were the Grand Central Terminal Complex, the Rockefeller Center and the World Trade Center.[118]

Also among these theories were two works from a very different perspective. The first was Robert Venturi's *Complexity and Contradiction in Architecture*,[119] in which architectural criticism was the focus, examining great architecture of the past in relation to the present. The theme, that complexity and contradiction are a good thing if competent and coherent, is based 'on the richness and ambiguity of the modern experience'.[120] Venturi believed that it was time to get away from the puritanism of modernism.[121] To him, modernism was too simplified. It required, he said, a separation of elements of 'less is more', justifying exclusion for expressive purposes. Venturi questioned whether exclusion was too selective. Aesthetic simplicity was possible with inner-complexity.[122] He added that the growing complexity of functional problems had widened the scope of architecture. Contradictory levels of meaning and use involve paradoxes, for example something that is closed yet open, or symmetrical yet asymmetrical.[123]

Venturi went on to say that playing with order and compromise supported the idea of evolution in city planning, a science developed by modifying the existing situation. Planners and architects who wanted to do away with conventional townscape could not succeed.[124] He believed that the answer lay in making slight adjustments, changing the context to achieve a better environment.

Adapting contradiction in design admits improvisation, making the design tolerant and pliable. Juxtaposing contradictions means the design will be unbending and too contrasting. Accommodation allows adaptation and new approaches. The idea of contradiction can be applied to the design and perception of cities, although in that case it becomes more complex. Ordered elements may be added to chaos or discordant elements to order, such as in Times Square, New York. Venturi remarked that cities today are either chaotic or monotonous, when they should be complex and contradictory. Juxtaposing contradictions can sometimes work. An example is the use of diagonals on a grid. In city planning this is done as a challenge to orthodox zoning.[125]

Lewis Mumford's *The Urban Prospect* gives a more historical perspective.[126] Mumford characterises the current urban situation in the US as 'the fourth migration'. The first was the movement westward, the second the movement into industrial cities and the third the movement to commercial centres. The current movement (at the time) was initiated by technological and automobile revolutions and could lead to a desirable future. The new pattern is dispersed, he said, and concentration of city form and functions are a thing of the past. Mumford acknowledges that many new urban problems have developed, such as sprawl and congestion. In a rhetorical statement he suggests that 'life has become too easy, while cities have become unfit for human habitation . . . city planning is only for adults without families. It is desirable to plan for all phases of life and planners must design for an environment suited to every phase of life and growth'.[127]

The late 1940s experienced the emergence of yet another planning concept – that of planning for neighbourhoods, an integral part of the city fabric. The basic idea was to have most functions within walking distance.[128] However, Mumford had some reservations about this idea and warned that this type of planning could lead to class and status segregation. He emphasised that open spaces are an important issue in urban and regional development – parks offset congestion and disorder in the city. Even at that time he recognised that private cars created a problem. Cars provide access, he said, but the more there are, the more congestion there is, and the less chance there is for alternative modes of transport.

Mumford defines megalopolis as an 'amoeboid nonentity'.[129] The reaction most people have is to escape to suburbia, with the idea that life there is more rural. Instead, Mumford says, it is a large-scale non-city. It has the worst aspects of Le Corbusier's *City of Tomorrow*.[130] The suburban concept of isolating functions resulted in a lot of space with no function and the anti-city has resulted from an overvaluation of mechanisation and standardisation.[131] Mumford also attacked the emerging strip development, saying: 'The city is decentralized with strip development – an urbanoid nonentity which dribbles over the landscape'.[132] He called development of a very low density the anti-city, with no urban attributes and confining people for hours each day inside their cars. He believed a new urban pattern was needed, writing: 'The key to a fresh architectural image of the city as a whole lies in working toward an organic unit of urban order, which will hold together its component parts through successive changes in function and purpose from generation to generation'.[133] He claimed that the British New Town movement succeeded at least in part in these goals.[134] The ideal city size, Mumford believed, has a population between 30,000 and 300,000. He viewed Radburn, New Jersey, as a good application of these principles, and especially admired the separation of pedestrians and cars. Other features of which Mumford approved were continuous greenbelts, parks and boulevards, and he advocated rerouting expressways. He identified the need for regional planning. The current practice was that plans were carried out by highway and housing departments that cancelled each other out. He cites the regional plan for New York as the first successful attempt at integrating the region. The plan was drawn up by the New York State Housing and Regional Planning Commission, with Henry Wright as consultant. While Mumford praised Jane Jacobs in many ways, he believed her ideas ultimately promoted chaos and disorder by examining only the micro scale of the city and street life.

The book concludes with the report made by Mumford to the Ribicoff Committee on government expenditure (Washington, DC, 21 April 1967), in which he said that the failure of the New York Regional Plan was due to indifference and the problems of government bureaucracy.

In September 1955, the American journal *Scientific American* published an entire issue with the title 'Cities'. It was to be a prophetic study. Contributors to this seminal publication included Kingsley Davis, Hans Blumenfeld, Lloyd Rodwin, Charles Abrams and Kevin Lynch. Lynch was to become the most prophetic among this list of distinguished academics. His article 'The city as environment' emphasised a new role for the city planner – that a city should not only be efficient, but humanised. He asked the question, 'If the world were covered with a single vast city, how would one achieve the felicitous contrasts of city and country? The metaphor dramatises the need for making the texture of great cities richer'.[135] Lynch believed that the first and most obvious problem was the burden of perceptual stress imposed by the city – the omnipresent noise and the uncomfortable climate (including polluted air) with the added problem of visual identity. He went on to say that a good environment was diverse, with its parts having a distinct identifiable character. Disagreeing with what was already occurring in the US in a popular movement to outer suburbs, he suggested that the city was inherently a much richer and more diverse habitat than rural areas.[136]

Lynch also said that a third cause of distress was illegibility. 'In order to feel at home and to function easily, we must be able to read the environment as a system of signs'.[137] Lynch proposed alternative plans for an 'inner ring expressway' for central Boston. This was constructed years later, but in the early 1990s the expressway, which separated downtown Boston from Boston Harbor, was demolished and, at the end of that decade, replaced with a subterranean route to restore the relationship of the city to the Harbor. However, Lynch's plan did include a short subterranean section in the southeastern section of Back Bay. The article included a number of interpretive drawings, which had also been prepared by his collaborators, Donald Appleyard and John Myer, in *The View From the Road*.[138] This emphasised a variety of sequences that could be played in a number of combinations. Some routes would be 'designed as pleasureways, planned more for the motion along them to be enjoyed than for the simple function of circulation. There would be direct lines for people in a hurry and slow leisurely journeys for people on tour'.[139]

URBAN DESIGN AND BUILT FORM:
THE SHOPPING MALL

The morphological change of cities during this decade took on a new form, that of the suburban shopping mall. This shift had a complex basis; social and economic conflict were only part of the equation. The new construction of the interstate highway system also had a major influence in the emphasis on the polycentric city as opposed to the central city.

Of all the new forms of shopping, the out-of-town shopping centres of the US were most dramatic in their novelty, growth and implications for the cities they served. Although the first centres of this type were built in the 1930s, real growth did not come about until the post-Second World War era. By 1965 there were an estimated 11,000 such centres. By the early 1970s they had captured half of the retail trade in the country and were growing at the rate of almost 20 million square metres (24 million square yards) each year.[140] Development on this scale had not simply modified a previous pattern or added a new element to it – it had transformed that pattern, extracting the retailing element from the commercial cores of cities on a large scale and relocating it in isolation from the city centres' elements with which it had previously been identified.

The characteristic form of the new centres was best captured in area photographs, and exercised an ambivalent fascination on European planners and developers who projected the car ownership and family expenditure patterns of their own countries and determined 'lessons to be learned'. Some were appalled by the development of an island building, comprising magnet department stores linked by a simple mall arrangement lined by small traders, and set in an enormous car-park adjacent to an intersection on the highway network and on the fringe of a populated area. Others suggested that here the modern shopping centre was achieving an 'ideal' form, derived purely from the laws that govern the process of retailing, unhindered by the traditional restraints imposed upon development in the urban centres.

Certainly the intensely competitive situation in North America quickly revealed the ground rules for the new shopping centres, and the logic of these has been found to apply equally in different contexts. Thus, the principle of using a few 'magnet' stores with great attraction for all shoppers in order to manipulate pedestrian movement through the centre (past shops of lower individual attraction, thus maximising the turnover for all tenants) was soon established, as was the consequent necessity of achieving a correct tenant mix. Similarly, the principles affecting the siting of centres was clarified and for the first time there was considerable effort in estimating population catchment areas, patterns of expenditure and the competitive positions of numbers of shopping centres within a region.

Such general lessons are now widely understood,[141] but it is necessary in considering North American suburban centres to remember that they have not produced a constant solution. Rather, they represent a continuous mutation as their competitive situation has changed along the lines of the 'spiral' theory.[142] First, the new type of shopping established itself as a low-cost operation; it then increased in size as competition forced it to seek economies in scale and labour costs;

competition subsequently caused it to widen its assortment of goods and, finally, to offer services. In the meantime, external factors were changing. The standard of living rose, car ownership and highway construction increased, and the range of mass-produced items extended from food and convenience goods to a durable range including, for example, electrical appliances.

However, the growth of the new supermarkets had left a gap elsewhere, leading to the appearance of another new shop type. The widened trading areas of the supermarket-led local centres and the consequent greater travelling distances to those facilities with diminishing cost advantages gave rise to hypermarkets such as Wal-Mart and, somewhat later, K-Mart. Other hypermarkets were to follow in the next decades and effectively brought about the destruction of downtown retail.[143] Stores like the European hypermarket Carrefour were monocellular as opposed to the multicellular North American shopping malls.

The most ambitious single highway programme, overshadowing all others, was the US National System of Interstate Highways, authorised by Congress in 1944, which apportioned a 90 per cent federal funding of $25 billion in 1956. The project envisaged the construction of 40,000 miles of express routes within 12 years. The programme was extended to 1974 by the Highways Act of 1968.

The implications of these intensifying nets of national and regional highways for the urban structure, and in particular for its retailing element, were enormous. At the same time as rising car ownership made the concentration points of the old routes increasingly congested, large, cheap sites on the outskirts of cities were made highly accessible. This coincided with an increasing demand for price competitiveness as standards of living rose. It is paradoxical that this should be so, and that out-of-town or suburban centres should be best placed to meet such a demand originating from precisely that section of the population which could afford the cars to reach them. The reason for this is perhaps that the rise in the standard of living and in the expectations deriving from this do not produce a smooth transition in family expenditure patterns. Rather, the requirement at a certain point in income growth, for a further range of durable or 'luxury' goods, causes the amount of income available for essential items at that time to drop. The suburban and out-of-town locations were therefore particularly suited to competitive food retailing operations, and this was reinforced by the growth in ownership of domestic refrigerators and freezers, enabling the consumer to match the new pattern of larger and more distant outlets with less frequent shopping trips. The rise of out-of-town shopping centres and malls also coincided with a general growth in population and a dramatic growth in suburban populations. In the US, the suburban populations trebled between 1960 and 1973 from 27 million to 76 million. This meant that in any case a general increase in retailing provision was required, but also that the growth areas requiring these facilities were further removed from the old city centres.

The forms were derived from the logic of all these factors: the growth of car ownership, highway systems, land availability, standard of living, cost emphasis, population and suburban development, all favoured out-of-town centres. So strong were these pressures that it was not necessary for all of them to coincide. The American centres, in particular, were able to successfully evolve under the spiral effect, away from the low-cost aspect and toward more elaborate and expensive building forms and ranges of goods, but remained viable due to the accessibility of their sites. Between 1940 and 1970, the population rose by 55 per cent in the US and by 15 per cent in the UK. The overall density of population in the US was 22 persons per square kilometre and in the UK 229 persons per square kilometre. The average American disposed of 2.5 times the income of his UK equivalent and owned 2.5 times as many cars – half, in fact, of the world's total.

THE ROLE OF THE DEVELOPER

A new kind of operator, the developer, was required in order to implement the new planned shopping centres. The developer's role was to assemble the finance, land, tenants and professional and building skills in such a way that a completed shopping centre would be produced by a certain date and thereafter function to provide a satisfactory return on the capital invested. This role is quite distinct from that of the banker, landowner, retailer, architect or contractor, although it could be undertaken by any one of these. For example, developers of American out-of-town centres have included insurance companies, contractors, architects and department stores, either individually, or in combination, as well as companies exclusively concerned with property development. The development team at the design stage might comprise four central parties: the developer, the architect, the contractor and the leasing agent. Structural, HVAC, electrical and soils engineers would also be brought in at appropriate stages and the contractor would then be involved as a cost consultant. Further contributors to the development team might be the centre managers of the developer's previous project. This pattern is complicated by the fact that the anchor department stores would probably have their own design teams, retaining the developer's architect as a coordinating consultant.

The developer generally acted as leader of the development team and exercised rigid control in the imposition of freeze dates related to the completion of design stages necessary for bidding and contractual negotiations to proceed. Leasing agreements by the developer related rental paid by shop units to their turnover. Thus, the developer had a direct financial interest in the way in which tenants competed against or complemented one another in the centre as a whole. It was for this reason that the merchandising plan, with its detailed tenant mix, was of such importance to the developer.

The number of these American regional shopping centres is so great that the choice of examples is necessarily arbitrary. The early centres developed during the mid-1950s were in the form of malls open to the weather with canopies extending out from the shop-front. Roosevelt Fields in Long Island was a complex plan of double main malls between magnet stores and a multiplicity of cross-malls and small squares. This development was

opened in 1955 on the site of a disused airfield, adjacent to Meadowbrook Parkway in Nassau County. Similar developments took place in the suburbs of Detroit such as Northland and Eastland, the architect for which was Victor Gruen, a pioneer in the design of early shopping centres.

However, the prototypical shopping centre, which can still be seen at the beginning of the twenty-first century, was the enclosed mall. The enclosure marked a fundamental change in the development of centres in the 1960s. Its implications were wide. For the developer it meant that the resection of the capital costs for which the developer did not directly gain rental was greatly increased, particularly in the field of service costs, since a large volume of public space had to be heated and air-conditioned. For the tenant it meant a corresponding increase in rental levels and a consequent increase in maintenance charges. The relationship between the mall and the shops was now dramatically changed. Instead of there being a separation between buildings, as in Skidmore Owings and Merrill's two-level Short Hills Center in New Jersey, opened in 1961, the enclosed mall represents the central, most densely used space of a single building. The natural environment stops at the building perimeter and all shops are turned in upon this central space, from which they no longer need to be separated by glass walls and doors. The department stores are simply extensions of this space, as the whole centre is like a department store.

Despite the additional costs of enclosing the malls, the increased attractiveness to shoppers was such that all new centres began to be developed in this way. Many early centres were forced to carry out modernisation programmes to roof their malls at considerable cost and inconvenience.[144] However, the increased costs persuaded developers and architects away from the complicated experiments of the earlier centres. Trucking tunnels under the building were less frequently used, servicing taking place in screened areas at the rear of the shops. This had the effect of reinforcing the introspective nature of the building. Except in the case of the department stores, the outside wall ceased to have any function as a shop window, and the shops presented their blank sides to the car-parks. Multilevel schemes were also abandoned[145] with the realisation that the secondary level, not being a part of the main pedestrian flow, was isolated and therefore unable to support the rental levels appropriate to the covered centres.

The basic layouts of the centres were finally simplified into a few standard patterns. The centres were still built around two or three magnet stores, and these were arranged simply to draw shoppers along a single main mall. A regional centre of 100,000 square metres (120,000 square yards) gross lettable area (GLA) would have half of this area occupied by magnet stores. The width of the cross-section of shop/mall/shop would be about 100 metres (110 yards), so that the 50,000m^2 (60,000 square yards) of smaller shops would require a mall about 500 metres (550 yards) long. The effective range of a magnet was only 90 to 120 metres (100 to 130 yards); however, this length of mall could only be sustained by at least three magnets, otherwise a weak zone would occur in the centre and the circulation would tend to occur in two independent circuits within the zones of each magnet. To break the monotony of a quarter of a mile

*Plan: Short Hills Shopping Center,
New Jersey (1961), Skidmore, Owings
and Merrill.*

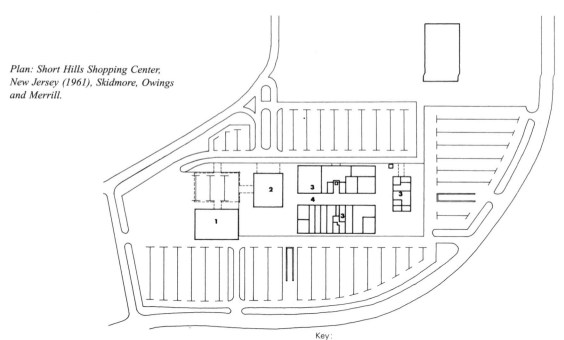

3·03 Short Hills shopping centre, New Jersey,
USA: mid-level plan
Architects: Skidmore, Owings and Merrill

Key:
1 Bloomingdale's department   3 Shops
   store (4 levels)   4 Mall
2 Bonwit Teller's department
   store (3 levels)   Scale: 1 : 4000

*Plan: North Park Shopping Center, Dallas,
Texas (1964), Harrell and Hamilton.*

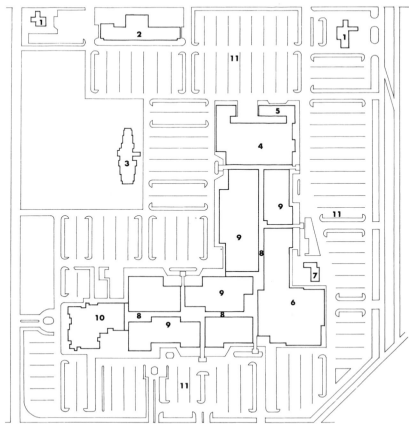

Key:
1 Service station   5 Penney's T B A   9 Shops
2 Convenience centre   6 Titche—Goettinger depart- 10 Nieman—Marcus depart-
3 Twin cinema   ment store (3 levels)   ment store (2 levels)
4 Penney's department store   7 Titche—Goettinger T B A   11 Parking
   (3 levels)   8 Mall   Scale: 1 : 4000

of mall, the layout could be broken at the point of the centre magnet to form an 'L', and this arrangement emerged as one of the classic forms of development of the period. North Park, Dallas (architects Harrell and Hamilton), with a total pedestrian circulation length of 790 metres (865 yards) and the largest air-conditioned mall area of any centre at the time of its opening in 1964, is a good example. *The Architectural Record* eulogised the new form in an article of the time: 'Not a "street of stores", but a flowing series of naturally lighted plazas is the enclosed mall of North Park. There are six such plazas, each with direct access from parking. The three largest with programmed fountains and plantings, mark the entrances to major stores but also provide visual contact with mall fronts of smaller tenants. Turning the "L" are two contiguous plazas which break the long vistas'.[146]

The architects describe their intentions thus:

> . . . to answer the problems of diverse, assertive occupancy and gigantic scale by recognizing we are dealing with one building. Our solution has attempted to create a sense of unity by the use of a single, simple palette of material (white brick, cast stone and concrete), and to manage the scale by variations in the form – establishing visual areas to which one can respond pleasantly at any point.

This quotation illustrates very well the new preoccupation with the building unity and the function of it within the mall. Certainly the malls at North Park, with their subdued range of materials, controlled bronze anodised aluminium framed shop-fronts, immaculate planters and seating units and 'programmed' fountains are apiece with the high-quality department stores they connect, and are some distance removed from the asphalt and concrete tiles and shrubbery beds of the earlier centres.

The 'rules' established for the design of covered centres in this period were:

1 Mall circulation should be as simple as possible, concentrating pedestrian movement along a single linear route and on one level only.
2 The simplicity of the straight mall should be broken only so far as to avoid monotony. Otherwise set-backs and other variations in the shop-front line should be avoided, so that each store is visible from the greatest area of the mall without being masked. For the same reason columns and other visual obstructions should be avoided in the malls.
3 Malls should be wide and brightly lighted.

There were, however, some interesting exceptions to the general pattern, an example of which is Randhurst, at Mount Prospect, Illinois. Designed by Victor Gruen for Victor Gruen Associates, this enclosed centre retains some of the complexity of the pioneering centres – it has an underground, half-mile-long service loop and a secondary lower-level mall without direct access from the car-parking areas. These features are brought together in a new way by virtue of the strongly centralised plan. Instead of disposing the three magnet stores along a linear route, they are used to generate a triple-arm pinwheel about a large central domed space at which point access is gained both down

to the secondary mall and up to a restaurant level. Although the malls are very wide (27 metres/30 yards), they have small kiosks scattered along the concourse and the department stores at the ends of the arms are visible from the central space. The geometric clarity of this scheme with its concentration in both plan and section upon a central place, equidistant from the magnet stores, foreshadows many later developments. This geometric completeness illustrates, better than any other centre so far considered, an essential characteristic of all these schemes – their close-endedness, their inability to grow, or to accept major programme changes, for example the number of magnet stores, without complete re-design. These were complete entities, made up of a specific range of components, and in the linear mall schemes the potentially extendible layout is stopped abruptly at each end by magnet stores. In such circumstances the centralised plan form of Randhurst seems particularly appropriate.

Built towards the end of this period, Willowbrook Mall in Wayne, New Jersey (opened in 1969) offers a transitional example into the last stage of mall development. The main problem with the schemes already discussed was the long mall lengths resulting from the simple arithmetic of providing a certain area within a length of section of fixed width. Willowbrook Mall attempted to overcome this difficulty in a number of ways. Welton, Becket and Associates, the architects, established the three-magnet arrangement based upon a 'T' rather than an 'L' mall form. Since the crossing of the 'T' is closer to the ends than is the angle of an 'L' of the same area, this device shortens apparent mall lengths from the mean point. In other words, the arrangement is centralised, reading as a cross with the fourth arm omitted and with a fourth department store, smaller than the three end magnet stores, located by the centroid.

The width of the section is increased to at least 120 metres (130 yards), decreasing the mall length enough to produce the required rental area. With fixed frontage/depth rations for most stores, this means the location of some shops with frontage to side malls only and a corresponding drop in passing customer traffic, and hence in turnover and rental potential. It also has the effect of greatly increasing the amount of service movement necessary across mall areas in order to reach units isolated within the depth of the section, particularly in the internal corners of the 'T' form.

The third device used to compress the plan form of this large centre was an upper mall level. Although this is still essentially secondary to the main ground-level malls and confined to one arm of the 'T', it is much more firmly integrated into the pedestrian system than was the case in the earlier centers. At Willowbrook Mall, despite a site area of 52 hectares (130 acres), a section of a two-storey car parking structure feeds shoppers directly into the secondary mall at the upper level. This mall is divided into perimeter routes along the shop frontages by large voids into the lower mall, providing visual connection between the two levels and accommodating escalator and stair connections between them. The upper mall also has a satisfactory circulation of its own, lying between one of the end department stores and the small central one and conforming to the 'dumb-bell' arrangement between the two magnets.

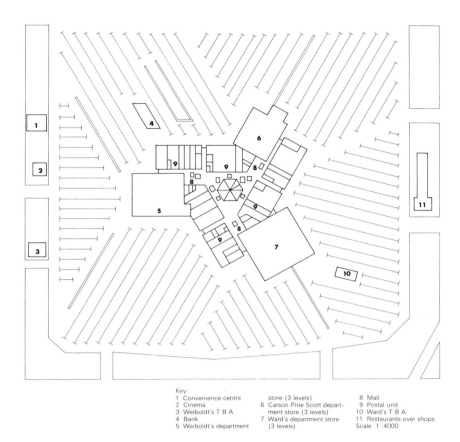

Plan: Randhurst Shopping Center, Mount Prospect, Illinois, Victor Gruen.

Key:
1 Convenience centre
2 Cinema
3 Weiboldt's T B A
4 Bank
5 Weiboldt's department

store (3 levels)
6 Carson Pirie Scott department store (3 levels)
7 Ward's department store (3 levels)

8 Mall
9 Postal unit
10 Ward's T B A
11 Restaurants over shops
Scale : 1 : 4000

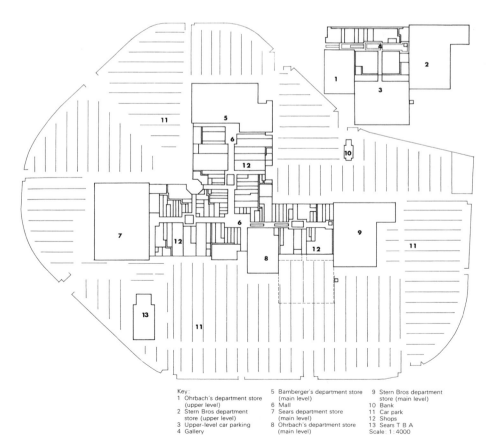

Plan: Willowbrook Mall, Wayne, New Jersey (1969), Welton, Becket and Associates.

Key:
1 Ohrbach's department store (upper level)
2 Stern Bros department store (upper level)
3 Upper-level car parking
4 Gallery

5 Bamberger's department store (main level)
6 Mall
7 Sears department store (main level)
8 Ohrbach's department store (main level)

9 Stern Bros department store (main level)
10 Bank
11 Car park
12 Shops
13 Sears T B A
Scale : 1 : 4000

The introduction of a second mall level in balance with the first, seen at Willowbrook in embryo form, is the most common mark of the archetypal centre at the end of the century. However, additional elements such as the 'food court' and 'multiplex' cinemas were to appear in the 1980s along with more exotic entertainment features including an internal theme park, for example that introduced at Mall of America outside Minneapolis-St Paul in Minnesota in the 1990s. Along with a tendency for centralised plans and more intensive site use, this is similarly a symptom of the spiral effect. By taking the next step in increased costs, the centres were able to grow still larger without falling apart through sheer inconvenience and without absorbing more of the site area, which in many regions was becoming increasingly expensive and difficult to obtain in competitive locations. The arithmetic of this problem is straightforward. A new centre of 150,000 square metres (180,000 square yards) GLA occupies perhaps 14 hectares (35 acres) with the building itself. At six cars per 100 metres (110 yards), it requires another 26 hectares (65 acres) for car parking, and with ancillary buildings, road junctions and inefficient parking layouts in the irregular areas between site and building perimeter, the total land take would probably be in excess of 50 hectares (125 acres). In the same issue of the *Architectural Record*[147] referred to above, this concern, when these later (stage three) centres were beginning to hit the drawing boards, was reflected in an article by Laurence J. Israel of the architectural firm of Copeland, Novak and Israel. Israel proposed that 'where the one-story shopping center is no longer economical . . . the multi-level

Willowbrook Mall, Wayne, New Jersey (1969), Welton, Becket and Associates: a) Interior of Connector Court, b) Interior of Central Court, c) Exterior view of Bamberger's department store.

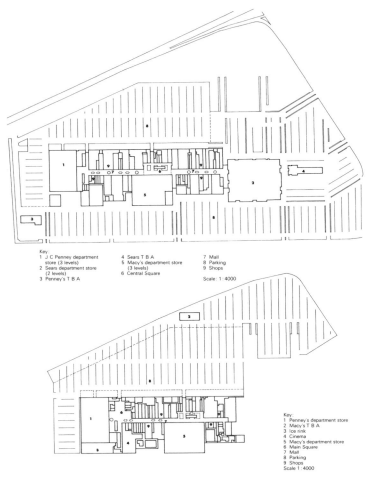

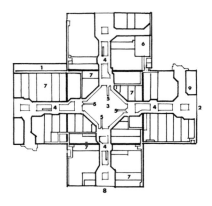

Key:
1 J C Penney department
  store (3 levels)
2 Sears department store
  (2 levels)
3 Penney's T B A

4 Sears T B A
5 Macy's department store
  (3 levels)
6 Central Square

7 Mall
8 Parking
9 Shops

Scale : 1 : 4000

Key:
1 Drug store
2 Penney's department store
3 Central Court
4 Upper-lever mall
5 Escalators
6 Restaurant
7 Shop units
8 Robinson's department store
Scale : Plan : 1 : 4000

Key:
1 Penney's department store
2 Macy's T B A
3 Ice rink
4 Cinema
5 Macy's department store
6 Main Square
7 Mall
8 Parking
9 Shops
Scale 1 : 4000

*Plans: Sun Valley, California (1967), Avner Nagger: a) upper-level plan,
b) lower-level plan.*

*Plan: Lakehurst Shopping Center,
Waukegan, Illinois (1971),
Victor Gruen.*

Key:
1 Wiedolot's department
  store (2 levels)
2 Carson, Pirie Scott
  department store (3 levels)
3 Penney's department store
  (2 levels)
4 Central Square

5 Mall
6 Upper-level parking
7 Lower-level parking
8 Future expansion
9 Penney's T B A
10 Bank
Scale : 1 : 4000

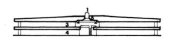

Diagonal section
Key:
1 Translucent plastic skylights
2 Air-conditioning slot
3 Upper-level
4 Lower-level
5 Escalators
6 Fountain
7 Plastic luminous ceiling
Sections : 1 : 2000

Cross section
Key:
1 Translucent plastic skylights
2 Air-conditioning slot
3 Upper-level
4 Lower-level
5 Fluorescent tubing light
  band with white acrylic lens

*Plans and sections, La Puente
Shopping Center, California.*

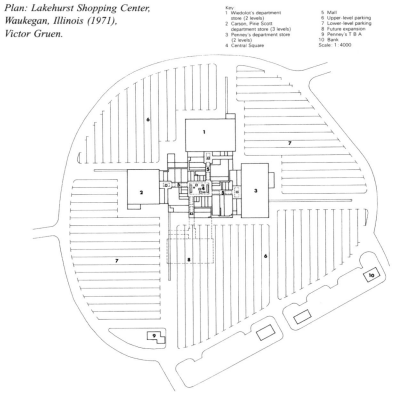

center is its logical and perhaps inevitable successor', and went on to suggest three alternative solutions in which both shopping and car-parking are on many levels and piled on top of one another. Sections of this complexity were only possible in urban areas of highest land costs and would have been inexplicable to the developers of the early out-of-town centres.

These later centres were not confined to tiny sites and their multilevel solutions generally comprised just two levels of shopping, equally served by a single level of car-parking. This was simply achieved on a site with a steady cross-fall by feeding the parking areas on the higher land into the upper mall on one side of the building, and those on the lower areas into the lower mall on the opposite side. An elaboration of this pattern could be seen in an early example of 1967 at Sun Valley in Concord, California, where the 'restricted' site area of 42 hectares (105 acres) has also meant the addition of a second car-parking level on the lower side of the site in order to reach the six cars per 100 square metres (120 square yards) figure of 9,000 spaces. Therefore, the upper mall had side malls feeding in from both natural ground level on the west and a parking deck on the east, while the lower mall had access from the east only, from parking areas cut in half by the slope. The stores at each end and one in the centre were linear with a magnet store at each end and one in the centre. However, the double-level arrangement meant that the mall length was kept to 335 metres (365 yards), with a 120-metre (130-yard) distance from the limit of Macy's frontage in the centre to either of the two end stores.

A sequence of three centres designed by Victor Gruen further developed the stage-three solution. The first of these was Yorktown at Lombard, Illinois, in 1968. This centre used the straight split-level idea and required no parking deck to accommodate the 9,000 cars. It was the first to have four major magnet stores. The result of the four equal-magnet programme was a struggle between the linear solution, like Sun Valley, with the axis lying along the 'fault' line between two levels of parking and a cruciform plan, generating a central node space.

The latter alternative was adopted in the second scheme, the Lakehurst Center in Waukegan, Illinois, which was completed in 1971. The third scheme was La Puente on the Pomona Freeway in California.

URBAN DESIGN AND BUILT FORM: THE NEW TOWNS

A more comprehensive and altruistic approach to urban design could be found in the construction of a new generation of new towns in this period. In Chapter 1 it was established that planned communities in the US extend back to the seventeenth and eighteenth centuries with the master plan for Philadelphia (1682) and James Oglethorpe's plan for Savannah, Georgia (1733). But it was through the influence of the garden city movement, emanating from the writings of the British visionary Ebenezer Howard at the beginning of the twentieth century, that true planned communities in their own right began to emerge across America. Among these early developments was Mariemont Garden City in Ohio (planned by New York architect John Nolan

in 1921), River Oaks in Texas, Palos Verdes in California, as well as Sunnyside Gardens, Long Island (planned in 1926 by Henry Wright and Clarence Stein). The Greenbelt New Towns of the US were part of a Federal Government programme started in 1935 as part of a quest for housing and community solutions for low- and middle-income families by the Roosevelt Administration's 'New Deal' policy.

There followed a hiatus during which neither the Federal Government nor private developers evinced any enthusiasm for planned communities. The National Housing Act of 1954 came into force in 1955 with Program 701. This legislation sought to encourage studies in planning by allowing states, regions, counties and towns to have two-thirds of their studies financed by the Federal Government.[148]

In *New Towns*,[149] Pierre Merlin suggested that 'new towns seem a natural product of the activities of the private promoter. These, having satisfied the demand for individual houses in the suburbs of the great cities, turned their attention to the wider market of upper-middle-income families. This wider market, with its demands for greater facilities than those of the suburbs, led to the planning of large-scale operations – consisting of over 10,000 dwellings – for which the term "new town" seemed the most appropriate'.[150]

Generally, the new towns were created by the acquisition of large areas of land developed by a single owner. This occurred at Reston, Foster City, Valencia and Redwood Shores. Of these, perhaps Reston was to become the most notable. Reston Virginia Incorporated became bankrupt in 1967 and was taken over by the Gulf Oil Company.

Merlin suggested that the new towns had a common planning policy – the aim of a true community – consisting of the following:

1   Development in small units (villages) in enclosed spaces as a reaction against the individualism or anonymity of the American suburbs, using terraced houses instead of individual plots.
2   The inclusion of leisure facilities in residential areas and great attention given to water spaces (Foster City and Reston), planned green spaces and recreation and sports areas.
3   Priority for pedestrian precincts, unusual in a country where priority was given to the car. The network of pedestrian-ways linked residential areas to the central village facilities, with a walking distance of no more than 400 metres (440 yards).[151]

These goals towards creating a true community provided a balance between public transport and the private car and attempted to create a high-quality environment borrowed from Mediterranean architectural design with piazzas, balconies, arcades, colonnades and patios. Some plans had conventional road systems (Valencia, Redwood Shores) while others (Foster City, Reston, Columbia) had freer systems without a gradation of road types.

The reaction of the press towards these new initiatives was enthusiastic. For example, *Time* magazine stated: 'Some 20 courageous developers have started new towns. But the unanswered question still is: will the independent (American) homeowner be willing to sacrifice a part of his backyard for the sake of more spacious community facilities? Will enough companies move out of the big cities into the new town's industrial park? For indications of how the future will go, the new town most closely watched by architects and developers alike is Reston, Virginia. It is probably the farthest along and architects agree that it is superbly designed'.[152] Architect Philip Johnson said: 'Reston is the most advanced planning in housing today'. In commenting on the residential and recreational aspects of the town, *Time* remarked: 'Situated on 6,800 acres [2,744 hectares] of rolling fox-hunting country, 18 miles [30 kilometres] west of Washington DC and 4 miles [6 kilometres] from the new Dulles International Airport, Reston is the brainchild of Robert Simon Jr., a New York entrepreneur. By its projected completion in 1980, it will house 75,000 people in seven villages, have over 1,600 acres [650 hectares] of recreational areas including two 18-hole and three 9-hole golf courses, a natural and artificial lake and a horse stable (the nearest village will have hitching posts in front of its stores) plus a plethora of community-owned swimming pools, tennis courts, playgrounds and hiking trails.[153]

'Residential and recreational will be woven together so closely that some Restonians will be able to chip onto a nearby green from their patio, others will watch their horses grazing a few steps away, still others cast off from their own bulkheads, motorboat across the lake, and moor a few feet away from their favorite store . . . Because no part of any village will be more than ten minutes away by foot, most travel will be confined to tree-lined walkways.

'The choice of residences is as wide as the choice of recreations. Prospective dwellings range from a one-room efficiency flat in a high-rise apartment building through a $25,400 three-bedroom town house to a custom-built home on a large lot for $60,000 or more. To avoid drab uniformity, Simon has assigned the designing responsibilities to five different architectural firms and they have come through with flying colors.[154] Instead of picture-window ranch houses or cramped Cape Cod saltboxes, Reston offers handsome modern architecture and quality construction found in few developments today.

'Almost 14 per cent of the land has been reserved for light industry plants and government agency buildings. To attract small companies, Simon is constructing a 132,000 square foot [12,260 square metres] office building that will rent out space, feature a common cafeteria, technical library and possibly a communal computer. The industrial park will restore to most residents the old fashioned pleasure of being able to walk to work.

'So far,' *Time* magazine went on, 'Reston's prognosis is good. Three companies . . . have already moved into the industrial park and another dozen are negotiating for space.'

Victor Gruen remarked that Reston was the most courageous effort toward building a new town that had yet been undertaken.

Construction of Reston commenced in 1963. By 1964, the Gulf Oil Corporation had lent Robert Simon $14 million and in 1966 John Hancock Insurance had lent him a further $15 million.

However, new towns like Simon's Reston or James Rouse's Columbia were not without their critics. Jane Jacobs sourly suggested that, 'They were really very nice towns if you were docile and had no plans of your own and did not mind spending your life among others with no plans of their own'.[155]

Financing was a major problem, because new towns needed much more land area and a much larger initial investment than conventional subdivisions. The economic success of new towns was mixed. Planners and the developers looked at new towns as a means of doing more than simply housing well-shaded suburbanites in congenial surroundings. They saw them as a means of restoring some social balance between city and suburb.

Nevertheless, the new towns did seem to remain as middle-income and upper-income projects with housing conventionally segregated by price. The then Secretary of Housing and Urban Development, Robert C. Weaver, remarked that the vast majority appeared destined to become country club communities for upper-income families.

This was not the view of the developers of Reston. In a 1998 interview with James Selonick, former Executive Vice-President of Simon Enterprises (The Reston Organization), it was emphatically clear that Robert Simon, James Selonick and Dr Carol Lubin, Community Planner, all had much wider objectives.[156] James Selonick said that both he and Simon wanted to establish a multi-ethnic, multi-income community, particularly because of its proximity to Washington, DC. The objectives were to draw 'blue-collar' and professional workers to establish a balanced social community. This social system worked in the early years but later, with growing property values, this was not the case – an issue not dissimilar from the garden cities earlier in the century.

James Rouse, who attained celebrity status as a banker, shopping centre impresario and civic leader, established Columbia, Maryland, as a parallel example to Reston. Rouse was determined not only to make a financial success of the new town, but a social breakthrough. Many experts considered that Columbia was the most soundly conceived and solidly financed of all of that generation of new towns.

Two important studies of Reston were made. The first, by the Washington Center for Metropolitan Studies,[157] was a critical review of the foundation and negotiations, financial, legal and communal which led to the establishment of the new town. The report suggested the significance of Reston lies in a number of quite different contexts. The goals set for Reston by Simon and his associates included:

- the widest choice of opportunities for the full use of leisure time;
- the possibility for anyone to remain in a single neighbourhood throughout his or her life, uprooting being neither inevitable nor always desirable, by providing the fullest possible range of housing styles and prices, from high-rise efficiencies to six-bedroom town houses and detached houses;
- the importance and dignity of each individual as the focal point for all planning;

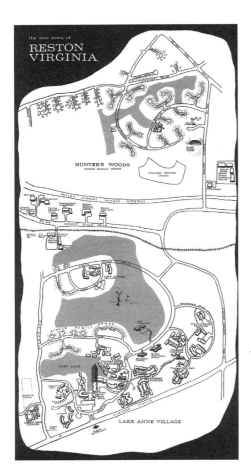

Map: Reston, Virginia.

Booklet cover: Reston, Virginia (1968).

Housing, Reston, Virginia (1970).

- that people should be able to work and live in the same community;
- that commercial, cultural and recreational facilities should be made available to the residents from the outset of the development, not years later; and
- that beauty (structural and natural) is a necessity of the good life.

Essentially, Reston was conceived as a socio-physical entity. The second report, by the Reston, Virginia, Foundation for Community Programs,[158] focused on the educational programmes of the new town. In the organisation of the community, the importance of the Home Owner's Association was stressed. The report suggested the success of Reston depended to a large part on the enlightened use of the community's beautiful land and water resources. Two homeowners' associations were established, one for each half of the town. The responsibilities of the associations were the operation and maintenance of parks, parking areas, streets, sidewalks and other facilities. All property owners were required to pay annual dues sufficient to pay all taxes, assessments and expenses.[159] This did not include charges for the swimming pool, tennis club and golf course maintenance – charges that were borne only by the people using those facilities. The associations were charged with enforcing the protective covenants including restrictions against exposing laundry to another lot, constructing fences, removing trees over a certain diameter, polluting air or water by using motor boats over 5.5 metres (18 feet) long on the lake and erecting television antennas or oversized signs.

Cultural organisations were encouraged. These included drama and singing groups, and a music society including a children's choir. The Reston Chapter of the Virginia Museum of Fine Arts was established, as was a multipurpose auditorium (Community Hall) for plays, concerts, dance classes, music lessons, lectures, films, meetings, conferences, parties and religious services. The Reston South Riding Stable provided riding instruction including jumping, dressage and polo.

The report said: 'Americans have more time to spend as they like than ever before. This increased time is often called a problem. Some housewives complain of boredom because they have nothing to do when they finish the day's chores. Some husbands spend their evenings in bars because no other social institutions serve their neighborhood. Some teenagers get into trouble because making mischief seems more interesting than doing nothing. But free time also represents a great opportunity. For the housewife, it can mean time to continue her education. For the husband, it can mean time to bring out an old trombone and join an amateur jazz band. For the teenager, it can mean time for active participation in sports'.[160]

This somewhat patronising and chauvinistic paragraph seems to imply an attitude of social engineering that some thirty years later was to be contradicted by a much more complex society of dual-income families and teenagers resorting to violence.

Nevertheless, the programme of pre-school education included a model facility in the form of a nursery-kindergarten completed in December 1965. Reston preferred the Montessori method of pre-school education, though this was only available to families with an adequate income to pay for nursery-school tuition.

Conditions made Reston particularly receptive to higher education. These included a fresh start, unusual cohesiveness of the community, a diversity of occupations, interests, backgrounds, income, ethnicity and education of a heterogeneous population living and working in the same community.[161] The plan included land for a major post-graduate facility in addition to 22 sites for the public schools of the Fairfax County school system, as well as a 22-hectare (55-acre) site for a college or university.

The article in *Time* magazine was preceded by a 1964 article in *Newsweek*,[162] which, unlike the *Time* article, recognised that the concept of new towns was not new, referring to Ebenezer Howard of the UK as the originator of garden cities at the turn of the twentieth century.[163]

Newsweek praised 'the 30-acre [12-hectare] artificial lake, already stocked with fish and the broad, brick-paved village center – designed by the New York architectural firm of Whittlesey and Conklin'. It mentions major technical innovations such as the community air-conditioning plant, which piped chilled water into basement coils in every house and shop.

In addition, *Newsweek* identified Simon Enterprises as pioneers who believed that it was possible to live an entire

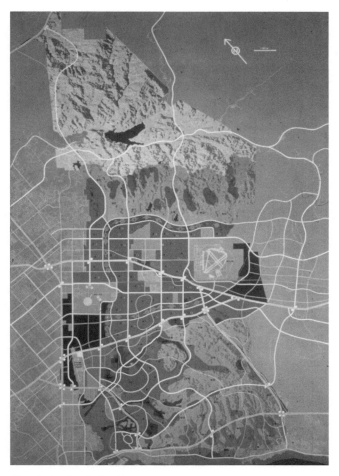

Plan: Irvine Ranch New Town, California.

lifecycle in a town, beginning in a high-rise as a single person, moving on to a town house as a married couple and to a detached house when children arrived. Permission would be required to chop down a tree more than 10 centimetres (4 inches) in diameter, or approval sought from an architectural review board for even the slightest change in a building facade.[164]

Most of this generation of new towns were in California where the population growth at the time was three times the rate of the rest of the US. Among them was Irvine Ranch New Town, 80 kilometres (50 miles) south of Los Angeles. William Pereira was the architect of this new town, one of the largest private developments in the world. Built on 35,610 hectares (88,000 acres), the three-city complex was to house 280,000 people, a number to be greatly exceeded by the end of the twentieth century. Like the university towns of Europe, *Newsweek* indicated, the focal point was the 400-hectare (1,000-acre) University of California's Irvine Campus. The residential areas branched outwards from the university, intertwined with high-tech industries. Similar to Reston, it incorporated a major section of public landscape – a 400-hectare (1,000-acre) green belt of lakes and woods.

A smaller development was Victor Gruen's 2,830-hectare (7,000-acre) community, Laguna Niguel, 70 kilometres (45 miles) southeast of Los Angeles, formed of seven self-contained neighbourhoods, with ocean and lakeside views.

Historically, it seemed that the American new towns appeared in 30-year cycles in the late 1930s, 1960s and 1990s for quite different social and economic reasons.

URBAN DESIGN AND BUILT FORM: NEW VILLAGES

Quite different from the major new towns of this decade were a number of settlements built along the California coast overlooking the Pacific Ocean. Sea Ranch, designed by Moore, Lyndon, Turnbull and Whitaker, is a 2,020-hectare (5,000-acre) development 145 kilometres (90 miles) north of San Francisco. The site runs along the coast between rocky cliffs and beaches on one side and steeply sloping meadows and moorlands on the other side of the Pacific Highway (California State Highway 1). The area was once covered with forests, but most of the trees were lost through logging and the area was subsequently used for sheep farming. The developers bought the land in the early 1960s for recreational use and by 1966 the first phases of Sea Ranch were completed.[165]

Lawrence Halprin and Partners, landscape and land planning consultants, were appointed to work with Moore, Lyndon, Turnbull and Whitaker as well as Joseph Esherick and Associates as architects. Halprin's analysis of the site was concerned with conserving and respecting existing conditions of its open character. The architectural form relates well to Frank Lloyd Wright's earlier theories of 'organic architecture', epitomised in Falling Water, completed in 1938 in Bear Run, Pennsylvania. The buildings were timber-framed and clad in vertical weathered cedarwood boarding and plate-glass windows, using mono-pitch shingle roofs skilfully related to the land form. Houses

were inserted into the hillsides with hedgerows for protection against the cool climate and prevailing sea breezes. Setbacks were included in the designs to maximise both close and distant sea views, and access roads were designed to minimise visual intrusion. Colour and materials were restricted to a limited palette.

Because of the nature of the site, the architects avoided overshadowing as far as possible and created outdoor spaces, generally in the form of courtyards. Six traditional-style houses were built first, followed by a condominium.

Donlyn Lyndon wrote the site criteria. Units had to identify with the site, ocean view, southern exposures and wind breaks. They were to be screened from the road with trees and walls and positioned in such a manner as to reinforce the natural landforms and scale. Cars were to be grouped in courtyards to simplify the road structure, and the units were intended, according to Lyndon, to work together to create a large-scale composition instead of using them as separate entities.

Clusters of ten to twenty units were laid out, starting with a demonstration model of ten units. These ten were all under the same large roof, which followed the slope of the site. A number of houses were designed for specific owners and located separately.

Commercially, the initiative was a great success and some of Halprin's ideas were relinquished as far as lot and density arrangements were concerned. A communal swimming pool and tennis courts were built, followed later by riding stables. The development proved so popular that eventually another recreational centre was built.

The main focus of the development has a major restaurant, lounge and bar overlooking the Pacific Ocean as well as a general store, community post office and gift shop.

The development has an indefinable quality beyond architectural seemliness. It can only be described by the Scandinavian term *'hygge'*,[166] suggesting a feeling of coziness, well-being and personal affinity, often experienced by the warmth of firelight and candles in the comfort of a log cabin during a cold winter. It represents a village quality that cannot really be achieved in larger developments such as new towns.

UTOPIAS

Less tangible than the new towns and new villages were the attempts at utopian settlements during this period. The social upheaval in the US by the newly emancipated generation of the early 1960s evolved into major political protests after 1968, particularly directed against the increasing military involvement of the US in the Vietnam War.

R. Buckminster Fuller, the visionary architect and inventor of geodisic structures, suggests that: '. . . within a few years we will be able to go in the morning to any part of the earth by public conveyance, do a day's work, and reach home again in the evening, and by the Treasury Department's income tax allowance for traveling expenses, we will not have been out of town. We will be realistically and legally in a one-town world for the first time in history'.[167] However, this utopian vision of

SITE PLAN

FIRST FLOOR PLAN

SECOND FLOOR PLAN

'Walk-in' cabins at Sea Ranch, California (1975),
Obie Bowman (architect).

the near future was not to be fulfilled. In the next decade, the 1973 energy crisis was to haunt the world of mega-utopians.

This sense of failure of technological utopia had already been evoked at the same time as its most confident assertions and in the same region as its final flowering in the southwestern US. In 1965, Paolo Soleri stubbornly insisted on building a city called Arcosanti. Although only a minuscule portion of this city was actually constructed, a different type of settlement appeared the same year. Drop City appeared ironically in a version of Fuller dome structures – fabricated from cannibalised components from the car industry that he studied so intently as a model for the new industrialised urbanism. To describe Drop City and similar communities as utopian would, no doubt, be as incorrect

as in the case of Marxian idealisations, for it lacked a formal utopian programme. Drop City, erected by well-educated young people generally emigrating from California to the deserts of Arizona and Colorado as a protest against a materialistic society and conservative politics was, for a time, a self-sufficient community of young adults and children who grew their own crops for food and rejected any hierarchical structure for their particular society. Indeed, its lack of an overt programme and its apparently unstructured appearance were essential parts of its message. 'The unspoken thing,' as Tom Wolfe observed, was a central feature of the open commune. 'They made a point of not putting it into words. That in itself was one of the unspoken rules . . . to define it was to limit it.' Nevertheless, this spontaneous

Drop City (1965).

flight of urban people to the land seemed to belong to a long-standing utopian tradition which acquired a new relevance as both the social and technical utopias became more self-embracing and, apparently, closer to implementation.

In this last tradition, which might be called consumer utopias, a major concern becomes that of limiting the powers concerning the density of urban development, which implies the need for centralised planning control. Thus, having abandoned his earlier enthusiasm for the Chicagoan machine city, Frank Lloyd Wright sought to overcome its problems by the reduction of its density to one acre per person – to the point where urban form, economics and control were dissolved away. Although he believed that new technology, in particular the motor car and telephone, favoured such a development in any case, it was the social implications of Broadacre City that were to be paramount. Through this decentralisation, society would be freed of the insidious controls and exploitation that urban life imposed on it, above all, the exaction of rent.

In utter contrast to the flight from the city to the countryside were attempts at brave reconstructions of the city centre itself. These included images of the Japanese architect, Kenzo Tange, in his plan for Tokyo Bay in 1960, in which the city structure left terra firma behind to spread across the water of the bay and expose its rationally ordered systems and elements – a city structure composed of cyclical transportation, civic axis and three-dimensional lattice-like spaces, unifying pilotis and service cores, a unified handling of city, transportation and architecture and a hierarchy of space from private spaces to social. The translation of the public/private, developer/tenant administrative separation of building roles into a powerful architectural language was relevant to another of Kenzo Tange's projects, the Yerba Buena Center in San Francisco, which he produced in association with McCue, Boone, Tomsick, Lawrence Halprin and Associates and John Bolles and Associates (URTEC). The Yerba Buena Center Redevelopment Plan, approved in 1966, called for the redevelopment of three major city blocks in the heart of San Francisco, in the Market South district, between Market Street to the north and Folsom Street to the south, and between Third and Fourth Streets including Mission Street. The area was to be divided into three superblocks, of which the nucleus was to be the YBC Center, a scheme for which was produced in 1969.

Tokyo Bay (1960), Kenzo Tange.

In this, a major element was the five-storey deep lattice structured car-park blocks, suspended five-and-a-half storeys above street level and served by tall drums of access ramps (not dissimilar from Louis Kahn's proposals for Philadelphia almost two decades earlier). These parking structures spanned the three city blocks of the site and had bridge connections across the flanking office and hotel slabs, with a discipline of vertical service cores running through both. Space frame roofs were to cover areas between and around these major elements to provide enclosed spaces for a sports arena, exhibition hall and other uses of the Central District. The concept was not dissimilar to Place Bonaventure in Montreal, Canada, which was completed in 1967. The San Francisco proposal emphasised shopping as an important part in the definition and generation of its pedestrian spaces and, in particular, the idea of shopping denoted by the pervasive and elastic term 'galleria'. This term was intended to denote not so much a precise physical model as a 'symbol' of life for the citizens, and was a measure of the understanding of the relationship between private and public enterprise. The YBC plan represented an important development from the pedestrian systems of Montreal, in which these became a controlled sequence of urban spaces and the form of the building elements of the megastructure began to indicate the novelty of its implications.

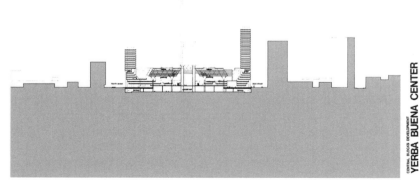

Yerba Buena Center, California (1969), Kenzo Tange.

Disneyland, California.

Had the Yerba Buena Center been constructed, it is debatable, in retrospect, whether it would now in fact seem to be beneficial to the city of San Francisco. The destruction of a historic core of the city would seem akin to the efforts of the city authorities about this time, just as it would have been in the elimination of the cable-car system, which has always proved to be a paramount tourist attraction, in the subsequent decade. The demolition of the Embarcadero Freeway, which separated the city from its waterfront, became symptomatic of changing public attitudes away from megastructures and high-tech built solutions towards a more likeable, humane environment.

UTOPIAS AND THE VIRTUAL CITY

This emerging attitude towards a more nostalgic view of the city was established by a new phenomenon. Tunnard and Pushkarev's *Man Made America*[168] had dismissed the prototypical commercial strip as a visually aggressive and ubiquitous feature that is sometimes considered to be typical, even inevitable, in the urban fringe.

One of the purest examples of the contention of the virtual city, and hence the most suggestive models for a formal consistency are provided in fun fair architecture. Travelling fun fairs have long been a cult subject among aficionados entranced with the decorative elements of the rides dating back to the nineteenth century. Surprisingly, little was said on the architecture of fun fairs, with the exception of a 1978 study by L. Wasserman, which subsequently received an award from

Progressive Architecture magazine in January 1979.[169] Wasserman, specifically seeking points of reference and lessons from fun fairs for application in architectural theory, was inspired by the quite phenomenal revival in fun fairs in the US, which, apart from Disneyland in California, had seen a decline in the 1950s and 1960s, including the closure of New York's Coney Island – the iconic example of the fun fair.

It is possible to consider, therefore, that the basis of fairground rides could be used as an analytical tool of total urban experience. At one level they provide a greatly heightened version of the everyday experience of sequential space, as described, for example, by Cullen, with experiences of danger, shock, surprise and changing light exploited in the fairground haunted rides. Alternatively they can be seen in terms of a broader experience of fantasy and idealism. The huge number of visitors to Disneyland may result from the basic need to create fantasy in a popular dream world of illusions, which for a day have more vivid reality than the monotonous environment they leave behind.

Opened in 1955, Disneyland was the first transformation of a fun fair such as Coney Island into an entirely different spatial and psychological experience. By the 1960s it had become the beginning of a renaissance of fun fairs. The magic kingdom, or miniature universe in Disneyland took the theme of popular fantasy based upon childhood memory much further and in a quite different way compared to the traditional fun fair. However, the element of danger and surprise was deliberately missing. Peter Blake, writing in *The Art of Disney*,[170] noted that Charles Eames had been the first designer to recognise its importance in the 1950s and that in Disneyland, Disney had produced something as yet unattainable in real life cities – a truly integrated scheme of multilevel transit systems comprising people-movers, non-polluting vehicles, pedestrian malls and vast urban infrastructures.

Walt Disney used cartoonists to colour-code buildings and drew upon the expertise of film-makers to chart the progression of pedestrians through a sequence of urban spaces. Above all else, he created an urban environment that endlessly fascinates and endlessly attracts. He deliberately used fake facades and a smaller-than-human scale. In Disneyland, the reduced scale at pedestrian level becomes further reduced above by the use of deliberately distorted perspective, so as to create the illusion of greater height as in Sleeping Beauty's Castle. Again, in Disneyland, use is made of specific themes to break down the scale of the overall experience into a series of small discrete worlds, such as the early twentieth-century Main Street, the nineteenth-century Mississippi riverboat area, or the medieval fairy castle.

It has been suggested by John Pastier[171] that both Disneyland and Las Vegas are colonies of Hollywood and that there are distinct parallels between the two. Both places are theatrical experiences, employing vivid characteristics – solid and wholesome in the first place, ephemeral and mysterious in the second. Perhaps, as Charles Moore has written, as we become more enlightened we will understand the multiple realities of Disneyland and come to enjoy our cities as giant theme parks.

NOTES

1. Lynch, Kevin, Trib Banerjee and M. Southworth (eds) (1990) *City Sense and City Design: Writings and Projects.* Cambridge, MA: MIT Press, pp. 12–18.
2. Ibid., p. 18.
3. Ibid., p. 19.
4. Ibid., p. 3.
5. Lynch, Kevin (1960) *The Image of the City.* Cambridge, MA: The Technology Press and Harvard University Press.
6. Lynch, Kevin (1957) 'Extracts from current research on the public image of Boston'. Unpublished paper, MIT (27 November). Given to the author, David Gosling, by Kevin Lynch.
7. Ibid., p. 1.
8. Ibid., p. 7.
9. Ibid., p. 8.
10. Ibid., pp. 26–28.
11. At the time, without the use of computer-generated data analysis, such a small survey control group was inevitably inadequate. Later, the size of an adequate control group of inhabitants, visitors and others would normally be between several hundred people and in excess of one thousand.
12. Ibid., p. 28.
13. Lynch, Kevin and M. Rivkin (1959) 'A Walk Around the Block', *Landscape*, vol. 8, no. 3, pp. 24–34.
14. Lynch, Banerjee and Southworth, op. cit., pp. 185–204.
15. Lynch, Kevin (1957) 'Go take a walk around the block'. Unpublished paper, MIT (November 1957), pp. 1–34. Given to the author, David Gosling, by Kevin Lynch.
16. Ibid., part 1, p. 1.
17. Ibid., p. 11.
18. Ibid., part 2, p. 17.
19. This was fundamental to the Bauhaus philosopher and particularly that of his mentor, Gyorgy Kepes.
20. This was also notable in the writings of the British theorist Gordon Cullen in his articles for *The Architectural Review.* Cullen, Gordon (1952) 'Focus on Floor', *The Architectural Review,* vol. III, no. 661 (January), pp. 33–42.
21. Lynch, Kevin (1960) *The Image of the City.* Cambridge, MA: The Technology Press and Harvard University Press, p. 34.
22. Gosling, D. (1960). Unpublished thesis, Manchester University, England (June), p. 15.
23. This was subsequently to be developed in the publication of a book: Appleyard, Donald, Kevin Lynch and John Meyer (1964) *The View from the Road.* Cambridge, MA: MIT Press.
24. Lynch, Kevin (1957) 'Introduction to the postgraduate study on The Boston Image', MIT (November): p. 1.
25. Bloomer, K. C. and C. W. Moore (1977) *Body, Memory, and Architecture.* New Haven, CT: Yale University Press, p. 79.
26. Norberg-Schulz, C. (1971) *Existence Space and Architecture Studio.* London: Vista.
27. Cullen, G. (1961) *Townscape.* London: Architectural Press.
28. Conversations between David Gosling and Kevin Lynch in early 1958.
29. Lynch, Kevin (1960) *The Image of the City.* Cambridge, MA: The Technology Press and Harvard University Press, pp. 145–52.
30. Ibid., pp. 9–10.
31. Ibid., p. 24.
32. Ibid., pp. 46–83.
33. Ibid., pp. 47–48.
34. Ibid., pp. 131 ff.
35. Groot, J. J. M. de. (1912) *Religion in China.* New York: GP Putnam. While this may be a pseudoscience, as Lynch suggests, geomantics are still taken seriously within Chinese culture. For example, in the 1980s Sir Norman Foster, in his design for the Hong Kong and Shanghai Bank, consulted geomancers through the design process. The design of the Bank of China, also in Hong Kong, by renowned Chinese American architect I. M. Pei, ignored such a philosophy with resulting sharp angular and triangular forms in the architecture. It is said that adjacent property values fell because such forms were considered to be 'unlucky'.
36. Lynch (1960), op. cit., p. 158. Lynch did not acknowledge, however, Cullen's earlier theories of serial vision.
37. Gosling, D. (1959) 'Rehabilitation area design plan – the Hill District'. New Haven, CT: official report, City Planning Commission (August).
38. See Garvin, A. (1995) *The American City.* New York: McGraw Hill, pp. 82, 212–13.
39. Geoffrey Baker of New Canaan, Connecticut, was an American authority on retail systems and should not be confused with Geoffry Baker, the British authority on Le Corbusier and professor at Tulane University, New Orleans.
40. Cullen, G. (1956) 'Alphabet as Image', *The Architectural Review,* vol. 120, no. 718, (October), pp. 240–47.
41. The interstate programme would eventually transform the landscape of the US. Built originally for military defence purposes under the Eisenhower administration, the interstate system allowed a mobility for individuals and families unknown in previous generations. It created the rapid growth of metropolitan areas in which mobility combined with inexpensive land caused an explosive growth into suburban and exurban areas. This was important since the interstate programme was in its infancy and the majority of inter-city traffic was on highways similar to the Berlin Turnpike in Connecticut. Nevertheless, uncontrolled commercial strip development on the edges of cities continues to this day.
42. Interstate highway signs are standardised, with major signs having white lettering on a green background and minor signs white on blue. Commercial development such as fast-food restaurants, motels and petrol stations are kept well in the background at the end of exit ramps. Most have clusters of high lighting columns with the firm's logo at the top of single columns.
43. It is interesting to note that the term 'civic design' was still in general usage in the US and UK at the time, though Lynch had already identified 'urban design' as representing something quite different.
44. Tunnard, Christopher and Boris Pushkarev (1963) *Man-Made America: Chaos or Control?* New Haven, CT: Yale University Press, p. 429.
45. Tunnard, op. cit., pp. ix–xii.
46. Ibid., p. ix.
47. Ibid., p. 13.
48. Ibid., pp. 72–80.
49. In the 1990s this trend was reversed, not only because land costs have risen, but because major demographic change has generated a market for relatively luxurious houses on comparatively small plots of land. This market addresses the need of retirees who do not want the burden of major yard maintenance.
50. Ibid., pp. 157–275.
51. Ibid., pp. 401–40.
52. Ibid., pp. 427–30.
53. Appleyard, D., K. Lynch and J. R. Myer (1964) *The View from the Road.* Cambridge, MA: MIT Press.
54. Ogilby, J. (1757) *Roads through England Survey of the Roads from Essex.* London: John Bowles and Son.
55. Appleyard, Lynch and Myer, op. cit., p. 63.
56. Ibid., p. 3.
57. Ibid., p. 57.
58. 'New Communities: One Alternative'. Proceedings of the Twelfth Urban Design Conference, 7–8 June 1968. Cambridge, MA: Harvard Graduate School of Design. The use of the expression 'one alternative' seems ambiguous. Alternative to what?
59. Ibid., p. 5.
60. Ibid., p. 9.
61. Ibid., p. 41.
62. Ibid., p. 55. Nash was incorrect. Though the new towns programme was a British government programme financed through the Department of the Environment, the new towns were self-governing under

separate Development Corporations. There was no 'Crown Corporation'. Eventually the British New Towns Commission was established and the tangible assets of each new town were sold by 1996.

63. Ibid., p. 58.

64. Ibid., p. 78. Prior to the conference, a hypothetical physical plan had been drawn up by the students with the title 'New communities: one alternative'. Unfortunately, the summary report was not included in the conference proceedings, but one extract from the report apparently claimed: '[T]he design is rather the result of many reflective sketches which presented provocative ideas. These were subjected to the professional scrutiny of the project staff working together with many other interested members of the university community . . . a preconceived master plan was resorted to' (p. 75). Neither did the proceedings provide illustrations of these proposals, though it is evident from the document that the plan was fashioned around the concept of a new town in the Boston area.

65. For a more substantial discussion of the relevance of semiotics to design, as also Gestalt psychology, see Norberg-Schulz, Christian (1963) *Intentions in Architecture*. London: London University Press, Allen & Unwin.

66. Cullen, G. (1974) 'Language of gestures', unpublished paper; but see Gosling, D. (1996) *Gordon Cullen: Visions of Urban Design*. London: Academy Editions, pp. 224–28; Broadbent, G., R. Bunt and C. Jencks (eds) (1980) *Signs, Symbols, and Architecture*. Chichester: John Wiley & Sons Ltd.

67. Calhoun, J. B. and A. H. Esser (eds) (1971) 'Space and the strategy of life', in *Behavior and Environment*. New York: Plenum Press.

68. Jacobs, J. (1961) *The Death and Life of Great American Cities*. New York: Modern Library.

69. Broadbent, G. (1990) *Emerging Concepts in Urban Space Design*. New York: Van Nostrand Reinhold, pp. 138–43.

70. Jacobs, op. cit., pp. 99–100.

71. Ibid., pp. 152–221. This is the central core of the book in which she describes chapter by chapter her 'four conditions' for socially successful cities.

72. Ibid., p. 153.

73. Alexander, C. (1965) 'A city is not a tree', *Architectural Forum* (April), pp. 58–62 and (May), pp. 58–61.

74. Alexander, C. (1969) *Notes on the Synthesis of Form*. Cambridge, MA: Harvard University Press.

75. Alexander, C. and S. Chermayeff (1963) *Community and Privacy*. Garden City, NY: Doubleday.

76. Alexander, op. cit.

77. During the middle of this decade, architectural schools in Europe and North America adapted a philosophy known as 'design methodology' – yet many results were arid. Design methodology precluded intuitive, inspirational or innovative design.

78. Alexander, C. (1966) *The City as a Mechanism for Sustaining Human Contact*. Berkeley, CA: University of California Center for Planning and Development.

79. Hanser, P. M., P. K. Hatt and A. J. Reisg (eds) (1957) 'The changing population of the modern city', *Cities and Society: the Revised Reader in Urban Design*. London: Collier Macmillan.

80. Sennett, Richard (1970) *The Uses of Disorder: Personal Identity and City Life*. Harmondsworth: Penguin Books, p. 53.

81. Harvey, David (1972) 'Social processes, spatial form and the redistribution of real income in an urban system', in Murray Stewart (ed.) *The City: Problems of Planning*. Harmondsworth: Penguin Books, p. 302.

82. Lupsha, P. (1969) 'On theories of urban violence', *Urban Affairs Quarterly*, vol. 4, pp. 273–96.

83. Harvey, David (1973) *Social Justice and the City*. London: E. Arnold, p. 95.

84. Ibid.

85. American R/UDAT.

86. R/UDAT Task Force of the Urban Planning and Design Committee of the American Institute of Architects (1983) *Urban Design, News From the Front*, Washington, DC.

87. Thiel, P. (1961) 'A sequence-experience notation for architectural and urban spaces', *Town Planning Review* (April), Liverpool: Liverpool University Press, pp. 36–52.

88. Ibid., p. 45, a quotation taken from Haroda, J. (1923) *The Gardens of Japan*. London: Studio Ltd.

89. Thiel, P. (1964) 'Movement in Japanese environmental representation', *Urban Planning/Development Series*, Seattle: University of Washington Press.

90. *Hishikawa Kichibei*, Tokaido Bunken no Ezu. (scaled illustrations of the Tokaido) Edo, Hichirobei, 1690.

91. Thiel, P. (1962) 'An experiment in space notation', *The Architectural Review* (May), pp. 325–27.

92. Eckbo, G. (1964) *Urban Landscape Design*. New York: McGraw-Hill.

93. Ibid., p. 18

94. Ibid., p. 178. Here again, as with many urban design theorists, the principle of serial vision is encountered.

95. Halprin, L. (1963) *Cities*. New York: Reinhold Publishing Corporation. Revised edition 1972, Cambridge, MA: MIT Press.

96. Ibid., p. 232–36.

97. Ibid., p. 233.

98. Halprin, L. and Associates (1968) *New York, New York: A Study of the Quality and Meaning of Open Space in Urban Design*. San Francisco: Chapman Press.

99. Rudofsky, B. (1964) *Architecture without Architects*. Garden City, NY: Doubleday.

100. Rudofsky, B. (1969) *Streets are for People: A Primer for Americans*. Garden City, NY: Doubleday.

101. Lewis, D. N. (1965) *The Pedestrian in the City*. Princeton, NJ: Van Nostrand Reinhold.

102. There were extensive pedestrianisation schemes built throughout the 1960s and 1970s in a number of American cities. Unlike Europe, however, where the pedestrianisation of shopping streets in cities like Copenhagen in Denmark, Munich in Germany or Norwich in England proved to be a major commercial success, the opposite was true in the US. Perhaps the increasing dominance of the motor car, the lateral spread of cities and the decline in public transport were all responsible for this.

103. Meier, Richard and Kenneth Frampton (intro.) (1976) *Architect*. New York: Oxford University Press, pp. 7–8.

104. Ibid., pp. 23–33.

105. Meier, R. L. (1962) *A Communication Theory of Urban Growth. The Joint Center for Urban Studies*. Cambridge, MA: MIT Press.

106. This was addressed in a special issue of *Scientific American* (September 1965) by Kevin Lynch and others. See later comments in this chapter.

107. Meier, R. L. (1965) *Megalopolis Formation in the Midwest*. Ann Arbor, Michigan: University of Michigan Press, p. l, ff.

108. Current government structure (1999) in a contemporary society illustrates the fallacy of such cooperation. Cincinnati as a medium-sized Midwestern city (with a metropolitan population of approximately 1.75 million) has a two-tier system. Within the innercity (population approximately 350,000 including approximately 50 per cent African-Americans) urban planning policy is controlled by the City Planning Commission. The surrounding affluent suburbs of towns and villages are controlled, in terms of land use and zoning, by the Hamilton County Regional Planning Commission. Historically, there has been little liaison between the two bodies until recently when the OKI (Ohio, Kentucky, Indiana) Regional Council of Government sought a coordinated policy for the Tri-State region.

109. Gruen, V. (1967) *The Heart of Our Cities*. New York: Simon and Schuster.

110. Ibid., p. 99.

111. Ibid., p. 102.

112. A curious assumption given that during that time the growth of manufacturing was essential to American prosperity. It was only towards the end of the twentieth century that the importance of traditional manufacturing was replaced to some extent by information technology, the banking and insurance industries and tourism.

113. Not dissimilar from Louis Kahn's earlier plan for downtown Philadelphia.

114. Such draconian social engineering would have been anathema in the US, given the focus within the American Constitution on the rights of the individual.

115. Okamoto, R. Y. (1969) *Urban Design Manhattan.* New York: Viking Press.

116. Ibid., p. 109.

117. Ibid., p. 115.

118. I would consider only the Rockefeller Center, of the three, as a good example of comprehensive urban design.

119. Venturi, R. (1966) *Complexity and Contradiction in Architecture.* New York: Museum of Modern Art. This was to be followed in the next decade by an equally seminal work by Venturi. *Learning from Las Vegas* was to give an entirely new emphasis and perspective on the American urban landscape.

120. Ibid., p. 16.

121. Perhaps this book heralded in the new architectural movement of post-modernism of which Venturi was to become one of the major protagonists.

122. Venturi, op.cit., p. 17.

123. Ibid., p. 23.

124. It is interesting to note here that Venturi uses the term first used by the British theorist Gordon Cullen. Generally speaking, Cullen's ideas were ignored in the US during this period.

125. Perhaps the best example is Manhattan, New York, where Broadway is a diagonal cutting right across Joseph Margin's 1811 plan for New York City, with Broadway extending from the southern tip of Manhattan northwest to Central Park.

126. Mumford, L. (1968) *The Urban Prospect.* New York: Harcourt Brace.

127. Ibid., p. 24.

128. Ibid., p. 79. This idea stems from the British theorist Ebenezer Howard, who, at the turn of the twentieth century, evolved the garden city movement.

129. Ibid., p. 116.

130. It is interesting to note here that Mumford vilified Le Corbusier's city planning theories at a time when Le Corbusier rivalled Frank Lloyd Wright as a major iconic architect.

131. Ibid., p. 125.

132. Ibid., p. 129.

133. Ibid., p. 163.

134. Mumford referred to the Mark I New Towns (1947–60) as 'prairie planning', a view not shared by writers Ian Nairn and Gordon Cullen on the editorial staff of *The Architectural Review.*

135. Lynch, Kevin (1965) 'The city as environment', *Scientific American,* vol. 213, no. 3. (September), pp. 209–19.

136. There is some irony in this statement since Lynch spent much of his time at his house in Martha's Vineyard off the coast of Massachusetts.

137. Lynch (1965) op. cit., p. 209. A theme later developed in the UK by Gordon Cullen as the theory of navigation. This was an emerging discipline to be analysed in the 1970s by Geoffrey Broadbent and Charles Jencks in their theory of semiotics.

138. Appleyard, Lynch and Myer. *The View from the Road* (1964). Cambridge, MA: MIT Press

139. Lynch (1965) op. cit., p. 219.

140. *Design for Shopping* (1970). Private publication. London: Capital and Counties Property Co., Ltd.

141. However, the potential for the decline in the traditional shopping centres and malls should not be underestimated. In the last part of the final decade of the twentieth century, the exponential growth of home computer use and the utilisation of the Internet have provided evidence of the rapid growth of online shopping where, in 1998, almost 25 per cent of Christmas shopping was carried out via the Internet. This statistic provides an interesting comparison with the same period a century ago, with the rapid population growth in the Midwest and beyond. At that time, shops in agricultural regions were rare and many families relied on the Sears Roebuck catalogue for their purchases.

142. This pattern was developed by Erik Agergard and Paul Anker Olsen (1968) *The Interaction Between Retailing and the Urban Center – A Theory of Spiral Movement.* The Institute for Center Planning (July). Agergard and Olson demonstrated the effect of the spiral movement of trading forms pictorially – the result of a circular movement in trading patterns coupled with a linear growth in the standard of living and urban framework with its hierarchy of shopping centres. The effect is one of instability with shopping centres themselves passing through transformations similar in pattern to those of individual shop types. In the US, older suburban department stores, located in the middle-tier district centres, were badly hit by the department store operations in the new out-of-town centres, which were bigger and offered greater variety.

143. An example of the closure of downtown retail in the last decade of the century can be seen in Lincoln, Nebraska, where one of the largest Wal-Mart stores in the country was opened on the edge of the downtown shopping district.

144. A late example of such modernisation was the hitherto successful early open mall, Tri-County in the northwest of metropolitan Cincinnati, Ohio. It was enclosed in late 1989, after the construction of a nearby enclosed mall, Forest Fair, earlier that year. Forest Fair was, as a result, never really successful since it was located only a couple of miles away from Tri-County Mall, and both competed for the same catchment population.

145. Though these were to return later, when developers experimented with building the malls on sloping sites.

146. *Architectural Record* USA (1968). 'A New Approach to Shopping Centers', pp. 167–180.

147. Ibid.

148. Merlin, Pierre (1971) *New Towns.* First published 1969 as *Les Villes Nouvelles* by Paris Press Universitaire de France. English language edition, London: Methuen and Co., Ltd., p. 177.

149. Ibid., pp. 178–79.

150. Though this was the opinion of Merlin, it contradicted the avowed intentions of the developers, Robert Simon (President) and James Selonick (Executive Vice-President). Their stated intention was to provide a multi-ethnic community of all income levels, not dissimilar with the intentions of Mary Emery some forty years previously in the establishment of Mariemont Garden City, Ohio.

151. Merlin, op. cit., p. 185.

152. 'Modern living: new towns', *Time* (21 May 1965), p. 77.

153. Reston was to become a model for new private residential developments across the US by the end of the twentieth century. The ubiquitous golf course/lakeside/clubhouse/swimming pool is the core of thousands of speculative owner-occupied housing developments throughout the country.

154. This policy was utilised in the construction of Mariemont Garden City, Ohio, from 1925 onwards, with John Nolan as coordinating architect.

155. Jacobs, J. (1966) 'Where city planners come down to earth', *Business Week.* (20 August), pp. 101–104.

156. Private interview between David Gosling and James Selonick in Cincinnati, Ohio.

157. The Washington Center of Metropolitan Studies (1964) *Reston, Virginia: A Study in Beginnings.* Washington, DC: The Washington Center of Metropolitan Studies, p. 373.

158. The Reston, Virginia, Foundation for Community Programs, Inc. (1967) *Social Planning and Programs for Reston, Virginia.* The Reston Virginia Foundation for Community Programs, Inc. (March).

159. Ibid., p. 19.

160. Ibid., p. 35. This prediction was clearly wrong. Leisure time over the next thirty years declined dramatically where financial necessity, as well as a true emancipation of women created dual-income families across the US. It had a darker side where it seems less importance was given among upper- and middle-income families for growing psychological problems in children and especially teenagers, which culminated in the deaths of 15 students and a teacher at Columbine High School, Colorado, in 1999.

161. This was the vision of both Simon and Selonick. In the early days of Reston there was a rich mixture of cultural and ethnic background, but inevitably this changed as the community became more prosperous and income levels changed. This also occurred in the garden cities established some forty years previously.

162. 'New towns: the shape of utopia?', *Newsweek*, 23 November 1964.

163. Chapter 5 addresses this historical issue in 'The Emergence of the New Urbanism', the phenomenon of the 1990s.

164. The Celebration new town near Orlando, Florida, under construction in 1998, had even more draconian regulations, improved by the Disney Corporation, but apparently fully acceptable to the inhabitants.

165. Moore, Lyndon, Turnbull and Whitaker, The Sea Ranch, California. ADA Edita, Tokyo, Japan 1966.

166. The Scandinavian term *hygge* is often used in Denmark. It cannot be directly translated because it describes a sense of psychological well-being in an abstract way. There are many parallels in other languages, such as the use of '*sympatico*' in Portuguese, which describes an ephemeral affinity with another person.

167. Buckminster Fuller, R. (1970) *Utopia as Oblivion: the Prospect for Humanity.* London: Allen Lane, The Penguin Press, p. 395.

168. Tunnard and Pushkarev, op. cit.

169. Wasserman, L. (1978) *Merchandising Architecture: the Architectural Implications and Applications of Amusement Parks*. Washington, DC: National Endowment for the Arts.

170. *The Architectural Forum* (August/September 1964), p. 114 ff.

171. Pastier, J. (1978) 'The architecture of escapism', *American Institute of Architects Journal* (December), pp. 26–37.

Chapter Four

1970–1980

THE SOCIAL CITY

The social unrest towards the end of the previous decade in large part manifested itself in the form of ethnic violence by African-Americans in cities such as Detroit, Pontiac (Michigan) and the Watts District of Los Angeles in 1968. Protests from many millions of Americans against the Vietnam War, which brought with it compulsory military draft for many young American males and what was perceived to be unfair exemption from military service for a privileged minority, was another sign of dissatisfaction with the 'American way of life'. This displeasure was displayed in the anti-war demonstration at Kent State University, Ohio, resulting in the killing of four students and the wounding of several others by the National Guard called in by the university authorities to quell the demonstrations.

THE SOCIAL CITY AND ECONOMIC ISSUES

Against this background there emerged new authors, influencing a change of direction in political thought. Richard Sennett, regarded as a leader of the New Left, published *The Uses of Disorder* in 1970. In his description of 'the city of necessity', Sennett analyses the function of innercity slums as the reception area for newcomers, which broke apart the self-contained qualities of the various ethnic groups. The groups were not small images massed together in one spot on the map; rather they penetrated into each other, so that the daily life of an individual was a journey between various kinds of group life, each one different in its function and character from the others.[1]

The economist J. K. Galbraith has remarked that all the problems of the city can be solved by the application of just one thing – money. Such a view of the city as something to be improved or cured by financial means hides the fact that the city itself is a financial device so important to the national economy that some authorities would regard the latter as little more than the sum of the urban economies it comprises. The economic functions of the city are so fundamental to its purposes that their symbolisation in terms of land values forms a precise shorthand description of its differentiated structure. It is commonplace that the form of the modern city tends towards a three-dimensional representation of land values, such as that suggested by Brian Berry,[2] and provides a vivid overall picture of the urban structure with ridges of higher value radiating from the centre, punctuated with local peaks along their way. Such a pattern draws attention to the tendency of high-value uses to cluster and to expose favoured positions within the circulation networks of the city or metropolitan region. At a more detailed level, the urban rent theory[3] provides a similarly graphic demonstration of the way in which central areas are used, offering a model closely related to both density of development and intensity of pedestrian flow.

Where the 'highest and best use' is shopping, the sensitivity of that use to subtle differentiations in pedestrian flows, influenced by visibility of attractions, shapes of streets, breaks in frontage and so on, produces a particularly intense interrelationship between urban form and land values, which can express itself in the smallest details of the building design. This responsiveness of shopping uses to surrounding pressures makes their distribution another important indicator of urban structure.

Urban design is concerned with the physical form of the public realm over a limited physical area of the city, and it therefore lies between the two well-established design scales of architecture (concerned with the physical form of the private realm of the individual building) and city planning (concerned with the organisation of the public realm in its wider context). Inadequate as this delimitation is, it does at least indicate the difficulty of defining specifically 'urban design problems'. On the one hand, material of urban design is the public aspect of private architecture, a notoriously diverse, multivalent thing, both art and science and as richly layered with social, economic and symbolic preoccupations as the personalities it serves. On the other hand, urban design is a particular issue within the context of the city, and indeed the words 'city' and 'problem' are practically synonymous.[4]

Nevertheless, in terms such as 'urban poverty', 'urban wasteland', or 'urban violence', the use of 'urban' is widely taken to be not simply a description of the location of a problem, but a deeply implicated factor. Given the circumstances of urban development in recent history, this suspicion is natural enough. The spectacular growth and subsequent metamorphosis of cities, which have universally accompanied the industrialisation of countries, form a background of such extensive disruption and change that discussion of urban problems becomes meaningless without some recognition of them. The distinctive S-curve of urbanisation was first exhibited in the UK, where a period of gradual city growth in the late eighteenth century was followed in the nineteenth century by dramatic increases, which, by the end of the century, had subsided. This cycle was also repeated in other industrialising countries. Thus, in Britain, the most rapid rise in the proportion of people living in cities of 100,000 people or more lasted from 1811 to 1851, whereas in the US it lasted from 1820 to 1890. In general, the rate of urbanisation has increased as time has passed, so that the change from 10 per cent to 30 per cent of the population living in cities of 100,000 people or more took 79 years in England and Wales, while it took only 66 years in the US.[5]

The urbanisation of a country is said to be completed when about 80 per cent of its population is accommodated in its cities. Yet the period of dramatic growth is not necessarily followed by stability; on the contrary, the cities of fully urbanised countries like the US have continued to undergo violent transformations as they have attempted both to contain internal contradictions inherited from the first stage and to accommodate new sources of instability.

If the city has thus come to be regarded as the focus of the most intractable of society's problems, and itself as a collective problem of unprecedented complexity and scale, it would be convenient if we could in some way isolate urban design questions from this context.

Two opposing views of the relevance of urban design do indeed offer such an escape. According to the first, the relationship between spatial and social order is so compelling that we may design an ideal society by designing an ideal city form for it. According to the second, the relationship is so weak as to make architectural solutions irrelevant to the solution of social issues. Both of these positions allow a limited view of urban design as a largely formal activity that can be pursued independently from the problematic context of existing cities.[6]

David Harvey writes that 'the urban system seems to have reacted very sluggishly indeed to the demand for low-income housing in suburban areas'. The difficulty of expanding the supply in the inner city (partly due to institutional constraints such as zoning regulations) means that poor-quality, low-income housing is relatively high-priced and more profitable for property owners than we would expect under true equilibrium conditions. Low-income families therefore have little option but to locate in the relatively high-priced (rental) inner city. In most American cities this condition has been exacerbated by the lack of an open housing market for the African-American population, which constitutes a large segment of the poor. Meanwhile, most of the growth in new employment has been in the suburban ring and hence low-income groups have gradually been cut off from new sources of employment.[7]

According to Melvin Webber,[8] in order to repair the shortcomings of the price mechanism, city planners should use the methods of civil engineers rather than those of economists, evolving three basic techniques directly analogous to those in engineering – the technical standard, the master plan and the land use regulations. The success of those methods in some areas of city design disguises the fact that they were appropriate only for what Rittel and Webber have described as 'tame problems' with clear ends in sight.[9] Most urban issues, however, are 'wicked' problems, impossible to formulate or to solve definitively, and thus, poor subjects for such methods.

The separation of interest groups in the modern city tended to occur with increasing affluence. If this social pattern arises, it reinforces the tendency to seek simplified design structure. This is further assisted by development convenience, for very often the structure of development agencies and their preferred areas of interest follow a similar dissociated pattern. According to Robert Goodman, the rent of explicability is relevant here, so that

the overall design grows from the need of one professional who doesn't live in the environment, to explain his design in simplistic terms, to groups of bureaucrats who also don't live in the environment (but control it through access to public funds). The need to *explain* the design thus becomes a prime motivation for what the design finally turns out to be.[10]

As urbanism forms the focus of so many aspects of society and is thus the valid territory of so many disciplines, Harvey has gone as far as to argue that 'we cannot promote an understanding of urbanism through interdisciplinary research, but we can promote an understanding of disciplinary contributions through a study of urbanism'.[11]

Design characteristics arising out of the nature of design itself may, of course, be beneficial, acting as a sort of third-party term of reference within which inherently unstable or irreconcilable elements of the urban designer's brief may be contained. However, urban design seems particularly to prove that condition which Ivan Illich describes as typical of 'manipulative' rather than 'convivial' tools, by which people's activities are arranged for the convenience of the institutional tool rather than the reverse. John Turner defines two kinds of approach to the provision of adequate housing – 'networks' and 'hierarchies'.[12] The former provides for user control and is characterised by a multiplicity of routes to the same end, while the latter centralises control in the hands of government or corporate producers. Although a choice between these methods is overtly a question of practical convenience or efficiency, Turner saw it as a deeper division between two ways of thinking about the problem – one convivial and the other manipulative. This was so fundamental that he described his conversion from the second approach (which he saw as the predominant philosophy of most contemporary planning) to the first as the 're-education of the professional'. The shift of design attitude alters the whole nature of the problem:

When dwellers control the major decisions and are free to make their own contributions in the design, construction or management of their housing, both this process and the environment produced stimulate individual and social well-being. When people have no control over nor responsibility for key decisions in the housing process, on the other hand, dwelling environments may become a barrier to personal fulfillment and a burden to the economy.[13]

A similar argument has been expressed by Colin Ward in his plea for an anarchic approach to housing and, here again, the attack upon institutional methods of solving a problem leads inevitably to a challenge of the planning professions, the role of which may be seen as superficial or sinister.[14] Robert Goodman castigated them on both counts, arguing that the language of aesthetic ideology acts as a smokescreen, an elaborate euphemism for the imposition of political ideology, while planning tools such as zoning regulations are used to enforce the status quo.[15]

Such criticisms have obliged urban designers to re-examine their relationship to the problems of the city and to admit the possibility that they are themselves an urban phenomenon and hence a part of the problem as much as the solution.

Against the relentless internal transformations of urban society, some would argue that the greatest failure of urban design has been its inability to supply a convincing image of a stable totality – an image that without sterilising those internal transformations shows the city as more than the haphazard outcome of economic competition for space, or semi-conscious and often malevolent social processes. The purpose of such a city image is, in Mumford's terms, 'to further man's conscious participation in the cosmic and historic process'.[16]

Such a view regards the city not as a passive vehicle of social forces, nor a simultaneous expression of them, but as an intermediary, making society explicable to itself, reminding it of its sources, and perhaps protecting it against the worst effects of those future and increasingly rapid transformations that authors such as Alvin Toffler envisaged.[17] Joseph Rykwert's account of the ancient city as a mnemonic and symbolic device in a wide range of cultures, rather than, as in modern society, 'an analogue of a pathological condition',[18] suggests this analysis, in which the urban designer's central problem (and perhaps the one which in the end makes others soluble) is to re-establish the public realm, fragmented by private interest and hostile forces, in a built form that liberates rather than represses the life of the city.

As much as Robert Goodman's *After the Planners* was a polemical attack on the injustices of society during this period,[19] Richard Sennett was equally critical of the increasing isolation from one another of socioeconomic communities.[20] Sennett described the events that led to the expulsion of an affluent African-American family from an elegant suburb in a Midwestern city. In this suburb the divorce rate was four times the national average, juvenile crime was getting close to the average in much poorer areas, and there was frequent incidence of psychiatric treatment for emotional problems. Nevertheless, according to Sennett, residents in that community united in their attempts to expel that family from their home some three days after they moved in, justifying this with remarks like 'we are a solid family community', 'this is a happy area without problem', 'we don't want the type of person who cannot keep a family together', and 'the character of the community has to remain wholesome'. The importance of these statements is not only that people lied, but that they lied in a specific way.

This sense of exclusion was emphasised by the appearance of 'gated' communities in the 1970s. A form of condominium development, this fortress-like mentality has continued to develop towards the end of the twentieth century. The condominium developments, sometimes surrounded by high walls, electronic entry gates and even security guards, were often built adjacent to golf courses and artificial lakes, perhaps with a community club-house, swimming pool, tennis courts and a fitness centre. This sends out the message that this kind of development is confined to a certain socioeconomic group. These developments across the US are enclaves separated from stretches of commercial development, concentrated in that singular suburban institution – the shopping centre. They are accessible only by car, and the lack of sidewalks (pavements) indicates that pedestrian movement was not a priority. Schools are isolated in a park-like landscape. In these controlled communities, where people are friendly and watch each other carefully, there is an eerie parallel to the patterns found in revolutionary regimes where the 'good life' is rigidly imposed as a disciplined life.

In contrast, in 1972, 11 years after the publication of Jane Jacobs' *The Death and Life of Great American Cities*,[21] came Oscar Newman's *Defensible Space*.[22] Like Jacobs' study, this was similarly based upon observations made in New York City, and again took crime and violence to be the most urgent symptoms of urban design failure. Newman, however, was able to include large-scale postwar development in his study, concentrating on the way that design features of buildings and neighbourhoods thoughtlessly undermine the checks and balances of social behaviour which, in traditional city forms, naturally accompany and make possible high-density life. His development of the concept of 'defensible space' as a principal allocation of responsibility for and supervision of territory in the highly artificial world of the city, implied a very strong connection between crime and poor design and drew attention to the fundamental characters of city space.

However, some of Newman's theories seem open to doubt. In a lecture at Sheffield University in 1973, Newman claimed that developments such as St. Francis Square, San Francisco, a medium-density low-rise ownership, would overcome many of the problems of social stress cited in his book. Each pedestrian square housed something in the order of a hundred families (at 37 dwellings per acre with a total of 299 houses). However, most of the families were lower-middle-income and had the use of a car. Many of the high-rise projects housed families who relied on public transport, and lack of mobility can, in itself, cause emotional stress.[23] If our instinctive appreciation of 'ownership' and 'occupation' of territory in the city is crucial to its success, the question of how we actually perceive and understand its complex variations is obviously important and has been one of the most active areas of interest for urban design theorists, bringing them into contact with a number of developments in the arts and sciences, including J. B. Calhoun's theory of territoriality.

Oscar Newman implies that an essential ingredient to urban understanding is 'territorial definition coupled with improvement in the capacity of the territorial occupants to survey their newly defined realm. Territorial definition may appear to be the antithesis of the open society, and surveillance a further restriction on its freedom'.[24] However, Calhoun accepted that territory and surveillance (including closed-circuit television cameras that were to be developed in the next decade) were traditionally devices of 'propertied classes and their agents and the police authority'. Newman argues that advocating territorial definition and the creation of surveillance opportunities allows the citizens of an open society to achieve control of their environment for the activities they wish to pursue, thus preventing others from destroying their habitat.

One of the iconic examples of the failure of public housing, cited by Newman, was the Pruitt-Igoe high-rise project (2,764 apartments built in 1955 with an overall vacancy rate in 1970 of 70 per cent). He asks why one cannot achieve thoughtful building groupings rather than having to resort to barbed-wire fencings. Furthermore, the design approach that produced Pruitt-Igoe in St. Louis, Columbus homes in Newark, Van Dyke in New York and Rosen Houses in Philadelphia had its roots in a compositional commitment with the architects conceiving each building as a complete formal entity, ignoring any consideration of the functional use of the grounds or the relationship of a building to the ground area it shared with other buildings. Newman suggested that the architect assumed the role of sculptor with the grounds little more than a surface for arranging a series of vertical elements within a 'compositionally pleasing whole'.

This lack of understanding was underlined by Minoru Yamasaki, the architect of Pruitt-Igoe, who said that if there were no economic or social limitations he would solve all his problems with one-storey building overlooking lovely gardens with flowers, but that within the framework of present cities this was impossible. The Pruitt-Igoe development was demolished a few years later.

The assumption that it is essential in such a context to find a solution compatible with high densities does, however, underlie the important contribution of Nicholas Habraken. In *Supports: An Alternative to Mass Housing*,[25] Habraken sets out a powerful argument against the philosophy and techniques of centrally controlled attempts to resolve the perennial housing problem. The result of these attempts – mass housing – is seen as essentially misconceived, itself exacerbating the problem it sets out to solve and in the process alienating the society that uses it and coarsening and corrupting the form of its cities. The root of the problem, according to Habraken, lay in the exclusion of the user from the process, resulting in a uniformity that is but a symptom of the wrongheadedness of the whole attempt:

> The greatest talents in the field of architecture and town planning have sought the liberating all-providing design. . . . The ideal which has been pursued is not only unattainable because, like all ideals, it is subject to the imperfection of man's existence, but especially because the posing of the problem in itself excludes a solution. . . . That is to say: matter is not manipulated in harmony with society, but society is forced to conform to a method which pretends to perform this task. . . . A town is not a thing without people; a town is man and matter together. . . . If a town is created before there is a population this fatal separation is implied. . . . But today we no longer think of a town as a unity of people, and while we should do all we can to stimulate the process, we spend our efforts in trying to reflect the form of the population. We are very busy arranging in advance conformity of towns

with their future populations because we do not understand that a town, a real town, can only emerge when this conformity already exists, and that it cannot be achieved by making a town, however, beautifully or skillfully.

Habraken was a professor of architectural design at the Technical University of Eindhoven in the Netherlands, and Director of the Foundation for Architectural Research. His book was quite remarkable in the sense that it had no illustrations, architectural or otherwise, but basically proposed a new modus operandi for public housing. The implication of his theory was that if authorities provided a skeletal structure for public housing, with an infrastructure of services, then the incoming tenants would have the freedom and choice to lay-out their own apartments according to individual family needs. He emphasises that 'a support structure is not the skeleton of a building, but all the dwellings together form the skeleton of a town; a framework for a living and complex organism'.[26]

It was suggested that with the appearance of support structures as the framework for a city, a clear line could be drawn between the activities of the city planner and the architect. The city planner could carry out his tasks in three dimensions,[27] despite the fact that many lacked a design education. 'By designing support structure ribbons in a certain pattern, he can organize the town as a network of mutually-related building plans and lay down scale and extent, determine closed spaces, outline green areas, give context to freestanding buildings and reach conclusions about main lines of development. . . . A great three dimensional mass has a totally different effect from the "two-dimensional street wall" of an old town, which forms, as it were, a décor'.[28]

By the time *Variations: the Systematic Design of Supports* was published in 1976,[29] Habraken was already a professor of architecture at MIT. The book was published by the MIT Laboratory of Architecture and Planning, a more prescriptive development in that much of this publication, unlike the original *Supports*, is richly illustrated, showing precisely how those theories could be put into practice. The authors emphasise that a support is not a structural framework and detachable units are not infill components. The support could be a structure that is designed and built in a specific place. It could be a traditional structure or the result of an industrialised system. Since the set of detachable units consisted of those units about which the user as an individual decides, it is clear that the question of what is or is not a detachable unit is a question of control. The authors ask the question: 'Which decisions should the user make for him or herself? As yet we have said nothing about what is technically possible. It could be that something easy to remove or rearrange would be outside the user's control. For instance, a lightweight partition must be considered as part of the support if the resident is not permitted to remove it. On the other hand, an internal brick wall could very well be a detachable unit if the resident had the opportunity to take it down or place it elsewhere as he or she pleased'.[30]

The majority of the illustrations in *Variations* show duplex apartments on two successive floors and a defined floor area, but with changes in internal arrangements of functional spaces according to the evolving life pattern of the resident or resident's family, taking it through the possibility of a complete lifecycle.

The residents as a whole, through group participation, are involved in the building process and have some control over the support design.[31] They may participate in the decision making at the community level concerning the design of the support and its immediate surroundings. In shaping the decision-making process there has to be a recognition of the distinction between participation and control. The next stage in this process is the participation of the individual family in the internal planning of their dwelling. The family has control over the division of rooms and may involve themselves in the building process by helping to make decisions that affect the number of units in a support. Finally, in an ideal situation, each member of the family has control over the planning of his or her own room and participates in the decisions concerning the laying out of that dwelling. Whether such a substantial piece of public hardware could actually separate the public and private realms as clearly as Habraken envisaged, or free the individual to the extent anticipated, is perhaps debatable. Two distinguished examples, albeit European rather than American, show the application of some of the theories of Habraken and his colleagues.

The Byker Wall (1973) by the Anglo-Swedish architect Ralph Erskine, with Vernon Gracie and Associates, is a sinuous block over a kilometre in length with access decks only on the south side. Erskine and his colleagues broke these down into identifiable sections. In attempting community participation, the architects set up shop in the adjacent slum that was to be progressively removed as the project was built and the families transferred to the new Byker housing. Future tenants of this public housing were invited to design their own facades, balconies and external porches in consultation with the architects, though not the internal arrangement of the apartments. The use of colour, organic materials and an emphasis on landscaping created a more sympathetic vocabulary, while a sound relationship was established between the architects and the community for which they were building through the operation of their site office as an advice and consultation centre. Perhaps such powerful urban gestures entail a correspondingly vivid identification of the communities that occupy them, whether just or unjust, so that it requires a certain added confidence to be a resident of the Byker Wall. Should that confidence diminish, the very boldness of the original gesture only exaggerates the inevitable cycle that results. Yet the curious instability in the appreciation of such large and apparently stable images cannot detract from the conviction they achieve when the urban form coincides with that of the community it serves.

The very considerable level of investigation and commitment that such methods may entail is also illustrated by the work of the Belgian architect Lucien Kroll, which similarly attempts to open up the design processes to users and place the designer in the role of orchestrator. Kroll's method of working with his medical student clients at the University of Louvain in 1976 resembled a gaming exercise in certain respects, particularly in its allocation of roles to distinct groups of students with instructions to consider specific areas of the brief, and then, when those

conflicts arose, to rearrange these groups with new interests. His simultaneous use of several building methods, and delegation of certain choices to the builder, were governed by rules of play, by which odd and unpredictable events occur spontaneously as the operations unfold.

Nicholas Negroponte has argued that this variety and sensitivity to particular, unique circumstances can be achieved in other ways: 'The industrial revolution brought sameness through repetition, amortization through duplication. In contrast information technologies – soft machines – afford opportunity for custom-made, personalized artifacts'.[32]

Thus, there can be a view of urban design as an essentially neutral technique, provided by a number of studies in which the problem of values is recognised by devising design methods that allow conflicts to be expressed and then resolved. Urban design is then seen as a 'forum' or 'ring', and the urban designer as a chairperson. Habraken's theory of 'supports' could be regarded in this way in that it sets out a literal framework of high-density housing within which a balanced reconciliation of public and private interests may be established.

The social issues and problems of urban design were summarised in 'The Social Impact of Urban Design', a collection of individual papers.[33] Lee Rainwater's essay identifies many of the same problems described earlier, mentioning the plight of African-Americans in the inner city, albeit with patronising overtones, describing this ethnic group as 'lower class negroes'. Rainwater indicates that the housing areas have poor maintenance and high vandalism, and also cites Pruitt-Igoe as one of the worst public housing projects ever designed, where exterior space was especially damaged. Physical design is indicated as being able to facilitate or interfere with the adaptation of housing projects[34] and this confirms Newman's theories concerning defensible space. Traditional problems such as vermin (rats, cockroaches), poison (lead paint), cold, thin walls, overcrowding and hostility create physical and psychological problems. In defensible space, people need friends, neighbours they trust, private entrances, front locks on the doors of buildings, and restricted circulation in public areas. Projects, the essay states, became 'icons', and not what the future residents wanted, and thus recommendations include low-income housing, rent subsidies and traditional style.

The other essays in the collection all painted a dismal portrait of the physical state of low-income housing, and the polemic contained within this publication did little to find applicable new solutions. In urban design, the social city paints a dismal picture of the physical reality of the low-income environment of this decade, and this belies the optimism expressed throughout the two previous decades.

THE COGNITIVE CITY

Following in the footsteps of Kevin Lynch, a new leader in the field of urban design, Christopher Alexander, portrayed a more optimistic vision of the future for the American city.

Alexander, Professor of Architecture at the University of California, Berkeley, and winner of the first medal for research awarded by the American Institute of Archives, was later to become Director of the Center for Environmental Structure at Berkeley. His first notable publication was *The Oregon Experiment*,[35] published in 1975. This was a master plan for the university of Oregon and it defined a process of master-planning that was applicable anywhere. Because of the rapid growth of a university in the relatively small city of Eugene (its population at the time was just 84,000), the need for growth control was paramount. The methods employed followed Alexander's *The Timeless Way of Building*,[36] the beginning of a series of six books published by Oxford University Press. Though *The Oregon Experiment* was not the first in the set of volumes, it nevertheless provided a link between *The Social City* and the *Cognitive City*. In *The Oregon Experiment* students, faculty and staff were involved in the development of the plan. Many of the buildings were designed schematically by students and staff, later to be executed by consultant architects. The new school of music began, in its schematic design, with a group of seven, comprising the Dean, three faculty members, one student and two architects. The plan for the campus emphasised the importance of organic growth, creating a natural order and, in a sense, allowing piecemeal growth. Some of the concepts applied were taken from Alexander's earlier *A Pattern Language*,[37] of which some two hundred 'patterns' were considered relevant, for example living and learning circles.

The Timeless Way of Building was Alexander's first major work, although the author had published a number of important essays during the previous decade. In 'The city is not a tree',[38] Alexander proposed a fundamental critique of attempts to solve the urban problem, in which he argued that attempts had been made based on a mistaken appreciation of the structural relationship of the city's elements, which typically take the form of semi-lattices. The tree-like structure of most modern plans, from Clarence Stein's Greenbelt, Maryland, and Tange's Tokyo Bay Plan to Le Corbusier's Chandigargh, represents a 'trivially simple' case of the semi-lattice structure, and one in which 'life will be cut to pieces'.

It has been argued earlier that the separation of interest groups in the modern city tends to occur with increasing affluence. If this social pattern does indeed arise, it reinforces the tendency to seek simplified design structures, which is often further abetted by development convenience, for very often the structure of development agencies and their preferred areas of interest follow a similar dissociated pattern.

In another early essay, published the following year,[39] Alexander proposed a theory of optimum road layouts – a road pattern of long straight avenues without cross-streets running the length of the rectangle. Across the neutral mesh thus set down (aligned to give each dwelling a precise orientation), hedgerows, trees, banks and other features of the natural landscape were allowed to run, flipping from 'ground' to 'figure' as they crossed the boundary between the developed rectangle and the surrounding fields, providing a chain of spaces through the community.

In his earlier *Notes on the Synthesis of Form*, Alexander followed the pursuit of Theil, Appleyard and others in striving for a more complete and precise method of describing the visual phenomena of the city, suggesting that an annotative method would lead to the reform of the subject of its study. In this essay he describes a process for the design of an Indian village that attempted to reconcile all the functional requirements of the problem by the meticulous breakdown into its most basic statements and their subsequent recomposition according to national, mathematical procedures.[40]

The Timeless Way of Building was abstract to a certain extent, implying that cities, towns and buildings grow from the inner nature of people, and that, as Rudofsky suggested, this could be achieved without architects and planners. The more living patterns there were in a place, the better the quality of life became. To attain this quality a living pattern language would be required as a gateway to show a rich and complex order within an urban environment, as well as a way to build that 'ideal' environment.[41]

If this work was to establish a new way of understanding the built environment, the second volume in the series, *A Pattern Language*, was a truly seminal work,[42] and more subtle, perhaps, than Habraken's 'supports' theory. Alexander's concept of an infrastructure of ideas, a detailed network of agreed solution-types, was consciously adopted by consumers to operate in both their own and the general interest. Although this approach requires none of the major engineering works of the previous two solutions, it does entail a far more comprehensive and pervasive shift of thought, for, rather than the demarcation of public and private interests, what is sought is their reintegration into a common, universal and interdependent network of preferred design solutions. Developing his earlier theoretical work on the structure of cities, Alexander and his collaborators produced an encyclopedic three-volume description of this 'pattern language', setting out the theory behind it, its method of use and an example of its application.

The ambition of these books is certainly utopian in scale: 'The books are intended to provide a complete working alternative to our present ideas about architecture, building and planning – an alternative which will, we hope, gradually replace current ideas and practices.' Ranging from the global arrangement of regions down to the minutia of domestic construction, they set out a menu of preferred solutions to the main design problems encountered through all the scales of environmental design. These 153 patterns are interrelated, not as a fixed sequence, but rather as a network in which each is contained by or related to a number of larger scale patterns 'up' the network, and in turn contains smaller-scale patterns 'below'. For example, pattern 31, 'Promenade', is related to the larger scale patterns: 8, Mosaic of subcultures; 12, Community of 7000; and 30, Activity Nodes. The statement on what makes pattern 31 necessary runs: 'Each subculture needs a center for its public life: a place where you can go and see people, and be seen'. A discussion of the problem then follows, concluding with a statement of the proposed instruction pattern 31: 'Encourage the gradual formation of a promenade at the heart of every community, linking the main activity nodes, and placed centrally, so that each point in the community is within 10 minutes walk of it. Put main points of attraction at the two ends, to keep a constant movement up and down'.

In turn, this leads to others in the network, including 32, Shopping Street; 33, Night Life; 58, Carnival; 63, Dancing in the Street; 100, Pedestrian Streets; 121, Path Shape, and so on. Arbitrary or even quirky as some of the individual patterns might appear, the mosaic they create, of humane injunctions logically interrelated, forms perhaps the most comprehensive and appealing of consumer utopias to date, possibly because 'these patterns can never be "designed" or "built" at once – but patient piecemeal growth, designed in such a way that every individual act is always helping to create or generate these larger global patterns, will slowly and surely, over the years, make a community that has these global patterns in it'.[43] Such optimism of the period was to be only partially fulfilled by the end of the century and then, in a somewhat distorted and artificial way, with the later rise of 'the new urbanism'.

Kevin Lynch's reputation in this area was already well established in this decade when he published *What Time is This Place?* His study concerns how 'the evidence of time' is manifest in the physical form of the urban structure. Personal images of time are affected by the external physical environment and perception of that environment and its preservation, while conceding that it may involve social upheaval with low-income people being forced from the older areas of the city. Lynch attempts to understand how people experience time, citing the number of clocks adjacent to the Scolley Square area of downtown Boston, and the fact that parking meters, shop signs and columns measure time and that trees measure seasons.[44]

The author's concern with time and its effect on people was reflected in his last book, *Wasting Away*, published posthumously in 1990.[45] While *Wasting Away* was a bleak view of the future in the US and the world in general, *What Time is this Place?* was generally an optimistic work, though it did focus on aspects of wasting in terms of perception and expression as well as the management of change in the environment. In the 'Managing Transitions' part of the study, Lynch implies that change could result in growth or decay but that, if well managed, change was desirable.

Professional planners who were more concerned with new growth and did not confront the problem of decay were criticised. Increasing mobility at the time was perceived to be a growing problem, for although travel was positive, involuntary migration was negative. In suggesting new policies, public and semi-public agencies should be responsible for the structuring and 'celebration' of the passage of time and there may be some way to change the conventional ways of measuring time and schedules to reflect biological time. All this, Lynch said, could remove rigidity and make journeys more memorable through improved highway design and outdoor spectacles of light, sound and action. In this model, city planners would provide information about the past and the future, including a public temporal model of the city and use of the environment. Written prior to the widespread use of computer-generated graphics, these objectives were to be achieved by verbal, graphic and 'dynamic' presentations in order to provide new ways of forecasting the middle-range future.[46]

The decision of MIT Press to publish a new edition of his *Site Planning*[47] (originally published in 1962) in 1971 reflected the growing interest in Lynch's theories. The title of the volume, which suggests an architectural engineering handbook, belies the highly original content. In the preface, Lynch states that site planning is the art of arranging buildings and other structures on the land in harmony with each other. It could be construed that what the author was attempting was a translation of the earlier research in *The Image of the City*[48] into a form of practical reality. The preface says: '... this book is intended to be an introduction to the art, an exposition of its principles, and a condensed technical reference'. The reason for the second edition was that, though the book had remained in continuous use as a reference and teaching textbook, it had become obsolete in the intervening ten years. In the new edition, new material included ecological issues[49] as well as psychosocial analyses and design methodology. Similar to techniques used previously in *The Image of the City*, the use of margins to drawings as a cross-reference system had limited application. As previously remarked, such drawings, if so abstract as to have little meaning, are not helpful to the lay reader.

'Technique: Site Form and Site Ecology' is surprisingly detailed in its scientific data.[50] The diagrams of the agricultural classification of soil[51] are perhaps of more use to the consultant structural or geotechnical engineer than to the architect or urban designer. Such voluminous data may be useful in the context of a technical handbook, and air movement and air flow may be relevant to the design of a building as groups of buildings, like the decided sources of noise ranging from the quiet 'rustle of leaves' (10 decibels) to the sound of a 'busy street' (70–80 decibels), but does not inspire the ultimate three-dimensional configuration of a neighbourhood. Lynch analyses movement patterns of people and in turn the 'localised behaviour', showing how people interact in a spatial setting as a whole, and, as in Gestalt studies earlier in the century as well as those of Philip Thiel, suggests that the graphic notation of dance can be useful here.[52] Lynch refers to this as a 'behaviour circuit', indicating the actions of an individual or small group carrying out some coherent purpose in space (obtaining food, going out for an evening's entertainment, doing a day's work).[53] Thus, in terms of spatial images, this may be applied to a person's sense of time, as embodied in the environment and used as in the previous study, respondents answering a direct set of questions: How do they act in the environment? Where do they go, what do they do there, why, when do they do it, what do they use, with whom do they interact?[54] In recommending the use of simulated environments such as photographs, drawings, models, films and verbal sketches, Lynch hoped that responses to these simulations would predict responses to reality. Giving a respondent tasks, problems or puzzles would reveal something about his or her mental structure of the world. By being asked to draw a freehand map of a large city or to make a model or sketch of a place as describing the route between two obscure locations, the respondent would reveal his or her cognitive map.[55]

Nevertheless, despite some technical shortcomings in interpretive methods, the publication provided a wide-ranging examination of techniques necessary in three-dimensional urban planning and included many other aspects such as movement systems, for example highways, and critical utilities.

Las Vegas strip, Nevada (1958/59).

Managing the Sense of the Region [56] was more of an essay than a compendium. Like *Site Planning,* this study enlarged upon Lynch's *What Time is This Place?,* which considered the perception of aging towns and enlarged the scale of his investigation in probing the psychology of the perception of the city and 'cognitive mapping'. Here Lynch turned his attention to a discussion of how human reactions should influence the planning of urban regions. [57] He defined the boundaries of the book as a focus upon the sensory qualities of large, complex areas that he believed could be managed at the scale of a city, substantial urban district, metropolitan region or rural countryside, with no separation between the issues of urban and rural areas. Lynch argued that they were part of the continuous spectrum of human habitats then becoming progressively more difficult to distinguish. *Managing the Sense of the Region* makes reference to the work of Michael and Susan Southworth in an article in the British journal *The Town Planning Review.* [58] Most of the studies cited, including Detroit, Brooklyn, Massachusetts and Minneapolis had commenced in the preceding decade. The study for San Francisco was published as a series of ten reports in 1971 resulting in the passage of a new ordinance to control building height and bulk, with the aim of encouraging conservation.

Southworth collaborated with Lynch on the joint study *Designing and Managing the Strip*.[59] Most shopping strips were considered to be environmentally offensive. The author identified the strip as the 'arterial street skeletal system of the American City',[60] but identified what they considered to be the many problems of such an environment – noise, confusion, monotony, hostility to pedestrians and ugliness. This was the creation of an automobile environment and they used a case study with, for example, Main Street, Waltham, Massachusetts, to illustrate these points. It was a fairly subjective study, for example in its criticism of the congregation of teenagers, but objective in the sense that clearly such strip malls were under the control of many conflicting agencies.

A quite contrary view was expressed in the iconoclastic book by Venturi, Scott-Brown and Izenour. *Learning from Las Vegas*, published in 1972, was to be a seminal work in altering attitudes concerning the cognitive city.[61] It contradicted the views expressed by both Lynch and Tunnard in their criticisms of the contemporary American urban landscape.

Learning from Las Vegas was a neatly subversive adaptation of the cognitive techniques devised at MIT. Venturi, Scott-Brown and a team from Yale University managed to turn the whole argument on its head. Selecting the most 'imageable' but least 'architectural' of American cities – Las Vegas – they used sequence illustrations and notated plans recording such environmental factors as neon lighting and frequency of wedding chapels to argue against the intentions of planning authorities to cultivate a 'coherent image' for the strip by such methods as trying 'to persuade the gasoline stations to imitate the architecture of casinos, in the interests of architectural unity'. Sadly, however, they found the techniques available still inadequate for their urban anti-design purposes: 'How do you represent The Strip as perceived by Mr. A. rather than as a piece of geometry? How do you show the quality of light – or qualities of form – in a plan at one inch to 100 feet scale? How do you show fluxes and flows or seasonal variation, or change with time?'.

Denise Scott-Brown had previously co-authored an article with British theorist Gordon Cullen, published in the American journal *Connections*,[62] in the spring of 1967. The article was one of the first major essays in semiotics, a field later developed by the British author Geoffrey Broadbent and the American author Charles Jencks.[63] Cullen and Scott-Brown examined the city as a 'message system', which could be functional – helping citizens to find their way and in general go about their daily business – or expressive, providing symbols for the citizen and others, of aspects of their civilization, its cultural values and aspirations, mysticism and philosophy, institutions and technology. The messages can be general ones, meaningful to all citizens, or specific to some groups, even personal and individual, and all these levels are interwoven.

The authors examined the various aspects of the message-giving system, the city's system of heraldry – its written and graphic signs. In the medieval city, few people could read and much use was made of visual symbolism for city signs; today, written signs have replaced picture imagery, and the authors believe that this modern system of signs and symbols in the US comes close to anarchy.

The physiognomy of the city is also important; in the medieval town there were strong differences between the main and secondary streets, while in the modern American gridiron city differences between streets could be sensed, not in width and alignment but through the nature of buildings along them, and, particularly, the movement within them. Architectural elements and styles have symbolic meaning in themselves, but there existed an additional way in which the city gave messages – the location pattern of buildings and spaces. The important civic building is placed at the end of an axis or on an eminence, with the market square and cathedral in the centre of the town. The ubiquitous 'corner stone' functioned in this way, positioning shopping centres at major highway interchange points. Symbolic messages in the medieval city formed a meaningful and perceivable whole, but in the contemporary city the messages are latent.

Learning from Las Vegas concluded that the 'commercial strip' and the elements that formed this part of the urban structure represented a significant part of the visual and physical environment of American cities. The more conventional view, shared by the majority of architects and planners, had been taken by Tunnard and Pushkarev's earlier study, which had dismissed the commercial strip as 'a visually aggressive and ubiquitous feature that is sometimes considered to be typical, even inevitable, in the urban fringe'. Venturi's view, by contrast, was that outdoor advertising provides the population with perhaps the most significant everyday visual experience, in which pictorial composition, colour relationships, graphics and visual metaphors represent the 'best popular art'. Sennett had supported this view, describing the southern entrance to Los Angeles as 'five miles of unrelenting neon, giving rise to the theory that electricity can induce an unending orgasm'.[64] We have Venturi's preference for the 'vital mess' and his model of 'the strip' draws precisely the opposite conclusion from the current unsatisfactory state of affairs: 'Henri Bergson called disorder an order we cannot see. The emerging order of the strip is a complex order. It is not the easy, rigid order of the urban renewal project or the fashionable "total design" of the megastructures'.[65] Las Vegas is to the strip what Rome was to the piazza. The strip developed over a very short period of time and became an archetype, with violent juxtapositions of use and scale. The visual image of the Las Vegas strip is chaotic and its order is not obvious. Neon negates the function of street lights.

What was notable about this study was its use as a teaching tool. The studio notes prepared by Denise Scott-Brown for the autumn of 1968 at Yale University were interesting inasmuch as they drew from the research of such people as Appleyard and Lynch, who held a very different polemical position. One of the notes referred to the 'architecture of persuasion' as the serial experience of movement along streets and highways, and also identified new graphic needs to analyse and understand Las Vegas (in terms of public and private space and system and order) and to make a composite 'pattern book'[66] showing schedules of building parts, signs and architectural monumentality in Las Vegas styles. Of more significance was the realisation of ugly and ordinary architecture, of the 'decorated shed'. Image, Scott-Brown wrote, was both process and form since it depended on perception and symbolism.

Las Vegas was a communication system showing the relationship between signs and buildings, architecture and symbolism, driver and road, form and meaning. Scott-Brown's preface to the revised edition in 1977 claimed that Las Vegas was 'not the subject of the book. The symbolism of architectural form is'. She said 'allegations that in studying Las Vegas we lacked social responsibility and concern[67] are answered in an article entitled "On architectural formalism and social concern; a discourse for social planners and radical chic architects".' The new revised edition had the subtitle 'The Forgotten Symbolism of Architectural Form' and attempted to be politically correct in omitting the use of the word 'he' as the main subject. Scott-Brown went on to say that since the first edition of *Learning from Las Vegas*, the lights of Las Vegas had gone out and Americans' confidence in the motor car and other resources had been rocked by the first of many crises, yet arguments of high energy expenditure and urban wastefulness were not seen as central to the arguments for symbolic architecture.

The gradual merging of interests in cognitive responses and environmental issues emerged with the publication of a series of papers edited by Gyorgy Kepes, the Bauhaus pioneer who came to the fore in the 1950s. Kepes' *Arts of the Environment*[68] focused on such issues as adaptations and ecological consciousness. In his own introductory essay, Kepes said that the man-made environment had shrunk space, dimmed light and bleached colour, expanded noise, speed and complexity. The changing fluidity of the man-made world was frightening to many people because it lacked a frame of reference and therefore a new set of 'coordinates' needed to be created. Nonetheless, Kepes appeared to be deliberately vague as to what these coordinates should be, and the suggestion that the 'artist' could move into a 'central position in the world to give sharpness and definition to a union and intimate involvement with (his) surroundings' defies the reality of society in the late twentieth century. Dennis Gubor, another essayist, presented a similarly pessimistic view with human boredom as a rife issue. Kevin Lynch's contribution on the *Openness of Public Space* presented a somewhat more optimistic view in his definition of open space as 'sports grounds, public spaces, unbuilt on land, natural areas, voids, places of outdoor assembly' – implying that public space in the city has value in extending the individual's choices with minimal social or economic constraints and that it could be relaxing, good for making acquaintances, and connection to the environment, providing choice, stimulus, contrast, social experiment, orientation and flexibility.

James Burns criticised the social and psychological implications of megastructures on architectural phenomena that had emerged in the late 1960s, and described them as 'three-dimensional matrix system(s) for the containment of man's activities'.[69] *The City as an Artwork* by PULSA had already predicted the major changes that were about to come about, regarding the city as the largest human artifact that would be overtaken by a global communications network[70] and other large-scale information systems as a flexible and mutating object.

THE ECOLOGICAL CITY

The image of the city as an uncontrollable, vastly powerful force dominating man, suggests parallels with the forces of nature to which phrases like the 'asphalt (or concrete) jungle' tend to conform. The metaphor also implies that, in supporting nature as man's customary habitat, this domination has been accompanied by a similar domination of nature itself, and it is the wider ecological consequences of that domination which form an important new source of problems for the urban designer.

To describe this as new may seem absurd. The epidemics of typhoid and cholera that followed the ecological failure of early European industrial cities, with their inadequate sewage treatment, record the long-standing nature of these problems. Pollution of all kinds is an established fact of urban life, causing extensive damage to all living things within the city area, as well as eroding its fabric. As recently as 1952, during the worst winter of London smog in England, the deaths of 12,000 people were directly attributed to the combination of sulphur and smoke (carbon dioxide and carbon monoxide) in the atmosphere.[71] But while internal ecological disorders of the industrialised city continue to present major local difficulties, a number of observers have concluded that in recent years the increasing scale of urbanisation threatens a larger and more catastrophic ecological failure. This arises in part from the sheer scale of contemporary global urbanisation. The French philosopher Jerome Dehusses has vividly depicted this expansion by pointing out that each year new concrete covers an area of pasture equal to the size of the Netherlands.[72] Yet it is not so much the physical extent of the cities themselves that poses the most alarming threat, but the increasingly demanding burden they place upon the hinterland. According to this view, the cities, through their ever increasing demands for water, energy, raw materials and food, act as the visible foci of a global system of natural exploitation, from which the huge scale of ecological disruption is only beginning to be apparent. It then becomes impossible to divorce urban problems from those arising from the deoxygenating and pollution of lakes such as the Great Lakes of North America, seas like the Baltic and Mediterranean, and ultimately our oceans.

If such global concerns seem remote from the more immediate difficulties of urban design, it is as well to recall that some of the most far-reaching contemporary attempts to alter nature are being conducted with urban development as an incipient feature, and one that is expected to play a key role in the future exploitation. One of the most dramatic examples of this is in the Amazon basin, which contains one-third of the world's remaining forests and supplies one-fifth of the world's oxygen. Ecologists have warned of the possibility of disaster following the government decision in 1968 to develop the Amazon by creating a network of highways criss-crossing the region.[73]

Though covered by dense forest, the subsoil is relatively thin and the ecological balance is delicate. Experience in the drought-stricken northeast of Brazil, in states like Ceará and Bahia, indicates that once the vegetation cover has been removed, the top soil is washed away in heavy tropical rainstorms, and a desert is formed, in turn lowering the rainfall. There are signs that linear strips of desert are already forming along these highways.[74]

Among the more radical publications of this era was the magazine *Shelter*.[75] This was a comprehensive overview of alternative lifestyles, anti-urban in any conventional sense and, reflecting the earlier rebellion against existing urban societies, epitomised in the communards in the Southwest US such as Drop City in 1965.[76] Following Rudofsky's *Architecture without Architects*,[77] this compendium examined many residential settlements ranging from North American barns, Adobe dwellings, Navajo and Hopi communities to the stone cottages of Ireland, from the cones of Cappadocia in the central region of Anatolia in Turkey to the widespread use of domed structures, including the geodisic domes invented by Buckminster Fuller. Based upon an icosahedron mathematical principle and patented in 1954, the 'Zomes', invented by Steve Baer and designed by John Martin in Placitas, New Mexico, were composed of ten 'exploded' rhombic dodecahedra fused to form different-sized rooms. The use of quite complicated mathematical formula and three-dimensional geometry may seem a curious contradiction to the radical political views of the inhabitants of these communities. Nevertheless, the ecological balance achieved by many of these self-sufficient structures using solar power was praiseworthy. Lloyd Kahn expressed the objectives thus: 'The choices are not clear-cut for these are complex times. But it is obvious that the more we can do for ourselves, the greater will our individual freedom be. This . . . is not about going off to live in a cave and growing *all* of one's food. It is not based on the idea that everyone can find an acre in the country, or upon a sentimental attachment to the past. It is rather about finding a new and necessary balance in our lives between what can be done by hand and what still must be done by machine'.[78]

It is strange when one views Richard Meier's recent vast and complex design for the Getty Art Museum in California, to note that during this earlier period he had devoted his attention to ecological balance in *Design of Resource-Conserving Cities*.[79] Meier formulated ideas about how to design resource conserving cities of the future from his experience of designing a new town in Venezuela. In this book, Meier redefined urban ecosystems and warned against massive urban sprawl, which has only recently been recognised. He said that cities were social reactors as 'an engine of socio-cultural and economic growth that works by expediting interaction between humans'.[80] Resource conservation should be a major element of city planning, especially in the 'third world'.

The proliferation of such ideas in the early part of the 1970s may be viewed cynically as a fashionable reaction motivated by popular sociopolitical ideas of the period. It was almost certainly motivated by the energy crisis of 1973. Had the oil embargo continued, perhaps there might have been a transformation in urban settlements in the US, but this was not to be. The cartel established by the major oil-producing countries of the Middle East fell apart as the embargo economically damaged the very countries that had imposed it.

Laurence Cutler's *Recycling Cities for People: the Urban Design Process*[81] was also a statement of the problem, quoting Mumford, Tunnard, Lynch and Le Corbusier. Cutler believed that political, social, technological and scientific, cultural and international revolutions were necessary for urban change. What was required, he indicated, was the development of ecological ethics. The study examined the emerging use of computers and certainly his technological and scientific revolution was partially fulfilled by the end of the twentieth century. However, the physical structure of the ecosystem worsened rather than improved during this period. Cutler's advocacy of prefabricated units and mobile homes did little to improve the socioeconomic conditions of the people who resided there and the preposterous suggestion of underwater habitats showed a lack of understanding and reality. New sources of energy were to include solid waste, nuclear power, solar power, geothermal and hydrothermal power, wind, tidal power and wood burning, all believed to have an ecological future, though the dichotomy between the usefulness of nuclear power and wood burning with solar energy, wind and tidal power, was puzzling. Cutler advocated the 'recycling of existing cities to retain the historical and social values of American civilization',[82] and the use of waterfronts in this regard in many of these cities came to fruition during the next decade.

There was a need for specific training in urban design, and the 'first' urban design course cited was that at Harvard Graduate School of Design in 1953. Cutler described examples of his own urban design projects in the small, historic coastal town of Newbury Port, Massachusetts; a proposal for a Personal Rapid Transit (PRT) system in Denver, and the small town of Gardiner, Maine.

URBAN DESIGN AND POSTMODERNISM

The prolific American writer Charles Jencks, who had settled in England during the previous decade, produced a number of seminal works, the most important of which was *The Language of Post-Modern Architecture*.[83] The earliest and most curious, *Architecture 2000: Predictions and Methods*, which will be the subject of commentary in the conclusions of this present work, suggested icons that were the very opposite of the ecological city.[84]

Nevertheless, there was a growing interest in self-sustainable cities. The case for improvisation, which was the subtitle of *Adhocism*, by Charles Jencks and Nathan Silver,[85] suggested that this was a term coined by Jencks and first used by him in architectural criticism in 1968. *Adhocism* maintains that, within many human endeavours, a principle of action has speed or economy and purpose or utility. The authors indicated the use of an available system or dealing with an existing system in a new way to solve a problem quickly and efficiently. The Charles Eames House in Pacific Palisades in Los Angeles, was, in the opinion of Jencks and Silver, a first polemical example of adhocism in architecture in the US, utilising catalogue industrial components. Yet its imagery is far from their message, and more akin to the contrived but aesthetically beautiful machine aesthetic of Mies van der Rohe in the same period. The architecture of Joseph Esherick's work in California or that of Charles Moore is also illustrated. More appropriate as an example was the more bizarre and eccentric architecture of Bruce Goff, which was to be represented in settlements such as Drop City built the previous decade.

Jencks' *The Language of Post-Modern Architecture*[86] was to have a profound influence over architecture and urban design during the next decade. Yet it had a very different message from *Adhocism*. It reflected a growing confusion in architectural direction that hitherto had been rooted in the modern movement and was now seen to be irrelevant to the needs and aspirations of the late twentieth century. In an apologia in his introduction, Jencks says: 'The phrase "postmodern" is not the most happy expression one can use concerning recent architecture. It is evasive, fashionable, and worst of all negative. . . . It doesn't say immediately, like a good slogan, what banner to follow'.[87] It is pluralistic with the idea that an architect must master several styles and codes of communication and vary these to suit the particular culture for which he or she is designing. Jencks said he had called this 'Adhocism in the past with the use of the term "radical eclecticism" and freely admits that this was, with rising vituperation, an attack on the modern movement'.

The criticism of formalism arising out of the modern movement is epitomised, Jencks says, in Frank Lloyd Wright's last work, the Marin County Civic Center in California, 'based on the endless repetition of various patterns (and their trans-

Bieneke Library, Yale University, Skidmore, Owings and Merrill.

formation) which are uncertain in their overtone. In its defense one can applaud its compelling surrealistic image, justifiable in terms of its Kitsch extravagance, but not much more'.[88] Similarly he criticises Skidmore, Owings and Merrill's Bieneke Library at Yale University, of which he says: 'This pompous temple looks extraordinary at night when the light shines through the translucent marble: the panels look like stacked television sets which have all gone on the blink'. The Rare Books collection of the Bieneke Library is set in a formalistic plaza within the heart of the campus and is not dissimilar to the lack of human scale and activity of the Lincoln Center, New York, designed by Catalano and others during that time.

The concluding chapter of this present book, defining post-modern architecture, will show how the work of Venturi and Rauch in their design for the Brandt house in Bermuda (1975),

Stern and Hagman's house in Washington, Connecticut (1974), and Charles Moore and William Turnbull's Faculty Club in Santa Barbara are among the most prominent examples of this new, ambiguous direction. But perhaps the most vivid example given by Jencks, an American author, was not American at all, but a Japanese building by a Japanese architect. The Omni-Rental stores in the Shinjuka Ward of Tokyo, designed by Minoru Takeyama in 1970, were truly the beginning of post-modernism in architecture, and related to the supergraphics movement in the US in the latter part of the previous decade. It was noted that: 'Retailing is holding out a welcoming hand to the objects of supermannerism'.[89] The two high-rise developments were indeed spectacular examples of supergraphics.

In Japan, unlike North America where strict zoning and building regulations militate against multi-use commercial

Omni-Rental Stores, Shinjuka Ward, Tokyo (1970), Minoru Takeyama.

circles and semi-circles, the other with straight lines in stripes and diagonals.[90]

Thus, the Omni-Rental stores became the iconic example of the 'new' postmodernism. According to Jencks: 'Architect's architecture and commercial motifs can be combined without compromising either code: in fact, their mutual confrontation is a positive gain for both sides. The resultant hybrid, like all inclusive architecture, is not easily subverted by an ironic attack, an unsympathetic viewpoint, because it balances and reconciles opposed meanings'.[91]

Given the exuberance of Jencks' example, the resulting influence was, in many instances, dismal as an urban design system. In the following years and into the next decade, postmodernism was to become a degraded form of architectural and urban design generally resulting in a pastiche of the reinterpretation of neoclassical motifs, resembling stage set design rather than true architecture, and degrading and relegating architectural design as a form of decorative art not dissimilar from 'the battle of the styles' a hundred years earlier.

URBAN DESIGN AS PUBLIC POLICY

The growing recognition of urban design as an integral part of public policy began during this period. Government policy already encouraged urban sprawl through easy mortgage availability for families wanting to move to the suburbs, thus exacerbating the problems of the inner city. Jonathan Barnett, in his book *Urban Design as Public Policy*, said: 'We cannot afford to write off the very substantial investment, social, financial, and cultural, in the existing fabric of our cities'.[92] Urban problems were heightened by the ideas of the modern movement and by government bureaucracy, while urban design tended to focus on antiquated solutions. Barnett argued that while city form was largely unintentional, it was not accidental since it resulted from numerous separate decisions by separate groups who did not consider the city as a whole. Urban designers avoided being involved in public policy, yet 'urban design can make a substantial difference to the welfare and livelihood of large segments of the population'.[93]

The Urban Design Group for New York was created in 1967, with Barnett as a member, and a number of special projects were initiated. One such project was a special graduate programme in urban design at City College, directed by Barnett, and urban design thus became an accepted part of New York government. Most large projects in New York, when constructed, looked nothing like their original design, as most were parcelled out to several developers, resulting in piecemeal development and little design integration.[94] The idea of planned unit development (PUD) then evolved, with cluster zoning using master plans to promote higher-density clusters as centres of activity. Another new method was urban renewal, which offered a high degree of design control as well as zoning incentives based on floor ratio bonuses. In New York, special zoning districts were introduced, the first of which was Greenwich Village and somewhat later Fifth Avenue, the goal of which was to control new buildings, to ensure that the district remained economically viable.

buildings, the tendency has been to encourage a complete mixture of residential, entertainment, shopping and other commercial use, not unlike the principles advocated by Jane Jacobs. The architect Minoru Takeyama thus proposed a development whereby each of the seven floors could serve as an independent building in its own right. Apart from shopping development at the lowest three levels, the upper floors included two clubs, a sauna, bar, restaurant and gaming rooms. The whole of the exterior was covered with supergraphic murals on an enormous scale, designed by Kiyashi Awazu using plastic spray-painted concrete. Huge numerals were applied to the top of both buildings, one of which had its blank walls painted with concentric

The Urban Design Group applied the principle of special zoning districts to Lower Manhattan, with the aim of surrounding the business centre with a ring of residential buildings on existing landfill. On the western side was a separate project, Battery City Park, which later became a major development. Among the Group's other initiatives were the introduction of advocacy planning, the object of which was to involve citizens in local decision-making by establishing neighbourhood working communities.

In Brooklyn, the business community appointed the Urban Design Group as consultants to prepare a plan for the downtown area. However, implementation proved difficult due to the large number of agencies operating in the area. The Office of Downtown Brooklyn Development was therefore created to facilitate decision-making, and the design plan was implemented ahead of schedule. It received the first Design Award from *Progressive Architecture* in 1973. *Progressive Design* magazine also ran a Design Awards programme, and it is interesting that the Brooklyn project was not placed in the urban design category but rather in the architectural category, and referred to as the Hoyt-Schemerhorn mezzanine project. Barnett also addressed other urban issues such as transportation, which he called 'the urban armature', suggesting that the 1970 Federal Highways Act required that new highways be planned in conjunction with new development. Underground transit, he said, while more expensive than highways, was a better alternative for the city. *Design Review* was, at this time, still in its infancy, though the danger of imposing design guidelines was seen to be too subjective.

From these new policies in urban planning and design came a new phenomenon – the architect as developer;[95] hitherto almost all major urban development and redevelopments were undertaken by entrepreneurial firms of developers who appointed architects and consultants to design their projects. John Portman was a pioneer architect in this field and became a real estate entrepreneur, developing projects and acting as his own architect. This changed the practice of both architecture and real estate development. In this way, Portman was able to undertake projects that would have been impossible for most architects working within the framework of conventional practice. He proved that his designs were profitable, and that communication between architects and developers was possible. Portman's theory was modelled after the concept of a 'coordinate unit' based upon the distance an average person is prepared to walk without seeking transportation.

Portman's first project was the Peachtree Plaza Hotel, a 70-storey building, then the tallest in Atlanta. It included retail stores, five office buildings, a shopping gallery, parking and another hotel, the Hyatt Regency. The scheme was Portman's first commercial success. Piranesi-like spaces were popular in the interior, as were the vertiginous glass elevators resembling the projected cities of the future in H. G. Wells' *The Shape of Things to Come*. Bridges connected hotels to other buildings in the complex.

Portman later designed other successful projects, including the Embarcadero Center in San Francisco. The Embarcadero Center was an urban renewal project with a multilevel circula-tion spine connected to four office buildings, retail stores and a hotel.

To Portman, architecture was a social art as environmental architecture, born of human needs responding to physical, social and economic circumstances. In a version of British theorist Gordon Cullen's theory of social vision, Portman said: 'Architects should articulate the journey into a sequence of spaces, ranging from tight enclosures to large volumes'.[96] The city was a living entity and could not be designed in the same way as an individual building. Design should be rooted in a cellular pattern based on a scale of distances that people are willing to walk; he claimed that the average American was only willing to walk between seven and ten metres (20 and 30 feet) without looking for transport. Portman's plan for Atlanta included a new rapid transit system (MARTA), the legislation for which was passed in 1971, which was to prove important during the 1996 Olympic Games.

Urban design as public policy was also identified in Joseph De Chiara's *Urban Planning and Design Criteria*.[97] This was a comprehensive source book for urban designers and planners, dealing with the physical aspects of the environment. Comprehensive community planning was seen to be a long-term 20-year plan including land use analysis, population studies,

Peachtree Plaza Hotel, Atlanta,
John Portman.

economic studies and community facility and transportation plans. 'Master plans' (by this time considered anathema in most western European countries as dictatorial impositions on the will of the communities that plans addressed) were seen to be smaller scale, containing population studies, housing studies, physical plans, land use plans, commercial development plans and specific plans for the central business district (CBD). The support for master plans was undiminished at the time, even though they were crystalline and the concept did not allow for changing circumstances.

De Chiara said that urban design existed as part of the comprehensive plan. 'Urban Design considers matters of space organization or commodity and efficiency, while at the same time seeking an aesthetic outcome'.[98] There were usually alternatives which appeared as part of the land use plan, plans for facilities and services, and a transportation plan, but all of these were essentially two-dimensional. Among the elements of urban design were definitions of types of single-use systems based on natural features or open-space development. Nevertheless, De Chiara's book seemed to confuse the fact that urban design, acting as a link between urban and community planning and architecture, was essentially three-dimensional. Included in the list of many things to be studied as part of the process were national population projections, statistical areas, educational facilities (but excluding higher education), industrial classification, issues of pollution, zoning and regulatory controls.

Gary Hack, a protégé of Kevin Lynch, introduced what was perhaps a more identifiable approach to urban design in addressing the issues of city streets at night.[99] Few designs had hitherto considered the different effects of night and day on the environment. Hack's study, between 1973 and 1974, was based on the Ghent Neighbourhood, an innercity part of Norfolk, Virginia, involving 19 adjacent environments. This was a low-income area with many buildings constructed in the late 1960s, although the neighbourhood did have a conservation area. The study raised the issues of security, safety, ambience and legibility, gathered from behavioural studies based on questionnaires, not dissimilar from Kevin Lynch's earlier studies. Subjects were asked to walk as well as drive through the selected study sites. Each site was rated according to forty dimensions. Pedestrian concerns were the most important in residential areas, though on main arteries the concerns of drivers were of equal importance in their need for legibility and safety.

At the opposite end of the spectrum to Hack's study was Kenneth Halpern's *Downtown USA*.[100] Halpern examined the major metropolitan areas of the US, which included New York, Chicago, Philadelphia, Houston, Washington, DC, San Francisco and Atlanta. Of these studies, perhaps the most interesting historically was the account of New York. Though Jonathan Barnett's book *Urban Design as Public Policy*[101] had been published four years earlier, Halpern provided a vivid account of the burgeoning public interest in urban design during this period. Though the Urban Design Group had been established in 1967 with six urban design offices as a response to the leadership of Mayor John Lindsay, the first project, Lincoln Center, would ultimately prove to be a less than satisfactory piece of

civic architecture. Using Rockefeller Center as a benchmark of successful civic design and emphasising the importance of Fifth Avenue and the Times Square theatre district, the founding of the Office of Lower Manhattan Development (OLMD) officially recognised urban design as public policy, creating guidelines requiring 'view corridors', pedestrian circulation patterns and historic preservation. At the same time, zoning amendments were made in historic districts allowing development rights from historic building parcels to be banked for future use. A goal of the 1975 zoning legislation was to provide people-oriented spaces in midtown Manhattan with the identification of three types of urban plaza. Houston, Texas, was cited as the only large city in the US with no effective planning control and the ideology that the private sector could perform more effectively was a political dogma that was to exist to the end of the twentieth century. This contrasted with Minneapolis and private partnerships for urban design in the country, using a skywalk system connecting all major buildings at the upper level as protection against severe winter weather conditions.

Professionally, urban design as a new profession was recognised by the American Institute of Architects in 1973.[102] The checklist provided by the Institute was bland and generalised, and touched not so much on the physical form of the city but rather emphasised a growing complexity in urban planning policy, such as the ecological framework of the city, regional economics and regional politics. In detail, it reiterated many of the issues raised by political activists of the previous decade, such as public participation in the planning process, open-space design, historical preservation, upgrading poor areas and rebuilding communities on a neighbourhood scale of between 500 and 3,000 dwellings each. All of this, the authors stated, should be paid for by state and federal agencies, and not property tax.

The most outstanding example of urban design as public policy was the plan for San Francisco in 1970. The San Francisco Department of City Planning, in its preparation of citywide urban design guidelines,[103] sought out aspects of development which might be encouraged and those which might be suppressed. It provided a framework for more detailed urban design plans at district and neighbourhood levels. The framework depended first upon an analysis of the city as a set of fairly discrete design units, identifiable by the distinctive natural or man-made character peculiar to each. This definition of 'visual districts' indicated the qualities of each part of the city that could be enhanced, and urban design guidelines were formulated to achieve this: 'Urban Design Guidelines for Open Space and Landscaping', 'Urban Design Guidelines for Streets', 'Urban Design Policy for Protecting Street Views and Street Space', 'Urban Design Guidelines for the Height of Buildings', and 'Urban Design Guidelines for the Bulk of Buildings'.

Such an approach, permitting exceptions but offering a consensus view of the particular qualities of a city that each new development should respect, was a more flexible form of urban design than, for example, that imposed by Lucio Costa and Oscar Niemeyer in their plan for Brasilia, the new capital of Brazil, ten years earlier. Like most regulatory documents, the

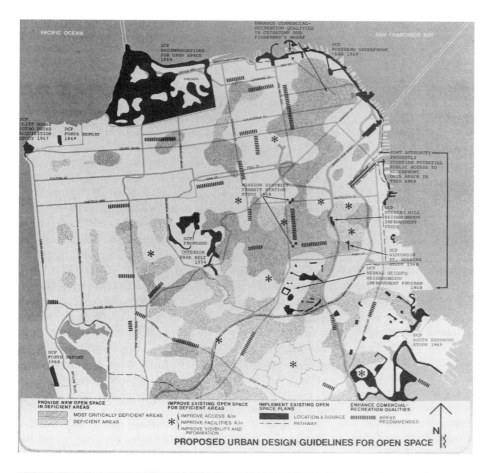

San Francisco Urban Design Plan (1970).

Bay Area Rapid Transport (BART), San Francisco (1971).

San Francisco plan shared some of the historical pessimism of such a policy, being based on the view that some distinctive quality had been, or was about to be lost, and that restrictive legislation would be necessary to save it. For San Francisco, and many other cities, it was primarily the eruption of high buildings in the downtown area in the 1960s that persuaded planners of the need for such a policy; however, this was not the only form of large-scale disruption to have such an effect.

Regional design policies were emerging, particularly in Europe, for example the Essex Design Guide, published in rural England in 1973.[104]

The San Francisco reports were integrated into the city's master plan in 1971. One of the aspects of San Francisco that aided the application of good urban design was the introduction of the rapid rail transit system – the Bay Area Rapid Transit (BART). The development of this had encouraged the rehabilitation of Market Street with small adjacent plazas, trams, widened pavements and tree planting.

URBAN DESIGN AS LANDSCAPE

The difference between urban design as public policy and urban design as landscape is that of implementation. One of the themes to be examined in this history of urban design is the extent to which ideas reach fruition. In 1972, Lawrence Halprin, the distinguished American landscape architect, compiled a history of his own works and ideas over the 12-year period between 1959 and 1971.[105] Halprin's notebooks were ways of expressing his ideas, and the book was a selection from between 4,000 and 5,000 pages of notes he had written during that time. In addition to comments on projects and about cities he had visited, there were also many sketches of nature and urban places. Halprin criticised the lateral spread of cities and the imposition of geometry on suburban communities. He said 'designers should design into the landscape in a naturalistic way so that communities merge and become landscape'.[106] Earlier communities had a quality of identity with natural landscapes due in part to available building materials such as stone and wood, but also because they were built slowly on a human scale.

Halprin defined the elements of a natural landscape as unpredictable rhythms and, echoing the work of Philip Thiel, suggested analysis using scores to identify design function in small environments. Among Halprin's built projects was Ghirardelli Square in San Francisco, with a restaurant in a tower, outdoor dining on the roof of the existing structure, and underground parking. He also cites his involvement in the Sea Ranch project designed by Moore, Lyndon and Turnbull. The notation system was described from a senior graduate seminar at Berkeley, as early as 1964, in which pedestrian priority was considered paramount.

THE CITY IN HISTORY

Many of Halprin's ideas were reflected in *The Growth of Cities,* edited by David Lewis.[107] Lewis rejected the idea of utopias as too simplistic and, following his earlier work in advocacy plan-

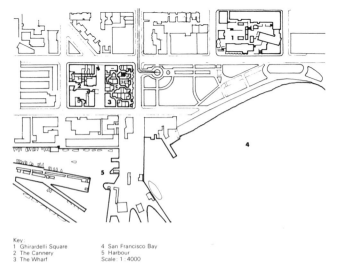

Key:
1 Ghirardelli Square
2 The Cannery
3 The Wharf
4 San Francisco Bay
5 Harbour
Scale: 1 : 4000

*The Cannery Plan (1971), Ghirardelli Square,
San Francisco, California.*

ning, suggested that architects should choose neighbourhood phenomena coupled with public participation. This series of essays followed Lewis' earlier *Urban Structure*, published in 1968, which included essays by Kenneth Frampton and Anthony Vidler, British expatriots who taught at Princeton University.[108] Many of the essays were critical of current American planning at that time, for example Hans Blumenfeld[109] claimed that planning in America had been unsuccessful, resulting in the unplanned modern metropolis with its freeways and skyscrapers. Design was the same thing as planning in the broad sense, because both are 'the mental anticipation of a combination of means to achieve a goal or set of goals'.[110] Denise Scott-Brown wrote that a non-judgemental attitude towards urban design, architecture and planning had developed.[111]

Edmond Bacon's *Design of Cities* explored the nature of the decisions that affected the building of cities, starting from the Periclean age in Athens.[112] The city, he said, should be a people's art and a shared experience. The final part of the book described Bacon's own experience as former Director of Planning in Philadelphia. Though Louis Kahn had provided the initial idea of three-dimensional movement patterns for Philadelphia, Bacon had expanded upon these, suggesting that different modes of travel offered different perceptions that would affect and have affected city building forms throughout history. Bacon also emphasised the way in which colour provided continuity and affected spatial experience.

A parallel study was Hans Blumenfeld's *The Modern Metropolis*,[113] a collection of essays in which he traced the theory of city form. Blumenfeld proposed that the most logical form was the star-shaped city, not dissimilar from the utopian models in Europe some four hundred years earlier, or even the technical utopia such as that described by Vitruvius in his *Ten Books on Architecture* as the epitome of Roman city planning.[114] Vitruvius' overriding preoccupation with the exposure of towns to winds, so as to give shelter but at the same time healthy ventilation, leads him to an unlikely piece of logic (contradicted by other Roman authorities)[115] – a polygonal form with 16 main radial streets, quite unlike the expectations of a Roman grid plan. Although Vitruvius' strange obsession with problems of ventilation was not shared by subsequent planners, his iconic solution proved serviceable for other cases where a single functional requirement dominated the programme, as did defence in the numerous projects for fortress towns devised during the Renaissance. In these designs for the city as a strategic unit we can see the expression of the public realm, not just in the imposition of an ordered pattern on the individual buildings, but in the development of major constructions that follow their own design logic, often quite independent of the pattern of elements they embrace. We might then trace the development of successive technical utopias as the increasingly ambitious attempt to envisage the city as a single piece of public hardware embedded with private components, and thus, to advance the design of its system.

The radial system, such as that advocated by Blumenfeld, was to be a natural, if somewhat haphazard, outcome for the twentieth-century European cities, with the outer suburbs housing the more affluent families. However, in both the nine-

The Cannery, San Francisco, California: two views of an urban renewal scheme with the adaptation of warehouse buildings into a shopping precinct.

teenth and twentieth centuries this was not to be the case in the US. Cities like New York evinced no such radial pattern, but rather the rigid imposition of a gridiron system following the Greek and Roman cities some 2,000 years earlier.

In seeking alternative solutions for metropolitan development, Blumenfeld rejected the idea of garden cities and new towns – slightly ironic given the popularity of such settlements devised by the new urbanists some thirty years later. Nevertheless, he believed that decentralisation was a modern trend that could not be reversed, and that the urban pattern was a dynamic and growing process, with metropolitan areas containing at least half a million people within a 50-kilometre (30-mile) radius, due to the mutual accessibility of places of residence and work. More curiously, the 'countryside' was seen to be the location of retired people, an oxymoron given the exponential growth of outer suburbs within Lewis Mumford's definition of the term 'conurbation'. Mumford had suggested that a conurbation contained many metropolitan areas and was a new form of settlement in the twentieth century, citing the northeast corridor of the US extending from Boston (in the north) to Washington, DC (in the south) and including New York City and Philadelphia.

In predictions for the future, there was the correct recogni-

tion that technology would improve communications, allowing meetings without travel, yet suggestions that transportation would maximise choices in employment and housing failed. There was, however, acknowledgement that low-density development could not support public transport: San Francisco, for example, with its BART system, was a new model of consumer choice that failed to fulfil its promise. *The Death and Life of American Cities,*[116] by Jane Jacobs, with its central idea of the 'good neighbourhood', was attacked by Blumenfeld as being an 'angry' book with sweeping generalisations and over-simplification. He claimed that the city was not a work of visual art but understood only by a series of perceptions.

Richard Sennett had described the pursuit of 'the urban whole' as a myth of purity by which imponderables, and particularly those arising from unpredictable urban growth and change, are transmuted into fixed, static objectives by the operation of techniques such as the statement of 'projective areas' as ambiguous as the contemporary 'vision statements'.[117] The dangers of applying what we have loosely called the 'engineering approach' to inappropriate 'wicked' problems is echoed in Sennett's analysis of the misleading use of the analogy of the city as a machine. Yet it must be said that the adaptation of this analysis is a symptom rather than a cause of the 'myth of purity'. Its place, for example in Le Corbusier's seminal urban projects, is illuminated by Colin Rowe and Fred Koetter's observations on the differences between the designer's stance as an urbanist and as an architect:

> There is Le Corbusier, the architect . . . who sets up elaborately pretended Platonic structures only to riddle them with equally elaborate pretenses of empirical detail, the Le Corbusier of multiple asides, cerebral references and complicated scherzi; and then there is Le Corbusier, the urbanist, the deadpan protagonist of completely different strategies who, at a large and public scale, has the minimum of use for all the dialectical tricks and spatial involutions which, invariably, he considered the appropriate adornment of a more private situation. The public world is simple, the private world is elaborate, and, if the private world affects a concern for contingency, the would-be public personality long maintained an almost too heroic disdain for any taint of the specific.[118]

This curious reservation of the simplest solutions for the most complex problems is a long-standing characteristic of much urban planning, and forms one basis of contemporary criticism of its results. It was zoning, among the earliest techniques used by planners to intervene in the development of the industrial city, which laid the basis for such an approach. For while the physical separation of land uses had undoubted environmental justifications, it also had the distinct advantage of achieving a radical simplification of the problem. Such concepts as land-use isolation and hierarchical community structures undoubtedly clarified the confusingly interdependent aspects of the problem to the point where a lucid design solution could be formulated, although critics have argued that such solutions were so sterile and so remote from the reality of the city that they were invalid. Attempts have thus been made to reinvest the end product with some of the functional and visual variety of pre-industrial or 'unplanned' cities, and many formulas for achieving this have been proposed. However, these formulas have the disadvantage that they appear only to make more acceptable the results of an initial faulty design decision, and thus they substantiate Papenek's accusation that 'so far the action of the [design] profession has been comparable to what would happen if all medical doctors were to forsake general practice and surgery, and concentrate exclusively on dermatology and cosmetics'.[119]

The approach investigated by Colin Rowe and Fred Koetter in 'Collage City' was to envisage a model of an idealised place by comparing two monumental palace complexes, the Villa Adriana at Tivoli and the Palace at Versailles. The second, controlled by a single conception, is complete and stands for the elusive purity and hegemony sought by many urban designers. The Villa Adriana, however, consists of a number of discrete component areas, each different in character and organisation – a fragment of some other whole – which are brought together in a fortuitous and pragmatic assembly, a collage in which the

dialectic between dissimilar components is as important as the parts themselves.

Rowe and Koetter go on to explore the implications of this idea and to draw upon related ideas that contribute to it. Claude Lévi-Strauss' notion of the *bricoleur* (handyman) for example, is invoked as a possible source of design attitudes for the urban collagist. In *The Savage Mind*, Lévi-Strauss distinguishes the *bricoleur* from the engineer or scientist 'by the inverse functions which they assign to events and structures as means and ends, the scientist creating events . . . by means of structures and the "bricoleur" creating structure by means of events'.[120] Again, their attitude to tools is contrasted, the engineer subordinating the task to the availability of raw materials and a purpose-designed set of tools, while the *bricoleur* improvises with a magpie collection of ready-made tools that will be reused for quite different projects.

Through such analogies and the investigation of the philosophical implications of the design principle, Rowe and Koetter developed an elaborate and subtle appreciation of the pluralist approach. Against this, one might object that this would hardly be amenable to prescription. Indeed, by its avoidance of simple and unitary goals it would be extraordinarily difficult for either lay or professional bureaucracies to control, and in place of the

Villa Adriana, Tivoli, Italy, from Collage City (1975),
Colin Rowe and Fred Koetter.

View of Versailles, from Collage City (1975),
Colin Rowe and Fred Koetter.

blinding self-righteousness of unitary conviction it would be necessary to recognise 'a more tragic cognition of the dazzling and scarcely to be resolved multiformity of experience'.[121] If the freedom is thus a demanding one, we can at least be comforted by Rowe's thought that it 'might be a means of permitting us the enjoyment of Utopian poetics without our being obliged to suffer the embarrassment of Utopian politics'.[122]

The Roma Interrotta competition was launched three years later. Although not strictly speaking a competition, the invitation to 12 well-known theorists and practitioners of architecture and urbanism to rework in whatever way they pleased a one-twelfth segment of Giovanni Battista Nolli's 1748 plan of Rome, produced a similar result in freezing, as it were, the state of the art as interpreted at one point in time by the contenders. The relaxed terms of the contest made it both more confusing and more revealing than a conventional competition, and although the participants tended to convey the impression that they saw the whole thing as a bit of a joke, it was apparent from the amount of work they devoted to their entries that they took the joke rather seriously. Thus, once the initial witty or self-conscious stance had been established by each, the opportunity to comment on what urban design might mean in 1978 produced some interesting results, which in the absence of a functional system concentrated on the questions of formal coherence.

The idea of the invitation came from the American architect Michael Graves, whose choice of Nolli's plan was not an arbitrary one. As he relates, Nolli's technique of drawing begins not at roof level, but at a horizontal plan section at ground-floor level, with commercial and residential buildings blocked in and spaces in public buildings shown as extensions of the outdoor streets and squares. He projects a particular view of the city as a complex sequence of rooms unlike, on the one hand, the rigid separation of inside and out shown on medieval representations, and, on the other, the spatial continuity implied in modern plans. This led Graves, in his own entry, to define four archetypal forms of urban organisation compatible with this view of the city, which he then combined and developed in his segment. The first four of these paradigms was 'the centroidal object in the landscape', a simple centralised mass outside, exemplified by the Temple of Minerva Medica, or Bramante's Tempietto. The second archetype is the 'figure-ground' antithesis of the first, a single space against a surrounding building, or building group, as at the Villa Madama. From these singular elements, the third and fourth archetypes build generic arrangements, the third being essentially a linear sequence of discrete spaces (as in the Villa Adriana), and the fourth a more fluid network of movements, as seen in the complex spaces forming the Church of the Trinità de Pellegrini.

Graves' careful definition of urban models and investigation of the subtle interrelationships possible between them was echoed in British architect James Stirling's (later Sir James Stirling) proposal which, paradoxically, started from precisely the opposite pole. Beginning with a proposition that he would bring together all of his various projects to populate his rather empty section of Nolli's plan, Stirling went on to cast them as generic urban types appropriate to their new location. Thus Stirling worked from a particular set of highly specific projects

to define, like Graves, some universal conditions of urban design. He likened his 'contextual associational' method to the historical process (in that any addition is seen as a confirmation and complement to that which exists), to Colin Rowe's and Fred Koetter's concept of 'Collage City', and to the working method of one or two other designers, such as O. M. Meyers. He contrasted this to the 'rational' methods of most post-Second World War planning by which sewers and roads determine the layouts of new buildings and 'expediency and commercialism' destroy existing cities.

This note of disgust at the state of contemporary urban development, and the part modern architecture played in it – here termed 'block modern' (cf. blockhouse, blockhead, blockbuster, blocked) – was shared by Colin Rowe and his team: 'We assume that on the whole, modern architecture was a major catastrophe – except as a terrible lesson – best to be forgotten; and though we sometimes wonder how an idea – apparently so good – could easily have been betrayed, we see no reason to indulge in pseudo regrets or quasi-satirical demonstrations'. Instead Rowe, in three richly worked compositions for the Aventine, Palatine and Celio Hills included in his sector, postulated a Rome that, with

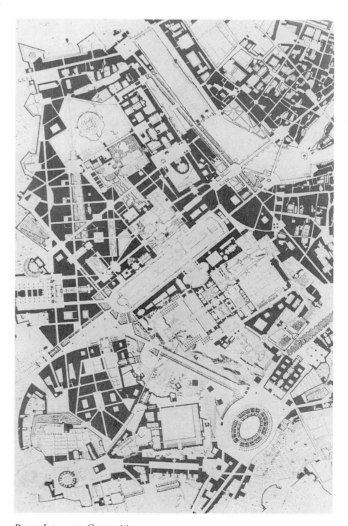

Roma Interrotta Competition,
Rowe (1978)

a little tinkering with history, might plausibly be interpolated as a natural extension of the old city. This suggestion of the search for improved urban form as the invention of an alternative, imaginary history, makes a fascinating contrast with Stirling's and Graves' 'endseeking' hunt for universal urban types, and is supported by an elaborate and learned guide to the alternative history of the area, supplied by an erudite (and imaginary) Jesuit scholar. The technique, though quite unlike the others, achieved results much in sympathy with them: 'We have attempted to constitute a fragment of . . . a city of discrete set pieces and interactive local incidents, a city which represents coalition of intentions rather than the singular presence of any immediately apparent all-coordinating ideas'.[123]

In 'Collage City', Rowe had already rejected modern architecture as little related to technological innovation or a formal vocabulary, claiming it was based on an idea to 'exhibit the virtues of an apostolic poverty'.[124] He believed that the tenets of this philosophy were quasi-religious, neither rational nor scientific. Architecture was seen, by both Frank Lloyd Wright and Le Corbusier, as the saviour of mankind. The classical utopian model was developed from concepts of a universal rational morality and ideas of justice, developing these ideas into an icon of a good society. To counter this, there developed an anti-utopian sentiment found in the works of such thinkers as Rousseau, Marx, Fourier and Burke. Eventually, futurism developed a frightening vision of a new world, derived from a Hegelian tradition, based partly on the thoughts of Nietzsche. Modern utopianism emerged from these ideas, formed both from avant-gardism and a liberal tradition. According to Rowe, this view was inadequate to deal with the modern world.

THE SYSTEMS CITY

A diametrically opposite point of view to historical references and procedure was represented by new technology in city structure. Following the energy crisis of 1973, the dominant role of motor cars in circulation-generated city plans came under more careful scrutiny, for example in Ulrich Franzen's 1975 plan for New York City.[125] Emphasising in his report the need for innovative attitudes toward improving the existing urban environment, Franzen's proposals included a linear support structure development along the East River, built in conjunction with the tradeway and through-traffic bypass and acting as an interchange system for different modes of travel. Thus, the conventional motor car would be stored in the interchange and small electric pool vehicles used on short distances across connecting bridges.[126] Franzen noted that the entire eastern (Queens) edge of the East River was largely under-utilised industrial land and suggested that the service structure would promote 'dynamic growth'. While not as visionary as Kahn's earlier plan for Philadelphia, the utilisation of small-scale transportation systems, such as electric cars in caravan formation or pneumatic tubes for mail and goods services, would require an equally ambitious, if more energy conscious, circulation network.

Since mechanical transportation systems sustain our present cities in terms of their size, distribution of uses and population, as well as determining much of their physical detail, any change in their form may be expected to have considerable implications for urban design. The recurrent scarcities and price increases of fuel for private cars at the time strengthened the argument in favour of alternatives to private transport in cities,

Transportation proposal, New York (1975), Ulrich Franzen.

whether of conventional or radically new types. For example, a number of planners have called for the reintroduction of a powerful public transport network for the city without the major expense of developing new vehicles and routes, and with the minimal of environmental impact.

Others have argued that such conventional systems have already demonstrated their limitations in that they inevitably come into conflict with other forms of traffic, particularly pedestrians (a German expert has described how 'hundreds' of Germans are mown down each year by fast, silent street railways). By the early 1970s, several companies in the US and Western Europe were investigating systems that would overcome these difficulties and, at the same time, provide a more flexible movement pattern for passengers used to the door-to-door convenience of the motor car.

The solution proposed by many was a variation of the PRT system, defined by Eino K. Latvala of Transportation Technology, Inc. as follows: 'In the completely automated, electrically powered, "Personal Rapid Transit" (PRT) systems demonstrated by TTI at Transpo '72, people ride in air conditioned, lightweight, low-profile, quiet running cars, each able to carry 6–12 seated passengers and their luggage. The cars move on a controlled right-of-way, or guideway, unimpeded by street or highway traffic, and it is possible for an individual passenger or family or other small group to have use of a car dedicated to a specific trip'.[127]

Although few of the many systems of the type proposed in the early 1970s made it beyond the experimental trade stage, LTV Aerospace Corporation's Airtrans System for Dallas/Fort Worth Airport demonstrated their possibilities. Using 68 rubber-tyred, steerable vehicles automatically controlled on a concrete U-shaped guideway, 21 kilometres (13 miles) in extent and running between 14 passenger stations, as well as additional pickup points for baggage, mail, and airport employees, the system was opened in 1973 to serve ten discretely scheduled routes within the airport complex.

Such a network could illustrate the technical implications of PRT, but in the special case of an airport context in which, for example, the special track could run for 80 per cent of its length at ground level, it did not really show the impact of such an installation on existing towns. In Europe, studies of the application of Cabtrack to Central London were carried out by Robert Matthew, Johnson-Marshall and Partners in 1971. The Cabtrack system, sponsored by the Transport Research Assessment Group of the Department of the Environment with the Royal Aircraft Establishment at Farnborough, investigated a network of largely elevated trackways offering a maximum distance of 250 metres (270 yards) from any point in the area covered to the nearest cab stop. The graphic use of photo montages and drawings to illustrate the impact of such a transport system upon an existing urban fabric caused much debate and controversy in the media. Although questions of cost and effectiveness were raised, it was primarily the visual intrusion of the elevated trackways that disturbed cities. In response, the

Cabtrack proposals for Central London (1971).

American Airtrans, Fort Worth Airport, Texas (1973), LTV Aerospace Corporation.

consultants pointed to the piecemeal intrusion of existing tactic, finding 'this an image for the future preferable to an acquiescence in a steadily deteriorating environmental situation. And Cabtrack, or something like it, is the only instrument in prospect which might bring it about'.[128]

If such systems are to be tailored to existing environments, then the great variety of the latter might be expected to foster a multiplicity of solutions. Certainly the argument raised against Cabtrack, that the centre of London, like New York with its subway systems (although both were under funded for many decades), was actually quite well served by public transport systems in comparison to the suburbs, which depended, and still depend, on private transport, was a relevant one. In the case of extensive lower residential areas, it has been argued that the solution lies not with elaborate new vehicles and trackways, but rather with a greater sophistication in the control and flexible routing of conventional vehicles. Thus, after the disappearance of trams in American cities post-1945, the light rail systems introduced in West Coast cities within the last 10 to 15 years have become increasingly popular as motorists living in the suburbs have become more frustrated by grid lock on interstate highways, metropolitan beltways and local freeways.

A 1978 study, *Systems of Cities*, edited by Bourne and Simmons,[129] presented a different viewpoint of the systems city, unconnected to issues of public transport. Seen more from a geographical science point of view, many of the essays addressed the issues of historical growth and urban systems. Jean Gottman recognised that the megalopolitan systems had arisen among polynuclear rather than elongated areas.[130] The author metaphorically described its function, in terms of trade, cultural, technological and population changes as 'the continent's economic hinge', citing the Boston–New York–Washington axis. It was suggested that a necessary condition of a megalopolis was a hinge, articulating two or more networks as well as an international and overseas network, hence the importance of the seaport function of some of the major bolts forming the network.[131] Gottman insisted on the importance of water transport, which now seems less than visionary. If anything, this major collection of essays addressed issues on a global scale and generally did little to expand information on the physical form of major cities at the time. The editors themselves noted that 'the development of new definitions of the city [were] particularly those with different spatial scales. The broader-scale definitions, because they internalize much of the hinterland economy by bringing it into the urban area, create very different impressions of that region's total economic base and of the factors affecting urban growth . . . the observed growth in the urban core appears simply to reflect a redistribution within the region, analogous to suburbanization, rather than an inter-regional shift of activities or population. The specification of the urban system is therefore a critical component of any analysis of population change and redistribution . . . the urban system also treats the city essentially as one point or node, within a large and complex network of external relationships'.[132]

A more definitive series of essays, at least in urban *design* terms, was published earlier in the decade by Wolf and Shinn.[133]

This mimeographed publication was funded by the relatively new US Department of Housing and Urban Development. The authors suggested that the term 'urban design' could lose some of the ambivalence of the past if changing urban patterns could be visualised in the context of design possibilities rather than design finalities – that considerations of parts of the city as they relate to the whole urban form should be shown 'more schematically to decision-makers while public policy is being considered'.[134] The intent was to produce a guideline document to give direction on the achievement of an urban design component within the planning process.

While much of the publication was illustrated by the use of flow charts showing the stages of public participation, the documents also included specific urban design proposals for the city of Bellingham in Washington State. These were, for the most part, fairly conventional proposals such as the Central Waterfront Design and Development Plan. Nevertheless, tackling waterfront development was then some ten years ahead of its time, after which, throughout the US, waterfronts were to become a major political issue. The notational system described[135] appeared to be developed from Lynch's earlier work, but graphics were somewhat easier to understand for the lay observer.

A more adventurous approach within the technological boundaries of the systems city was Nicholas Negroponte's *Soft Architecture Machines*.[136] Seen as a development of Negroponte's earlier *The Architecture Machine*,[137] published between 1970 and 1971 in architectural journals such as *Werk* (Germany); *Techniques and Architecture* (France); *Architecture and Urbanism* (Japan); *Architectural Forum* (USA) and *Architectural Design* (UK), *Soft Architecture Machines* was a visionary study.

Recognising that computer applications in urban design would become universal, Negroponte said that it required 'passing from an idiom to a reality following (not necessarily consciously) notions set down in *The Architecture Magazine* with an uncanny precision. The prognostications of hardware enumerated in wanton fantasy have been achieved and even superseded.' *Soft Architecture Machines*, Negroponte claimed, proposed a 'new kind of architecture without architects and even without surrogate architects'. However, this somewhat arrogant assumption failed to provide evidence that 'attractive environments' would emerge merely from the use of computers. Indeed, in the author's final note in the preface, written in August 1972, he remarked that 'the writing of this book was completed in the summer of 1972. By fall it had advanced to a computer-readable format (paper tape). It is appearing only now, in 1975, for a number of reasons related to its production. The author and the publisher share the embarrassment that most of the delays were caused by the use of automation'.

Negroponte was, however, correct in the assumption that if computers were to aid the evolution of architecture, they would have to be a class of machine that exhibited intelligent behaviour. In 1968 one could read all existing literature on the subject of 'artificial intelligence' within one month, by 1972 it would take six months.

The conclusion of the study goes beyond the architect and, in Negroponte's terms, beyond the need for an outside designer's intervention between our needs and their fulfilment. He asserts that each individual should be the best architect for his own needs and does not require a paternalistic human or mechanical architect to dictate his final decisions. The book ends with a vision of the distant future, as it was seen then, looking beyond the architect and beyond architecture as it was known. In a sense, Negroponte was accurate in one of his predictions, that 'architecture machines' would not simply be used as aids in the design of buildings, but would serve as buildings in themselves – the so-called intelligent building found particularly in office structures at the end of the twentieth century. Man would live in living, intelligent machines or cognitive physical environments that could immediately respond to his needs, whiles or whims. Yet this almost anarchistic view begs the question why Nicholas Negroponte was a professor in the school of architecture at MIT where he was presumably engaged, in part, in educating students who wished to become architects and, above all, designers. A parallel could be seen in the UK at the University of London, where for a period of time drawing boards were eliminated from the school of urban planning. Architecture, which draws both from the arts and sciences, has throughout history been an important part of the *creative* arts.

Soft Architecture Machines suggests that the use of the highly cumbersome FORTRAN software introduced by Oliver Selfridge in 1972 was a desirable route forward. Since that time, the application of three-dimensional computer-generated simulation of the urban environment has advanced significantly, and certainly commercially available current software programs have increased in speed and efficiency, eliminating the need to write individual software programs using FORTRAN.

THE MYTH OF FUTURISM

If Negroponte's important contribution was a visionary step towards an urban design world some thirty years hence, many other studies of this period were deeply flawed in predicting the future shape of cities. As Charles Jencks said in his foreword to *Architecture 2000: Predictions and Methods*: 'To give a series of specific predictions for the future, cut away from their context and ideology, is next to useless. . . . Anticipating the future is as unavoidable and commonplace as breathing'.[138] Many of these views of the future were indeed erroneous or only partially accurate, as was the case of novels of the future by distinguished British fiction writers in the earlier part of the twentieth century.[139]

Jencks' account of the construction of the new capital of Brazil, Brasilia, by Lucio Costa and Oscar Niemeyer between 1956 and 1960 was erroneous.[140] According to Jencks, 'another example of unifying visual and social forces into one, total, overpowering direction which allows no dissent, ambiguity or memory' is both unfair and inaccurate. The decision to build the new capital was by then President Juscelino Kubitschek, freely elected within a democratic society at the time. Kubitschek's visionary idea, developed from those of predecessors and constructed at great cost to the economy of the nation, was to relieve the overpowering physical, ecological,

economic and social pressures on the huge metropolitan areas of the east coast of Brazil, namely Rio de Janeiro and São Paulo, and also to open up the resource-rich hinterland on the central plateau of Minas Gerais.

Mistaken by many observers and critics as a beaux-arts solution, Costa's plan, the result of a 1957 national competition with an international jury, was, in fact, an interesting proposal for a linear city. The crescent-shaped linear development was based on high-speed public and private transport using an urban expressway as its spire. Both Costa and Niemeyer, who had firmly held democratic socialist beliefs, saw the city as one of mixed socioeconomic groups and hoped that low-income workers would live in the *superquadras* (superblocks) of the *plano-piloto* (central zone) in the same way that other *superquadras* would house the higher-paid civil servants. Following the military takeover, government policy determined this was not to be, and lower-paid workers were destined to live in the 'planned' *cidades satélites* (satellite towns).[141]

The mean-spirited indictment of Brasilia was continued in the architectural criticism of the Presidential Palace in Brasilia as 'a classical building whose over-simplification and gross detailing betray its subsequent political usage',[142] when, in fact, the lyrical lines of the buildings could be seen as distinct in lineage to the curvilinear architecture of the Brazilian baroque in cities such as Oruo Preto and Congonhas in Minas Gerais, as well as the more immediate influences of Le Corbusier.

On the same page were the wildly inaccurate world population projections of 7.2 billion people for the year 2000, quoted from Kahn and Weiner.[143] On the other hand, R. Buckminster Fuller's proposal for an air-conditioned dome covering much of the lower part of Manhattan, viewed as 'an unconscious trend towards increased efficiency made into a conscious goal',[144] was apparently an acceptable idea imposed with reference to the thousands of New York citizens who would live beneath it.

On the other hand, the diagram of the Delphi Technique graph,[145] which predicted inventions and discoveries with the high points on the bars showing the date most favoured by experts, was surprisingly accurate. Examples were the feasibility of genetic engineering (2000), the economic feasibility of synthetic protein for food (1990) and biochemical immunisation against bacterial and viral diseases (1995), although all of this had little to do with the future form of cities. Another table, 'Evolutionary Tree to the Year 2000',[146] was a method based upon a structural analysis by Claude Lévi-Strauss. It referred to megastructures, tensile bridges (Calatrava), holographic design, electronic highways, design by computer light-pen (mouse), super sprawl, a third-world ghetto between 1980 and 1990 and later information-rich laser 'pipes' and androids and biological engineering between 1990 and 2000 – all correct predictions!

Indeed, the combination of the personal computer and light-pen, which would allow 'the individual to sit in one place daydreaming about a project, calling up product after product to see how it suits his taste',[147] was reality by the late 1990s due to the worldwide explosion in the use of the Internet, which began to make redundant such vast out-of-town shopping centres as Roosevelt Field, New York. The rise in affluence, particularly in the US, would not alter the growing inequitable distribution of income: by the year 2000, the concept of the service state, it was said, would not be guaranteed by providing 'free' medical care and housing, since all services have to be paid for by someone, but by giving everyone the purchasing power to select what they want within the restored free marketplace. Such a myth is contradicted by the collapse of communism in the last decade of the twentieth century and the rise of capitalism in such major societies as the former Soviet Union, which teeters on the edge of anarchy. Equally the prediction that the prototypical 'Drop City' would emerge as a major social alternative in the thirty years from 1970 was proved wrong by a new generation totally committed to a consumer society.[148]

The idea of megastructures at this time was described in Reyner Banham's *Megastructure* with the enigmatic sub-title *Urban Futures of the Recent Past*.[149] Prior to his death, Banham had been a professor of Architecture History at University College, London, and later Professor of History and Theory of Architecture at the State University of New York. He had been deeply involved in North American design theory, which was included in *Theory and Design in the First Machine Age* (1960) and, more particularly, in *Los Angeles: the Architecture of Four Ecologies* (1971). Megastructures were the essential concept of massive, multifunctional buildings of the 1960s. Usually, with a disregard for individual human involvement in these super-monuments matching the scale of the modern city, they were considered a new form of adaptable architecture suggesting that citizens would create their own small-scale environments within the huge frameworks. Such ideas of the future were gradually abandoned in the next decade as increasing alarm after the 1973 energy crisis created a more ecologically and socially friendly environment with more modest solutions.

The megastructure solutions were both popular and fashionable in architectural schools around the world, and many city centres, universities and public housing projects reflected this interest. The projects of the Japanese Metabolist Group, led by such architects as Kikutake and Kurokawa or the Archigram Group in the UK, were never built.[150]

As his frontispiece, Banham chose the Lower Manhattan Expressway by Paul Rudolph for New York City in 1970, in which Rudolph cited the medieval structure of the Ponte Vecchio in Florence, Italy, as its precedent. It is also worth noting Banham's declaration that no designed twentieth-century megastructures existed before 1966,[151] as this was not true.

The author's ambivalent attitude towards the central concept of megastructures as the key to the city's future in the late twentieth century is surprising. The Milan Central Station project, designed by Sant' Elia in 1914, was a generator of future machine/city analogies. Sant' Elia was a pioneer of the futurist movement, which was limited to the philosophical ideas of suprematism and those of Nietzsche, and later the fascist movement in Italy.

Also mentioned in Banham's work are Kenzo Tange's ambitious Tokyo Bay project of 1960, preceded by the Boston Harbor development project designed by Kenzo Tange and MIT students in 1959. Like Jencks, Banham criticised Lucio Costa's 1956 master plan for Brasilia as 'the best that conventional Modern Movement planning wisdom had achieved before 1960 but timid and constrained by comparison with Tange's gigantic vision for Tokyo'.[152] The Tokyo proposal was never built, Brasilia was. The Yamanishi Communications Center, Kofu Tokyo, designed by Tange in 1967, was the best example of Tange's built result of a megastructure, albeit on a relatively small scale.

Victor Gruen's earlier Fort Worth scheme in Texas was, in a sense, a megastructure prototype as long ago as 1956. His East Island project in New York City was the first of a series of designs that could have resulted in New York's Welfare Island (later Roosevelt Island) being made into a residential megastructure. Of greater interest was the design submission for the housing competition Welfare Island in 1975 by O. M. Ungers and the Office for Metropolitan Architecture (OMA). In this, Ungers proposed urban blocks as a 'fixed typological unit' in a series of standard variants of a generic theme. Victor Gruen was later joined by Cesar Pelli and participated in the United Nations City Competition for Vienna in 1969. Though never built, their design won first prize. It used two ordering principles from the field of urban commercial architecture and combined them in an original way. The first of these was the tower and podium arrangement of office and supporting buildings familiar from Skidmore Owings and Merrill's much earlier Lever Building on Park Avenue in New York. The second was the use of a spine wall as an ordering element for a series of irregular horizontal elements. The latter theme was used by Pelli in a number of later projects, such as that for the Santa Anita Fashion Park shopping centre in Arcadia, California, where the conventional shopping mall, which normally formed a subservient link between major department stores, emerged out of the building mass to become a large, extruded, open-ended and asymmetric glazed section into the sides of which were plugged the one-off elements.

The Vienna project was much larger in scale, with the major circulation spine supplemented by secondary spurs; against the horizontal extension of these elements were set the offices, not in one tower, but in a whole series of butting towers of varying height. The two ordering ideas were then welded together by locating the range of towers directly over the mall, like the spinal plates of a Stegosaurus, so that the central route also became the generator of the spurs of vertical circulation rising up through the offices.

The scheme that took second place was by the British practice Building Design Partnership, and offered perhaps an even greater coherent image, seen by its designers as a linear city and a microcosm of life and movement.

A more extreme version of the megastructure idea could be seen in the 1968 film *Barbarella*, with Jane Fonda in the leading role. Directed by Roger Vadim, with production design by Mario Garbuglia, and based upon Jean-Claude Forest's intellectual comic strip, this was a science fiction space-opera with strong sexual overtones. The city of Sogo (the city of evil) was an organic form of the megastructure portraying life in a labyrinth as a biomorphic existence. In utter contrast to these organic forms was Stanley Kubrick's version of Arthur C. Clarke's *2001: A Space Odyssey*, produced a year or two later,

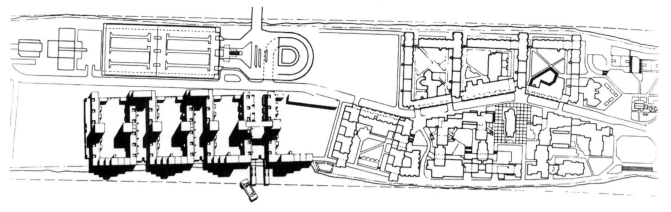

Roosevelt Island, New York (1975), O. M. Ungers.

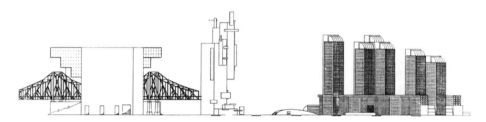

*Cornell University Project,
O. M. Ungers and Rem Koolhaas.*

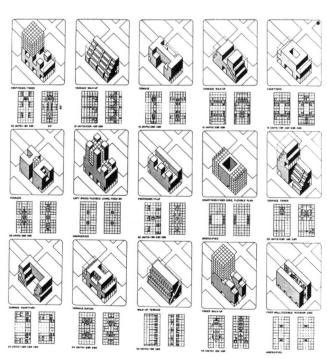

*Welfare Island Competition, New York (1975),
O. M. Ungers.*

in which the imagery of the space station was uncannily like the space station Mir, constructed by Russian scientists and engineers in 1986 with purist, functionalistic hardware.

The 1967 exhibition at the Museum of Modern Art in New York reflected the commitment of architectural students to the ideology of the megastructure. The four schools represented were Cornell, California, Princeton and MIT. The distinguished faculty included David Lewis, Colin Rowe, Fred Koetter, Jonathan Barnett, Peter Eisenman, Stanford Anderson, Michael Graves and Robert Goodman, all of whom later eschewed the relevance of megastructures. It could be said that of these teachers only Peter Eisenman pursued an extension of megastructure ideas in his folded plate systems for Frankfurt and the College of DAAP at the University of Cincinnati in 1997.

URBAN DESIGN AND BUILT FORM

The majority of megastructure designs were never built, and within the same decade there began a transition away from those ideas and towards a growing interest in urban renewal and rehabilitation. Such manifestations were strongest, paradoxically, in retail systems, where the rejection of out-of-town shopping malls resulted in a return to city centres.

The best example of this was perhaps San Francisco, where there were numerous and successful examples of conversion and rehabilitation in relation to shopping. Of these, three were developed in old industrial buildings around Fisherman's Wharf. Ghirardelli Square[153] was formed within a city block of low brick buildings which had formerly housed the Ghirardelli chocolate factory. Demolishing only one wooden structure, a four-storey underground car-park was inserted in the complex of old buildings and a terraced square formed above. Around this, the brick buildings were sand-blasted, gutted and internally arranged to accommodate shops, cafés and offices. Nearby, the Del Monte Fruit Cannery, a building that had survived the 1906 earthquake and fire, was similarly converted. Within the old brick shell the new three-storey structure of the cannery was erected with a maze-like variety of horizontal and vertical, interior and exterior spaces. Across the street, a four-storey warehouse was converted by the same architects, Esherick, Homsey, Dodge and Davis (though for different clients) into two office floors above two levels of fashion shops, restaurants and museums, and the latter again evolved into a network of meandering, intricate routes and spaces threaded through the old structural brick walls and timber columns.

These conversions shared a refreshingly unacademic approach to the old standards upon which they were based. Of the cannery, its architects wrote: 'To us there is too much beady-eyed, dead serious restoration going on, much of which isn't all that good. Old buildings such as this center should be approached with a sense of humor – a common sense approach that acknowledges the building's anachronistic aspects'.

Interesting and useful fragments of the old were seized upon, for example the huge Ghirardelli sign that previously advertised the chocolate factory was illuminated and restored by the architects of the conversion, Wurster, Bernardi and Eammons. New work was carried out in materials sympathetic to the old, although retaining strange elements such as an escalator sliding up the exterior of a brick wall at the cannery. The tenants of these buildings, who were subject to careful control, produced anachronisms of their own. Thus, at the cannery, the 'English Restaurant' reconstructed the long gallery of Albyn's Hall, in England, which was 29 metres (95 feet) long and dated from 1620, a Jacobean staircase and two Elizabethan upper rooms, all authentic and obtained from the William Randolph Hearst estate where they had been in storage.

In Boston, Ben Thompson, designer of the unique Design Research building in Cambridge, Massachusetts, published a rehabilitation plan for the Faneuil Hall Quincy Market Area, Boston, in 1971.[154] The development was composed of three long parallel buildings, of which the centre is the 1824 Quincy Market. The proposal retained the open street character around the block and pedestrian priority. Sheltered arcades contained outdoor traders and sidewalk cafés with continuous shopping and restaurant development along pedestrianised streets, so as to generate both daytime and nighttime activity. The Quincy Market became a food market at second floor level with specialist food trading along an internal street. The central dome of the building became the focal space, with balconies around the rotunda housing specialist shops overlooking the 'crossroads' of the marketplace. The north and south buildings on either side of Quincy Market housed restaurants, nightclubs and boutiques, with emphasis on local restaurants, clubs and cafés under owner management.

Ben Thompson was chairman of the Department of Architecture at the Harvard Graduate School of Design between 1963 and 1967. His Design Research shops were all located in traditional congenial settings: in the Ghirardelli Square complex in the harbour (San Francisco), in an elegant town house in New York, and in a wooden three-storey house in Cambridge. In the US, Design Research became the domestic equivalent of Knoll International. In 1971 it opened a small store, designed by Benjamin Thompson Associates, to market its own particular type of furnishing merchandise. The clientele appeared to be composed of young families with little or no domestic help, and the merchandise was to absorb the clutter of young family life with natural timber finishes, heavy, simple pottery and glassware, vivid, heavy fabrics of cotton or wool and a preference for natural materials over synthetic materials.

The building was planned on seven levels with four floors above ground level and one sunken level visible and accessible from the street. The impact of the building, in urban design terms, is quite remarkable. It is, in a sense, a transparent non-building that utilises both reflection and the absorption of light. Because of its faceted plan, it creates an image of constantly changing volumes as one moves around the building, inside or outside. In daytime it reads as a shimmering opaque shape depending in colour upon the sky and the surrounding landscape. At night, the colour and movement are inside, creating kaleidoscopic patterns; here the designs are brilliant, making the customer more aware of the merchandise on sale than of the display techniques or architectural background.[155]

Ghirardelli Square, San Francisco, California: general view of the urban renewal scheme with the adaptation of a chocolate factory into a shopping centre.

Fisherman's Wharf, San Francisco, California (1958).

Faneuil Hall Market Place, Boston, Massachusetts (1971), Ben Thompson.

*Design Research Building
(1971), Ben Thompson
Associates.*

SUPERGRAPHICS

The impact of supergraphics, particularly in the realm of retail design, has been remarked upon in Charles Jencks' *The Language of Post-Modern Architecture*.[156] The emergence of supergraphics in various forms of retailing was described in *Progressive Architecture* in April 1969: 'retailing is holding out a welcoming hand to the effects of supermannerism . . . in increasing numbers, shops are appearing with ambiguous environment and with a permissive attitude toward customer involvement. Some are kinetic boutiques that offer electrically changing devices to bring the customer closer to the merchandise. Other stores shout for attention with supergraphics. A third direction in store design evidences an interest in systems and construction kits'.[157]

Ulrich Franzen's design for the Paraphernalia group of shops in New York, published in 1969 and completed in 1970, did not use painted or applied supergraphics, but relied entirely on the use of projections. The two sections of the shop-front comprised an opening that extended the full width of the shop and the shop sign, which used white letters on a black background. The illuminated sign flashed a sequence of alternating red and white letters across the name 'Paraphernalia', travelling in the same direction as the traffic along the one-way street. Inside, a screen on the rear wall displayed colour projections of clothing, girls and accessories from three overhead, continuous projectors. Everything else was unobtrusive, the side walls clad in shiny black acrylic and the shop-front glazed with minimal framing. The ceiling was black and the carpet dark brown. The women's clothing on sale could not be seen from the outside and was instead concealed on low racks within circular or semi-circular island units clad in stainless steel. The projections and continuous music had all the atmosphere of a discotheque of the era. Franzen described his design thus: 'The work was an experiment in electrographic architecture. The basic notion was to create a magic box on the sidewalk with moving images illustrating the clothing for sale. Upon entering the store, each customer was handed a remote control for the various projectors to enable her to run through the entire line of products in the hope that this would be of enough interest and stimulus to then lead her to the racks of clothing contained in the stainless steel half cylinders'.[158]

Many of the early interior designs for retail in the late 1960s and early 1970s were carried out entirely with applied paint as this was the least expensive medium. The increasingly sophisticated use of materials from then on included mirror, polyethylene sheetings and silver mylar. Painted mirror images and painted shadows of real objects were also used to extend space and confuse the experience. It was suggested that ultimately a feeling of weightlessness and the hallucination of infinity might be achieved. Synthetic materials such as epoxy resin coating were also used extensively. Electric lighting was developed to produce kinetic experiences in these environments, using neon and tungsten as well as stroboscopic effects. A further development was the use of lasers and holograms for projecting three-dimensional images on walls or even empty space. Jack Larson, an American designer, suggested that 'interior design using an ever changing array of projected color and pattern can be universally and inexpensively available as recorded music'. In combination, a series of mirrors, a laser and a single lamp might fill an entire building with light. At its simplest, automatic slide, film or video projection (then in its infancy) was being used. Retail displays also included the use of sound-controlled lighting in clothing boutiques, which made extensive use of recorded music. There were kaleidoscopic silent projectors as well as liquid light projectors using multicoloured liquids sealed within a projector to create kinetic light shows.

The November 1967 issue of *Progressive Architecture* had already introduced the topic of supergraphics, in which it had praised the use of bold stripes, geometric forms and three-dimensional images at a superscale.[159] It was traced back in the US to Charles Moore's interior designs in 1965 for the Sea Ranch condominium. The techniques used the painted application of giant forms as two-dimensional typefaces and signs on architectural surfaces.

> The aim in using such graphic devices is to produce optical effects that destroy architectural planes, distort corners and explode rectangular boxes that we construct as rooms. . . . Discordant scale is the fundamental force of this graphics technique.[160]

The following year, *Progressive Architecture* was to devote an entire issue to an examination of supergraphics, referring to this new design form as 'mega-decoration of supermannerism'.[161]

THE NEW GALLERIAS

The idea of developing a dense shopping centre form on several levels around one large, full height space appeared in the Galleria at City Post Oak, a rapidly expanding area on the western edge of Houston, Texas. Here, the shopping structure was developed on three levels within a single rectangular block, with a single independent department store located at one end of the major axis. The main mall circulation occupied a zone along the length of this axis, with a large space protruding the full height of the building in its centre and knots of vertical circulation linking the shopping levels at its ends. Gallery malls on the upper levels cantilevered into the central space, overlooking an ice-skating rink at the lowest level and rooted by a glazed barrel vault. This was a twentieth-century interpretation of the famed nineteenth-century Galleria Vittorio Emanuele, Milan, circa 1865–67.[162] External ground level corresponded to the middle of the three shopping levels, at which a single, central cross-mall, with a bridge across the central space, provided a main access to the building. In addition, large multistorey parking garages flanking both long sides of the centre provided direct access to the upper and lower malls. Servicing was accommodated in a continuous route at the lowest level from which there was freight elevator access to service corridors on upper floors.

Designed as 'a total and environmental complex whose key element contained all the vital ingredients of a planned city core', the simple and compact disposition of shopping and parking uses in the Galleria development was supplemented by two office towers and a hotel. The density of site use and the urban quality of its central shopping space gave this develop-

ment a place among integrated centre forms, although its location at the time was less truly urban than most downtown sites, arising from Houston's laissez-faire approach to planning, which 'can be as heartening as a barbecue'.

In terms of its tenant mix, the Galleria was quite unlike any of its European counterparts and was unusual even in North America. The 'compelling opulence' of the Neiman-Marcus department store was matched in the finish of the malls and the list of the other tenancies, which included no less than five art galleries.

Designed by Hellmuth, Obata and Kassabaum for Gerald D. Hines, the Galleria mall was completed in 1970, with further development continuing until 1973.[163]

Other downtown centres in the US included two in the Broadway Plaza area in Los Angeles, incorporating a hotel, office tower, multistorey parking garage, shopping facilities and a mall square arrangement, again christened the 'Galleria'. This term was shared by a number of other developments and was to become almost synonymous with 'mall' for this type of central space in an urban development. The designers' intention was to create 'a lively meeting place with the atmosphere of an old-world street with sidewalk cafés, boutiques, trees, flowers, flowing fountains, graphic displays, benches and antique paving tiles'.[164]

Galleria, Houston, Texas (1970), Hellmuth, Obata and Kassabaum.

The view of urban design as a true representation of the social system and as an expression of choice of use can be represented by the idea of the city as a battleground of competing private interests. The problem of most urban spaces is not how to control unbridled vitality, but how to restore real signs of life.

In retail design this could be said of SITE (Sculpture in the Environment), whose first experiments for the Best Products company depended upon destabilising the predictable image of a supermarket shed by signs of spectacular building failure – a brick outer leaf peeling away, a parapet collapsing in a pile of bricks over the entrance canopy or an entrance formed within the jagged opening at opening time. These architectural jokes worked more dramatically than conventional signs and evoked widespread reactions: 'Police and a frantic motorist bang at the door: "The wind is tearing apart your building!" A local structural engineer, after careful study of the project: "I have dedicated my whole life to preventing things like this". Customer to the store manager: "Your building is shrinking!". I knew I was on the right track when a Texan came along as we were building it and said "That's what I always wanted to do – kick the shit out of it."'[165]

James Wines, Alison Sky and their group went on to explore other surreal architectural devices, reversing wall and ground elements in a project for the Molino Stucky Mills in Venice, Italy, and inserting the building under an undulating asphalt car-park in a showroom proposal for Best Products in Los Angeles. Besides acting as startlingly effective signs, these inversions also probe customary expectations of commercial commentary on the assumptions of planning control. For example, one of SITE's proposals for a Best supermarket involved burying it in a grove of trees. The policy of calling for landscaping to hide obtrusive buildings commonly applied by city and regional planning commissions in the US resulted in buildings being designed with a surrounding trellis structure on outriggers from the main envelope to support a masking screen of creepers, or the more conventional use of earth and grass beams to create a fortification surrounding the retail outlet. But while the purpose of this vegetation was normally one of elaborately contrived camouflage, in the SITE project it was precisely the opposite, since no architectural device could

Ghost parking lot, Hamden Plaza, Connecticut (1977), James Wines and Emilio Sousa.

Indeterminate design, Best supermarket, Texas (1975), James Wines.

York Rest Stop, Interstate 80, Nebraska (1974), Alison Sky.

Undulating car park, Los Angeles, California (1975), James Wines.

have been more obtrusively unexpected in the middle of a car-park than a rural copse.

Robert Venturi's position emanating from *Learning From Las Vegas* in 1972, concluding with a theory of the 'ugly and ordinary architecture,' in which the characteristics of the commercial strip and modern architecture were contrasted, was somewhat different from that of Wines and his team. Both made compelling visual images using dramatic variations of the conventional language of architecture. SITE's images of reversal and collapse, for instance, were witty and artistic manipulations of the spectator's expectations, much as were Giulio Romano's disturbances of the classical language of Renaissance architecture four centuries earlier. While Wines' jokes are more effective for being unexpected and uncommon, Venturi's strip is offered as a universal, generic model of one possible form of urbanism.

SOCIAL SOLUTIONS: THE CITY AS AN EXPRESSION OF SOCIAL ORDER

The apparent impossibility of making any technical decision about the city without thereby implying a corresponding social structure has persuaded many designers of the primacy of the social programme. Urban design is thus seen essentially as the attempt to find an appropriate form to sustain this programme or perhaps, more actively, to reinforce or even induce it.

A few examples have been chosen here, from innumerable possibilities, beginning with the work of a Massachusetts design group of this period. Arrowstreet, Inc.'s projects for relatively prosperous coastal communities in California and Aquitaine, France, explored the possibilities, through design, for reconciling conflict within the social programme and for developing an appropriate formal vocabulary from it. Through these case studies we can examine examples of particular social organisation types.

Although the coastal suburbs of Los Angeles serve one of the most affluent communities, their development still involves the usual reconciliation of public and private interests into coherent and appropriate social patterns. In 1972, a project at Laguna Niguel was halted by such a problem, arising from Proposition 20 and the establishment of the California Coastal Commission. This statement of public interest in preserving the integrity of the coastal strip, and public access to it, was in conflict with the established pattern of suburban sprawl; in 1979, the State Commission accepted a new plan, prepared by John Myer, Richard Krauss and Robert Slattery of Arrowstreet, as a basis for accommodating the various demands upon the site.

Arrowstreet's plan adopted all the specific topographical and landscape features of the site, and used these to orchestrate the patterns of density of occupation and land use – including a commercial centre, school, golf course and beachside hotel complex that were required in addition to the dominant residential use. Thus the housing increased in density as the land rose away from the beach, and followed corresponding changes in the character of the vegetation, from low, dense, evergreens providing protection from the wind and views along the ocean front, to the tall, dense grove planting along the hilltops behind. Similarly, the destination resort hotel, associated with a public park route leading from the centre of the site down to the beach, was designed with a terraced form that adapted itself to the natural bluffs overlooking the ocean.

The Laguna Niguel project thus used landscape as a metaphor and prescription for social harmony, in which the civilised, unassertive accommodation of each private need, hidden under 'a green mantle of vines, trees and green tiled roofs' does not intrude upon the primary communion between each individual resident or visitor and the beach, framed by its 'natural' hinterland. The solution contrasted neatly with a second project by Arrowstreet, for Port d'Albret New Town on the Aquitaine coast of France, in which the metaphor is urban rather than natural, and for which a more explicit statement of the rules governing development became necessary.

This master plan for a holiday community, designed for a consortium of the French government, a private developer and a tourism cooperative, again required the acknowledgement of an existing context, in this case the timber-frame architectural tradition of the Landes region. The requirements, which also placed emphasis on the expression and personalisation of the individual units, tended to clash with both the process of implementation and the desire to emulate the visual creation of the traditional architecture of the region. The balance between public order and private freedom, between community and privacy, takes on a particularly illuminating aspect here.

The Laguna Niguel project of Arrowstreet in 1979 also had an interesting parallel in an earlier proposal by Kevin Lynch and Donald Appleyard for the San Diego regional study in Mission Valley, California, in 1975.

THE DESIGN OF VILLAGES

In addition to being, in practical terms, a special case of certain general urban design problems, the village has also provided a metaphor for the larger town. This sense of compacted scale is particularly evoked in the most artful of villages, Portmeirion, built by Clough Williams-Ellis for himself on the North Wales coast of the UK. Williams-Ellis was a close friend of Frank Lloyd Wright who shared with him a Welsh ancestry. Portmeirion provided a key to other projects for which the idea of 'village' is a central reference.

An excellent example of this was provided by the design of Charles Moore and William Turnbull for Kresge College, part of the Santa Cruz campus of the University of California. Completed in 1974, and built in a secluded forest setting, the community for resident students with its library, dining hall and other common facilities was housed in an irregularly grouped sequence of stuccoed wood-frame buildings along a meandering street. The street was structured, first by the disposition of the main common buildings at its ends, like magnet stores in a shopping centre, and then by a series of 'idiosyncratic landmarks', or 'trivial monuments' as the architects called them, set out along its length – an entrance gate, fountain,

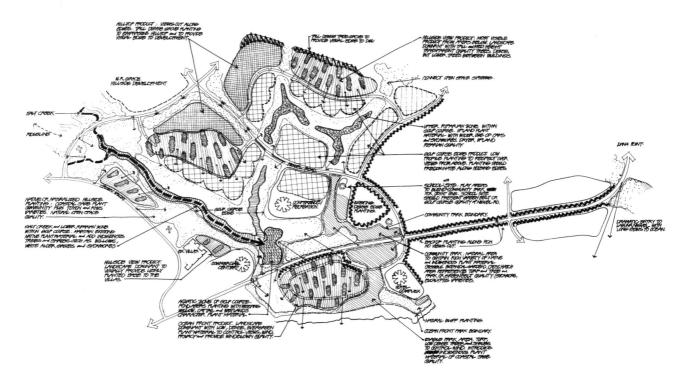

Laguna Niguel, Los Angeles, California (1979),
Arrowstreet, Inc.

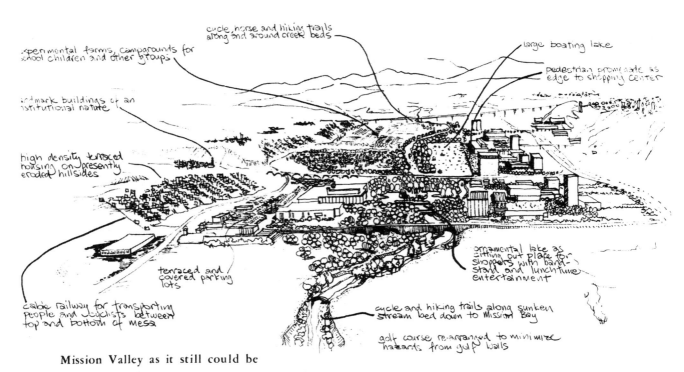

Mission Valley as it still could be

Plan: San Diego, Mission Valley, California (1975),
Donald Appleyard.

speaker's rostrum painted red, white and blue, and so on. 'These are meant, without prejudicing the freedom of students to make their own institutions, to signal to them where they are'. The jokey, theatrical element that this project shares with Portmeirion is not accidental. It makes it possible for the designer to offer an ordering framework without seeming to impose it and to enrich his settings with historical or memorial anecdotes that everyone knows, without loss of pleasure, to have been made only yesterday. Perhaps for the city dweller it is almost impossible to approach the village in any other way.

The links between Kresge College and other village developments can also be traced to the world of Obie Bowman (at Sea Ranch in California, 1975), which Moore had initiated. The 'Walk-in' cabins received the American Institute of Architects twentieth annual award that year. Following the general philosophy of Sea Ranch, the development was not on the edge of the Pacific coast, but on a rugged hillside where the primary concern was minimising the visual and physical impact on the land. The developer's wish was to provide retreats that would increase an experience of the natural environment. As at Sea Ranch, cars were restricted to a single parking area, and access was by means of a series of foot trails. The two-storey dwellings maximised the volume of enclosed structure relative to the floor area in simple unpretentious forms covered by natural redwood boards and shingles.[166]

Such an approach was also evident in the 1976 study on the East Coast in Martha's Vineyard.[167] While this was not a proposal for a new village, it was a proposal to preserve the rural qualities for which Martha's Vineyard was famous. The introduction to the report stated that: 'A special feature of Martha's Vineyard has long been the freedom of movement across the island, along quiet roads and on paths through fields and wood-

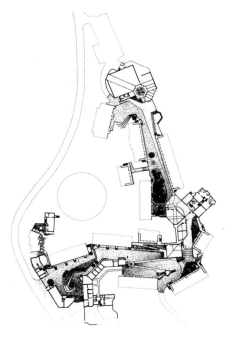

Kresge College, University of California (1974), Charles Moore and William Turnbull.

land. This opportunity is threatened by the pressures of an ever expanding recreational and residential community. As the landscape changes, many of the old trails are disappearing'.[168]

Emphasis on horse-riding along the trails gave 'an ideal opportunity for enjoying the island's richly varied terrain. Abandoned roads lead the rider through dense woodland, next to stone walls and across hilly meadows, affording perhaps a special glimpse of the sea. Fall and spring are the best months for riding in the woods and along the edges of open fields. Summer equestrian outings often take the form of long beach rides'.[169] Among the consultants for this study was Kevin Lynch, and though his contribution is hard to determine, as a resident of the island, it seems possible that his own passionate beliefs were present here.

The problem with the trails was that riders lacked a continuous system of riding loops in their neighbourhoods and of connecting links giving access to the State Forest and other connecting trails. Road shoulders are often not wide enough for safe travel on narrow roads.

Nature trails were equally important. Martha's Vineyard had over 530 hectares (1,300 acres) of open space reserved and open to the public for learning and enjoyment. In addition to protecting the fragile natural areas and wildlife habitats, the sanctuaries provided the walker and rider with the opportunity to discover the island's varied landscape and see birds and other wildlife in their natural habitats.

The vivid and evocative sketches contained within the report illustrated the way in which trail design could be improved, for example by aligning trails near streams, ponds or by the edge of woods, to emphasise the edge. Where a trail passed close to home, the trail should be aligned to take advantage of a physical or visual buffer.

The report also identified cycle trails. Martha's Vineyard had always been a special place for cyclists. The island's narrow scenic roads that wind through the gently rolling countryside connecting the historic villages were always popular for this recreational sport; however, there was growing conflict between motorists and cyclists, who were more numerous than horse riders. It was not until the late 1960s that the bicycle returned to Martha's Vineyard as a necessary part of the island's transportation system. Among the criticism of cycle trails was that their current 2.5-metre (8-feet) width did not allow cyclists riding two abreast to pass other cyclists. The report noted that cycling is a congenial activity and riders tend to talk and ride side by side.[170]

The Martha's Vineyard study was not about built form, but the preservation of a heavily used rural landscape. A central reason for the popularity of the island was its rural character and the village-like quality of its settlements.

A more curious contribution by American designers to the concept of village settlements was the Manila International Competition in the Philippines in 1976.[171] This was to coincide with the United Nations Habitat Conference. Sponsored by the Chicago-based Graham Foundation for Advanced Studies in the Fine Arts, the Rockefeller Foundation, the International Development Research Center of Canada and the National Endowment for the Arts among many other North American

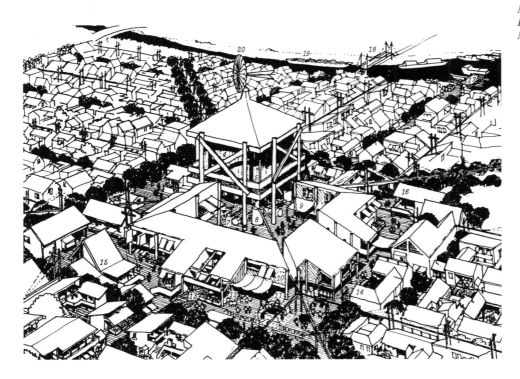

Manila International Competition, Freebairn Smith, Crane, Grundstein, Meier, Philippines (1976).

contributors, it was intended to assemble designs for low-cost settlements in order to meet the problems of rapid and uncontrolled urbanisation around major cities in developing countries, this time based on a site in the Tondo freeshore of Manila. It became apparent from the competition conditions issued by the sponsoring body, the International Architectural Foundation (formed by the two architectural magazines *Architectural Record* (USA) and *L'Architecture d'Aujourd'hui* (France)) and from subsequent events, that the attitude of the international architectural community and of the proposed recipients of such designs had changed. As the sponsors noted: 'The world's urbanization problems are such that it is not possible to talk of an "architectural solution" or perhaps of any "solution", although it is possible for architects to make their contribution'.

Although the competition conditions were broadly similar, indicating low-rise, high-density, low-cost solutions for the planning of 500 dwellings on a five-hectare (12-acre) site, greater emphasis than before was placed on the need for establishing the self-sufficiency of the community in terms of public services, employment and construction effort. Although the site was already occupied by a squatter settlement operating at a density more than 50 per cent higher than that of the competition brief, the plan was to involve the minimum relocation of residents, who were also to be consulted on its implementation (though not on the choice of the competition winner). The main design problems seemed to be those of appropriate building technology and community form, but in practice both sponsors and competitors seemed much more conscious of another problem underlying both of these – the degree to which any design could be imposed from outside. What precisely did 476 design teams from around the world have to offer their 3,500 user-clients in Manila? This was a question asked by the squatters themselves when many of them were arrested for protesting against the refusal of the Philippine authorities to allow a group of their representatives to visit the Habitat Forum in Vancouver, where the competition entries were displayed.

It was perhaps a sensitivity to this issue that principally distinguished the winning entry by the New Zealander, Ian Athfield, since it comprised in essence a system of almost defensive enclosures within which community subdivisions of the whole town could operate with a high degree of autonomy.

There was considerable disagreement among the competitors over just how much of such planning was necessary for the community. The Californian team of Freebairn-Smith, Crane, Grundstein and Meier, for instance, while accepting the *baranguay* (500–750 families) subdivision of the town, and the idea of a focal centre, advocated as little further control as possible. In particular, they disagreed with Athfield's control of building materials 'to give visual unity to the *baranguay*', advocating rather that 'restricted only by lot configuration', every family would build according to its immediate needs and its resources'.

Of the other American entries, an honourable mention was awarded to Steven Hall, James Tanner and John Cropper of San Francisco.[172] Perhaps less imaginative than the submission by Freebairn-Smith *et. al.*, the designers offered a highly structured overall site plan with a great degree of flexibility for the individual and the family with their 'spontaneous' house plans.[173] Other American entries to receive honourable mention were those of Jim Fong and Robert Olwell, and Helmuth, Obata and Kassabaum, both of San Francisco.

A final ironic comment on the competition was provided by Mrs Imelda Marcos, first lady of the Philippines and Governor of Metropolitan Manila, who, concurrently with the competition, ordered the construction of 500 housing units in the area of the site as a demonstration project. Too expensive for the Tondo squatters, and diametrically opposed in philosophy and approach to the intentions of the competition sponsors, it was attacked by confused critics of the competition who assumed that it was Athfield's prize-winning design, which in fact was never built.

URBAN DESIGN AS TECHNIQUE

The pursuit by Thiel, Appleyard and others of a more complete and precise method of describing the visual phenomena of the city, suggested that an annotative method would itself lead to the reform of the subject of its study. As mentioned earlier, the line of enquiry begun at MIT in the 1950s was further developed by Appleyard in his Environmental Simulation Laboratory at the University of California, Berkeley, during the 1970s. There, the search for an accurate method of simulating and testing alternative planning proposals was substantially achieved via extremely realistic models through which a periscope with a tiny movable lens, mounted on an elaborate overhead gantry system, was remotely controlled in response to either hand or computer directions. Thus film of a simulated walk or drive through a familiar environment incorporating proposed developments could be debated by interested parties.

At MIT, the Architecture Machine Group developed two extraordinary mixed-media projects, 'Movie Map' and 'Dataland', which used responsive computer techniques to provide a detailed journey through a chosen area. Seated before a 2.4 × 3.3 metre (8 × 12 feet) screen in an armchair equipped with joystick controls and touch-sensitive monitor screens, the viewer could zoom down from satellite pictures of, say, the East Coast of the US into a particular city area and then proceed along its streets. The observer could stop and look into or out of nearby buildings and add sound to the experience (provided, of course, the computer had previously been supplied with the appropriate slides and film). The first Movie Map was made in Aspen, Colorado, for a conference, and further developed in the more elaborate Dataland project. This could add 'virtual' objects to the screen to support the visual programme, for instance a calculator or reference book that could be manipulated by normal hand movements to the touch-sensitive monitors (to 'turn the pages' of a book for example).

By means of such techniques, the urban designer could perform the main function, which was presumably seen as formulating and presenting the problem as accurately and vividly as possible. In this, the approach is similar to other investigations of design methods in the 1960s. Christopher Alexander's *Notes on the Synthesis of Form*,[174] for example, described a process for the design of an Indian village that attempted to reconcile all the functional requirements of the problem by its meticulous breakdown into its most basic statements and their subsequent recomposition according to rational, mathematical procedures. Again, to take an example which, if less intellectually rigorous, resulted in a considerably greater volume of building, Skidmore, Owings and Merrill's use of

'Field Theory' in the late 1960s generated plans with highly elaborate octagonal geometries from the application of overtly natural methods of activity analysis and grid overlays.[175]

It may be objected, however, that while an accurate statement of the problem is invaluable, and may lead to a more rational debate, it cannot in itself provide solutions. Further, the pursuit of apparently authoritative and neutral techniques may mask those value judgements that urban design problems invariably entail. A rhetorical commentary on the search for new descriptive and analytical methods to pin down such elusive problems is provided by those who have presented the record of the act of creating the work of art as the work itself. An example of this is Bernard Tschumi, whose exhibition 'Manhattan Transcripts', held at Artists Space, New York, in April 1978, set out to represent, by methods not dissimilar to those earlier identified at MIT, an urban sequence of events. In this case, however, the photographs, plans and schematic diagrams of movement recorded not a progression of landmarks, nodes and paths, but a violent crime and the murderer's subsequent movements to evade capture.[176]

Bernard Tschumi, later Dean of Architecture at Columbia University, New York, was to become renowned for his prize-winning entry for La Villette competition in Paris in 1983. Prior to that he had been a tutor at the Architectural Association School in London among distinguished company including Rem Koolhaas, Leon Krier, Peter Cook and Ron Herron. In his 'Advertisements for architecture' in 1978 he said: 'The game of architecture is an intricate play with rules that you may break or accept. These rules, like so many knots that cannot be untied, have the erotic significance of bondage: the more numerous and sophisticated the restraints, the greater the pleasure'.

PROFESSIONAL RECOGNITION OF URBAN DESIGN

The periodical *Progressive Architecture* had long been known for its annual design awards programme for future building projects. Surprisingly, the urban design category was not introduced until the 1970s, and a mean-spirited attitude on the part of the 1972 jury resulted in neither award nor citations. The 1973 jury of Edward Logue, Archibald Rogos and Rai Okamoto (who had been joint author of the 1970 San Francisco Urban Design Study) gave three awards and five citations. Their concerns were much more pragmatic and their evaluation of projects had less to do with relating programme information to solutions than that of the previous year's jurors.

Edward Logue, President and Chief Executive Officer of the New York State Development Corporation, questioned whether the proposal was appropriate and, pertinently, whether it was likely to be built. Most of the designs submitted were low-key and anti-monumental. Such was the case of Michael and Susan Southworth's 'Lowell Discovery Network', which was intended to be a total learning environment in Lowell, Massachusetts, aiming to provide an opportunity for economic rejuvenation and create an attraction for tourists. The solution was to provide a continuous open-space system centred on the historic canal system, with cycle and pedestrian paths passing through, along with discovery centres and historic and industrial sites.[177]

The following year the format had changed to a confusing division of 'Recycle', 'Environmental Response', 'Machines', 'The Planning Jury: Issues Not Answers', and 'The Research Jury: Establishing the Program'. Such confusion was compounded by the inclusion of the BOSTCO project (Boston), the Metropolitan Bikeway (Atlanta), and the Design Review Massachusetts General Hospital in the category of research, and of the Lower Manhattan Waterfront (New York City) and the Oak Park Community Development Plan (Ventura County, California), as 'issues' for the planning jury.

The urban planning jury (there was no urban design jury) was composed of distinguished practitioners and academicians Denise Scott-Brown and Jaquelin Robertson. Over a hundred submissions were considered and the two jurors admitted bias in that they felt that learning from developers' language (dealing with image and design of the mass market) was a new role for the architect. Of these, the San Antonio River Corridor Study was probably the most fruitful, given the distinguished record of that city from the 1930s in recognising its most important physical attribute.[178] The report by Skidmore, Owings and Merrill with Kaplan, Gans and Kahn resulted in a planning framework allowing for large- and small-scale steps effecting a remarkable riverfront growth that was largely implemented.

The evident problem in most of the *Progressive Architecture*'s design award juries over the years was a cantankerous disposition in which everything seemed to be wrong and little right. In 1975, only three projects were recognised, and only one award and two citations were given. The jurors, Joyce Whiteley and Lee Copeland, reviewed 104 submissions, which were listed by the magazine as 'Urban Design and Planning' awards (though the distinction between urban design and planning was not made clear). The jurors felt that few of the design or planning proposals addressed all the issues they considered necessary. There was an 'absence of proposals that acknowledge the entire scope of planning and design considerations, including defining the problem'. The new open-ended flexible approach resulted in a number of planning studies that avoided concrete conclusions and tangible solutions. Rather, many urban design and planning studies were concerned with compiling inventories of the existing environments. The sole award that year[179] was a study by Warren W. Gran and Associates for a new zoning district in Clinton in the west mid-town section of New York City, to preserve a low-rise, low-income neighbourhood while allowing for high-density development.

In 1976, the urban design and planning awards and citations were much more imaginative. The jurors were Donald Appleyard and Raquel Ramati. Paramount in their considerations was the idea that schemes should be realisable not only in physical terms but specifically in that they are modified and conditioned by the economic and social realities of the day.[180] Of these, the most notable was the Piazza d'Italia in New Orleans, which reused old commercial structures to commemorate the achievements of the Italian community. The architects August Perez and Associates involved Charles Moore in the

planning and execution of this public space between 1975 and 1978. As Geoffrey Broadbent noted in his book, *Emerging Concepts in Urban Space Design*,[181] Charles Moore had gained second place in the competition by focusing on a fountain, designed by Moore as a map of Italy in relief and providing a sense of magic. Such a focus had been lacking in the scheme by Perez and Associates.

A completely different direction was seen in 1977 in the twenty-fourth awards programme.[182] The jurors, Raymond Affleck and Ernest Bonner, awarded a citation to the Community Design Center in San Francisco, California. This was not a tangible project in itself but the forerunner of an idea that was to gain momentum the following decade. The Yerba Buena Planning Ballot gave the public a voice regarding decisions for a controversial urban renewal project. Located in the Market Street neighbourhood of downtown San Francisco, it was intended to provide an effective way for citizens to make decisions, register opinions or select ideas from the multitude of proposals made. There was no physical plan but rather a ballot divided into three parts, as a means of expressing preferences on the most important facets of the projects. Other awards and citations were made to the Massachusetts Audubon Society, in the Great Miami River project, Dayton, Ohio, and Arrowstreet's Bicentennial Celebration in Boston.

The schemes acknowledged the following year were curious. Given the revolutionary turmoil that was about to erupt in Iran, proposals for a new city centre for Tehran as well as a new town

Piazza d'Italia, New Orleans, Louisiana (1973), Charles Moore.

proposal seemed, perhaps, inappropriate. The first award in the category, by Sanoff, Smith, Liberatore, and Polston, for plan alternatives for the National Register Historic District in Murfreesboro, North Carolina, was more realistic in providing a workbook to aid citizens of a small town to make decisions about preservation, restoration, and future growth.[183]

At the close of the decade, the 1979 awards featured one of the best collaborative schemes by Donald Appleyard and his original tutor, Kevin Lynch.[184] This was their project for the San Diego region in California, entitled 'Temporary Paradise: A Look at the Special Landscape of the San Diego Region'. The jury noted: 'It is interesting at a time when we emphasize inter-disciplinary team work, two people can come up with a poetic and personal kind of statement, speaking very much as individuals, but without sacrificing their sense of community needs'.

ARCADIA AND THE MULTI-TECHNIC CITY

Designer Emilio Ambasz has provided some ingenious clues as to how a soft urban technology might operate in his remark, 'Europe's eternal quest remains Utopia, the myth of the end. America's returning myth is Arcadia, the eternal beginning'.[185] Ambasz's designs for the latter, in a project for a cooperative of Mexican grape growers in California, emphasises the interdependence of natural, cultivated and built structures, with the grapevines, suspended on wire grids, forming a shady 'roof' to

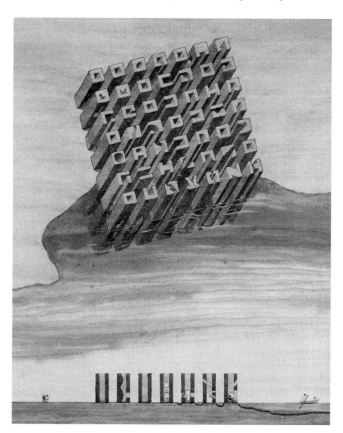

Mexican-American grape growers cooperative, Southern California (1979), Emilio Ambasz.

areas of settlement and cultivation below. While the pursuit of the 'eternal beginning' may be appropriate for the citizens of California, its offer by a government agency to the poverty-stricken aboriginal population of the Peruvian Andes must seem ironic. Nevertheless, Ambasz's project for the Commision de Integración Nacional demonstrates a similar novelty of approach. The 'hard technology' response to the problems of the inhabitants of the high Valle de Huallanco – isolation, illiteracy, disease, poverty, and periodic devastation by sudden river floods – might have taken the form of a major dam-building project or the resettlement of the population elsewhere. Instead, Ambasz proposed the construction of a series of 12 square metre (130 square feet) barges in Peru's idle shipyards, and towing these upstream to be anchored in one of a variety of appropriate configurations at each existing village, providing classrooms and communal areas and places of refuge at flood time. His strategy of 'making peace with the river' was further developed by equipping some barges with paddle wheels to generate electricity from the river's current, mainly to refrigerate food and to receive UNESCO's satellite-linked educational television broadcasts. Finally, two-year-old river gun-boats were to be refitted, one as a hospital ship and the other as an educational ship, first to tow the barges into position and then to visit the villages in rotation.

Ambasz also used the idea of the barge as a building that does not impose itself too permanently on the landscape in a design for the Center for Applied Computer Research and Planning (Centro Mexicano de Cálculo Aplicado SA) outside Mexico City. Here, a 150 square metre (1,600 square feet) water basin would be required for site drainage and would act as the location for the office work spaces required by the programme, provided by barges floated into appropriate positions and then settled in shallow water by flooding their ballast tanks. Two large walls 28 metres (90 feet) high and 150 metres (500 feet) long contain two adjacent sides of the lagoon and act as a 'site mark' for further developments on the estate. One wall is a solar energy gathering device and the other is an information wall displaying messages and information on current research projects. Above the platform hovers a cloud, 'conceived as an architectural element', created by pressurising water through specially designed nozzles and then pumping by windmills around the centre, and which cools the outdoor climate. Ambasz provided his own commentary on the transitional nature of this design on the road to Arcadia: 'The users understand the architect's basic premise that "Nobody should have to work. If present circumstances so constrain us, at least it should be possible to do it from home.[186] There is not, therefore, a real need for a large building but for a relatively small installation to house the computer and receive messages". But the users also feel they are not yet ready for such a radical arrangement. The building has been conceived, therefore, as composed of elements which may be progressively removed, as courage grows and the need for physical space diminishes. Then, only the silent walls and a single barge turned into an island of flowers will remain'.[187]

Ambasz's idyllic evocation of an alternative soft urban technology remains in the polarised forms of hardware comprising on the one hand the bristling high-tech hardware offered by the

Center for Applied Computer Research, Mexico City (1975), Emilio Ambasz.

Pompidou Centre in Paris by Renzo Piano and Richard Rogers (1971–77), and on the other the gentle low-tech Arcadia.

It could be argued that a mono-technic city, such as was implied by the modern movement, is a functionally inappropriate concept, better replaced by the notion of a bi-technic city comprising two distinct technological zones. Such was the basis of the otherwise repulsive Nazi *Blut und Boden* philosophy in which the monumental and technically advanced places of work and public ritual envisaged for the city centre by Albert Speer or Ernst Sagebiel contrasted with the vernacular hearth-and-home associations of the residential *Schaffendes Volk* estates. This is surely the case with the actual condition of most Western cities, particularly in North America, divided into the technological zones of the commercial downtown or central business districts on the one hand, and on the other, suburban 'houses with clapboard siding and a high-pitched roof and shingles and gaslight-style front porch lamps and mail boxes set on top of stiffened chain that seemed to defy gravity'.[188] It could further be argued that such a bi-technic division is itself a crude simplification of the ancient association of the most advanced and expensive technology with the most powerful building types, which themselves tend to congregate in the areas of highest land value. This suggests a picture of the city as a spectrum of technologies, hierarchically ordered from the most exotic house of God, king, state, or business corporation, to the most modest structure for the domestic pet.

The idealisation of a mono-technic city can also be challenged by the reality of a multi-technic one in the sense that at any one moment a city in fact comprises comparatively few examples of newly formed, precisely contemporary construction, together with a huge mass of steadily obsolescent material that is undergoing, to a greater or lesser extent, a continual process of modification. We may recognise this as a matter of fact, but we may also welcome it as a fundamental characteristic of a valid urban design approach in which the city is seen as an unpredictable compound of technologies. Banal as this truism may be, there are few examples of designs that suggest where such an approach might lead. While designers have

readily accepted fragments, or indeed whole envelopes of existing older structures into their compositions, they have generally regarded the technological purity of the new element to be sacrosanct.

It must be said, however, that for most urbanists the question of appropriate technology is not considered so much a matter of survival, as Buckminster Fuller would regard it, but rather as a route to the discovery, or authorisation, of an appropriate formal language for the city, the problem of which forms a second common preoccupation among designers. Thus in the conventional development control debate between private interest and public authority, materials, forms and patterns of elements may be sought to be 'in keeping' with existing models – that is to say to 'represent' an equivalent technology to that used elsewhere.

One way out of the impasse of a messy environment that immediately loses its saving characteristic (its vitality) as soon as one attempts to regulate it or absorb it into a public culture, is to regard the public presence not as an ordering discipline for private display, but simply as a third party – a connective theme that surfaces from time to time at significant points in the city. This approach was suggested by Emilio Ambasz in his 1975 project for Grand Rapids, Michigan, in which an abandoned federal building was rehabilitated as a new Community Arts Center. Between the wings of the beaux-arts building, Ambasz proposed the insertion of a large inclined plane acting both as a translucent canopy to the enclosed forecourt and as a monumental flight of steps up to the grand foyer at first-floor level. On either side of this stairway, it was intended that water would flow down the inclined surface as a silent cascade visible from across the public space facing the building. Apart from these specific functions, however, the tilted plane was envisaged as the first of a series and 'as an architectural sign whenever there is a need to identify other abandoned city buildings recovered by and for the Community Arts Center'.[189]

Quite the opposite was true of Richard Meier's Bronx Developmental Center in New York City in 1975. Not an Arcadian philosophy, it demonstrated the ability of a clear social programme to evoke a correspondingly lucid architectural solu-

*Community Arts Center, Grand Rapids, Michigan (1975–79),
Emilio Ambasz.*

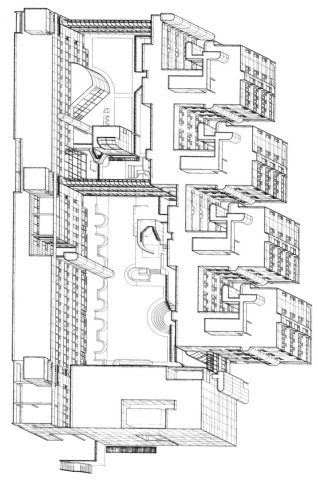

*Bronx Development Center, New York City (1975),
Richard Meier.*

tion. Architecture at its highest level was a very specialised case of a medium-density neighbourhood, and provided an excellent illustration of the way in which a highly architectonic solution can be generated by the structure of the programme and its hierarchies of public and private space. Accommodating 350 resident physically and mentally handicapped children as well as providing outpatient and extensive technical support facilities, the Bronx Developmental Center is situated in a blighted industrial area and is also concerned with the creation of a sense of place. Its success in doing so makes it a relevant source for the urban designer, and not least because it derived both its social and its architectural form precisely from 'the rational and schematic ordination of territory'.

The complex is organised in two parallel spines with sheltered courtyard space between. The western spine block, containing support services, forms a neutral screen to the site approach and car-parking areas. It is linked by bridges, one open and one glazed, across the courtyard to the parallel eastern block, from which the L-shaped residential groups grow out to the east in echelon formation, defining small, partially enclosed courtyards along the eastern edge of the complex. There is thus a layering of functions across the building from west to east,

from public to private, enlivened by the introduction of specialist elements along the way. The uses and organisation of the building thus elegantly correspond. The organising principle of zones layered one on another is reflected in the detailed architectural treatment. The sense of order, unity, and yet of great formal richness and invention offers an unsentimental model for architecture as an ordering, yet liberating, social framework.

Fascinating as this range of opinions on the questions of technology and formal language may be, it is difficult to adopt a coherent position without considering a third area of common concern, as most statements of technical or formal position beg further questions about the scope and purpose of urban design itself: What is the nature of the design problem posed by urban design? What are the aims and limitations of the urban designer's activity? If we consider these questions while studying the proposals and statements of designers, we must soon conclude that their arguments develop from very different assumptions as to the nature of their task. The identification of these attitudes may thus provide us with a useful appraisal of alternative future directions for urban design. In each case the initial premises lead to specific implications for the designer and are open to particular critiques.

NOTES

1. Sennett, Richard (1970) *The Uses of Disorder: Personal Identity and City Life.* Harmondsworth: Penguin Books, p. 53.

2. Berry, Brian and Larry S. Bourne (eds) (1971) 'General features of urban commercial structure', in *International Structure of the City.* New York: Oxford University Press, pp. 361–67.

3. See Alonso, William. 'A theory of the urban land market', Berry and Bourne, ibid., pp. 154–59.

4. Davidoff, Paul and S. Anderson (eds) (1968) 'Normative planning', in *Planning for Diversity and Choice.* Cambridge, MA: MIT Press, pp. 173–79.

5. Abrams, Charles (1965) *The City is the Frontier.* New York: Harper Colophon Books, p. 3.

6. See Gosling, D. and B. Maitland (1984) *Concepts of Urban Design*, Part One: 'The Nature of the Problem'. London: Academy Editions, p. 9, ff.

7. Harvey, David (1973) *Social Justice and the City.* London: E Arnold pp. 61–62.

8. Webber, Melvin, A. Blowers, C. Hamnet and P. Sarre (eds) (1974) *'Permissive Planning' in the Future of Cities.* London: Hutchison Educational and Open University Press, p. 223.

9. Rittel, J., W. Horst, Melvin Webber, N. Cross, D. Elliott, and R. Roy (eds) (1974) *Wicked Problems in Man-Made Futures.* London: Hutchinson Educational and Open University Press, p. 272.

10. Goodman, Robert (1972) *After the Planners.* Harmondsworth: Pelican Books, p. 163.

11. Harvey (1972). 'Social processes, spatial form and the redistribution of real income in an urban system', in Murray Stewart (ed.) *The City: Problems of Planning.* Harmondsworth: Penguin Books, p. 302.

12. Turner, John and Robert Fichter (eds) (1972) *Freedom to Build.* New York: Macmillan, p. 250.

13. Ibid., p. 241.

14. Ward, Colin (1974) *Tenants Take Over.* London: Architectural Press Limited.

15. Goodman, op.cit.

16. Mumford, Lewis (1966) *The City in History.* Harmondsworth: Penguin Books, pp. 655–56.

17. Toffler, Alvin (1970) *Future Shock.* London: The Bodley Head. Predictions of the future were numerous during this period. However, the amazing transformations that occurred at the end of the twentieth century from 1990 onwards – in particular the growing sophistication of information technology and the Internet – were to suggest the first implosion of the traditional city in history and a lifestyle pattern that was unpredictable even as recently as 1970.

18. Rykwert, Joseph (1976) *The Idea of a Town.* London: Faber and Faber, p.190.

19. Robert Goodman was an Associate Professor of Architecture when he wrote *After the Planners.* Goodman was particularly virulent in his comments against Daniel P. Moynihan who, ironically, given his later liberal views, as he stepped down as a Democratic Senator in the year 2000, was in 1969 President Nixon's chief planner in residence. He had previously served under President Kennedy as Assistant Secretary of Labor. In a memo, according to Goodman, to President-elect Nixon, he said of African-Americans that 'they are not going to become capitalists, nor even middle-class functionaries. But it is fully reasonable to conceive them being transformed into a stable working class population . . . people with dignity, purpose, and, in the United States, a very good standard of living indeed'. Goodman also states that Moynihan, in referring to urban design, suggested that political leaders in the US had an inability to insist on the right kinds of architecture which had led to 'a steady deterioration in the quality of public buildings and spaces, and with it a decline in the symbols of public unity and common purpose with which the citizen can identify.' This was a view expressed some years earlier in Adolf Hitler's views on city design in *Mein Kampf*: '[O]ur cities of the present lack the outstand-ing symbol of national community which, we must therefore not be surprised to find, sees no symbol of itself in the cities. The inevitable result is a desolation whose practical effect is the total indifference of the big-city dweller to the density of the city'. Hitler, Adolf (1943) *Mein Kampf.* Boston: Houghton Mifflin, p. 266.

20. Sennett, op. cit.

21. Jacobs, Jane (1961) *The Death and Life of Great American Cities.* New York: Modern Library.

22. Newman, Oscar (1972) *Defensible Space: People and Design in the Violent City.* London: The Architectural Press.

23. In 1969, a public housing project was completed in Irvine new town, Scotland. This was not dissimilar from the later San Francisco project cited by Newman. In Pennyburn, designed by David Gosling, the two-storey row of houses were developed around pedestrian squares with vehicular entry only at the head of each square and pedestrian-only access at the rear of each house. Surveillance was possible from the first-floor living room at the front of the house so that children playing in the square could be watched over. The designer lived in one of these houses for two-and-a-half years as an experiment in understanding the issues of public housing with a family of very young children. The scheme failed, ironically, because of lack of privacy. The density was considered too high, the private backyards too small, and the lack of mobility (where car ownership was minimal) of the Scottish low-income families as opposed to their American counterparts meant that recreational opportunities were limited. Too many children played in the communal square and landscaping deteriorated. It was thus falla-cious on the part of the architect to assume that low-income families with a lack of mobility could deal with an urban environment in which higher-income families with cars could live happily. Privacy should have been a greater priority. See Gosling and Maitland, op. cit. Also Gosling, D. (ed.) 'Irvine New Town Plan', Irvine Development Corporation, Scotland.

24. Newman, op. cit., p. 204, ff.

25. Habraken, Nicholas and B. Valkenburg (trans.) (1972) *Supports: An Alternative to Mass Housing.* London: The Architectural Press, pp. 10–29.

26. Ibid., p. 69.

27. Clearly this should have been the case, and the city planner would have become the urban designer. By the 1990s computer-generated, ani-mated three-dimensional images of urban environments became a reality. The weakness in Habraken's argument is his acceptance of the division between architecture and city planning. Most employees of city or regional planning commissions in the US occupy most of their time with zoning and land use issues, addressing them with (albeit computer-generated) two-dimensional plans. Many of them lack any architectural design education.

28. Habraken, op. cit., p. 69.

29. Habraken, Nicholas J., J. Boekholt, P. Dinjens and A. Thijseen, and Wim Wiewel (trans.) (1976) *Variations: the Systematic Design of Supports.* Cambridge, MA: MIT Press.

30. Ibid., p. 22.

31. Ibid., p. 77.

32. Negroponte, Nicholas (1975) *Soft Architecture Machines.* Cambridge, MA: MIT Press, p. 145.

33. 'The Social Impact of Urban Design', Center for Policy Study, University of Chicago, 1971.

34. Ibid., p. 8.

35. Alexander, Christopher (1975) *The Oregon Experiment.* New York: Oxford University Press.

36. Alexander, Christopher (1979) *The Timeless Way of Building.* New York: Oxford University Press.

37. Alexander, Christopher *et al.* (1977) *A Pattern Language.* (Series 2 of 6). New York: Oxford University Press.

38. Alexander, Christopher (1965) 'The city is not a tree', *The Architectural Forum* (April/May).

39. Alexander, Christopher (1966) 'The pattern of streets', *Journal of the American Institute of Planners*, vol. 32, no. 5 (September).

40. Alexander, Christopher (1964) *Notes on the Synthesis of Form.* Cambridge, MA: Harvard University Press.
41. Alexander (1979) op. cit.
42. This is not exactly new. Such a theory is not dissimilar from the design of shopping malls discussed previously though the ten-minute walk suggested from any point in the community contradicts the age of the automobile. Alexander *et al.* (1977) op. cit., pp. 168–73.
43. Ibid., p. xix.
44. Lynch, Kevin (1972) *What Time is this Place?*. Cambridge, MA: MIT Press.
45. Lynch, Kevin (1990) *Wasting Away.* San Francisco: Sierra Club Books.
46. Ibid., p. 224.
47. Lynch, Kevin (1962) *Site Planning.* Cambridge, MA: MIT Press.
48. Lynch, Kevin (1960) *The Image of the City.* Cambridge, MA: The Technology Press and Harvard University Press.
49. Issues of the sustainability of urban environments became of increasing interest to planners and architects, generated in part by the 1973 energy crisis.
50. Lynch (1962) op. cit., pp. 45–94.
51. Ibid., p. 52.
52. Ibid., Chapter 5, pp. 95–117.
53. Ibid., p. 105.
54. Ibid., p. 109.
55. The efficacy of these methods largely depends upon a respondent's graphic ability. Many lay persons do not have such skills, which brings into doubt how a response might be interpreted.
56. Lynch, Kevin (1976) *Managing the Sense of the Region.* Cambridge, MA: MIT Press.
57. In addressing regional planning Lynch entered a more difficult arena. Attempts to coordinate regional plans as 'collaborative' proposals of many cities, townships and regions inevitably have met with failure. The Western Hamilton County Regional Plan (Ohio), July 1999, met with such a failure because each entity did not want to accept the influence of interests of adjoining communities. The articulate protests of local branches of the Sierra Club, in their attempts to protect the natural environment of the western hills of Cincinnati metropolitan area, met with fierce opposition (see Chapter 6.)
58. Southworth, Michael and Susan Southworth (1973) *Environmental Quality Analysis and Management for Cities and Regions: A Review of Work in the United States, Town Planning Review.* Liverpool: Liverpool University Press.
59. Southworth, Michael and Kevin Lynch (1974) *Designing and Managing the Strip.* Cambridge, MA: Joint Center for Urban Studies MIT and Harvard University.
60. Ibid., p. 1.
61. Venturi, Robert, Denise Scott-Brown and Steven Izenour (1972) *Learning from Las Vegas.* Cambridge, MA: MIT Press.
62. Scott-Brown, Denise and Gordon Cullen (1967) 'Messages', *Connections* (Communication Special Issue), vol. 4 (Spring), pp. 12–15.
63. Broadbent, G., R. Bunt and C. Jencks (1980) *Signs, Symbols, and Architecture.* Chichester: John Wiley and Sons Ltd.
64. Sennett, op. cit.
65. Venturi, op. cit. Second edition, 1977, p. 52.
66. Patterns books were used extensively in Europe in the eighteenth century by British architects such as Robert Adam, John Nash and John Wood who created an urban order from their neo-classical designs.
67. This was at a time in that decade when there was intense criticism against what was seen to be social irresponsibility.
68. Kepes, Gyorgy (ed.) (1972) *Arts of the Environment.* New York: George Braziller.
69. Burns, James, ibid., p 135.
70. In the middle of the 1990s the Internet became a reality with web sites across the entire planet.
71. This series of fogs was not caused by emissions of gasoline exhaust from cars and trucks, as became the case thirty or forty years later. Car ownership figures at the time were relatively low and most of the atmospheric pollution was caused by the burning of fossil fuels (such as coal in open fireplaces) to heat homes and supply industries such as steel manufacturing, which later became redundant.
72. Dehusses, Jerome (1979) *Delivrez Promethée.* Paris: Flammarion.
73. The Brazilian regime during the period 1964 to 1984 (during a period of political repression which also occurred in other South American countries such as Chile and Argentina), actively encouraged the commercial exploitation of mineral and natural resources, mostly by North American companies.
74. This is not unlike the 'dust-bowl' phenomenon that occurred in the Great Plain states of Iowa, Nebraska, and the Dakotas in the 1920s and early 1930s, where over-production farming methods eroded much of the fertile top-soil and sub-soil.
75. Kahn, Lloyd (ed.) (1973) *Shelter.* Bolinas, CA: Shelter Publications.
76. Rabbit, Peter (1971) *Drop City.* Paris: Olympia Press.
77. Rudofsky, B. (1964) *Architecture without Architects.* Garden City, NY: Doubleday.
78. Kahn, op. cit., p. 3.
79. Meier, Richard (1973) *Design of Resource-Conserving Cities.* Berkeley, CA: Institute of Urban Regional Development, University of California.
80. Ibid., p. 27.
81. Cutler, Laurence (1976) *Recycling Cities for People: the Urban Design Process.* Boston, MA: Cahers Books International.
82. Ibid., p. 67.
83. Jencks, Charles (1977) *The Language of Post-Modern Architecture.* London: Academy Editions. Many architects and architectural students have considered *The Language of Post-Modern Architecture* as an invention of architectural thought. Post-modernism had its derivation in earlier European linguistic theory, which had evolved from the various theories of semiotics. Post-modernism, as part of linguistic theory, was developed by such European writers and philosophers as Jacques Derrida.
84. Jencks, Charles (1971) *Architecture 2000: Predictions and Methods.* London: Studio Vista.
85. Jencks, Charles and Nathan Silver (1973) *Adhocism: the Case for Improvisation.* Garden City, NY: Anchor Books.
86. Jencks (1977) op. cit.
87. Ibid., p. 7.
88. Ibid., p. 19.
89. The development of supergraphics into various forms of retailing was described in *Progressive Architecture*, April 1969.
90. Ni-ban-Kahn (1970) 'Omni-Rental Stores', *Japan Architect* (August).
91. Jencks (1977) op. cit., p. 90.
92. Barnett, Jonathan (1974) *Urban Design and Public Policy: Practical Methods for Improving Cities.* New York: Architectural Record Books, p. 3
93. Ibid., p. 7.
94. This can still be seen more than twenty years later in the Canary Wharf development in the London Docklands, UK. The master-planners were the Chicago Office of Skidmore, Owings and Merrill, but the architectural design of the various buildings was executed by many different practices, both American and British.
95. Barnett, Jonathan and John Portman (1976) *The Architect as Developer.* New York: McGraw-Hill.
96. Ibid., p. 74.
97. De Chiara, Joseph (1975) *Urban Planning and Design Criteria.* New York: Van Nostrand Reinhold.
98. Ibid., p. 27.
99. Hack, Gary (1974) *Improving City Streets for Use at Night: the Norfolk Experiment.* Cambridge, MA: MIT Press.
100. Halpern, Kenneth (1978) *Downtown USA: Urban Design in American Cities.* New York: Whitney Library of Design.
101. Barnett, op. cit.
102. American Institute of Architects, Committee on Urban Design (1973) 'Checklist for Cities: Local Action Guides for improving Urban Design'. Washington, DC: AIA.

103. San Francisco Department of City Planning. Preliminary Report no. 8. Urban Design Plans, 1970. See also Zucker, Paul (1959) *Town and Square*. New York: Columbia University Press.
104. County Council of Essex, England. 'A Design Guide for Residential Areas', 1973.
105. Halprin, Lawrence (1972) *Lawrence Halprin Notebooks 1959–1971*. Cambridge, MA: MIT Press.
106. Ibid., p. 33.
107. Lewis, David N.(ed.) (1971) *The Growth of Cities*. London: Elek Books.
108. Lewis, David N. (1968) *Urban Structure*.
109. Lewis, David N. (ed.) (1971) *The Growth of Cities*. London: Elek Books, p. 14.
110. Ibid.
111. Scott-Brown, Denise, ibid. 'On pop art, permissiveness and planning'.
112. Bacon, Edmond (1976) *Design of Cities*. New York: Penguin.
113. Blumenfeld, Hans (1971) *The Modern Metropolis: Its Origins, Characteristics, and Planning*. Cambridge, MA: MIT Press.
114. Vitruvius, Morris Hickey Morgan (trans.) (1960) *The Ten Books on Architecture*. New York: Dover Publications.
115. See Rykwert, Joseph (1976) *The Idea of a Town*. London: Faber and Faber, p. 42.
116. Jacobs, op. cit.
117. Sennett, Richard (1970) *The Uses of Disorder: Personal Identity and City Life*. Harmondsworth: Penguin Books, pp. 53 and 81.
118. Rowe, Colin and Fred Koetter (1975) 'Collage City', *Architectural Review*, vol. 158, no. 942 (August), p. 81 ff.
119. Papenek, Victor (1972) *Design for the Real World*. London: Thames and Hudson.
120. Lévi-Strauss, Claude (1969) *The Savage Mind*. Chicago, p. 16., quoted by Rowe and Koetter, op. cit., p. 83.
121. Rowe and Koetter, op. cit., p. 86.
122. Ibid., p. 90.
123. Roma Interrotta. Catalogue of exhibition in Rome, 1978, originated and promoted by Incontri Internazionali D'Arte, Rome. See also 'Roma Interrotta', *Architectural Design*, vol. 49, nos 3–4 (1979).
124. Rowe and Koetter, op. cit., p. 10.
125. Franzen, Ulrich (1975) 'Urban design for New York', *Architectural Record* (September).
126. Twenty-five years later this seems a utopian proposition for Manhattan, where the movement system copes, albeit inadequately. Most inhabitants either walk or use the relatively efficient subway system. The more affluent may use taxi cabs manned by drivers, the majority of whom speak poor English, and the wealthy may use their own limousines.
127. Latvala, Eino K (1973) *The TTI Hovair PRT System*. Society of Automotive Engineers, Inc. By the end of the twentieth century, the reintroduction of systems known as 'light rail' was not only widespread in Europe (particularly in Germany, the Netherlands, France, Denmark and the UK) but also in the US in Portland, Oregon, and San Diego, California.
128. LTV Aerospace Corporation (1971) 'Fact Sheet: Airtrans System', *The Architects' Journal*, vol. 153, no. 20 (19 May), pp. 1112–23.
129. Bourne, L. S. and L. W. Simmons (eds) (1978) *Systems of Cities: Readings on Structure, Growth, and Policy*. New York: Oxford University Press.
130. Jean Gottman, ibid., pp. 53–60.
131. Over the next thirty years the seaport function appeared to become less important. Instead, the airport's function as a hub for major airlines produced major regional growth. Delta Airlines, the nation's third most important airline, established its main hub in Atlanta, followed by Cincinnati and Dallas-Fort Worth, none of which were seaports.
132. Bourne and Simmons, op. cit., pp. 25–26.
133. Wolf, M. R. and R. D. Shinn (1970) *Urban Design Within the Comprehensive Planning Process*. Seattle: University of Washington Press.
134. Ibid., p. 202.
135. Ibid., pp. 70–74.
136. Negroponte, Nicholas (1975) *Soft Architecture Machines*. Cambridge, MA: MIT Press.
137. Negroponte, Nicholas (1970) *The Architecture Machine*. Cambridge, MA: MIT Press.
138. Jencks, Charles (1971) *Architecture 2000*. London: Studio Vista.
139. Three renowned British fictional writers of the future in the twentieth century were H. G. Wells (*War of the Worlds*), Aldous Huxley (*Brave New World*) and George Orwell (*1984*). Of these, George Orwell's prediction of a world separated into three totalitarian states, with complete surveillance of the individual, was probably the most accurate. However, the fall of fascism in Europe after 1945 and the collapse of the Soviet Union from 1989 onwards, to be replaced by the domination of world capitalism, was to belie his impression that this would be permanent. Czechoslovakian author Franz Kafka's novels *The Trial* and *The Castle*, though more abstract and less descriptive than the British writers, from a psychological point of view, pinpointed the isolation and persecution of the individual.
140. Jencks (1971) op. cit., p. 10.
141. See Gosling and Maitland (1984) op. cit.
142. Jencks (1971) op. cit., p. 12.
143. Kahn, Herman and Anthony J. Weiner (1967) *Year 2000*. London: Macmillan.
144. Jencks (1971) op. cit., p. 14.
145. 'Delphi Technique', *Science Journal* (October 1967).
146. Jencks (1971) op. cit., pp. 43 and 46–47.
147. Ibid., p. 55.
148. Lundberg, Ferdinand (1968) *The Rich and the Super-Rich*. New York: Lyle Stuart.
149. Banham, Reyner (1976) *Megastructure: Urban Futures of the Recent Past*. London: Thames and Hudson.
150. Ibid., pp. 12–13.
151. Banham made a number of factual inaccuracies in this study. Elsewhere he mentions the town centre project for Cumbernauld New Town in Scotland, designed by Geoffrey Copcult as project architect in 1961, the first stage of which was completed long before 1966. (Sir) Hugh Wilson, though chief architect, had little to do with the design, which, it is said, he disliked, and Copcult resigned shortly after its completion. Similarly, Banham attributes the design for the town centre of Runcorn New Town in England, completed in 1971 and influenced by Copcult's earlier designs, to chief architect Roger Harrison. In fact, the design was completed long before Harrison took office; at the time Harrison was a principal architect in charge of the housing division, but was under the direction of his predecessor, F. Lloyd Roche, with the design team composed of David Gosling as team leader with Keith Smith, John Randle and Peter Edwards, among others. These inaccuracies are surprising given Banham's reputation as a historian.
152. Banham (1976) op. cit., p. 51.
153. 'San Francisco: Ghirardelli Square' (Architects: Wurster, Bernardi, Eammons), *Interiors* (July 1970), pp. 73–76.
154. 'Faneuil Hall Market' (Boston), *Progressive Architecture* (January 1975), p. 61.
155. Thompson, Benjamin (1971) 'Design Store', *Boston Sunday Globe* (4 July). See also *Architectural Record*, vol. 147, no. 5 (May 1970), pp. 105–112; *Interiors* (May 1970), pp. 108–117; *Contract* (July 1970).
156. Jencks, Charles. (1977) *The Language of Post-Modern Architecture*. London: Academy Editions.
157. 'Kinetic boutiques and campopop shops', *Progressive Architecture*, no. 4 (April 1969), pp. 148–207.
158. 'Revolution in interior design', *Progressive Architecture*, vol. XLIX, no. 10 (October 1968), pp. 148–207.
159. 'Supergraphics', *Progressive Architecture* (November 1967).
160. This was later to be reflected in the deconstructivist movement of the late 1980s and early 1990s.
161. *Progressive Architecture*, op. cit. (October 1968).

162. The Urban Land Institute. Project Reference File vol. 1, no. 9; see also *Architectural Forum* (April 1972).

163. Though the scope of this present study does not include Canada, the Houston Galleria was paralleled by Place Ville Marie and Place Bonaventure (designed by architects Affleck, Desbarats, Dimako-polous, Leibensold and Sise) in Montreal, which were on a much vaster scale.

164. Broadway Plaza brochure by Odyer Development Corporation, 1973.

165. Six projects by SITE Environmental Communications, Venice, California, 1974.

166. Marsh, Peter (1977) 'Vintage year', *Building Design* (18 November).

167. Sunset Cabins and Vacation Houses, 1975.

168. Vineyard Open Land Foundation. 'The Martha's Vineyard Byways Study', consultants: Kevin Lynch, Vera Pratt, Lyle Brecht, Benjamin Moore and the Conservation Law Foundation of New England, 1976.

169. Ibid., p. 1.

170. Ibid., p. 6.

171. Seelig, Peter (1978) *The Architecture of Self-Help Communities (The First International Design Competition for the Urban Environment of Developing Countries)*. New York: Architectural Record Books.

172. Ibid., p. 66.

173. Ibid., p. 69.

174. Alexander, Christopher (1964) *Notes on the Synthesis of Form*. Cambridge, MA: Harvard University Press.

175. *Progressive Architecture* (March 1969), pp. 94–113.

176. Tschumi, Bernard (1981) 'The Manhattan Transcripts', *Architectural Design*, London: Special Profile.

177. *Progressive Architecture* (January 1973), p. 104.

178. *Progressive Architecture* (January 1974), p. 76.

179. *Progressive Architecture* (January 1975), p. 68.

180. *Progressive Architecture* (January 1976), p. 82.

181. Broadbent, Geoffrey (1990) *Emerging Concepts in Urban Space Design*. London: Van Nostrand Reinhold, pp. 260–61.

182. *Progressive Architecture* (January 1977), p. 83.

183. *Progressive Architecture* (January 1978), p. 92.

184. *Progressive Architecture* (January 1979), pp. 104–105.

185. Translated from the introduction to the monograph *Arquitectura Alternative de Emilio Ambasz* by Marina Waisman. Editorial Summa, Buenos Aires, Argentina, September 1977, p. 15.

186. And, of course, this became an accurate prophecy. With the advent of the Internet, twenty years later, many people across the world do exactly that.

187. Waisman, op. cit., p. 11.

188. Wolfe, Tom (1977) 'The "Me" Decade'. New York: *Harpers and Queen* (January), p. 48.

189. Ambasz, Emilio. 'Notes on Project: Community Arts Center, Grand Rapids, Michigan', 1975.

Chapter Five

1980–1990

THE SOCIAL CITY: CITIZEN PARTICIPATION AND ADVOCACY PLANNING

Among efforts to combat the decline of major US cities following the 1967 urban riots (a result, many believed, of the growing poverty, social deprivation and racial segregation) were the Council on Urban Design, set up by Mayor John Lindsay in New York, the community design centres that spread across the country with volunteer architects, teachers and students, as well as the Regional/Urban Design Assistance Teams (R/UDAT) (see Chapter 3), which published a major report in 1983.[1]

The Community Design Centres

The Community Design Center Directors' Association was established in 1977. Here, directors from community design centres met to exchange ideas concerning the provision of urban design services for moderate- to low-income communities. However, by the mid-1980s, community design centres were experiencing major financial hardships due to lack of funding and, in part, to prevailing political antagonism towards such ventures. With declining government funding, many centres found a new stability in working directly with colleges and universities. The State Board of Regents in Ohio, for example, funded three design centres working within the university sector, and the Center for Community Development and Design served as a public outreach component of the University of Colorado in Denver.[2]

A survey published in 1988[3] revealed seventeen community design centres nationwide. These ranged from the Community Design Center for Environmental Change at the University of California, Berkeley, to the Columbus Neighborhood Design Assistance in Ohio, as well as the Community Planning and Design Center in Cincinnati, Ohio. The majority of funding came from the Pratt Institute for Community and Environmental Development in New York, under the direction of Ron Shiftman. The Institute had an annual budget at the time of slightly under $2 million and, with 24 full-time staff, it addressed the needs of developing new methods for financing low-income housing. Among its programmes were planning technical assistance for groups in the greater New York City metropolitan area (including Brooklyn), developing neighbourhood plans and surveys, and assisting local groups in building evaluation, rehabilitation, new construction design, contract documentation and financial services.

The substantial media coverage of the success of urban design or community development centres was exemplified in a *New York Times* article in October 1987.[4] Although the problem of unemployed had been identified the previous decade, homeless people remained largely ignored until tangible results were revealed in the 1980s. The *New York Times* reported that in August 1985, squatters, advised by community organisers, seized 25 vacant, city-owned buildings in the East New York section of Brooklyn. It became a fundamental political issue in the Democratic primary that year between Mayor Koch and City Council President Carol Bellamy. Eventually, the New York City Board of Estimate unanimously approved a programme to give the illegal squatters, transformed into homesteaders and incorporated as the Mutual Housing Association of New York, 58 city-owned buildings and funds for technical and architectural aid, as well as a $2.7 million revolving loan fund for rehabilitation.

It was the first test in New York of a much discussed model for low-income housing development, a neighbourhood collective of homesteaders given money and technical help by the city in return for restricted rights of resale. It was believed that it held promise for a city that owned 4,500 vacant buildings and had, at the time, 200,000 families waiting for public housing.

The Pratt Institute, which had a long history of dealings with the city, was asked to mediate, and director Ronald Shiffman persuaded ACORN[5] to abandon squatting. Pratt and Shiffman were crucial agents in countering ACORN's confrontational and illegal tactics, and were aided by the New York Foundation, a philanthropic organisation that agreed to serve as the project's banker, as well as the Consumer-Farmer Foundation, which originated in the mid-1970s as the Banana Kelly, organising housing protests in the South Bronx. Harold De Rienzo, one of the latter's founders, suggested that in a mutual housing association, neighbourhood residents form a collective, contributing money and a lot of 'sweat equity' to rehabilitate buildings for their own use in return for public support and limited ownership. The Mutual Housing Association of New York retained title to the land. The basis of this was that if owners chose to sell, the association had the right to repurchase for an agreed price reflecting individual investment, not the market.

Mutual housing was seen as representing a new form of social contract between the city and its poorer residents. Critics were sceptical, claiming that mutual housing required a high level of community organisation and sustained commitment.

However, a location map of community design centres in the lower 48 states of the US indicated the burgeoning success of these ventures. The map (1989) shows the major concentration of centres in the Eastern sector of the country, along the East Coast in New York State, Massachusetts and Pennsylvania, as well as Illinois, Indiana, Minnesota and Ohio in the Midwest. Elsewhere, they were concentrated on the West Coast, particularly in Washington State and Oregon. Many of the centres were associated with or attached to universities or other academic centres.

However, the R/UDAT, established through the auspices of the American Institute of Architects (AIA), experienced, on occasion, quite different results. The following case study, albeit atypical, illustrates the fairly distinctive social and economic forces involved.

The Pittsburgh Experiment

The so-called rust belt cities of the American Midwest had suffered the same terminal decline in their manufacturing base as that of their counterparts in Western Europe. The years of divestment in heavy industry, combined with competition from Japan, South Korea, Taiwan and elsewhere in the Pacific Rim, had created the partial collapse of the automobile industry in Detroit, the steel industry in Cleveland and the coal and steel industry in Pittsburgh. In Michigan, Ohio and Pennsylvania, there was much agonising and introspective self-examination as to what the future held.

The 1988 Pittsburgh R/UDAT study, 'Remaking the Monongahela Valley',[6] warned that there would be no 'white knight' in the form of alternative heavy industrial users who might arrive in these depressed regions to hire the many thousands of redundant workers. Neither would vast new highway networks regenerate obsolete industry.

The Pittsburgh study was a unique example in a number of ways. It was the ninety-eighth venture of R/UDAT since the assistance teams were formed by David Lewis and others in 1967, and differed from preceding studies in that it was the first Anglo-American initiative, timed to coincide with the 'Remaking Cities' International Conference in 1988 (organised for the AIA by David Lewis and addressed by Prince Charles), at which its conclusions were presented.[7] The study was carried out at the invitation of the Allegheny County Board of Commissioners of Greater Pittsburgh, which consisted of 16 members, including representatives of the unemployed, the steel industry, the business community, trade unions, churches, local government and chambers of commerce, as well as teachers, social workers and retraining personnel. The international team included twelve American experts from a wide range of professional disciplines and six Britons, all of whom, except for the charismatic community leader, Tony McGann, from the Eldonians of Liverpool, were architects. Twelve volunteer architectural students from Carnegie-Mellon University joined the process.

Travel costs, accommodation and subsistence were provided by the elected Board of County Commissioners. Additional assistance was voluntary. Team members provided their expertise free of charge and agreed not to accept architectural or planning commissions connected with the visit.

In the six months prior to the team's visit, much of the preparatory work was carried out by a smaller team from the AIA in Washington, DC.[8] During this period, some fifty meetings were held with two hundred local people. The Monongahela Valley Commission published its preliminary report in 1987.

Local residents also played a key and sometimes vociferous role in the intensive five-day visit by the main R/UDAT team in March 1988. This included a public meeting on the Saturday morning, which served as an opportunity for local residents to express their opinions, with the proposals re-presented at a second public meeting the following Monday evening.

The studies were, therefore, to a large extent prescriptive, with the R/UDAT proposals stemming from grass roots initiatives.

One criticism of the R/UDAT study is that the team was a superficial group, unable to address a problem such as that of terminal industrial decline in the rust belt of the American Midwest in a weekend study. However, such criticism is misplaced. The intervention was not imposed upon the community; through action groups, elected councils, or even chambers of commerce it sought the voluntary assistance of teams in an attempt to address complex and seemingly insoluble issues.

The problems of the Monongahela Valley were serious, with 30,000 jobs in Pittsburgh industry lost since 1979 and the consequent high unemployment, decline in family income, loss of population and the near bankruptcy of the steel towns. The contrast with downtown Pittsburgh could not have been more poignant. The 'golden triangle', or corporate headquarters such as architect Philip Johnson's glittering neo-gothic towers for Pittsburgh Plate Glass and the associated renaissance affluence of the downtown area, contrasted vividly with the dead steel towns of the valley itself where row upon row of houses in the small river towns lay deserted. The public meetings were full of people who appeared to be in a state of traumatic shock over what had happened to their communities.

Some of the British members of the study team appeared to exhibit a patronising attitude towards the decline of formidable communities of steelworkers and their families; these communities were seeking new solutions for the regeneration of industry and employment, not theme parks, 'garden festivals', or antique fairs. In addition, the situation was not helped by the sycophantic attitude of both American and British team members towards Prince Charles, who, upon visiting the final presentation of the study during the Pittsburgh conference, was seen by some as the patron of the entire affair.

The structure of the Pittsburgh study inevitably created ideological and philosophical differences of approach between urban designers, who prepared tangible paper proposals, vague public relations exercises and tactical and strategic policies. It mirrored the schism that existed between architects and planners in the UK as well as, possibly, in the US at the time. The educational system over the previous two decades had resulted in a growing proportion of planners emerging from backgrounds of geography and economics, as well as sociology and civil engineering, some of whom, according to Gordon Cullen, were 'visually illiterate'.[9] Their dreams and goals were quite different from those of architects and designers.

In constrast to the Pittsburgh studies, the magic of advocacy planning, led by David Lewis and others in the 1960s, was conducted in dangerous, tense and frightening environments against a background of urban riots. The teams were smaller than those used in the later studies, though this was not a significant factor. Perhaps the difference was the political commitment and passion felt by the Pittsburgh team members. Their public meetings were interesting and informative. Views of the unemployed ranged from bewilderment and sadness to anger and desperation, and were complemented by input from high-school children, teachers, priests, politicians and even uninvited anarchists.

The Monongahela Valley study, initially published in February 1987, focused on redevelopment issues in the Lower Monongahela Valley towns of West Homestead, Munhall, Duquesne, Swissvale, Rankin and McKeesport. Strategies for the reuse of the four abandoned steel sites included land use, density, marketing, development, site access, open space and relationship to the river. Location and historical sites were also taken into account. The redevelopment of the mill sites and the adjoining towns was important.

In regional terms, major difficulties were the diverse policies of county, public and private agencies. It was necessary to define a comprehensive riverfront development policy as well as improving transportation, sewage and other infrastructure issues. In the past, all development decisions had been made by the United States Steel Corporation (later known as USX) and there had been little or no consultation with the community regarding 'development objectives'. However, the redevelopment of more than 400 hectares (1,000 acres) of former steel mill property could not take place simultaneously. Redevelopment of industrial wastelands is a slow process and therefore low-budget, high-profile results on various sites needed to be achieved in the short term in order to maintain the confidence of affected communities. This would include low-density development and the demolition of redundant buildings, along with the reclamation and installation of a basic infrastructure. In the medium term, there should be a response to light and moderate scale industrial needs, the reuse of appropriate existing structures, and the addition of support facilities.

The sites were not all equally attractive, and development potential would have to be realistic. Various aspects of development would advance more quickly in some towns than others. The R/UDAT team's approach to site planning was to provide a basic framework of streets and open spaces to organise new development. Within that framework, a variety of uses produced by different developers at different times could be implemented, to result in a unified, attractive valley community. For many years, the steel mills had prevented all access between river and town.[10] The Monongahela River was perceived as a tremendous asset for development, and public access to the riverfront itself was therefore a primary consideration.

The interviews and investigations revealed several recurrent themes, which were often erroneous and counterproductive. Such points of view included: 'someone holds a magic key', 'we are unable to control our destiny', 'we are unique in our plight' and 'development of the mill sites will save our valley'.

However, no single activity could result in turning the economy around any more than could a new superhighway system. Ending the deficiencies in the existing road system could cure economic ills, and regional access was an important consideration, but the Monongahela Valley was not in need of massive transportation investment near the industrial sites themselves. The perception that the steel industry could and would return as a major economic factor was also unlikely, since there was little viability for steel production. And the myth that an alternative major industrial user would appear as the 'white knight', was allowing a sense of inertia and lethargy to grip the valley.[11] New industries suggested the inclusion of a large-scale, industrial, multi-state waste recycling and energy cooperative.

The study identified the need for re-education of citizens and officials as to the way they viewed their role in influencing the future, and how formal and informal governmental and community mechanisms could be used in doing so. Towns needed to develop a joint land-use policy aimed at mutual interests and benefits.

However, it should be noted that the Monongahela Valley was not unique in such problems. The evolution, transformation and transfer of heavy manufacturing has also been the plight of many older industrial centres throughout the world.

THE EMERGENCE OF THE NEW URBANISM

Studies in social justice, exemplified in the 'Pittsburgh Experiment', were to develop into an entirely new wave of urban design thinking, which in the following decade was to become known as 'the new urbanism'.

A pioneer of this movement was Peter Calthorpe. His book *Sustainable Communities*,[12] based on a 1980 Solar City Design Workshop in Sonoma, California, was an attempt to create a plan for three prototype communities based upon East Coast cities, post-Second World War western cities and new development in growing metropolitan areas. Under the heading 'The Urban Context', Calthorpe suggested that older cities had an efficient framework that could be modified to meet modern needs. The urbanisation pattern of the US was different to that of Europe, particularly in its use of the gridiron system. Somerset Parkside, Sacramento, was cited as a progressive development utilising solar heating and cooling. In contemplating this approach, Calthorpe said that orientation of streets was critical, but added that workplaces should also be redesigned as part of the neighbourhood in a variety of types and sizes. This clearly reflected the earlier writings of Jane Jacobs but ignored, to some extent, the operation of a market economy and capitalism espoused during this period by the Reagan administration. A second case study was Philadelphia. Though this did not relate to the better-known earlier studies of Louis Kahn and Edmond Bacon, the site, adjacent to the University of Pennsylvania, was a neighbourhood that required rehabilitation and better public transit. The first stage of this involved making the houses more energy efficient, improving parking and creating a traffic hierarchy. An urban garden programme was introduced sometime later.

In the suburban context was a case study of Sunnyvale, a mature suburb of San Jose, California. Among the recommendations was the narrowing of neighbourhood streets with dense tree planting to provide summer shade. Commercial development (retail) needed to be more dense, with pedestrian-oriented activity nodes at major intersections, though the study was not explicit concerning the nature of these nodes. Again, the recommendations emphasised energy-efficiency with the future use of solar energy.

Calthorpe's publication contained contributions from a number of authors, but demonstrated a consistency of philosophy concerning energy efficiency and the evolving structure of the American family, particularly the needs of working women. In an essay by John Todd, the emphasis was on adaptable design, self-sufficient power supply, solar-based technology, water purification, waste recycling, internal agriculture and aquaculture.

Peter Katz,[13] a leader of the new urbanism movement, proposed that farming on small plots could be introduced in the cities.[14] This, according to Katz, was more sustainable than relying on commercial agriculture. Planting would improve the microclimate and reduce pollution, and watershed development could be incorporated to use plants to preserve water. Other essays (for example the proposals by F. A. Reid) suggested alternatives to the motor car, such as electric vehicles and light rail systems in urban areas, bus-only lanes, park-and-ride, as well as pedestrian links.[15]

However, Peter Calthorpe's later book, *The Pedestrian Pocket Book*,[16] was perhaps more influential. Calthorpe observed that emerging households in the US were composed of single, rather than married people, yet suburbs were still being constructed for the prototypical American family of the mid-century. The book was based on a charrette held at the University of Washington in Seattle during Spring of 1988. Pedestrian pockets were described as 'simple clusters of housing, retail space and offices within a quarter mile radius of a transit station'.[17]

Auburn, Washington, some 40 kilometres (25 miles) south of Seattle, was selected as the site for this development. Calthorpe and his team felt that contemporary planning strategies were outdated. Their approach offered an alternative method, allowing choice, affordable housing and reduction in car usage, and it could be executed in stages allowing for incremental growth.

The jury, which included Anne Vernez Moudon and Gary Pivo, concluded that the diversity of choice offered a good alternative to urban sprawl. Calthorpe described pedestrian pockets as post-industrial suburbs, to become known a few years later as 'edge cities'. With more people working from home and major suburban urban growth, pedestrian pockets provided a mixed use of housing (approximately 2,000 houses of various types), daycare, recreation, parks, retail and even offices within 20 to 40 hectares (50 to 100 acres) of zoned land. There would be parking and transit in the form of metro-buses and light rail. Housing should be affordable for all household incomes and should include housing for the elderly. Everything (as recommended by the garden city movement) would be within walking distance.[18]

The pockets were intended to form a network for long range growth in a region. Each might have a different focus, perhaps acting as a catalyst for growth in a poor area or as a cultural centre in a wealthier one. One study was of a sprawl area in Sonoma County, north of San Francisco. Uncontrolled development was a problem, so a county proposal of twenty pedestrian pockets was presented along a light rail line, preserving land, energy and resources, reducing traffic and providing easier access. This would reduce commuting time and, returning to Radburn principles of the early twentieth century, emphasise pedestrian access and safety with the use of pedestrian paths, three related housing neighbourhoods and a hierarchy of open spaces.[19]

The connection between the social city and behavioural sciences became evident at the beginning of the 1980s. In an important work published in 1980, authors Rubin and Elder emphasised the significance of man/environment relationships. Behavioural researchers and architects, they claimed, had much in common.[20]

Quoted in this context are F. Ladd and Michael Southworth. In her study of the way in which African-American youths viewed their environment, Ladd asked the interviewees to describe this environment and then draw a map.[21] The maps were analysed and placed into four categories: pictorial representations of houses, buildings and other street elements; schematic representations of independent places; features of a map without identifiable landmarks; and a map containing identifiable landmarks. The study was a gaming simulation technique, popular among urban researchers in the late 1960s and early 1970s. In this, representatives from the low-income group made up one team and the middle-income group formed the other. The two teams were asked to discuss their differences about the project and agree upon a recommendation to city council.[22]

Michael Southworth's study explored a new notion in urban design – 'soundscape'.[23] The study explored two questions. First, what is the perceived variety and character of city sounds and, second, how do sounds influence perception of the visible city? To investigate changes in the soundscape over time and under varied weather conditions, the researchers took blindfolded subjects on trips through various parts of the city. Though such an experiment may be considered slightly bizarre, the analysis of the interactions between the visual and auditory indicated that without sound/visual perception, environments have fewer attention-demanding qualities and convey less information. Southworth suggested two steps towards improving the city soundscape. The first would be to reduce and control noise and the second would be to increase the amount of information provided by city sound.[24]

A less sanguine point of view towards the aspects of the social city within the context of urban design was expressed in a somewhat acerbic article by Leon Krier in the pages of *Art and Design*.[25] Krier was taking a defensive stand against his critics who had claimed his work to be 'ultimately reactionary' and that the invitation to donate his drawings to an American group known as Architects for Social Responsibility was tempting. Krier responded by saying that 'Architects for Responsibility was akin to the British organization, Architects for Peace', and that 'neither organization was merely moved by a professed love for peace and universal brotherhood, but an ever present urge to participate in other people's business'.[26] 'Participation,' Krier said, 'had become the central demand in all overdeveloped industrial democracies'.

In this piece of polemicism, Krier suggested that the ever-present urge to participate in matters of environmental design and policy was not an outburst of creative grassroots energy, but a lack of confidence in modernist architecture and planning (presumably referring to much of the public architecture of the 1960s). He concluded by saying that if modernist architects and artists now opened their doors to participation, it was not because of democratic concern and altruism, but because the modernist movement no longer had an artistic or cultural base or a cultural or social foundation.

EDUCATION FOR URBAN DESIGN

The Institute for Urban Design was founded in New York City in 1979 as a successor to the Urban Design Group. In 1982 Anne Ferebee, as proceedings editor, published a selection of papers from an Urban Design Educators' Retreat held in Puerto Rico between 30 April and 2 May 1981.[27] In her introduction, Ferebee said the retreat was funded by the National Endowment for the Arts (NEA), and the application for that funding stated that

there is a crisis in urban design education. While the teaching of city planning has focused on policy planning, and architectural education has continued to emphasize the design of individual buildings, education for the emerging field of urban design has attempted to bridge the gap. However, these efforts have been scattered, diverse and uncoordinated. If urban design is to better respond to new opportunities, a common effort will be needed to identify the objectives of urban design education, the substantive areas to be taught and the best pedagogical means to be used.[28]

Once the application was approved, Michael Pittas, director of the NEA's Design Arts Program, assumed responsibility for the retreat programme. In his preface, Pittas addressed his words to an invisible prospective student of urban design: 'Let's [sic] consider city and regional planning curriculums in many American universities. While you might expect to find most planning students draped over their drafting boards, developing vast visionary schemes for future cities, nothing could be further from the truth. Despite the name "city planning" such work is not very concerned with the physical or visual qualities of the built environment. Instead you will find courses on economics, sociology, law, public policy and statistical analysis; aspects and parameters which only influence built form'.[29] Among other suggestions, Pittas said that urban design had a civic dimension and whether it was practised in the public arena or in private development, its principal focus was the public environment. It was concerned more with the ensemble of build-ings in the urban fabric and their relationship to public space than with the building of a particular artifact.

The list of participants contained many of the most respected authorities in the field of urban design. In a paper entitled 'Current crisis of disorder',[30] Jaquelin Robertson, who had formerly worked for the New York Office of Midtown Redevelopment, said (perhaps erroneously): 'Urban design is not a separate area of study and concern, an elective if you will. Rather it is precisely what architecture and planning and development are concerned with'.[31] He goes on to say, as did the British architect Michael Wilford in 1984, that 'cities are urban design'. Whereas Robertson's article did not really address the issues of urban design education as such, and the title was something of a misnomer, it did imply that the length of time required in conceiving, and even partially achieving urban design work allowed little room for testing the work as it progressed. In a contradictory suggestion to that of Michael Pittas, he asserted that the key ingredient affecting the delivery or implementation of urban design ideas was the complexity of the support system such as social, political and economic support.

Jon Lang, who was then chairman of the urban design programme at the University of Pennsylvania and author of a significant book, *Urban Design: the American Experience* (1988), addressed studio methods of teaching. A pivotal part of the teaching framework, as described by Lang, was the attempt to unite architecture and city planning. There were three programmes: Master of Architecture with an emphasis on Urban Design; Master of City Planning also with an emphasis on urban design; and a Joint Program in Architecture and City and Regional Planning.[32] Of the three, the last programme was probably the most important. The objective of this programme of studies, according to Lang, was to educate architects and planners who would be able to plan and design and assume responsible roles in governmental agencies, consulting firms and education. A strenuous effort was made to run specific courses parallel to specific studios, but this seemed to work only when the courses and studios were taught by the same person. The studio sequence was intended to develop a student's ability to understand the decision process and policies that would meet specific ends. A secondary purpose was to enhance students' graphic and verbal communication skills.[33]

Lang emphasised the importance of professional internships to give students work experience in urban design. He admitted that this requirement was not rigorously enforced,[34] but examples of studio projects, illustrated by Lang, indicated a high degree of professionalism such as a three-dimensional urban design controls system proposed for the South Street Seaport Area in New York City.[35] Past students, Lang claimed, strongly endorsed this structure as providing a rich educational environment and enhancing their knowledge, skills and self-confidence.

The theme for internships and case studies was also taken up by Jonathan Barnett, Director of the Graduate Program in Urban Design at the City College of New York.[36] Urban design, Barnett stated, required a different process from designing a landscape or building (a process involving government, communities, investment and entrepreneurs). The sequence of events was more complex than the creation of a single structure, and this was, Barnett said, difficult to simulate in an academic setting. Traditional studio methods of teaching design did not work well in this context.

The urban designer should have enough knowledge of the social sciences to be able to make diagnoses about the social dynamics of the community. Yet, the urban designer had less need of some of the planning specialities such as social service delivery systems, capital budgeting or even transportation planning and ecology. Barnett believed that even highly pertinent areas of expertise such as historic preservation would be available to the urban designer through specialist consultants in the same way that the architects hired acoustic specialists and structural and mechanical engineers.

Case studies emphasised analysis of completed designs rather than the synthesis of completed design by the student. Internships at City College were offered in public and private offices in the region. Practical experience provided an intellectual framework for assimilating specific material offered in courses.

Kevin Lynch also attended the San Jose Retreat. Lynch suggested that city design was a more developed, more focused version of city planning. It was interesting to note that throughout his paper, Lynch used the term 'city design' rather than 'urban design', though he was partly credited with inventing the latter term. City design seemed to imply that only the issues of big cities, such as Boston, should be addressed and not the design issues of smaller townships and villages. City design, Lynch stated, was no longer confined to the public regulation of private action, or the design of public works but should include programmes for 'activity and character and the making of framework plans engaging in environmental education and participatory design'.

Like other participants, Lynch agreed that education in this field was ambiguous, lying between city planning, architecture and landscape architecture. He described the typical urban design school as a two-year graduate course for architects that gave students studio experience in dealing with large, complex projects such as new towns, urban renewal and downtown rehabilitation, which he opposed.

City design, he said, should not be restricted to architects and landscape architects. 'I am fearful of the human consequences of "big architecture"',[37] later to become known in the US as 'signature architecture'. Most urban design departments at the time were in an uneasy marginal position, bedevilled by isolation, lacking support or critical mass, worried about accreditation and the fluctuations of student interest, and deprived of a sure institutional basis for implementing their designs.

Some of the first to show an interest in the city design programme at MIT were apparently from the city planning department,[38] some of whom sought a joint masters degree and a few who sought a doctoral degree in planning. This was a liberal programme with three full-time and four part-time faculty members. There was no separate degree or formal control over budgets, and no staff appointments or admissions. There did exist a vocal lobby, and this informality led to a strong group spirit and easy intercommunication. However, an interdepartmental group would always be exposed to departmental shifts.

According to Lynch: 'A common place is extremely important: a single location for faculty offices, studio space, student desks or lockers, secretary, lobby, small seminar (space), coffee, mail pickup (all with a single entrance)'.[39] Most good teaching was informal and personal; it happened in the halls and on the stairs.

Three central skills were described. The first was a sharp and sympathetic eye for the interaction between people, places, place events and the institutions that manage them. The focus of intervention was place. A knowledge of environmental psychology and microsociology was useful but not truly central. One acquired the habit of wandering through a city for the joy of discovering places. The second skill was a grounding in the theory, technique and values of city design. Designers were too often taught to be egocentric and prize originality. City design should use images of process, management and four-dimensional form in active use. Finally, the city designer should be skilled in communication. This was crucial for someone who would spend his or her life exchanging ideas with clients, residents, opponents and decision-makers. These represented four social languages: written words, spoken words, mathematics and graphic images. To be fluent in all four, Lynch said, meant being fluent in sending and receiving; writing and reading; speaking and listening; computing and understanding numbers; and drawing and seeing.

Such a centre should be engaged in research of its own with a connection in other fields. City design research would connect with other fields, but its central concern would be with imaginative responsibilities for the form and management of the everyday urban habitat.

In one of the final papers published, Denise Scott-Brown, discussing her experience teaching urban design at the University of Pennsylvania from 1960 onwards, said that over the following years a consensus developed among planning faculty to abolish studio teaching.[40] By 1963, the social revolution had changed planning education at the university. In fact, Paul Daindoff, a lawyer, planner and an ardent warrior for the poor, was to campaign for a new method and philosophy of planning. His Theory of Planning course, according to Scott-Brown, had a strong following among the students. The planning theory espoused was to ensure the democratic participation of those for whom planning systems were intended, and to promote a rationale while in the process of arriving at decisions.

In describing her later work at UCLA, establishing a new school of architecture and urban planning with Henry Liu, Scott-Brown decried the lack of knowledge of the English language by European students from Italy and Germany. Yet her assistant, Francis Ventre, used such terms as 'Now I'm going to give you the break-out on the housing starts'.[41] What did this mean – even to an English speaker?

An appendix to the collection of papers included a directory of graduate programmes in Urban Design (compiled from May through November 1981). Many of the courses were either masters degrees in architecture and planning, with an emphasis on urban design, architecture in urban design or landscape architecture in urban design, though Washington University, St. Louis, had a combined Master of Architecture and Urban Design.

One of the most eminent teachers in the field of urban design during this decade was Colin Rowe, who died in 1999. In 1948, after British army service during the Second World War, Rowe joined the Faculty of Liverpool University School of Architecture. He had previously studied at the Warburg Institute in London under Rudolf Wittkower, who was to have a lasting influence on his teaching methods.[42] His lectures on Palladio, Michelangelo and Italian Mannerism were much admired. He eventually moved to the US, where he became a faculty member in the Department of Architecture at Cornell University in 1963.

Rowe directed the graduate urban design studio at Cornell, and according to Jerry Wells, chairman of the architecture department, though the work of the studio was highly theoretical, it contained many instances full of fantasy. The outcome of these studios was published in the second issue of *The Cornell Journal of Architecture*.[43] In this, the editor, D. B. Middleton, whose 1980 graduate thesis design for a Capital District development strategy for Providence, Rhode Island, was published in this volume,[44] said that since 'the publication of "Collage City", by Colin Rowe and Fred Koetter in 1978, many ideas implicit in studio work have gained wider exposure ... Ideas first hatched and developed through studio design projects inspired the concepts found in "Collage City"'.[45] The issue concentrated on a comprehensive survey of design projects and theories emanating from the graduate level studio since its formation in 1963, and the publication of the exhibition catalogue for the 1980 show.

Much of this studio work dated from the turbulent period from 1965 to 1975, when many urban design departments emphasised the abstract analyses of urban infrastructures and social policy planning, including the location of low-income housing, neighbourhood preservation and urban renewal.

Colin Rowe's essay 'Program versus paradigm' criticised two dominant forms of problem-solving: the reliance on the programme as an empirical and neutral generator of subsequent design decisions and the use of the paradigm (the typological model for building and city plan form).

The fourth volume of the Cornell journal was published at the end of the decade.[46] Colin Rowe's essay, 'Grid/Frame/Lattice/Web'[47] drew heavily upon his earlier teachings on the sixteenth-century works of Giulio Romano, in particular Rome's Palazzo Maccarani. In a subsequent essay, Andrea Simitch extends urban design theory somewhat further.[48] In 'Exploring the periphery: parallel perceptions in the design studio', it is suggested that the 'realization of an idea is manifested by the sequence of images (episodes). Each is composed of a collection of details: "suggestions". Architectural form can be generated by a series of unfolding images that mark an impression, uncovered through a narrative, an awareness emerges of the function of *narrative* in architecture'. The essay goes on to say that there is a critical relationship between two-dimensional representation and three-dimensional actuality – the illusion of the single two-dimensional illusory images into the third-dimension. The constant transformation of what is perceived as static defines the potential of in architecture. The resultant third dimension decodes the illusion. The spectator (investigator) reintroduces illusion through motion.[49]

Notable among Rowe's contribution to urban design studio techniques was the extensive use of figure-ground studies.[50] Wayne Copper, in Volume 2, had referred to the argument for using figure-ground plans as an abstract representational technique for urban form and analysis and design. The conceptual reversibility of buildings and spaces, either of which could

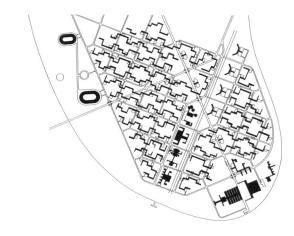

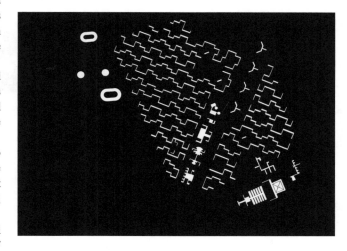

Figure-ground studies (1965–75),
Wayne Copper.

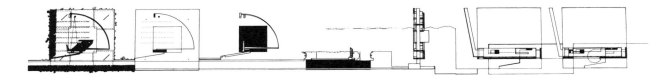

the RECORDING of these IMAGES reveals a constant adjustment and re-alignment of each element relative to every other element.

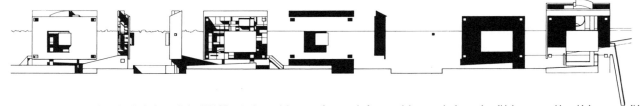

the cone of vision determines the limitations of the IMAGE. background becomes foreground, foreground becomes background, solid becomes void, void becomes solid.

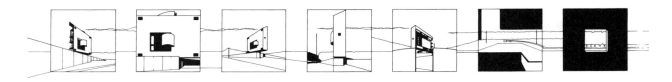

a three-dimensional actuality can be recorded or discovered through a series of unfolding IMAGES that mark an impression. it is the juxtaposition of these IMAGES in memory that produces an understanding of the form(s).

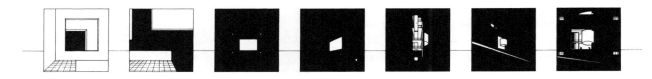

Cornell urban design studio (1990),
Andrea Simitch.

be highly defined or ambiguous, demonstrated their interdependence, yet offered through such graphic techniques a perception of the urbanistic whole. The antecedents, as noted in Chapter 4, extended as far back as Nolli's 1748 plan for Rome and Sitte's analyses for Vienna. Copper's 1967 thesis, though relatively unknown, was to have a major impact on subsequent studio projects.

Figure-ground studies often dominated Colin Rowe's urban design studios at Cornell. According to Copper, three ideas dominated such studies: that of figure-ground reversibility; the definition, structuring and zoning of a field; and the application of two orders of hierarchical ranking to the elements within a city. These remain primary considerations in contemporary urban design problems. A comparison between Le Corbusier's 1945 plan for St. Die, France, showing a fragmented urban form composed of *unités d'habitation*, revealed how the twentieth- century city had been dispersed in a fragmented way, unlike the medieval Piazza San Marco in Florence where dominant voids were shaped by solids. To operate correctly, a dominant-subordinate schema must rely on the clearly perceptible dominance of the object over what must surround it and be subordinate to it. Gestalt philosophy indicated a noticeable difference between objects being compared. They should be exceeded several times before a perceptible

hierarchy could be created. An examination of late twentieth-century mid-sized cities in the American Midwest reveals this problem. Here, with the decline of downtown retail and commercial offices from the mid-century onwards, there is a distressingly fragmented physical structure, where, on the periphery of the central business district, demolished buildings have given way to surface car-parks like so many broken teeth in a jaw.

Steven Hurtt gave a more detailed account of Rowe's Cornell urban design studios between 1963 and 1982.[51] He stated that urban design emerged in the early 1960s as a reaction to the urbanistic shortcomings of modern architecture. Urban design was initially created as a programme within architecture, not planning schools (with the exception of MIT). Urban design was not a separate department, degree or programme. Comparatively, there was little literature and no known method, and it was under these conditions that Rowe was invited to initiate and develop urban design as a post-professional degree programme at Cornell in 1963. The methods and theories of the Cornell programme linked studio projects with the evolution of theories of contextualism as well as the 'Collision City' and 'Collage City'.

The Graduate Studio of Urban Design at Cornell University was formed by Rowe's attitudes and beliefs regarding architectural education. Hurtt said that 'Rowe's attitude toward the studio effort needs to be distinguished from a profile that treats architecture as what in scientific or mathematical terms might be called a proof. Proofs are offered only after a hypothesis has been proven, not before. Rowe was not so much interested in proofs but in projects that explored or elucidated problems, however vague or undefined'.[52] Hurtt suggested that what had been written about the Cornell Urban Design Studio created the misimpression that the theories and methods were formed in Rowe's mind from the beginning. He felt uncomfortable that there should be an entity called urban design that was distinguishable from architecture. Rowe proposed that the city had to be considered as a whole (a Gestalt).

Rowe's study method, as previously noted, was the reduction of the complex form of the city to black and white drawings that delineated mass and space (the figure-ground drawings). Taken from Gestalt philosophy, they polarised space and mass, each reciprocal, and the relationships of figure, field, texture, pattern edge and axis parallel to but not dissimilar in many ways to Lynch's visual analysis. Figure-ground drawings allowed the morphological comparison of cities and building groupings. It is suggested that this was a conscious rejection of both townscape theory, invented by Gordon Cullen, as an indulgence in neo-historicism, nostalgia and the picturesque, and the science-fiction visions of megastructures espoused by the British group, Archigram. In 'Collage City', Rowe and Koetter remarked that both were nostalgic, one for the past and the other for the future.[53]

It was apparent that such an abstract method could not discern the range of compositional qualities in figure-ground drawings and that the correlation between actual experience and the drawing was not possible. Despite the rejection of Cullen's theories of the picturesque in *Townscape* theories, one of his strengths was his theory of 'serial vision' or sequential three-dimensional experience by moving through the city and annotating these experiences in the form of sequential perspectives. Figure-ground drawings were largely two-dimensional, though a number of the studio projects were also expressed in three-dimensional block models, orthographic shadow projections on plan and occasionally axonometric drawings of the city.

However, Rowe and his students were generally of the opposite assumption. Cities with high experiential quality were deliberately selected to be examined through figure-ground plans in order to understand complex order and experiential richness. Hurtt indicated that in the studio, figure-ground plans became a design shorthand, carrying rich perceptual potential recalling exemplary urban conditions represented by the figure-ground drawings of Copper.[54] In the early years there was a unanimous feeling that 'the figure-ground plan carried crucial information [as a] genetic code for future design decisions. Three-dimensional implications were only explored to make a case to planners and developers that schemes could be realized with standard technology and building types'. Sites were often assigned without preset programmes. It was, in a sense, an antagonistic rejection of what was seen as deterministic, socio-economic, programme-dominated thinking that had become so pervasive in American society, with a dismissal of the antiurban

Visual illustrations: the Cube (1949), Gordon Cullen.

dogma of modern architecture.

Against the Cornell school of thinking were the schools stemming from the École des Beaux Arts pedagogy engaging, ironically, in the presumptions and procedures of the Bauhaus. Such was the case in the school of architecture (but not the school of planning) at MIT during the late 1950s and early 1960s. The Gestalt emphasis and figure-ground methods encouraged the study of figure-field structures including textures and edges by which such figure-fields were perceived. Hurtt claimed that 'correlations were easily established between traditional urban design principles and those of Gestalt perception[55] at the same time rejecting Cullen's theories which were entirely based on traditional urban design principles and included clear references to the Gestalt theory, including Cullen's 1949 exposition of viewing a hollowed cube in two opposite ways'.[56] 'Hierarchy and focus,' Hurtt went on, 'could be equated to figure, enclosure to closure [another Cullen term] and edge to contour.'

Among Rowe's three major principles, perhaps contextualism is the most important. Contextualism relates closely to the new urbanism theories of the 1990s. Rowe perceived that everything was wrong with the modern movement (of object buildings, surrounded by open space and designed in isolation from both place and cultural history).[57] He created a reaction against figural and anticontext bias and composite buildings and promoted the relation of figure to context in studio work. Hurtt wrote that 'as long ago as 1967, the studio shared the feeling that it had become privy to a new theory of architecture (urbanism). They intended Contextualism to convey the values of the theory as an antithesis to Modern Architecture'.[58] It has been argued that contextualism was intended to reconcile the ideas of Rowe and Venturi as antithetical, and Rowe's ideas, extrapolated from studio projects, were regarded as formalistic and lacking ideality.[59] Rowe's studio projects, notwithstanding, were considered to exhibit an interest in place and continuity of urban form. Venturi was seen as obsessed with the iconography of popular culture. To Rowe and Koetter the idea was not simply an interaction of type and context but of interaction between *ideal* type and context.

The early studios focused on physical context and the deformation of building types rather than on ideal types. 'Collision City' and 'Collage City' attempted to counter the overemphasis of interest in the spatial field and insufficient interest in the psychocultural field.

'Collision City' could be described as a common situation in American cities in which grids of different alignments would abut, join or collide and include the 'broken teeth' syndrome of surface car-parks in downtown areas where buildings had been demolished. Rowe indicated that there was no hierarchy of urban space and no integration. These collision sites were often underdeveloped or deteriorated, and it was suggested that they offered the opportunity to create hierarchy and focus in a way that the regular grid system could not.

Rowe and Koetter went on to explore the implications of this idea and to draw upon related ideas that contributed to it. Claude Lévi-Strauss's notion of the *bricoleur* is invoked as a possible source of design attitudes for the urban collagist. In *The Savage Mind*, Lévi-Strauss distinguishes the *bricoleur* from the engineer and scientist 'by the inverse functions which they assign to events and structures as means and ends, the scientist creating events . . . by means of structures and the "bricoleur" creating structures by means of events'.[60] Again, their attitude to tools is contrasted, the engineer subordinating the task to the availability of raw materials and a purpose-designed set of tools, while the *bricoleur* improvises with a magpie collection of ready-made tools that will be reused for quite different projects.

Through such analogies, and by the investigation of the philosophical implications of the design principle, Rowe and Koetter developed an elaborate and subtle appreciation of the pluralist approach. Against it, one might object that it would hardly be amenable to prescription. By its avoidance of simple and unitary goals, it would be peculiarly difficult for either lay or professional bureaucracies to control, in place of 'the blinding self-righteousness of unitary conviction'.[61] If the freedom is thus a demanding one, we can at least be comforted by Rowe's thought that it might be a means of permitting us the enjoyment of Utopian poetics without our being obliged to suffer the embarrassment of Utopian politics.[62]

Donald Schon, in his 1985 study of the application of design studios,[63] suggested that the idea that professions other than architecture and planning taught in institutions of higher learning had much to learn from architectural education, was a radical – if not unique – point of view. He pointed to the architectural studio as a quite special form of education in the creative arts, drawing upon precedent in the craft system of the medieval guilds as well as the nineteenth-century École des Beaux Arts. The greatest of the European architects in the early part of the twentieth century used the atelier system, and this strongly influenced the organisation of schools of architecture both in Europe and North America. Yet it was also true that studio work in schools of architecture sometimes bore little resemblance to conventional architectural practice, particularly with regard to what Schon described as 'the laborious rendering of technical detail'. The advocates of computer-aided design in architecture would argue that it is precisely by the extensive utilisation of computers that the need for laborious technical details could be obviated, and that the creative aspects of the architectural studio would then be more closely reflected in practice.

Schon's study drew comparisons between the architectural profession and its use of design 'language', as in Rowe's studios of Cornell and parallels in other professions such as law and medicine. It has been argued elsewhere, however, that 'learning-by-doing' in architecture draws upon the experience of medical teaching rather than vice versa.

This detailed account and case study of studio presentation by an individual makes fascinating reading with graphical descriptions in each design review. Such an analysis is of interest to any architectural teacher in assessing comparative processes in other schools of architecture. There is still a persistent emphasis on spatial relationships in which a particular student in the case study and the teacher seem to reject some of the functional requirements of cost and programme usual in architectural practice. Schon acknowledges this in accepting that designers might differ with respect to the priorities assigned to 'design domains'.

Schon also emphasises a further problem. Contrary to previous doctrines of architectural education, architectural design later comprised an extremely complex pluralistic approach with the danger of the architect becoming merely a designer of facades and styles, such as the postmodern movement, not dissimilar to that of a hundred years earlier in the late nineteenth century. The analysis of design evaluation provided independence from stylistic considerations. Such an evaluation, based upon a form of objectivity, allowed the architect to fulfil new and demanding roles, for example the architect/developer.

New roles now require an even wider base of knowledge and it is difficult to see how these new fields of knowledge can be taught within the conventional system of architectural education. One idea was the possibility of architectural education incorporating units of research-based theory and technique while retaining the traditions of the studio as the 'heart' of the curriculum. Schon cited two examples concerning solar research at the University of Southern California and interactions of urban design at the Harvard Graduate School of Design. But, generally, the situation of medical students in the clinic, the engineers in the laboratory or the social workers in the field does not yet apply comprehensively in architecture. The proposal for a 'reflective practicum' suggested a way forward in integrating newfound theories and techniques within the advantages of a studio system.

TRANSITIONS FROM EDUCATION TO PRACTICE

During this time there was a growing number of urban design texts that linked education with theory and practice. Among the more important publications was Jonathan Barnett's *An Introduction to Urban Design*.[64] In his introduction, Barnett stated that this study evolved from a previous 1974 publication, *Urban Design as Public Policy*. While this latter work addressed the issues of New York City, *An Introduction to Urban Design* was much broader in context. Until recently, Barnett was the director of the graduate programme in urban design at the City College of New York and a consultant to such authorities as the New York State Development Corporation.

One of Barnett's most telling comments was that since the inception of the urban design teaching programme in New York, 'no course was taught the same way two years in a row'. The secret of success in urban design education is the recognition of rapidly evolving and often conflicting theories. It was argued that Environmental Impact Analysis, required by Title One of the National Environmental Policy Act of 1969, changed the way in which the government made decisions. Such a requirement had to identify the environmental impact of any proposal, urban action together with adverse environmental effects, and alternatives to the proposed action. Barnett criticised such legislation as a 'process of institutionalized neurosis'. On the other hand, he acknowledged the positive effect created by the energy crisis of the mid-1970s – using less fossil fuel and diminishing the potential of outlying suburbs. Community participation in urban design decisions was also acknowledged as essential and pointed to the previous confrontation between angry citizens and well-established plans (where change had not been possible), which created a sense of helpless anger and alienation. Barnett, in particular, mentions a dysfunctional planning process in the city of Cincinnati, Ohio. Cincinnati had originally developed an excellent master plan for the downtown area in 1948, yet between 1961 and 1963 it had produced three new downtown conventional renewal plans, all of which had failed. According to Barnett, in 1963, Herbert Stevens, the planning director at the time, wrote the following to the City Manager: 'It will be a waste of time to work on a new plan without a process for resolving differences . . . consequently a process should be established whereby the City Planning Commission and City Council can work together . . . in creating a new plan which will lead up a ladder of planning decisions'.[65] By the turn of the century, some fifty years after the 1948 master plans, the downtown area of Cincinnati (unlike Boston, Baltimore, Portland, San Francisco, San Diego and Cincinnati's northern Ohio rival, Cleveland) is still without a comprehensive downtown plan.[66]

Equally, Barnett stressed the need to link urban design policy with preservation movements. Looking back to 1962, we can see the protest against the demolition of one of New York City's most important historical buildings, Pennsylvania Station, which represented the nadir in the public recognition of important architecture. Ironically, this was to contrast with the construction of the new office tower over New York's Grand Central Station. Though it was designated as a landmark in 1967, the design of the tower was one of the worst urban design aberrations of the twentieth century, utilising the transfer of 'air rights' from the landmark itself. The subsequent litigation, which was finally determined by the Supreme Court of the United States in 1978, indicated that the New York City Landmarks Preservation Law did not have the effect of the condemnation of private property for public use without compensation.

Barnett advanced the principle that urban design was a separate and emerging discipline by suggesting that cities could be designed without the design of individual buildings. City planning courses, he said, taught that zoning regulations represented the sole means for implementing master plans, and in New York City, as exemplified in the masterly architectural perspectives of Hugh Ferris,[67] zoning setback lines modelled and created the three-dimensional forms of skyscrapers. Planned unit development (PUD), a technique evolved to create cluster zoning in rural and suburban neighbourhoods, was still actively used at the end of the twentieth century. Zoning regulations were extended in the late 1960s to produce new urban design objectives by the designation of special zoning districts in New York City, in particular Manhattan. This zoning included the Theater District around Times Square in 1967 during the administration of Mayor John Lindsay and while Jaquelin Robertson was director of the Mayor's Office of Midtown Planning and Development. Fifth Avenue was included to preserve the integrity of Manhattan's major shopping street, and Greenwich Street was also designated a special district.

In terms of architectural and urban design education, the third part of Barnett's book is probably the most vital. Its study of land use strategies challenged the basis of zoning as the separation of land uses. It was argued that public policies of a city or small community can produce a more acceptable human environment. An urban design strategy including more traditional land use and transportation planning would be able to provide a more effective guide to development, including the coordination of public parks and public spaces in privately financed buildings as part of public space policy.[68]

An example was the prototypical legislation for more usable public plazas enacted by New York City in 1975 and 1976[69] and prepared by the Urban Design Group of the City Planning Department with William Whyte as consultant. Here, the plaza itself was categorised as primary space, residual space and 'plaza'. However, one of the best examples cited by Barnett was the Citicorp building in mid-Manhattan. Designed by Hugh Stubbins and Associates, this is a remarkable building of its time. The skyscraper, crowned by a monopitch roof (originally intended to house solar panels), is an icon of this section of the city. It is notable because the tower itself commences some eight storeys above street level, close to Park Avenue. The site, occupied by St. Peter's Church, allowed the construction of the massive tower on four giant 'pilotis' above the church itself. It includes a sunken plaza with a subway system entrance but allows for a public plaza at several levels (containing surrounding retail), and with the office block below it soars

Citicorp building, New York (1970), Hugh Stubbins and Associates.

Barnett recognised that the traditional studio form of teaching in architectural schools did not meet the needs of teaching urban design. The cooperative educational programme at the City College of New York offered internships in a professional environment instead of a studio.

Christopher Alexander took this argument somewhat further. *A New Theory of Urban Design*[71] by Alexander and his associates from the Center for Environmental Structure at the University of California, Berkeley, was the sixth in a series concerning urban design issues. Of these, *A Pattern Language*[72] established Alexander's international reputation. Here, Alexander had put forward an infrastructure of ideas with a detailed network of agreed solution types, which was subsequently to be consciously adopted by consumers to operate their own and the general interest. It had entailed a comprehensive and pervasive shift of thought. Rather than the demarcation of public and private interest, it sought their reintegration into a common, universal and interdependent network of preferred design solutions and ranged from the global arrangement of regions down to the most minute of domestic constriction. It had formed, perhaps, the most comprehensive and appealing of consumer utopias to date.

A New Theory of Urban Design was part of an experiment going back some ten years to 1978. Its title acts as something of a challenge to the reader in accepting that it is as radical as it sounds. The precursor to the book was a paper published by Alexander in 1982.[73] The central theme was that cities had been destroyed by modern growth, and it promoted the notion of piecemeal development, a system of emerging wholes, the creation of positive urban space and the centrality of urban growth with five entities that make up cities: buildings, pedestrian spaces, gardens, roads and parking.

Such a simplistic formula was better developed in *A New Theory of Urban Design*. Urban design as 'process' may be taken, in the economic sense, as the response to the power of economic forces shaping the structure of the city not as a physical end but rather as part of a dynamic process.

Alexander maintained that it was the process, above all, which was responsible for wholeness, not merely the form. In creating a suitable process there should be hope that the city might become whole again. This 'wholeness', Alexander said, can be provided by the definition of a number of geometric properties with a centring process. In this, it was recognised that there were many conflicting aims and requirements involved in the changing nature of the city, but that the single overriding rule should be concerned with the 'healing' of the city – perhaps the layering process advocated by urban morphologists such as Leon Krier or even Aldo Rossi. The vivid historical images used in the development of this theme were not identified for the reader and, therefore, lost a certain validity. Equally, the enigmatic use of language in the definition of intermediate rules of growth confused rather than enlightened. Detailed rules of growth became almost too explicit and precise in the allocation of building uses at each stage of a particular project. Roughly drawn examples from the San Francisco harbour area showing such apparently arbitrary growth were followed by photographs of the Ponte Vecchio in Florence, as well as early twentieth-

above on a Piranesi-like scale. Though it reflects earlier nearby public space developments such as Lever House and the Seagram Building on Park Avenue, the Citicorp building has a grandeur of public open space unmatched in twentieth-century Manhattan.

Barnett concluded his study by posing a rhetorical question regarding the difference between an urban designer and an urban planner. He argued that a city planner's job was concerned with the allocation of resources for future need. The implication of this was that the city planner's function was not necessarily creative in a functional sense. Architects were primarily concerned with the design of individual buildings, whereas planners regarded land use as an allocation of resources, of land for zoning purposes without much regard for the three-dimensional characteristics of the city. This seemed to produce zoning ordinances and land use plans that produced 'stereotyped and unimaginative buildings'.[70] Good architecture, he suggested, related buildings to their surroundings. Urban design was within the control of local government, which commissioned a high proportion of urban design studies. But such polemicism often belies the truth. During that decade and throughout the late twentieth century (as we shall see), a relatively small proportion of urban design schemes, per se, were actually implemented.

century photographs of New York and a drawing of Les Halles, Paris, a necessary vision of the powerful imagery to be sought. As in Colin Rowe's precedents, positive urban space was exemplified by a segment of Giambattista Nolli's 1748 plan of Rome, yet this was contrasted with a hazy aerial view of suburban strip development.

In the seven detailed rules of growth, the prescriptive process included building design guidelines, which at this particular point in history could be paralleled by Skidmore, Owings and Merrill's Chicago office's prescriptive urban design guidelines for the London Docklands Canary Wharf project. Base storey, roof line, window area and bay sizes were all included. But whether such a prescriptive urban framework is positive or negative in encouraging good urban design is open to question.

A majority of the study was devoted to the experiment itself, based upon a portion of the San Francisco waterfront north of the Bay Bridge with its existing mixed use. The simulation of developer/community group situations by the students was accepted practice, though it seemed to emulate gaming simulation techniques evolved some twenty years previously.

A 1984 American Planning Association publication by Richard Hedman and Andrew Jaszewski tended to follow a more secular and less academic point of view.[74] Richard Hedman had been a member of the San Francisco Department of City Planning from 1968 onwards, and was one of the leaders in the pioneer San Francisco urban design plan. The authors reasoned for harmonious building relationships rather than disharmony, yet the whole idea of 'good neighbours' is full of anomalies. The attraction of central San Francisco, in particular Nob Hill, is the eclectic mix of architecture. To achieve design unity involved the establishment of eleven rules:[75] building silhouette; spaces between buildings; setback from street property lines; proportions of windows, bays and doorways; massing of building form; location and treatment of entryways; surface material, finish and texture; shadow patterns from massing and decorative features; building scale; architectural style; and landscaping. Yet if these rules were established as part of mandatory urban design guidelines in a city like San Francisco, where would be the place of visual urban variety?

The text suggests that 'contextualism is one of the current trends'.[76] The authors recognised the need for understanding visual perception of urban spaces, both in sequence and the constantly changing field of vision of the observer passing through that space. Again, in terms of urban design education, the authors argued strongly against the placing of urban design education in city planning schools, which did not demand particularly strong architectural skills.

Nicholas Habraken, whose 1976 book, *Supports: An Alternative to Mass Housing*[77] had advocated an argument against centrally controlled attempts to solve low-income housing problems, later developed this theory during his tenure at MIT. The *Grunsfeld Variations*,[78] published in 1981, further developed his work at the Stichting Architecten Research (Foundation for Architects Research) in the Netherlands (SAR methods) between 1965 and 1975. They were based upon an attempt, through studio teachings, to produce a thematic

development of an urban tissue. The graduate students in the programme, drawn from many different countries including Mexico, South Africa, Japan and Puerto Rico, as well as the US, drew up a series of proposals for low-income housing. Habraken suggested that the terms 'theme' and 'variations' were ways of indicating an environment in which specific elements relate to each other according to specific rules. The system depended on 'agreements' expressed in the selection of elements and the distribution of space, not dissimilar from the 'patterns' proposed by Christopher Alexander and parallel to the ideas of advocacy planning of the late 1960s and early 1970s. Habraken indicated the replacement of the term 'theme' with the more specific concept of 'system', with built forms and spaces producing spatial relationships. Thus, he said, they were not variations within a theme, but 'variants within a system'.

The interpretation of this somewhat opaque theory produced results which, in some cases, could only be described as mundane. Unlike *Supports*, which had no illustrations, this study was amply portrayed visually in both two and three dimensions. Students within the team were drawn from the Master of Architecture professional degree programme as well as the Master of Science in Architecture Studies programme. In the synthesis of the study, the team was given a schematic plan in which the tissue theme in question was applied to a fictitious urban context.[79] Habraken said 'the particular merits of the tissue represented by the theme are *insignificant* for the purposes of this work'.[80]

While the 'tissue' level was regarded as no-man's land, urban structure was firmly rooted in urban physical planning with issues like traffic circulation, road network capacity, services infrastructure, green areas and densities. These issues were quantifiable. Urban tissue, it was said, was a field of intervention and exploration in its own right. It was claimed that the development and testing of a valid tissue concept could be quantified and evaluated just as much as the development of an urban structure.

Tissue types cited included the late Georgian terraces of London and the boulevards of Paris, which were seen as 'oppressively monotonous'. Yet the monotony of urban structure proposed by Martha Lampkin and Anthony Mallows with its plethora of statistical data, or the rigid design guidelines for urban streets by Tutaka Takase (albeit creative in their own right) seem to belie the whole idea of the flexibility of 'urban tissue'. The multi-family housing prototypes illustrated by Paula Krugmeier seemed to ignore the need for individual family privacy. Visually, the elevational variations, suggested by José Aldrete-Haas, Andrés Mignucci and Tom Hille did not seem to fulfil the promise of Habraken's *Supports* theory in providing a spectrum of flexibility similar to the work of Lucien Kroll in Belgium. Nevertheless, the exercise was an interesting experiment in urban design studio teaching.

In the same school, the imaginative studios at MIT, started by Kevin Lynch in the late 1950s, had continued. The third edition of *Site Planning*, by Kevin Lynch and Gary Hack, was published in 1984. [81] This study stretched back almost twenty years, and the 1984 edition was extensively revised to include much of the experience of Gary Hack. What was notable about this publication was that it had provided a valuable resource book, not just in the field of urban design (linking architecture and urban planning), but extending into landscape architecture. There had long been a dichotomy between landscape architecture and city planning where landscape architecture was seen as a discrete field of study, an adjunct to architectural design but not part of it. Frank Lloyd Wright was one of the few visionaries to connect the two. The emigré architect, Richard Neutra, in California, also recognised the connection.

According to Lynch and Hack: 'Site planning is the art of arranging structures on the land and shaping the spaces between, on art linked to architecture, engineering, landscape, architecture and city planning'.[82] Theirs is a highly analytical work including politically charged examples of site-planning issues. The explicit studies for the chemical industries of ARCO are a model of this kind. The sequential diagrams of the relationship between the two research centres for chemicals and polymers raises the issues in diagrammatic form of the reuse of existing buildings, including a school campus, open space proposals utilising English landscape ideas and a projection of future building needs.[83]

In many ways, *Site Planning* is highly technical and stands out from many of the other urban design texts discussed previously. It included, for example, soil surveys, water tables, subsurface problems, landforms and plant cover, which form part of the larger landscape in a subcontinent. It also addressed social issues, a recurring theme of Lynch throughout his years of research.

Access was regarded as a key element of urban design, though, in a sense, it was a reiteration of the themes of many other writers. The analysis of street systems was useful in this context. It ranged from grid patterns, which were criticised for monotony, to radial and linear patterns. Superblocks, a theory developed by Le Corbusier some fifty years earlier, was criticised for imposing a more circuitous path on local traffic and impeding pedestrian access with the lack of crosswalks and peripheral road systems, as opposed to central road systems, analysed in terms of minimising the cost of urban development.

A surprising section was on 'The Moving View'. Though Lynch had denied the relevance of Cullen and serial vision, this publication argued that: 'People in motion are oriented to the forward direction and a focusing of paths gives us the feeling of a strategic common point.'[84]

The concluding chapter was 'Other Uses'.[85] One of the best examples was the University of Virginia, designed by Thomas Jefferson as a prototype of an ordered American university campus. Trinity College in Cambridge, England, was also illustrated as an example of a consistent spatial vocabulary despite a much greater variation in age and styles of building than the University of Virginia.

This extension of landscape architecture into the realm of urban design was taken even further by Barrie Greenbie in *Spaces: Dimensions of the Human Landscape*.[86] In a profusely illustrated book, Greenbie uses examples from both private and public domains. The most important message is the way in which man-made environments either constrain or facilitate social interaction. Such a humanitarian objective is praiseworthy. The many illustrations are, for the large part, photographs taken by the author that give a useful visual analysis of major American cities such as New York, Boston, Atlanta, St. Louis and New Orleans. But equally important were the small towns of New England including Massachusetts, Connecticut and Maine.

In his analysis of Boston, for example, Greenbie makes the distinction between a 'distemic' (see below) urban centre and proximic neighbourhoods. In reference to Lynch's much earlier studies of the Boston downtown peninsula as well as his studies of Jersey City and Los Angeles, Greenbie suggested that many Boston neighbourhoods had low imageability in terms of Lynch's 'middle-class subjects'.[87] In a romantic reference to American history, and the American Revolution in particular, the imagery of Paul Revere and the North End of Boston are recalled. In 1776, most of Boston was under water, but the symbolism was important. Symbolism, as Lynch had already stated some twenty years earlier, was important in terms of the smaller New England cities. The 'common' was a functional node and symbolic nucleus, just as it was in the UK some five hundred years earlier. Though few large cities in New England had retained their 'common', Boston was an exception. The Statehouse, determined by Lynch, was a major landmark. Designed by Charles Bullfinch and constructed in 1799, it had become, with its gilded dome, a major landmark assisting pedestrian navigation in the city, according to both Lynch and Greenbie. In the latter part of the twentieth century, the construction of new skyscrapers in the financial district had destroyed much of its impact. Greenbie lamented the violent visual contrasts which had occurred in contemporary downtown Boston and suggested that 'the little old Statehouse sits like a piece of a child's toy village among the grown-up furniture in the heart of the financial district . . . this absurd violation of scale and inversion of symbolic importance'.[88]

In addressing the issues of the city of New York, Greenbie argued that in terms of symbolic meaning, the Statue of Liberty in New York harbour was more imbued with distemic meaning for travellers arriving in the US than any other symbol. Roebling's historic Brooklyn Bridge, opened in 1883 and preceded by his Cincinnati suspension bridge (the model for the Brooklyn Bridge), was equally symbolic. The Empire State Building in mid-Manhattan was also cited as an important icon. Yet it was the Rockefeller Center that was to become the most important connection between urban landscape design and urban architecture created in the US. This brilliant piece of urban intervention, built during the Great Depression, was to take urban design a major step further into the future. It is not the architecture of the buildings but the magnificently articulated outdoor space that makes it such a wonderful experience. Raymond Hood was a 'mid-modern' architect of the fashionable art deco style and a follower of the strict height-to-width ratios demanded by building regulations. The unity *and* variety of Hoods facades provided a complex juxtaposition of building forms, planting, street furniture and, above all, activities, which made it the heart of social life in Manhattan.

In the contemporary late twentieth century, another dimension is exposed. It is not only the sunken plaza which is revealed, alternating between a skating rink in winter and café square in summer, but the much more visually startling roof gardens on the ascending setbacks of the various skyscrapers that form the composite whole. The contrast between the life of the Rockefeller Center Plaza and the sterile Lincoln Center complex, also in mid-Manhattan, west of Rockefeller Plaza, could not be more poignant. The Lincoln Center – probably the most prestigious centre of the performing arts in the world – is, apart from the performances, devoid of human activity, and its 1960s architecture can only be described as banal.

One of the main themes in Greenbie's comprehensive study is what he calls distemics. Greenbie establishes an important differentiation between proxemics and distemics.[89] He says that the term 'proxemics' was defined by Edward T. Hall in 'The hidden dimension',[90] with the etymological explanation of the word explained as a combination of 'proxemal', or near, with the suffix '-emic' used by anthropologists to describe a system viewed from the inside. Greenbie took the term proxemic as an adjective to describe culturally homogeneous urban communities or city neighbourhoods. While acknowledging that spatial behaviour is unconscious, conflict is lessened if a group of people of the same culture share (and control) the same area. On the other hand, he recognised that in the contemporary twentieth- or twenty-first-century city, areas are shared by people with different cultural values and codes of conduct. In this way he coined the term 'distemics' to pair it with 'proxemics'. He criticises the view of sociologists in using the terms 'primary group' and 'secondary group' as a difference between intimate and other relationships. Levels of intimacy within a culture are quite distinct from members of different classes or cultures.

To illustrate this, of all distemic public places, the oldest in accommodating social diversity is the market place, which overcomes the natural reaction of xenophobia within any given cultural group. Thus Times Square and Rockefeller Plaza in New York are distemic public spaces. Greenbie cites Jane Jacobs' theory that the essential characteristic of the city is a 'community of strangers'.

In 1986, Roger Trancick published *Finding Lost Space: Theories of Urban Design*.[91] Like Greenbie, Trancick examined traditional urban space in terms of the theories, vocabularies and issues of urban spatial design. In so doing, he proposed a method that lay between site-specific design and urban land use plans, based on the concept of urbanism, not master-planning. Lost space is left over at the base of high-rise buildings, unused sunken plazas, surface car-parks, unused land alongside freeways, abandoned areas, brownfield sites of derelict industry and blight clearance sites that remained undeveloped. Resulting from this was a need for design in which plans are themselves generators of context, in which building defines public exterior space instead of displacing it, and the sequence of space, and not individual pieces of it, should be emphasised.

Trancick criticised the garden city concept, suburbia and new towns, which was contrary to the new urbanist movement and Seaside, Florida, in particular. He urged the reuse and readoption of existing areas, and correctly observed that many new

towns were merely dormitories. A successful public space was City Hall Plaza in Boston, designed by Kallmann and McKinnell; although public reaction to it was at first negative, the square acted as a stage for circulation and public events. Construction made the urban fabric more dense, suggesting that large public spaces at the base of monuments can work if there are enough public services and if the area is dense enough to generate activity.[92]

Trancick propounded three theories of urban spatial design. First was the recognition of figure-ground studies based on the environmental pattern of solids and voids, with voids as entry or foyer space, inner block voids, streets, squares, parks, gardens and linear open space. Second, the 'linkage theory' is based on lines connecting objects such as streets and other linear open spaces. The system of connections is thus created in a network that establishes a structure of ordering space. Finally, 'place theory' adds the component of human needs and culture to physical design, taken from Lynch's theory of continuity with the past and the response to time and place.

Urban Design: the American Experience[93] was a wide-ranging study of American urbanism. Author John Lang was Director for Urban Design of the Environmental Research Group at the University of Pennsylvania, Philadelphia, where he taught from 1970 to 1990. An Australian and Professor of Architecture at the University of New South Wales in Sydney, he continued his association with the University of Pennsylvania until 1993.

Unlike the studies of Greenbie and Trancick, which examined the social and environmental issues within the context of American urban history, Lang's concern was with the creation of liveable, and especially enjoyable, built urban environments. Lynch, Trancick, Greenbie and Lang were all concerned with a user-oriented approach in achieving a higher quality of life in human settlements.

Thus, Lang's major work examined twentieth-century American urban design within a socio-political context. Though spanning the twentieth century, including Burnham's City Beautiful movement in Chicago, the emphasis of this study was on developments after the Second World War and the latter half of the twentieth century. Discussing neo-modernism, as well as rationalism and empiricism, Lang created an understanding of how people experience the environment and the implications of experiencing architectural and urban design. While it points to design methodology (a fashionable issue of the 1960s), there were in fact many other issues to be considered in creating optimal urban environments.

Lang reiterates the fact that urban design in America was influenced by theories and practices from Europe and, in this, the public sector in the US had an important role in developing urban design. Attempting to integrate the social sciences with behavioural systems, he indicated that these aspects were necessary in the development of architectural theory. He criticised projects based upon intuitive processes but avoided pursuing new paradigms that redefined urban design and constructed theories on empirical bases such as neo-functionalism. Psychological, aesthetic and cognitive methods are also discussed. Here it is suggested that urban design has become a part of architectural theory existing both in rationalism and empiricism (Le Corbusier versus Radburn) and the basic belief seems to be the need for pragmatic empiricist solutions for adapting to changing cities. However, whether Lang's definitions are accurate is questionable. Seaside, Florida, and Laguna West (Peter Calthorpe) are defined as postmodern urban design. Bernard Tschumi's plan for Corona Park, Flushing, New York, and Peter Eisenman's Visual Arts Center at Ohio State University are defined not as deconstructivist theory, but as neo-rationalist. Christopher Alexander and Charles Moore are seen as neo-empiricist.

THE COGNITIVE CITY

Kevin Lynch expanded his previous theories on the cognitive city with his *Theory of Good City Form*.[94] This was somewhat more vague in its intentions than previous work, or, at least, it was more abstract. The study posited that there were three basic planning theories: the environmental decision-making process; the social, biological and physical forces that created the elements of city form; and 'normative theory', which examined spatial policies concerning growth, migration and the creation of new towns in terms of implicit and explicit values of these policies. Utopian visions are considered, including Shaker settlement in states such as northwestern Kentucky, and contrasted with the visions of 'Superstudio',[95] a contemporary European (Italian) vision of utopias. Lynch referred to this as a 'cacotopian' as opposed to a utopian vision. Good planning policy should be on the boundaries of dream and reality.

On the other hand, it is questionable whether a normative theory is possible, since at the time there was no adequate normative theory on city form. Perhaps it is not possible to create such a theory because physical form has little role in satisfying human values unless it is extreme. Lynch argued that orientation of time and place were important and have a congruence between environmental structure, on the one hand, and non-spatial structure on the other. This thought was concerned with earlier theories of legibility and the utilisation of symbolism referring to the significance of place that is difficult to design. In the final part of the study, it seems that Lynch fell into the trap of social engineering, for although agreeing that there was no optimum size for a city (and indeed in a democracy there is little that can be done to determine this), he suggested 'self-governing' units of between twenty and forty thousand people as an ideal city size, a concept that harks back to the utopian theories of the eighteenth, nineteenth and early twentieth centuries in proposals such as J. S. Buckingham's 1849 plan for Victoria in England.

Lynch's personal utopia was an urban countryside, which was neither urban nor rural (but also not suburban). Streets would be set among trees with small, intense urban centres.[96] However, this seems contradictory since his manifesto said there would be no cities surrounded by suburbs. This new form would evolve from previous foundations, with old cores retained and rebuilt, with no private ownership but only lease-holds. In further flight of fancy, Lynch suggested basic needs would be cheap and the standard of living simple. Thus there would be less luxury and less consumption, which would result in little theft or vandalism; all people would be responsible for the land and each other, with a reduction in the amount of meat eaten, everything recycled and everyone with a role in society.[97] This optimistic vision, ideal as it may sound, did not make it into the twenty-first century.

To some extent, this utopian vision was developed by Richard Meier in *Ecological Planning and Design*.[98] It is suggested that community ecology could provide an understanding of nature and that this allows planning problems to be broken down into small components. Yet again, like Lynch, Meier seemed to be suggesting a form of social engineering in stating that there was a need to plan for the future life of the community through the neighbourhood organisation of cities. He speaks of a hierarchical system from single room, house, housing group, small neighbourhood, large neighbourhood, small polis up to the largest, the ecumenopolis of 50 million people. Boundaries, Meier said, should be mapped, and changes decided upon if deemed necessary. But this begs the question as to who is responsible for these decisions. Resource conservation, he correctly observed, should be a part of the plan.

Perhaps a less ambitious but more relevant study of the cognitive city was that by Philip Thiel in *Visual Awareness and Design*.[99] A student of both Lynch and Kepes, Thiel said the study owed more to Kepes than Lynch. It was an approach to visual design inspired by the work of Kepes. Much of communication is either verbal or visual and the environment is full of visual methods. The basis of the book was a course programme developed after interaction with undergraduates in urban planning, architecture and management. The course was non-competitive with students working in cross-disciplinary groups in the studio. Thiel's study emphasised the importance of the sight and flow charts produced, identifying problems, constraints, goals, hypothesis, simulation, testing criteria, comparison of solutions, implementation, evaluation and management.

Most of the exercises were simple and focused on the identification of visual criteria. Thiel says the city is generated by a stochastic process, which he defines as 'a sequence of probabilistic operations that produce a series of unprecedented individual events with a predictable overall character'.[100] Within these constraints occur the random actions of many different individuals and groups over long periods of time. The confusion of the city lies not in its form, but in the mind of the viewer.[101] Some say that professional difficulties in coping with large-scale environments are due to a historical preoccupation with iconic single buildings or traditional compositional forms and groups.[102]

Similar analytical approaches appear in Allen Jacobs' book *Looking at Cities* (1985)[103] and his earlier study *Observing and Interpreting the Urban Environment* (1982).[104] The earlier work suggests it is possible to learn a lot about a city by looking at its physical environment. This was a student project to test a technique for observing and diagnosing change in the urban environment. Similar to some of Lynch's earlier techniques, the case study was accomplished by walking in an environment unfamiliar to the observers but organised by a group who knew the area well. The area selected was Naglee Park, San Jose.[105] Jacobs stated that many of the observations and assumptions proved to be correct, but there were also misconceptions. 'Correct' observations related to the history of the area, changes, current characteristics and the dynamics of change. Among the misconceptions was a failure to perceive that gentrification had taken place, as well as the growth of a strong community organisation with changes in zoning laws.

Looking at Cities related to the earlier University of California study. It also offered ways to look at a city and begins with a walk around San Francisco with observations of architecture, street signs and people. The book also refers to the earlier Naglee Park study and a section called 'Clues' is the visual recognition of signs and symbols such as the number of doorbells on a house, architectural style, age, function and condition. Change can be seen in the physical, social and wealth (presumably upward and downward). A proliferation of 'For Sale' signs is a clue to rapid change. In the conclusion, a pertinent observation was that observers of visual urban design were often made to feel like intruders and challenged where walking was considered inappropriate, and sketching was more acceptable.[106] Cars should be used instead of walking, or even bicycles. Observation should take place only when an area was busy, and there should be at least two observers. Talking to inhabitants was useful.

Similarly, Donald Appleyard and Allen Jacobs' *Toward an Urban Design Manifesto*[107] supported the phenomenological views espoused by Kepes and Lynch, while at the same time rejecting not only the manifesto of the CIAM (Congrés International d'Architecture Moderne) and the modernist movement but also the garden city ideals.[108] Their new manifesto looked at contemporary problems: poor living environments, large-scale development, loss of control, large-scale privatisation, loss of public life, decentralisaiton, placelessness, injustice, inequality and susceptibility to fashion. The modern movement and the garden city movement, it was claimed, did not produce 'good' environments because they did not look at the design of public spaces and ignored the positive physical and social attributes of existing cities.

Appleyard and Jacobs suggested that new goals of liveability, identity and control by the inhabitants could be achieved by providing six physical characteristics: liveable streets and neighbourhoods with sunlight, clean air, landscaping and open spaces; a minimum density of fifteen dwellings per acre up to a maximum of forty-eight units per acre; integration of activities; buildings arranged to define public space; public places and a public way system especially for pedestrians; and different buildings and spaces within a complex arrangement and relationship.

URBAN DESIGN GUIDELINES: DESIGN REVIEW AND DEVELOPMENT CONTROL

What emerged from these views of the cognitive city was the perceived need for a new mechanism in city planning. Yet in contemporary American practice all of these proposed systems are flawed. Urban design guidelines are only helpful if they are utilised in urban development plans. But too often, with notable exceptions such as San Francisco, Portland, Oregon, Boston, Baltimore, Denver and San Diego, most developers and their architects choose to ignore them since they have no legal standing in most cities. Design review is an even more pernicious system. Urban design review panels for urban areas mainly consist of designers and architects sitting as peers reviewing the design proposals of their professional colleagues. The system usually fails because the development applications are often examined on a block by block basis, ignoring the adjacent four blocks (in a gridiron city) without the benefit of an urban design plan. In essence, they are architectural, not urban design review panels. Development control in the European sense is little used.

In the UK, for example, development control examines not only land use and zoning, but also the aesthetic merits of the proposal. This is the subject of much controversy, of appeals and legal action. Planning officials are more likely to seek positions in strategic and economic planning, while the junior staff oversee development control (often with little or no training in three-dimensional architectural design and a bias toward neo-historicist solutions). In the US the situation is worse. City planning commissions and regional planning commissions usually examine planning applications within the strict confines of zoning laws and land use policy. Architectural and urban design considerations are held to be beyond the remit of the commissioners and, therefore, three-dimensional and contextual issues are often overlooked, including such important factors as topography. Proposals are presented as two-dimensional flat plans.

Thus Richard Bender in *Design Review*[109] argues, somewhat inaccurately, that such a process has always existed in some form and that it has been intended to create good design. However, he acknowledges that in contemporary America the public has little influence and the clients and investors have the most control over design. Certainly community empowerment projects in the 1960s increased public interest in controlling their environment. A design review, Bender claims, extends this influence, though he suggests that design control can be achieved through zoning. Design review is usually initiated by local government and not grassroots organisations. In defending zoning as an urban design control mechanism, he indicates that New York City zoning has been used creatively. Architectural urban design competitions are an alternative way to ensure good design, but these are used more in European countries (especially Germany), and relatively few are implemented in the US. Private review of private development occurs in the case of major university campuses. The University of Washington in Seattle, the University of California at Berkeley and the University of San Diego all have design review boards. A notable example is the University of Cincinnati, Ohio, which has had a design review board over the last decade (1990s) and has implemented architecture by Peter Eisenman, Frank Gehry, Michael Graves, I. M. Pei (Cobb) and Rudolfo and Machado among others, as well as a campus-wide landscape plan by Michael Hargreaves. Bender says that design review is best when it is integrated into the planning process. Standards can be laid down after a panel makes architectural surveys of an area, in the same way that historic district preservation plans are drawn up.

The enforcement of a design review is more difficult. It may be linked to the building permit and other discretionary actions. Design review boards are mostly composed of specialists in architectural and urban design as well as some members of the local community, usually volunteers. And most prescriptive guidelines do not carry the weight of law.

Donald Appleyard and Peter Bosselmann's *Urban Design Guidelines for Street Management*[110] addresses the issue of what is popularly known as 'traffic calming'. Liveable streets evolved in Europe, particularly in the Netherlands (Woonerf) and in Germany (Woonerven). The authors say that drivers are slowed by the streets being made 'visible' for pedestrians, through the use of raised crosswalks, sidewalks (pavements) covering the whole street space and 'chicanes' (or curvilinear geometry) to slow down traffic speed. Parking is at right angles to the street, cycling facilities are provided and attention is paid to surface materials, natural landscaping and street furniture, including signs.

The authors argue that crime is reduced because more people use the street, whereas in the US streets are deliberately designed to encourage fast traffic. Recommended techniques in residential areas should be extensive planting, hidden parked cars and textured surfaces, such as brick, employed throughout.

Among other recommended measures are the planting of tall trees with space for growth, street plazas, speed bumps and sidewalk crossings lowered for the handicapped. Street activities, such as skateboarding and rollerblading, should be encouraged, and parks, places for ballgames and for sitting and talking should be provided. Are these eighteen-year-old recommendations applicable to contemporary America at the turn of the century? Casual observation suggests that these activities, desirable as they may be, have been superseded by more intense pressure on daily living, where a multiplicity of pedestrians use mobile phones and eat or drink while walking (euphemistically referred to as 'grazing').

Urban environmental design was introduced by the Department of Housing and Urban Development (HUD) as an eligible cost for community development. Genevieve Ray describes the application of this policy in the US in *City Sampler*.[111] A general view is that American cities grow in response to economic forces, contrary to the concept of urban design. By the use of comprehensive planning, zoning, urban design, engineering and urban law, urban environmental design is achievable as part of community development. The HUD saw this as a response to the need for urban design administration. In examples cited, Baltimore pioneered the employment of urban designers to coordinate activities in urban renewal districts. In Minneapolis, the urban design division of the department of planning and development provided design review services for neighbourhood projects, development districts, special projects and historic preservation. In New York, an urban design team in the planning department provided design expertise to other city agencies in setting physical development policy and regulations. In San Diego, urban design staff provided appraisals of city policy. The University of Wisconsin provides design and planning assistance to small, rural communities.

Tools include design review, design controls and design incentives such as the use of design guidelines in Portland, Oregon (for historic preservation districts and conservation districts) and Seattle (using an environmental review committee to assess the impact of new development). In Baltimore, residents help in the creation of urban design guidelines for homes and neighbourhoods, including a design advisory panel of experts, a special area review board, a civic design commission and a review panel commission for historical and architectural designation. Implementation can be achieved through historic preservation, waterfront development and pedestrian and street design.

The necessity for urban design guidelines was also expressed by Wayne Attoe.[112] Most urban design in America, he said, was pragmatic instead of idealistic, as in Europe, and driven by market economics. Pragmatism only works if revitalisation is created in the long term. Yet Attoe seems to contradict this by claiming American urban design is based upon European values without an American vision: mixed-use development, buildings and spaces as building blocks, the importance of history, public spaces and streets, the incorporation of different forms of transit and citizen involvement. Urban designers, Attoe says, should arrange 'catalytic reactions' that result in the incremental regeneration of the urban fabric.

URBAN DESIGN AND BUILT FORM

Tall buildings emerged in American cities in the late nineteenth century. The Alphabetical City[113] was composed of buildings that developed from gridiron plans in the shape of the letters U, E, L and T. Such buildings depended on adjacent structures for meaning. Between the 1880s and 1940s the American city became more vertical with the invention of the elevator, steel frames and electricity. The emerging skyscrapers, nevertheless, developed on the existing grid, allowing the continuation of the urban fabric.

Rodolfo Machado and Jorge Silvetti presented a different historical perspective, albeit within a different and shorter time span.[114] They argued that two schools of thought in urban design had developed over the last 25 years (from 1965 onwards) on how cities should be understood and made. The positivist model focused on categorisation such as land use, infrastructure and urban systems. This led to urban-architectural formalism. Urban design was seen as physical, based on type, morphology and the urban fabric with phenomenological descriptions. The other was more poetic, with an interest in the invention and search for a more responsive urban architecture. Cities should be appreciated subjectively, with site-specific design less important. The formal organisation is based on the image of the city. Machado and Silvetti claimed that they did not distinguish between the realm of architectural fact and the public realm of the city.

This emphasis on the importance of the public realm can be seen in the Steps of Providence for the Rhode Island School of Design. The school uses existing buildings, part of the urban fabric, many of which are of historical importance. In creating a tangible, positive urban space, the steps themselves are not just functional but also create a tangible, positive urban space. They tie the dislocated campus together, beginning at the bottom of the hill as a 'grand urban staircase' that becomes smaller as they move uphill. In Pioneer Courthouse Square, Portland, Oregon, the design proposal was intended to create an exemplary American urban public space that would be flexible, legible and durable. The imagery of the courthouse was strengthened by placing a greenhouse (conservatory) at the opposite end of the square. The conservatory had a central open gateway and the square had four flagpoles at the corners combined with pergolas and shelters.

One possible view of urban design, as a true representation of the social system and as an expression of user choice, is provided by the idea of the city as a battleground of competing private interests. There are obvious historical precedents for such a notion, as, for example, in the skyline of San Gimignano and, to a lesser extent, Bologna, which are still dominated by the unlikely towers competitively erected by feuding medieval families. Today, competition is widely accepted, at least within the confines of shopping streets and shopping centres where considerable freedom for display is permitted within the boundaries of shop windows, and rather less beyond them.

Nor could it be argued that the controls that customarily limit such display and restrict its proliferation in signs and advertisements beyond the shop window are misguided. Traditionally, highly regarded spaces such as Times Square, New York, are remembered for their unconstrained display of those elements that elsewhere are restricted in the interests of urban design. Not only do these restrictions prevent the development of new and unexpected urban forms (the contemporary equivalents of the San Gimignano towers), they tend to promote unimaginative, conforming solutions, the banality of which invites further controls.

The investigation of private display as urban design was *Learning from Las Vegas*, published in 1972 by Robert Venturi, Denise Scott-Brown and Steve Izenour and based upon a Yale University School of Architecture study in 1968. Venturi and his colleagues developed a critique of architecture and urban design that paralleled that offered by Rudofsky and others in respect of vernacular success by opposing an alternative, apparently unselfconscious and vital tradition to the conventional culture of professional architecture. Their theory of 'Ugly and Ordinary Architecture' in which characteristics of the strip and modern architecture were contrasted: 'Decoration by the attaching of superficial elements' in the former against 'Unadmitted decoration by the articulation of integral elements' in the latter could be expressed by such terms as 'Symbolism' against 'Abstraction' and 'Expedient' against 'Heroic.'

Venturi's position on the exuberant display of the strip is somewhat different to that of Wines, both of whom make compelling visual images of their buildings using dramatic variations of the conventional language of architecture. SITE' s images of reversal and collapse, for instance, are witty and artistic manipulations of the spectator's expectations. Venturi, on the other hand, proposed a new insight, a ready-made collection of values and techniques quite different from those normally adopted by architects. While Wines's jokes are more

Molino Stucky Mills, Venice, Italy, James Wines/SITE.

effective for being unexpected and uncommon, Venturi's strip was offered as a universal, a generic model of one possible form of urbanism.[115]

And yet it is difficult to see what kind of relationship this model could strike up with conventional modes of architecture. Venturi castigates the efforts of the 'Strip Beautification Committee' for applying conventional notions of improvement such as tree planting and unification of building treatments, since these misunderstand and compromise its real character. But if the efforts to make the strip conform to 'architecture' are doomed, the converse seems hardly more promising. Venturi catalogued the efforts of modern architecture to absorb earlier models, such as industrial buildings, Italian hill towns and Cape Kennedy, and ranges these as symptomatic of the architectural method with which the 'vital mess' of the strip contrasts. And if these sources could not be enlisted without some loss of their original virtue, it seems hardly possible that assimilation of the strip would be more successful.

If Venturi's message is difficult for architects to apply, and perhaps more exhilarating in its iconoclasm than its formulation of new models, it does carry for the urban designer one straightforward exhortation that contrasts with other views considered here:

> The commercial strip . . . challenges the architect to take a positive non-chip-on-the-shoulder view. Architects are out of the habit of looking non-judgmentally at the environment because orthodox Modern architecture is progressive, if not revolutionary utopian and puristic; it is dissatisfied with existing conditions. Modern Architecture has been anything but permissive: Architects have preferred to change the existing environment rather than enhance what is there. For the artist, creating the new may mean choosing the old or the existing. Pop artists have relearned this. Our acknowledgment of existing commercial architecture at the scale of the highway is within this tradition.[116]

Thus Wines' iconoclastic architecture is very different from the views expressed by Venturi and his colleagues. Bruno Zevi, in his introduction to *SITE: Architecture as Art*,[117] suggests Wines and his colleagues provide results that 'no doubt have a humorous connotation, but behind them, there is a notable toil of inventiveness and critical intelligence. Clearly the polemic is against the "finite object"'. Levi says that the beauxarts approach had canonised the 'finite' ideology, such as the Seagram Building and the remainder of New York's Park Avenue towers and boxes. Positing that de-architecture is an answer to the present state of foolishness, cynicism and laziness, it provokes simply because it offends academic common sense. It states that the finite building box, before being functionally absurd, is visually ridiculous. SITE's philosophy was an extension of the most authentic American culture in that it was heretical and realistic at the same time.

SITE's use of the term 'de-architecture' from 1972 onwards presaged, perhaps, the term 'deconstruction' a decade later. The theory was intended to challenge the notion of a building as the product of insular hypotheses, while acknowledging that it was one of a number of philosophical viewpoints that had emerged during the 1970s, each also acknowledging that the crisis of communication is a crisis of sources and available alternatives to the senile repetition of modernist formulas. Postmodernism declared that architecture had to be salvaged from the dehumanising legacy of modernism by the inclusion of anecdotal references to historical and popular imagery and by metaphorical allusion and a new plurality of sources.[118]

The basic purpose of de-architecture, in both theoretical and built form, was to explore new possibilities for changing professional and popular response to the sociological, psychological and aesthetic significance of architecture and public space. Rather than treat art as a decorative accessory to architecture, SITE's work has been a hybrid fusion of both disciplines.

James Wines returns to these theories in a later publication, *De-architecture*,[119] in which he classified it as a frame of reference for questioning the nature and practice of architecture. Again, Wines suggests that there is a crisis in communication. Postmodernism is seen as a land of non-communication, while modernism lacks an iconographic potency due to its inappropriate imagery in a disordered, pluralistic world.[120] Postmodernism, epitomised in the works of Stern and Graves, was considered by Wines as eclectic.

URBAN DESIGN AS INVERSION AND ICONOGRAPHY

Despite his criticism of over-diversification, Wines' own proposal for the Paz Building in Brooklyn, New York, is itself highly eclectic.

SITE's proposal in 1983 to convert an 80-year-old YMCA building into a multi-use commercial space showed a continuation of the group's powerful use of imagery. The designers said that this imagery should reflect the general spirit of the community with its conditions of contrast. Themes such as old/new, decay/rebirth, worldly/religious and closed/expansive are visually evident in the neighbourhood. In contrast to the entertaining 'building failure' structures of its earlier work, SITE produced an impressive, if somewhat sombre emergence of a new building from the ruins of the old.

Another project for the Frankfurt Museum of Modern Art is perhaps more interesting for its use of interpenetrating structures, a device used elsewhere in the work of Ungers and others. While in a sense it was a historic study using a German factory prototype, it contradicts the view of the urban morphologists in actually distorting, or at least disturbing, the fabric upon which it is placed.

In addition, in 1983 Emilio Ambasz had produced a design for Houston Center Plaza in Texas in a more sophisticated essay on the same theme. This garden, with its powerful imagery, reversed the normal role of the city centre, with its underground theatre, restaurants and exhibition areas. Ambasz saw the solution as a physical, metaphorical and spiritual image of the city of Houston. The dominant feature of the proposal was its square grid, the strength of which lay in the fact that it (apparently) permitted endless expansion. Its weakness was that it did not allow for the definition of a well-defined centre. Yet it had potential, since the purity of the grid could be used as a backdrop against which the urban interventions could be read. Thus, the grid of the city was transformed into the grid of the plaza, with a rough edge on the outside representing the incomplete nature of the growing city, and the square pool in the centre representing the plaza in the city.

The plaza was also meant to show various aspects of Houston on a metaphorical level. The culture of the city is represented by the theatres and galleries, the commerce by the shops, the advanced technology by the laser exhibitions, the life and energy of the city by the life of the atrium at the heart of the shops and galleries.

But most important of all was the spiritual quality of the space. The outer part of the plaza consisted of an array of trellises on a square grid covered by vines, with colourful, fragrant flowers growing between them. The ground sloped down from the edge of the plaza to the large square pool in the centre with its circular opening above the atrium. The taller trellises towards the centre were like gazebos with portals and seating. Each enclosure was to have mist emanating from the top, thereby cooling the surroundings. The gazebos were seen as social spaces, for relaxation from office work, places to talk and meet friends or for quiet contemplation amid green shade.

The work of Ambasz was celebrated in 1989 at an exhibition at the Museum of Modern Art, New York.[121] This compared or contrasted Ambasz with Steven Holl. Both architects were seen to represent a generation formed during the collapse of modern ideology, searching for meaning and symbol by a return to historic models of architectural education. Ambasz looked towards the archaic and primitive, while Holl looked to the anonymous vernacular of the city and small town. Both shared a strong sense of the need for architecture rooted in place.

Ambasz created the virtual integration of buildings and earth, and Holl connected existing culture and the physical markings of the site. Ambasz emphasised the importance of landscape by bringing the gardens into the city, using the traditional urban square as a point of departure. Holl's theoretical and experimental urban design was intended to provide an alternative to modernist planning and historical methods, by seeking a new urban landscape based on the notion of a psychological urban space that 'would allow the modern soul to emerge'. His technique was to compose urban spaces and ensembles in perspective before a three-dimensional creation was projected into two-dimensional plan fragments. At the end of the design process, the designed fragments were brought together as a master plan.

A final example of this design philosophy is Coop Himmelblau's *Architecture is Now*.[122] Coop Himmelblau was founded in 1968 in Austria by Wolf D. Prix, Helmut Swiczinsky and Michael Holzer. Their uncompromising goal was to create 'architecture . . . that bleeds, exhausts, that whirls and even breaks'.[123] Their designs became, in a sense, increasingly aggressive – theirs was a radical shift in architecture. They saw the city as empty and banal, and while most of their early works were sculptures in the city, the two most relevant to urban design were The Skin of this City in 1982 and City and Utopia, a model of an urban building intervention – walls of nerves without urban skin. This bore no resemblance to any existing urban form. A scheme for an Apartment Complex in Vienna, in 1983, was for 50 two-storey, partially finished apartments to be altered and changed by the occupants, not dissimilar in ideas to those of John Habraken in the Netherlands with his theory of supports and those of Belgian architect Lucien Kroll. Wolf Prix later established practice and teaching in Southern California.

URBAN MANIFESTOS

Quite different from the espoused theories of Wines, Ambasz and Prix were the more abstract and perhaps more complex manifestos of Bernard Tschumi and Rem Koolhaas. Tschumi rose to prominence with his well-publicised winning design for the La Villette, Paris, competition in 1983. At two separate levels, the project reflects, perhaps accidentally, design antecedents from elsewhere and certainly from outside Europe. Significantly, one of the competition assessors was the talented Brazilian architect Roberto Burle-Marx, whose exotic tropical designs complemented the modern urban architecture in Brazil. Indeed, the modern baroque forms of Oscar Niemeyer, Alfonso Reidy and others required the dazzling colours and curvilinear forms of Burle-Marx's gardens. In the same vein, the dramatic forms envisaged by Tschumi for the urban park of La Villette do not summarise the grand formal tradition of French landscape architecture and can in no way be considered historicist.

Another analogy occurs in the curvilinear forms of the late twentieth-century fun fair or theme park. The interlocking geometries of highly complex gravity rides, when seen on engineering drawings, have a startling resemblance to Tschumi's plans. The casual observer may be forgiven for thinking at first sight that they are indeed the plans of an urban fun fair, similar to parts of Copenhagen's Tivoli Gardens.

However, Tschumi had more profound objectives than this. He believed that the park formed part of the vision of the city:

> The competition for the Park of La Villette is the first in recent architectural history to set forth a new program, that of the 'Urban Park', proposing that the juxtaposition and combination of a variety of activities will encourage new attitudes and perspectives. This program represents an important breakthrough. The 1970s witnessed a period of renewed interest in the formal constitution of the city, its typologies and its morphologies. While developing analyses focused on the history of the city, this attention was largely devoid of programmatic justification. No analysis addressed the issues of the activities that were to occur in the city. Nor did any properly address the fact that the organization of functions and events was as much an architectural concern as an elaboration of forms and styles. The Park of La Villette, in contrast, represents an open-air cultural centre, encouraging an integrated programmatic policy related both to the city's needs and its limitations.[124]

In *Manhattan Transcripts*,[125] published in 1981, Tschumi writes: 'Books of architecture, as opposed to books about architecture, develop their own existence and logic. They are not directed at illustrating buildings or cities, but at searching for the ideas that underlie them. Inevitably, their content is given rhythm by the turning of pages, by the time and motion this suggests. The books may be read as sequences, but they do not necessarily imply narratives'. The transcripts consist of frame-by-frame descriptions of an architectural inquest, but 'by no means do they comprise a definitive statement'.[126] The transcripts were mainly composed of drawings, though other forms of notation were devised at various stages of the project.

The Manhattan Transcripts, Tschumi claimed, were neither real projects nor mere fantasies.[127] The book included a mixture of elegant drawings by Tschumi counterbalanced by photographs of New York. He describes this as an architectural interpretation of reality, with the photographs witnessing events, while the drawn plans, sections and diagrams indicate the movements of the different protagonists – people intruding into the architectural 'stage set'. While Tschumi correctly acknowledges the influence of Sergei Eisenstein in his film scripts or Laszlo Moholy-Nagy in stage directions, there is no reference to Cullen's serial vision, the goal Tschumi was seemingly endeavouring to attain. Apparently, the explicit purpose was to transcribe those things normally removed from conventional architectural representation: the complex relationship between spaces and their use.

Composed as a series of essays, sequences defined as MT1, MT2, MT3 and MT4 are discrete episodes in themselves. MT1, for example, is composed of 24 sheets illustrating the drawn and photographic notation of a murderer. The plot describes the lone figure stalking its victim, the murder, and, finally, the capture of the murderer.

MT1 is based on Manhattan's Central Park; MT2 is based on a typical street – 42nd Street (notorious at the time for the selling of pornography, strip clubs, peepshows and prostitution). MT3, The Tower, refers to home, office, prison, hotel and asylum as common denominators and MT4 shows five inner courtyards in the city with contradictory events.

The brilliance of such a totally new and radical system of urban design analysis is without question. As Tschumi himself states: 'The original purpose of the tripartite mode of notation (events, movements, spaces) was to introduce the order of experience, the order of time – moments, intervals, sequences – for all inevitably intervene in the reading of the city'.[128] As such, they surpass the earlier techniques used by Lynch, Appleyard and others some twenty years previously. The narratives implied by the composite sequences could be linear, deconstructed or dissociated.

In MT4, each horizontal sequence (made of five frames notated A, B, C, D, E) is part of a simultaneous vertical relation that contains the three equal conditions of object, movement and event (notated 1, 2, 3). Tschumi correctly observes that the movement notation is an extension from the drawn conventions of choreography, eliminating preconceived meanings given to particular actions, so as to concentrate on spatial effects, the movement of bodies in space.

Tschumi's pursuit of the interpretation of the city through time and space, as well as those of Thiel, Appleyard and others seeking a more complete and precise method of describing the visual phenomena of the city, suggests that these annotative methods would themselves lead to the reform of the subject of their study. This line of inquiry, begun at MIT in the 1950s, was further developed by Appleyard in his Environmental Simulation laboratory at the University of California, Berkeley, during the 1970s.

By the end of the 1990s, the development of virtual reality and the Internet presented boundless opportunities. By means of such techniques, the urban designer can perform his or her main function, which is presumably seen as being able to formulate and present the problem as accurately and vividly as possible.[129]

However, it may be objected that while an accurate statement of the problem is invaluable and may lead to a more rational debate, it cannot in itself provide solutions. Further, the pursuit of apparently authoritative and neutral techniques may mask those value judgments which urban design problems invariably entail. A rhetorical commentary on the search for new descriptive and analytical methods to pin down such elusive problems is provided by those artists who have presented the record of the act of creating a work of art as the work itself.

The work of Rem Koolhaas is different. It might be argued that the rationalist movement in Europe had developed what will be referred to here as the 'third typology'. The new rationalist analysis was selective in its approach to the third typology in that it seems, in practice, to show a preference for a specific urban prototype, the nineteenth-century European city with an orthogonal street pattern. This preference is heavily reinforced by the use of an architectural language, which Colin Rowe aptly described as 'the tricking out of Beaux-Arts plans with neo-primitive facades'.[130] Although by no means an inevitable accompaniment of the original analytical intention to seek basic urban solution types, the choice is not an arbitrary one but, as Leon Krier has set out, forms part of a package of social and architectural intention, which together constitute the great themes of this movement:

1   The physical and social conservation of the historical centers as desirable models of collective life.
2   The conception of urban space as the primary organizing element of the urban morphology.
3   Typological and morphological studies as the basis for a new architectural discipline.
4   The growing conscience that the history of the city delivers precise facts, which permits one to engage in immediate and precise action in the reconstruction of the street, the square and the quartier.
5   The transformation of housing zones (dormitory cities or suburbs) into complex parts of the city, cities within the city and quartiers, which integrate all the functions of urban life.
6   The rediscovery of the primary elements of architecture, the column, the wall, the roof etc.[131]

The conviction and consistency with which this programme presented itself should not prevent us from examining the logic of its urban design component, and, in particular, its assertion that the study of historical form-types provides us with a relevant and useful basis on which to proceed. It is, after all, not long ago that those same form-types were being condemned as 'a picture of the seventh circle of Dante's inferno' and the nineteenth-century city 'as it exists in actuality' as 'an absurdity'.[132]

It might be argued that the particular model of the third typology has been undermined by forces additional to the preferences of the modern movement and that these must be recognised in any new approach. This argument was developed in a project run by Cornell University with O. M. Ungers, Rem Koolhaas and others at the Sommer Akademie of Berlin in 1977, where they sought to define an effective urban design strategy for that city. Here it was concluded that 'the current opinion whereby the historic quarters of the city can be preserved and saved only through additional and integrant building stems from erroneous assumptions and is therefore illusory'.[133] The fallacy arises from the depopulation of the city that undermines all the bases upon which a return to the historic forms ignore the activities and events that the city contains (except perhaps those that celebrate the virtues of 'collective life') in defiance of the view expressed by Tschumi that 'What matters is that there is no architecture without the relationship between live actions and the spaces themselves'. By contrast, one might compare Venturi's strip, which although generated by private display, works as an overall system to identify variations in intensity of use and points of focus of activity as they come into effect. One might suggest, then, that the new rationalist analysis of existing city form has identified those formal elements and structures that tend to stability and uniformity, but has omitted those equally pervasive structuring principles that tend to variety and change. This does not diminish the value of the first analysis, but might reinforce the argument that the analysis can be separated from the formal preferences that the new rationalists attach to it. If Tschumi's manifestos were seen to be radical, perhaps those of Rem Koolhaas were even more extreme.

Koolhaas's *Delirious New York* was published in 1978.[134] Koolhaas was born in Amsterdam in 1944, studied architecture in London and later moved to New York as a Harkness Fellow in 1972. In 1973 he was a Visiting Fellow at Manhattan's Institute for Architecture and Urban Studies and later became a co-founder of the office for Metropolitan Architecture (OMA), which produced the notable competition design for Welfare Island, New York, in 1975, with O .M. Ungers as team leader. The design bore certain similarities to Tschumi's designs elsewhere. Koolhaas had proposed that the urban block should be reinvestigated as the 'fixed typological unit' in a series of standard variants on a generic theme. Such a large-scale type of study was also accompanied by local but no less generic manifestations of the public realm.[135]

Perhaps this pursued as ruthless a disregard for the surrounding urban fabric as the redevelopment projects condemned by Ungers, Leon Krier, Rob Krier and other rationalists. The obsessive concern for the character, shape and organisation of public space gave the vision of the meaning of the term 'urban design' a particular urgency. It was expressed in terms familiar enough to those who, having developed doubts about the efficacy of the modern movement, nevertheless felt unable to abandon its rigorous climate in favour of the more soporific alternatives of conservation.

Delirious New York suggested that there was a consistency and coherence to the unrelated episodes of Manhattan's urbanism. It was an interpretation of Manhattan as the product of unformulated movement, the true programme of which was so outrageous that, in order for it to be realised, it could never be declared. This was a retroactive manifesto of Manhattan's architectural enterprise, untangling theories, tactics and dissimulations within the grid. The Office of Metropolitan Architecture developed a theory of a Culture of Congestion with a polemical investigation of Manhattan and its symbiotic relationship between a mutant metropolitan culture and its unique architecture.

In its subtitle, the book was defined by Koolhaas, as 'a retroactive manifesto for Manhattan'. In the ten or so years since its publication, the OMA has designed major urbanisation projects in Amsterdam, Rotterdam and Lille, as well as Atlanta and Tokyo.

A 1989 preview of Koolhaas's 'The Contemporary City'[136] included an interview in which Koolhaas surprisingly said that the 'most visionary architect, the one who best understood the ineluctable disorder in which we live, remains Frank Lloyd Wright and his Broadacre City'. In addition he said that 'the projects I have been working on have been situated in a territory that can no longer be called suburbia but must be referred to as the borders or limits of the periphery. It is here, on the edge of the periphery, that we should observe how things take shape'. If the periphery became important to Koolhaas, it had yielded a form of manifesto in some ways similar to Wright's Broadacre City or Joel Garreau's *Edge City*, first published in 1991.

Koolhaas, in a sense, seems to celebrate the concept of urban sprawl by indicating that his models are not Paris or Amsterdam, but Atlanta (that contemporary American city), though at the same time he contradicts this by saying that *except* for 'certain airports and a few patches of urban peripheries', the image of the modern city has 'nowhere been realized'.[137] The resulting stratum of neo-modern negates the traditional city as much as it negates the original ideas of modernity. He referred to the IBA in Berlin in 1977, where he believed himself and Ungers to be dissenting voices from Krier, Rossi, Kleihues and other rationalists.

THE ARCHITECTURE OF EXCITEMENT

According to Koolhaas, the city was home to 'architectural mutations' (Central Park and the skyscrapers), 'utopian fragments' (the Rockefeller Centre and the UN Building) and 'irrational phenomena' (Radio City Music Hall). In addition, it was seen as 'several layers of phantom architecture in the form of past occupancies, aborted projects and popular fantasies'.[138] In stressing the fact that the metropolitan condition is one of hyperdensity, Koolhaas believes that Manhattan's architecture is a paradigm for the exploitation of 'congestion'.

Yet the most prominent celebration was not of Manhattan itself but of Coney Island, to which Koolhaas refers as 'The Technology of the Fantastic'. Coney Island was, apparently, discovered one day before Manhattan in 1609 and inhabited by the Canarsie Indians who named it Narrioch, meaning 'place without shadows'. In 1885, the first railway extended to the centre of the island along the beach. An infrastructure developed with bathhouses, food, supplies (including the 1871 invention of the hot dog) and accommodation. The 90-metre (300-foot) tower that celebrated the centennial in Philadelphia was moved in 1876 and reassembled in the centre of Coney Island. In 1883, the anti-gravitational theme initiated one of America's first Loop-the-Loop railways, though the technology for this was flawed, resulting in a number of serious accidents. The roller coaster that replaced it in 1884 was the first fun fair roller coaster in the US, though not a new invention – having been developed in Russia in the fifteenth century as an ice slide in St. Petersburg. This was known as the Flying Mountain, and by the eighteenth century it became the first roller coaster to use wheels. Later, a device called the Switchback was developed for the Gardens of Orienbaum, using vehicles with small wheels that ran in shallow grooves down a sloping track with gentle hills. In 1804, another roller coaster with wheels, Les Montagnes Russes (Russian Mountains), was constructed in Paris, France.

Early rollercoasters, Coney Island, New York.

The first-ever roller coaster built in the US came from the coal-mining hills of Mauch Chunk, Pennsylvania, where Josiah White, a mining company executive at Summit Hill, needed a way to transport coal down the mountain. This railway system became known as the Gravity Road, in which trains filled with coal would be sent down the mountainside – a 30-minute journey – with one brakeman sitting in the last car. Mules would haul the cars back to the mine – a three-hour journey. By 1845 White had completed a return track on which the cars would be pushed back by steam engine. The 30-kilometre (18-mile) circuit became known as the Mauch Chunk Switchback Railway, and by 1873 it attracted more than 35,000 tourists annually.

The Coney Island fun fair roller coaster of 1884 was designed by an Indiana inventor, La Marcus Thompson, and constructed on 10th Avenue in Coney Island. It was 600 feet long and cost five cents a ride. Thompson's Switchback Railway was followed by the Serpentine Railway, designed by Charles Alocoke, which eliminated the need for the switchback process. The third Coney Island roller coaster, with taller and faster hills than its two predecessors, followed in 1885, and was designed by Philip Hinkle. The number of roller coasters in America reached its peak of 1,500 by 1929.[139]

But Coney Island's reputation declined as quickly as its popularity had risen; it was sometimes referred to as 'Sodom and Gomorrah', although George Tilyou had pioneered new rides in the 1890s, including a Ferris wheel and the Steeplechase. The Steeplechase was ridden on mechanical horses on 'an automatic racetrack with gravitation as its motive Power', the walled enclosure of which was to become known as Steeplechase Park, and later Luna Park, operated by Frederic Thompson and Elmer Dundy.

Thompson, who had trained as an architect and later rejected the formalism of a beaux-arts architectural education, became, wrote Koolhaas, 'a financial genius and entertainment professional'. He had borrowed from Tilyou's park-enclave model for Luna Park. According to Tschumi: 'The lake is lined by a forest of needle-like structures, specimens of Moon architecture'. Thompson's own comments indicate the acuteness of his private rebellion against beaux-arts repression: 'You see I have built Luna Park on a definite architectural plan . . . I have eliminated all classical conventional forms of its structure and taken a sort of free renaissance . . . the (skyline) is an ensemble of snow-white pinnacles and towers lined against the blue firmament'.[140] Thompson, Tschumi suggested, had designed and built the appearance, the exterior of a magic city. Dreamland, Thompson's subsequent development that opened seven years after Steeplechase, was to be built in Manhattan itself on 6th Avenue between 43rd and 44th Streets as a 'post-proletarian' park, with the backing of Senator William Reynolds. It included park rides such as the Canals of Venice and the Tunnels of Love. In contrast to the two other parks, the whole of Dreamland was painted white.

However, the Great Depression and the Second World War were about to bring the demise of the Coney Island Complex, exacerbated by the impact of television. Coney Island, in totality, closed for good in the early 1960s.

EPCOT (Disney), Florida (1982).

Other examples of this type of urban entertainment development included the opening of Disneyland in Anaheim, California. Around the same time that Koolhaas had published *Delirious New York*, the Disney Corporation had taken such a venture to further limits, with the construction of EPCOT (Experimental Prototype Community of Tomorrow) in Florida. Overleaf, the EPCOT Center is illustrated in an aerial photograph, under construction in 1982. EPCOT may be said to fall precisely into the category of urban utopias, but it remains, nevertheless, as a utopian concept rather a blueprint for the future.

Walt Disney's original vision for EPCOT was not as a fun fair, as Disneyland, but as an ideal community with parallels and analogies to many of the nineteenth-century utopias in Europe and North America. Disney's view was that 'People actually live a life they can't find anywhere else in the world today. EPCOT will be a "living blueprint" for the future . . . a fully operating community with a population of more than 20,000. Here American free enterprise will constantly introduce, test and demonstrate new concepts and technologies years ahead of their application elsewhere'.[141]

The reality is sadly different. EPCOT never became the ideal community or the urban utopia.[142] Instead it was developed by Disney's successors as a gigantic theme park or even a world trade fair. Construction commenced in 1976 and was nearing completion by 1982. Certainly the project perspectives and progress photographs show an uncanny similarity, but neither reflected the utopian framework suggested in Disney's early statements. Perhaps the sponsorship by American industry did much to distort the original idealism and, for all the advanced technology employed in the entertainment and movement systems, the suggestion that EPCOT reflects an ideal world is somewhat far from the truth. Finance may or may not represent the participation of such countries as Japan, Germany or the UK, but it undoubtedly left a notable gap concerning the views of the then eastern European block of communist nations or many third-world countries. Similar to the market-economy view of enterprise zones in England at the time, EPCOT tended to turn its back on the world of reality. As a fun fair, such a disregard for reality can lead to enchantment; as an urban utopia, such a view is unacceptable.

Nevertheless, by the beginning of the twenty-first century, the Disney Corporation was to produce an ideal utopian settlement, matching Seaside, Florida in the form of the new town of Celebration, also located in Florida.

CELEBRATION OF THE SKYSCRAPER

Another important development at the time was that special and peculiar American architectural invention, the skyscraper. Koolhaas suggests that the Manhattan skyscraper, born between 1900 and 1910, had evolved since the 1870s with the invention of the elevator and the use of the steel frame in building construction. The 'Globe Tower', a hypothetical skyscraper published as a cartoon in *Life* magazine in 1909 was, he said, a theorem that described the skyscraper supporting 84 horizontal planes.[143]

The Flatiron Building in mid-Manhattan, built in 1902 and designed by Daniel Burnham, has always been an original icon of this building type, some 22 storeys high. The 1913 Woolworth Building, much taller with some 60 storeys, is less elegant but was the forerunner of all subsequent skyscrapers. The 1916 New York City Zoning Law used an imaginary envelope to define the outlines of maximum allowable construction and clearly influenced the later skyscrapers of the 1930s, such as the Empire State Building, the Chrysler Building and the Rockefeller Center, all in Manhattan. Koolhaas points to the magnificent yet eerie perspectives by Hugh Ferris, illustrating these laws in an almost surrealist way.

In 1929 Ferris published these visions in *The Metropolis of Tomorrow*.[144] Celebrated, too, was Radio City Music Hall with its equally eerie, syncopated, automated dancing of the Rockettes. But most curious of all was Koolhaas's description of another peculiarly American phenomenon, the Downtown Athletic Club. Built in 1931 shortly after the Wall Street Stock Exchange Crash, this enormous structure of 38 storeys on the banks of the Hudson River near Battery Park was a building of enormous complexity. It included an interior golf course, complete with the transplantation of an 'English' landscape, as well as a Turkish bath for massage and, according to Koolhaas, it catered for 'puritanical hedonists',[145] where men could finally confront the opposite sex on a small dance floor located on a seventeenth-storey roof garden. Yet one curious illustration of the oyster bar adjacent to the locker rooms was of three naked athletes wearing boxing gloves and eating oysters. Such homoerotic imagery seems at variance with the proclaimed objectives of the club itself. The Downtown Athletic Club was a 'machine for metropolitan bachelors whose ultimate "peak" condition lifted them beyond the reach of fertile brides'.[146]

Towards the end of Koolhaas's startling book there are beautiful drawings of unbuilt skyscraper designs. The constant, ongoing political battle of Times Square and adjacent 42nd Street had still not been adequately resolved by the beginning of the twenty-first century. Yet Koolhaas's design for the Hotel Sphinx on a corner of Times Square (1975–76) could have created a new, and perhaps appropriate urban typology for mid-Manhattan. The building was to straddle two blocks at the intersection of Broadway and 7th Avenue. The idea behind this proposal was that it was a 'luxury hotel as a model for mass housing'. Such an enigmatic statement is puzzling, and the complexity of the connection between all the subway stations adds to the contradictions. Nevertheless, the imagery shown in the drawings is breathtaking, with its twin towers that contained double-height studio apartments, creating an architectural duality in opposition to classical and neoclassical architectural principles. Like his historic model of the Downtown Athletic Club some 45 years earlier, the design emphasised physical culture and relaxation in the phallic representation of the head of the Sphinx as a domed structure at the top of an enormously tall circular base.

Another version of Koolhaas's celebration of the New York skyscraper is a contemporaneous design (1975–76) for Welfare (now Roosevelt) Island in the East River, parallel to Manhattan. Unlike Ungers' proposals, Koolhaas suggested that all the high-

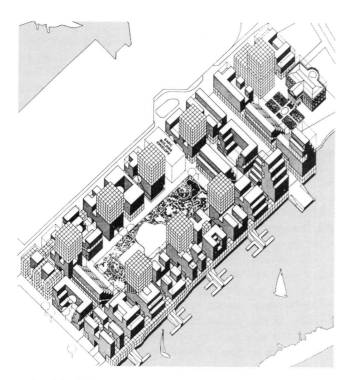

*Welfare Island Competition, New York (1975),
O. M. Ungers.*

rise blocks would be connected by an elevated horizontal travelator from the river bridge southward down the centre of the island, which he described as an 'accelerated architectural promenade'.

Finally, Koolhaas illustrates his Welfare Palace Hotel (1976), in which he proposed a city within a city, also on the southern tip of the island site, with towers increasing in height as they move away from Manhattan.

URBAN DESIGN AND ACTUAL BUILT FORM

While the fantastic designs of Tschumi, Ungers and Koolhaas represented a visionary future, the reality of what was happening in the US during this decade was somewhat more mundane.

Urban renewal was experiencing a new phenomenon. Revolutionary changes in freight transportation technology such as containerisation made many seaports and docks across the world redundant. New transoceanic ships of huge proportions were replacing the multitudes of former small cargo ships, resulting in the decline of labour-intensive dockside industry. Hence, ports like London, Boston and even New York were no longer significant.

The emerging public and political concern with the issues and problems of the inner city led to many radical proposals including community architecture initiatives, advocacy planning and enterprise zones. But these proposals, mainly politically based, tended to disregard the urgent necessity for rational physical planning structures for the public and private realms. Examples of this are the missed opportunities that involved

notable firms of American architects and planners in London Docklands.

It is interesting to note that the need to renew nineteenth-century docklands was by no means confined to the newer derelict parts of London and Liverpool in the UK. Probably the most notable achievements in the revitalisation of waterfront areas in the latter part of the twentieth century were to be found in the US. Most planning trends, whether in retail systems, transportation, engineering or commercial development, seem to have originated in the US some ten to fifteen years before similar trends began in Western Europe; the waterfront developments found in San Francisco, Boston, Baltimore and New York are no exception. American architects and planners appeared, by and large, to recognise the importance of urban context, a factor that has been sadly lacking in the plethora of widely differing proposals by developers in the London Docklands.

The methodical systems used by American planners in seeking the best possible development within the urban context contrasts sadly with the British approach, which, during the 1980s, took a much looser and more pragmatic view. The result was that the visual coherence and unity noticeable in developments in the US was not reciprocated in the UK.

The London Docklands Development Corporation (LDDC) was established in 1981, following the closure of the West India and Millwall Docks. The LDDC was the first Urban Development Corporation established by the Thatcher Administration. The important difference between these and the former New Towns Development Corporations established from 1947 was that the new later corporations were not only the planning authority of the designated areas with the statutory right to produce a development plan, but also had the implementation authority for subsequent design and construction. The LDDC was believed to be an enabling authority within a strict market economy, responsible only for assembling sites through the purchase and sale of land and providing infrastructure renewal (including transportation systems) as well as incentives to maximise private investment.

However, though the LDDC was charged with development control, it lacked the statutory authority to prepare a conventional development plan. This, combined with the designation of an Enterprise Zone with *no* formal planning controls, local tax exemptions including 100 per cent capital allowances on new construction and no development land tax, created a recipe for visual anarchy and ad-hoc development Such an economic atmosphere encouraged inflationary land prices and property values with the corporation continually seeking higher and higher prices for land to pay for the infrastructure provision. Housing land in the Isle of Dogs, where the North American investment for Canary Wharf was situated, rose from around $60,000 per acre in 1982 to $7 million per acre five years later.

The inevitability of the redevelopment of the London Docklands was always clear. Encouraged by the deregulation of the London Stock Exchange in 1986/87, as well as the revolution in information technology, it created a subsequent demand for office space of an entirely new type. Such inevitable financial success could have been foreseen. Once success was experienced, it was hard to understand why there was not greater effort in seeking to satisfy the government's Department of the Environment remit that 'regeneration should be secured by creating the ability to attract substantial private investment, especially in industrial, recreational and affordable housing development ... and that ... the highest architectural and environmental standards in built form should be sought'.

The subsequent ad-hoc development was a result of the negation of the urban design plans drawn up by David Gosling and Gordon Cullen in 1982 as 'too prescriptive', and it was the Canary Wharf proposal that was to really change planning attitudes in the Isle of Dogs. The initial Canary Wharf master plan was presented in September 1985 by an American consortium led by G. Ware Travelstead and architects Skidmore, Owings and Merrill of Chicago.[147] The proposal was to construct a 10 million square foot financial development on a 70-acre site in the West India Docks. This included three towers, 790 feet tall. It is ironic that LDDC had previously rejected the concept of an urban design plan as an example of prescriptive planning, but welcomed a master plan with strict design guidelines produced by an outside agency. An office workforce of 40,000 was projected for Canary Wharf alone, presenting a major transportation problem in terms of model split. The design guidelines produced by Skidmore, Owings and Merrill[148] to ensure the development of individual parcels by different architects and developers would reflect the intentions of the master plan.

The guidelines were the subject of analysis and appraisal by consultants and the technical staff in LDDC. Gordon Cullen questioned the unusual height (for London), haphazard siting of the three towers and conflict between these and the Greenwich Axis, which is regarded as one of the finest urban vistas in Europe. Cullen suggested that, instead of three large and disparate towers, a cluster of medium-height towers at the eastern end of Canary Wharf would be more appropriate. A more significant analogy for the development would be to envisage it as a miniature Manhattan rather than a vertical nineteenth-century neoclassical city. Cullen also pointed to the reduction of the water areas as a result of this proposal, saying that there was an even greater urgency to conserve and accentuate other adjacent water basins and proposing a water square at the eastern end.

In 1987, David Gosling, Stephen Proctor and John Ferguson drew up an alternative proposal for the eastern end (Phase 2) of Canary Wharf, eliminating two of the skyscrapers and retaining only the major one (later to be designed by Cesar Pelli) on the north–south axis of the Docklands Light Railway system. The public spaces and squares were seen in a more formal relationship and the eastern end terminated by two smaller gateway towers on the east–west axis. The proposal was incorporated in a revised scheme drawn up by Skidmore, Owings and Merrill for the subsequent developers after mid-1987 by Olympia and York of Canada.

The LDDC also, albeit belatedly, recognised the need to generally review the planning proposals for the Isle of Dogs. Although by January 1987 much development had already taken place, the rapidly rising land values, demolition and redevelopment within only four or five years, implied that such a review was necessary. A new plan included the Canary Wharf revisions and the northern water court proposals, relating them to the possible redevelopment of the Millwall Docks, with air space studies over and above existing development where low-rise development was no longer financially viable. This, together with the growing shortage of land, implied the use of air rights above the first wave of industrial buildings, such as the Olsen Lines shipping terminal designed by Norman Foster, constructed from 1982 onwards.

The pressure to build to greater densities and greater heights had grave implications on future developments to the east, down river. These hitherto undeveloped areas, including the East India Docks and the Royal Docks, have been the subject of a variety of planning proposals, including one by Benjamin Thompson of the US.

In 1986, Janet Abrams, writing in *Progressive Architecture*,[149] said: 'The buildings erected since the publication [of the original plan by Cullen and Gosling, 1982] bear out [Michael] Wilford's contention that few developers would pay much attention to the guide's recommendations, since it lacked the authority of a statutory development plan.[150] By pitching its objectives so low, the corporation has denied itself the opportunity of achieving anything but a mediocre visual and experiential environment. Wilford agreed with Gosling's own conceptual studies, relegated by Hollamby and Ward to the Guide's Appendix, which emphasized the need for a well defined public realm to pull together the inevitable variety of architectural form and quality entailed in the Enterprise Zone concept'.

In an earlier article Michael Wilford wrote: 'The conceptual studies prepared by David Gosling represent approaches based on clearer urban structures and stronger relationships between the public and private realms than those indicated in the Conceptual Diagram (a pragmatic plan). His options advocate the strong and coherent public realm necessary to organize the inevitable variety of architectural form entailed in the Enterprise Zone concept'.[151]

The planning potential of the Greenwich Axis, connecting Nicholas Hawksmoor's eighteenth-century St. Anne's Church, Limehouse, Inigo Jones' Queen's House, Vanbrugh's Greenwich Palace (The Royal Naval College), the Greenwich Observatory and All Saint's Church, Blackheath, is now irrevocably lost, and the elevated track of the Docklands Light Railway, which carves a crooked path across the Isle of Dogs with the futuristic pathos of a World's Fair monorail, did nothing to solve the public transportation issue. Indeed, the provision of mass public transport, advocated by planning and engineering consultants in 1982, was not completed until 1999. The Jubilee Line extension, which is now built, an extension of the London Underground system, would have provided access for the tens of thousands of office workers predicted for the Canary Wharf Development.

In the early 1990s, Olympia and York filed for bankruptcy, a contrast with the similar but much more successful Battery Park City development on the southern tip of Manhattan with a master plan also by Skidmore, Owings and Merrill. The imagery of Canary Wharf was not assisted by the terrorist acts of the IRA during this decade.

Heron Quays Urban Design Guideline Study,
Gosling, Proctor et al. 1988.

Heron Quays Urban Design Guideline Study,
David Gosling, Stephen Proctor et al.

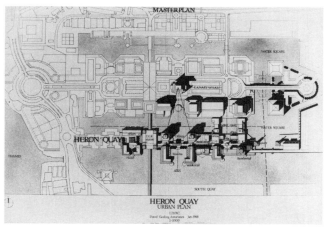

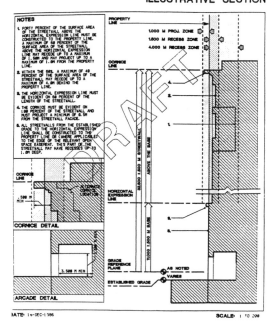

Street wall condition. Canary Wharf Guidelines, 1986.

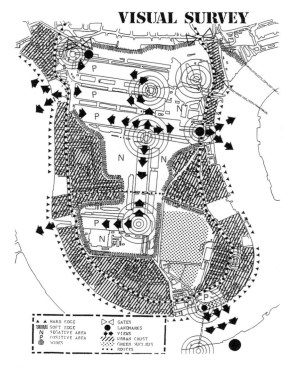

Isle of Dogs, visual analysis.

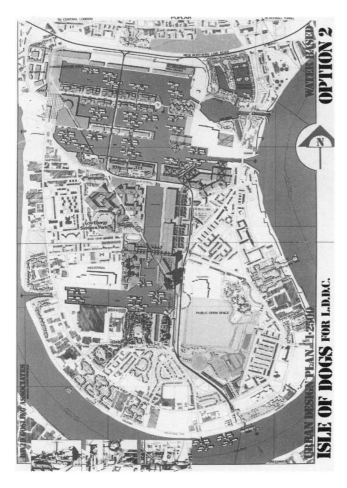

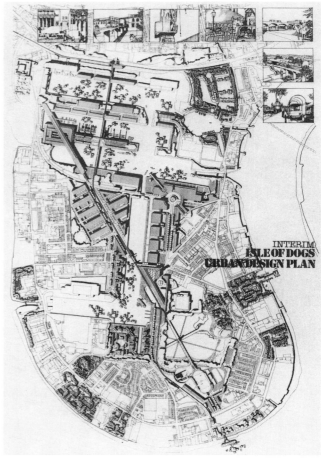

Isle of Dogs Urban Design Proposal, Option 2,
David Gosling and John Ferguson.

Isle of Dogs, Interim Option,
David Gosling and John Ferguson.

Waterfront development in the US was less controversial; it emerged up to fifteen years before this type of development in the UK, and included the notable Quincy Market redevelopment in Boston, which had an obvious influence on the subsequent Covent Garden Centre in London.

A publication by Douglas Wrenn and others for the Urban Land Institute is a comprehensive survey of American achievements.[152] The study, as an account of built projects, also included a historical survey of the original role of waterfronts in both inland and coastal ports. Technically, it included geographic locations, analyses of water and land resources as well as climatic effect. Equally relevant was the assessment of the effect of government legislation at both state and local levels. The authors recognised the importance of the urban context sadly lacking in the plethora of widely differing proposals from developers in the London Docklands. The methodical systems used by American planners in seeking the best possible development within the urban context extends from project planning and initiation through project analysis, preferred development programmes and finance and leasing arrangements. Of the case studies, Union Wharf in Boston, the

Embarcadero in San Diego and the Inner Harbor in Baltimore are models of their kind.

One of the most significant statements in Wrenn's book was that

Citizen participation is necessary to ensure that public sector values are not sacrificed in order to accommodate private development. The public and private sectors must work together to create a manageable community involvement process that respects both public objectives and private property rights . . . Major waterfront redevelopment programs such as the Inner Harbor in Baltimore require several years to plan and implement. For such an undertaking to be successful, there must be a strong public sector commitment (and investment) to carry the program through to completion . . . the amenity of the water's edge will not compensate for poor judgment and bad management in developing urban waterfront sites. In fact, the difficulties of shoreline development will only be exacerbated by incompetent development efforts. The Thatcher Administration, which sponsored the establishment of the London Docklands Development Corporation in 1980 and greatly admired the US achievement, should have realized that public investment, planning, design and commitment was needed just as much as the injection of private capital.[153]

Many of the contributors to a later study, published in 1988 by Hoyle, Pinder and Hussein,[154] were geographers who drew a very different perspective from Douglas Wrenn's earlier publication. Much of the polemic was based in the realm of economics and physical planning and did not really address urban design issues. In a carefully structured book of 'Frameworks for Analysis', 'Policy and Practice' and 'Strategic Planning Issues', it logically took the reader through the process of such a specialised development. Typical examples, described by John Turnbridge, were, predictably, Harbor Place, Baltimore and Quincy Market, Boston. These examples pointed to the conflicts that had emerged later in the decade between profit-oriented development and concerns for social justice with the need for conservation policies.

A positive urban design plan was that commissioned in 1985 by the City of Ithaca, New York, and Cornell University. Sir James Stirling, Michael Wilford and Associates and British architectural consultants in London prepared the Collegetown Urban Design Study in February 1985.[155] The report was to determine how the area of Ithaca surrounding Cornell University might develop in the future, and recommended criteria for the formulation of appropriate zoning ordinance revisions. In the introduction, Wilford reiterated his statement, published elsewhere, that urban design *is* (or should be) architecture and not a separate activity mediating between planning and building. In retrospect, this might be seen as wishful thinking since, like Gosling and Cullen's design guidelines for the Isle of Dogs, London, it was never implemented, though the Performing Arts Center, commissioned by Cornell University, was built, and is an outstanding example of urban design within a conglomerate of adjacent buildings.

Wilford went on to say that urban design was the physical expression of society's hopes and intentions and a means of using and developing human and architectural potential, involving areas of concern that do not recognise boundaries between public and private domains. 'Currently architecture deals primarily with individual owners and properties', he said, 'and unfortunately, rarely crosses ownership boundaries. Planning is concerned with land use and public expenditure policy and rarely involves three-dimensional physical solutions. Urban design should integrate physical design with the power of policy making to shape the large-scale public/private environment and manage its growth and change'.[156]

Collegetown was not an easy case for Ithaca's design review board. It was neither an identifiable historic district nor a coherent area of similar buildings and unique characters. Including Cornell University, it is situated in a beautiful location adjacent to the Cascadilla gorge high on a plateau with views to the north, south and west at the southern end of Lake Cayuga, and adjacent to the university campus itself. In the analysis, the elements accessible for interpretation were separated into layers of different systems, which had clarity and logic when studied individually. These were represented as abstract diagrams to convey particular qualities and were progressively combined to demonstrate interrelationships. The street pattern was characterised by a break in the city grid, resulting from typographical conditions. Using figure-ground studies espoused by Cohn Rowe, who was teaching at Cornell at that time, the original pattern of individual freestanding buildings spaced out at regular intervals was still visible in the southern part of the neighbourhood.

Various strategies were explored in Stirling and Wilford's proposals, and examples were shown in both plan form and three dimensions. In the first proposal, the undeveloped inner area of the Dryden Street block would have become an informal, landscaped park within which would be a series of free-standing buildings, different in nature from those on the perimeter. Dryden Street itself would become a boulevard-type street. The second envisaged the inner block as a formal park enclosed by predominantly residential buildings.

The third proposal was more complex, based upon a 'slipped' square responding to the diagonal movement of Dryden Street. Both parts of the square were to be developed as a public plaza enclosed by commercial and residential buildings. The stepped market square on the inner area of the Dryden block was the generating idea of their design concept and used to accommodate festivals, concerts, rallies and other community activities, including a regular farmer's market. Three quadrants of the square would be enclosed by stores, cafés and pubs, with offices and residential accommodation above. The buildings were to be three storeys high with pavilions and towers to emphasise entrances and corners.[157] Stepped passageways and glass-roofed arcades through the enclosing buildings would have connected the square to College Avenue and Eddy Street. The southern end of the block would have accommodated a larger commercial building, accessible through an archway to the square, below which a garage would have been built to utilise the sloping terrain.

Though this plan was never implemented, the Performing Arts Center for Cornell University, developed and built between 1983 and 1988, was the epitome of the application of urban design to architecture – not dissimilar to the application applied by Peter Eisenman in his design for the Wexner Center for the creative arts at Ohio State University, Columbus, completed between 1990 and 1991.

Critics have suggested that the Cornell Performing Arts Center represented Stirling's major move away from modernism.[158] However, it may be argued in reviewing the work of the practice over a 30-year period (until Stirling's death in 1992) that a number of specific projects, both before and after Wilford/Stirling partnership, demonstrate this shift away from modernism.

The Cornell Center for dance, music and theatre illustrates Wilford's commitment to urban design and the public realm as much as the unbuilt Collegetown plan. The centre is viewed by critics as an evocation of Italian architecture and Italian hill towns. Certainly the typography of Ithaca assisted in the germination of these influences. Girouard identifies a campanile (the

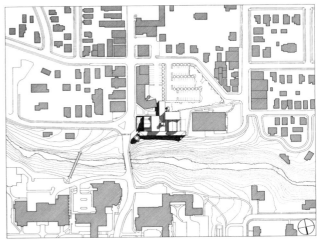

Site plan: Cornell Performing Arts Center, New York (1983–88), Stirling and Wilford.

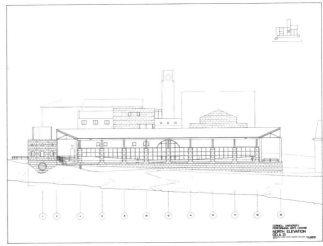

North elevation, Cornell Performing Arts Center, New York (1983–88), Stirling and Wilford.

Cornell Performing Arts Center, New York (1983–88), Stirling and Wilford.

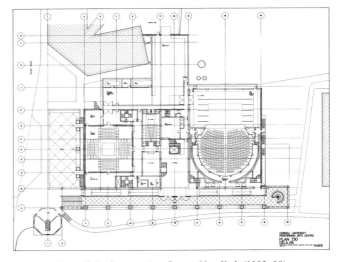

Site plan: Cornell Performing Arts Center, New York (1983–88), Stirling and Wilford.

elevator tower), a baptistery (information kiosk), the silhouette of two basilicas (auditorium and studios) and a loggia. The loggia element is perhaps the most significant, though Maxwell describes it as a 'colonnade [facing] the gorge'.[159]

In American and British schools of architecture there seems to be some confusion as to the exact functions of colonnade, arcade and loggia, but it does seem that Girouard's definition is the most accurate. The loggia is a public realm route linking the different and sometimes complex functions of the centre as a 'street'. Situated on a podium of stone, the supporting columns of what is mostly a timber-trussed monopitch roof create a great sense of elegance in the transition from solid podium to stone piers, which, in turn, support the reinforced concrete columns and hence the roof.

Equally important is the entrance to the arcade, which, in true urban design terms, is marked by an octagonal 'gateway' building that also identifies the bridge over the gorge and defines a small urban square. Maxwell suggests that this is Tuscany rather than New York State, upon overhearing a visitor say, 'it's some sort of Florentine rip-off', which Stirling regarded as a compliment.

Girouard identifies the clock tower as the central feature, inspired by a campanile, but criticises the centre as a 'stage-set' Italian town rather than a real one. A parsimonious view, perhaps, given the dire results of postmodernism during the same period. The stone, used at the request of President Rhodes of Cornell University (English by birth), was a type of Vermont marble in contrast to Stirling's original suggestion of alternating stripes of red brick and grey stone. With cost overruns, the years following 1979 were complex and frustrating, and internal university faculty battles ensued. The project was overseen by the American firm of Wank, Adams and Slavin of New York, but the design was finally accepted, though some of the marble was replaced by rendered surfaces which, in the opinion of Girouard, 'added to the stage-set effect'.[160] The building was completed in 1988.

AWARDS FOR URBAN DESIGN: UNBUILT AND BUILT PROJECTS

Progressive Architecture magazine's annual design awards were probably the most prestigious in the architectural profession, but it was not until the 1970s that urban design studies were to be regarded as a separate design issue from that of individual buildings. Indeed, in 1972, though the urban design category had been introduced, no awards were made, seeming to display the intention on the part of the jury of that year to deny that any urban design submission was worthy.

By 1981, *Progressive Architecture*'s Annual Awards programme received more than a thousand entries,[161] from which two were selected for first awards: one in urban design/planning and one in research. The urban design award was interesting in the context of the Stirling/Wilford proposal for Ithaca. Steven Peterson had been commissioned by the Schickel Design and Development Corporation, the Ithaca City Planning Department and America the Beautiful Incorporated to undertake a study for University Avenue. Like the Stirling/Wilford proposal, it was on a sloping site on the East Hill between the Cornell University campus (at the top of the slope) and the town of Ithaca. The intention of the plan was to link the two existing areas in a formal arrangement, establishing continuity of space with new housing in the form of walk-up garden apartments, pedestrian walks and steps parallel to the slope. The plan used a series of horizontal reference planes extending across the face of the hill with buildings both perpendicular and parallel to the slope.

Of the eight jury members for the 28th Awards Program, Edmond Bacon (the executive director of the Philadelphia City Planning Commission between 1949 and 1970) and Jacques Brownson formed a subcommittee set up to examine the 123 submissions in the urban design category. Their unreserved praise for Peterson's proposal is summarised in Bacon's comments: 'I am astounded by the proposal. It is a very carefully conceived extension of history. Look at the way it seizes the tower of the university library as the focal landmark at the top of the hill and then carries the axial organization down to the town of Ithaca on the flatlands through a series of buildings, terraces and courts. It is very extraordinary'.[162]

In discussion with the rest of the jury, however, while Bacon and Brownson acknowledged, with surprise, the quality of entries in the urban design category and said that they demonstrated a sense of larger structures in a real way as well as relating to the historical context of existing urban form, they also criticised the extensive verbiage and the exploration of side issues.

A more curious winner was that of Venturi, Ravich and Scott-Brown for the preservation and commercial revitalisation of the historic district of Jim Thorpe, a mining town in Pennsylvania noted for its switchback railway conveying coal to the base of the mountain. The plan retained the Victorian heritage of the once thriving mining town served by canals and railways. The thorough study addressed both economic and design issues in the Old Mauch Chunk Historic District. The design team went through a process of citizen participation with small business areas, proposing modest, incremental development. Bacon and Brownson agreed that the sensitivity towards old buildings was exemplary, particularly in the use of sequential photography.

The following year, in 1982, the urban design jury included David Childs, partner in the Washington, DC office of Skidmore, Owings and Merrill, and Dolores Hayden, associate professor of urban planning at UCLA. Professing a disappointment in the overall quality of the submissions they did however say that the winning schemes were 'exceptionally good'. Of the 79 schemes submitted, their main criticism was the poverty of the visual presentations. Preservation seemed to be the dominant issue, but even the award-winning projects were ordinary, if not mediocre. Hayden said: '[from] the borrowings of Europe, I was really heartened to see how many submissions were trying to deal in an extremely earnest and knowledgeable way with the American built environment. How many people who presented their work were struggling to come to terms with the American vernacular: not simply Main Street, but small towns, rural house types, in many different parts of the country from New England to the South to the West'.[163] Childs lamented the lack of international projects such as new towns in Saudi Arabia, for which Skidmore, Owings and Merrill had won an award in the previous year.

Despite the praise for the high quality of the submissions, the works illustrated seemed mundane, including the historic district renewal of Miami Beach, which certainly celebrated the restoration of its art-deco architecture but from its cartoon-like perspectives did little to reassure the reader, just as the orthogonal grid application for Chestertown, Maryland, did little to reassure that the proposed residential commons surrounded by new detached residences would actually form new public spaces.

The jury for the 1983 urban design awards was composed of Stanton Eckstut and John Woodbridge. They echoed a growing view towards the new urbanism that was to follow in the next decade. As Woodbridge explained: 'Especially in reaction to the megastructure days in urban design, a project was felt to merit an award if it was pragmatic and realizable'. [164] Eckstut said: 'Well developed management tools were also considered sufficient grounds for recognition. Now we demand the basics and look for more'. [165]

Nevertheless, some of the projects that were presented were praiseworthy. The Richmond, Virginia project by UDA Architects, led by David Lewis and Raymond Gindroz of Pittsburgh, was a classic example of urban revitalisation in rebuilding an area for dislocated residents. The 30-hectare (76-acre) site had been cleared in the late 1960s and early 1970s and was separated from downtown Richmond by an expressway. Lewis and Gindroz proposed a separation from the expressway by a linear park with two small parks to the east and west to 'create a peaceful and separate enclave, with short blocks patterned after healthy neighborhood(s)'.

The most notable entry in 1984[166] was by Andres Duany and Elizabeth Plater-Zyberk for the town of Seaside, Florida. Seaside was to become the quintessential icon of the new urbanism movement. Unlike many other urban design projects, it was actually constructed. Situated on an 32-hectare (80-acre) site in Northwest Florida on the Gulf of Mexico, the project could not be termed a new town as such, built as it was as a vacation resort of 350 dwellings, 200 lodging units, a shopping centre, conference facilities and a tennis club. The authors suggested the focus was upon American urban typologies, particularly those of small southern towns before the Second World War, yet the plan seems to draw upon much earlier garden cities, such as Mariemont, Ohio, built at the beginning of the twentieth century. The jury praised the high intensity of land use and the proportions of squares, avenues, streets and alleys. Given the subsequent worldwide publicity this project received, it seems strange that it received a citation rather than an award. Michael Kirkland, one of the jurors, remarked that: 'It is far less convincing in its detail propositions, which are overworked but ineffectual'. The final built form belies this, however. Despite its theatrical appearance, the detailed architectural design, though strange, is often exquisite.

Also receiving a citation was the Arcadia Creek Urban Design Plan for Kalamazoo, Michigan, by a team from Skidmore, Owings and Merrill's Chicago office, led by Kim Goluska. This addressed the periodic flooding of Arcadia Creek as well as the general decline of the northern section of downtown Kalamazoo. The plan was more formalistic and axial than Seaside but identified two distinctive public arenas linked by a watercourse. Goluska cited as inspiration the San Antonio riverwalk, and one of the jurors suggested comparisons with John Nash's early nineteenth-century Regent's Park development in London. The proposed conservatory and garden trellis system did have analogies with regency landscape design.

Of the awards given, another example that was actually built was the Banfield Transit Way in Portland, Oregon. Designed by Zimmer, Gunsul and Frasca of Portland, it was a 24-kilometre (15-mile) segment of a proposed region-wide light rail transit system that is still notable today. As well as the public transportation role, relieving traffic congestion, it was intended as a focus for regional development on a neighbourhood basis. The project design was also environmentally friendly, passing through sensitive areas with minimal or no impact.

The Banfield Transit Way was a model of its kind in terms of professional planning. Policies and strategies included economic analyses, market studies, transportation and parking management programmes as well as architectural urban design standards. At the detailed level, the guidelines included vehicular and pedestrian flow patterns, as well as visual and perceptual effects.

The jury praised this project as a good example of streetscape (or townscape) revitalisation in its use of highly detailed drawings of the public elements. It was not intended to be spectacular, but in its fine detail it was quite beautiful. The first segment of a regional network that was to establish Portland as one of America's premier cities in urban design policy and implementation, it was estimated that there would be 5,000 riders a day. However, the debut of the system, with free rides over a three-day period, attracted 200,000 riders, and a year later the average paid daily ridership was 19,900.

Another award-winner was the submission by Beckley/Myers of Milwaukee for the Milwaukee Theater District. This was an ambitious programme for the creation of a new theatre district in the downtown area of the city, intended as a catalyst for attracting public and private investment. The plan proposed 'nodes of activity' with an arcade system on a north–south axis.

The following year, the number of submissions was reduced for reasons that were not clear. The jury that year (Reginald Griffith and Peter Walker) rejected plazas and pedestrian-scaled elements, with Walker remarking that urban design needed to play a political role.[167] Perhaps this was so, but as has been remarked elsewhere, urban design proposals are too often used for purposes of political manipulation, and far too many never implemented once the ambitions of politicians in promoting such ventures have been satisfied.

Typical of this was the award-winning scheme for Jerusalem – The Seam: Urban Design of No Man's Land – by Gene Dyer, Todd Johnson and Clifton Page (of Cambridge, Massachusetts), with Moshe Safdie, Fred Koetter and Gerald U. McCue of Harvard as consultants. Even today it appears that the warring factions of Jerusalem have found little common ground.[168] Nevertheless, the plan was highly imaginative. It consisted of two detailed three-dimensional plans showing 'the seam' before and after, and is quite lyrical. The programme was to reintegrate the politically separated sections of the ancient land by developing a comprehensive plan that anticipated modern traffic requirements, new buildings and circulation patterns with the praiseworthy notion of implying a non-aligned public identity. The new circulation system wove the halves of the city together with a new entrance as a processional vehicular path to the central city. The Old City via Damascus Gate would create a multi-use zone.[169]

Other schemes receiving awards and citations in 1985 included the Chicago Central Area Plan, by Thomas Beeby/ University of Illinois and Skidmore, Owings, and Merrill, which was vast in scale. The team also included Helmut Jahn and Carter Manny (renowned for his work with the Graham Foundation) as well as Stanley Tigerman. The initiative came from the projected Chicago World's Fair in 1992, and among the goals were the encouragement of economic growth, enriching land use and linkages between major activity centres. This was promoted by a citizens group in Chicago and was a good example of participatory planning.

Also worthy of note was a proposal for North Austin Town Center in Austin, Texas, by Black, Atkinson and Vernooy. The project was unusual in that it proposed a dense urban pedestrian-scale neighbourhood in a suburban area with a public park in the tradition of the 'picturesque' of English eighteenth-century landscape design or Cullen's later townscape theories, with an intricate system of courts, paths and gardens connecting the park with the centre.

The 1986 award-winning projects were more mundane. The contrast between each successive year seemed to imply that the personal agenda of each jury member played a large part in the selection. Perhaps instead of the division of categories with, say, two jury members for the urban design submissions, the entire jury ought to have been involved in the selection for each category. Though creating a more combative atmosphere, a broader perspective of opinions would have been useful.

That year there appeared yet another plan for downtown San Francisco, repeating many such plans generated over the previous twenty years that were yet to be implemented. Similar remarks could be applied to the Union Station Redevelopment proposals for Seattle.[170] However, both plans were praiseworthy.

The most noteworthy submission in 1987 was probably the Flats-Oxbow Development Plan for Cleveland, Ohio, by James Boniface and Freeman-White Associates. At the time, Cleveland, regarded as one of the 'rust belt' cities of the Midwest, was the butt of many jokes for reasons including the spontaneous fire in the river estuary to Lake Erie. Nevertheless, in the next decade it had transformed its riverfront and lakefront into a model for its southern Ohio neighbour, Cincinnati, which at the beginning of the twenty-first century is still arguing policy over riverfront development.[171]

In 1988, the Architectural Design Awards displayed a major breakthrough in recognising much more radical architects such as Thom Mayne and Michael Rotundi of Morphosis, as well as Peter Eisenman and Steven Holl. However, the urban design submissions were again not particularly challenging.

The two-person jury comprised Peter Calthorpe and Diana Balmori. Calthorpe addressed the issue of the problems of suburban growth and the lack of solutions. Balmori had referred to 'galactic' cities that could no longer depend on nineteenth-century models.[172] Calthorpe pointed out the tendency towards beaux-arts master-planning as a reaction to modernism, and the shift of planning methodology towards building typology instead of zoning envelopes. The Main Street design by Pereira Associates for the University of California at Irvine probably confirmed these views with a central spine that was primarily pedestrian.

San Francisco again figured in the citations, with the plan for Mission Bay, for which a previous plan by I. M. Pei and Partners had received a *Progressive Architecture* citation in 1984, confining the impression of the recycling of ideas for specific cities. Certainly the designers of the 1988 submission, EPAW Inc., followed a rigid beaux-arts plan aligned on axial grids, which seemed in contradiction to the much looser urban framework of the city. The residential guidelines for the city of San Jose, California, by Daniel Solomon and Associates, seemed to be statements of the obvious, though Calthorpe praised them as fine-grained analyses of standard suburban housing, meticulous and realistically innovative, which, from the diagrams, seems unlikely.

In 1989, the awards jury, Alexander Cooper and Don Logan, rejected schemes that emphasised public participation, Logan describing them as 'too vague or generalized to evaluate seriously. They are more like political documents . . . What we're missing is suburban town planning'.[173] Cooper said: 'We got a number of guidelines, which are very *au courant*. They are a substitute for zoning, which is very prescriptive'.[174]

Among the selected schemes that year was West Hollywood Civic Center, a reasonably elegant interpretation of postmodernism. However, the most impressive project was probably the Design Guidelines for Highway 11 in Indian Wells, California, by Johnson Fain and Pereira Associates. This was for a 5.5-kilometre (3.5-mile) highway corridor in a desert resort and followed a city council decision to limit future commercial development of highway frontage. The plan sought to enhance what was left of the desert landscape within town boundaries. It embodied many of the perceptual theories of Kevin Lynch some three decades earlier, including the concept of gateways, which in this instance was marked by a 'grove gate' incorporating a historic date palm grove symbol of the town's former industry. Another natural gateway was the spur of the Santa Rosa Mountains. A new community centre housing a Cahuilla Indian Interpretive Center located on the site of an eighteenth-century Indian village was also included. It was, as the jury remarked, a heroic public works project unsurpassed since the creation of parkways in the 1930s. The sequential perspectives, rendered in masterful watercolours by Norman Kondy (project designer Stephen Levine), were a paradigm of urban design presentation.

THE EMERGENCE OF PLURALISM

With the rejection of the modern movement and the eruption of postmodernism, the 1980s was a period of various new factions in architecture and urban design. It was Charles Jencks who was responsible for the introduction of the concept of postmodernism to the architectural world. Jencks had delivered a paper[175] at a conference on postmodernism at Northwestern University in Illinois in 1985,[176] and claimed that postmodernism was defined in the writings of John Barth and Umberto Eco.[177] According to Jencks, postmodernism was a 'paradoxical dualism or double coding', which is perhaps defined in the emergence of pluralistic thinking in architecture. More ambiguous was his remark that this hybrid was 'a continuation of Modernism in exaggerated form'. Certainly in architectural design it was no such thing, given the neo-historical references of postmodern architecture, and in these terms it was retrogressive. Berthold Lubetkin, a Russian émigré and leader of the modern movement in pre-Second World War Britain, linked postmodernism with 'transvestite architecture'.[178] According to Jencks, Lubetkin compared postmodernism with Nazi Kitsch and equated Prince Charles with Stalin for his attack on modernism.

Postmodernism was also reflecting in painting. Peter Blake's representational painting 'The Meeting', or 'Have a Nice Day Mr Hockney' (1983) portrayed the photorealism of the representational artists Howard Hodgkin and David Hockney (an English immigré to California). There is an eerie similarity, stylistically, in this California setting between Peter Blake's techniques and those of Hockney, evident in paintings such as 'A Greater Splash'.

The May 1985 issue of *Art and Design*[179] drew up a table establishing the differences between modern and postmodern in philosophical terms: idealist versus pragmatist; utopian and elitist versus pluralist and popular; universal as opposed to contextual; rejecting historical memory instead of using historical memory; and international uniformity as opposed to regional diversity. Stylistically, purist was compared to the eclectic, simplicity to complexity, explicit to rhetorical and a rejection of humour to the enjoyment of humour.

The International Building Exhibition in Berlin, 1984, was a vast undertaking that took place prior to the fall of communism and the Berlin Wall. Located in what was then West Berlin, it sought to establish a built form of ideal cities. Whether it was successful in terms of such a lofty dream is, perhaps, debatable. Nevertheless, the international competition attracted a significant number of North American entries as well as entries from internationally known architectural practices such as James Stirling, Michael Wilford, Mario Botta, Rob Krier, Gregotti Associates, OMA and O. M. Ungers. Other entries came from Ralph Erskine, Arata Isozaki, Leon Krier, Oriel Bohigas, Kisho Kirokawa, Aldo Rossi and Maurice Culot.

An American entry by Charles Moore with John Ruble and Buzz Yudell, won first prize for the development of the Tegel harbour area of the city. Based upon a series of promenade proposals, it included a cultural centre as well as recreational and residential centres in the form of multi-unit housing. The cultural, recreational and residential uses were positioned as discrete building elements with all the water edges maintained as public spaces. While not as coherent as Moore's earlier Kresge College plan in California, it did return to the public realm, though the architectural imagery with postmodernism was somewhat more dubious.[180]

Peter Eisenman and Jaquelin Robertson won a special prize for the Koch/Freidrichstrass Block Five. This was a notable entry because it introduced Eisenman's growing interest in shifting grids in urban design.[181] Eisenman and Robertson's design was based on a concept called 'anti-memory'. This was distinct from sentimental or nostalgic memory, since it ignored both past and future. At the time (1983) it was suggested that the act of memory obscured the reality of the present as, specifically, the presence of the Berlin Wall. Instead of historical allusion, it involved 'the making of a place that derives its order from obscuring its own recollected past', though this obscure allusion was difficult to apply to the proposal itself. Described as a site with three semi-ruined existing buildings with the Berlin Wall to the north, the ground was considered as an archeological site with a universal geometric pattern without history or specificity. Using the Mercator Grid (geographically), anti-memory was developed as a second set of walls upon the historical walls, built to the same height as the Berlin Wall. In this way, the artificial or neutral walls would erase the physical presence of the historical walls. Urban grids, Eisenman said, generally mark out negative spaces, the streets, between the positive spaces of building. However, such a sweeping comment might not apply to the grid system of Manhattan or, for that matter, Savannah. L-shaped plans were proposed and the squares had a rotational symmetry around corners rather than centres.

Another American architect, John Hejduk, won a special prize for the Wilhelmstrasse, Block Nineteen, which included some extraordinary architectural imagery with a wind tower, observation tower and great guest towers. These towers, in themselves, were not particularly high, ranging from 21 metres (70 feet) for the bell tower to 55 metres (180 feet) for the observation tower, all juxtaposed with a tiny public theatre, book market, maze and reading theatre.[182]

In a celebration of American Architecture,[183] Demetri Porphyrios and Charles Jencks analysed the rapidly changing theoretical stances in design. For example, Jencks, a prolific writer, indicated three mainstreams in American architecture with a development away from modernism, epitomised only by Eisenman's subsequent work. There were also architects committed to technology, as Helmut Jahn with his 'high-tech' architecture, parallel to architects in the UK such as Norman Foster and Richard Rogers (later to be translated into minimalism and employed by other art forms such as music), and the architecture of Billie Tsien in New York City. The work of Allan Greenberg, Tim Vreeland and Robert Stern was, Jencks thought, a return to the City Beautiful syntax, depending on a modified traditionalism and the more 'radical camp' (not really radical) of Duany and Robertson, which rediscovered the equivalent of the New England Village.

Of the illuminated projects that might be considered urban design, albeit in a rural setting, the Clos Pegase Winery in the Napa Valley, California, by Michael Graves in 1984, is an outstanding combination of urban elements. In terms of sequential space, it takes the visitor on a procession through a sculpture park, beginning with a stepped circular building, seen by the designer as a symbolic mountain of Pegasus.[184] This journey from a man-made to a romantic and natural landscape, through winding, tree-lined zigzag paths up the natural hillside, provides excellent views of the sculpture, and leads up to a grotto and a water course dividing the two sides of the site. The use of pergolas, winter gardens, planted staircases, watercourses and an aqueduct all contribute to the visual experience.

Though Frank Gehry was not to become renowned for his major architectural achievements until almost a decade later, his compositional abilities were nevertheless evident in his work during the early 1980s, for example in the new buildings for the Loyola Law School in Los Angeles.

Peter Eisenman's design for Ohio State University's Wexner Center for the Visual Arts, completed in 1989/90 in Columbus, Ohio, is also a major urban design statement on a university campus. Located on a difficult urban site, the Wexner Center skilfully welds together disparate pieces of existing architecture spanning over a hundred years. The magical combination of a white pergola/arcade/colonnade and trellis is a unique artifact of its kind. The implication to the angular orientations of this system was considered by Eisenman to be a type of lay-line system as in Stonehenge and other 'standing circles' throughout England, as well as in South America, particularly in Peru.

The Wexner Center was designed specifically to house the avant-garde and experimental arts, including new art forms involving laser, computer and video technologies. It integrated the geometries of the street grid of Columbus and the central oval of the campus. It became the generator of a new pedestrian path within the campus. According to Eisenman: 'This path projects a trajectory that extends along the ragged northern edge of the oval, reinforcing its form through the main tower of University Hall all the way to the flat end of the oval-shaped Ohio Stadium'.[185] He continued:

The new crossing which we have created as the intersection of these two 'found' axes is not simply a route, but an event, literally a center for the visual arts. It defines the intersection of the university grid with the city grid, and thus symbolizes the intersection of the arts with the community. The extension of the axes of the Columbus grid into the campus, and the use of these to mark an important symbolic route on the campus . . . Thus conceived, the site itself becomes the new architecture, and the massing concept of our building is that of an archaeological earthwork whose essential elements are scaffolding and landscaping . . . the latent patterns and discontinuities, which make something specific and real. The 'scaffolding' [the pergola/colonnade] of the intersecting grids inscribed on the plan provides a matrix connecting all the arts buildings and structures with a series of functional links to the various entries into the public and private functions.

It is interesting to compare Eisenman's design for the Wexner Center with his later building for the College of Design, Architecture, Art and Planning at the University of Cincinnati,

Wexner Center, Ohio State University, Columbus (1989), Peter Eisenman.

completed in the middle of the next decade. If the Wexner Center can be seen as a brilliant paradigm of urban design, some observers have suggested that the interior is too exuberant for an art museum, where the works of art should take precedence over the 'background' architecture. In the case of the Cincinnati structure, the interior of the building is probably the best part of the design, with a cascading staircase over five floors creating a *promenade architecturale* in a visual experience similar to the drawings of Piranesi.

In contrast to Eisenman's emergence in deconstructivism theory, works by Michael Graves and Charles Moore during the same period are paradigms of postmodernism. Graves' Portland Public Service Building in Portland, Oregon, designed in 1980, was the result of an international competition.[186] It was regarded as the first postmodern high-rise building at twenty storeys high, a multi-use building with wide plinths at its base and a clearly defined tip. The base contains public arcades and small shops and, of course, a main bulk of offices. The top is defined by a paradoxical keystone. Graves' original proposal, vetoed by city authorities, might have defined the public realm further with a group of pavilions for the top as a 'city within the city', which he compared to the agoras of ancient Greece at the Forum Romanum. This was a new typology of the skyscraper some time before Cesar Pelli's bulky building at Canary Wharf in London, which responded to new market requirements for information technology and provided massive floor footprints to accommodate financial brokerage layouts.

In the debate on pluralism, Christian Norberg-Schulz suggested that postmodern architecture was the result of a reaction to the limitations of modernism.[187] He observed that in the absence of meaning in modern architecture, postmodern architecture was a quest for 'communicative, meaningful architecture', comparing it, however, to a set of 'Janus heads', one looking back to seek origins and the other looking forward, advocating nihilism. His reference to the earlier theories of semiology and sign language include the fictional works of Umberto Eco, with the quotation that only truths that are useful are instruments to be thrown away.[188]

The growing popularity of the work of Martin Heidegger[189] among the teachers of theory in American schools of architecture (despite his dubious political background) reflected, according to Norberg-Schulz, the concept of 'Thing' in what it 'gathers'. Thus, a generally understood language of form allows for a meaningful expression of the inherent order of things and draws from Nietzsche's nihilistic philosophies as well as those of Kant.[190] Norberg-Schulz concludes by suggesting that the nihilistic face of postmodernism represents a 'late modern' outlook, by posing the problem of meaning to negate meaning, regarding forms as arbitrary instruments and reducing architecture to fashion.

The emergence of a new design theory, deconstruction (see below), perhaps best epitomised in the work of Eisenman and Gehry, may be based on the critical philosophy of the French writer, Jacques Derrida,[191] which drew upon structuralism and phenomenology in a post-Nietzschean world. The work of Eisenman and Gehry may be linked to that of others such as Daniel Libeskind, Bernard Tschumi or even Michael Sorkin. It did not appear to have formal or ideological goals, however Sheenan claims that it returns to the early twentieth-century Russian avant-garde of constructivism displayed in the designs of architects such as Chernekov. Therefore, all of the past may be rhetorically deconstructed in literature, art and architecture to expose its contradictions.[192]

'The Architecture of Pluralism' was celebrated at a symposium of the Academy Forum in London on 3 October 1988, connecting the three architectural movements of postmodernism, deconstruction and the new classicism. John Melvin drew parallels with Mikhail Gorbachev, then leader of the declining Soviet Union and head of a dramatically controlled state, who had embraced pluralism at this time in the form of *glasnost* and *perestroika*.[193] This provided a vivid image, although the comparison of politics with design requires a leap of the imagination. Melvin reports, somewhat erroneously in the context of Western European history, that such pluralism had existed in politics for the previous two hundred years because of consumerism and market economy. The history of Victorian England a hundred years previously hardly confirms this. He suggests that the repudiation of the 'monotheism of the International Style' was recognised by Robert Stern in the US, who welcomed the idea of pluralism. While this may be partially true, Robert Stern's earlier buildings were large houses for individual clients, which naturally would reflect the tastes and even eccentricities of those families.

The symposium was illustrated by a galaxy of architects including Leon and Rob Krier, Norman Foster, Richard Meier, Robert Venturi, Michael Graves, Frank Gehry, Terry Farrell, OMA and Aldo Rossi (the name of Peter Eisenman is strangely missing), and discussed Robert Stern's Observatory Hill Dining Hall at the University of Virginia. The University of Virginia at Charlottesville, designed originally by Thomas Jefferson, is possibly the most beautiful university campus in the US. Thus, the challenge of building within such a context of neoclassical architecture was formidable. Stern remarked: 'It has been my privilege to build in places where inherited and borrowed forms have been successfully cross-pollinated with deep-rooted local traditions'.[194] Suggesting that he is a modern architect rather than a modernist, Stern recognised that Jefferson's university campus was a paradigm for American architecture: not merely the use of the elements of the classical tradition of ancient Greece and Rome but a liberation of American architecture from the European past. Built between 1982 and 1984, the Observatory Dining Hall was Stern's first significant building beyond his designs for private houses, and it was certainly contextual in the urban design sense in that it masked some of the more mundane twentieth-century facilities built in the 1970s.

Deconstruction

Within this environment of pluralism, deconstruction was to become a major movement both in architecture and urban design by the end of the twentieth century. The exposition of this movement was illustrated in a special issue of *Architectural Design* magazine in mid-1988.[195] A major exhibition,

'Deconstructivist Architecture', organised by Philip Johnson and Mark Wigley at the Museum of Modern Art in New York in June 1988, suggests that, indeed, deconstruction had, in itself, become a movement. Parallel to this was the celebration of deconstruction at the Tate Gallery in London, organised by the Academy Forum.

Peter Eisenman and Bernard Tschumi were most closely identified with the writings of French philosopher Jacques Derrida. Mark Wigley, however, indicated at the time that deconstruction was non-Derridean in that it was not avant-garde but disturbing, conservative architectural thought 'challenging harmony, drawing out repressed impurities and internal violence'. While Derrida was moving away from deconstructivist theory, some ten years later the architectural profession (after much debate) was taking it up.

The writer Andrew Benjamin[196] referred to the writings of Descartes.[197] He said that Descartes' aim was twofold: establishing a total and unified system as well as one that breaks fundamentally with past philosophical systems. He extended the range of the metaphor from a single construction to the city, and identified two built-form models: the city of natural accretion over a long period of time and a city conceived at a single moment in time.

Regarding the latter, many cities owe their foundation to a specific event, a 'big bang' origin, the result of a self-conscious design decision that exists as a concept before it is realised. Most of the settlements of the 'New World' (whether North or South America) were of this type, and even in Europe the bastides of France and Wales, and the Zähringer towns of Switzerland and South Germany were established in this way. Further back in time, the Roman colonial cities of Europe and North Africa (such as Tripoli in Libya or Djemila in Algeria) were explicit examples with 'big bang' foundations, a notation following twentieth-century theories of the origin of the universe. Such cities provided standard plans and carefully specified ritual to impose these plans upon the land.

The first of Benjamin's 'beginnings' has no such definition. In this case, the moment of birth or the culture to which a society belongs is more complex. Again, borrowing the term from science, 'steady-state' settlements have grown organically with that culture. The medieval cities of Europe, which emerged during a population explosion in the twelfth and thirteenth centuries, had no master plan and produced an irregular geometry of a different origin.

In the twentieth century and beyond, cities in the US are often composites of these two types of formation. In Europe, 'big bang' Roman grids can be seen through the later steady-state medieval accretions and *artificial* sectors are added to *natural* cores.[198]

Benjamin identified Descartes' architectural metaphor as having two components: the functional opposition between reason and chance (reason and madness), and a more complex opposition between the inside and the outside. The metaphor of the city, in order that it furthers Descartes' philosophical end, must be understood as a structured space and therefore as a place to be redeployed in the construction of the city of reason.[199]

Jacques Derrida described the oppositions created by the force of deconstruction:

De-construction . . . analyzes and compares conceptual pairs which are currently accepted as self-evident and natural, as if they had not been institutionalized at some precise moment, as if they had no history. Because of being taken for granted, they restrict thinking.[200]

He comments on the work of Bernard Tschumi, particularly Parc de la Villette in Paris, and especially on constructed elements of the Park, which he refers to as 'Les Folies'. In his writings on architecture, Derrida attempts to show a philosophical argument and denies that, despite their appearance, the buildings of deconstruction are not in themselves an architectural metaphor and do not amount to a simplistic dismantling of elements. He says that, in a Nietzschean sense, it is affirmative.

There is a relationship between Derrida's theories on architecture and literature. Both, he indicates, can be logocentric. He cites another French writer, Roger Laport: 'In inscribing itself in an historically, libidinally, economically, politically determined field . . . no meta-language is powerful enough today to dominate the progress (*la marche*) or rather the unfolding (*la dé-marche*) of this writing'.[201]

Derrida says of Tschumi's 'follies' that 'Tschumi's "first" concern will no longer be to organize space as a function or in view of economic, aesthetic, epiphanic, or techno-utilitarian norms. These norms will be taken into consideration, but they will find themselves subordinated and reinscribed in one place in a text and in a space that they no longer command in the final instance'.[202] Derrida denies Cartesian philosophy in the search for the new and unique as an impossibility.

Benjamin suggests that the challenge presented by deconstruction is that which it presents to all the arts, including philosophy and literary criticism, and quotes Eisenman as saying: 'What is proposed is an expansion beyond the limitation presented by the classical mode'.[203]

The relationship between deconstruction architecture and the original Russian avant-garde architecture of the early twentieth century was outlined by Catherine Cooke as a point of departure for formal language.[204] Cooke says that Rem Koolhaas visited the former Soviet Union to see drawn and painted examples of the Moscow constructivist Ivan Leonidov. Zaha Hadid, a pupil of Koolhaas in London, acknowledged the influence of Leonidov, who vehemently pronounced that constructivism was 'not a style but a method'. Cooke maintains that the 'high-tech' stylisation swept 'Soviet architectural schools with the same mindlessness that characterized neo-Constructivism of European and North American schools of the present day'.[205] OMA's designs were a reworking of Leonidov's synthesis of constructivism and suprematism with Bernard Tschumi's pursuit of those two paradigms, which, Cooke claims, resulted in a language that is clearly 'constructive', following that of the Leningrad architect Iaakov Chernikov.[206] Cooke went on to say that Koolhaas and Hadid 'used' the work of Leonidov as a repertoire of formal systems in questions of planning and urban design, borrowing from his

Atlantis Condominium (1982), Arquitectonica,
Laurinda Spear and Bernardo Fort-Brescia.

formal experience in the social realist period.[207] Constructivism was based on three-dimensional space in, Cooke says, measurable 'real' time whereas suprematism asserted the integral and equivalent position of an experiential time. This was not dissimilar in concept to Giedion's ideas of 'space-time'.

Cooke's penetrating analysis indicated that the tactile 'objects' of modernism provided a paradigm of a space-time universe and, in a deconstructivist context, a new perception of the cognitive and phenomenal world of the late twentieth century. In the struggle between the urbanists and disurbanists of the early 1920s in the former Soviet Union, the disurbanists, exemplified by Miliutin, suggested that as a result of new communication technologies, 'distance would now be measured by time' and 'proximity' or 'connectivity between individuals would no longer correlate spatial continuity'.[208] Such a prophecy was to be fulfilled in computer science with the development of the Internet and web sites almost a century later.

Koolhaas's ideas were translated into reality by, according to Jencks, the American architectural practice Arquitectonica. The firm, based in Miami, Florida, developed a style that Jencks refers to as 'skyscraper deco'. The principals, Laurinda Spear and Bernardo Fort-Brescia, used modernist typologies in the work, which made a radical change to the city. In the Biscayne Bay area, on Brickell Avenue, the Atlantis, the Babylon, the Imperial, the Palace and the Helmsley Center, started in the early 1980s, were examples of startling architecture.

The use of modernist motifs like the glass box were deconstructed in the case of the Atlantis, Arquitectonica's first major building, in 1982. The amazing central void in the facade of a luxury condominium development and the use of what Jencks refers to as 'cocktail colours' of red triangle, yellow balcony and the blue square halfway up the block (referred to as the 'skycourt') create a series of dichotomies with the functionalist basis of the architecture.[209] Jencks compares this with contemporary Brazilian architecture and calls it 'Miami-Niemeyer'. However, Oscar Niemeyer's architecture clearly follows the precepts of Le Corbusier, with Lucio Costa, Alfonso Reidy and others, in the design of the Ministry of Education in Rio de Janeiro in 1937. His subsequent buildings in Brasilia suggest a new adaptation of the curvilinear forms of the colonial Brazilian neo-Baroque in such cities as Ouro Preto in Minas Gerais, but with an originality that has little to do with the conceits of deconstruction. Jencks is, however, correct in saying that Spear and Fort-Brescia turn modernism on its head in a subversive sort of way, and that this commercial architecture, in playing with social responsibility, 'deconstructs'.

Nevertheless, the work of Arquitectonica is breathtaking in its visual impact. Examples such as Emilio Ambasz's building for the San Antonio Botanical Conservatory in Texas provided a solution for a greenhouse in a hot, dry climate, at the same time recognising regional vernacular in the relatively complex organisation of building. Also, the Sixth Street project in Los Angeles by Morphosis recognised the 'Detritus and Flotsam' of the city in which, according to Thomas Mayne, 'discrete pieces manipulated independently, simultaneously separated and associated through a geometric order, describe a vision of the world which is neither fragment nor whole. Beauty and ugliness blur . . . These examples display an extended vocabulary of Deconstruction. The 6th Street project was an impacted building and a metaphor for veils and walls as protection against the world'.[210]

In an interview with Jacques Derrida in Paris in March 1988, reported in *Architectural Design* in 1989,[211] it was proposed that the term 'deconstruction' might have applied to much earlier artists like Duchamp, Jasper Johns and Francis Bacon. Derrida also mentioned Magritte in the deconstruction of 'mimetic illusion through effects of juxtaposed image and text'. Interviewer Christopher Norris posed the question as to whether there was such a thing as deconstructive art or even deconstructive architecture, to which Derrida replied: 'Well, I don't know'. Deconstruction, Derrida said, was not simply a matter of discourse or a matter of displacing the semantic content of the discourse. Deconstruction, he thought, went through certain social and political structures. He regarded deconstruction in architecture as an architectural metaphor and believed that the architects involved were deconstructing the essentials of tradition, to free architecture from external finalities, including assumptions of beauty, usefulness and functionality. Peter Eisenman suggests that the displacement concerns the role of the architect and the design process. It may be only an expression, a mannerist distortion of an essentially stable language. There was a need for other than intuition, of 'I like this' or 'I like that'. Intuitive design never produces a state of uncertainty.[212]

Eisenman's project for the Bio-centrum in Frankfurt, Germany, had certain programmatic requirements not dissimilar from Frank Gehry's Microbiology Research Centre at the University of Cincinnati. Eisenman stated that current biological research dislocated the traditions of science, and similarly the Bio-centrum design dislocated the traditions of architecture; it articulated the research processes themselves. In a stretch of his imagination, Eisenman suggested a departure from the traditional representation of architecture into an architectural reading of the biological concepts of DNA processes by interpreting them in terms of geometrical processes. He saw the similarity between the processes of fractal geometry and the geometry of DNA processes as an analogy between architectural processes and biological processes.

Eisenman's project for the Carnegie-Mellon Research Institute took similar cues. Using a Boolean cube, or N-geometric figure, the cube becomes a structure with an infinite N-number of geometries. The function of the building as a model for computer design in the field of artificial intelligence[213] provided an opportunity for the computer to move beyond a simple information frame, by allowing the multiplication of N-geometries for information movement so that, from any point in a 1,000-N cube a move could be made in a thousand different directions within the information matrix.

The Third Typology

Whilst recognising pluralism, an argument arose within rationalist theories (particularly in Italy) for a third typology with a central concern for the morphology of the city. In the modern movement, urban design had adopted a functionalist view of the city as a homogeneous product in formal terms.

The functionalist theory blamed city chaos on a lack of clarity in the subdivision of the city by functions – such an indiscriminate mixture could only favour chaos (a view vehemently opposed by Jane Jacobs). Le Corbusier had said, referring to the construction of new city blocks in the centre of Paris that were to replace obsolete structures, that: 'Nobody interferes. On the site of the old city, which was so destructive to life, a new city is rising. Which will be even more deadly to life, in that it is creating real centers of congestion without any modification of the street'. This comment could be taken as a curious contradiction by Le Corbusier, since his own urban design proposals ignored the morphology of nineteenth-century Paris.[214]

Standards were used for analytical measure and as criteria for future proposals, researching the different functions within the city. The city then achieved the second typology, that of the industrial order symbolised by the machine (*machine à habiter*). The city is divided into its constituent parts, for living, working, shopping, recreation and transportation, and the city itself becomes part of a larger structure within the territory, which might include university cities or industrial cities. A late twentieth-century example of this early twentieth-century dream is the aberration of central Brasilia, originally planned and constructed within a democracy but curiously reflecting the aspirations of the military regime that followed in the late 1960s.[215]

The 'mono-technic' city implied by the modern movement is functionally inappropriate. The 'bi-technic' city comprises two distinct technological zones. The Nazi *Blut und Boden* philosophy was based on this, in which monumental and technically advanced places of work and public ritual envisaged for the city centre by Albert Speer or Ernst Sagebiel contrasted with the vernacular hearth and home associations of the residential *Schaffendes Volk* estates. But this interpretation was by no means confined to societies of the far right. An examination of the 'Third Phase' new towns in the UK showed a similar dichotomy between town centre uses and residential areas, albeit within the more benign influence of a welfare state. If the town centres reflected an attempt to incorporate the highest degree of technological innovation into the concept of 'a town which is enclosed', the housing areas were intended to reflect the aspirations of the inhabitants who hoped for privacy in an arcadian and traditional setting. Certainly the early privately financed new towns of the US reflected this philosophy.

At a more mundane level, the actuality of cities in the industrial or postwar world is also divided into the technological zones of the central business district or the outlying business/high-tech industrial parks on the one hand, and on the other hand the 'suburban houses with clapboard siding and high-pitched roof with shingles and gaslight style front porch lamps and mailboxes set up on top of lengths of stiffened chain that seems to defy gravity',[216] as any viewer of current American television soap operas will confirm.

Such a bi-technic division could be described as a crude simplification of the ancient association of the most advanced and expensive technology with the most powerful building types, which themselves tend to congregate in areas of the highest land value. This suggests a picture of the city as a spectrum of technologies, hierarchically ordered, from the most exotic house of god, king, state or business corporation, to the most modest structure for the domestic pet.[217]

The idealisation of a mono-technic city can be challenged by the reality of a multi-technic one. The city undergoes a continual process of modification because of the huge areas of steadily obsolescing material. We may recognise this as a matter of fact, but we may also welcome it as a fundamental characteristic of a valid urban design approach in which the city is seen as an unpredictable compound of technologies.

Maui discusses Anthony Vidler's notion of a third typology,[218] where the city itself was to be the source of legitimate architectural design. The Princeton University teacher indicated that history, rather than Corbusian function or economy, would thus have been a source of urban types. Nonetheless, there was a declining interest in historical models as sole exemplars of urban order. The examples from this decade united under the topic 'Urbanism' were neither arbitrary nor a deliberate attempt devoted to the third typology. Rather it is an attempt to include a diverse, even disparate group of internationally acknowledged urban designers to display previously unpublished projects in order to discover whether there was a shift away from the third typology towards new directions.

It may be useful to reiterate some principles associated with the third typology. If the historicism of such writers as Lewis Mumford or Chueca-Goitia[219] is based upon a generalist approach to cultural historical periods, that of the writers concerned with urban morphology and building typologies is specialist in approach and more directly related to design theory. Architecture is considered here as the primary element in the construction of the city, through history, with a sense of permanence, locus, monument and memory.[220]

In history, separate building typologies are identified with different cultural periods and locations. These typologies determine the form of the city within a total infrastructure, including the transportation network and urban spaces (the public realm of places and squares) and the containers (the private realm of buildings). Thus:

1 Typology is concerned with construction types in a particular urban situation.
2 Morphology is the formal expression of the construction types taken individually or as a whole.[221]
3 Open space is the container, the 'rest of the urban form' or the public realm. It is this public realm that provides the

semiology, the system of orientation for the inhabitants of the city. They perceive the city through the public realm as a coherent entity, or they do not if the public realm is imprecise.

Notes

1. American Regional/Urban Design Assistance Teams (R/UDAT). 'Urban Design, News from the Front'. The News of the Art. R/UDAT Task Force of the Urban Planning and Design Committee of the American Institute of Architects, February 1983.
2. Community Design Center. News. Washington, DC: Community Design Center Directors' Association, February 1986.
3. National Community Design Center Directors' Association (1988) *Survey of Members*. New York: Pratt Institute for Community and Environmental Development.
4. Erlanger, Steven (1987) 'New York turns squatters into homeowners', *The New York Times*, 12 October, p. A-1 ff. and D-11 ff.
5. ACORN was formed by a community-based organising group – The Association of Community Organizations for Reform Now (ACORN) – founded in Arkansas in 1970, with 75,000 members in 27 states. A paid organiser for ACORN, Francine Streich, came to Brooklyn in 1982 to organise a branch that by 1987 had 4,000 members. Streich suggested that homesteading was an 'obvious issue'.
6. R/UDAT: A Service of the American Institute of Architects. 'Remaking the Monongahela Valley' (March 1988), p. 120.
7. Lewis, David (conference chairman) and Barbara Davis (ed.) (1989) Pittsburgh chapter of the American Institute of Architects, 'Remaking Cities: Proceedings of the 1988 International Conference in Pittsburgh'. Pittsburgh, PA: University of Pittsburgh Press.
8. For a detailed account of their study see Gosling, David (1989) 'Public Participation and Urban Development: the Pittsburgh Experiment'. Second International Convention on Urban Planning, Housing and Design proceedings. Singapore Institute of Planners, Applied Technology PTE LTP. Singapore (27–29 July), pp. 539–62.
9. Gosling, David (1996) *Gordon Cullen: Visions of Urban Design*. London: Academy Editions, pp. 147, 226 and 228.
10. This situation was by no means unique in the rust belt of the Midwest. Cleveland, Ohio, suffered similar problems at this time, but within a ten-year period the river estuary and the shoreline of Lake Erie were transformed. The same could not be said of Cincinnati, Ohio, where, over the same period of time, constant bickering between elected county commissioners, elected city council members, city officials and the private sector resulted in little except for the construction of a gargantuan megastructure for the football team and a proposed megastructure for the baseball team. The limited space that is left on the Ohio riverside was still awaiting development in 2000.
11. Although it is true to say that in the Ohio Valley the Toyota Corporation of Japan appeared as the 'white knight' during the following decade in Northern Kentucky, Ohio and Indiana.
12. Calthorpe, Peter and Sim Van der Ryn (eds) (1986) *Sustainable Communities: A New Design Synthesis for Cities, Towns and Suburbs*. San Francisco: Sierra Club Books.
13. Peter Katz was to become known in 1994 as the author of the highly influential book *The New Urbanism*, published by McGraw Hill, Inc. New York.
14. This reflected the original theories, almost a hundred years earlier, of Ebenezer Howard's garden city movement. During the 1939–1945 period of the Second World War, this idea was implemented in the UK because of food shortages, with the allocation of allotments to families to grow their own produce of fruit and vegetables.
15. Many of these ideas were introduced within a short period of time, particularly on the West Coast of the US in cities such as Portland, Oregon, Seattle, Washington and San Diego, California.
16. Calthorpe, Peter (1989) *The Pedestrian Pocket Book: A New Urban Strategy*. New York: Princeton Architectural Press.

17. Ibid., p. 3.

18. Ibid. See plan of central area, p. 16.

19. Ibid. See plans pp. 44 ff.

20. Rubin, Arthur and Jacqueline Elder (1980) *Building For People*. Washington, DC: Environmental Research Division Center for Building Technology, National Engineering Laboratory, US Department of Commerce.

21. Ladd, F. (1970) 'Black youths view their environment: neighborhood maps', *Environment and Behavior* (June), vol. 2, no. 1, pp. 74–99.

22. Rubin and Elder, op. cit., p. 72.

23. Southworth, Michael (1969) 'The sonic environment of cities', *Environment and Behavior* (June), vol. 1, no. 1, pp. 49–70.

24. In encompassing these studies within the subheading of the social city, it may be argued that they are also relevant to the subheading of the cognitive city in chapters 3 and 4.

25. Krier, Leon (1985) 'The urge to participate', *Art and Design* (April), vol. 1, no. 3, pp. 4–8.

26. Ibid., p. 5.

27. Pittas, Michael (Retreat Chairman) and Ann Ferebee (Proceedings Editor) (1982) *Education For Urban Design*. New York: Institute for Urban Design.

28. Ibid., p. 14.

29. Ibid., p. 11.

30. Ibid., pp. 3 and 5–58. However, Robertson's paper was not connected with the manifesto of Richard Sennett in *The Uses of Disorder: Personal Identity and City Life*, published in 1970 and espousing two main themes: 'A New Puritanism' and 'A New Anarchism'. Sennett, Richard (1970) *The Uses of Disorder: Personal Identity and City Life*. Harmondsworth: Penguin Books.

31. Ibid., p. 37.

32. Ibid., p. 74.

33. During the next decade, graphic communication skills were to become enhanced through the use of computer graphics and electronic computer projection techniques in which the computer itself replaced 35mm-slide projection and video presentations. However, verbal communication skills have not improved. This is an important factor, since contemporary urban design proposals are seldom presented to individual clients but rather to committees, in both the public and private arenas.

34. The College of Design, Architecture, Art and Planning at the University of Cincinnati has required a mandatory cooperative programme (co-op) in which, during the six-year course, students in both the planning and architecture schools spend six months in practice and six months in the university each year (co-op programme). The success of this educational structure is confirmed by the high degree of professionalism once the students graduate. (It could be argued that the practices employing students gave a better education than that provided theoretically by faculty within the universities!)

35. Ibid., p. 83.

36. Ibid., pp. 85–89.

37. Ibid., p. 106.

38. This was certainly true in the late 1950s and early 1960s. The most visionary teachers were in the city planning department, including Lynch, Mumford and Rodwin. The architecture programme was much more concerned with modernist iconic architecture of individual monumental pieces of architecture.

39. Ibid., p. 107.

40. Ibid., pp. 132–72. 'Between three stools: a personal view of urban design and pedagogy'.

41. Ibid., p. 156.

42. Girouard, Mark (1998) *Big Jim: The Life and Work of James Stirling*. London: Chatto and Windus, p. 39.

43. Middleton, D. B. (ed.) (1982) *The Cornell Journal of Architecture*.

44. Ibid., pp. 128–29.

45. Ibid., p. 3.

46. Ahmed, Imran and Merritt Bucholz (eds) (1990–91) *The Cornell Journal of Architecture*, vol. 2.

47. Ibid., pp. 6–19.

48. Ibid., pp. 122–131.

49. Ibid., p. 127. Of course, this idea of experiencing the city through sequential experience was by no means new and was fully expounded by Gordon Cullen some thirty years earlier. Narrative architecture, too, was explored by Bernard Tschumi in his *Advertisements for Architecture* in 1978, as well as Rem Koolhaas in *Delirious New York*, also published in 1978.

50. Op. cit., p. 42. *The Cornell Journal of Architecture*, vol. 2.

51. Ibid., pp. 54–78.

52. Ibid., p. 55.

53. Rowe, Colin and Fred Koetter (1975) 'Collage City', *Architectural Review*, vol. 158, no. 942 (August), p. 81 ff.

54. Ibid., p. 56. See also in same volume Wayne Copper's graduate thesis, prepared in 1967, entitled 'The Figure-Grounds' pp. 42–53.

55. Ibid., p. 58.

56. Gosling, David (1996) *Gordon Cullen: Visions of Urban Design*. London: Academy Editions, p. 216.

57. An example of this is the abhorrent term 'signature architects', used frequently in the 1990s. Although during this decade such architecture relates little to the modern movement, in terms of deconstruction or postmodernism, most structures have little to do with contextualism. However, exceptions may be found. Michael Graves' Engineering Research Laboratory (postmodernism) and Frank Gehry's Vontz Center for Molecular Research (deconstructivism) both built at the University of Cincinnati during this period show a laudable degree of contextualism.

58. This philosophy was quite different from another emerging trend in the late 1980s and early 1990s, that of neo-historicism, parallel to similar trends at the end of the nineteenth century – the so-called 'battle of the styles' between Greek revivalism and neo-gothic styles. Neo-historicism has little to do with contextual theory as such. Examples of neoclassical themes may be seen in Skidmore, Owings and Merrill's (Chicago) designs for the Canary Wharf development in London Docklands during the 1980s.

59. The Museum of Modern Art, New York, commissioned four university teams in 1967 to prepare urban design schemes for the Harlem area of Manhattan. The schemes of the universities of Princeton, Columbia, MIT and Cornell were seen to be, according to Richard Hatch in *Architectural Forum* magazine (vol. 126, no. 2, March 1967): 'Not specific enough to qualify as serious contenders for construction, the proposals all lack the vision of social place and purpose which would qualify them as utopian'.

60. Lévi-Strauss, Claude. *The Savage Mind* (1975) Chicago, p 16. Quoted by Rowe, Colin, and Fred Koetter. 'Collage City'. *Architectural Review* (1979).

61. Rowe and Koetter, ibid., p 86.

62. Ibid., p 90.

63. Schon, Donald (1985) *The Design Studio (Architecture and the Higher Learning)*. London: MIT Cambridge Massachusetts/RIBA Building Industry Trust.

64. Barnett, Jonathan (1982) *An Introduction to Urban Design*. New York: Harper & Row.

65. Ibid., p. 29.

66. See reporter Tonya Albert in *The Cincinnati Enquirer*, 14 January 2000.

67. These visionary drawings by Hugh Ferris go as far back as 1916.

68. These ideas presaged the ideas of Peter Katz and Peter Calthorpe in the following decade, including Calthorpe's 'pocket parks'.

69. Barnett, op. cit., pp. 179 ff.

70. Ibid., p. 238.

71. Alexander, C., H. Neis, A. Anninou and I. King (1987) *A New Theory of Urban Design*. New York: Oxford University Press.

72. Alexander, Christopher *et al.* (1977) *A Pattern Language*. (Series 2 of 6). New York: Oxford University Press.

73. Alexander, C. (1982) *Wholeness in the Structure of the City*. Berkeley, CA: University of California Center for Environmental Structure.

74. Hedman, R. and A. Jaszewski (1984) 'Fundamentals of urban design', in *Planners Press,* Washington, DC: American Planning Association.
75. Ibid., p. 14.
76. Ibid., p. 26.
77. Habraken, N. J. and B. Valkenburg (trans.) (1972) *Supports: An Alternative to Mass Housing.* London: The Architectural Press.
78. Habraken, N. J. *et al.* (1981) *The Grunsfeld Variations: A Report on the Thematic Development of an Urban Tissue.* Cambridge, MA: MIT Department of Architecture.
79. This technique pervades studio teaching to this day. If context is an important element in urban design, how can a lack of a real, physical site give value to the final outcome of the studio?
80. Habraken *et al., op. cit.,* p. 5.
81. Lynch, Kevin and Gary Hack (1984) *Site Planning.* Cambridge, MA: MIT Press.
82. Ibid., p. 1.
83. Ibid., pp. 14–15.
84. Ibid., p. 205.
85. Ibid., p. 295 ff.
86. Greenbie, Barry (1981) *Spaces: Dimensions of the Human Landscape.* New Haven, CT: Yale University Press.
87. Ibid., p. 122.
88. Ibid., p. 127.
89. Greenbie, op. cit., pp. 112–116.
90. Hall, Edward T. (1968) 'The hidden dimension and "proximics"', *Current Anthropology* 9, nos. 2–3, pp. 83–102. Also Hall, Edward T. (1974) *The Handbook of Proximic Research.* Washington, DC: Society for the Anthropology of Visual Communication.
91. Trancick, Roger (1986) *Finding Lost Space: Theories of Urban Design.* New York: Van Nostrand Reinhold.
92. Ibid., p. 83, figure 3–27.
93. Lang, John T. (1993) *Urban Design: The American Experience.* New York: Van Nostrand Reinhold.
94. Lynch, Kevin *A Theory of Good City Form.* Cambridge, MA: MIT Press.
95. Superstudio studies were European, not American visions of utopian settlements, and appeared in the cartoon strips in the Italian architectural magazine *Casabella,* no. 367, (1972), pp. 15–26. The cartoon strip *Vita, Educazione, Cerimonia, Amore, Morte – Cinque stone del Superstudio* was subtitled 'Superface – an alternative model of life on earth' as the ultimate statement of postindustrial urbanism.
96. Not unlike the ideas of the new urbanists twenty years later in build projects designed and developed by Peter Calthorpe and Peter Katz on the West Coast of the US.
97. This vision was to culminate in Kevin Lynch's last book (published posthumously). Lynch, Kevin and Michael Southworth (eds) (1990) *Wasting Away.* San Francisco: Sierra Books. This was to be a much gloomier prognostication of the American city of the future.
98. Meier, Richard L. (1988) *Ecological Planning and Design: How to Achieve Sustainable Communities.* University of California Center for Environmental Design Research.
99. Thiel, Philip (1981) *Visual Awareness and Design: An Introductory Program in Conceptual Awareness, Perceptual Sensitivity and Basic Design Skills.* Seattle: University of Washington Press.
100. Ibid., p. 118.
101. Ibid., p. 119.
102. Ibid., p. 122.
103. Jacobs, Allen B. (1985) *Looking at Cities.* Cambridge, MA: MIT Press.
104. Jacobs, Allen B. (1982) *Observing and Interpreting the Urban Environment.* Berkeley, CA: University of California, Berkeley's Institute of Urban and Regional Development.
105. Ibid., map, p. 6.
106. A British colleague of one of the authors visited Radburn, New Jersey, in the 1980s as part of his research on public housing design. He walked two miles from the motel and was stopped and questioned by police (Highway Patrol). Though the street was not a freeway, in keeping with twentieth-century highway design, it had no sidewalks.
107. Appleyard, Donald and Allen Jacobs (1982) *Toward an Urban Design Manifesto.* Berkeley, CA: University of California, Berkeley's Institute of Urban and Regional Development.
108. Congrés International d'Architecture Moderne. In rejecting the CIAM manifesto and, at the same time, the garden city movement, the authors presented an unusual dichotomy. These two theoretical stances were almost the diametric opposite of one another and the rejection of the garden city movement in 1982 seemed to contradict the emerging new urbanism of Peter Calthorpe, Peter Katz and others.
109. Bender, Richard (1989) *Design Review: A Review of the Processes, Procedures and Potentials.* Berkeley, CA: College of Environmental Design, University of California.
110. Appleyard, Donald and Peter Bosselmann (1982) *Urban Design Guidelines for Street Management.* Berkeley, CA: Institute of Urban and Regional Development, University of California.
111. Ray, Genevieve H. (1984) *City Sampler: A Catalogue of Urban Environmental Design Tools and Techniques in Local Government.* Washington, DC: Community Design Exchange.
112. Attoe, Wayne (1989) *American Urban Architecture: Catalysts in the Design of Cities.* Berkeley, CA: University of California Press.
113. Holl, Steven (1980) *The Alphabetical City.* New York: Pamphlet Architecture.
114. Machado, Rodolfo (1989) *Rodolfo Machado and Jorge Silvetti: Buildings for Cities.* New York: Rizzoli.
115. Marsh, Peter (1977) 'Vintage year', in *Building Design* (18 November).
116. Venturi, Robert, Denise Scott-Brown and Steven Izenour (1977) *Learning from Las Vegas.* Cambridge, MA: MIT Press, pp. 3–6.
117. Zevi, Bruno and Pierre Restany (1980) 'The poetics of the unfinished', in *SITE: Architecture as Art.* London: Academy Editions, pp. 9–11.
118. Ibid., p. 14. While the critique of postmodernism is correct, there has been little mention of the multiplicity of mediocre buildings in which the designer has simplistically adapted this idea and produced architecture that has all the impermanence of stage sets in the theatre.
119. Wines, James (1987) *De-architecture.* New York: Rizzoli.
120. Ibid., p. 37.
121. Ambasz, Emilio and Steven Holl (1989) Architecture, 4th Exhibition of Gerald D. Hinds. 'Interest in Architecture Program', New York, Museum of Modern Art.
122. Himmelblau, Coop (1983) *Architecture is Now: Projects, (Un)buildings, Actions, Statements, Sketches, Commentaries 1968–1983.* New York: Rizzoli.
123. Ibid., p. 5.
124. Tschumi, Bernard (1983) 'Un Parc Urban Pour le 21e Siécié Competition Report', Paris.
125. Tschumi, Bernard (1981) *Manhattan Transcripts: Theoretical Projects.* London: Academy Editions and New York: St. Martin's Press.
126. Ibid., p.6.
127. Ibid., p.7.
128. Ibid., p.9.
129. Ibid., p. 10.
130. Krier, Rob and Colin Rowe (foreword) (1979) *Urban Space.* London: Academy Editions, p. 9.
131. 'Rational Architecture', *Editions des Archives d'Architecture Moderne* (Brussels: 1978), p. 41. Also see Colot, Maurice, *The Survey and Four Projects of the Archives d'Architecture Moderne* (Brussels: 1983) and others for the Bureau d'Urbanisme de l'Agglomeration of Brussels.
132. Le Corbusier (1971) *The City of Tomorrow.* London: The Architectural Press. Originally published as *Urbanisme* Paris, 1924.
133. 'Cities within the city', *Lotus International 19*, June 1978, pp. 82–97.
134. Koolhaas, Rem (1978) *Delirious New York.* London: Academy Editions.
135. Gosling, David and Barry Maitland (1984) *Concepts of Urban Design.* London: Academy Editions and New York: St. Martin's Press, pp. 104–105.

136. Koolhaas, Rem (1989) 'The Contemporary City' (preview), *Design Book Review*, vol. 17 (winter). Originally published in *L 'Architecture d'Aujourdhui.* (April 1989).

137. Ibid., p. 15.

138. Koolhaas (1978) op. cit., p. 6.

139. Wyatt, Mark (1996) *White Knuckle Ride.* London: Salamander Books, pp. 7–10. See also, Throgmorton, Todd (1994) *Rollercoasters of America.* Osceola, WI: Motorbooks International.

140. Koolhaas (1978) op. cit., p. 33.

141. Walker, Derek (1982) 'Epcot 82' *Architectural Design*, vol 52, no. 9–10.

142. Yet, in fairness, it must be said that Disney Corporation's venture in the late 1990s in the construction of Celebration in Florida, perhaps emulating the earlier Seaside new community in Florida, was close to the concept of a utopian community.

143. Koolhaas (1978) op. cit., p. 69.

144. Ferris, Hugh (1929) *The Metropolis of Tomorrow.* New York, Iven Washburn. See also Ferris, Hugh (1953) *Power in Buildings.* Columbia University Press.

145. Koolhaas (1978) op. cit., p. 130.

146. Ibid., p. 133.

147. See Gosling, David (1988) 'Urban forms and spaces: waterfront development', in *Urban Futures*, vol. 1, no. 1, pp. 18–33.

148. Skidmore, Owings, and Merrill. 'Canary Wharf Design Guidelines' (April–December 1986).

149. Abrams, Janet (1986) 'Dockland demise', *Progressive Architecture*, no. 2. (February), pp. 4–7.

150. Gosling, Cullen, Hollamby *et al.* 'Urban Design Study: A Guide to Development, The Isle of Dogs', London Docklands Development Corporation, November 1982.

151. Wilford, Michael (1984) 'Off to the races or going to the dogs', *Architectural Design,* Special Issue: 'Urbanism', vol. 54, no. 1/2, p. 12.

152. Wrenn, Douglas (in association with John Casazza and Eric Smart) (1983) *Urban Waterfront Development.* Washington, DC: Urban Land Institute.

153. Ibid., pp. 212–17. Citizen Participation: Major Development Lessons: Future Development Opportunities.

154. Hoyle, B. S., D. A. Pinder and M. S. Hussein (eds) (1988) *Revitalizing the Waterfront: International Dimensions of Docklands Redevelopment.* England: Bellhaven Press.

155. Stirling, James, Michael Wilford and Associates. 'Collegetown Urban Design Study'. City of Ithaca, New York and Cornell University, February 1985.

156. Ibid., p. 1.

157. Ibid., p. 18.

158. Girouard, Mark (1998) *Big Jim: The Life and Work of James Stirling* London: Chatto and Windus, p. 226.

159. Maxwell, op. cit., p. 101.

160. Girouard, op. cit., pp. 228–29.

161. Annual Design Awards. *Progressive Architecture*, January 1981.

162. *Progressive Architecture*, January, 1981, pp. 90–92.

163. *Progressive Architecture*, January, 1982, p. 173.

164. Annual Design Awards. *Progressive Architecture*, January 1983, p. 119. This remark was strange, since Woodbridge had worked for the San Francisco office of Skidmore, Owings and Merrill between 1965 and 1973, when the firm was paramount in the design of megastructure, culminating in some of Gordon Munschaft's last projects in Saudi Arabia, including the Haj Pilgrim's impressive terminal in Jeddah.

165. Ibid., p. 119.

166. Annual Design Awards. *Progressive Architecture*, January 1984, p. 138.

167. Urban Design Awards Program. *Progressive Architecture*, January 1985, p. 131.

168. Despite Pope John Paul II's pilgrimage to the Holy Land and Jerusalem in March 2000, little seems to have been resolved.

169. *Progressive Architecture*, January 1985, p. 133.

170. Annual Design Awards. *Progressive Architecture*, January 1986, p. 122.

171. Annual Design Awards. *Progressive Architecture*, January 1987, p. 123.

172. Annual Design Awards. *Progressive Architecture*, January 1988, p. 124.

173. Urban Design Awards. *Progressive Architecture*, January 1989, p. 106.

174. Ibid., p. 106. Cooper's remark seems contradictory since American planning legislation seemed to be confined to land use and zoning and not three-dimensional design as anything but prescriptive.

175. Jencks, Charles (1985) 'Post Modernism'. Evanston, Illinois: Northwestern University conference (October). This was followed by another conference in Hanover, Germany, organised by Dr Peter Kolowski for Cintas.

176. This paper, published by *Art and Design* (London) in 1986, also makes references to other articles such as: Howe, Irving (1970) 'Mass society and post modern fiction', *Decline of the New.* New York: Harcourt Brace; and Graff, Gerald (1979) 'The myth of the post modern breakthrough', *Literature Against Itself.* Chicago: University of Chicago Press.

177. Barth, John (1980) 'The literature of replenishment, post modern fiction', *The Atlantic Magazine*, pp. 65–71. Eco, Umberto (1984) 'Post modernism, irony, the enjoyable', postscript to *The Name of the Rose.* New York: Harcourt Brace Jovanovich. This was a major work of fiction as an example of postmodernism in literature.

178. Lubetkin, Berthold (1985) Royal Gold Medal Address. Royal Institute of British Architects. *Transactions II*, vol. 1, no. 2 (May), p. 9.

179. Editorial (1985) 'Peter Blake and Post-Modernism', *Art and Design*, vol. 1, no. 4 (May), p. 9.

180. AD Profile (1983) 'Architecture in Progress', *Architectural Design.* 'Architecture in Progress IBA Berlin 1984', vol. 53, no. 1/2 , p. 42–43.

181. Ibid., p. 91–93.

182. Ibid., p. 109–111.

183. 'Cross currents of American architecture', *Architectural Design*, vol. 55, no. 1/2, 1985.

184. Ibid., p. 11–19.

185. Ibid., p.46.

186. Klotz, Heinrich (guest ed.) (1985) 'Revision of the modern', *Architectural Design*, vol. 55, no. 3/4, p. 45.

187. Norberg-Schulz, Christian (1988) 'The two faces of post modernism', *Architectural Design*, vol. 58, no. 7/8, pp. 11–15.

188. Eco, op. cit.

189. Heidegger, Martin (1971) 'The Thing', *Poetry, Language, Thought.* New York. Norberg-Schulz, Christian (1983) 'Heidegger's thinking on art', *Perspecta 20.* Yale University Press.

190. Kant, I (1965) *Critique of Pure Reason.* New York: publisher unknown, p. 513. Nietzsche, F. (1967) *The Will to Power.* New York: publisher unknown, p. 301.

191. Sheenan, J., *Architectural Design*, (1988) vol. 58, no. 7/8, pp. 21–23.

192. Ibid., p.21.

193. Melvin, John (1988) 'The architecture of pluralism', *Architectural Design*, vol. 58, no. 9/10, p. xi.

194. Ibid., p.21.

195. 'Deconstruction in architecture', *Architectural Design*, vol. 58, no. 3/4, 1988.

196. Ibid., p.8.

197. Descartes, R. (1985) 'Discourse on method', *The Philosophical Writings of Descartes.* Cambridge: Cambridge University Press, vol. 1.

198. See Gosling and Maitland, op. cit., p. 26.

199. 'Deconstruction in Architecture', *Architectural Design*, op. cit., p. 9.

200. Derrida, J. (1986) Interview. 'Architecture Ove il Desiderio Può Abitare' *Domus* (Italy), no. 671 (April).

201. Derrida, J. (1987) 'Ce Qui Reste à Force de Musiquè Psyche' Galilee, p. 96. See also Gaschè, R. (n.d.) *The Train of the Mirror.* Cambridge, MA: Harvard University Press, pp. 225–318, and Benjamin, Andrew (1988) 'Naming deconstruction', *History of Human Sciences*, vol. 1, no. 2.

202. Such an argument might be applied to Frank Gehry's Microbiology Research Center at the University of Cincinatti, completed in 1999. To the casual observer, the complex, leaning and interlocking external geometry of the building belies the orderly, highly functional laboratory research spaces within the envelope.

203. Eisenman, Peter (1984) 'The end of the classical', *Perspecta no. 21*. See also Eisenman's contributions in 'Investigations in Architecture: Eisenman Studies at the Graduate School of Design (1983–1985)', Harvard University (1986).

204. Cooke, Catherine (1988) 'The lessons of the Russian avant-garde', *Architectural Design*, vol. 58, no. 3/4, pp. 13–15. Gozak, Andrei, Andre Leonidov and Catherine Cooke (eds) (1988) *Ivan Leonidov: The Complete Works*. London: Academy Editions.

205. Cooke (1988) op. cit., p. 14.

206. See, for example, Chernikov's 'Coordinated Volumetric Planning' of the late 1920s and Leonidov's project for a new linear city at Magnitogorsk, 1929, also attributed to Ernst May and Miliutin. Cooke, Catherine (1986) 'Vision and historicism', *Architectural Design*, no. 6., pp. 12–21.

207. Cooke, Catherine (1988) 'Russian constructionism and the city', *International Union of Architects (UJA) Journal*, vol. 1, no. 1, pp. 16–25.

208. 'Deconstruction in Architecture', *Architectural Design*, op. cit., 1988, p. 21.

209. Ibid., p. 77.

210. *Architectural Design*, vol. 58, no. 1/2, 1989.

211. Ibid., p. 42.

212. Ibid., p. 51.

213. 'Such a concept of function, taken from physiology, assimilates the form of an organ, in which the functions justify the form and the variations of the functions mean the change of the form. So, functionalism and organism, the two main streams that have presided over modern architecture, show the common root, the cause of their weakness and fundamental misunderstanding.' Rossi, Aldo (1966) *L'Architettura della Città*. Italy: Marsilio.

214. The classification of cities in this way is by no means a twentieth-century phenomenon. Jacques Francois Blondel in his *Cours d'Architecture* listed the various kinds of buildings in the architect's repertory and these were classified according to the dominant function to which the building was dedicated. However, the idea of the separation of functions (land use) and later zoning was a city planning device introduced in the US in the latter part of the twentieth century.

215. Wolfe, Tom 'The Me Decade', *Harpers and Queen*, January 1977, p. 48.

216. See Gosling and Maitland. op. cit. See also Gosling, David (1984) 'Definitions of urban design', *Architectural Design*, Special issue: 'Urbanism', vol. 54, no. 1/2, pp. 16–25.

217. Ibid., Maitland, Barry (1984) 'The uses of history', *Architectural Design*, Special issue: 'Urbanism', vol. 54, no. 1/2, pp. 4–7.

218. Vidler, Anthony (1978) 'The Third Typology', *Rational Architecture*. Brussels: Editions des Archives d'Architecture Moderne, pp. 28–32.

219. See: Mumford, Lewis (1938) *The Culture of Cities*. New York, republished in expanded form as *The City in History* (Harmondsworth: Penguin Books, 1961) and Chueca-Goitia, *Introduction al Urbanismo* (Madrid, 1970).

220. There are even differences between some of the main representatives of this movement such as Rossi and Aymomino. For Aymomino the architecture of the city is a continuous demonstration of the relationship between the parts, and constitutes a precise operation included within a spatial structure. For Aldo Rossi in his Gallaratese project in Milan, Italy, in 1973, a linear residential building is placed beside a building designed by Carlo Aymomino: the architecture does not need to have an immediate contextual relationship. (Aldo Rossi displayed this in his *Citta Analoga*, Tavola, *Lotus International*, no. 13, Milan, 1976, p. 5.) For Rossi, Gina Conforto, Gabrielle de Giogi, Allesandra Muntoni, Marcello Pazzaglini, in # *Il dibattito archittorico in Italia, 1945–1975*. (Roma: Bulzoni Editore, 1977).

221. Morphology or urban morphology was defined by Carlo Aymomino as 'The study of built form considered from the point of view of its production in relation to the urban structure. In *La Città di Padova*, 1970, C. Aymomino, M. Brusatin, G. Fabri, M. Lena, P. Lovero, S. Lucianetti, and A. Rossi.

Chapter Six

1990–2000

CONTRADICTIONS: THE CELEBRATION OF CENTRAL CITY AND THE EMERGING EXTERNAL CITY

Two polemic works, published in 1988[1] and 1991,[2] represent two opposing views regarding the future of the American city, though neither reflects the inward-looking pluralism of such theories as deconstruction of the previous decade.

William Whyte's *City* was to become a manual among elected officials, city planning commissions and professionals across the country in rediscovering the qualities of traditional city centres. Whyte's research, 'Street Life Project', examined urban space from a social standpoint. This is not to say that he ignored physical design but rather related those aspects to both positive and negative social behaviour. However, suggesting that there had been an increase in the number of people using city centre spaces perhaps belies the reality. There is of course the proliferation of outdoor cafés, but in actual fact such activity is mainly confined to Southern cities such as San Antonio, New Orleans or Fort Lauderdale rather than cities of the Midwest with their violently contrasting harsh climates.

In Whyte's previous work with the New York City Planning Commission, the emphasis had been on urban design and the use of incentive zoning to provide new parks and plazas. The entire study was carried out by direct observation, including extensive use of photography: 35mm slides, Super 8 video (for time-lapse photography) and 16mm movie cameras. The use of a telephoto lens precluded observation of the photographer. Interviewing, though part of the study, was not extensive; this contrasted with Kevin Lynch's previous techniques where street interviews were of paramount importance.

Whyte refers to the social life of the street, not dissimilar from Jane Jacobs' studies some thirty years previously. If people conversed on the street they did not move out of the main pedestrian flow. Street corners were considered the best places. Whyte refers to the Yiddish term *Schmoozing*, which, though not directly translatable, apparently relates to 'nothing talk' or chat. Certainly observation of human behaviour outside central city street life would confirm this, particularly in the US. 'Break-out' sessions at major conferences are examples of delegates enthusiastically participating in this practice within the conference centre, in this context often referred to as 'networking', an abhorrent term that also applies to cocktail parties. In this respect, Whyte's photographs are vivid, and reference is made to similar encounters in London's Financial District or Milan's Galleria. As part of the social commentary, Whyte remarked upon the presence of street vendors, despite their illegality in most instances. In Manhattan, the ubiquitous presence of street vendors, particularly food vendors, is obvious, and though not part of the urban fabric, it creates nodal points at intersections, particularly along the Avenue of the Americas (6th Avenue). Other insertions of human behaviour as part of the urban fabric include street entertainers, card players and even bag ladies. On the darker side are drug dealers, prostitutes and their promoters, though such operators of street corners are confined to specific neighbourhoods not identified by Whyte.

In addressing the physical street, Whyte emphasises the priority given to vehicular traffic over pedestrians. The dictatorial flashing, electronic crossing signs, 'Walk' and 'Don't Walk', confirm this by creating nervousness and erratic behaviour among pedestrians.

Like other observers, Whyte notes that Lexington Avenue in Manhattan between 57th and 61st Streets is heavily used by pedestrians despite its decrepit condition of narrow, cracked and broken sidewalks (pavements), a proliferation of parking signs, rubbish containers and advertising displays.[3] This begs the question, 'Why?', the answer to which, according to Whyte, is 'second storeyness'.[4] This is a useful observation considering that most observers walking down any downtown street have a range of vision probably not more than four storeys vertically and 180 degrees horizontally. Only tourists, and particularly architects, will look beyond that vertical and horizontal range. On Lexington Avenue, Whyte points out, there are a plethora of second-storey users including dance studios, karate academies, Chinese restaurants, palmists, hair stylists and so forth. Window shopping also adds to activity along the street.

The plaza is a major contribution to the urban design fabric in terms of social spaces used by couples, groups and, as Whyte says, 'lovers' who embrace each other fervently. Yet, the celebration of urban plazas as an important part of the public realm is not necessarily consistent in New York. Though not demonstrated by Whyte, there exists a contrast between crowd activity in the plaza on Park Avenue beneath the Seagram building, where activity is relatively low-key, and the intense activity in front of the Rockefeller Plaza, particularly in winter during the ice-skating season. Observing these skaters (mostly amateurs) from above provides some of the best experiences of free urban theatre.

Whyte refers to the behavior of 'winos' in Chapter 11, under the heading 'The Undesirables',[5] where he indicates that winos in public places are feared by other citizens more than are drug dealers. Given that alcoholism is a complex mixture of both a psychological and a physical disease (parallel to similar problems of anorexia and bulimia), this irrational fear is widespread; however, it is true that the behaviour of such individuals is often intrusive. Whyte argues that the best way of dealing with this problem is to make the public space more attractive to everyone else, an example, perhaps, of wishful thinking.

Good places, he thought, are largely self-policing, with a building guard, news stand operator or food vendor acting as an unappointed supervisor.

The dancer Marilyn Wood, who has staged choreographic celebrations in public spaces, nominates the Seagram Plaza in Manhattan and Fountain Square in Cincinnati as two of the best public spaces in the country. While this may be true, perhaps, of Seagram, the same cannot be said of Fountain Square. Cincinnati has one of the lowest proportions of public open space per head of population in the Midwest – far worse than Columbus, Ohio, Cleveland, Ohio, Louisville, Kentucky or Indianapolis. For example, on major public occasions, such as the winning of the World Series baseball in 1990 by the local Cincinnati Reds, capacity for public celebration was not available.

The Plaza in front of the Seagram building is praised as having the best public steps of any major office building. Different levels are an integral part of urban design. Whyte refers to Mies van der Rohe's design as meticulous in both appearance and functions, not only in terms of ease of use (5-inch riser, 14-inch tread)[6] but also in appearance. The nearby Citicorp building is also praised, though the pitch is somewhat steeper. Subway steps are far less comfortable. The steps in the plaza behind Michael Graves' Engineering Research building at the University of Cincinnati, completed in 1998, are intended more as a sitting area than a functional transition between different levels. This design by Wes Jones can be compared with other earlier examples such as Robert Venturi's design for Wu Hall at Princeton or Gund Hall at Harvard's Graduate School of Design.

Another component of townscape design in the US are 'skyways', second- and third-floor public walkways connecting downtown buildings such as offices, hotels and department stores, introduced in cold winter cities such as Montreal and Minneapolis. Though the skyways here work well, this is not the case for cities further south in the North American continent. Cincinnati, for example, though it has harsh winters, also experiences extremely warm summers. The skywalks in Cincinnati are perceived as threatening public spaces and are therefore under-utilised. Not only are they confusing in that they often traverse hotel lobbies where people may be eating breakfast (for example the Hyatt hotel), but the bridges can be of different designs, adding to the visual chaos of the urban fabric.

Another drawback to the skyway concept is that it removes people from the public realm, that is to say, the street. This, as Whyte suggests, is to establish the primacy of vehicular traffic. However, with the establishment of skywalks and adjacent enclosed shopping centres, it often appears as though some gigantic vacuum cleaner has literally swept all the people from the streets. Indeed, cities such as Seattle, with steep topography, have rejected skyways mainly on aesthetic grounds.

Regarding the issues of megastructures within downtown areas, Whyte praises the Citicorp building in mid-Manhattan. Hugh Stubbins' design, which raises the skyscraper on four giant pilotis five storeys above street level, was regarded by Whyte as 'notably hospitable'. Sheltering the existing church below it, it also provides spaces within which people can eat their lunch, talk and read. Better still, it is not surrounded by an antiseptic mall but rather a mix of small stores, Irish bars, flower shops, news stands and lunch counters.[7]

Whyte also addresses the issue of sunlight and shadow in the central city. This is an important factor given the height of skyscrapers in most American cities, but is it really important? A University of Cincinnati study of shadow patterns in Fountain Square revealed no real problems in that particular location. Whyte suggests that the most pervasive loss has been of secondary light, but he acknowledges that in New York, for instance, zoning did make provisions for sun and light, resulting in the curious 'wedding cake' architecture of strange setbacks in that city during the skyscraper construction of the 1930s.

In his conclusion, Whyte makes the case for gentrification in pulling the more affluent people back to the city centre. With the exception of mid-Manhattan, where some of the wealthiest people remained, high-income families from other major cities had long ago fled to the suburbs. This issue is controversial as it raises the question of where the displaced poor will live once gentrification takes place (for further discussion of this see Chapter 7).

Joel Garreau was a senior reporter for the *Washington Post*, and his text has been attacked by some critics as too journalistic, with interviews and an undeniable celebration of booming suburban centres.[8] In his *Edge City* Garreau examines the transformation of major American metropolitan areas. His seminal work addresses a late-twentieth-century phenomenon in American metropolitan areas – the transition from the central city of the late nineteenth and early twentieth centuries towards the polycentric city. The polycentric city, generated by the mid-twentieth-century construction of interstate highways initiated by the Eisenhower administration in the 1950s at the height of the Cold War, caused the exponential growth of the suburbs on cheap land and the flight of the more affluent from the central city.

However, the completely different phenomenon of 'edge cities' did not appear until the end of the twentieth century, due to the increasing traffic gridlock in metropolitan areas – a direct result of the creation of polycentric cities. Most major US cities now have peripheral freeways, or beltways (ring roads) to deal with this problem.[9]

Edge cities are a new urban design phenomenon in the sense that new office complexes, usually sleek if somewhat anonymous examples of architecture of horizontal, low-rise design, with dark tinted plate-glass bands alternating with gleaming white stove enamelled panels in parkland settings, are now being built outside the beltway. The implication of this is that those who had originally fled to the suburbs were no longer commuting to the city centre as their main place of employment (excluding industrial plants) but beyond their place of residence. Silicon Valley, south of San Francisco, is a case in point.

Garreau's edge cities are seen as external retail and office developments that have proliferated along the beltways in most major cities. He defines an edge city as an agglomeration that has more than five million square feet of office space, over half a million square feet of retail space and more jobs than housing, which defies the definition of a conventional city.

Critics such as Terry Christensen of San Jose State University in California suggest that Garreau was not actually discovering something new in his edge cities, but was describing the multinucleated city and the deconcentration of the metropolis discussed by urban theorists such as Lewis Mumford some forty years earlier. Other critics, for example Stephanie Stubbs, proclaim admiration for Garreau, in that his journalistic style makes for a readable book.

There were two hundred edge cities around the country when Garreau's book was published in 1991. Sixteen surrounded Washington, DC, and it was only New York, supposedly Manhattan, and possibly Queens, Brooklyn, and the Bronx as well as the core of San Francisco where urban living was still vibrant, yet 88 per cent of all Americans were living outside the traditional city. Stubbs identifies the implications for the built environment with shorter travel distances to replace long commuting time.[10] This is only partially true as the majority of the population still commute to their places of work in the city centre and relatively few are employed beyond the beltway. But what if Stubbs' hypothesis were correct? If people no longer commute to the city centre for their place of employment, this conjures up an Orwellian vision[11] or even that of the cult movie *Bladerunner*, of total decay and the residue of the urban poor with anarchy and repression controlled only by brutal security forces.[12]

Again, while Garreau claimed in his address to the 1990 American Institute of Architects convention in Houston, Texas, that 'one of his first genuine surprises was to discover how little architects had to do with the appearance of these places', such a remark is patently untrue and the office complexes and shopping malls, as well as the speculative housing developments of transitional style homes, complete with community club, swimming pool and golf course, have everything to do with the perhaps cynical architects obeying the orders of Mammon. The brilliant, streamlined white and black tinted glass of the offices are a paradigm of this architectural approach and were certainly not built by speculators without the assistance of architectural designers, contradicting Stubbs' final plea to 'the wheeler-dealers tycooning Edge City, USA: To hell with the clowns – send in the architects. Please!'.

In his review of *Edge City*, Martin Zimmerman noted that Garreau does not refer to the term 'urban design' although this was clearly what the book was all about.[13] Edge cities are bland, surreal and discomforting. Zimmerman considered Garreau's defence of edge cities as ambivalent and confused, yet he refers to a 350-year-old culture. However, the culture is either slightly more than 200 years old, since the American Revolution of the British colonies, or well over a thousand years old, stretching back to the Anasazi tribes and later the Hopi and Navajo tribes in what is now the Southwest of the US.

Zimmerman is correct in saying that society has been incapable of sustaining an equilibrium between the dualities of city and country and technology and nature, yet the resolution of whether edge cities are a beginning or an end is questionable because, in Garreau's definition, edge cities are a fact. Zimmerman is also correct in criticising Garreau as saying, 'I have a healthy regard for greed as a social motivator'. This is a reflection of the politics of the 1980s, whether it was the Reagan administration in the US or the Thatcher administration in the UK (the so-called 'me' decade). Perhaps of greater importance is Zimmerman's criticism of Garreau's lack of concern for public sector planning, of architectural design review, growth management and zoning, and his lack of answers towards the end of his book.

In the introduction to *Edge City,* Garreau writes: 'Most of us spend our entire lives in and around these Edge Cities, yet we barely recognize them for what they are . . . Edge Cities are tied together not by locomotives and subways, but by freeways, jetways and jogging paths . . . an atrium shielding trees perpetually in leaf at the cores of our corporate headquarters, fitness centers and shopping plazas'. Yet surely this celebration of edge city is misplaced. It ignores the fact that the cores of most major urban metropolitan areas are still inhabited by the urban poor and ethnic minorities, and are likely to remain so in an increasingly divisive society with growing differentiation between affluent and high-income families and the rest who earn minimum wages of between $5 and $7 per hour. Given his journalistic knowledge of the contemporary structure of American society, Garreau cannot possibly claim that most of us spend our entire lives in and around edge cities. Visit a suburban shopping mall, and it is overwhelmingly populated by Caucasians.

However, *Edge City* is a challenging and extremely well written piece of literature. In his analysis of Boston, Garreau cites five edge city limits as 'Insurmountability, Affordability, Mobility, Accessibility and Nice'.[14]

The US city of Boston, which in the middle of the twentieth century was the closest to a European city such as Amsterdam or Munich, had only one skyscraper (the John Hancock Insurance headquarters). Garreau quotes William Whyte as saying that the average distance to downtown from a CEO's home is eight miles, in a circle about four miles in diameter bounded by country clubs, and adds that 'Nice' includes high schools with astonishingly high SAT (Scholastic Assessment Test) scores.[15] In this contradictory celebration, he also mentions that horses drive up land prices. For example, near Far Hills in New Jersey, where the US Olympic Equestrian Team rides, or in California around Santa Barbara, horse country is a great asset in the eyes of real estate agents. This is another example of Garreau's fifth definition of 'Nice'.[16]

The greatest contradiction in the Boston study was the attempt by the developer Mortimer Zuckerman, led by one of his managers, Jim Rosenfield, to build a 13,750 square metre (148,000 square feet) office building overlooking Walden Pond.

Walden, or *Life in the Woods*, was a celebration of tranquillity written by Thoreau in 1854. Rosenfield claimed he had read 'parts' of Thoreau's book. Thoreau had written: 'The mass of men lead lives of quiet desperation ... I went to the woods because I wished to live deliberately.'[17]

In the context of Detroit, Garreau mentions FAR (floor-to-area ratio) indicating that 100,000 square feet on 100,000 square feet of land gives a FAR of 1.0, but 40 square feet of office space on 100,000 square feet of land give a FAR of 0.4.[18] This is simplistic, and 'plot ratio', which is the equivalent of FAR, is far more complex in both the developers' calculations as well as the zoning and land use regulations of city and regional governments. Another set of calculations important to developers is the ratio of rental floor space to circulation, such as elevators and fire escape staircases in the vertical sense or access corridors in the horizontal sense. The use of open office floor plans, which arose from the German *Burolandschaft* idea, eliminated separate rooms for office employees and replaced them with five-foot screens forming cubicles in which individual computer terminals were placed. This new configuration became far more profitable for developers as it reduced the horizontal circulation space to the elevator lobbies and eliminated corridors. The ratio of rental space to circulation was formerly in the range of 75 to 25 per cent or at best 80 to 20 per cent. The new configuration gave much more efficient figures approaching 90 to 10 per cent.[19]

Garreau mentioned that a FAR of 0.4 per cent assumes that the configuration devotes one and a half times as much land to the parking of cars as the space occupied by office workers, assuming flat car parks. Such an absurd land use is the very image of edge cities, though Garreau refers to parking garages (presumably subterranean) as a solution as an 'expensive, dense, but potentially more urbane and civilized, edge city'.[20] Civilised?

Perhaps the most potent parts of Garreau's commentary are his chapters on Southern California and the San Francisco Bay Area. Though these two regions are quite different in character they certainly represent the epitome if not the beginnings of the edge city phenomenon. In Southern California, the new town of Irvine becomes a paradigm. As Garreau says, Irvine is the largest edge city landscape designed by a single company. The median home prices are the third highest in America. Irvine is 56 kilometres (35 miles) southeast of downtown Los Angeles. It spans Orange County between San Diego and Los Angeles with 25,900 hectares (64,000 acres) of land, with plots selling for as much as $1 million. It is no Levittown. It is segmented into subdivisions with bizarre names like Irvine Spectrum and Newport Center-Fashion Island or, worse, John Wayne and Orange County itself, the birthplace of Richard Nixon. All of this with, at the time Garreau wrote his book, a population of over 200,000,[21] of which the high-technology job base was 150,000. It is also significant that Irvine is 16 kilometres (10 miles) south of Disneyland, the very first theme park, in Anaheim. Garreau is incorrect in saying that the Mediterranean-style homes are more repetitive than those in the old post-Second World War Levittown. Certainly, people in Levittown made additions to their houses and individually landscaped their backyards, but

though Irvine had deed restrictions, not dissimilar to later developments like Seaside or Celebration in Florida, the architectural variety was much richer.

The San Francisco Bay Area is a contrast. The largest edge city was the 237-hectare (585-acre) ranch in the San Ramon Valley developed by Alex Mehran, who lived in San Francisco in the elegant Presidio Heights, a round trip commute of 110 kilometres (70 miles). The Urban Land Institute, which seems to have a schizophrenic attitude toward urban design, gave Bishop Ranch an award as a model of 'foresight, planning and partnership between public and private interests',[22] following a previous award for Disneyland. But equal control over public and private landscape is omnipresent as much as it is in Southern California. The interior trees of the three identical office buildings are planted in the floor (not tubs) of the central atria because Mehran believed they added to the 'quality of life', although he concedes that he and his family would not want to live there. He prefers downtown San Francisco, excluding the neighbourhoods of Berkeley and Oakland across the bay. Michael Barone[23] suggested that the coasts of California belonged to liberal democrats, inland to conservative republicans, with the San Pablo Ridge serving as the cultural divide. Silicon Valley is, naturally, the cause of the edge city phenomenon whether it is to the north, south of San Francisco, or closer to the area between Los Angeles and San Diego. But San Francisco has survived as an entity, Garreau suggests, because of geo-physical conditions of undeveloped land such as wetlands, floodplains, mountains and ridges. Petulama, north of San Francisco and south of Santa Rosa, severely restricted growth from 1972 onwards, and Santa Rosa and its adjacent communities still have the qualities of small-scale American towns.

The eccentric conclusion to Garreau's eloquent work is a glossary of terms, quite unlike any formal architectural list. He defines, for instance, amenities as 'frills', for example, trees.[24] 'Ample parking' is defined as the singular distinction between edge city and downtown, a 'beautiful building' as one that is fully leased, and an 'attitude' (a non-architectural term) as a negative mindset. All of these may represent a certain cynical humour, but the reader gets the impression that there is seriousness behind them. Most are drawn not from architectural language but from the language of the developer's corporate boardroom. The terms are chilling, the worst example of which, 'value engineering', is often cynically used to eliminate design refinements in favour of functional necessity and ignores the value added benefits of thoughtful aesthetic design.

A subsequent appendix, 'The Laws', makes even more cynical reading, for example: the definition of a 'prime location' is the commuting time of the chief executive officer; the function of a glass elevator is to make women feel safe since rapes rarely occur within such a facility.[25]

One is left with the feeling that Garreau himself is ambivalent about edge cities. At first the reader may think that the book is a celebration of urban life, but will eventually reach the conclusion that it is in fact an acerbic criticism of urban life at the turn of the twenty-first century.

A more passive view of the contemporary American city is, perhaps, *The American City,* by Alexander Garvin.[26] Garvin portrays a less vivid but more technical analysis of the contemporary city. Though the subtitle 'What Works and What Doesn't' seems demeaning and slightly frivolous, this is a scholarly work between the polemicism of both Whyte and Garreau. Garvin's work is a very comprehensive reference on many aspects of city planning legislation and administration, and draws not only on his teaching at Yale University but also on his experience as a New York City Planning Commissioner. He correctly claims that most source books focus on only one issue, such as housing or historic preservation, one discipline, such as architecture or even law, or a particular city. Garvin's research is examined on a multi-disciplinary basis and though it may emphasise market economics, it does examine many other issues including utopian visions, pedestrianisation, housing supply and demand, rehabilitation, neighbourhood revitalisation, slum clearance and suburbia.

In expressing the widespread disillusionment with urban planning, Garvin cites cities that have achieved major success: Chicago's 37 kilometres (23 miles) of shoreline along Lake Michigan;[27] Charleston, South Carolina; Pittsburgh, Pennsylvania; and Portland, Oregon. In the case of the latter example, he praises the pedestrian environment, the reclamation of its riverfront and the light rail system.

Garvin's arguments regarding market economics are more dubious in suggesting that the formula may be market, location, design, financing and entrepreneurship. This may seem to be an over-simplistic formula. On the other hand, he refers to stillborn projects that have a long record in the latter part of the twentieth century. Whether his prescription is correct is debatable. For example, the 6-hectare (15-acre) Pulaski Ward in Savannah began rehabilitation in 1964, and revitalisation had become successful by the mid 1970s, but the same strategy had not worked with the 150 blocks of Savannah's Victorian District, using federal subsidies. By 1992, Garvin reports that the neighbourhood remained riddled with vacant and deteriorating structures,[28] possibly as a result of the curtailment of federal funds during the 1980s.

In his comprehensive study, Garvin emphasises the importance of pedestrianisation in the context of urban design policy. Pedestrianisation during the 1970s had been regarded as somewhat of a failure in American cities due to the increasing dominance of the motor car. Nevertheless, Portland in Oregon and Denver in Colorado are examples of successful strategies. Contrary to national trends, Portland emphasised pedestrianisation and mass transit during the 1970s with a high-density office district, overlapping retail core, two transitways and a suburban light rail system.[29] The integration of pedestrian systems and light rail has made Portland one of the most successful cities in the US in creating a pleasing downtown urban environment and increasing the downtown workforce and retail sales.

At the same time, it must be recognised that downtown pedestrianisation in attracting retail is inevitably facing suburban competition. In addressing the issue of slum clearance, Garvin seemed to accept that demolishing a slum and removing its people was not that simplistic. The opponents to clearance believed that the new buildings of redevelopment projects had little reference to historical precedent and traditional architecture. Vincent Scully, a distinguished professor of architectural

history at the time, referred to the redevelopment plan for the hill neighbourhood of New Haven, Connecticut, by saying it 'had a purism and a distaste for life's messy multiplicity [that] could go no further'.[30]

Thus, slum clearance was also linked to the revitalisation of neighbourhoods. Garvin distinguished slum clearance from attempts to combat deterioration. Topography such as San Francisco's Nob Hill or Pacific Heights or the historical housing stock of Boston's Beacon Hill or Back Bay were examples of continuing preservation and revitalisation. But, suggesting that Congress should enact legislation that provides (financial) assistance to localities to achieve this avoids the social issues of gentrification. Indeed, current legislation aids only those owners of revenue-producing commercial properties and it is unlikely that the owner of a house designed by Frank Lloyd Wright, for example, would receive any public financial assistance in the process of restoration. Wooster Square, New Haven, was presented as an example of the successful rehabilitation of an Italian-American neighbourhood with Mayor Lee and Administrator Logue maximising Title One, non-cash credits. The illustrated plan was given as 1965, but the original plan, also under the direction of Christopher Tunnard and prepared by David Gosling, was published in 1959. An equally successful restoration was the Ansonborough neighbourhood of Charleston, South Carolina, which had been fully restored by 1980, tripling property values.

Cluster zoning, or planned unit development (PUD) was already being adopted in the 1960s. Garvin refers to this as an 'alternative to cookie-cutter suburban subdivisions'.[31] This planning mechanism had emerged from the 1960s onwards, though cluster zoning was not dissimilar from much earlier garden city examples such as Mariemont and Greenhills in Ohio or Radburn. Garvin suggests that in areas without zoning regulations (presumably in suburban or ex-urban areas), the only way to create a cluster community with common open space relating to topography and other natural features should be done outside traditional zoning requirements. Yet PUD proposals are considered by most regional planning commissions only in terms of land use and not the three-dimensional aspects of the proposal. Garvin acknowledges that such efforts are not necessarily self-executing, that approval is discretionary, and that such projects are often viewed by authorities in an entirely subjective way. In addition, he intimates that these projects may result in bribery and political pay-offs.

Elsewhere, Garvin refers to new-towns-in-town and new-towns-in-the-country such as Battery Park City in New York or Portland's riverfront esplanade as examples of the former, and Seaside, Florida or Sea Ranch, California, as examples of the latter.

At the end of each section of his study, Garvin summarises the issues categorised by different headings, including market, location, design, financing and entrepreneurship, under the general term 'Ingredients of Success'. The implication that all can be solved within the pursuit of market economics is, perhaps, debatable.

John Lang's book *Urban Design: The American Experience*[32] is quite different from Garvin's work, *The American City,* which might be perceived as pragmatic in approach. Lang's study includes four parts, the first of which, 'Urban Design in Context',[33] is perhaps the most vivid. Contextual design is the most important element in urban design because without context, the city becomes fragmented. In the criticism of the modern movement, Lang rightly argued that the modernists failed to understand the richness of human needs and the environment.

Lang's major work, unlike the studies of Greenbie and Tancick, examines the social and environmental issues within the context of American urban history. Like Lynch, he was concerned with the creation of liveable, and especially enjoyable built urban environments. Lynch, Trancick, Greenbie and Lang have all been concerned with a user-oriented approach in achieving a higher quality of life in human settlements.

Thus Lang's work examined twentieth-century American urban design within a socio-political context. Though spanning the twentieth century, including Burnham's City Beautiful movement in Chicago, the emphasis of the study was on developments after the Second World War and towards the latter half of the twentieth century. Discussing neo-modernism, as well as rationalism and empiricism, he created an understanding of how the environment is experienced by people and the implications of experiencing architectural and urban design. Though there were many other issues in creating optimal urban environments, Lang concentrates on design methodology, a fashionable issue of the 1960s now considered somewhat outmoded.

Lang reiterates the fact that theories and practices from Europe influenced urban design, and the important role of the public sector in the US in its development. Attempting to integrate the social sciences with behavioural systems, he indicates that these aspects were necessary in the development of architectural theory. He criticises projects based upon intuitive processes but avoids pursuing new paradigms that redefined urban design and constructed theories on empirical bases such as neo-functionalism. Psychological, aesthetic and cognitive methods are also discussed, and it is suggested that urban design has become a part of architectural theory existing both in rationalism and empiricism (Le Corbusier versus Radburn). The basic belief seems to be the need for pragmatic empiricist solutions in adapting to changing cities. However, whether these definitions are accurate is questionable. Seaside, Florida (Duany E. Plater Zyberk) and Laguna West (Peter Calthorpe) are defined as postmodern urban design. Bernard Tschumi's plan for Corona Park in Flushing, New York, and Peter Eisenman's Visual Arts Center at Ohio State University are defined not as deconstructivist theory, but as neo-rationalist. Christopher Alexander and Charles Moore are seen as neo-empiricist.

Suggesting that each American city is unique, Los Angeles, Houston and Phoenix are cited as examples of major cities emerging as a result of 'independent decisions' with emphasis on the motor car. A curious comment is that Los Angeles was provided for by an extensive light rail system but still somehow became a city dependent on the motor car. Yet there is little evidence that any light rail system was ever provided extensively in this city, and in any case light rail in itself is a late-twentieth-century invention.[34]

An apposite, and justifiable, comment is that any new piece of architecture or landscape architecture is urban design in that it changes the city, and urban design has come to have this meaning. It is also true that the majority of the *Progressive Architecture* urban design awards were for individual buildings, and that it was never entirely clear whether there was any differentiation between the architectural awards and the urban design awards. Lang suggests otherwise. Urban design, he says, was a planned intervention in the marketplace of combinations of land, building uses and building configurations constituting the three-dimensional physical nature of human settlements.[35] This is a satisfactory definition.

Of particular importance in Lang's text is his remark that 'the urban designer is never really in complete control of the decision-making process that initiates a project and brings it to fruition'.[36] He also identifies the social implications of urban design and the lack of clarity with which urban designers address these issues. Le Corbusier in particular stated that though modernists in the past, their theories were intended to solve social issues of the twentieth century, and the social objectives of their generic designs were often deliberately vague. Colin Rowe and Fred Koetter, in *Collage City*, criticised such amateur social engineering as resulting in disastrous urbanism and total design.

Lang suggests that all designs have been both social and aesthetic statements. Four types of urban design work were proposed, and though these subdivisions were somewhat clumsy in their nomenclature, they were, nevertheless, a clear analysis of the activities of the urban designer. 'The urban designer as a total designer'[37] represented a situation in which a single designer, or at least the head of a design team, would make decisions concerning the proposed built environment, from the largest to the smallest scale. Quoting Vignelli Associates in 1990, who said: 'We believe that a designer should be able to design anything from a spoon to a city because the basic discipline of design is one, the only thing that changes are the specifics . . . We strongly believe in the social responsibility of the designer', Lang wrote that a more likely scenario was that while urban designers may play a major role, with other consultants they would have control only of the translation of the programme into physical form. Total control was seen in only a relatively small number of built examples, such as Radburn, New Jersey, and the greenbelt towns of the 1930s.

A second category was 'All-of-a-Piece Urban Design'. This was the use of overall illustrative design carried out by a single architectural practice, with the urban designer acting as the reviewer of each sub-proposal. Examples cited include Columbia, Maryland, developed by the Rouse Company in the 1960s, and the relatively recent Las Colinas near Dallas. But perhaps a more contradictory example is that of Parc de la Villette, designed by Bernard Tschumi in the 1980s. While acknowledging that Tschumi's design was based on a single architectural idea and was one of the best examples of deconstruction, Lang hardly justifies his categorisation of 'All-of-a-Piece Urban Design' with Tschumi as a design shepherd. Since this many layered example of deconstructionist philosophy in its three superimposed grids was clearly the inspiration of

Tschumi and Tschumi alone, one or two single pieces were allocated to other designers, including John Hedjuck and Peter Eisenman.

Lang's third category was 'The Urban Designer as the Designer of Infrastructure', which recognised that much of the built environment consists of public spaces. Roads, parks, plazas and public facilities create the character of any urban space.[38] Elements of the infrastructure create a catalytic effect in the juxtaposition of land use, building and open space configurations.

The final category, 'The Urban Designer as Designer of Guidelines for Design', is perhaps the most contentious. Design guidelines were seen as links between public policy statements and the physical design of an area. They set parameters within which a design is acceptable regardless of other questions. Prescriptive guidelines establish the limits or envelope framework within which buildings must be built.[39] Performance guidelines provide the criteria whereby the impact of a proposal will be assessed, an example of which is plot ratio (or American floor area ratio) – floor area of any structure related to the size of the site – and might also examine the amount of sunlight on a particular site between certain hours at the winter solstice (though the summer solstice is equally relevant).

However, a problem with urban design guidelines is that unless they have statutory authority, they are of little use. Of much greater effect are prescriptive urban design guidelines prepared for the developer client who has purchased the site, for example Battery Park City, New York, or Canary Wharf in London.

PESSIMISTIC VIEWS OF THE FUTURE CITY

Kevin Lynch's last major work, *Wasting Away*, was nearing completion before his untimely death in 1984.[40] Lynch, whose seminal studies spanned twenty years, was a man of great humanitarian values. His influence on architects and planners throughout the world was profound, and his first book, *The Image of the City*, published in 1961,[41] was also the first step towards an understanding of how citizens perceived their environments, good or bad, rather than how they were perceived by architects.

Such humanism was a powerful influence at MIT during that period, embodied in the seminars of such giants of architectural history as Lynch and Lewis Mumford, who contributed much to the department of city planning in contrast to the more dogmatic and somewhat arid philosophies of the school of architecture at the time.

Lynch followed *The Image of the City* with a number of equally important books including *What Time Is This Place,*[42] *Site Planning*[43] and *A Theory of Good City Form*.[44] All these works on the theory of urban design could be described as optimistic, and were certainly highly influential. However, *Wasting Away* does not share the same optimism, and perhaps it is no coincidence that it was Lynch's last work. It is, in some ways, a dark study showing a growing recognition by Lynch, at least, that decay and waste are a necessary part of contemporary life.

Editor Michael Southworth points out in his introduction that since Lynch's death in 1984, the world has been rocked by man-made disasters such as the Chernobyl nuclear accident in the former USSR, the Bhopal chemical explosion in India and the Exxon Valdez oil tanker spill in Alaska. The former two had disastrous effects on many thousands of people; the third was a total ecological disaster for the natural habitat.

Despite the lack of obvious connections with Lynch's earlier work, Southworth suggests that the book is a natural progression in Lynch's consideration of all aspects of urban life. Its structure is fascinating, based upon an unfinished manuscript without references, illustrations or final editing. Sections of the book, finally published in 1990, were much to the credit of Southworth, a former student of Lynch, and contributions from Lynch's family.

The way in which the book commences is curious, as Lynch predicts an urban scene of the near future that is not dissimilar from George Orwell's or Franz Kafka's pessimistic visions earlier in the twentieth century. Recognising the greenhouse effect of a polluted atmosphere some years before it became imperative to do so, the author portrays a vivid scenario illustrating the destruction of entire countries, such as Holland, as a result. Though Richard Sennett's *The Uses of Disorder*[45] does not appear in the bibliography, it too includes a description of the fortressed enclaves of the rich surrounded by increasing chaos further down the income scale. The following chapter, with many literary illusions to detritus, seems to emphasise this in our individual needs for cleanliness and order. A vast and complex hierarchy of chaos and disorder forms an essential part of our daily lives, and, indeed, clutter and chaos may be celebrated in a high art form such as Rodia's Watts Towers in Los Angeles.

Neither the way in which waste is disposed of in the thousands of gigantic, relatively inexpensive landfills, nor the use of the internal combustion engine motor car for selfish individual mobility has been answered with realistic alternatives. Partial answers include the recycling of manufactured materials or even 'remanufacturing' itself. Yet the problems of the disposal of toxic, hazardous waste have been only partly addressed in the developed world and not really addressed at all in the developing world. The same can be said of the permanent dereliction caused by strip (opencast) mining, such as that from the vast coal fields in the southwest US.

The ways forward, according to Lynch, might be the planning of new settlements to include patterns of decline, with planned obsolescence and the reuse of building structures a realistic possibility. The ultimate abandonment of the motor car would demand new uses for redundant freeways, the vast linear strips of which have been the cause of so much adjacent urban blight. Strip mines in the UK, unlike those elsewhere, including the US, pay recovery costs. Durability of goods, rather than expendability, should be a central objective.

Wasting Away was a remarkable, controversial and thought-provoking work, and a fitting tribute and monument to Lynch's life endeavours and passionately held beliefs. In his task of completing the unfinished manuscript, the editor, Michael Southworth, clearly turned it into a labour of love, and in doing so extended the spectrum of the study. For example, it is doubtful that Lynch would have included facsimiles of the hand-written manuscript notes; Southworth describes these in his notes on editorial methodology, providing the reader with further insights into the thoughts of the author.

Chapter 4 contains 25 pages of photographs and provides some encouraging sunlight and optimism among the contrasting images of a grim world and a potentially bleak future.[46]

A massive work by Tridib Banerjee and Michael Southworth, *City Sense and City Design: Writings and Projects of Kevin Lynch,* was also published in 1990.[47] This was the final collection of Lynch's remaining unpublished work. It included professional design and planning projects, though due to their lack of specificity these may be viewed as the weaker side of Lynch's career, his theoretical writings being the more powerful. The editors, both of whom studied under Kevin Lynch, had prepared a massive and devoted work dedicated to Lynch's contribution in transforming the urban design profession from the 1950s onwards.

In their foreword, the editors acknowledged the role of Mrs Anne Lynch in the creation of the book. Anne Lynch had rightly influenced them in their focus on the early life of Kevin Lynch within a biographical context. The book focuses first on the original premises of Lynch's work, that is to say his unique reading of large-scale built environments and the theory that the design of an urban landscape should be as relevant as design theories for the natural landscape. Second, drawing from Lynch's travel journals, it looks at the perception of how people (and most importantly children) view their cities, related to environmental-perception research. This is followed by both small- and large-scale analyses of the visual form of the city, and more theoretical writings on city design.

The final essays are curious in many ways. Lynch describes the fantasies of utopian settlements and dire warnings of caco-topias. As long ago as 1961 he had acknowledged the edge city condition in what he referred to in the *Pattern of the Metropolis*[48] as the dispersed sheet. He also identified Frank Lloyd Wright's Broadacre City, which he erroneously believed solved traffic congestion through total dispersion and the balancing of loads, raising flexibility, local participation, personal comfort and independence to a maximum. In reference to the Galaxy of Settlements, he suggests that instead of guiding growth into an even distribution, development should be bunched into relatively small units, each with an internal peak of density and each separated from the next by a zone of low or zero structural density.[49] The core city, the urban star and the ring were seen as further options. Yet these made no sense in a contemporary, democratic twentieth-century society. However, Lynch did recognise what was about to evolve in American urban structure with a population of perhaps 20 million as the polycentric net (or polycentric city), with dense clusters served by transportation networks or grids organised in three dimensions, like a skeletal framework in space. Thus, the Interstate Freeway System, with its multilevel interchanges, adapted to local configurations in topography.

In a 1965 article in *Scientific American* on 'The City as Environment',[50] Lynch produced diagrams of spatial sequences

in central Boston with graphic notations that were confusing. Lynch never acknowledged Cullen's theories of 'serial vision', which were published in England much earlier in 1947 and were, graphically at least, far more evocative than Lynch's own two-dimensional diagrams. In a letter to Frank Lloyd Wright in 1935 he had said: 'One of my major deficiencies is the lack of ability in drawing and I imagine that it is only a technique I can master with hard work'.[51]

Banerjee and Southworth's book also included Lynch's previously unpublished 'A Walk Around the Block', co-authored with Malcolm Rivkin, which was part of a research project at MIT.[52] The three-dimensional sketches of Boylston, Arlington and Newberry Streets can hardly be described as evocative, though the written commentary is particularly vivid. Similarly, such comments might apply to his urban landscape plan of San Salvador in 1968.

However, his Rio Saludo Development Plan showed changes in temperament. Stephen Carr was the project director, though other distinguished professionals such as Gary Hack were also involved in the Carr/Lynch Associates collaboration. Reprinted from an article, 'Collaboration and Context in Urban Design',[53] the taped record showed an irritation on the part of Lynch with the flood-control expert referred to as 'CB'. The last of Lynch's major professional works, this was an extremely difficult project, dealing with the flood plains of the Salt River in Arizona, which runs through the Phoenix metropolitan area. Mostly dry throughout the year, the plains formed a barren wasteland, but with occasional spasmodic periods of flooding. The flood-control expert had disagreed with Lynch's suggestion of lakes in the channel. Lynch had envisioned bringing the natural landscape into the city in the form of an oasis, to which Stephen Carr added that the problem with an oasis was that people would not think of it as different. Kevin Lynch replied 'Uh hum'. The flood-control expert said that the primary flow channel had landscape and trees and comparisons were drawn with Turtle Creek in Dallas. Lynch's reply was 'Yeah, um hum'.[54] In the opinion of Banerjee and Southworth, Lynch's rich imagination provided a critical role as senior designer, but just as important was his role of conflict resolution in group discussions. The concluding chapter of the book was Lynch's paper 'The Possible City', published in 1968.

Banerjee and Southworth thought that Lynch's cacotopias were educational in purpose, yet with an admission that they were imaginary descriptions of the horrifying worlds to come, as suggested in *A Theory of Good City Form*. Utopias, they thought, were a recital of wishes and hopes for the future.

Lynch rightly questioned the absurd suggestion of the Reagan administration of a 'limited' nuclear war and 'survivable' atomic exchanges. The essays 'What Will Happen to Us' and 'Coming Home' were intended to mobilise public opinion against such a foolish nuclear defence policy. The then presidential candidate George Bush Jr. was still perpetuating these ideas at the turn of the twenty-first century with the resurrection of Reagan's 'Star Wars' policy in 2000. Of the two essays, 'What Will Happen to Us', with co-authors Tunney Lee and Peter Droege, is a manual to help communities cope with the disaster of limited nuclear engagement. Yet recent events in Iraq and elsewhere suggest a more potent and deadlier threat in germ warfare, the weapons of which can be produced at a fraction of the cost of nuclear weapons.

In 'The Possible City', Lynch indicates that in any event, social changes cause environmental problems such as congestion, discomfort, obsolescence, pollution and abandonment. Such changes are disturbing as landmarks are swept away. This observation is certainly true in the context of the image of the city. The metropolis is seen as the normal environment of the future, with the prediction that 80 per cent of the population in the US would be living in such regions (megalopolises divided into four giant megalopolitan regions – the Atlantic seaboard and the lower Great Lakes, which may join, Florida and California) by the year 2000. While this prediction is partially true, Lynch did not foresee the growth of other metropolitan areas such as Atlanta, Georgia and Dallas, Fort Worth and Austin in Texas. The movement of high-tech industries to such cities in the south denied the permanence of Silicon Valley, California, and the establishment of Seattle, Washington, with the emergence of Microsoft and the Boeing Company.

Lynch's suggestion was that public power could be used to reduce the segregation of the population by race and class. This has not been the case. African-Americans are still segregated by income and race, and the Hispanics, through much illegal immigration into the Southwestern part of the US, have overtaken, numerically, the African-American population. The disparity between the very wealthy and the urban poor in the last decade of the twentieth century has been greater than it has ever been since the late nineteenth and early twentieth centuries.

In a vision of the future, Lynch predicted that new technology would soon allow the occupation of marginal areas on which increasing wealth and population would place mounting pressure. The national exploitation of these areas, he thought, would apply to areas previously considered waste lands. Experiments for desert settlements, on water or under water, in swamps and on high mountains, in arctic regions and underground, seemed to contradict his earlier visions of the celebration of the contemporary city. Why would the future populations be content to conquer the wilds and eliminate them? In such an essay on futurism, he seemed to conduct an Orwellian, Wellsian or Huxleyian[55] vision of a new world, in which, he acknowledged: 'Experimental communities might become laboratories of our society, a new sort of university, where people are not experimented upon, but join in conducting experiments in which they learn about themselves and their own possibilities'.[56]

In 'Grounds for Utopia', published in 1975, Lynch justifiably criticises the architectural visions of Soleri, Le Corbusier and Fuller as indulging in the fantasies of architectural form,[57] as opposed to Goodman's 'Communities'. Instead, social utopias were based upon the creation of new social structures, which hardly address the issues of the physical environment. Instead Lynch argues that an urban countryside would be a continuous, highly varied and humanised landscape, neither urban nor rural in the conventional meaning, envisaged within an Arcadian setting of houses, workplaces and so forth, and set among trees, farms and streams, with a moderate to low population density.

Perhaps this was to predict the rise of the new urbanism, which was to occur some twenty years after his essay.

Nevertheless, Lynch's social engineering seemed unrealistic within the context of American democratic society, for example no rent required for few permanent assignments of land with no rents at all for residential spaces allotted to individuals and small groups.[58] The growth of recycled materials was equally visionary, including the conversion of wastes, but the low density of such an Arcadian environment seems contradictory in that it necessarily generates a much more extensive network of surface travel, by whatever mode.

Much more gloomy was one of Lynch's final essays, published in 1983, a year before his death. 'What Will Happen to Us'[59] was directed towards the survival of the US in the event of nuclear war with (presumably) the former USSR. But this alarming view seemed unrealistic.[60] The alarmist vision of this final essay seemed to deny all of Lynch's previous optimism. He describes, vividly, the effects of a nuclear detonation, including blast, thermal radiation and fire, direct nuclear radiation from ionising radiation, causing fatal cancers as well as radioactive fall-out. It would take between two and three years to disappear on the ellipse of the explosion and ten years within the city. The evacuation of urban areas would be an incredible problem in terms of street and highway movement.

The ultimate essay, published in 1984,[61] studies the aftereffects of a nuclear holocaust and examines ways in which the few survivors might rebuild America. The appalling description of the survivors of Hiroshima rebuilding their city, which, by 1984, was only 50 per cent resettled, is an agonising read.

The conclusions in City Sense and City Design are sombre indeed, and beg the question, 'What went wrong?'. As one of the greatest urban theorists of the twentieth century, the optimism and vision of Lynch, which began with The Image of the City in 1961, was dissipated in utter pessimism at the end of his life in 1984, when the Cold War was virtually over. It would take volumes to explain this, but Lynch, nevertheless, left a great legacy that established the discipline of urban design.

Lynch invariably made a major distinction between city design and urban design. City design, he said, was no longer confined to the public regulation of private actions or to the design of public works or land-use plans. It created prototypes used in making framework plans (though without statutory authority such framework plans are useless as they are seldom implemented). Urban renewal, coastal management, energy conservation, downtown revitalisation, transport schemes and housing rehabilitation all fall within its orbit.[62] He acknowledged that city design was not very different from the term urban design, which, he believed, was concerned with the large-scale field of project design. Thus, the field is ambiguous, in that it lies between the fields of city planning, architecture and landscape design.

According to Lynch, urban design courses in the US were taught as a one- or two-year graduate course, and with this he disagreed, suggesting that city design should not be restricted to architecture. But perhaps many graduate students outside the field of architecture do not have the requisite skills in manual drawing and computer graphics to translate ideas into three-dimensional frameworks, which is surely what urban design is all about.

An equally pessimistic view of the future was published in 1992, with Michael Sorkin as editor.[63] *Variations on a Theme Park* is a remarkable collection of essays, and of these Sorkin's introduction and concluding essays are perhaps the most telling. In envisaging the universal use of mobile phones, which were developing rapidly in the middle of the 1990s, Sorkin opined, quoting Walter Wriston, former CEO of Citicorp, that such devices had made time and space obsolete.

The use of computers, credit cards, mobile phones and faxes, which produce instant artificial adjacency, create, as Sorkin suggests, the ageographical city. Recognising, like Garreau, the edge city condition, Sorkin laments the clusters of skyscrapers adjacent to the interstates as well as huge shopping malls and atrium hotels, identical from coast to coast (or continent to continent for that matter). The phone and the modem render the city street irrelevant with the use of fibre-optic cables. The new city, Sorkin says, is marketed by three salient characteristics: the dissipation of stable relationships in local physical and cultural geography, globalised electronic means of production and the uniform mass culture.

Sorkin presents a more sinister view of the obsession with 'security' using massive surveillance techniques and new methods of segregation. In his final statement concerning this bleak view of the future city, he suggests that worst of all, the new public realm is a city of simulations – the city as a theme park. It may be the unreal simulation of Main Street in Disneyland or the false historic celebration in a Rouse market-place, or the gentrification of the Lower East Side in Manhattan, though this is near where Sorkin has an office (Tribeca). The theme park, he says, is the ageographia, surveillance and control. A regulated vision of pleasure, which, taken to its ulti-mate form of absurdity, is seen in Las Vegas at the beginning of the twenty-first century. Now one of the US' most popular tourist destinations, Las Vegas presents the most preposterous of urban visions – people like it.

In his acerbic concluding essay, 'See You in Disneyland', Sorkin describes Disney World in Florida as the ultimate of theme parks in the form of Elysium. He quotes serial killer Richard Ramirez, 'The Night Stalker', as he snarled at the court-room, 'See You in Disneyland'. It is suggested here that Disney World is an American substitute for Elysium, with Orlando welcoming over 30 million visitors a year and containing more hotels than Chicago, Los Angeles or New York.

Seeking an artificial utopia, wrote Sorkin, is a confusion of goals and ideals, and he describes the culmination of Walt Disney's fantasies of transport and transportation in 1955 with the opening of Disneyland at Anaheim in California. An interesting counterpoint is his description of the 1851 Great Exhibition in London as the first utopia of global capital, sponsored by Queen Victoria's consort, Prince Albert.[64] Prince Albert's speech evoked a world shrunk by technology – an eerie prophecy of current opinions 150 years later. Thus, the 1892 fair in Chicago presaged the City Beautiful movement of Daniel Burnham and others.

The essay draws comparison with the garden city move-ment of Ebenezer Howard at the beginning of the twentieth century. It argues that the organisation and scale of Disneyland in California and, later, Disney World in Florida, Disneyland in Tokyo, and Eurodisney in Paris, are those of the garden city, located on metropolitan perimeters, which Sorkin likens to office complexes on the edges of the Interstate Highway System, not dissimilar to Garreau's theories. However, Disneyland was not alone in its fantasia. Busch Gardens, a theme park in Williamsburg, Virginia, is an equal indulgence in nostalgia.

Public transport to the theme parks is also an anachronism. Access to the original Disneyland is via an exit from the freeway. Access to Eurodisney outside Paris is via the TGV (Trem de Grande Vitesse) system, one of the fastest railways in the world. In a perceptive observation, Sorkin points out that the main reason why visitors circulate on foot at Disneyland is so that they can go on the rides – and that most of the rides, such as Space Mountain, are indoors.

Disney locations in the US are accessible by air with Delta Airlines acting as 'official' carrier. The hub is based in Hartsdale, Atlanta, and has an automated 'people-mover' transit system linking its terminal concourses with small, autonomous, silent transit cars on elevated tracks. Yet, on arriving in Orlando, one still needs to rent a car or use a taxi to get to the hotel or the theme park itself.

Sorkin opines that Disneyzone is not urban at all, in invoking an urbanism without producing a city. Margaret Crawford, in the same volume, gives an equally bleak view of the world of the shopping mall.[65] West Edmonton Mall, at the time the essay was published, was the largest shopping mall in the world (according to the *Guinness Book of Records*). It was later surpassed in size by Mall of America, built in the middle of the decade in the suburbs of Minneapolis. It consisted of office towers, three hotels, a convention centre and a Knott's Berry theme park. This last element is important since the introduction of amusement rides, including roller coasters, added a new dimension to retail attractions. Crawford lists a horrific spectacle of the elements of West Edmonton Mall (Alberta, Canada) as the World's Largest Indoor Amusement Park, Water Park and (unbelievably) the World's Largest Parking Lot. All of this replete with 800 shops, 110 restaurants, 20 cinemas, imitation nineteenth-century Parisian boulevards and so forth. Architecturally, seen from the outside, it is a series of huge boxes in an asphalt landscape. Within there is a replica of Christopher Columbus' *Santa Maria* floating in an artificial lagoon with a seascape of plastic seaweed and electronically controlled rubber sharks.

Whether such dinosaurs will survive the twentieth century is open to question, as is the future of the 28,500 shopping malls across North America with the exponential rise of shop-ping on the Internet. Crawford suggests that the formula of finance and marketing was established between 1960 and 1980 when the basic regional mall paradigm was perfected. But this belies, as she acknowledges, the uneven and complex over-lapping pattern of circles. Neglecting the strict formula of catch-ment area, population size, travel distance, and spending power in particular, many adjacent malls are eventually doomed to failure.

Similarly, Langdon Winner questions the mirage of Silicon Valley in California.[66] Microelectronics is the dominant industry south of San Francisco in Santa Clara County. Over a million residents live here, of which more than a quarter are employed in semiconductor, computer, software and communications industries. The remainder appear to be in supplemental service industries ranging from house repair to financial and legal consultation. However, there is no centre, only the blurring of settlements from San Jose to Santa Clara to Palo Alto. San Francisco, 50 kilometres (30 miles) north, has no relevance as a hub. The futurist view of employees at IBM wearing sanitised white clothing and masks to ensure no contamination of circuitry is set in bizarre fashion among immaculate rows of non-producing fruit trees and no grass.

Winner also mentions Stanford University as being 'modeled upon a business firm', and Hewlett-Packard as being modelled after a university with campus-like architecture. The workforces are mostly white, male graduates of MIT, Cal Tech and Berkeley, enjoying working prodigiously long hours. However, inequalities do exist. According to Winner, East Palo Alto is a black ghetto with insoluble problems of deep poverty, which can be seen from neighbouring Stanford University. There is an astonishing gap in income between the rich and the poor in this region, yet, on average, it has the highest house prices in the US.

Published in 1992, Sorkin's edited work foresaw the exclusion of all individuals who were computer illiterate, creating a separate and privileged world. As Winner remarks: 'To enter the digital city one must be first granted access. Having "logged-on" one's quality of participation is determined by the architecture of the network ... (with) technical professionals ... greeted by a computerized version of the social matrix'.[67]

Overall, this bleak view of an increasingly divisive society where 'ordinary' workers become the objects of top-down managerial control augurs ill for the future health of democracy.

Other contributors to Sorkin's volume included Neil Smith, who commented on the Lower East Side in New York, Edward Soja who discussed Orange County's right-wing political traditions, and William Pereira with his 30-year-old vision of Irvine Ranch new town as a university campus – all presenting a grave view of the exclusion of urban design in the American cities of the twenty-first century.

THE TRANSITION FROM OPTIMISTIC TO PESSIMISTIC VIEWS OF THE FUTURE

An authoritative view of emerging theories in urban design was *Postmodern Urbanism* by Nan Ellin.[68] The title is, perhaps, a misnomer, as postmodernist theory emerged in the 1970s first as linguistic theory and later as architectural theory, from such writers as Charles Jencks.

Ellin's work covers a vast spectrum of twentieth-century theory prior to that decade, for example, the townscape movement in England, with Gordon Cullen as the clear leader, which has been referred to by Geoffrey Broadbent and others as neo-empiricism. Thus, Chapter 3, 'Urban Design Theory: the Anglo-American Axis' preceded postmodernism by some thirty

years.[69] It is also curious that a subsection of this chapter includes edge cities, since this phenomenon, as described earlier, had little to do with postmodern theories. Certainly all the constituents described by Ellin were quite unrelated to, and were even antagonistic towards the earlier modernist movement in the construction of cities.

Cullen's view of the city was simultaneously embraced on the other side of the Atlantic by Paul Goodman, Kevin Lynch and Jane Jacobs. Whereas this might have been true of Jane Jacobs (a sociologist, and not an architect), who certainly embraced a humanistic approach to the central city, it was not true of Kevin Lynch who refuted any influence of Cullen and has dismissed him as irrelevant in conversations with the author.

Ellin examines an amazing range of theorists, ranging from Lewis Mumford and Richard Sennett to Serge Chermayeff and Christopher Alexander to Buckminster Fuller and the British group Archigram. Advocacy planning and community participation are also mentioned, including the work of the American Institute of Architects Regional/Urban Design Assistance Teams (RUDAT), which evolved into the sustainability programmes developed by Peter Calthorpe and others in the 1980s.

Ellin describes Robert Venturi as the father of postmodern architecture and urban design in both the US and Europe. While this is certainly true as far as the US is concerned, the claim is more dubious for Europe. The issue of master-planned and gated communities in terms of the translation of postmodern theories into built form is certainly apposite. Ellin correctly points out that planned unit developments (PUDs), though housing 10 per cent of the American population by the mid-1990s, have been virtually ignored by design journals (presumably architecture). Most telling is the fact that each PUD contains 'households on the same rung of the socio-economic ladder ... and [these] are homes to the middle class and up'.[70] This is a manifestation of an increasingly divisive American society at the turn of the twenty-first century. Also mentioned in this context are second-home markets with a resort environment, such as 'equestrian communities' (Palm Beach Polo) or golf communities (Polo Club Boca Raton), though perhaps Seaside, Florida, is the most significant example.

Gated communities present more sinister examples, with volunteer neighbourhood block watches to professional security companies. In postmodern urbanism, mention is made of crime prevention through environmental design, and a chilling photograph illustrates such a gated community.[71] Ellin attributes the proliferation of these types of gated communities to riots such as that in Los Angeles in 1992 (the Rodney King riot). Oscar Newman, the author of *Defensible Space* in 1971, is apparently consultant to 50 neighbourhoods across the US with financial support from the US Justice Department. Shopping centres, particularly those in South Central Los Angeles, surrounded by iron fences and policed by a private security force, were not affected by the 1992 riots. Public toilets are often not provided because they are regarded as magnets for transients. This form of defensive architecture, which is a repetition of older typologies such as courtyard architecture, particularly in the Iberian Peninsula of Europe or parts of Central and South America, represents a new late-twentieth-century form for urban fabric.

Though Ellin makes passing reference to the subsequent ideology of deconstruction,[72] following the linguistic theories of structuralism and semiology developed from the writings of Jacques Derrida, who in turn was inspired by Heidegger, the next stage of lateral thinking in this decade is scarcely acknowledged.

Towards the end of the work, the scholarly twentieth-century historical accounts are replaced by more polemical writing. For example, the 'Significance of Urban Design' is appropriately questioned. It is doubtful, however, that 'Recent urban design . . . advances the modern project because it refuses to relinquish the vast possibilities offered by new technologies and because it is embedded in larger market forces'. The claim that post-modernism may be regarded as 'another swing on the pendulum' may be so, and the counteraction of minimalist architecture in the US, Japan and the UK may bear witness to this.

DECONSTRUCTION THEORIES AT THE END OF THE TWENTIETH CENTURY

Two giants of deconstructivist theory of the 1990s are Peter Eisenman and Frank Gehry. Charles Jencks suggests that Eisenman's Aronoff Center at the University of Cincinnati, and Gehry's Bilbao Museum in Spain, both completed in the late 1990s, were, together with Daniel Libeskinds' Jewish Museum, the major buildings of the period.[73] With their work referred to as cosmogenic design, non-linear architecture, or the architecture of emergence, Eisenman and Gehry are seen as organic-tech architects. Nevertheless, Eisenman's Aronoff Center can hardly be described as non-linear.

The Aronoff Center is part of a visionary though highly controversial development of the University of Cincinnati campus, engaging the services of some of the most renowned American architects. It may be argued that an essentially 1960s campus (although the early nineteenth-century buildings are elegant) could not be welded together to form a coherent whole. The European idea of the American university campus is that of manicured lawns, mature trees and a feeling of Arcadia epitomised in the campuses of Harvard, Yale and Princeton. Perhaps one great architect should have been invited to design the whole of the university campus, like Maki at Keio University in Japan, Isozaki at Bond University in Australia, or even Thomas Jefferson at the University of Virginia, though these projects were built on virgin sites.

Instead, in 1991, George Hargreaves, the San Francisco landscape architect, was invited to prepare a campus master plan – something of a misnomer as this was really a comprehensive landscape design. By the turn of the twenty-first century, Hargreaves' intricate designs of braids, lay-lines and references to American Indian burial mounds form the framework of a powerfully vivid natural setting. Michael Graves' design for the College of Engineering Research Center is a surprisingly contextual success and one of powerful architectural imagery. The campus power plant was designed by the Cambridge Seven; the Sigma Sigma tower by Machado and Silvetti; the Swing

Building (constructed for overflow accommodation while other structures were being built) by David Childs of Skidmore, Owings and Merrill; the outdoor terrace plaza by Wes Jones; and the extensions to the nationally renowned College Conservatory of Music by Pei, Cobb and Freed. Most notable was the Vontz Center for Molecular Studies by Frank Gehry, completed in 1999. All these mostly iconoclastic structures bring together spectacular aspects of late-twentieth-century architecture and urban design.

The University of Cincinnati is a large Midwestern university with some 35,000 students. Founded in 1815, it is an urban university of an 85-hectare (212-acre) campus, 5 kilometres (3 miles) from the city centre. Its explosive growth during the 1960s led to the building of some of the unsightly architecture of that decade – concrete structures rooted firmly in the modernist movement. Peter Eisenman's design for the addition to the College of Design, Architecture, Art and Planning (DAAP), later referred to as the Aronoff Center, linked three existing buildings of around 16,000 square metres (19,130 square yards). Eisenman's brief was to double this. The new building opened in October 1996. DAAP could and should have been the Bauhaus of the late twentieth century with its departments of architecture, interior design, urban planning, fine art, industrial design, graphic design, fashion design and art history. But like universities throughout the world, internecine rivalries between academic factions have always precluded this. The objective of the new building was to bring these factions and the students together, and in the first months of its use it appeared, in a modest way, to have succeeded.

Attention was first drawn to Eisenman's design when he won the *Progressive Architecture* Award in January 1991.[74] Eisenman described his design thus:

[Located] on the north side of the existing college, three structures end to end in chevron pattern stand at the top of a knoll sloping east. Library, administration offices, auditorium, photo lab, café, additional studios, laboratories, together with multi-purpose spaces for juries and exhibits.

The solution:

The building was conceived as a symbol of the new cosmology of man and information. Just as information comes to us in the media in a fragmented, ambiguous manner, so does this building arise out of a series of formal transformations that fracture and blur traditional architectural dichotomies such as old and new, inside and outside, structure and infill. The form of this architecture school addition takes its cue from the chevron shape of the existing building. [We] torqued, tilted and shifted this shape out of phase, resulting in an architecture that carries within its plans and elevations the trace of these formal moves like the after-image on a television screen or the interpretation of radio frequencies. The chevron shape finally becomes so fuzzy that it takes on the undulating quality of the site. Captured between the space between the new building and the old is a complex skylighted atrium. Walkways and bridges overlook this public space.

It is interesting to note the jury's response. Adele Santos commented: 'Its response to the sloping site is really quite nice. It also has some very fine sections. I think the way the light will come filtering down into the walkways will be very beautiful. What astounds me is that the school of architecture would pick an architect whose work is going to be so clearly defined at a point in time, knowing that would be the image of the school forevermore. This is precisely one of the building types that requires a certain type of neutrality, flexibility and open-endedness. This is an enormously particular and highly personal statement'. Ralph Johnson agreed, saying, 'This is true. Architecture schools tend towards more neutral types of spaces'. (However, this comment is hardly correct in the context of Louis Kahn's Art Gallery and School of Fine Art, or Paul Rudolph's School of Architecture, both built at Yale University in the middle of the twentieth century.) Rem Koolhaas continued: 'Yes, but this building is quite clever in terms of organizing the utilitarian parts in a utilitarian way. Only with the public spaces does it become expressive', a comment concurred by Dana Cuff: 'The existing buildings are pretty awful'. Ralph Johnson asserted, 'It has an extremely skillful definition of public spaces and a beautiful treatment of the public corridor'.

What is most remarkable about the design drawings shown in *Progressive Architecture* is that the final built form, externally and especially internally, is astonishingly faithful. Rarely has any radical architect achieved this, and on a comparative basis one can think only of the extreme tenacity of Frank Lloyd Wright.

As Peter Eisenman began the design of the DAAP building, a commentary on his work in general appeared in an *Architectural Design* special edition on 'Deconstruction Theory'.[75] Andrew Benjamin argues that in examining the architectural metaphor in Descartes,[76] a series of oppositions has emerged, creating a structural role within this philosophical position. Benjamin further suggests that it is in relation to these oppositions that the force of deconstruction can be located. Jacques Derrida proposes that in deconstruction, analysis and comparative conceptual pairs, which are currently accepted as self-evident and natural, appear as if they have not been institutionalised at some point, as if they had no history. Derrida considers the work of Tschumi in his plan of the Parc de la Vilette in Paris,[77] especially the series of constructs known as Les Folies (an architectural expression commonly misused in the nineteenth century). Derrida makes the point that they are not 'madness' (la folie) and that, despite appearance, deconstruction is not in itself an architectural metaphor. Benjamin goes on to say that 'the challenge presented by deconstruction is the same philosophy, literary criticism, linguistic theory and so forth. It is a challenge that initially takes place on the level of thinking – here in the example of architecture'. Thinking becomes enacted in the architectural work of both Eisenman and Tschumi.

Charles Jencks refers to Eisenman as the 'positive nihilist',[78] implying that the latter became a disciple of deconstruction at the same time that he was undergoing personal trauma and psychoanalysis. In the 1970s, Eisenman was a member of a group known as the New York Five (Eisenman, Meier, Graves, Gwathmey and Hejduk) and founder of the Institute for Architecture and Urban Studies in New York City, which reached its zenith between 1976 and 1978, before closing in 1984. These facts are pertinent in a special way.

The jewel-like villas built by the New York Five owed much to neo-Corbusian philosophy and, to a lesser extent, Terragni. Eisenman's earlier house designs such as House 1 (Princeton, New Jersey, 1967), House II (Hardwick, Vermont, 1970), House III (Lakeville, Connecticut, 1971) and House IV (Cornwall, Connecticut, 1975) were not really precursors of his later exuberance, displayed in the much larger deconstructionist buildings in Ohio (The Wexner Center for the Visual Arts 1983–89), the Greater Columbus Convention Center (1989–93) and the University of Cincinnati DAAP building (1988–96). The villas explored rectilinear spatial sequences and interpenetrating volumes and planes with consummate skill. Although House III showed a distinct shift in complexity and contradiction, deliberately lacking the apparent serenity of the other houses, in 1971 it perhaps foreshadowed Eisenman's major change in direction. Later, theoretical house studies such as the *Fin d'Ou T Hou S* in 1984 for the Venice Cannaregio, or House X, demonstrated, albeit through orthogonal grids, a different form of complexity.[79]

Philip Johnson selected two American architects for the Fifth International Exhibition of Architecture at the Venice Biennial in 1991, organised by Francesco Dalco.[80] The two (representing the US) were architects who were challenging their discipline in an aggressive way and challenging dogma above all else. Johnson said that there were, however, great differences in their personalities: Eisenman, as the East Coast intellectual, and Gehry, as an intuitive anti-intellectual West Coast savant. Eisenman's key display at the Biennial were the design drawings for the DAAP building.

And yet, for all the praise showered on Eisenman as the leader of deconstruction theory and its architectural application, far less is known about his formidable talents as an urban designer. According to Jencks in *The Architecture of the Jumping Universe*, no individual has looked at the lessons of emerging sciences more strenuously than Eisenman.[81]

Alongside Peter Eisenman's shift to the non-linear sciences was the beginning of the new urbanism in 1987, for example his Rebstock Housing Project in Frankfurt, which made extensive use of the 'fold'. In Cincinnati, Eisenman had introduced the waveform as a transformation of the zigzag rectangles of the three existing buildings. This was referred to by Jencks as a shift of the non-linear sciences and a new urbanism, yet this terminology is confusing because the new urbanism, eloquently explained in a book by Peter Katz,[82] is generated in part by the forces of conservatism and reaction. Seaside by Andres Duany and Elizabeth Plater-Zyberk, for all its romanticism and elegance, has little to do with urban exploration or 'real' communities for that matter. For the Frankfurt project,

Eisenman, on the other hand, explored ways of developing new communities of social housing on a major scale, in collaboration with Albert Speer and Partners (Germany) and landscape architects Hanna/Olin of Philadelphia. The site was a vast tract of land to the north of major railway marshalling yards. The plan, starting with orthogonal grids, transformed subsequently into warped folds and twisted grids or torques, the initial studies showing a mixture of low- and medium-rise housing.

These observations of the Frankfurt project are relevant since the DAAP building is essentially more about urban design, both within (with great success) and without (with lesser success) than a single building or even a group of buildings. Benjamin Forey, writing in the *Washington Post*, remarked that although Eisenman was not great in the way of Frank Lloyd Wright and Le Corbusier, who changed the fundamentals of architectural design, his design emphasises the importance of route, which neither great twentieth-century master had confronted. Forley believed that the design was intended to be a polemical statement – sometimes to invigorate, sometimes to annoy. An open-closed-open spatial sequence clothed in unconventional forms intended to heighten surprise and pleasure, snakes up the hill; the more conventional spaces, such as the classrooms, studios, library and offices, tended to be left-over spaces – little nooks and crannies. He argued that 'Eisenman identified himself as a radical avant-gardist, critical of mainstream architecture'. Yet Eisenman's Convention Center in Columbus, Ohio's state capital, is a totally mainstream building, though the Wexner Center at Ohio State University in Columbus is not. Forey commented on Eisenman's sources, archaeological excavations, as a fascination shared with the landscape architect George Hargreaves (the triangulated Indian Burial Mounds are an integral part of the DAAP design), mathematical models, the Boolean cube used in computer modelling, chemical compounds such as DNA, geometrical conundrums and philosophers as diverse as Noam Chomsky and Jacques Derrida.

Each of the three Ohio buildings mentioned above is quite different. DAAP was Eisenman's first truly curvilinear building of Dryvit-rendered panels, glass and steel, with dramatic grids, diagonal lines and towers together with lay-lines or lines of force of the Dryvits (referred to as 'braids' in the landscape design for the University).

In a parallel appraisal by Kurt Foster in *Casabella*[83] 'the total design is like a gently orchestrated earthquake'. The building, Eisenman claims, is like the plates of an armadillo or the segments of an airport baggage terminal.

Paul Goldberger, writing in the *New York Times,* opined that Eisenman treats this design as the most important event in American architecture since Frank Lloyd Wright was able to convince the Solomon Guggenheim Foundation that pictures look good in round places. Philip Johnson announced that it had 'no equal in American architecture'. Goldberger described it thus: 'Few walls are perpendicular; three bland institutional buildings are joined together, frozen after the first shocks of an earthquake (one of the authors with an office in the new structure feels, on occasions, a sense of vertigo and seasickness in some spaces)'.[84] Is this, Goldberger asked, the final gasp of modernism and the beginning of something else? Was it

intended simply to grab attention? Was the breaking of barriers between inside and outside the blurring of form and function? These questions can be answered only by studying Eisenman's design process.

In an elegant limited-edition book edited by Cynthia Davidson, *Eleven Authors in Search of a Building,*[85] an essay by Donna Barry (a key project architect) explains this succinctly by offering an insight into the process. Eisenman is not the director of a huge practice that delegates design. Like Frank Lloyd Wright, he is the designer. Nevertheless, Wright influenced the impressive architecture of Fay Jones, a former Taliesin apprentice. Barry summarises the Eisenman design process as follows:

> The strategy was to react to the fundamental rules of construction while creating a space that appears to contradict or ignore them. For example, in science, the process of symmetry breaking explains observed complexity within a non-linear system. Space can be curved, mass is not constant and the relative position of the body affects the measurement of the space between the object and the body. The building represents a process of symmetry breaking in the design process of the building, providing a new awareness of the human experience in space by disrupting the conventional relationships between form, function and meaning. The idea of self-similarity is an example of a process analogous to symmetry breaking. Self-similarity is a process of repetition that produces an asymmetry. Self-similarity sets up a duality between the original form and the copy or trace of that form. The original and the trace are then superimposed to create a third form that incorporates them both. The resulting design is based on a dynamic mathematical non-linear design process. The series of displacements attempt to redefine the human experience of space.

She concludes her analysis with: 'The space of this project has a labyrinthine quality. It is experimented as a logical but not easily read path, a discovered path'.

Cynthia Davidson refers to Colin Rowe's 'Promenade Architecturale',[86] suggesting that the building climbs a hill, a route, giving continuously unfolding views, talks of chevrons, x-y-z coordinates, symptotic tilts and torquing, and no facade. The entry at the 300 level reveals no promenade architecturale and there is reentry at the 400 level. However, this is what the design is all about and analogies with the theories of Gordon Cullen's serial vision and Frank Lloyd Wright's organic architecture and the Usonian House seem pertinent, though it is unlikely that all three – Wright, Cullen and Eisenman – would agree!

Cullen believes that the perception of the town as a piece of moving scenery hardly enters the head of the person in the street, yet, this is what the town is – a moving set. This he demonstrated in a remarkably evocative way, illustrating an uninterrupted sequence of views that would unfold themselves like stills from a movie.[87]

Many theories of the modern movement,[88] including two important concepts that came together in the 1920s, are relevant to urban designers. The first of these, with origins in De Stijl paintings and the architecture of Frank Lloyd Wright, was the idea of space as a natural continuum, with no distinction between external and internal spaces. Both Sigfried Giedion's 'space-time' and Moholy Nagy's *Vision in Motion* drew attention to a more dynamic approach to visual understanding, which seemed to offer new insights into the process of describing and analysing urban environments.

Peter Eisenman's DAAP building is a lesson in space-time. Modest on the exterior, half-buried in the hillside landscape, it reveals little of the dazzling interior. In seeking analogies with Frank Lloyd Wright, America's greatest organic architect says: 'Plasticity was a familiar term, but something I had seen in no buildings whatsoever . . . You may see the appearance of the thing in the surface of your hand as contrasted with the articulation of the bony skeleton itself. This ideal, profound in its architectural implications, soon took another conscious stride forward in a new aesthetic. I called it continuity (it is easy to see it as a "folded plane"). Continuity in this aesthetic sense appeared to me as the natural means to achieve truly organic architecture.'[89]

Externally, Eisenman's design, in its sinuous curvilinear way, exemplifies in its relationship to the hillside most of what was true about Wright's organic architecture. It grows out of, and is part of, the landscape. It is surprisingly reticent. And yet, the only point of the building that is separated from its predecessors is the northwest corner (ignored by architectural photographers). It is the one point, externally, where serial vision, space-time and sequential spaces between outside and inside come into play, separated here from the chevron or the three existing buildings.

However, the real magic of the DAAP building is its interior public space. It is one of the rare occasions of serial vision as an urban design concept. The continuous cascade of stairs and platforms from the 300 level at the eastern end to the 600 level at the western end is breathtaking. It does not end at street level, as other critics have suggested, but 12 metres (40 feet) above it.

The contrast between the Wexner Center and DAAP is interesting. The Wexner Center has been criticised for its internal exuberant architecture. As an art gallery, one might expect it to be reticent like the admirable Van Gogh Museum in Amsterdam (before the recent additions). But as a piece of urban design, the Wexner, with its delicate, white pergolas-cum-arcade-cum-colonnade welding together disparate pieces of academic architecture spanning a century, is a stroke of genius. Externally, DAAP has no such pyrotechnics. It is certainly not contextual. On the other hand, the surrounding urban context is visually mediocre.

Internally, the spatial experience of ascending (or descending) from level 300 to level 600 is breathtaking. At the 400 level, the atrium breaks into a public space, gathering ground, social meeting space, café and party space, attempting to fulfil the requirement of bringing the schools of the College together. It is interesting to note that most of the architectural photographers, following the example of their Japanese peers, do not include people in their photographs. Yet the DAAP atrium is a rare contradiction. At an opening celebration in 1996, the atrium was packed with people and it looked marvellous, as a town centre. It needed to be populated as Eisenman surely intended. Its Piranesi-like qualities with its soaring criss-cross bridges and overlooking galleries make it a procession, a promenade architecturale, a serial vision, a space-time experience to be treasured.

Eisenman describes the philosophy behind this major urban design project in an unpublished paper, 'Folding in Time: the Singularity of Rebstok'.[90] He acknowledged different building typologies such as the high-rise or point block, the piloti of the horizontally extruded block and the *Siedlung*, all of which played a dominant role in the development of the city in the twentieth century. His theory was that whereas the unit in the perimeter block retained its individuality due to specific character and configuration, in the *Siedlung*, the block lost its identity and created a change in the role of individual expression. Repetition involves space and time. Time in the mechanical paradigm was narrative, linear and sequential. In the electronic paradigm, it was argued, time lost its immediacy (capable of being speeded up, slowed down, replayed or fast-forwarded). A photograph is mechanically produced (a product of repetition) but can be manipulated to accentuate contrast, texture and tone. In electronic repetition, the telefax has no original negative, and the original material may be on a computer disk as a series of electronic impulses stored in a matrix. As a disk is modified by corrections, a unique original is hardly ever retained.[91]

Traditionally, Eisenman argues, Cartesian architecture is conceptualised as Cartesian space. Thus Mies van der Rohe's 1940 master plan for the Illinois Institute of Technology in Chicago proposed a structure of buildings as a manifestation of an implicit Cartesian grid pervading the whole area. Eisenman describes planning envelopes as volumes of Cartesian space that 'seem to be neutral'. These platonic solids contain images of classical, modern and postmodern space. Thus, he argues, the notion of the 'fold' as a crossing or extension from a particular point is another kind of neutrality. Place and time, when no longer defined by the grid but rather by the fold, will exist but not as place and time in their former context. Narrative time is consequently altered.

The folded ground of Rebstok inhabits a netherworld of a time between the organic and the crystal, between surface and depth. The mediating device between the organism and the crystal is the idea of the membrane and, in the case of Rebstok, it is the folded surface. The fold is never the same in space or time. A folded surface maps relationships without recourse to size and distance, but, according to Eisenman, it is conceptualised in the difference between a topological and a Euclidean surface. The Rebstok project uses the fold as an attempt to produce conditions of a singularity of place and time by using the *Siedlung*. Here, the topological event, the dissolution of figure and ground into a continuum, resides physically in the fold, no longer in the point or the grid. The ground surface as a membrane (becoming a topological event or structure) is also simultaneously the building form.

In his summary of the Rebstok Park master plan for Frankfurt, Eisenman describes how late eighteenth- and early nineteenth-century perimeter housing or commerce defined both the street space and interior court as positive. This is in the sense that spaces seem to have been carved out of a solid block of the urban condition.[92] In the nineteenth century, Eisenman continues, the development of the grand boulevards and alleys in Europe presented a new kind of urban structure. The streets were positive spaces lined with ribbon buildings, and he thought that the rear yards were 'left-over' spaces. The development of the German *Siedlung* resulted from a situation where no streets were adjacent to the buildings. All of the open space was, in a sense, left over.[93] The ground became a wasteland, and object buildings seemed detached, floating on a ground that was no longer active.

Thus, Eisenman believed that a *Siedlung* urbanism was prevalent in the centre of Frankfurt. His Rebstock Park tries to reassess the entire idea of a static urbanism, dealing with objectives rather than events.

Framed by segments of the Mercator Grid, the Rebstock Park master plan floats within a rectilinear container to obscure the residual position it occupies along Frankfurt's third green belt. Compressing the large grid segment on to the site perimeter and compressing the small-scale grid on to the close site, contingent readings emerge as the two site figures fold and unfold, each relative to its expanded position. The idea of the fold gives the traditional edge a new dimension. Rather than being seen as an abrupt line, this dimension provides both mediation and a reframing of conditions such as old and new, transport and arrival and commerce and housing. Thus, the idea of folding was used on the site to initiate new social organisations of urban space.

This project, the master plan guidelines for which were completed in 1992 as the result of an international competition, raises some interesting questions. Previous commentary has indicated the problems of social engineering in the context of public housing and the clear failure of Corbusian philosophy in this context during the mid-twentieth century. Here Eisenman has produced a highly original urban typology. Whether it succeeds is in the hands of the tenants.[94]

Of the many major buildings designed by Frank Gehry, probably the Guggenheim Museum in Bilbao, Spain, is the most outstanding. Though Gehry refutes identification with the deconstructivist movement (in much the same way that James Stirling rejected identification with postmodernism during the 1980s), certainly many of the precepts of his designs have clear links with deconstruction.

It may be said on reading critical accounts of the Bilbao Guggenheim that it is often viewed as an amazing piece of iconoclastic architecture. Yet its location in an essentially industrial city in northern Spain suggests that Gehry fully understood its urban context. The site of the museum is prominently located on the edge of the riverbank where the main road bridge crossing is positioned between City Hall and the Museo de Bellas Artes. It is also significant that it is in the central business district rather than in a parkland setting. The city centre has a grid of contextual urban grain, based upon the nineteenth-century street pattern. This has established a series of connections in the city with tree-lined boulevards and walkways, public spaces and piazzas, as well as the river promenade itself. In addition, Gehry created vistas to and from the city, so that the river is visible through the buildings.

Gehry describes the design development in the following terms: 'The scale of the expressed building parts relates to the existing buildings across the road and river, while the height of the atrium roof relates to the adjacent rooftops. The tall tower at the East End of the scheme captures the bridge and makes it a part of the building composition. Bilbao's river has been very important in its history and this is reflected in the introduction of the large areas of water in the project'.[95]

The complex composition of the museum includes three different types of exhibition space: site for the permanent collection, specific installations and temporary exhibition galleries, as well as a 400-seat auditorium, a restaurant, café, retail space and a large central atrium, which Gehry envisioned as a public town square.[96] The museum is therefore distributed across the site in several interconnected buildings, the large central atrium space with its 'figural' roof unifying the composition. The entry plaza leads into the central space, which is surrounded on all four sides by galleries and has a large glass wall facing the river.

Jencks differentiates between the folded plates and staccato cubes of Eisenman and Gehry's fast-developing vocabulary of undulating surfaces. Herbert Muschamp, writing in the *New York Times*,[97] recognised Gehry's Bilbao Museum as 'A Masterpiece for Now', in that many people made pilgrimages to see the Guggenheim in the two years before its official opening on 19 October 1997. He was correct in his belief that Gehry's aim was not to found a school or to create a style. A visit to any major architectural school in the US will reveal many second-rate imitations, just as postmodernism had its imitators a decade earlier.

The approach to Bilbao is via a chaotic mess of urban industry before the emergence of the valley and its river (the Nervíon), almost like a mirage or a 'dreamscape', as Muschamp describes the experience. His most important observation is that the Guggenheim 'flashes briefly into view, its curving walls of titanium steel glinting unmistakably welcome. The taxi plunges into the city and the river disappears, the museum vanishes.'[98] This illustrates the importance of the museum as a piece of urban design, not merely iconoclastic architecture. Again, the experience is one of serial vision, and is not dissimilar to the approach to the medieval cathedral of Chartres. Travelling south across Central France, the cathedral appears as a mirage on the horizon then disappears behind the ramparts of the city, only to reappear at the last moment as a visual explosion.

Muschamp remarks that Gehry's architectural contributions came too late to have an impact on New York City, and that rather his influence was in the Midwest, for example in Toledo, Minneapolis and Cincinnati. Gehry, he says, epitomises the transformation of the industrial metropolis into the post-industrial urban centre with the exit of former industries to the third world.

It is interesting to compare the Bilbao Museum with Gehry's later design for the Vontz Center for Molecular Studies at the

University of Cincinnati. Opened in 1999, this building is a pivotal element in urban design terms on the East Campus of the university, which houses the College of Medicine, the University Teaching Hospital, Children's Hospital and many other buildings, most of which visually provide a pyramidal agglomeration of mediocre architecture. However, the Vontz Center is an example of outstanding architecture. Its curvilinear and tilted volumes clad in brick and glass make it a singular gateway building to the medical campus. Though the interior atrium space has none of the panache of Bilbao, externally it is highly organic and melds with Hargreaves' surrounding landscape. A permanent exhibit honours Albert B. Sabin, the University of Cincinnati researcher who developed the live oral polio vaccine.

According to Marisa Bartolucci: 'Serving as a gateway to UC's top-ranked Medical Center [the Vontz Center] is an animated multi-angled fungiform'.[99] Although Gehry detests the term 'signature architect', this is undeniably a signature piece. Gehry sits on the board of a hereditary disease foundation and enjoys being around scientists ('I love their ability to soar, to go where angels fear to tread'). The Vontz Center was Gehry's first design for a major laboratory, in collaboration with Earl Walls, an expert in laboratory design who had consulted on the laboratories designed by Louis Kahn at the Salk Institute. Bartolucci praises Gehry for the building's 'soaring, enthrallingly awry skylit atrium [as] a marvelous antidote to the tedium of geometrically predictable lab modules',[100] and praises the abundance of natural light.

Of even more startling impact and in contrast to both Bilbao and Cincinnati, is Gehry's recently completed design for two office buildings in Prague. Considered to be the cultural capital of Eastern and Central Europe, Prague was witness to the construction of Bauhaus-inspired designs during the 1930s. Like Krakow in Poland, also a major historic city with medieval roots, Prague survived the Nazi invasion in the late 1930s, and both cities survived communist domination from the former Soviet Union until the return to democracy over a decade ago. Though a particularly beautiful city, the liberalisation of the economy and privatisation of industries in Prague led, to some extent, to the destruction of its urban fabric, which had survived for almost a millennium. Nevertheless, central Prague's medieval city, Staré Mesto, remains intact.

The Czech architect Vladimir Milunic, though born in Zagreb, Croatia, spent his life in Prague. After the Velvet Revolution of 1989, Vaclav Havel, now president of the Czech Republic, sought the services of Milunic as a consultant for a site on the banks of the river Vistula. The site was bought by a Dutch firm of developers (Nationale Nederlanden ING Real Estate) who wanted to use a non-Czech architect, and Milunic therefore approached Frank Gehry, whom he had met in 1992. Gehry apparently accepted the invitation with enthusiasm, and the twin office blocks on this tight riverside site on the Raisin embankment, sometimes pejoratively referred to as 'Fred and Ginger', were based on Milunic's original concept.

Certainly the juxtaposition of these two extraordinary short towers of some ten storeys, one in a concrete cladding with deep projecting windows and the other, more delicate, in collapsing

Zentralsparkasse bank, Vienna, Austria (1979), Gunther Domenig.

(visually) glass curtain wall, seems to be in constant motion. However, the Nationale-Nederlanden towers do have a curious precedent. The banks in Prague resemble Gunther Domenig's design for the Zentralsparkasse bank in Vienna. Completed in 1979, this bears resemblance to the wilder fantasies of the Swiss artist H. R. Giger (set designer of early scenes in the horror movie *Alien*). The building resolutely rejects conventions of structure, form, permanence and security normally associated with a city bank building.[101] Comparisons might also be drawn with Gaudi or Van der Velde earlier in the century, but this design has a different intent as a theatrical statement. The incredible appearance of the street facade, paralleled by Gehry's later work, is surpassed by the interior design with its connotations of the human organism. Gehry's interiors, in this sense, are less flamboyant. Public reaction to Domenig's Vienna building has been surprisingly mixed rather than, as one might have supposed, uniformly hostile, with comments ranging from 'a disgrace to the district' to 'a super-style building'. Perhaps it achieved the same impact intended by Prague's most famous son, writer Franz Kafka, in his 1936 short story *Metamorphosis*,[102] which describes the transformation of a human being into a giant insect, a reaction of shock but not necessarily a lack of acceptance.

Though close friends, Frank Gehry and Peter Eisenman come from quite different educational backgrounds, and have been described by Philip Johnson in the following terms: 'Perhaps more interesting than their similarities, however, are their differences. I am not too interested in the public persona that each of these architects go to such pains to present. Mr. Eisnemann's image as East Coast intellectual extraordinaire and Mr. Gehry's role as the intuitive, anti-intellectual West Coast savant are too carefully wrought and too finally cultivated to be persuasive'.[103]

Frank Gehry was born in Toronto in 1928, studied architecture at UCLA and, after working for large commercial firms in the Los Angeles area established his own practice in Santa Monica in 1962. Most architects ignored his early career, and he was drawn to the culture of fine art and artists such as Robert Rauschenberg, Richard Serra and Claes Oldenburg, even claiming that some of his floor plans were inspired by the paintings of Hieronymus Bosch. Given his talent, Gehry is a very modest man and a person with a life-long commitment to social justice. His original interest was in urban planning, which he abandoned out of sheer frustration with the vacillations and inaction so prevalent in that field.

Peter Eisenman was born in 1932 and studied architecture at Cornell University, Columbia University and the University of Cambridge in England. Between 1963 and 1967 he was a faculty member at Princeton University, where he became a renowned teacher, and later founded the Institute for Architecture and Urban Studies in New York. Like Gehry, his involvement with major buildings began late, his first being the Wexner Center for the Visual Arts in Columbus, Ohio, which was completed in 1989.

THE WEST COAST PROPHETS OF DECONSTRUCTION

Peter Eisenman as the East Cost intellectual, together with Michael Sorkin, might be regarded as exceptions in the general development of deconstruction. But apart from the giant works of Frank Gehry, the Los Angeles area, in particular, was represented by many other significant designers.

Eric Owen Moss established his practice in 1976 and since 1978 has won numerous *Progressive Architecture* and American Institute of Architects Awards. In Culver City, a declining industrial suburb of central Los Angeles, Moss has designed and built a series of impressive buildings near his office. For the last ten years, his developer patrons Fred and Laurie Samitur Smith have devoted their financial resources and expertise to the reconfiguration of the empty shell of redundant warehouses, providing in their place flexible office and studio spaces for media companies.

In this, Moss's work differs from that of Gehry, who designs new iconoclastic major buildings such as his notable museums. In terms of deconstruction, Moss has disjointed geometries like Gehry; however, they are different, and perhaps in urban design terms they may be regarded as more pertinent. Cannibalised warehouses may be seen as more relevant in a post-industrial society (or at least in a post-heavy-industrial society) and Moss presents visionary alternative strategies for urban redevelopment.

His offices for a digital film and graphic design studio, completed in 1998, are the first project in which Moss eliminated existing ancillary structures, the new building occupying a northern section of the site. Unfortunately, though, the remainder appears to be taken over by the typical blacktop car-park. The original brick wall of the warehouse was retained, as were the timber trusses. In the organisation of the new building, all functions are welded by four floors of spine corridors and, though open-plan, Moss has created a sense of territory with what has been described as 'nooks and crannies'.[104] This latter factor is important because in the age of rapidly advancing information technology, the coziness and privacy of individual workspaces have become increasingly important.

> Like a stage set, the building becomes an adaptable armature of events, capable of accommodating corporate muscle and individual creativity. It is a brave move that adds a much-needed shot of vigour to a desolate part of LA, worlds away from the city's slick, sanitized Central Business District.[105]

Coop Himmelblau, a partnership between Helmut Swiczinsky and Wolf Prix, is also on the West Coast. Prix is perhaps better known in the US than is his partner. Educated at the Technische Universität in Vienna, and later at the Southern California Institute of Architecture (Sci-Arc), he has taught both at Harvard and at Columbia University, New York. The practice was founded in 1968 in Vienna and the second office established in Los Angeles in 1988. One of its most recent interesting works is the 1995–2000 proposal for the rehabilitation of the Gasometer Project in Vienna. This is perhaps even more remarkable than the projects of Moss in terms of urban rehabilitation. Though it could hardly be classified as deconstructivist in motivation, the design nevertheless shows how the use of huge, redundant industrial structures could be managed.

The four historical gasholders (or gasometers) originally supplied gas for the city of Vienna. The interior elements were dismantled and the original nineteenth-century neo-classical facades were maintained. Like Culver City, this project is located on an industrial site, with the four huge cylinders creating unusual resultant spaces.

Other teams were involved in proposals for the reuse of the gasometers. Gasometer B adds three new volumes to the existing facade – the cylinder inside the gasometer, the shield as a visible addition outside and the multi-functional event hall situated at the base. Apartments and offices are situated inside the cylinder and shield. Natural light is provided through a conical inner court and through the historical outer wall. A total of 360 apartments have differentiated living arrangements ranging from two-storey duplex and loft apartments to small student apartments. Office space and apartments are combined – presumably based on current predictions on the growth of home-based workplaces. A shopping mall at street level links all four gasometers and the subway station. At the seventh floor level a social space is created in the 'sky-lobby'.[106]

Thom Mayne, founder of Morphosis (his erstwhile partner, Michael Rotondi, was a co-founder) said that the 'modernist penchant for unification and simplification must be broken'.

The work of the Morphosis group therefore recognised the changes in society at the end of the twentieth century and the emerging phenomenon of electronic communications. More disturbing was the view of Morphosis that there was to be, inevitably, a breakdown of a conventional notion of community.

Some commentators have said that, like some Japanese architects, Morphosis has insisted on breaking down the separation of boundaries between the interior and the exterior of buildings.[107] But surely such a precept was not new. Frank Lloyd Wright's pursuit of 'organic architecture' from the prairie style to the usonian visions during the first part of the twentieth century was well established. Philip Vodidio confuses this further by saying that Morphosis had a similar interest to that of Peter Eisenman in *Chaos Theory,* thought to justify the diversity and apparently disordered forms that they generated.[108] Thom Mayne is quoted as saying: 'Our work transcribes the fragmented, dispersed, and detached nature of existence'.[109]

In 1992, Morphosis produced designs for a huge golf club complex in the prefecture of Chiba, Tokyo. The Chiba project concerned itself with the interaction between architecture and the natural landscape. The design attempted to break down the demarcations between the man-made and the natural by developing a strategy that linked site investigations to an architectural language: 'The focus was directed to the whole of the physical and draws on all senses, producing an architecture which is engaged in making environmental processes self-evident and connected to one's day-to-day life . . . The entire program with its emphasis on the game [golf] is about movement, the rhythm of walking the arch of an arm in full swing, the nature and sequence of physical spaces, the narrative and diversity of place and the dynamic and connective nature of a complex organization.'[110] The basic 'parti' is made up of four elements, a curved wall for the arrival of motor cars, a linear sequence of alternating volumes accommodating most of the programme, a second circular wall embracing the larger site and a circular partition for dining and social events. The configuration of the two curved walls is described as containing the 'more static and platonic inner spaces which are introspective and contemplative in character . . . the realized or built environment seeks more than just a truce with nature'. Yet the imagery of the twelve pavilions (a group of ten separated from the remaining two conjure up designs of a previous generation, of Paul Rudolph and the Yale University School of Architecture and the 'new brutalism' of the 1950s and 1960s) is very eloquent in urban design configuration.

About the same time was a proposal for a Performing Arts Pavilion in Los Angeles. Like the Chiba project, the Morphosis designers emphasised the importance of establishing a correspondence between the aspects of the site in its broader geographic context. The concept arose, so the designers claimed, from a response to the relentless uniformity and energy of the grid organisation that was intrinsic to the suburban condition (presumably a reference to the Los Angeles street pattern). Taking the x-y component and producing three intersections to create systems for the distribution of people and cars, the three elements were perceived as figures giving a primary order on the connections and intersections by which the buildings themselves assumed a secondary hierarchical role. This reversal placed a fundamental emphasis on the sequence of events including arrival and movement towards activities – a theme of serial vision.[111] The designers went on to suggest that the predominance of the three reiterations of the grid put the focus upon the landscape and park, providing a system to bring order and focus to the individual building complexes and their respective activities. The Performing Arts Pavilion was to become the generator of this new order.

Thom Mayne, in his essay 'Connected Isolation',[112] argued that the relationship of architecture to its immediate political and economic context is elusive and complicated and, therefore, we need to assert a position that redefines our intentions and methods of intervention.[113] He goes on to say that the lure of the city in the nineteenth century emptied rural space of its social and cultural substance, and by the end of the twentieth century it was urban space that was losing its geographical reality. With the modern, post-industrial destabilising influences the old city disappears, and one of the consequences of this breakdown of a conventional notion of community is the individual's loss of a clear concept of his or her public role.

Of completed projects, perhaps one of the most notable was the Cedar's Sinai Comprehensive Cancer Center. Linear in design, Morphosis said that its primary focus was on the public armature as an organisational strategy that emphasised the discrete nature of public spaces, which oriented the user to the multidimensional facility, made up of five specialities and their various secondary functional elements. The continuum of public space had characteristics of depth and intricacy contrasting with the generic qualities of the specialised treatment spaces. Above all, the decision to build a healing environment in a subterranean space was to resolve the contradiction inherent in this – that perception was an experience of travelling through, or even of ascension. Such a statement may seem preposterous since it is unlikely that the cancer patients were concerned with sequential spatial experience. Yet the designers argued that they were intent on challenging a traditional hospital architectural language based upon a clinical antiseptic environment and replacing it with 'an illusion of space, openness, movement, freedom and growth'. The architecture of the vertical, or z-axis, created a ground-sky dialogue and the 'play structure' – resembling a glass-enclosed elevator shaft topped by a tree – may be seen by some as merely architectural conceit.

Equally, the 1991 Disney Town Center and Educational Institute, with both Thom Mayne and Michael Rotondi as principals, was to be a city of the twenty-first century, based on a series of interactive systems producing a diversity that would 'mirror a future cultural environment'. Though never built (and presumably replaced by the new town of Celebration, which reflected the safer ideals of the new urbanism), it was deliberately intended to explore a multitude of complex, diverse and contradictory demands of indeterminate programmes. The location of a linear park on a wetland flat site was in the form of a snake, ribbon or river producing its own sequences of spaces. The juxtaposition of circulation elements, entertainment, commerce, education and water spaces created a suggested movement and fluidity connecting all elements of the development as interpenetrating organisations that contradicted the more traditional, monolithic character of urban development.

In 1997, when Morphosis became Ro-To, led by Michael Rotondi, a more modest scale reflected a change in direction.[114] Noteworthy in terms of urban rehabilitation was a derelict power station conversion in Los Angeles, which involved remodelling the machine shop of Los Angeles' first electrical power station in a former industrial sector near the city centre. This may seem the most challenging and frustrating of downtown renewal schemes, but nevertheless Ro-To succeeded in providing a vivid, even revolutionary vision of what could be achieved, given far-sighted clients. It has been suggested[115] that the transformation from a railway and recycled materials yard emulated 'any house Frank Lloyd Wright built into a bucolic slope'. Such a proposition is tenuous, however the recycling of industrial trusses, beams and staircases was to provide a new form of architecture. The standardised systems of the former building were re-assembled in non-standardised ways.

Like much of the philosophy of Morphosis and, later, Ro-To, the visual relationships between the building, the near and distant landscape were of paramount importance in creating the centres of several arcs instead of one geometric centre, and the language of non-Euclidean forms contrasted with the original neo-classical shell. The house that emerged was remarkable.

A more recent example of the work of Michael Rotondi is the KZF/Morphosis proposal for the Student Recreation Center at the University of Cincinnati. As yet unbuilt, the complex project on a complex site presents new ideas on street development. The initial designs, presented in June 2000, indicate a major curvilinear block of dormitory rooms above a complex agglomeration of basketball courts, a swimming pool, food courts and so forth. Envisaged as the future 'image centre' of university student life, the formation links Pei's and Cobb's new buildings for the Conservatory of Music to the south and Michael Graves' Engineering Research building to the north.

Both Thom Mayne and Michael Rotondi were key teachers at Sci-Arc. Though the school did not receive professional accreditation until September 1990, it had existed since the mid-1970s and had attracted the more revolutionary architectural educators, competing with UCLA and Berkeley. Much smaller in scale than the latter two behemoths, its student programmes were exciting. A studio held in the autumn of 1994 by Margaret Crawford and John Kaliski focused on Culver City, to the east of Sci-Arc, in a area where Moss designed and/or constructed his projects.[116] Fox Hills was described as an 'in-town edge city' with its shopping centre, strip clubs, office complexes, townhouses and freeways. The students were asked to confront this paradoxical landscape. The tutors wished to eliminate the distinction between theory and practice with a rigorous critical framework. More questionable was the pursuit of the practices of surrealism, intended to encourage experimentation, and the contradictory statement that it was, nevertheless, initiated in the theory of the ordinary. Dividing the studio into different components, 'Urban Facts', Week 2 (or 'Material Gathering'), contrasted with 'Urban Fantasies', Week 3. Reference was inevitably made to the writings of Venturi and others in 'redefining the popular'. More opaque was Week 7, 'Detournement and Heteroglossia', followed by the remaining weeks of 'The Everyday' with reading from Henri Lefebvre and Michel de Certeau. Yet despite these questions of structure and direction, such studios as Sci-Arc were a refreshing change in urban design.

THE PURSUIT OF MODERNISM, HIGH-TECH AND WHITE ARCHITECTURE

Though the interest of students of architecture and urban design was centred during this decade on deconstruction, a strong parallel movement in both philosophy and architectural imagery continued.

Richard Meier's work exemplified the concepts of modernism and 'white architecture'. Meier was a member of the New York Five (formed in the early 1970s), the other members of which were John Hejduk, Michael Graves, Peter Eisenman and Charles Gwathmey. In 1972, their work was published in *Five Architects*. The book outlined their manifesto, based upon the philosophies of Le Corbusier and contemporary French philosophy in general. Of the other four members, John Hejduk built little but, prior to his death in 2000, he was a highly regarded educator, serving as Dean of Architecture at the Cooper Union Institute in New York City. Michael Graves' later work was firmly rooted in the philosophies of postmodernism, whereas Peter Eisenman, who did not build much until the late 1980s, developed complex deconstructivist theories. Charles Gwathmey's work remained relatively close to the precepts of modernism but was not as faithful as that of Meier. However, one of his most notable and challenging works was the extension to Frank Lloyd Wright's Guggenheim Museum in New York City (1992), executed with consummate skill. Recognising the icon of Frank Lloyd Wright's work, the expansion at the rear of the original structure was modest and reticent (though some critics have said that Wright would have rejected it). Gwathmey's work in 1991 for the Disney Contemporary Resort at Disney World, Lake Buena Vista, Florida, was much closer to the postmodernism of Michael Graves, also in Disney World.[117]

Richard Meier's early work was epitomised in two projects. Though both could hardly be classified as urban design (and are probably the opposite), they nonetheless set the precedent for his major work. The Smith House, situated on Long Island Sound in Darien, Connecticut, and completed in 1967, can only be described as a serene piece of architecture. On a steep site, surrounded by dense evergreens, the house was designed as a series of layers but, more importantly, it provided a sense of progression, moving from the entrance down to the shore. This line of progression determined the major site axis.

As already mentioned, though it could be argued that this icon of architecture has absolutely nothing to do with urban design (located as it is in a rural, privileged setting, a single piece of domestic architecture related solely to the natural landscape), the line of progression with the intersecting planes of the house responded to various rhythms of gradient, rock outcrops, shoreline and trees.[118] According to Meier: 'As the site plan indicates, the approach, entrance, access and view are organized to cross the contours of the site, and thus afford an unusual prospect of landscape and water. The angle of the garage to the path leading to the front facade and the curved wall on one side of the door help to draw one through the open zone of the house'.[119] He went on to say that the entry facade was treated as an opaque screen that had to be penetrated to reveal the view of the water lying beyond, with the separation between public and private areas (each family member had a private space for sleeping, bathing and retirement) contrasting with the public spaces where the family would meet and entertain. Thus, the private sector was constructed as a series of closed cellular spaces on three levels and the public sector as three separate platforms within the glass enclosure.

The Athenaeum at New Harmony, Indiana, completed in 1975, moved many of Meier's ideas of sequential space on to another level. Historically, New Harmony was an important Utopian community in America. The Phalanstery, by the American architect Stedman Whitwell, was unique and based on the beliefs of the Welsh social reformer Robert Owen, who advocated principles for an ideal society in 1824. Owen was in turn inspired by the earlier writings of Charles Fourier in France who proposed a social revolution 'leading humanity towards Harmonic periods'. Meier detected a contradiction in Owen's thinking, creating a conflict between an 'ordered' Utopia and a 'disordered' reality and, unlike many of his peers, he perceived a dichotomy inherent in the ideas of architects who attempted to solve real problems with ideal solutions.

The Athenaeum, which could be described as a literary or scientific association, was intended as a centre for community cultural events. Unlike Meier's earlier Smith House in Connecticut, New Harmony was built on a flood plain that determined the design solution. The building accorded with the existing street grid, but all the public spaces related to the water. It was seen as a plane of arrival, interpretation and orientation – the commencement of a tour of the town of New Harmony. Meier describes it thus:

Movement spaces can be places of initiation: This is the beginning of a route. The intention of the design solution is to function as a transitional element, a link between two different worlds – even a link between past and present. The entire movement system is a continuous experience, in which the building is a space of social interaction that is finally linked with the town of New Harmony itself. The building complex has two dispositions. Its predominant order is orthogonal, in response to the existing street grid of the town, as every new structure should respect the presence of the grid in the landscape.[120]

Though the 'white architecture' of Meier was quite revolutionary in the existing urban structure of the town, his concern with context is interesting. He went on to say that the form of the building was also influenced by the diagonal random edge of the town itself.

These two early precedents of Meier were to presage his gargantuan work for the Getty Center in Los Angeles, which was opened to the public in December 1997. This can be interpreted as a truly major piece of urban design. Nearly fourteen years in design, the Getty Center paralleled Frank Gehry's Guggenheim Museum in Bilbao. Though often compared, both are quite different. Gehry's design for Bilbao is iconoclastic, jewel-like and singular. Meier's is iconic with the modernist idiom, is not singular and is, in effect, a city. The context, too, was quite different. Bilbao was within a decaying urban situation. The Getty was on a pristine hilltop site in one of the wealthiest sectors of Los Angeles, adjacent to the suburbs of Bel Air and Brentwood. According to Meier:

The spectacular site . . . invites the architect to search out a precise and exquisitely reciprocal relationship between built architecture and natural topography. This implies a harmony of parts: a rational procedure; concern for the qualities of proportion, rhythm and repose, precision of detail, constructional integrity, programmatic appropriateness and, not least, a respect for human scale . . . In my mind's eye I see a classic structure, elegant and timeless, emerging serene and ideal, from the rough hillside, a kind of Aristotelian structure within the landscape.[121]

Thus Meier's Getty Center may be regarded as a rejection or challenge to the many other abundant theories at the very end of the twentieth century. It was classical in the true sense of the term, using classical materials such as Italian travertine. A complex grouping of buildings at the top of a mountain with a controlled sequence of public space, it provided distant views of the surrounding landscape.

In their commentary on the design, Thomas and Carol Reese affirmed that Meier was inspired by classical Italy (though it might be seen as more relevant to the Acropolis at Athens).[122] It was clear, they said, that Meier's design was a monument to 'static', whereas Gehry's was one of 'becoming'. Recognising the dichotomy between these two paradigms, they acknowledged that both Bilbao and the Getty are works of extraordinary architectural achievement.

Nevertheless, an examination of Meier's exquisitely drawn site plans undoubtedly indicates a city. The grids, geometries and paths were the flux of the entire composition. It is said that Meier always established two overlapping grids in an urban and geographical context – the grid of the city of Los Angeles and the diagonal of the San Diego Freeway. Reese mentions figure-ground studies including the art of Rauschenberg, Johns and Stella, yet curiously omits reference to Colin Rowe. Seen as layerings, transparencies and collages rather than true figure-ground relationships, the compositions were conceived as integral units.

Whether Meier's drawings invoked archeological drawings is a more dubious argument. Certainly much of the organisation is subterranean with interconnecting passageways, though whether this reflected the ordering of the Roman fora rather than the Greek Acropolis is debatable. It is also suggested that the architectural forms above ground level reflected Aalto, Neutra, Schindler and even Wright, as well as the geometries of Kahn. This is patently incorrect. The crystalline forms of Meier's architecture are unique. Based though they are on modernist theories, they owe little to previous models. In fact Meier acknowledged historic precedent in suggesting that Hadrian's Villa and Caprarola, with sequential space, thick walls and a sense of order, had inspired him.

Thomas and Carol Reese identified the Getty as an evocation of a hill town or citadel image in the tightly clustered masses seen from the north, south and east, and this is certainly so, though Meier's fascination with processional space created many external views. The access to the complex via automated tram to the crest of the hill gives a further experiential dimension of sequence, at a different speed, to the Arrival Plaza.[123] The Plaza seemed to represent the dilemma of the Getty Foundation – there were distinctions between the private collection and research facilities and the public functions. Many alternative designs were produced to resolve these problems, and finally the Museum itself was to be the principal site of destination, its backlighted lobby defined by a series of circular forms in an embracing and welcoming way.

Noriko Takiguchi said that though Meier's trademark material was the white aluminium panel, the decision to use travertine stone as well (imported from quarries near Tivoli, Italy) was also significant.[124] The effect was to create a sense of permanence, of buildings growing out of the hilltop itself. Takiguchi does not believe that the Getty Center was the execution of a grand plan, as was the case with the temples of Rome, but the result of complex interactions between the roles and expectations of a contemporary arts foundation, yet in its final result it is indeed a true citadel.

The relative obscurity of the Getty Trust is an anomaly in itself. Despite its enormous private wealth, it was an elite community of scholarship and research, self-funded and not dependent on public resources. The results of its research and scholarship were disseminated through the art history community and the works of art in the collection were available to the public free of charge.

The Getty in Los Angeles is not about Hollywood or Disneyland but the creation of a 'feeling of eternity,' as Meier himself describes it. The use of neutral white boxes created dramatic controversy among the design team but Meier believed this was essential for a background for works of art. In this he was correct, and though the white panels became off-white and similar in tone to the travertine slabs, the reciprocal relationship was unobtrusive. The setting of the building in a vast Los Angeles landscape was not, as Takiguchi suggests, reflective of the framed ocean views of Louis Kahn's Salk Institute, but dynamic with a kaleidoscope of foreground and background views. The hilltop location created an urban masterpiece.

Rafael Viñoly's Tokyo International Forum complex, though not directly relating to Meier's aesthetic, produced a complex on an equally heroic scale. The Forum has been described by Herbert Muschamp as 'a crystal palace of culture and commerce' and 'such a perfectly realized building that you may actually find yourself hoping that a flaw will turn up'.[125] More reminiscent of the drawings of Piranesi, its *tour-de-force* is the central galleria or 'glass hall' criss-crossed with dizzying glass bridges and flooded with natural daylight.

Designed in his New York office in 1989, the result of winning an international competition of 395 entries, the Tokyo International Forum was Viñoly's first major project. Muschamp suggests that it contradicts many of the preoccupations of contemporary American architects, but in a way quite different from that of Richard Meier.

Though in the past such a design might have been described by critics such as Rayner Banham as a 'megastructure', the Forum is in fact much more than that. Indeed it is a huge structure, but beyond this it has major cultural significance in both Japanese and international terms. The Japanese architect Fumihiko Maki, on seeing the winning design in 1993, said: 'When a significant spatial experience is shared by a number of people, this is the genesis of public space'.[126] This remark is significant in the sense that the public space or public realm is the foundation of urban design. Though the design has its roots in modernism, it could hardly be classified as 'white architecture', as was Richard Meier's work. Rather, it has analogies with the high-tech architecture of British designers such as Norman Foster, Richard Rogers and Nicholas Grimshaw.

The creation of a new urban space in a world city like Tokyo owes much of its success to Viñoly's clarity in the interpretation of the programme, three-dimensionally, in plan and section – the design was considered not to emphasise form hierarchies but a juxtaposition of complex spaces with different elements forming filters, gateways and barriers.[127]

The site, occupying two city blocks in the Marunouchi central business district, is literally adjacent to the main railway station and close to Tokyo's Imperial Palace Gardens. As with Brazilian architect Oscar Niemeyer's collaboration with his structural adviser Joaquin Cardoso, so Viñoly's collaboration with Kunio Watanabe has produced a crystal palace with the same impact that Joseph Paxton's building of the same name must have produced in London in 1851.[128] In a simplistic analysis it is two structures linking a major public space. The latter acts as a pedestrian promenade, and Muschamp describes this as 'an oasis for office workers in the financial district . . . The visual effect of this outdoor space is of a man-made ravine, a portage between rippling glass reflections and a cliff of faceted gray stone'.[129]

The external plaza controls the entries to the glass hall. The great halls include a 5,000-seat theatre used as both a symphony concert hall and a conference hall. Controlled by an electronic system, this auditorium produces possibly the best acoustic results of any auditorium in the world.

PROFESSIONAL RECOGNITION OF BUILT AND UNBUILT PROJECTS

The plurality of design philosophies described above is reflected in many of the design awards programmes of this decade (though by the middle of the decade *Progressive Architecture's* 40-year-old Awards Program had come to a close). The urban design awards programme was now significant, and in January 1991 the major award for architecture was given to Peter Eisenman, architect (together with executive architects Lorens and Williams) for the extension to the College of Design, Architecture Art and Planning (DAAP) at the University of Cincinnati.

However, the problem of expanding the scope of the *Progressive Architecture* awards programme beyond architectural design to urban design (and indeed research), was that, to the casual observer, the boundaries were blurred.

As illustrated above, the DAAP project could be considered an urban design project rather than architecture. Equally, the design by Holt, Grimshaw, Pfan, Jones for a 'House for a Corporate Family' exemplifies the ideal of a hill town rather than an individual structure. Like many other proposals in the awards programme, it did not seem to reach fruition in its original form.

On the other hand, the Davids-Killory design for housing for homeless mothers and children (which was awarded a citation in 1991) was eventually built and could truly have been classified as 'urban design'.[130] Fulfilling an important social programme, the project was constructed in Escondido, Southern California, and is composed of 13 two-bedroom units for single mothers and their children, with shared service and play areas. The apartments enclose three sides of a courtyard with the intention of fostering a sense of community, once typical of Hispanic culture. This proposal was highly praised by the jury. In the words of Adele Santos: 'It is a fabulous program, if you think about the idea of all these single mothers with this giant program'. While Rem Koolhaas thought it too rigid, Santos went on to praise the idea of connected units – which really became little houses with a front porch, living room and private patio with the kitchen looking out on to the play spaces – that yet provided the mothers with some privacy.

The following year, Davids-Killory received another *Progressive Architecture* Design Award for a project with a similar social agenda. Also located in Escondido, California, this was an interim housing programme for eight homeless families. Though both the 1991 and 1992 designs hardly scratch the surface of homelessness and poverty in California they nevertheless present a breakthrough in architectural design seriously addressing social problems. According to Davids-Killory:

This pilot project was adapted from bungalow courts common to Southwestern California, integrated layers of open and enclosed space with patterns appropriate for the automotive city. Twelve cars can be parked in a shaded court that is on axis with a protected pedestrian area, flanked by the two-floor apartments. This courtyard is a private street for the residents with palm trees and movable canvas shades which extend across the rowhouses, like the 'toldos' typical of a street in a Latin American town. Here they cover the play area while channeling cool air into the apartments. Each household is entered from this oasis, which features a laundromat, a children's play area and a small theater . . . Because this prototype is designed for a small number of families, it should be more readily accepted in an established neighborhood.[131]

One of the jurors, Steve Holl, commented: 'For the sort of people who are falling through the cracks in our society, here's something that can be done on a small scale . . . small pockets that reintegrate with the network of the city'.

Other architectural citations in the 1991 awards included a project by Valerio Associates for Colton Palms, California, an urban design proposal for the Redevelopment Agency of the City of Colton and Cooperative Services, Inc. Through a national open competition, community participation resulted in a new village centre which the jury (Santos and Koolhaas) thought was 'too cute'. But such observations raise other questions in the context of urban design – why shouldn't public housing proposals be 'pretty', as per the Colton Palms proposal? Steven Holl's own proposal for a housing project in Fukuoka, Japan, which also received a citation that year, was much more serious in image.

When the 1991 urban design awards were published, an outstanding proposal was that from Machado and Silvetti for the Piazza Dante in Genoa, Italy, the result of a city-sponsored international design competition in 1990. The reconstruction of the Piazza Dante was intended to create an oasis as a commemoration of Christopher Columbus on the 500th anniversary of the discovery of America. The elimination of vehicular traffic, the construction of the fountain and stairways connecting the old city with the more recent, created a central space in the true tradition of the Italian metropolis, and particularly the hill-towns of northern Italy.

Among the other urban design awards was the Carr's Hill precinct study for the University of Virginia by Michael Dennis and Associates. This was a challenging project in many ways, not least in that it was located adjacent to one of the finest campus designs in the US. The original design by Thomas Jefferson was on a formal, neo-classical axis and is possibly the most beautiful campus in the country. This proposal was for the creation of an 'acropolis for the arts,' which would include architecture and drama facilities as well as music, TV/film and studio arts. It created a densely defined central court, connected to the existing campus by a new street. The architectural imagery was certainly sympathetic towards Jefferson's eighteenth-century building and though the axes of the original campus were respected, the inevitable asymmetrical development is questionable.

Also included was Bernard Tschumi's proposal for Future Park in Flushing Meadow, Queen's, New York. Executed in collaboration with Skidmore, Owings and Merrill, including Alan Plattus, it was a further development of Tschumi's Parc de La Villette in Paris, France. On 485 hectares (1,200 acres) of reclaimed land, the site housed the 1939 and 1964 World Fairs. The ordering devices of Tschumi used enhanced green areas called 'the Meadows' and a mall running the full length of the park, protected by heavily planted edges to provide a visible linear element. Tschumi, in terms of serial vision ideas, considered that this should be an episodic and meandering formal walk, with an emphasis on entry points and other pedestrian pathways.

In 1992, the *Progressive Architecture* awards were to produce one of the most significant schemes of the late twentieth century.

In Boston, the harbour had been long cut off from the rest of the peninsula by eastern freeways, and the Boston Redevelopment Authority subsequently proposed urban design guidelines for the central artery air rights. Still under construction in 2001, this project is perhaps the largest implemented scheme ever illustrated in the Awards' 40-year history.

A team led by Eric Schmidt for the Boston Redevelopment Authority created a proposal for a one-and-a-half-mile strip through downtown Boston. At the time, the land was occupied by an elevated expressway, cutting off the waterfront from the rest of downtown. This problem was not dissimilar to the Embarcadero expressway along San Francisco's harbour. The demolition of the Embarcadero expressway, which preceded the Boston project, was less radical and less costly but achieved the same objectives. The project, illustrated in *Progressive Architecture*,[132] proposed a tunnel underneath the city – eliminating the elevated expressway – and a comprehensive redevelopment programme for 20 hectares (50 acres) of reclaimed land, establishing a linear system of public activities. The plan indicated a series of parks and spaces with two boulevards in parallel running the entire length of the artery tunnel. The reconstruction of a historic district (the Bullfinch Triangle) was considered to be a key element. The ideas referenced half-century-old theories of mixed uses of retail, offices and housing, maintaining strong street wall conditions. A community park would serve the North End neighbourhood, originally settled by Italian immigrants. The open and interconnected blocks in the waterfront district would include a park with amenities like a carousel, skating rink and botanical gardens, as well as a 'gateway' for Chinatown (with some of the best Chinese restaurants in the US).

The jurors (Baldwin and Silvetti) seemed sceptical. Baldwin commented: 'We were very concerned that the good intentions of the design are implemented. So as we considered project entries, we looked at them to see what it would take to get them built. I think the Central Artery is one of the best projects in that regard. It also assumes a great deal of responsibility. It is going to build something that is very alien to the traditional city . . . The project has been a little more egalitarian than I would like, and, in my mind, goes overboard in soliciting good advice from a lot of people'.[133] To this Silvetti added: 'I think there is hardly a city with more people with opinions on the design process than Boston. The fact that these people after four years have been able to articulate guidelines that are very clear and sensible and intelligent deserves rewarding'. Some twelve years and $13.5 billion later the project is still not complete and has amassed significant cost overruns. Yet, as a textbook example of public participation and visionary design, it is probably without parallel at the turn of the twenty-first century. Why this proposal received a citation rather than an award is puzzling.

A citation was also awarded to the Gateway Project for Cleveland, Ohio, by Sasaki Associates. This is another major urban design project that was, by and large, implemented. In contrast to its major rival, Cincinnati in southwestern Ohio, Cleveland, in the northeast, had achieved a major reconstruction of its riverfront by 2000. (Though Cincinnati is finally addressing the issue of its Ohio riverfront, the construction of

two behemoths – in the form of two stadia – illustrates a lack of vision in the so-called Banks project.) Sasaki's plan for the 11-hectare (28-acre) site at the southern entry point to Cleveland's downtown included a 45,000-seat baseball stadium and a 20,000-seat indoor arena, forming an edge to the city and creating a destination drawing people through the existing streets and landmark arcades.

The final *Progressive Architecture* awards in urban design were announced in January 1995.[134] An award was given for the Lower Manhattan Urban Design Plan by Peterson/Littenburg Architects, New York, with the Battery City Authority, the Port of New York Authority and the New York Landmarks Conservancy as clients. The site of over a square mile is a major downtown business district but at the time had a 28 per cent vacancy rate. The problems identified included a 'flawed street network, confusing and discontinuous; restricted transportation connections; insufficient housing to support round-the-clock use of the infrastructure', which needed to go beyond the expanding housing programme of Battery Park City and Tribeca.

Among the jury opinions was that of Michael Dennis who said: 'If you asked someone what they were doing and they told you that they were working on a plan for Lower Manhattan, you would think they were onto something pretty strong'. It was the sheer audacity of the plan that startled the jury, and as British architect-juror Nicholas Grimshaw suggested, 'the term megalomania comes to mind'.[135] But six years later, in 2001, the proposal had still not been built. Though the design itself had merit, the construction of Battery Park City, already underway, conflicted with such a comprehensive solution.

The following year the awards programme experienced a hiatus. Penton Publishing of Connecticut, the parent company of *Progressive Architecture*, closed the magazine and brought to a close the history of probably the most distinguished of American architectural journals.

However, the awards programme was resurrected by the American Institute of Architects' *Architecture* journal. In January 1997, *Architecture* created a new image for itself with radically changed graphics and new, controversial writers. Acknowledging the importance of the *Progressive Architecture* awards, the new editor, Reed Kroloff, said in the annual awards issue of 1998 that it gave pleasure to continue that tradition.[136]

Yet that issue demonstrated a substantial difference in philosophy from previous awards issues. The 1998 jury was composed of radical jurors including Sheila Kennedy (a partner in Kennedy/Violich in Boston), Carlos Jimenez of Houston, Dan Hanganan of Montreal, Zaha Hadid of London and James Cutler of Washington. It was clear that their agenda did not include urban design – indeed, there was no urban design category in 1998.

That year there were two awards and four citations together with research awards out of 400 entries. In 1997, there had been four awards and fifteen citations. Whether this was significant is debatable. What was significant was the polemicism of the jurors. It appears that the jury was satisfied that no 'big-name' firms appeared among the 1998 winners. No honours went to major projects, though perhaps this was a good thing as although the procedure had always required anonymous entries,

entries from majors such as Eisenman or Morphosis were certainly recognisable.

Aaron Betsky, a contributing editor, said at the time that 'if this year's batch of winners of the P/A awards are any indications, we now aspire to skewing, warping, unfolding and exposing the status quo'.[137] At least he acknowledged that 'some of the work looks strange'. But was this about real architecture, let alone urban design? Hadid remarked that the programme was a place to look at new ideas that may at first seem marginal and Hanganan commented that 'visionary has several components: future, fantasy and optimism'. An examination of the award winners reveals small projects such as the Zahedi house by Office dA, the Woman Suffrage Memorial by Loom, and the House on a Terminal Line by Preston Scott Cohen.

If urban design had any place it was probably represented in the Water Garden in Columbus, Ohio, by RUR Architecture. Whether a result of the graphic representation (which included computer renderings), the designs had the opaque obscurity of philosophical writings emanating from some East Coast American schools of architecture that often appeared to be a navel-gazing inner circle preaching to the converted in an unknown language. However, the city proposal for West Hollywood, by Studio Words, though obscure in its message, was the only urban design project to receive a citation. Situated on the eastern section of Santa Monica Boulevard, it was titled 'Seven Diagrams for Seeing a City, 29 City Proposals, Five Projects for Faith Plating'.[138] An analysis of the seven plan diagrams of the boulevard documented existing scale, variations of the street grid, topography, local landmarks, building placement and views. From these analyses 29 recommendations attempted to manipulate, correct and enhance existing uniformities and anomalies. The procedures had links to Christopher Alexander's earlier work, and among the radical ideas was the creation of translucent walls on the top of single-storey buildings, and new street furniture ranging from gigantic to miniature in scale.

It should perhaps be noted that the research awards that year also had some connection with urban design. The jury of Robert Beckley, Susan Maxman and Alan Plattus selected projects such as the Living Learning Communities Study by Angelini and Associates and the University of Michigan. Also noteworthy was the Cultural Form and Process in Building at the Zuni Pueblo in New Mexico by a team from the University of Pennsylvania.

PARALLEL URBAN DESIGN INITIATIVES

Koetter, Kim, Agrest and Gandelsonas became increasingly well-known authorities on urban design theory and practice. In 1992 *Progressive Architecture* printed an analytical article by Alex Kreiger on three different approaches to urban design.[139] These were Asbury Park, New Jersey, by Koetter, Kim and Associates, and the same practice's plan for the Surrey Quays in London, as well as the Vision Plan for Des Moines, Iowa, by Agrest and Gandelsonas. The latter differed from the first two projects in that the analytical studies, a consolidation of two

decades of developing urban design, resulted in a proposal that built upon the original new-classical gridiron plan of Des Moines and the City Beautiful movement. Agrest and Gandelsonas had developed a scholarship of writings on semiotics and architecture, and the adaptation of linguistic theory to city structure is interesting. Yet it does not impinge on the experience of movement and vision through the city. Like the new rationalists, Agrest and Gandelsonas based their strategy on the premise that 'the American city is the modern city', with the belief that the gridiron system of streets is the city's main asset. The computer-generated analytical drawings of Des Moines, referred to by Gandelsonas as a 'de-layering', suggested a shift in the downtown street grid, defining the axis between the state capitol and the business district.

Koetter, Kim and Associates had a different approach in the Asbury Park waterfront proposal in New Jersey, but parallel to the work of Agrest and Gandelsonas, they also thought that urban design should be used to reinforce street life and the integration of new development into existing street patterns. Asbury Park was originally an important seaside resort with avenues on axes towards the Atlantic Ocean. In their proposal, they emphasised the street edges and, though it may be seen as romantic thinking, reinforced the former resort function, proposing new entertainment pavilions with arcades and 'light towers' and a reconstructed broadwalk.

The work of Fred Koetter and Susie Kim was further expanded in an article in the Japanese Journal *A+U*:[140] 'In America, what is left of traditional urban patterns – the old city centers – have been transformed into special enclaves of business and selective habitation, or, in the terms of current journalistic usage [1993] – theme parks for yuppies'. They continue: 'Many attempts in recent times to redefine the terms of the city, to illustrate the "new urbanism" . . . have failed to result in any comprehensive models or results'.[141] Whether this was fulfilled or not is open to question. Certainly, the East London proposals for the Limehouse Urban Infill and the Surrey Quays could be regarded as a monument to conservative politics of the time, corporate greed and the elimination of deeply rooted communities. Koetter and Kim do acknowledge this, however, in saying that typical modes of development had resulted in patterns of isolated and aggressive self-interest and that the public structure of the city in theorems of social and spatial meaning had been reduced to a barren and pathetic social reminder. Their laudable goals for 're-establishing in East London reasonable and salubrious places of human endeavor, a celebration of public commitment and private opportunity' might be seen as empty promises, given the increasing divisiveness of British society (or, for that matter, society in the US) with the growing and alarming gap between its high-income and low-income members. Such divisions cannot be mended by physical planning alone.

A more rational argument could be made for the Boston plan described as Little Cities within the City. Historically the American city had presented itself as a composite of 'little cities', such as New York with its Greenwich Village, SoHo, Little Italy and Chinatown, and thus Boston had its Back Bay, Beacon Hill, North End, Chinatown, Bay Village and South

End. The imaginative proposal by the authors to unite some of these disparate elements was praiseworthy. The urban design plan for Allston Landing was a light industry-based mixed-use development on a 15-hectare (38-acre) site situated along the Charles River, adjacent to the Harvard Business School. It created a series of interrelated spaces giving spatial focus to the site, and provided connections from the presently isolated community to the more developed parts of the city. The urban design guidelines established controls for the development of primary public spaces and promoted development flexibility within the parcels.

It is interesting to note here that graphically there were strong similarities between the early analytical diagrams of Gandelsonas for the Boston peninsula and the three-dimensional structure diagrams of Koetter and Kim.

ALTERNATIVE URBAN DESIGN SYSTEMS

In 1990, Skidmore, Owings and Merrill of Chicago published a series of urban design plans that introduced the use of computer applications in urban design.[142] In the introduction, the firm stated that:

> The computer allows effective analyses of a virtually unlimited number of alternative shapes, forms and massings to be studied. Perhaps even more importantly, it allows the urban designer, as well as the client and the public, to enter the space being studied and/or created together to facilitate interactive discussion and evaluation.

In the description of their urban design systems, Skidmore, Owings and Merrill indicate that hitherto the acceptance and application of computer technology focused mostly on areas of architectural detailing, repetition and mathematical calculation. But during the 1980s, computer applications to urban design and urban planning in general created a need for software and hardware specifically intended to analyse and evaluate the urban spatial environment. The computer could thus provide for the unique issues arising from the complexities of urban problems.

The key element to urban design applications was the ability to physically and three-dimensionally place the designer, the client and, ultimately, the public into the space being analysed and evaluated. Skidmore, Owings and Merrill recognised that this design process utilised plans, hand-drawn perspectives and architectural models, but that these were seen as having limited success in approximating the intended 'sense of place'. Unlike an architectural medium that communicates the intention of a particular design, the ability to physically represent in three dimensions was originally limited to hand-drawn three-dimensional plans, which could be manipulated to communicate a false sense of spatial relationships. Thus, architecturally constructed models of balsa, plywood, Plexiglas and hardwood created a miniaturised version of the proposal, which though endearing, often belied the reality of the final built structure.

The ability to accurately simulate any and all views (perspectives) of urban design solutions gave the designer an invaluable tool that could evaluate historically important settings, vistas (or what are popularly known as 'new corridors') as well as pedestrian-level scale, daylight and air rights implications and other relevant analyses in plan and section experienced by entering the space as a user. The computer's ability to animate the urban landscape, therefore, gave the profession one of its most important urban design tools for the future.

One of the more dramatic examples of this technique was a study by Skidmore, Owings, and Merrill for a downtown site analysis along the Chicago River. The proposal for a major office building on the Jaymont site used three-dimensional computer images to identify critical elements of the urban

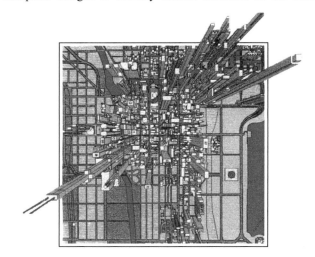

COMPUTER APPLICATIONS
in
URBAN DESIGN

Skidmore, Owings & Merrill
Chicago

1990

Computer applications in urban design (1990), Skidmore, Owings and Merrill.

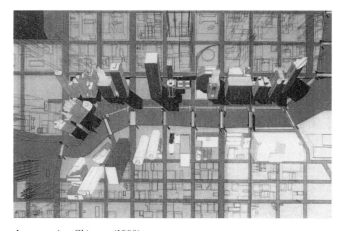

Jaymont site, Chicago (1990), Skidmore, Owings and Merrill.

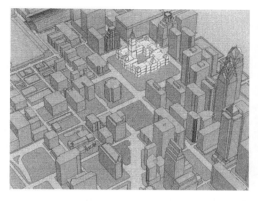

Philadelphia view corridor study (1988), Skidmore, Owings and Merrill.

Existing View from Museum View Corridor 1

Hypothetical Form for Skyline Silhouette

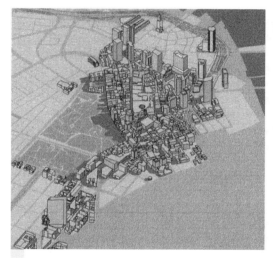

Rowes Wharf, Boston, Massachusetts (1990), Skidmore, Owings and Merrill.

design context and provide a variety of views into and from the site. Through the urban design analysis, it was determined that the architecture for the parcel should respond to three basic urban design issues or layers: 1) the formal monochromatic edge of Wacker Drive, 2) Clark Street as a major entry into the Loop, and 3) the silhouettes that would provide these buildings with an image and identity with the downtown. The layers were studied and evaluated according to the site's unique interpretation. Massing studies explored potential development scenarios using a zoning analysis to calculate the maximum floor area ratio (FAR) with the buildable area of the site. They also determined the required parking and loading capacities for a variety of building configurations defined by the Chicago zoning ordinance.

A parallel study by Skidmore, Owings and Merrill was Rowes Wharf in Boston for the Beacon Companies. Located in Boston Harbor, the proposed private development of offices, condominiums, hotels, restaurants, shops and parking was also intended to create new downtown public space. The Boston Midtown/Cultural District study, commissioned by the Boston Redevelopment Authority, produced a master plan, urban analysis and design guidelines for the Midtown office and theatre district. The overall district plan created a guide for the growth of the area from a citywide perspective and used (then) state-of-the-art computer technology for environmental analyses and massing studies for twenty separate land parcels. This included shadow studies and analyses of building heights and massing from critical viewpoints in the city. The Boston Redevelopment Authority also commissioned the firm to study South Boston and provide a master plan for the overall framework and guidelines for a multi-district area to include the Boston waterfront, Historic Wharf District, and South Boston neighbourhoods, as well as existing maritime industrial uses. The consensus plan resulting from the study involved many Boston residents' groups as well as over a hundred manufacturers, businesses and local and regional authorities.

THE FUTURE OF THE SYSTEMS CITY

Alongside the evolution of urban design systems with their increasingly sophisticated use of three-dimensional computer graphics, movement systems were to become equally sophisticated. It was the city of Portland, Oregon, that was to serve as the role model for integrated city planning and public transportation in the US. From the 1970s onwards the city replanned its vehicular and pedestrian circulation and established a light rail transit system serving the suburbs to downtown. Pedestrian precincts, which were introduced in many other cities during that time, though many of these did not succeed, were an outstanding success in Portland. A riverfront park was created, downtown streets were repaved in brick and transformed into transitways, and new public parks were established.

This public investment generated more retail shopping in downtown Portland, including the establishment of a prestigious Nordstrom store and investment by the Rouse Company in the conversion of redundant old buildings into a galleria, and the opening of Saks Fifth Avenue. All of this was achieved against a background of neither population growth nor economic growth, which had been experienced in many cities elsewhere on the West Coast. The construction of an inner expressway loop in 1973 eliminated the need for the major Harbor Drive expressway along the Willamette River and the Harbor Drive was transformed into McCall Waterfront Park. The use of the interstate highway fund reservation financed the suburban light rail system and the eleven-block pedestrian transit mall that opened in 1977.[143]

In the eleven blocks along Fifth and Sixth Avenues, the landscaping is impressive, with new trees, flower planting, fountains, sculptures and brick paving. The transit system is free to riders anywhere within the 300 blocks that form the core of downtown Portland. Buses connect with this core, linking the entire metropolitan area with television monitors displaying timetables and routes in each bus shelter. The original 24-kilometre (15-mile) light rail system, with 27 stations, connected with suburban Gresham. According to statistics, the use of mass transit increased from 10 per cent of the population in 1971 to 25 per cent in 1978, with a growth in the downtown work force from 50,000 in 1960 to 80,000 in 1980.[144] Since that time, the expansion of the transit system has stimulated the growth of new inner-city neighbourhoods for middle-income families, changing the daily patterns of people walking to local shops and using the transit system to get to work.

Though some second- and third-tier cities, like Cincinnati, are still hesitant regarding the introduction of light rail systems, many others, such as Cleveland, San Jose, San Diego and Denver have adopted them with alacrity and subsequent success.

The introduction of light rail in San Francisco may be seen as something of an anomaly. The ancient cable-car system in the city centre was threatened with closure in the late 1970s and early 1980s; however, a public outcry resulted in its preservation. The Bay Area Rapid Transit System (BART) has always been one of the great tourist attractions of the city and it is now designated a National Historic Landmark. Constructed during the 1970s, it has become one of the most effective transit systems in the US, linking Daly City south of San Francisco, through the city itself, via a tunnel beneath San Francisco Bay, with Oakland and Berkeley to the northwest and Fremont to the southeast. An extension is currently under construction to extend the Daly City route to San Francisco International Airport. The surface light rail system is comparatively new[145] and provides short-distance rides within the city itself.

In Contra Costa County, five suburban communities flourished during the 1980s with a growth in office space from 353,020 square metres (3.8 million square feet) in 1980 to 3 million square metres (32.5 million feet) by 1990. The suburban communities included Walnut Creek, San Ramon, Concord, Pleasant Hill and Pleasanton. These are connected both by the freeway system and BART to San Francisco and Oakland, and each has a well-defined form. McGovern identifies these as 'edge cites',[146] though this is probably not exact. 'Edge cities' in Garreau's terms are ex-urban communities, usually located beyond peripheral beltways and served only by

Proposed magnetic levitation rapid transit, Bradley International Airport

expressways or interstate highways: the communities in the Bay Area are served by a highly efficient public transit system and perform in a quite different way.

One of the more interesting facts about the introduction of light rail systems in the US (of which there were more than 30 by 1999) is that contrary to economic predictions, the intrusion of light rail was not detrimental to property values. Recently constructed light rail systems such as that in St. Louis had produced interesting property values near to station stops in the suburbs. Far from the declining residential property values during the 1990s, new housing developments near (within a 10-minute walk) these station stops have shown escalating prices above the national average. Nancy Houston, regional director of the Florida Department of Transportation for Central Florida, affirms that light rail is fast and efficient reaching speeds of up to 105 kph (65 mph) and carrying 420 passengers on a three-car train with one driver[147] (though newer versions are driverless – entirely computer controlled with smart-card entry). Houston suggests that it would require eight buses, each with its own driver, to provide the same carrying capacity (equivalent to a six-lane freeway) at far slower speeds. The trains can operate at five-minute intervals with crossing paths every 2½ minutes during peak hours.

There are also more exotic proposals for public transport, including former MIT research scientist Henry Kolm's magnetic levitation (MAGLEV) train system. The fifty-ton vehicle he proposed would use magnetism, not aerodynamics, to lift the vehicle six inches from the ground.[148] Such a system would have little relevance to city transit but perhaps a great deal of relevance to inter-city travel. MAGLEV is by no means new; its roots extend back to research in the early 1950s at the Manchester University Institute of Technology in England, and since that time the idea has been developed in Germany and France. In 1991, Senator Daniel Patrick Moynihan of New York

inserted a $725 million provision for MAGLEV development in the $151 billion highway bill during the last days of the former Bush administration.

Japanese test tracks in Southwest Japan by the Railway Technical Research Institute in the Miyazake Prefecture have tested a vehicle that can run at 500 kph (310 mph) and carry 10,000 people per hour in trains of 14 cars long. Envisaged for the busy Tokyo–Osaka route, this would replace the 'bullet' trains introduced into service in 1964. Its linear synchronous motor employs alternating current to generate a magnetic wave that travels along with the vehicle. These time-varying fields interact with vehicle magnets to push and pull the vehicle along.

The impact of such a system on inter-city travel is obvious. Travelling from one city centre to another at such speeds could make air travel for these routes, with its attendant delays, almost obsolete.

In Europe the French Train á Grand Vitesse (TGV) has already carried millions of passengers at top speeds approaching 320 kph (200 mph). Indeed, across the Continent inter-city travel by train, including the more modest high-speed trains in the UK that average 200 kph (125 mph), has proved faster and more efficient than using the motorways.

However, new prototypes for inter-city travel, quite different from those described above, have emerged more recently. The concept of personal rapid transit (PRT) is relatively new. J. Edward Anderson, president and CEO of Taxi 2000 of Minneapolis suggests that PRT solves the problem of precise longitudinal control of vehicles following predetermined time-varying speeds and position.[149] He says that the control of vehicles of close headway of 0.5 seconds is different from, but no less rigorous than, that of conventional railways, and refers to the control strategy as an 'asynchronous point follower'. This requires no clock synchronisation, is flexible in unusual conditions and requires minimum manoeuvring and minimum software. Wayside zone controllers have their own memory with manoeuvre equations the same as the on-board computers in each unit.

Anderson's paper describes the problem of closed-loop automatic longitudinal control of a single vehicle following a guideway at specified time-varying speed and positions. The PRT, he proposes, would control a large fleet of three-passenger vehicles operating on a fractional-second headway, merging in and out of stations and between separate branches in a network of guideways with safety, comfort and dependability. The simplest interchange is a Y, with either two lines entering and one exiting or vice versa. Such an interchange gives the least visual impact at any point. The Aerospace Corporation, in its prototype, used two-in, two-out multilevel interchanges that allowed vehicles to diverge first and then merge. The three-passenger vehicles are driverless and computer controlled with smart-cards to predetermine users' routes in much the same way that they would use a conventional taxi.

In railway practice, according to Anderson, if a conventional train is to stop instantaneously, the train behind must be able to stop within a short enough distance to avoid collision. He describes a journey on the PRT as follows:

> Let's join a group traveling together to the same destination by choice. We either have a magnetically coded ticket with the destination recorded on it because we take the same trip every day, or we must approach a ticket machine to punch in the destination, pay a fare and receive a ticket. With a valid ticket we approach the forward-most available vehicle in a line of vehicles and insert a ticket into the stopped and ready vehicle. This action flashes the origin and destination station to a central computer that has in its memory the estimated arrival times of all vehicles moving through the system. If our vehicle is expected to arrive at its destination at a time when the station is full and cannot receive a vehicle, we are informed that we must wait a specified time before we can try again.[150]

The Rayteon Corporation completed a test-engineering model in June 1997 on a 0.5-kilometre (0.3-mile) test track with three simulated stations in Marlborough, Massachusetts.

The concept of 'transit villages', however, is not new and relates not only to the theories of the new urbanism but back to Ebenezer Howard's ideas of a century ago in his proposals for garden cities orbiting London, protected by greenbelts and connected to inter-municipal rail tracks.[151] Although Back Bay, Boston, Riverside, Chicago and Roland Park in Baltimore introduced early streetcar neighbourhoods depending on pedestrian access to transit for downtown employment or neighbourhood services, these were largely constructed before the widespread use of the motor car. Europe, according to Robert Server, provides better, more recent examples, with interlinked communities in metropolitan regions such as Stockholm served by rapid transit. In 1990, 38 per cent of residents and 53 per cent of workers in Stockholm used transit systems from the new towns. Nevertheless, in San Francisco, those using the BART system with no free parking account for nine out of ten work trips.[152] For trips to secondary urban centres like Oakland and Berkeley, half of all commuters travel by BART. The signing of California's Transit Village Act (AB3152) in September 1994 was an important step towards promoting the transit village and included special legislation for the assembly of land and tax increment privileges as well as a density bonus of a minimum of 50 per cent.

Architecturally, the resurgence in the use of public rail transportation has resulted in some well-designed stations, for example the new MTA line developed in Boston during the late 1980s has produced some notable buildings.[153] The Orange Line within a single right-of-way is a new rapid transit line almost 8 kilometres (5 miles) long, uniting a commuter line with the long-distance Amtrak. Its effect is enhanced by the landscape forming an unbroken linear green park, extending from the city centre to Forest Hills and the adjacent Franklin Park. It forms an addition to the networks of parks, referred to as the Emerald Necklace and designed by Frederick Law Olmstead. Each of the nine stations along the line is designed by a different architect (similar to the extension of the Jubilee underground line in London, which included such architects as Norman Foster). The stations act as interchanges between local buses, Amtrak and rapid transit.

Of these stations, perhaps the most notable in terms of architectural design are Back Bay station by Kallman, McKinnel and Wood, and Ruggles station by Stull and Lee. Back Bay brings many disparate functions together in its major attractive concourse with its great roof of laminated timber arches evoking the grandeur of Victorian railway stations like St. Pancras in London. Like York station in the north of England, the concourse curves, tracing the century-old curve of the rail line beneath it. The ticket lobby has the same magnificence of Grand Central station in New York but as urban design, it is the external twin brick tower (which is merely an air exhaust ventilation shaft) with its divided shaft and pedimental truss that serves as a major visual marker of Back Bay's townscape. Its vivid juxtaposition with Boston Public Library, designed by Charles McKim, acts as a visual link or picture framework with the John Hancock Tower some distance away. Robert Campbell considers the architecture to be eclectic, though not, like so much postmodernism, pastiche. It is in the same tradition of heroic architecture as Kallman, McKinnel and Knowles' first design some thirty years earlier – the new Boston City Hall.

THE URBAN LANGUAGE AND THE COGNITIVE CITY

The impact of new ideas and theories such as deconstruction during this last decade perhaps overshadowed parallel movements of architecture theory which continued not only the development of the understanding of city imagery but also of advocacy planning and community design.

Though complex, linguistic theory has major applications in urban design. The distinguished American writer on the English language William Safire suggests that the ideas of icon (used extensively in architectural language) have their roots 'in semiotics, the theory of the relationships of signs in language . . . an icon is a sign chosen to stand for its object because it looks like or triggers an association with, the thing it represents'.[154]Safire points out that a gas (petrol) station may have a star as its sign but, unless you are a Texan, you are unlikely to associate the symbol with the name Texaco. However, the symbol used by the Shell Oil Company is familiar to all and is an icon of semiotics.

The city as a cultural investment tends to be imbued with meaning for its inhabitants and is similar to a language in terms of syntactic structure, or through the study of the meaning of signs as in semiotics.[155]

Mario Gandelsonas is a leading theorist on the visual understanding of the city. The Urban Text[156] shows how Gandelsonas adopts many of Sigmund Freud's ideas of floating attention to urban systems. The computer-generated images produce a 'de-layering' process as a way of reading the plan of the city. This analysis is particularly relevant to the traditional gridiron plan of the American city. It reflects the design process itself with the overlapping of different layers, which in turn create the final architectural composition. The Urban Text has as its focus central Chicago, and explores the spatial relationships between the physical and abstract realities of the Chicago River. Gandelsonas uses a one-mile grid and its subdivisions; inevitably, there are anomalies and contradictions in the grid. More controversially, Gandelsonas identifies an invisible, implied wall that divides north Chicago and south Chicago, or rather, white Chicago from black Chicago. Whether the de-layering process of the diagonal and orthogonal streets scrutinised by Gandelsonas produces answers is, perhaps, debatable.

The study is divided into ten basic elements, referred to as Series 1–10. All are computer generated. In Series 1, the two drawings describe the one-mile grid of the Chicago River in a combination of three layers. In Series 2, four quadrants are represented in which the regularity of three quadrants are recognised in contrast to the chaotic nature of the fourth, which reveals a diagonal organisation. In Series 4, the de-layering of the four quadrants in the horizontal (east–west) streets and vertical (north–south) streets and the diagonal streets contrast with what Gandelsonas calls 'leftovers', implying that the city

could be seen as a series of overlapping formal layers with internal consistency. In Series 5, the Invisible Walls elucidate an element not perceptible in the 'real' plan. These walls are horizontal and vertical streets creating discontinuities in the ghost of the Chicago River, and relate to the implied ethnic separations between north and south Chicago. The only three-dimensional computer-generated graphic images are in Series 10. It is not made clear why this was the only study in the series to be produced three-dimensionally, however 'City Views' does provide a more vivid understanding of the city of Chicago, exposing the landscape resulting from the extrusion of the diagonals and the irregular streets and valley: a city of voids as opposed to solids.

Catherine Ingraham, in her essay in Gandelsonas' The Urban Text, refers to Freud's floating attention of the analyst in that the architect or urban designer looks with a floating gaze at the city's 'data' in order to understand the city's morphology and ideology. Suggesting that the architect is normally hypnotised by the regularity of the grid, the failures of the grid become more provocative. Joan Copjec, in her essay, said that there was no consensus of opinion about whether the regular and systematic disposition of streets 'logicizes' space[157] and renders it intelligible, or creates a monotonous sameness that detracts from spatial intelligibility. John Whiteman[158] refers to the practice of drawing an urban design, suggesting that the city itself in its entirety cannot be made the object of a designer's attention or covered by a single design action. Lacking control, urban design is often considered to be futile, 'but the drawing may act as an alternate object in the debates about urban development and act as a surrogate for the city itself. The drawing may revise the city itself'. Though perhaps unrealistic, he says that 'the drawing may actually enter the city and act as a thesaurus from which senses the city can be retrieved at a later date'.[159]

Prior to the publication of The Urban Text, Gandelsonas delivered a lecture in London for the Annual Discourse at the Royal Institute of British Architects (RIBA).[160] He described the development of Boston (beginning in 1986), as revealing the 'head' of the city as opposed to the 'neck'. The head is a European-type fabric; the neck is made out of American grids, overlapped by different types of collisions. The head had 'been

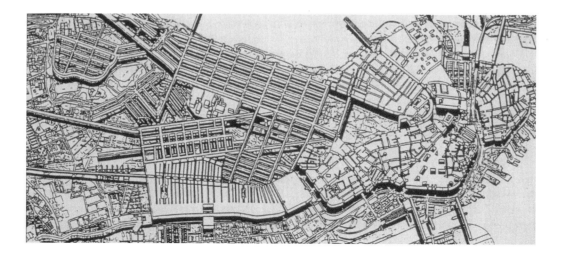

Visual/structural analysis of Boston Peninsula, Gandelsonas RIBA lecture (1989).

surgically operated on leaving different sectors separated by open spaces, fields and buildings, so presenting an alternative fabric space; a fabric field which explains the nature of this city transformed by the urban interventions of the sixties. The drawings describe the radial-concentric nature of Boston, showing that the head and the neck belong to the same structure'.[161]

Throughout this contemporary history of urban design, one name appears many times. Philip Thiel, now Professor Emeritus at the University of Washington, Seattle, began his academic career as a student of Kevin Lynch at the Massachusetts Institute of Technology. In 1990, prior to the publication of his major work *People, Paths and Purposes* (see below), Thiel published an essay, 'Starting Off on the Right Foot'.[162] In architectural education, he suggests that not only the time-honoured precepts of 'commodity', 'firmness' and 'delight should be recognised, but that the end result should be the satisfaction of the users.

In such an architectural education structure, small-scale problems with explicit performance specifications and objective acceptance criteria would be grouped in the three subject areas, quoted above, with what Thiel described as the rubric of technology, behaviour and communication (which involves visual perception). This would be carried out within the traditional university setting of three ten-week sessions (or quarters). Each ten-week segment would be regarded as an independent entity involving concepts or principles with a specific problem or exercise to provide a case study with a group review and evaluation. Thus under the category of Firmness (Technology) the first problem might include shop procedures, the use of standard hand or power tools, safety and maintenance procedures. Another problem concerning visual representation would examine the availability of graphic media. Under the heading Commodity (to which he gives the subheading 'Behaviour') Thiel cites user participation, performance specification and simulation or remodelling. The more complex or even contradictory term Delight concerns the visual field, basic pattern areas, visual attributes and visual communication using different types of graphic media. Reference is made to Gestalt laws, colour attributes of the Munsell System, colour expression and colour harmony.

In a subsequent paper,[163] Thiel takes the theme further, suggesting that public evaluation of interventions in the physical environment now involves the public to an unprecedented extent as participants in the design process. Thiel believes that such participation is not necessarily regressive in reducing design decisions to the lowest common denominator and he rejects the concept of design review, describing it as: 'the charade of the so-called architectural "honor awards" in which committees of architects' peers view artful unpeopled photographs and small scale drawings as the evidence for their design merit'.[164]

Thiel describes discrete categories of user participation in the design process: the resident, the employee, the customer, the manager, the janitor, the servicer, the neighbour and the passerby. Of course, other control groups in this process have already been described in this volume – the designers (architects, urban designers, city planners, highway engineers),

residents of the city, elected city officials, visitors including tourists and those attending conventions and sports. Given such a matrix, Thiel devises a system within a 24-hour period summarising the human presence in the project.

This research culminated in his major work *People, Paths and Purposes*.[165] The study is divided into a number of sections including 'User Participation', 'Experience Notation', 'Environment Notation', 'Environtectural Theater', 'Experiential Envirotecture', as well as 'Techniques'. The research extends back as far as 1951, commencing with an urban design thesis at MIT, and is one of the most comprehensive in notation analysis. Drawing from extensive study in Japan in collaboration with Kiyosi Seike, and financed by the Graham Foundation for Advanced Studies in the Fine Arts and the Nippon Kotsu Bunka Kyokai, the book unites analytical techniques of urban space exploration in Japan with parallel studies in the US.

Notations are described thus: 'We are concerned here with the development of systems of graphic notation for (a) the multipartite polyphonic description of actual (or proposed) real-time sequences of concurrent actions, feeling, and thoughts associated with given behavior patterns and given users and (b) the real-time sequential description of multi-sensory physical environments as experienced . . . in movement along given routes'.[166]

In a description of the user-participant condition, Thiel uses an illustration of a cube divided into four quadrants: the summation, on-line, real, virtual. These are divided into free (active) and constrained (passive). Thus the real includes the pedestrian and the vehicle driver; the virtual is the new technology of the holograph, the head-mounted TV camera and the computer, but the passive is the vehicle passenger, traditional film and slide shows.[167]

However, the most important section of Thiel's work is in Chapter 6, 'Environment Notation'.[168] Reference is made to the phenomenological frame of reference by establishing user-participant coordinates. Thiel states that with the phenomenological experience of the environment, the representation of the environment is seen from an egocentric point of view. User-participant reference coordinates may be seen as a mobile transducer moving through variable fields. Since the human transducer elements are inevitably asymmetrical, there is differentiation between before and behind, left or right, above or below. For these reasons it seems necessary to establish a set of reference coordinates for the instantaneous position and heading (direction) of the subject mapping the environment: 'We assume first that the ego is localized at the point midway between the eyes and then provide a set of orthogonal coordinates between this point for the most general condition: in motion along a path in three dimensions'.[169] 'Fish-eye' projections, either through a camera lens or substitute drawing, give a form of a 360-degree representation of the immediate surroundings. It is, however, artificial since the human eye is unable to operate in this manner.

In 'User-Participant Orientation',[170] reference is made to the original notational methods of Kevin Lynch, though these were limited to physical, perceptible objects and patterns with just six iconic symbols of path, edge, district, node, landmark and sign (or symbol). However, in user-participant orientation this fairly rigid (or simplistic) terminology may be expanded, as Thiel's accompanying diagrams suggest. These include position indicators – the movement of the head (eyes) including ahead, 90 degrees on left, 60 degrees on right, directly above, coordinated with a 'time-line' of 'district crossed', 'edge followed', 'path followed', 'node reached' and so on. The extension, then, of Lynch's static symbols into 'space-time' was a major step forward. An illustration of such a comprehensive analysis of route in linear, graphic form expands this notion with clarity.[171]

COMMUNITY DESIGN AND DEVELOPMENT

The comprehensive research of Philip Thiel in the perception of the city through user-participation was linked to the continued growth of advocacy planning and citizen participation in the 1990s. The Community and Urban Design Centers, which had burgeoned during the late 1960s and early 1970s went through a hiatus, only to re-emerge in stronger though different forms in the 1990s.

A link between visual perception and community development can be seen in the seminal works of Spiro Kostoff. Kostoff's brilliant career at the College of Environmental Design at the University of California, Berkeley, ended prematurely with his death in December 1991. His last book, *The City Shaped,*[172] published just before his death, examined urban patterns and meanings. It spanned many periods of history and was by no means confined to the US. Also among his achievements was the television series 'America by Design'.

The City Shaped was a book of immense horizons. Like Gallion before him, Kostoff used the term 'urban patterns' to establish subheadings of 'The Grid', 'Organic Patterns', 'The City as Diagram' and 'The Urban Skyline'. According to Kostoff, such patterns could be used effectively in urban analysis. Decision and order applied to apparently organic plans, though whether he implied that this involved citizen participation is not clear. Yet in discussing the gridiron of the American cities he pointed out that the geometric system was constantly reorganised with the changing impact of public input. In concert with public involvement, Kostoff did not believe that the initial urban form of a city created limits to the forces of change, and cites a variety of historical precedents in Europe, such as the Roman military cities in England and the Norman builders of Wales, the Spanish conquerors in Mexico and, later, the imposition of gridiron systems with the construction of the railways in the Midwest US during the nineteenth and early twentieth centuries.

Kostoff's final work, posthumously published, *The City Assembled,* took his arguments a step further.[173] This work, edited by Greg Castillo, continued his investigation of how cities were established, and connected the language and forms of urban structures. The question of city edges, streets and public places is addressed within typological analysis and visual form. But Kostoff also saw them as an expression of particular societies. Like Lynch in his last work, *Wasting Away*, Kostoff had an equally uncanny vision of the present and near future.

Although it certainly did not pervade his career, Kostoff's pessimism is evident in a description of cycles of destruction and reconstruction whether by war or natural disasters. Urban design is placed within the structure of political and economic power as well as within a sociological matrix.

The social matrix has been key in the work of William Morrish and Catherine Brown at the University of Minnesota in Minneapolis. Morrish and Brown created a new type of community design centre, which was praised by Herbert Muschamp writing in the *New York Times* in 1994.[174] The two met in 1976 as students at Harvard's Graduate School of Design, and went on to establish the Design Center for American Urban Landscape (DCAUL) in 1988, addressing social and environmental issues and funded initially by the Dayton Hudson Foundation. Citing its Phoenix public art plan, Muschamp said of the Design Center that though its work was on 'big picture lines' it was also along pragmatic microcosmic lines.

One of the centre's notable studies was 'The Fourth Coast: An Expedition on the Mississippi River'.[175] In the summer of 1990, Morrish conducted a group of twenty students and thirty professionals and scholars on one-week visits on an eight-week trip up the length of the Mississippi River, starting at the mouth and finishing at the river's source in Lake Hasca in Minnesota. The combination of teaching, scholarship and practice set new standards for the evolving community design centres. Morrish considered this to be a response to the contemporary condition of urban design in the US, in terms of both built form and theoretical studies. The concern was with the land at the river's edges, constantly subject to disastrous flooding that had never been properly addressed. He rejected the European-influenced 'figure-ground' studies in creating public space. Simple geometric forms such as the American grid ignore the geographic structure of the nation's landscape – a powerful design resource, which, if utilised in the early process of urban design could create a genuine framework for place and could counteract the current sprawl of the urban landscape. Morrish's plea was for a broader definition of urban design to include the heterogeneous environment.

The Mississippi is, of course, the longest river in North America, some 4,100 kilometres (2,552 miles) in length, and such an expedition was an awesome task. The starting point at Pilot Tow, Louisiana, a small community mostly standing on stilts in the flood waters, provided the southern urban gateway. The 'Fourth Coast' is described as a waterway joining the western edge of the East Coast with the eastern edge of the West Coast – an element of confrontation and transformation. St. Louis forms a gigantic interchange of the Ohio, Missouri, Illinois and Mississippi Rivers. In each of the smaller river towns, the length of the Mississippi, most were organised into gridded blocks, often oriented towards the river. At eye level, within the river corridor, Morrish said that 'the points that appear on the horizon are the result of a collision of the plan grid organization of buildings and gardens and the topography of the river valley ... church steeples, county courthouse domes, industrial smokestacks and parks carved from the outcroppings of river bluffs'.[176]

The theme was taken further in 1996 with the publication of *Civilizing Terrains*.[177] A collection of forty-nine beautifully drawn sketches illustrates the connection between prehistoric and ancient structures with the immediate landscape. In his introduction, Morrish says that the sketches portray a story concerning the role of the sacred mountain within our formal and spatial thinking. South Mountain, above the city of Phoenix, Arizona, is described as a powerful geomorphic landscape that no longer plays a role in the city's morphology. Yet 1,500 years ago, the valley was inhabited by the Hohokam Indians, and the sketchy remains indicate the presence of major irrigation systems and village centres on earthen platforms, elevating the settlements skywards. Reference is also made to Frank Lloyd Wright's appraisal of the Arizona desert as an astounding landscape with natural masonry rising from the mesa floor.

Morrish laments the loss of meaning in such places, for example the vantage point from the mountain which was established by the citizens of a former community as their terrain or place. The loss, too, of the sacred mountain as a utopian place and finally the idea of earth, mountain, place, site and centre as self-supporting and sustaining entities are also mentioned.

Though the examples stretch across the world, drawing from ancient Japan, Europe, the Middle East and South America, the American-Indian mounds of the Mississippi Valley and Eastern seaboard suggest a connection with earlier studies. These earth mounds once served religious and celebratory functions as well as boundary demarcation. For example the serpent snake mound in Ohio parallels the shape of a life-giving river.

In contrast with this inspection of vast early man-made landscapes, the microcosm would be the publication of 'Public Art Works: the Arizona Models'.[178] This study, funded by the City of Phoenix, the Dayton Hudson Foundation, the Arizona Commission for the Arts and the DCAUL, and published in 1992, was innovative in being one of the first comprehensive public art master plans. It went beyond the usual framework of public art (usually sculpture) in public spaces in its study on the entire urban infrastructure and was seen as a language that could transform the ordinary into the extraordinary.

Such a public arts master plan presented new challenges, including the wider application of the term 'infrastructure'. It contained formal elements similar to, or parallel with public works infrastructure systems, and the cultural infrastructure recognised historic urban patterns, urban topography and the public cognitive map. Stormwater drainage was seen as a primary concern in Arizona, providing on the one hand impressive spectacles but on the other major functional problems. The cognitive map is more ethereal as an 'invisible language of the imagination'. The drawings were divided into five spatial components: water systems, park and open space systems, vehicular systems, landmark systems and pedestrian systems. In the final stages of the study, the urban design framework for Phoenix was created within 'working zones', described as natural points of concentration and based on new capital construction projects incorporating the Per Cent for Art elements used in other American cities. These focused on highly visible spaces involving both public and private expenditure. Fifteen working zones were designated and included downtown

pedestrian paths, baseline scenic parkway, Central Avenue from South Mountain Park to Arizona Canal, village cores, neighbourhood parks, mountain parks and canals.

The DCAUL also concerned itself with neighbourhood planning. In 1994, *Planning to Stay* by William Morrish and Catherine Brown[179] addressed the retention and preservation of existing city residential neighbourhoods. Almost a manifesto, it implicitly rejects unfettered individualism. Neal Pierce in his foreword says that the study is a radical assertion of the polar opposite. A neighbourhood need not succumb to special interest groups, city bureaucracies or politicians, as the residents and merchants can map their own destiny. The study focuses on the neighbourhood issues – physical, social and economic – of the twin cities of St. Paul and Minneapolis.

The Design Center's framework uses a vocabulary of five physical features and five organising themes. The physical features are:

- Homes and Gardens – the spaces where we rear our families, often sharing spaces with friends and neighbours.
- Community Streets – lanes that supply an equable balance between motor cars and pedestrians but provide significant social spaces for sidewalk conversations, walking the dog, and strolling the baby.
- Neighbourhood niches – not downtown but rather places where neighbours can buy basic goods and services as well as occasional speciality items. These might include haircuts and hardware, pizza and pastries and birthday cards.
- Anchoring institutions – the cultural, educational and social traditions such as the elementary school, parish church, library, and community recreation centre.
- Public Gardens – distinct from major city parks in that they are smaller and allow people of many ages, ethnic origins and economic circumstances to gather together.

The five organising themes included:

- Location – the relationship of individual homes and other physical features. St. Paul Cathedral was seen as an integral feature of its neighbourhood but also a visible symbol of the entire city.
- Scale – important in sensing whether a building is too large, a store is too distant, streets too busy, paths too narrow or the playground inadequate.
- Mix – a constant theme in this volume, concerned with the uses and activities that make a neighbourhood liveable.
- Time – a more abstract concept including day and night routines, seasonal changes and a sense of continuity.
- Movement – considering accessibility to physical features within the neighbourhood.

Morrish and Brown conclude the study by a checklist entitled 'taking action'.[180] This establishes priorities for neighbourhood groups such as forming discussion meetings, gathering broad community support for the plan and action programme, meeting public officials, non-profit organisations and members of the private sector, as well as the importance of making agreements, arrangements and accommodations including investment strategies.

In the summary, Morrish produces cartoon drawings describing organising, gathering, ordering, making, taking action and sustaining.

A more prescriptive study, 'Making Housing Home',[181] logically follows from the preceding study. A design guide for site planning of housing, it was produced in association with the Minneapolis Public Housing Authority (with Cora McCorvey as executive director) and with many neighbourhood community groups. The study suggests that 'quality housing' is intended to foster a sense of ownership, security and belonging responding to the life-cycle needs of a diverse and changing community. Livable neighbourhoods are seen as 'single family houses on continuous tree-lined, sidewalked streets, interconnected to an extensive system of parks and lakes spread throughout the area'.[182]

In the drawings, the description of the individual house block shows the gradation from front to back, beginning with the street, the boulevard of trees, the sidewalk, the front yard, the front porch, the facade, the interior of the house, the backyard, the garage and, finally, the alley. This, then, is the public-to-private hierarchy of space of the traditional neighbourhood, and not new neighbourhoods where double or triple garages facing the street are the dominant architectural elements.

Natural systems such a topography, soil and vegetation are considered as well as circulation in the network of streets, cycle paths and sidewalks that connect to the surrounding neighbourhood, and proximity to public transportation lines for access to goods, services, amenities and jobs. 'Making Housing Home' was not about the suburbs but about the existing city. The site development guidelines include an appraisal of the immediate neighbourhood subdivided into the private domain (what is mine) – outdoor space, pedestrian walkways, cars and car parking. The quality of life issues – ownership, use, security and image – cross-reference with the physical features of this private domain. Though they may be seen as nostalgic or even romantic, the plea of the design guidelines for a return to community neighbourhood living certainly relates to the wave of the new urbanism subsequently discussed.

A broader view of the city of Minneapolis can be seen in another publication, the result of an invited, limited architectural competition organised by the Cunningham Group of Minneapolis[183] in 1996. Carried out with the support of Paul Farmer, Minneapolis Director of City Planning, the goal was to represent a synthesis of a process and efforts by several Minneapolis public agencies. 'The Minneapolis Riverfront: Vision and Implementation' not only involved local urban designers but also designers from San Diego, Fargo, Santa Monica, New York, Cincinnati and Marina del Rey, as well as the Netherlands.

Though the designation of the Mississippi as an industrial-only corridor began to disappear from 1965 onwards, the potential of the river basin in Minneapolis for residential and commercial development had never been fully realised, much as was the case with the Ohio River basin in Cincinnati. Between 1980 and 1990, the downtown office core of Minneapolis experienced a major expansion of office towers, and the downtown residential population grew from 18,000 to 24,000, with 140,000 working in the downtown area.

The competition study area was anchored on the northwest by the southern tip of Nicollet Island, including land from the original Minneapolis and St. Anthony settlements. The development site faced St. Anthony Falls and extended upstream between the river and Washington Avenue. The land, mostly owned by the city, comprised some 30 hectares (80 acres). The focus for the fourteen firms invited to take part in the competition was on the Central Riverfront Regional Park uniting historical districts on the river with the St. Anthony Falls Heritage Trail.

The intention of the competition was to avoid a single-use ghetto but explore issues of mixed-use and mixed-income groups, mixed working/living quarters, age-integrated communities and cultural, commercial, recreational and educational components, all of which might create a vibrant urban neighbourhood. The model for the Minneapolis study was Amsterdam in the Netherlands: the city's Eastern Harborlands, Ceramique in Maastricht and Kop van Zind in Rotterdam were seen as models of public/private partnerships.

The competition organisers said in their report that all fourteen urban designs linked the city core to the Mississippi River, embracing natural urban and industrial archeology of the river and its banks.[184] Suggestions included extending the river park into the city fabric. All submissions, according to Victor Calliandro of the Cunningham Group, celebrated public access to the river, including public transit as part of the network access, recognising that the universal reliance on the motor car destroyed public parks and the city fabric. Safe streets created safe neighbourhoods with parks and water basins located in each. Calliandro said that 'taken as a group, these proposals suggest a collective vision of a community based on propinquity, where the role of natural elements is integral to the form of the built fabric, where connections are multiple, where convenience is based on the pedestrian's abilities and is supported by amenities and where memory is the springboard to the creation of a unique place'.[185]

Among the entries, Davids-Killory appropriately recognised the replacement of the hierarchy of centre and periphery by a diffuse complex connected by TV cables, telephone wires and computer links. The Netherlands team of Sijoerd Soeters Architecten and Stadsantwerp Urban Design identified three neighbourhood squares, each with its own character, with the boundary between city grid and river valley having broad walkways for city and river views. Parsons and Fernandez-Casteleiro of New York presented a more complex proposal with overlapping city grids not dissimilar from Eisenman's Frankfurt proposals. This included a light rail system connecting the Metrodome with the city and the river with vertical transitions between light rail and the ubiquitous skywalk system of Minneapolis. The most pyrotechnic scheme, visually, was proposed by Shea Architects of Minneapolis with the aim of bringing the Minneapolis riverfront to life, with a marina, water features including fountains and a major waterfall, a Ferris wheel, lighthouse and cable ride as well as a floating stage and water sports park.

Narrow-gauge railway proposal, Cincinnati, Ohio (1994),
David Gosling.

The scheme by David Gosling, John Ferguson and James Foster of Cincinnati and Sheffield, in the UK, recognised that waterfronts are one of America's greatest urban assets. The nature reserve in the north should be preserved with additional trails and a nature learning centre for children. Using the existing railroad rights of way, a narrow gauge railway would cross directly across the falls and traverse the nature reserves. The creation of a linear curve of river islands could enclose a lagoon with housing and shops built on stilts, linked to the mainland by floating bridges. Twin apartment towers, floodlit at night, would create a waterside focal point on the southwest bank, and a landmark tower with radial viewing platforms and laser lights would illuminate the riverfront. River Road would be replaced by a corniche with a landscaped road within a linear park.

In his summary of the competition schemes, Calliandro identified those that met certain goals and objectives and concluded that these were the creation of value faster than costs were increasing, a movement away from 'us' versus 'them', shared ownership and active participation in neighbourhood-based planning.[186]

In neighbourhood participatory planning, a short report in 1994 broke new ground with regard to public information.[187] Most urban design reports had lacked a certain degree of levity and their impact upon citizens has often created a certain lack of response and even resentment. However, this report on planning needs for the Snohomish County Transportation Authority for the Puget Sound Regional Council in Seattle used drawn cartoons to explain the process. The use of cartoons in comic books and newspapers has a distinguished history throughout the twentieth century, for example political cartoons in prominent newspapers have had major influence, particularly through the use of 'speech bubbles'.

Washington State's Puget Sound region is attempting to structure new growth in a way that preserves forest and farmlands and builds strong communities. The strategy of growth management is predicated on the creation of vital urban centres. Such growth would focus on compact, liveable, mixed-use neighbourhoods served by multi-model transportation systems.

Such urban centres would be full-service communities providing transportation connections with housing and lifestyle choices.

The report, through its cartoons, illustrated the evolution of the rapidly growing suburban communities on the outskirts of a metropolitan centre. It featured the mall, convenience centres, business parks and freeway interchanges. The speech bubbles have captions like 'Herb, would you drive the kids to day care? The next bus won't come for an hour'. Or 'Great! Another freeway backup . . . late to work again'. Proposals included the revitalisation of the central city with true mixed-use, pedestrian-oriented centres. Suggesting the development of a plan with the involvement of citizens, business people and developers, the community's goals and objectives would be refined. Captions here included 'Even the kids got in the act' or 'Hey! How about a pedestrian spine connecting transit to the mall?'.

Potential conflict was also reflected in the report, for example the response from the transit authority: 'We can't provide better transit until the ridership goes up', and 'We can't build our new neighbourhood without better transit service. Who will take the first step?', 'Why don't you go first?', 'Oh, I insist, after you'. And, in the city finance department: 'Uh, oh. Sounds like real troubles in the department. Maybe I'd better polish up the old resume', 'Sounds like you got a problem. Say, want to do lunch? Sure'.

This witty way of presenting urgent city planning issues may be seen as a better method of communicating with citizens, replacing the ponderous methods used hitherto.

The clarity and explicit nature of the two studies in community planning described above is contradicted by an important and highly publicised document and exhibition in 1994 – *Urban Revisions: Current Projects for the Public Realm.*[188] Following current fashions in magazine graphic design and typography, this may be seen as a model in obfuscation and opacity. With poor typography in the introductory essays (almost invisible to a reader with mediocre sight) and chaotic overlays, the presentation of this publication virtually negates the important messages of people like Mike Davis, Richard Sennett and Elizabeth Smith. Indeed, the projects in the touring exhibition were equally hard to decipher.

Morris Newman, writing in *Progressive Architecture*[189] said much the same: that viewers of 'Urban Revisions' may wonder what this important show is trying to say. Newman acknowledges, however, that this was, perhaps, the most important contribution to urban thinking in North American museums. He suggests that Michael Rotondi and April Greiman sought to create an enigmatic art installation rather than a public forum of ideas. Such navel-gazing is not uncommon in some East Coast universities. The display of plans, elevations and models appeared without informing spectators what the urban planners were seeking to achieve, and therefore became unintelligible to the lay observer. Virtually all eighteen displays were North American in origin, and the implication that most would eventually be built suggested a potpourri of current urban thinking.

If one can penetrate the chaotic graphics, it is apparent that many of the projects are important in late-twentieth-century urban design, but as Newman pointed out, 'The show has some misfires, such as the ill-conceived Steel Cloud West Coast Gateway by Rashid and Couture (as) a deconstructivist praying mantis that architects propose to set atop an L.A. freeway'.[190] Although he praised the essays by Mike Davis and Richard Sennett, Newman added that there was 'something ultimately ironic about a show that celebrates the reinvention of the city as a place for people and pedestrian movement and yet shows such calculated indifference to its audience. Work dedicated to making the city usable and intelligible deserves an exhibition that does not contradict the values of the projects on display'.[191]

The Central Artery Corridor Plan for Boston by Chan Krieger is notable, as well as that by Michael Sorkin for a proposed military base conversion in the southwestern US and Agrest and Gandelsonas' vision plan for Des Moines. Calthorpe Associates' Region 2040 study for Portland, Oregon is also interesting. But many of these projects (like other urban design proposals) beg the question as to their implementation. The Watts, Los Angeles Uhuru Gardens by Achua, Benzinberg, Stein, BLS Environmental Planning and Design is praiseworthy, as are the other community-based projects in Los Angeles, for example the Greenshaw Neighborhood Plan for South Central, Koreatown and Pico-Union. But will they ever be built?

The implementation of urban design projects is an important issue. In 1993, *Progressive Architecture* published an interesting survey of the first forty years of its design awards programme,[192] stating that, 'In 1953, the editors of P/A had a bright idea that has become an architectural institution. They turned their annual survey of work "on the boards" into a competition and invited some renowned architects to be the judges'.

In reviewing the period between 1954 and 1962, modern architecture (or modernism) had become established as *the* idiom for serious corporate architecture. It is suggested that the triumph of modernism opened new avenues in the arena of urban design, symbolised by the works of Le Corbusier. Urban planning had been viewed as a suspect left-wing political issue, but had begun to flourish under Federal urban renewal programmes. The Boston Back Bay project by Belluschi and others (see Chapter 2), was the First Award-winning project of P/A's first awards programme. Though it was believed to have pioneered mixed-uses and the reuse of old railyards (rather than slum clearance) it was, nevertheless, never built. Neither was Yamasaki, Stonorov and Gruen's plan for the gigantic Gratiot-Orleans, which received a First Award in 1956. On the other hand, Yamasaki's folded-plate concrete structure for the American Concrete Institute in Detroit was constructed after his 1957 award, despite being denounced by some members of the jury. Other built examples included Pietro Belluschi' dormitory development for the Rhode Island School of Design, which reflected the growing popularity of vernacular design, as well as Eero Saarinen's village of gable structures for Concordia College in Fort Wayne, Indiana. The 1961 jury alluded, for the first time, to the term 'new brutalism', as explained by Philip Johnson.

From 1963 to 1972, preservation and contextualism became more important, as reflected in a scheme for an Engineering Sciences Center by a team that included Belluschi and Sasaki.

Best of the built projects was the 1965 award for the Sea Ranch condominiums in California by Moore, Lyndon, Turnbull and Whittaker. On the other hand, DMJM's megastructure Sunset Mountain, with Cesar Pelli as design director, was never built. The political upheaval and urban riots of the late 1960s could be said to represent a growing concern with social and environmental issues, as in Charles Moore and Donlyn Lyndon's built Kresge College at the University of California, Santa Cruz. In 1972, an award went to a 'Don't Build' project on 22 hectares (55 acres) of rolling landscape, representing a counter movement against establishment architecture, one in which the natural environment should be left alone. More bizarre that year was a proposal that involved inmates in the redesign of their own prison.

As the energy crisis emerged in 1973, there was increasing emphasis among juries on 'issues' and, in 1974, the category of research joined architecture and urban design within the *Progressive Architecture* programme. Charles Moore received an urban design citation in 1976 for his built Piazza d'Italia in New Orleans. The previous year, Benjamin Thompson received a citation for the restoration of Faneuil Hall Market in Boston, probably one of the most successful urban renewal projects in the country. Similarly, in urban design, the Inner Harbor in Baltimore by Wallace, McHarg, Roberts and Todd, which received a citation in 1973, became America's first major waterfront renewal project. Yet there was also among the jurors a backlash against urban design, with awards to individual house designs such as Michael Graves' private residence in Pocantico Hills, New York. Those urban design projects that did appear, such as the Community Map in the Hill District of Pittsburgh by Community Design Associates (developed for citizen participation through a 'walk-on map'), seemed to have been designed more for the sake of political expediency.

In the final period of *Progressive Architecture's* awards from 1983 to 1992, architectural design rather than comprehensive urban design seemed to dominate. However, this period did see the emergence of neo-traditionalist urban design, such as Battery Park City, New York, by Cooper, Eckstut and Associates, or Hammond, Beeby and Babka's 1983 design for the Chicago Public Library. More significant in the urban design category of built projects was the proposal for Seaside, Florida, by Duany and Plater-Zyberk.

Deconstruction was reflected in built terms in two internationally significant projects: Peter Eisenman's Wexner Arts Center in Columbus, Ohio, and Bernard Tschumi's Parc de la Villette in Paris. The growing rejection of corporate and individual greed during the latter part of the 1980s was the recognition of socially responsible architects like Davids-Killory for housing developments in Southern California and the Comprehensive Cancer Center in Los Angeles by Morphosis.

Shortly before its demise, *Progressive Architecture* magazine launched a quite different type of awards competition. Published in the October 1992 issue, 'The First Public Realm Competition' coincided with the following month's presidential election, resulting in a change from a conservative to a more liberal administration. In his editorial, Thomas Fisher said that the purpose of the competition was to add to the current political debate about the nation's infrastructure and 'to demonstrate that the design professions have much to contribute to any national reconstruction efforts'.[193]

There were 232 entries and equal awards were given to ten submissions. The distinguished jury included David Lee, partner in the firm of Stull and Lee, Boston, and adjunct professor at Harvard; Harvey Gantt, two-term mayor of Charlotte; Susana Torre, chair of Environmental Design at Parsons School of Design in New York and board member of Architects/Designers/Planners for Social Responsibility; and Robert Yaro, senior vice president of the Regional Plan Association, New York. It was clear that this jury's agenda differed from that of the design juries. According to Fisher, expectations were high, as were the quality and substance of the entries submitted.

There was real complexity in considering the public realm. Submissions dealt with the infrastructure of roads, highways and bridges and, in particular, vacant space under freeways. The integration of new, affordable housing under highway overpasses, within cloverleaves, was also an issue. Recreational space among bridges, highways and dams was considered favourably. Other entries focused on the gigantic and under-utilised spaces in cities such as the 'broken teeth' syndrome of vacant downtown car parks and derelict landscape along railways and canals. Among the more imaginative submissions was a proposal for a series of 'urban follies' containing cooking facilities, showers and toilets to provide the homeless with some of the comforts of home. The practicality of this is debatable. Many submissions made the important statement that after a decade of financial starvation, the public realm needed not so much expansion as a redefinition to address the exponentially increasing gap between the rich and the poor, the skilled and the unskilled.[194] The jury tended to reject submissions in the high technology arena of high-speed computers and invisible infrastructure that invoked a 'Big Brother' type quality.[195] In addition, the jury mentioned that one of the great obstacles were current zoning laws that divided the city into single uses – a contradiction of Jane Jacobs' writing some thirty years earlier.

The jury's discussion revolved around the distinction between the public realm, identified with 'contested territory, strife, competition and danger' (Susana Torre), and the civic realm, which they saw as the embodiment of a commonality of purpose. Most entries were seen as addressing the public realm and not the civic realm. The Los Angeles riots that year were seen by Harvey Gantt as also significant.

The chaos of the suburbs – car parks, strip malls, office parks and residential subdivisions – was hardly addressed.

Of the ten award-winning submissions, perhaps the most imaginative was San Francisco's 'Sutro Baths: A New Public Room' by Tanner, Leddy Maytum, Stacy Architects,[196] which was illustrated on the front cover of the magazine. The original Sutro Baths were completed in 1894 but closed in 1966. A fire during demolition left a few ruins, including a giant saltwater pool on a steep slope overlooking the Pacific. The laudable aim was to create an urban space that addressed the physical and spiritual needs of the city by integrating civic gathering spaces with facilities for alternative energy generation and desalination of ocean water. The main saltwater pool would be reclaimed for recreational use with desalination facilities located above the pool and, above that, wind generators at the top of the hill. The triangular trusses of the composite structure would serve as water conduits bringing seawater to the desalination stills.

The jury admired the scheme for its consistency and the use of public investment for the public good. The presentation was also admired for its success in communicating to the public its creative intentions for the public realm.

The Mississippi River Bridge Corridor in New Orleans by Michael Stanton and Scott Wall, with a team from the Tulane University School of Architecture, was the largest scheme among the award-winning submissions. Taking a two-mile-long division of abandoned railyards, factories and the substructures of the Greater New Orleans Bridge, the urban designers suggested ways of reclaiming this wasteland and reintegrating it with the city. This urban wasteland was representative of the desolate residual areas in many American cities.[197]

A similar project among the ten award-recipients was the Rust Belt Renewal proposal for the rehabilitation of vacant steel mills in Duquesne, Pennsylvania, across the Monongahela River Valley from Pittsburgh.[198] The scheme, by David Gosling, Maria-Cristina Gosling and Stephen Proctor, was based upon a much larger community study developed by a Regional/Urban Design Assistance Team (R/UDAT) of the American Institute of Architects, which included other communities along the river valley, including McKeesport and Homestead. As part of the original study in 1988,[199] the Duquesne proposals were now divided into three parts[200] and, presented as a triptych, ranged from relatively modest proposals to a high-technology proposal addressing the closure of virtually all the steel plants (with the exception of CSX) that had been the crucible of Second World War armaments production.

Option 1 proposed that the major industrial elements at the northern end of the site would be retained, but only as structural shells. This skeletal system could be used to incorporate semi-permanent studio workshops, emulating the work of John Habraken. Option 2 proposed a major resource recovery (recycling) plant with cogeneration of electric power capabilities. Tertiary industry/high technology units were seen as a new-generation spin-off industry from the Mellon (Carnegie-Mellon University) Institute Science Park research activities. The derelict Dorothy 6 furnace at the southern end could be refurbished as an industrial heritage museum. Option 3 was the most ambitious, envisioning the virtual redevelopment of the site. Though new housing was a controversial issue due to the high vacancy rates in the three towns, the riverside seemed to present a unique opportunity for attractive development. It was suggested that Carnegie Mellon University and the Mellon Institute might transfer all their research activities from overcrowded sites across the river given tax incentives to re-establish in Duquesne.

The scheme as a public/private collaboration to recycle a lapsed infrastructure had a two-fold appeal to the jury. Duquesne could develop jobs as well as an alternative to typical zoned development. David Lee thought it had 'a romantic quality to it'. Harvey Gantt feared that the environmental clean-up of the site might be formidable, though Robert Yaro said that

Existing derelict mill building and steel rolling plant, Monongahela Valley, Pennsylvania.

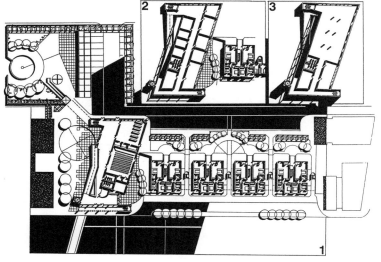

Alternative proposals for housing and Appalachian Heritage Museum, Lower Price Hill, Cincinnati, Ohio (1991), D. Gosling et al.

Stage 5 (design process), detailed schematic of urban Appalachian Heritage Museum and affordable housing, Lower Price Hill, Cincinnati, Ohio (1991), D. Gosling et al.

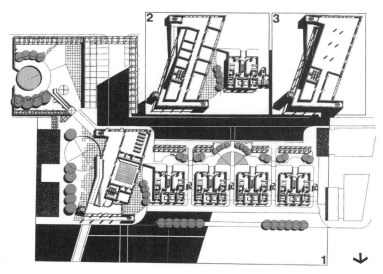

the scheme could create market forces that would allow that, in part, to happen, adding that refitting the structures was only part of the challenge and that cities like Duquesne might be forced to develop a new set of jobs.

Urban design in Cincinnati

The US has a fairly dismal record of implementation of urban design schemes, whether prize-winning or not. Examples abound, but the city of Cincinnati in particular has a poor record of neighbourhood renewal.

Some 52 neighbourhoods make up the city and although many urban design studies have, over the years, been commissioned by the city or the county, few have ever been implemented. What has been implemented – a fine architectural design on the downtown riverfront, the Paul Brown Stadium, completed in 2000 for the under-performing Bengals football team – has been financed by the raising of the sales tax by the county commissioners. Cincinnati's better-performing baseball team, the Reds, will have their own megastructure on the riverfront by 2003, by which time taxpayers will have paid a figure approaching a billion dollars with little going towards the much-needed neighbourhood renewal. This lack of attention to the city's neighbourhoods can only exacerbate migration to the suburbs, for example those in Warren County.

Nevertheless, in July 1993 a contract was awarded to the Center for Urban Design at the University of Cincinnati for a year-long study (funded by the Department of Neighborhood Housing) and a printed report (funded by the Department of Economic Development) on the Ludlow Avenue business district. The study involved full community participation including residents, merchants, business and property owners in the Clifton neighbourhood, which includes the main campus of the 35,000-student University of Cincinnati. The scheme

received approval from the neighbourhood groups in June 1994.[201] Sadly, six years later in June 2000 precisely nothing had happened. At the presentation of the final study report, 196 people had been for the proposals, and only 2 against. But the Center for Urban Design was nevertheless disbanded by the University College of DAAP administration in 1996.

As far back as 1978, Cincinnati's City Council had approved the designation of the Ludlow Avenue Business District as an Environmental Quality District, though this also accomplished little beyond improving car park access, planting some trees and restoring gas lamps along the streets.

The urban design proposals had been preceded by an economic survey, identity study and a marketing/management programme. The erosion of traditional city neighbourhoods created major problems as the fiscal base eroded, while services (police, fire, libraries and parks) did not decline in cost. Property taxes replaced income taxes to pay for city services, thus encouraging companies to move outside city boundaries into areas with lower taxes. A strategy of creating an environment in which it is pleasant to live through sound neighbourhood business districts is clearly significant in quality-of-life decisions for many households. Neighbourhood business districts were seen as one of the best indicators of the health of an entire neighbourhood. Clifton was fortunate in two ways. First, it still had a vital business district with a 'village' character and, second, it seemed that the city was willing to help preserve and improve the business area. The second of these assumptions proved not to be true.

Clifton had an unusually high proportion of pedestrians relative to other neighbourhood business districts, perhaps due to its high concentration of students who tend to walk further than many other customers. Further, the business area contained restaurants, bars and a cinema (The Esquire Theater)

Lower Price Hill, Cincinnati, Ohio (1991), Gosling et al.

Ludlow Avenue urban design study, Cincinnati, Ohio (1994) (Nos. 2B and 3B), D. Gosling et al.

Lower Price Hill, urban design study, Cincinnati, Ohio, Gosling et al.

Lower Price Hill, urban design study, Cincinnati, Ohio, serial vision studies (1991), Gosling et al.

that showed 'art' films, all of which made it an ideal destination for an evening out. In terms of housing quality, rehabilitation had occurred faster than deterioration.

The Clifton Neighborhood Business District is located in the 'uptown' residential area, 5 kilometres (3 miles) north of downtown Cincinnati. It includes two major city parks – Mount Storm and Burnet Woods. The 'gaslight' district is home to most high-income residents, many of whom are employed by the nearby cluster of teaching hospitals or the university.

The study included a diagram that established the lack of adequate parking, traffic congestion, including vehicular and pedestrian conflict, and visual clutter. Specifically, there was the lack of focus at two major nodal points, poor facade quality (in terms of both maintenance and architectural character), absence of gateway indicators at entries into the business district and the lack of a perceived centre. Ludlow Avenue bisected the district between the affluent historic gaslight district of old villas to the north and the university district to the south.

In the year-long advocacy planning process, eight major public meetings were held from November 1993 to June 1994. All residents, business and property owners were invited to attend, through direct mail and public notices.

The urban design policies established by the plan included the following components:

1 Car Parking. The creation of a new parking structure in tiered decks utilizing a change of level between Ludlow Avenue and Howell Avenue. The decks would be staggered with planting on each parapet forming a "hanging garden" and floodlit at night. Other existing surface lots would emulate West Coast cities such as Santa Monica, with pergolas, blossom/shade trees and trellises.

2 Lighting. Façade lighting for all buildings along Ludlow Avenue to draw attention to historic façades and enliven the nighttime environment. There would be gateway flood-lighting of entry signage on freestanding structures and low-level lighting on the proposed new village green on the top deck of the parking structure.

3 New landscaping. All public spaces would be landscaped with flowering trees and shrubs, including a boulevard of trees along Clifton Avenue.

4 New paving. Using brick pavers for new crosswalks in Ludlow Avenue to create "traffic calming" with special paving in all public open spaces particularly at major intersections or nodes.

5 Pedestrian amenities would be through the creation of connectors to existing parking lots and new public spaces with ten-foot-high pergolas and trellises. A new village green, a public square, a vending area and a public garden would be created within Burnet Woods Park.

6 The construction of a needed small public library on top of the parking structure which would also serve as a community center facing the village green where music could be played during the summer months. A new illuminated clock tower, with chimes and moving figures in the German tradition would be placed at the intersection between the village green and the public square.

7 Burnet Woods would be opened up for more public use with a narrow gauge railroad (allowing riders to view the migratory geese on the lake) and a fountain at the entrance to the park.

The total cost, required as an estimate by the city, was more than $18.8 million, and budget application was made for the 1995–97 fiscal period. The city offered $300,000, and nothing happened.[202]

THE NEW URBANISM

In the closing years of the twentieth century, of all the movements in urban design so far reviewed, it is possible that the new urbanism was to become the most influential. However, the term the 'new' urbanism is perhaps a misnomer, as it refers to old values and standards established almost a hundred years ago with the garden city movement.[203]

It was the author of *The New Urbanism*, Peter Katz, who in 1994 brought this movement to the nation's attention.[204] Katz is a design and marketing consultant based in San Francisco in association with his colleague Steve Price of Oakland, California. He also studies architecture and graphic design at Cooper Union in New York City. His book gives an explanation of great clarity espousing the principles of the new urbanism, and the twenty-four case studies include the best-known and perhaps most controversial development of the new town of Florida, Seaside, by Andres Duany and Elizabeth Plater-Zyberk. *Time* magazine had referred to Seaside as part of a growing movement to replace 'charmless' suburban sprawl with civilised, familiar places that people love. This urban design revolution proposed a vision of the future, combining concepts of the past with the realities and convenience of the closing years of the century.

According to Katz, his recognition of this new movement began in 1991 when it was termed 'neo-traditional', though much of the architectural press was slow to recognise it. The suburban paradigm that dominated the mid-twentieth century could no longer be realistically sustained. While the new urbanism may not entirely fulfil the American Dream, it was seen as a better option for the Baby Boom generation. Its theories borrow heavily from the period between 1900 and 1920, but at the same time the new urbanism does not turn its back on the technological revolution of the twentieth century, recognising that telecommuting using computers, modems and the Internet is possible from a home office or neighbourhood work centre.

Peter Calthorpe, one of the leading practitioners of the new urbanism, says that the relationship between architecture and public space can be 'urban' regardless of building height or mass.[205] While such a statement is of dubious value, equally dubious is the suggestion that spatial hierarchy and connectedness can be rendered regardless of land-use intensity.

Calthorpe cites Portland, Oregon, as an example of a city that goes beyond the traditional programmes for urban infill and revitalisation in its use of an urban growth boundary and zoning, which allows a transit system to focus on the central city.[206] This strategy, Calthorpe believes, is central to the thesis of the new urbanism – a regional system of open space and transit complemented by pedestrian-friendly development patterns. In its use of the relatively new light rail system, Portland allowed for sensitive urban planning, creating a thriving downtown.

Urban sprawl, on the other hand, is rightly seen by Calthorpe as destructive in any growth strategy, lacking the fundamental qualities of towns such as pedestrian scale, identifiable centres and edges and diversity of use, which are further negated by the dominance of the private motor car.

Before the publication of *The New Urbanism*, the construction of Seaside in Florida's panhandle on the Gulf Coast was already under way. In the publication *Seaside: Making a Town in America*,[207] the architects acknowledged the influence of various precedents, including Venice, Florida, in 1926, and Mariemont, Ohio, in 1923. The book also included the precedent of the work of Arquitectonica of Florida – where both Duany and Plater-Zyberk had worked – the international style of which was to differ substantially from the subsequent architecture of Seaside. Also acknowledged were the urban design theories of European architect Leon Krier.

Seaside progressed slowly, building of the first half of the project spanning ten years. Kurt Anderson said that Duany and Plater-Zyberk represented a new generation after Robert Venturi, who had made vernacular forms respectable.[208] Though Seaside had met with opposition, particularly among the modernists who rejected such traditional forms, it nevertheless also met with some admiration. The idiosyncratic architecture of Steven Holl and Deborah Burke operating within the strict architectural code elicited grudging respect. Indeed, the project

has been criticised as elitist – a settlement of second homes for the wealthy, rather than a true community, under a tyrannical code of good taste.

The importance of Seaside was in its reintroduction of the public realm in the form of street and square, recalling the American City Beautiful and garden city movements. The radial plan of Seaside, illustrated in 1983, reflects, to some extent, John Nolan's 1921 plan for Mariemont, Ohio, albeit covering a smaller land area. At 30 hectares (80 acres), it establishes easy walking distances, following the same principles as Radburn, New Jersey. The coherence of the urban code for Seaside – down to finite details such as yard layout, porch and balcony design, outbuildings, parking and height – produced a quite remarkable harmonic relationship given the diversity of the architectural designers who contributed to the urban system. For example, Type 1 zoning was intended for retail uses at street level with residential above, and Type 2, based upon the Vieux Carre district of New Orleans, defines the pedestrian square with the town hall surrounded by four-storey buildings with courtyards and specific requirements for arcades and silhouettes. Thus, the urban design plan is developed into eight different types of zoning, ranging from the highly restrictive to the more liberal, dispersed throughout the residential areas of the town. Prototypical street sections, such as the Town Square, City Hall Square, Schoolhouse Square, Church Square, Beach Front Square, Market Square as well as cross-sections of the avenues, large streets, small streets, alleyways and footpaths, are illustrated in the plan. In 1991, Duany and Plater-Zyberk produced an extension plan with the addition of three neighbourhoods separated by greenbelts with maximum five-minute walking distances. Of the first architectural designs to be built, the house design by Robert Davis, the Averett Tower and Gray House by Deborah Burke, are notable.

The frequent use of timber colonnades, arcades and balconies surrounding these structures, albeit designed by different architects, creates an unusual visual unity. Robert Stern's Seaside Hotel, on a larger scale, was one of the earliest projects. In this design, Stern used large verandahs and overhanging eaves that reflected the residential architecture elsewhere in the town. The main wing runs parallel with the beach and another wing defines the town square. The final built structure followed Stern's original design on the beachfront site, but the secondary wing was designed by Steven Holl. Holl also designed the Hybrid Building, which incorporated mixed uses of commercial spaces at street level, offices on the second-floor level and apartments on the third and fourth levels. Apparently, Holl accompanied his design with a written narrative suggesting that west-facing apartments would be for 'boisterous types' while those facing east and the rising sun would be for 'melancholic types', suggesting that such people might be mathematicians, musicians (presumably classical) and 'tragic poets'.

The restaurant pavilion by Joan Chan and David Mohney is a gazebo in European, eighteenth-century landscape design traditions. Many such gazebos permeated the town of Seaside, for example the Odessa Street Beach Pavilion by Roger Ferri.

But of all the icons, the most vivid contributions were made by the European architect Leon Krier, whose writings on urban design in the 1980s were to have enormous influence world-wide. Pursuing the writing of Camillo Sitte almost a century earlier, with pleas for a return to the pedestrian scale, Krier, a self-taught architect, did not actually build anything until 1989, despite his many beautiful drawings. Duany and Plater-Zyberk regarded him as a mentor and he clearly influenced the general morphology of Seaside's plan. His first design was for a tower in the town square, followed by his own house at Seaside, composed of porches, a tower and a core of rooms. Constructed of wood, as are the majority of buildings at Seaside, the architecture, nevertheless, follows the aesthetics of traditional stone construction.

Kurt Anderson, writing in the *Princeton Architectural Journal*, asked the question 'Is Seaside too Good to be True?'.[209] He rightly observes that, like many such aberrations in the history of architecture, if the story of the creation of Seaside were fiction it would certainly be regarded as facile and over-romantic. As an example of the pervasive American system of planned unit development (PUD), which now houses 10 per cent of the population, it has become a rejection of twentieth-century suburbia. Anderson acknowledges the influence of Leon Krier and Jane Jacobs but suggests that much of Krier's thinking, which he describes as Luddite, was a reaction to student rebellion in both Europe and the US in 1968. More significantly, he says, 'the archetypal residents now manifest themselves in Seaside's quasi-populist architectural style; in its celebration of community and nature; in its affluent, overeducated, hang-loose, good vibes'. Such a statement could be read to have chilling overtones.

Critiques of Seaside include that by Julie Iovine, who, writing in the *New York Times,* says that 'probably no eighty-acre patch of America has been more heavily styled, or scrutinized, in recent years than Seaside . . . a small town planning revolution . . . Envisioned as the kind of town a well-mannered Tom Sawyer or Huck Finn would appreciate – where every house was required to have a porch and where bicycle paths and picket fences were written into the urban code – Seaside is growing up and taking on a life of its own'.[210] Pointing to recent urban expansion to the west, Iovine observes that it threatens the small scale of Seaside itself with its much larger residences.

Seaside has now become an exclusive resort community, though some of the wealthy residents claim that it is a real year-round community. The larger houses are to be found in the urban hub around such squares as Ruskin Place, with smaller houses on the edge. Yet even the largest houses rarely exceed 230 square metres (2,500 square feet) with 170–200 square metres (1,800–2,200 square feet) being considered large and the average floor area of the first houses as small as 55 square metres (600 square feet). By mid-1997 nearly three hundred lots had been sold with average land value appreciation averaging 25 per cent a year since 1982, compared with 5 per cent a year elsewhere in this part of Florida.

The universal use of painted shutters provides unity, but with various colours allowing for differing identities and appropriate to the climate of sea breezes and surf. As in most sub-tropical climates, the indigenous plant growth has been prolific and the stark early photographs of the town are now belied by a mature landscape, which was the intent of the much earlier garden cities, though here the palm and the myrtle are the indigenous plants. Often overwhelmed with sightseers, the town actively discourages such visitors.

A more chilling critique of Seaside is found not in newspapers, magazine or books, but in the release of the film *The Truman Show* in mid-1998.[211] Paramount Pictures selected Seaside to describe the story of a man going through life without realising his world had been scripted for a continuous television show. The town is a set, and its inhabitants are fellow actors. The division between television and reality is deliberately blurred. It is a pinnacle in high-concept ingenuity and Jim Carrey brilliantly plays the part as a guinea pig for a television nation obsessed by soap operas and voyeurism. The surrealistic fraud produces an intensity reaching into science fiction – of a perfect world of beautiful people and pretty architecture which, in fact, is a huge prison-like enclosure. The message is subtle but clear: Seaside is a human trap.

An interesting aspect to Duany and Plater-Zyberk's work is that in their design process they rely not on computer-generated plans and illustrations but rather upon immaculate and rendered drawings, generally in watercolours and coloured crayon. Todd Bressi in Katz's *The New Urbanism*[212] says that they place enormous importance on communicating their proposals so that both elected officials and citizens can easily grasp the perspectives, which might be perceived by some as overly romantic. The illustrations, drawn by Charles Barrett and coloured by Manuel Fernandez-Nobal, emphasise the picturesque qualities of the proposals. Much of the process is carried out through intensive charters involving local officials and community leaders, and reflects the advocacy planning methods of thirty years previously.

Laguna West in Sacramento County, California, was produced by Calthorpe Associates in 1990 and defines a much larger site – over 400 hectares (1,000 acres). This was the first of Peter Calthorpe's transit-oriented developments. Serving 3,400 residential units and a one-hundred-acre town centre including a village green, town hall, main street and neighbourhood parks, Laguna West was believed to have sufficient density to justify a transit service. However, though embraced in the plan, the transit was not at the time linked up. Calthorpe's design plan incorporates some highly prescriptive proposals with porches and elevated stoops, the sharing of single driveways between pairs of houses and a car-parking court.

Other Calthorpe urban design plans include South Brentwood village in California (1991).[213] Less lyrical than Laguna West, Brentwood nevertheless incorporated many of the same elements. A mixed-use community of five hundred detached houses, it provides for 30 per cent on-site employment-generating uses such as light industry, offices and retail, with a village green, small parks and a church. The houses are built on alley lots with accessory apartments over garages providing affordable accommodation. The tree-lined streets are again accompanied by design guidelines for the neighbourhood parks, village green, gated cul-de-sacs, rotaries to provide traffic calming and sound walls created by dense tree planting.

In his *The New Urbanism*, Katz also includes the example of Riviera Beach, part of Palm Beach County in Florida. Despite its wealthy neighbours, Riviera Beach had a negative image as one of the poorest cities in Palm Beach, housing the regional power plant as well as boat yards and commercial fishing facilities. The 650-hectare (1,600-acre) site was selected because of its reasonable land prices and waterfront location, and the urban design plan proposals in 1991 were by Mark Schimmenti working with Dover, Corra, Kohl, Cockshutt and Valle in a citizen-driven planning initiative through Riviera Beach's Community Redevelopment Agency. The plan has nine mixed-use neighbourhoods, each with separate identities with a neighbourhood centre and town square, but is unlike Seaside and other new urbanist communities in that it is not a greenfield site.

Most notable about the citizen-sponsored initiative at Riviera Beach are the photomontage illustrations allowing those at the public meetings to compare a series of simulations of the main street, Broadway (the principal north–south route), with the master plan proposals. Significantly, the presentations are sequential diagrams illustrating the consequences of Riviera Beach's present and proposed codes as opposing scenarios. The existing codes required excessive setbacks and parking requirements forcing buildings back from the street and away from each other. The proposed code aligns buildings of various sizes with the street edge and parking to the rear. It also introduces, in true Italian classical fashion, a continuous arcade above the sidewalk, recreating the traditional Main Street of small-town America. Geoffrey Ferrell's proposed code is simplicity itself, printed on one large sheet accompanied by a hierarchy of street types.

The final pages of Katz's book include a proposal for the Clinton neighbourhood of Manhattan. Designed by Steven Peterson and Barbara Littenburg in 1986, it is substantially different in concept than the later work of Duany and Plater-Zyberk. Clinton in mid-Manhattan is a neighbourhood with a distinct identity. The city-supported plan of two huge new apartment towers was countered by a community-sponsored plan consistent with the scale and character of the adjacent developments. The new plan saved all existing housing and provided much more affordable and modest-income housing units, preserving the neighbourhood's authentic urban fabric. The master plan, presented eloquently as a three-dimensional axonometric drawing, took advantage of undeveloped tracts of land – a strange phenomenon in mid-Manhattan.

The New Urbanism concludes with an essay, 'The Architecture of Community', by the renowned architectural historian Vincent Scully.[214] Some of Scully's observations were acerbic. He says that 'the historic preservation of neighborhoods and their inhabitants . . . cannot help but seem overly comprehensive. The New Suburbanism might be a truer label'. He suggests that terms such as 'historicism' were not relevant and that the Zeitgeist mentality is 'historicist'. Scully wonders what the input of Frank Gehry, with his love of American wood-frame construction, might have been within the code of Seaside. He also criticises the tendency of Duany and Plater-Zyberk in addressing the new modernism to use vernacular images because it appeals to clients. He refers to this as buffoonery, though 'genial', leaving a possible charge of pandering to the public. However, such a criticism seems a little harsh, given the message of the new urbanism that is precisely that – of appealing to the public and not the navel-gazing of the inner circles of academic architecture. Interestingly, Scully cites Oak Park, Chicago, with its plethora of Frank Lloyd Wright-designed residences and directly connected to the elevated suburban train and downtown Chicago, as an implied example of Peter Calthorpe's 'pocket park' communities.

Scully ends his essay with an important rhetorical question, 'So the rich, who can choose, choose community, or at least its image. How much more must the poor, who must depend on it for their lives, want community? If Seaside and the others cannot in the end offer viable models for that, they will remain entirely beautiful but rather sad'.[215]

Such allegations have been made against a more recent new urbanist development in Florida. The town of Celebration, outside Orlando and sponsored by the Disney Corporation, has attracted criticism not dissimilar to that levelled against Seaside. In an article in the *New York Times,* Michael Pollan indicates that the central control of the Disney Corporation cannot necessarily 'create a script it can only partly control'.[216] In 1995, the site was only a cypress swamp on the borders of Walt Disney World. With a planned population of 20,000 people and 1,500 residents in 1997, Pollan saw it as a way of transforming isolated and disaffected American suburbanites into civic-minded members of a community – not dissimilar from the portrait presented in *The Truman Show*. He suggests in a rather mean-spirited way that Celebration had become a ground for a luxuriant growth of scout troops, religious groups and hobbyist clubs, and refers to the omnipresent Rotarians.

Disney's theme parks since the mid 1950s had nurtured the propagation of America's vernacular architecture and the concept of Main Street in particular – of walkable streets and attractive public spaces. The difference was that theme parks were for paying 'guests', not for citizens who would inhabit the town.

Among the architects involved was Robert Stern who observed that: 'The street is the key to everything else we are trying to accomplish here'. The master plan for Celebration was prepared by Stern together with Jaquelin Robertson (the two are, respectively, Dean of Architecture at Yale University and Professor of Architecture at Harvard). The network of streets, the downtown and the parks are skilful examples of urban design principles. It is a neo-traditional town like Seaside. It has narrow streets deliberately designed to slow down traffic giving clear priority to pedestrians. The houses are close together, creating a sequential and pleasant rhythm though on small lots. Pollan observes that the sociable front porches did not have porch sitters, though Stern sees the importance of the street as an outdoor room, not just a connector. The planting of thousands of mature trees creates unified street walls with garages at the rear of the houses, not the front. There are, as Pollan observed, no poor people in Celebration, as in Seaside, and in ethnic terms it is overwhelmingly white, reaffirming a common rule in real estate that people will live next door to neighbours of the same class (with the implication that ethnic minorities are not as wealthy as the white majority). Yet it appears that the service alleys deliberately mix high- and lower-income families (albeit white) to attempt cross-social mingling. As Stern said, 'Design can help to orchestrate community'.

The mid-1960s Disney experiment of Epcot (Experimental Prototype Community of Tomorrow) for 20,000 residents never really succeeded after company founder Walt Disney's death in 1966. Michael Eisner, the current company chairman, was very clear about his goals of 'improving American family life, education and health', making Celebration a form of social engineering. The financial success of Celebration parallels the other new urbanist models in Florida and elsewhere, fulfilling Walt Disney's original dream of becoming a world attraction for 'architectural' tourists. The codes imposed upon the residents are draconian and include such things as a precise ratio of lawn to perennials.

Celebration's pattern book was produced in fine detail, not dissimilar from the pattern books of the eighteenth-century architects in Europe – particularly in England and Italy. A galaxy of famous architects was appointed for individual buildings. Unlike the younger group of architects nominated by Duany and Plater-Zyberk for Seaside, these designers were part of a respected establishment and included Philip Johnson for the Town Hall, Michael Graves for the Post Office, Venturi and Scott Brown for the bank, Cesar Pelli for the cinema, Graham Gund for the inn, William Rawn for the school, and Moore/Anderson (the firm of the late Charles Moore) for the preview centre, possibly the most lyrical of the buildings. The strong framework of the Stern/Cooper/Robertson plan works well in providing a strong sense of community.[217]

In March 1998, on a tour around the town as part of a major national urban design conference organised by the American Institute of Architects, Committee on Design,[218] a disgruntled delegate interrupted the Disney tour guide to challenge her description of the development as a 'multi-income social community' by asking the price of the smallest house of two bedrooms on a street frontage. The answer was $200,000.

Pollan's criticisms of Celebration in the New York Times[219] drew subsequent observations from many readers. One, Michael Costello, said: 'I found little to celebrate . . . the community spirit touted by Disney is more about real-estate cynicism and opportunism marked by clever public relations playing into utopian daydreams than about the true spirit of civic participation. Diversity does not mean the choice of false architectural styles in the middle of a reclaimed swamp. Nor does it mean corporate engineering of the "American Hometown"'. Other remarks included that given Disney's meticulous planning of its town, a more fitting name might be 'Calibration' (Mark Sydel) and, 'Are some of the disgruntled inhabitants of Celebration now realising that to privatise all is to sell all and that the price may have been too high?' (Lelde Gilman).

But despite these criticisms, the author's visit to Celebration as a delegate at the AIA conference revealed the beginnings of a town with beauty and almost dreamlike qualities.

Clearly the new urbanism movement is a strong force.[220] The establishment of the Congress for the New Urbanism is significant. Founded in 1996, the Charter for the congress was signed by CNU in Charleston, South Carolina that year.[221] In its mani-festo, it states that transit, pedestrian and cycle systems should maximise access and mobility throughout a region, while reducing dependence on the motor car, and that neighbourhoods should be compact, pedestrian-friendly and mixed-use, with many activities of daily living occurring within walking distance, allowing independence for those who do not drive. Streets and public spaces should be safe and comfortable, encouraging walking and cycling and enabling neighbours to know one another.

NOTES

1. Whyte, William (1988) City: Rediscovering the Center. New York: Doubleday. Reprinted by Anchor Books, New York.
2. Garreau, Joel (1991) Edge City: Life on the New Frontier. New York: Doubleday. Reprinted by Anchor Books, New York.
3. Whyte, op. cit., pp. 79–102.
4. Ibid., p. 111.
5. Ibid., p. 157 ff.
6. Recent studies on the design of staircases in the public realm have indicated that staircase designs of previous centuries are now inadequate because of the growing size of human beings. For example, human feet are now much larger, and need to be accommodated by the horizontal component of steps.
7. Despite this vivid mixture, the author of this book, taking admiring photographs of the Citicorp building, was suddenly seized by an elderly lady in an expensive fur coat who berated him for photographing 'crap' architecture. The screaming attracted quite a large crowd of bemused onlookers.
8. See Terry Christensen's critique of Edge City in Cities, November 1993, pp. 343–44.
9. The problem is not solved by beltway systems. The most alarming proposal for Madrid, Spain, was the proposal in the 1990s to create a fifth beltway enclosing the four other concentric beltways.
10. Stubbs, Stephanie (1991) 'Edge City, here we come', American Institute of Architects Journal, November/December, pp. 6–7.
11. Orwell, George (1948) 1984. London: Penguin Books.
12. This is to some extent happening today. Accusations of police brutality and the shooting of unarmed African and African-American citizens, whether in New York or Cincinnati, has become increasingly reported over the last several years.
13. Zimmerman, Martin (1992) Review of Edge City in Blueprints, National Building Museum, Washington, D.C., vol. X, no.1 (Winter), p. 8.
14. Garreau, op. cit., p. 81.
15. Ibid., p. 93.
16. Such a popularity for horseback riding in upper-income enclaves is not the same as trail riding. Trail riding in the US goes back to the nineteenth century with the expansion of the population towards the Midwest and later the far west, with the establishment of cattle ranches in particular. The large Western saddle is far different to the European saddle in size and configuration, and is designed for comfort. It evolved for long journeys, and cowboys dressed in a relaxed fashion of shirts, denim jeans and short cowboy boots (concealed beneath the jeans). In Olympic competitions, it is more formal and in Europe, more popular among women than men. The dress is composed of tailored black hacking jacket, a black velvet helmet and skin-tight white jodphurs (breeches) accompanied by knee-high, gleaming black leather boots. Such horse riding is concerned with show-jumping and dressage, not long-distance riding, and indicates social success among women residents in edge cities.
17. Thoreau, Henry David (1960) Walden. New York: New American Library. Originally published in 1854.
18. Garreau, op. cit., p. 121.

19. Such an example was a built design by the author in the late 1960s of the Victoria Bridge office tower, thirty storeys high, in Manchester, England. Inspired by Louis Kahn's 'served and servant spaces' theory, and applied to the Richards Medical Research laboratories and the University of Pennsylvania, the office slab itself was entirely rental space served by a connecting but separate service tower with elevators except for fire escape staircases at each end of the slender office slab.

20. Garreau, op. cit., p. 121.

21. Compare this with Irvine New Town, Scotland, on the Ayrshire coast, which on completion had a total population of under 100,000.

22. Garreau, op. cit., p. 308.

23. Barone, Michael and Grant Ujifusa (1990) 'The almanac of American politics', *Washington, D.C. National Journal*, p. 55.

24. Garreau, op. cit., pp. 443–59.

25. Ibid., p. 468.

26. Garvin, Alexander (1996) *The American City: What Works, What Doesn't*. New York: McGraw Hill.

27. Ibid., p. 1.

28. Ibid., p. 11.

29. Ibid., pp. 146–47. Garvin refers in his text to Carl Abott's (1983) *Portland: Planning, Politics and Growth in a Twentieth Century City* (Lincoln, NE: University of Nebraska Press), and John R. Post's (1988) 'The Portland Light Rail Experience' in, Wayne Attoe, ed. *Transit, Land Use and Urban Form*. Austin, TX: Center for the Study of American Architecture, University of Texas, pp. 63–72.

30. Scully, Vincent (1988) *American Architecture and Urbanism*. New York: Henry Holt, pp. 250–51. While this observation in 1988 may have been true, after constant revisions of the Hill District redevelopment plan, the original proposals (proposed under the direction of Christopher Tunnard some thirty years earlier in 1958–59) emphasised the importance of the retention and restoration of existing housing fabric.

31. Garvin, op. cit., p. 230.

32. Lang, John (1994) *Urban Design: The American Experience*. New York: Van Nostrand Reinhold.

33. Ibid., pp. 13–135.

34. Ibid., p. 66.

35. Ibid., p. 70.

36. Ibid., p. 73.

37. Ibid., p. 79.

38. See Chapter 1, 'Definitions of Urban Design' and reference to the public and private realm.

39. Such an example of prescriptive guidelines was utilised by the Chicago Office of Skidmore, Owings and Merrill in the Canary Wharf Development in London during the mid- to late-1980s.

40. Lynch, Kevin (1990) *Wasting Away*, ed. Michael Southworth. San Francisco: Sierra Club Books.

41. Lynch, Kevin (1961) *The Image of the City*. Cambridge, MA: The Technology Press and Harvard University Press.

42. Lynch, Kevin (1972) *What Time is this Place?*. Cambridge, MA: MIT Press.

43. Lynch, Kevin (1962) *Site Planning*. Cambridge, MA: MIT Press.

44. Lynch, Kevin (1984) *A Theory of Good City Form*. Cambridge, MA: MIT Press.

45. Sennett, Richard (1971) *The Uses of Disorder: Personal Identity and City Life*. Harmondsworth: Pelican. First published in the US, 1970.

46. Lynch, Kevin (1990) *Wasting Away*, ed. Michael Southworth. San Francisco: Sierra Club Books, pp. 119–45.

47. Banerjee, Tridib and Michael Southworth (1990) *City Sense and City Design: Writings and Projects by Kevin Lynch*. Cambridge, MA: MIT Press, p. 853.

48. Lynch, Kevin, 'Pattern of the Metropolis', in Banerjee and Southworth (1990) op. cit.

49. Banerjee and Southworth, op. cit., p. 51.

50. Lynch, Kevin (1958) 'The City as Environment', *Scientific American*, 213, no. 3, pp. 209–14.

51. Banerjee and Southworth, op. cit., p. 12.

52. Ibid., p. 200–203.

53. Carr/Lynch Associates (1968) 'Collaboration and Context in Urban Design', *Design Studies* 5, no. 9, pp. 178–84.

54. Banerjee and Southworth, op. cit., pp. 711–13.

55. References to George Orwell's *1984*, Aldous Huxley's *Brave New World* and H. G. Wells' *War of the Worlds* – all British authors who predicted the future during the twentieth century.

56. Banerjee and Southworth, op. cit., p. 783.

57. Lynch, Kevin (1975) *Responding to Social Change*, ed. Basil Honkiman. Stroudsburg, PA: Dowden, Hutchinson and Ross.

58. Banerjee and Southworth, op. cit., p. 795.

59. Lynch, Kevin with Tunney Lee and Peter Droege 'What Will Happen to Us', *Space and Society*, no. 22, pp. 87–97.

60. One of the authors of this work visited the Soviet Union in September 1979 as a Technical Specialist under the Anglo-Soviet Cultural Agreement, Article III (3)c to visit the new towns encompassing Moscow, most of which were related to scientific research. It was obvious that the Soviet economy was already on the verge of collapse and that any nuclear threat was negligible. The Soviet Union therefore presented little threat and the subsequent growth of other nuclear powers like Pakistan and India posed much greater instability.

61. Lynch, Kevin (1984) 'Coming Home: the Urban Environment After Nuclear War', from 'The Counterfeit Ark: Crisis Relocation for Nuclear War', J. Leaning and L. Keyes (eds) *Physicians for Social Responsibility*, Ballinger Publishing Co.

62. Lynch, Kevin 'City Design: What It Is and How It Might Be Taught', *Urban Design International*, I, no. 2, pp. 48–53.

63. Sorkin, Michael (ed.) (1992) *Variations on a Theme Park*. New York: Noonday Press.

64. The Great Exhibition of the Works of Industry of All Nations was held in London in 1851. It was built within an enormous cast iron and glass hall, designed by Joseph Paxton, and referred to as the Crystal Palace.

65. Sorkin, op. cit., pp. 3–30.

66. Ibid., pp. 31–60.

67. Ibid.

68. Ellin, Nan (1996) *Postmodern Urbanism*. Cambridge, MA: Blackwell Publishers.

69. Ibid., pp. 44–89.

70. Ibid., p. 69.

71. Ibid., p. 71.

72. Ibid., p. 254.

73. Jencks Charles (1997) 'Landform Architecture: Emergent in the Nineties', *Architectural Design*, vol. 67, no. 9/10 (September/October), pp. 15–31.

74. *Progressive Architecture 01–09* Progressive Architecture Awards, January 1991, pp. 82–83.

75. Editorial, pp. 7–11, Andrew Benjamin, *Architectural Design*, vol. 158, no. 314.

76. Descartes, R. (1985) 'Discourse on Method', *The Philosophical Writings of Descartes, vol. 1*. Cambridge: Cambridge University Press.

77. Derrida, Jacques 'Architecture ove I'desiderio puo' arbitare', *Domus*, no. 671.

78. Jencks, Charles *Architectural Design*, vol. 158, no. 314, pp. 26–31 and 49–61.

79. Eisenman, Peter (1987) *House of Cards*. Oxford: Oxford University Press.

80. *Architectural Design*, (1992) vol. 162, no. 1–2.

81. Jencks, Charles (1995) *The Architecture of the Jumping Universe*. London: Academy Editions.

82. Katz, Peter (1994) *The New Urbanism: Toward an Architecture of Community*. New York: McGraw-Hill.

83. Foster, Kurt (1996) *Casabella*, no. 638 (October), pp. 12–16.

84. Goldberger, Paul (1996) *New York Times*, Monday 14 October, pp. B-1, B-5.

85. Davidson, Cynthia (ed.) (1996) *Eleven Authors in Search of a Building*. New York: Monacelli Press, Inc., pp. 48–95.

86. Ibid., p. 14.

87. See Gosling, David (1996) *Gordon Cullen: Visions of Urban Design*. London: Academy Editions, p. 26.

88. Gosling, David and Barry Maitland (1984) *Concepts of Urban Design*. London: Academy Editions, pp. 42–43.

89. Wright, Frank Lloyd (1954) *The Natural House*. New York: Horizon Press, p. 18.

90. Eisenman, Peter, 'Folding in Time: the Singularity of Rebstock', unpublished paper.

91. Such an observation has recently (July 2000) been made by a number of commentators with the phenomenal success of the 'Harry Potter' series of children's books by British author J. K. Rowling. The point made here is that in recent years children rarely read books for pleasure. Books, however, are tangible but electronic data are not. Much of electronic data on disk has been eliminated and replaced and thus, the original is lost.

92. The return to this typology espoused by the neo-rationalists of the 1970s and 1980s by such European urban designers as Leon Krier, Rob Krier and Aldo Rossi, is a reversal back to perceived nineteenth-century urban design values.

93. Such an observation harks back to the editorial pages of the *Architectural Review* in the 1960s and 1970s, where commentators like Kenneth Browne coined the term 'SLOAP' (space left over after planning), and is reflected in Colin Rowe's critique of Le Corbusier's city planning ideas where urban configurations, in terms of figure-ground, dissolved any discernible city structure.

94. See also Eisenman Architects (1991) *Unfolding Frankfurt*. Berlin: Ernst & Sohn.

95. See *Architectural Design Profile* no. 129 (1997) 'New Science = New Architecture', *Architectural Design*, vol. 67, no. 9/10 (September/October), pp. 32–35.

96. It may be recalled that Giambattista Nolli's figure-ground plan of Rome in 1748 indicated that the interiors at street level for the great basilicas and temples were an extension of public space and, therefore, were part of the public realm.

97. Muschamp, Herbert (1997) 'The Miracle in Bilbao', *New York Times Magazine* (7 September), pp. 54–59.

98. Ibid., p. 58. The affirmation of the Guggenheim's urban qualities can be seen (p. 54) in a photograph by David Heald of the termination of a nineteenth-century street vista as a gleaming jewel.

99. Bartolucci, Marisa (1999) 'Development by Degrees: the Reinvention of the University of Cincinnati', *World Architecture*, no. 79 (September), pp. 56–60.

100. Ibid., p. 58.

101. 'Banca Viennese', *Domus*, no. 602, January 1980, pp. 14–19.

102. Kafka, Franz (1936) *Collected Short Stories*. Prague: Heinrich M. Sohn.

103. Johnson, Philip (1992) 'On Eisenman and Gehry', *Architectural Design*, vol. 162, no. 1–2, pp. xxv–xlviii.

104. See *The Architectural Review*, vol. CCVI, no. 1232, October 1999, pp. 56–59.

105. Ibid., p. 59.

106. See *A+U*, no. 347, pp. 66–73.

107. Vodidio, Philip (1993) *Contemporary American Architects*. Cologne: Taschen, p. 116.

108. Ibid.

109. *Architectural Design Profile,* vol. 62, no. 1–2, pp. 46–53.

110. Ibid., p. 47.

111. Ibid., p. 55.

112. Mayne, Thom (1993) *Morphosis: Connected Isolation*, London: Academy Editions; New York: St. Martin's Press, pp. 6–19.

113. Ibid., p. 6.

114. Giovanni, Joseph (1998) 'Powered-Up', *Architecture*, vol. 87, no. 2 (February), pp. 64–73.

115. Ibid., p. 69.

116. Crawford, Margaret and John Kaliski (1994) 'Quotidian Bricolage: Retrofitting Fox Hills', Southern California Institute of Architecture (Fall).

117. Much more startling than Gwathmey's extension to Wright's Guggenheim of Fifth Avenue was a proposal by Frank Gehry for another Guggenheim Museum on the Lower East Side of New York City. This design, released in April 2000, created images that developed many of the ideas of Bilbao in an even more vivid manner.

118. Muschamp, Herbert (2000) 'The Guggenheim's East Side Vision', *New York Times*, 17 April, p. A-23. This design, developed as an entirely speculative idea, seems not to address the context of the site in the same way as Bilbao.

119. Ibid., p. 23.

120. Ibid., pp. 200–201.

121. Gerace, Gloria (ed.) (1991) *The Getty Design Process*. Los Angeles: the Paul Getty Trust, p. 19.

122. Reese, Thomas F. and Carol McMichael Reese (1998) 'Richard Meier's New Getty Center in Los Angeles', *A+U*, no. 328 (January), pp. 6–8.

123. Though many visitors at the opening in 1998 complained about the tram access: 'When people saw the lines at the tram station, few were willing to make a pit stop for fear of the long wait in getting up to the complex . . . It took me so long to get up here that I'm not going to walk halfway across this place and lose that time . . . I don't really know what to do. I love this place. It's beautiful, really beautiful. But I didn't come here to see the bathrooms. It's like a rock concert or something. That's the price you have to pay'. Carla Sherman, *New York Times*, 2 April 1998, pp. B-1 and B-10.

124. *A+U*, no. 328 (January) 1998, pp. 58–61.

125. Muschamp, Herbert (1997) 'A Crystal Palace of Culture and Commerce', *New York Times*, 12 January, p. H-45.

126. Maki, Fumihiko (1993) 'Tokyo International Forum: A Work in Progress: The Birth of a New Public Place'.

127. Ibid. Essay by Rafael Viñoly, 'Making a Building: Notes on an Architectural Process'.

128. The Crystal Palace in London no longer exists, destroyed by fire in the 1920s.

129. Muschamp, Herbert (1997) 'A Crystal Palace of Culture and Commerce', *New York Times*, 12 January, p. H-45.

130. *Progressive Architecture*, 38th Annual Awards Program, January 1991, pp. 77–133.

131. *Progressive Architecture*, 39th Annual Awards Program, January 1992, pp. 54–56.

132. Ibid., pp. 85–87.

133. Ibid., p. 87.

134. *Progressive Architecture*, 42nd Annual Awards Program, January 1995, pp. 68 ff.

135. Ibid., p. 68.

136. *Architecture*, vol. 87, no. 4, p. 11.

137. Ibid., p. 62.

138. Ibid., p. 86.

139. Alex Kreiger (1992) 'Projects: Three Approaches to Urban Design', *Progressive Architecture* (February).

140. Koetter, Fred and Susie Kim (1993) 'Commentary: Urban Design', *A+U* (December), pp. 102–114.

141. Ibid., p. 102.

142. Skidmore, Owings and Merrill, 'Report: Computer Applications in Urban Design'.

143. Abbott, Carl (1983) *Portland: Planning, Politics and Growth in a Twentieth-Century City*. Lincoln, NE: University of Nebraska Press, pp. 248–66.

144. Post, John (1988) 'The Portland Light Rail Experience', in Wayne Attoe (ed.) *Transit, Land Use and Urban Form*. Texas: University of Texas, pp. 63–72.

145. Lindsey, Robert (1978) 'New Transit Chief Praised for Role in Portland', *New York Times* (August).

146. See McGovern, Patrick (1998) 'San Francisco Gay Area Edge Cities', *Journal of Planning, Education and Research*, vol. 17, no. 3 (Spring), pp. 246–58..

147. Houston, Nancy (1998) 'Is Light Rail on the Right Track?', *Orlando Sentinel*, 22 February, Section G1–5.

148. See *Scientific American*, August 1992, p. 103.

149. Anderson, J. Edward 'Control of Personal Rapid Transit Systems', *Journal of Advanced Transportation*, vol. 32, no. 1, pp. 57–74.

150. Ibid., p. 65. See also, Anderson, J. E. 'Safe Design of Personal Rapid Transit Systems', *Journal of Advanced Transportation*, no. 28, pp. 1–15, and Anderson, J. E. 'Synchronous or Clear-Path Control in Personal Rapid Transit Systems', *Journal of Advanced Transportation*, no. 30, pp. 1–3.

151. Cevero, Robert 'Transit Villages', *Access: Research at the University of California Transportation Center*, Berkeley, no. 5, pp. 8–13.

152. Ibid., p. 12.

153. See Campbell, Robert (1988) 'Architecture Along a Transportation Spine', *Architecture* (December), pp. 99 ff.

154. Safire, William (1990) 'On Language', *New York Times*, 4 February, pp. 12–14.

155. Gosling, David (1993) 'The Spaces in Between', in Ben Farmer and Hentie Low (eds) *Companion to Contemporary Architectural Thought*. London: Routledge, pp. 349–56.

156. Gandelsonas, Mario (1991) *The Urban Text,* with essays by Joan Copjec, Catherine Ingraham and John Whiteman. Cambridge, MA: MIT Press.

157. Ibid., p. 13.

158. Ibid., p. 19.

159. Ibid., p. 20.

160. Gandelsonas, Mario (1989) 'The Order of the Modern City', RIBA Annual Discourse, *RIBA Journal* (December), pp. 48–55.

161. Ibid., p. 52.

162. Thiel, Philip (1990) 'Starting Off on the Right Foot: An Incremental Approach to Design Education for Responsible Public Service', March.

163. Thiel, Philip (1992) 'Beyond Design Review: Implications for Design Practice, Education and Research', *Environment and Behavior*, vol. 26, no. 3 (May), pp. 363–76.

164. Thiel, Philip (1990) 'Starting Off on the Right Foot: An Incremental Approach to Design Education for Responsible Public Service' (March), p. 10.

165. Thiel, Philip (1997) *People, Paths and Purposes: Notations for a Participatory Envirotecture*. Seattle: University of Washington Press.

166. Ibid., p. 3.

167. Ibid., p. 79.

168. Ibid., p. 201, ff.

169. Ibid., p. 202.

170. Ibid., p. 218.

171. Ibid., p. 221.

172. Kostoff, Spiro (1991) *The City Shaped: Urban Patterns and Meaning Through History*. Boston: Little Brown.

173. Kostoff, Spiro (1998) *The City Assembled: the Elements of Urban Form Through History*. London: Thames and Hudson.

174. Muschamp, Herbert (1994) 'Two for the Roads: Morrish and Brown, Urban Visionaries', *New York Times*, 13 February, pp. 1 and 33.

175. Brown, Catherine and William Morrish (1991) 'The Fourth Coast: An Expedition on the Mississippi River (8 June–22 July 1990)', ed. Mildred Friedman, *Design Quarterly*, pp. 1–32.

176. Ibid., p. 26.

177. Morrish, William (1996) *Civilizing Terrains: Mountains, Mounds and Mesas*. San Francisco: William Stout.

178. The Phoenix Arts Commission (1992) 'Public Art Works: the Arizona Models', in Catherine Brown and William Morrish, *Making a Public Art Master Plan*, pp. 12–31.

179. Morrish, William and Catherine Brown (1994) *Planning to Stay*. Minneapolis: Milkweed.

180. Ibid., pp. 106–107

181. Design Center for American Urban Landscape (1996) 'Making Housing Home: A Design Guide for Site Planning Quality Housing', University of Minnesota.

182. Ibid., p. 5.

183. The Cunningham Group (1996) 'The Minneapolis Riverfront: Vision and Implementation'.

184. Ibid., p. 19.

185. Ibid.

186. Ibid., p. 47.

187. Urban Center for Incremental Development Strategy (UCIDS) (1994) 'UCIDS to the Rescue', vol. 1, no. 1 (December).

188. Smith, Elizabeth and Russell Ferguson (1994) *Urban Revisions: Current Projects for the Public Realm*. Cambridge, MA: MIT Press.

189. Newman, Morris (1994) 'City Design: For Insiders Only', *Progressive Architecture* (October), pp. 41–42.

190. Ibid., p. 42.

191. Ibid.

192. Dixon, John Morris (1993) 'The First Forty Years (Forty Years of P/A Awards)', *Progressive Architecture* (January), pp. 94–105.

193. Fisher, Thomas (1992) 'The New Public Realm', *Progressive Architecture* (October), pp. 74–75.

194. Ibid., p. 74.

195. See Orwell, George (1948) *1984*. Harmondsworth: Penguin.

196. *Progressive Architecture*, January 1993, p. 76.

197. Ibid., p. 84.

198. Ibid., p. 86.

199. American Institute of Architects Regional/Urban Design Assistance Team (1988) 'Remaking the Monongahela Valley: An Examination of the Declining Steel Manufacturing Communities of the Monongahela Valley', March, pp. 80–91.

200. See Gosling, David, Maria Cristina Gosling and Stephen Proctor (1992) 'The New Public Realm Competition Winners', *Progressive Architecture* (October), pp. 1–4.

201. Center for Urban Design, University of Cincinnati, 'Ludlow Avenue in Clifton', August 1994.

202. See also Center for Urban Design, University of Cincinnati (1994) 'Ludlow Avenue Urban Design Plan', July 1994; City of Cincinnati, 'North Avondale Urban Design Plan', December 1992; City of Cincinnati, 'Lower Price Hill, West 8th Street Urban Design Proposals', January 1991; City of Cincinnati, 'Plan 2000 Urban Design Guidelines, Downtown Cincinnati', October 1990. None of the above-funded projects were ever implemented.

203. Howard, Ebenezer (1902) *Garden Cities of Tomorrow*, first published as *Tomorrow: A Peaceful Path to Real Reform*. London: Faber & Faber.

204. Katz, Peter (1994) *The New Urbanism: Toward an Architecture of Community*. New York: McGraw-Hill.

205. Ibid., p. xi. Calthorpe's view of the lack of importance of building height and mass contradicts many of the principles found in the best examples of Renaissance architecture whether they are the Georgian terraces of London by John Nash, or the Georgian crescents of Bath by John Wood the Younger.

206. Ibid., p. xiv.

207. Mohney, David and Keller Easterling (1991) *Seaside: Making a Town in America*. New York: Princeton Architectural Press.

208. Ibid., quoting Kurt Anderson, p. 44.

209. Kurt Anderson (1985) 'Landscape', *Princeton Architectural Journal*, vol. 2, pp. 35–43.

210. Iovine, Julie V. (1997) 'A Matter of Boom vs. Bungalow in Seaside, Fla.', *New York Times*, 10 July, pp. B-1 and B-7.

211. *The Truman Show*, 1998. Peter Weir, the Australian director, directed other notable films such as *Gallipolis*, *Fearless*, *Witness*, *Dead Poets Society*, *Picnic at Hanging Rock*. However, the idea of setting a film in such an artificial and almost surreal setting is not new. 'The Prisoner' was a British television series in the 1960s. Highly praised for its analogies to the writings of Franz Kafka, the episodes are set in Portmeirion on the coast of Wales, designed by Sir Clough Williams-Ellis. Like California's Disneyland, here was a deliberate use of fake facades, distorted perspectives and smaller than human scale. Portmeirion was described in *Concepts of Urban Design* (Gosling and Maitland 1984) as urban design as theatre. Built between 1925 and 1975, it attracts well over 100,000 visitors per year. As a piece of urban design and what was essentially a private collection of buildings by Williams-Ellis, it is certainly theatrical, portrayed as a medley of Italy,

Wales, pirate's lair, Cornwall, Baroque, reason and romance. The theme of 'The Prisoner' was essentially the same as that of *The Truman Show*, the central character being trapped in what appears to be a benign, isolated environment, eventually becoming ever more sinister.

212. Katz, op. cit., p. xxxvi.
213. Ibid., pp. 47–51.
214. Ibid., pp. 221–30.
215. Ibid., p. 230.
216. Pollan, Michael (1997) 'Town-Building Is Not Mickey Mouse Operation', *New York Times*, 14 December, pp. 56–63.
217. See also 'Workbook: Themes and Issues', American Institute of Architects, 1998.
218. 'Celebration 98: Time and Space', American Institute of Architects, 1998.
219. See *New York Times*, 11 January 1998, pp. 6 and 10.
220. See Muschamp, Herbert (1996) 'Can New Urbanism Find Room for the Old?', *New York Times*, 2 June, p. H-27.
221. See Congress for the New Urbanism, History and Membership Information, San Francisco, California.

Chapter Seven

CONCLUSIONS: LESSONS FOR THE URBAN FUTURE

PRECEDENTS OF THE NEW URBANISM

It may seem appropriate that this present study should be published at the turn of the twenty-first century. Ebenezer Howard's *Garden Cities of Tomorrow* was published almost a hundred years ago in 1902, following his original publication of *Tomorrow: A Peaceful Path to Reform* in 1898.[1]

Howard was born in London in 1850 and educated privately in Suffolk and Hertfordshire. In 1871 he emigrated to the US where he joined a firm of stenographers reporting the proceedings of the Chicago Law Courts, returning to England in 1876 to become an official reporter to the Houses of Parliament. As a freelance writer until his retirement in 1920, he was influenced by Edward Bellamy's book *Looking Backward,*[2] which resulted in his own book, *Tomorrow*. In 1899, Howard founded the Garden Cities Association and in 1903 formed the first Garden City Company. Land was acquired in Hertfordshire to construct the new town of Letchworth in England, followed by Welwyn Garden City, which led to the establishment of the International Garden Cities and Town Planning Association in 1909. Howard died in 1928 and his reputation was founded on his solutions to urban problems through the idea of garden cities, which would eventually lead to the development of 'sustainable communities'.[3]

Thus the inheritance of Howard's ideas led directly to the American Greenbelt towns of the 1930s and the British New Towns programme after the Second World War. Reston and Columbia new towns followed in the US, and in turn heralded the new urbanist movement. Radburn, in New Jersey, was more of a prototypical garden suburb than a new town, with the innovative ideas of Clarence Stein and Henry Wright and their proposals for pedestrian/vehicular segregation. Howard could be considered a socialist, a term which would probably not usually have applied to the new urbanists. He believed that private land ownership was an inequity and that land should be owned cooperatively by all the residents of a garden city with rent funding pensions, healthcare and civic improvements.

In urban design, Howard contributed little except in the form of planning diagrams, and it was Raymond Unwin and Barry Parker, advocates of the arts and crafts movement at the turn of the twentieth century, who turned Letchworth into an architectural reality. Howard lived in Letchworth until 1921, before moving to England's second garden city, Welwyn, where he died a few years later.

Within the last hundred years, the urban design concept has come full circle. Yet in a 1998 conference sponsored by the American Planning Association[4] few of the new urbanists would acknowledge any connection with the garden city ideals. Alexander Garvin said that the concept of the garden city was 'an idea . . . irrelevant today. With trucking, it is cheaper to bring food from other parts of the country. Why would you give up inexpensive food in order to have an agricultural belt?'. But fossil fuels are finite, and the oil crisis of mid-2000 with its major protests against escalating petroleum and diesel costs in the US and Europe (including violent protests in France, Belgium and the UK) demonstrates that exclusive reliance on trucking does not auger well for the future.[5] Even Peter Calthorpe was ambivalent towards the ideas of garden cities, saying, 'We still do some greenfield new towns but most of our work is infill around transit . . . We don't need more new towns, but we do need more transit-oriented, walkable infill development'.[6]

It is hard to understand the negative attitude of the new urbanists towards garden cities when that is precisely why they are building a hundred years later. James Hoben, community planner at the federal Housing and Urban Development agency (HUD), has suggested that no one is interested in building new towns from this perspective. It would mean managing the market more than we traditionally do – espousing the free-market economic philosophies perhaps too cavalierly. But what is more controlling than Celebration or Seaside in Florida?

Mariemont, in Ohio, is cited by Ruth Knack as an '*upper class* community that illustrates such basic Garden City principles as a central focus and a connected series of green spaces'.[7] However, this description is inaccurate. Mariemont, to the east of Cincinnati, was envisioned by its founder, Mary Emery, as a 'national exemplar' in town planning. A visionary and philanthropist whose wealth was based on an industrial empire in the Midwest, Emery believed that congestion and poor housing were the result of poor planning. Though it was not entirely a philanthropic venture, Emery was motivated by a dream to better the environment and living conditions for her family's blue-collar workers. Certainly it was not intended for the benefit of the upper classes. The fact that by the end of the twentieth century Mariemont had become an exclusive residential neighbourhood was the result of the decline of public transport and the exponential popularity of the private motor car, generating ever-increasing property values.

Emery acknowledged the models of Letchworth and Port Sunlight (built by the Lever Brothers in New Liverpool, England). Designer John Nolan was considered one of America's outstanding city planners of his day and he, like Duany and Plater-Zyberk at Seaside, Florida, engaged the services of the leading American architects of his time.

The village of Mariemont issued strict design guidelines after it was incorporated in 1941 (it was listed on the National Register of Historic Places in 1979). The guidelines covered such areas as pet control, removal of snow and ice, parking restrictions, waste containers, minimum heat requirements, a zoning code, and architectural review board, and a planning commission as well as a weekly street maintenance programme. The architectural review board determined height, building volume, window treatment, exterior details, roof shape, materials, signage, use of property, removal of original materials, colour selection and approval,[8] setting the precedent for the new urbanism movement at the end of the twentieth century.

In 1986, *Lotus International*, the distinguished Italian quarterly architectural review, devoted an entire issue to the emergence of the new urbanism.[9] An article by Janet Abrams on the form of the (American) city illustrated two projects by Duany and Plater-Zyberk. Abrams acknowledged the examplars of the garden city not only by Raymond Unwin but, in particular, by John Nolan. Suggesting that Duany and Plater-Zyberk demonstrated 'the fruits of their research into what constitutes the archetypal American Small Town',[10] she reasserted that theirs was a rejection of statistics-based planning and recreated nostalgically a kind of community that reached its apogee towards the end of the nineteenth century (according to Duany) and remained intact in the US until around 1940.

Many of the projects illustrated in *Lotus International* were clearly intended for the affluent, and possibly resulted in the further segregation, if not necessarily racial, of socio-economic classes. The issue captured equally significant designs, including that of Michael Graves for Grand Reel, Galveston East Beach, Texas, as well as the Municipal Center for Phoenix, Arizona, the Venturi Ranch and Scott Brown proposal for Welcome Park, Philadelphia, and their design for the Republic Square District in Austin, Texas, Machade and Silvetti's design for Deep Ellum, Dallas, as well as one by Agrest and Gandelsonas for the same site.

Editor Pierluigi Nicolin asked the question, 'In what directions is the construction of urban America moving?'.[11] This particular issue of *Lotus International* was the fiftieth issue, which coincided (whether relevantly or not) with the fiftieth anniversary of the invention of the board game Monopoly. Nicolin suggested that Europeans had the image of the American city regulated by the games of stock exchange trading, however there was something else about the American city beyond these simple games of speculation.

HOMELESSNESS IN INDUSTRIALISED COUNTRIES: POVERTY AND HOMELESSNESS IN THE UNITED STATES[12]

The above examples may be viewed as an indulgence of an affluent economy and their relevance to the urban problems of the majority of the world's population in South America, Africa or Asia questioned.

As early as 1971, the United Nations Children's Fund (UNICEF) stated that only 10 per cent of the children in developing countries ever receive medical attention of any sort. In such a world, do we need designers and urban planners when adequate food and shelter are lacking? In underdeveloped or developing countries, perhaps more self-determination for the urban poor, rather than less, is called for.

The lessons in Latin America, described by John Turner and others, indicate that reconstruction and self-determination are often a more satisfactory answer (in psychological and practical terms) for the inhabitants of squatter settlements than the forceful removal of families to government-controlled housing projects. It is a case of the citizens creating their own urban design schema. This is not to deny that many of these groups received technical help from architects and others, but the final decision of the form of their urban complexes lay with the residents and not the technicians. Nor is self-determination necessarily confined to developing nations. Cooperatives in Glasgow, Scotland, and the northeast of England, or protest groups in the black ghettoes of North America are all indications of an alternative approach to urban development. Jane Jacobs, in her analysis of American cities,[13] and, more forcibly, Richard Sennet in *The Uses of Disorder,*[14] make the case for an almost anarchistic variety and degree of self-determination.

Events in mainland Britain during the summer of 1981 mirrored the street violence of Belfast, Northern Ireland, in the preceding decade. But in the predominantly black areas of London's Brixton, Liverpool's Toxteth, or Manchester's Moss Side, the root causes were not sectarian, political or even tribal (as some observers have described the civil disturbances of Belfast). Though strenuously denied as the basic underlying cause, it is evident that bad housing conditions, social and economic deprivation, and the spectre of permanent unemployment for the uneducated young all contributed to the explosion of violence. This, combined with an antagonism between the police and the people, has brought frightening visions that George Orwell's prophecies[15] might yet be fulfilled. The confrontation between police and the population of ghettoes in the inner neighbourhoods of American cities is pandemic, an example of which was the Rodney King riots in Los Angeles in the early 1990s.

In 1992, the International Year of Shelter for the Homeless, the International Federation of Housing and Planning (IFHP) published *Homelessness in Industrialized Countries.*[16] The IFHP revealed that homelessness was barely recognised as a problem, and despite apparent economic prosperity, homelessness in industrialised countries was in fact rapidly increasing. The working party members were Michael Lachambre (Paris), John Lane (London), Gisela Schuler-Wallner (Darmstadt),

Wolfgang Vormbrock (Hamburg) and Neils Salicath (Copenhagen). Reports were received from Denmark, France, Germany, Ireland, the Netherlands, the UK and the US. (Although the study was to primarily address the problems of the European Community, it was felt that a parallel study from the US was of equal relevance.) All these countries might be regarded as prosperous.

Neils Salicath tried to define homelessness, suggesting that it was not a fixed situation, but rather a process to which individuals are exposed. The homeless comprise people who are roofless, sleeping rough, living in shelters or hostels, or other places not intended for dwellings, such as car parks, bus and railway stations, airport terminals, 'cardboard' cities and so on. Homelessness may also be applied to residents of psychiatric units without any place to go if they are discharged, those who are discharged from prison after serving their sentences, pensioners waiting for accommodation in a nursing home, or those who occupy accommodation illegally – 'squatters'. It may also include individuals threatened by violence (battered women and children, for example) who need temporary shelter, and there are also those who may have a dwelling, but for economic and financial reasons may be dispossessed of their home. Economic vulnerability is often the main problem and homelessness frequently strikes in socially weak groups such as single-parent families (mostly women with small children), young isolated and alienated people, illegal immigrants and refugees. The crises that can result in these dire circumstances, for example disease (AIDS), divorce, unemployment, alcohol or drug addiction, are seldom addressed.

The reduction of existing rental housing due to demolition, urban renewal and transition to owner occupation, eliminating affordable single-room occupancy – particularly in the US – is an important factor, as are increases in rent above the annual inflation rate.

'Poverty and Homelessness in the United States' was the concluding chapter of the 1992 report,[17] yet it is ironic that the most affluent and politically powerful nation on earth confronts a growing problem of poverty and homelessness on an unprecedented scale. It is not the intention here to analyse the underlying political causes of the crisis, which grew from a relatively minor social issue to an imminent social catastrophe during the 1980s. Rather, the aim is to provide a factual account of the problem as it existed during the rise of the new urbanism movement.

A series of articles entitled *Opposing Viewpoints* appeared in the US during this period, investigating various crises relating to AIDS, drug abuse, violence, the health crisis, social justice and poverty. 'The Homeless', edited by the publisher, David Bender,[18] is an impressive attempt to give an accurate, factual account of these issues.

The authors describe the ways in which almost 50 per cent of single-room occupancy in the country have been demolished. This was largely due to the decrease of federal involvement in the creation and maintenance of subsidised housing during the Reagan administration, during which funding was reduced from $32 billion in 1981 to $9 billion in 1985. In addition to depriving poor families of adequate housing, the situation was exacerbated by the wholesale depopulation of the nation's psychiatric hospitals, resulting in the release to the streets of formerly institutionalised patients. It is worth noting that the Conservative Thatcher administration in the UK during the same period applied similar policies in its reduction of financial support for the National Health Service.

It has been argued by Carl Horowitz[19] that the statistical claim that there were at the time three million homeless in the US was exaggerated and largely dependent on a study by Hombs and Snyder of the Community for Creative Non-Violence. Entitled 'Homelessness: A Forced March to Nowhere', and published in 1982, the study was based on a detailed survey of shelters operated for the homeless across the US. However, the survey was later challenged by the HUD, which carried out its own survey in 1985, claiming that the number of homeless was in the range of 250,000 to 350,000.

It is clear from the above discrepancies in estimates that the homeless typically slip throught the net of conventional census samples, and it is suggested by Rossi[20] that most national estimates are based on compilations and/or extrapolations from local estimates of individual cities. The literally homeless are those who sleep in shelters provided for homeless persons or in places, private and public, not intended for dwellings – the 'hidden homeless'.

Rossi cites his own study (Rossi, Fisher and Willis, 'Chicago Homeless Study', 1986) as the only accurate study based upon a strategy of sampling both sheltered and unsheltered people in all areas of a major city.[21] He suggests that locating and interviewing the homeless is best done when most citizens would normally be at home in bed. His Chicago study, for example, was conducted in the middle of the night between 1 am and 6 am, but even this does not take into account night workers and those travelling between cities. The results are listed in the table below.

The seasonal pattern reflects the harshness of the Chicago winters and the responsiveness of its shelter supply. The shelters listed in the table were provided by Chicago's social service agencies for only a bare majority of the city's homeless. Most

Interview location	Survey source		
	Fall	**Winter**	**Combined**
Shelters	39.4%	73.9%	55%
Public buildings (bus/train stations, airports, building lobbies, bars, all-night cinemas)	16.4%	24.6%	20.1%
Sidewalks, streets, alleys	13.9%	0.8%	8.0%
Parks	0.8%	0.0%	0.4%
Abandoned buildings	1.6%	0.3%	1.0%
Under bridges or viaducts	0.8%	0.0%	0.6%
Parked cars, vans, trucks	0.0%	0.3%	0.1%
Unspecified non-shelter locations	27.0%	0.0%	14.8%

Pattern of homelessness	Street	Shelter	Combined
Homeless continuously	13.5%	9.4%	11.2%
Homeless once, less than one year	29.2%	43.6%	37.2%
Homeless once, more than one year	17.6%	21.8%	19.9%
Homeless more than once	39.7%	25.3%	31.7%

Source	Percentage of total income
Economic activity	29.0%
Pensions and disability	21.0%
Welfare	30.2%
Family and friends	2.9%
Charity	5.1%
Other	1.8%

shelters, especially those for homeless men, provide dormitories with many beds in each room, spartan bath and toilet facilities, and modest eating arrangements where food is offered. Privacy and comfort are minimal.

Just as it is difficult to compare the homeless and the extremely poor, it is also difficult to distinguish between being homeless and living in a conventional dwelling. Rossi's Chicago study identified categories of the homeless in terms of the length of time spent without adequate shelter (1980–85) (see the table above left).

Up to a few decades ago, in most cities like Chicago, private enterprise provided lodging at very nominal rents in the form of rooms in inexpensive hotels or 'flophouses'. Spurred by downtown urban renewal, most were condemned and razed, and were virtually non-existent in Chicago by 1986.

Present-day shelters, with subsidies from both city and state, are nearly all run by private sector groups, such as Catholic Charities. Many shelters have rules concerning conduct and prohibit drinking, drug use, disruptive behaviour and smoking. Explicitly barred persons include those with chronic mental illness and, though dress and appearance are not prescribed, probability of admission clearly takes this into account.

Sources of income derived by the homeless are as shown in the table above (right).

Though homelessness may afflict males more often than females (and this is increasingly not the case), this is not true of extreme poverty, especially for single parents. Single mothers take on responsibility for feeding, clothing and housing their children, and their poverty is more extreme than that of men, few of whom take on such responsibility. Unlike the current situation in Latin America, most homeless people in the US are long-term residents of the major cities. Chicago's homeless, for example, are not the migratory workers who occupied the skid row (a dilapidated section of the city inhabited by vagrants) of history. Some homeless are migrants: about 11 per cent have lived in Chicago for less than a year, although it should be noted that only 7 per cent of all Chicagoans have lived there for less than five years.

Rossi suggests that a major factor for the decline of skid rows in the 1960s and 1970s was the shrinkage of the casual labour market in urban economies. The changing technology in materials-handling equipment meant that the demand for unskilled labour or 'muscle power' disappeared, though this applied generally to the traditionally male labour demand and not the demand for unskilled or semi-skilled labour traditionally performed by females. Exacerbating this was the erosion of public welfare during the 1980s and 1990s.

Many of the extreme poor have been supplied by welfare Aid to Families with Dependent Children (AFDC). These payments have now declined to 63 per cent of their 1968 value, resulting directly in the appearance of female-headed households among the homeless. In 1986, a typical Illinois AFDC household comprising a mother and her 1.5 children was expected to live on $4,014 a year in direct cash payments and $1,798 in food stamps.

In an earlier work, Chester Hartman[22] resurrected the possibility of the resurgence of tenants' movements – last seen in the closing years of the 1960s. Hartman says that with nationwide rental vacancy rates at their lowest point in three decades, and the construction of new rental housing at a standstill, this, combined with escalating rental levels, has deprived tenants of their option to move. He suggests that affordable housing should be a basic right, like healthcare. (The collapse of affordable healthcare in 1991 indicates the espousal of a different set of priorities nationwide.) Indeed, during the 1980s some tenant groups did react against involuntary displacement due to gentrification, where private developers (with the aid of public subsidy and tax advantages) build office complexes, luxury residential condominiums or hotels, which, Hartman asserts, displace low- and moderate-income tenants, either directly by demolishing their housing or by attracting higher-income residents and boosting rental levels.

Atlas and Drier[23] maintain that the tenants' movement builds grassroots organisations and wins victories, developing leaders with political skills. Rent control, they say, keeps costs down, and anti-eviction laws and control over condominium conversion can give security and stability. However, their argument is weak in that it does not solve the problems of the truly homeless as defined by Rossi. Nevertheless, it does at least defend those lower-income families who are currently housed.

Later in Hartman's edited work, Paul Davidoff[24] suggested that three policies should be established:

1 a legal entitlement for all Americans to decent housing;
2 the employment of resources in the development of housing for lower-income families;
3 and the legal right not to be removed from a preferred place of residence.

However, the Reagan administration made it abundantly clear that it did not accept the concept of entitlement. Davidoff says that in the light of America's relative affluence, entitlement should be a reality. He quotes Michael Store's 1982 estimate of $55–77 billion to provide decent housing that meets higher construction and maintenance standards, and compares this figure with the elimination of a hundred B-1 bombers from the military budget at a total cost of $20 billion.

In another book, published in 1989,[25] Rossi described a new form of homelessness, markedly different from the skid row of the 1950s or even the 1960s. Skid row was replaced by 'new' homeless sleeping in doorways, cardboard boxes, abandoned cars, or resting in rail or bus stations. This was a vision not dissimilar to scenes in Europe. For example, in London, in particular, it was ironic to see during the Thatcher government – a period of economic affluence and spiralling property values – a veritable city of cardboard boxes in the Charing Cross Station/Leicester Square area of the West End of the city, in full sight of tourists and theatre-goers. The aggressive behaviour of beggars in major American cities and in particular New York, generated violence and even killings. New York responded by being one of the first municipal governments to provide shelters for the homeless. An alternative was to shelter families in so-called welfare hotels.

The Interagency Council on the Homeless in the US was founded by congressional legislation in 1987.[26] In 1991, its annual report insisted that programmes for the homeless included Federal Shelter Assistance, Food and Nutrition Assistance (including Special Nutrition Assistance for Home-less Children and Mothers), as well as programmes reaching the mentally and physically ill homeless. Many cities provided such support, including Atlanta and Detroit. However, the inescapable conclusion that arose from the report was that there was no coordinated programme to provide affordable housing on a national scale. This suggests an inexorable slide into an anarchical situation by the beginning of the twenty-first century. Funding for two major states during the period between 1987 and 1990 period was $205 million in California and $163 million in New York. A poorer state, West Virginia, where there is a more serious problem of homelessness, received a meagre $12 million during that three-year period.

In a study edited by Jurgen Freidrichs,[27] Elizabeth Huttman identifies the American problem. Like other cited examples, she describes how San Francisco has suffered a major loss of cheap housing units in the city, especially residency occupancy (SRO) hotels, most of which disappeared in the 1970s.

William Tucker, in a controversial work on homelessness,[28] describes the 1986 New York City Plan (under Mayor Edward Koch) to confront the problem of homelessness. The total programme amounted to $5.1 billion in 1990 figures for the provision of 252,000 units targeted at low-income families with an income up to $15,000, with the reconstruction of vacant buildings, the preservation of units from abandonment and the rehabilitation of occupied units of city-owned housing providing a total of 126,000 units. For moderate-income hous-ing with a family income of $15,000 to $25,000 there would be a total of 93,000 units, and for middle-income housing for those with an annual family income of $25,000 to $48,000 a total of 33,000 units. Tucker asked the question, 'Where does the $5.1 billion come from?'. The answer was the taxpayers. The financial crisis for New York City in 1991 was that nothing became of the programme. It is clear in the current political and economic framework of the US that such massive government intervention is an impossibility.

However, a number of private organisations do have an im-pact, in specific ways. The Association for Community Design, for example, is a group of non-profit architectural and planning technical assistance centres based in various cities across the US and frequently attached to universities. The centres limit their activities to the services of low-income people. They facilitate the volunteer efforts of private practitioners, and provide direct professional services to hundreds of self-help efforts generated by community- and neighbourhood-based organisations across the nation.

The Association includes Assist, Inc. of Salt Lake City; the Chicago Architectural Assistance Center; City College Archi-tectural Center, New York City; Community Design Center, San Francisco; Community Design Center, Minneapolis; Com-munity Design Center, Pittsburgh; Columbus Neighbourhood Design Assistance Center, Ohio; Environmental Works, Seattle; East Tennessee Community Design Center; Community Plan-ning and Design Center, Cincinnati; Los Angeles Community Design Center; Neighborhood Design Center, Baltimore; Pratt Architectural Collaborative, New York.

But not all of the centres listed above have received funding from their respective universities. The Community Planning and Design Center of Cincinnati had its funding withdrawn by the University of Cincinnati and is now an independent entity known as the Community Design and Development Center. This non-university entity has a considerable spectrum of ideas and projects, and its publication of the *Cincinnati Information Note* is one of the first attempts to implement the National Community Information Exchange Program of interconnected computers, augmenting the national framework of community-based organisations. The Cincinnati Neighborhoods Database is a system that warehouses graphic displays of land-use and building characteristics of neighbourhoods. A study of single-room occupancy in the northern sector of Cincinnati's Central Business District included housing for the Thirteenth Street Tenants' Association and rehabilitation for the Carthage District; rehabilitation of residences for the mentally disabled on behalf of Catholic Charities; housing rehabilitation for the physically handicapped; and housing design and construction for the homeless in Over-the-Rhine, one of Cincinnati's poorest innercity neighbourhoods.

The findings of these studies present a sombre picture of the homeless in the US. It is evident that political and economic change during the previous two decades has been responsible, in part at least, for the dramatic increase in the number of home-less. Equally disturbing is the lack of agreement between authoritative groups as to the true extent of homeless people across the nation. Advocacy planning and grassroots move-ments have played a significant role in changing public attitudes and awareness towards the problem, but again, such voluntary efforts like the community design centres cannot be expected to bring about major change without adequate funding. Affordable housing programmes need to be accepted as a necessity if social disruption and disintegration are to be avoided.

Yet if all the statistics above reflect an era during the 1980s and early 1990s when the US economy could be seen to be in decline, more recent investigations regarding poverty and the homeless equally give little cause for celebration.

In 1991, with the beginning of a transition towards a booming economy that was indeed sustained throughout the Clinton administration, the existence of homeless families remained a canker. In an article in *Scientific American,* Ellen Bassuk pointed to single women with young children as constituting the most rapidly growing segment of homeless persons.[29] Bassuk was, at the time, president of the Better Homes Foundation, a non-profit organisation serving homeless families. Her study, conducted with colleagues in psychiatric medicine at Harvard University, identified this group as the most urgent issue with regard to homelessness. It was revealed that every night between 61,500 and 100,000 homeless children sleep in welfare hotels, abandoned buildings or cars, the consequences of which are dire. During their formative years, Bassuk points out, homeless children lack the basic resources needed for normal development, which in turn causes medical, emotional, behavioural and educational problems. Their mothers are often the victims of abuse.

The increase in social security expenditures during the 1980s was seen as helping only the elderly. In 1970, one in ten families were headed by women; by 1989 this figure was more than one in five.

A 1990 survey published in *Time* magazine[30] from the State Office for Children's Defense Fund, US Department of Agriculture, revealed the following disturbing cost statistics under the title of 'The Economy of Intervention'.

Prenatal care for a pregnant woman for nine months	$600
Medical care for a premature baby for one day	$2,500
A small child's nutritious diet for one year	$842
Special education for a child with a mild learning disability for one year	$4,000
A measles shot	$8
Hospitalisation for a child with measles	$5,000
Drug treatment for an addicted mother for nine months	$5,000
Medical care for a drug-exposed baby for twenty days	$30,000
School-based sex education per pupil for one year	$135
Public assistance for a teenage parent's child for twenty years	$50,000
Six weeks of support services so parents and children stay together	$2,000
Foster care for a child for eighteen months	$10,000

Bassuk concludes her paper by saying: 'The serious systemic ills plaguing this country virtually ensure homelessness for a growing number of families'.[31]

Though much of the material cited above belongs to the previous decade of the 1980s, the record-breaking economy of the 1990s with increasing family affluence at every level, seems to ignore the whole issue of the need for stable housing to keep the working poor in their jobs, their children in school, and families out of shelters.

Jason De Parle reiterates the point made by the other observers that low-wage jobs of the new economy cannot pay the rent. The government, he claims, has now let new aid drop to zero, and he suggests that 1996 was 'the year that housing died'.[32]

De Parle's article implies that the federal government had conceded defeat in its drive over the last half-century to make housing affordable to low-income Americans. There was sufficient precedent. The Reagan administration had cut the number of new families receiving help from previous levels of 400,000 a year to 40,000. The Clinton administration dropped the number to zero. Housing, De Parle says, has 'simply evaporated as a political issue'.

More than five million households at that time in the mid-1990s paid more than half of their pretax income for shelter, with food becoming a lower priority. The government view, apparently, was that shelter was 'affordable' if rent and utilities consumed no more than 30 per cent of a household's income. This is a new situation: a generation ago, there were more cheap apartments than poor families. De Parle considers that as many as 15 million families qualify for federal housing assistance, but only 4.5 million receive it (a third live in government-run projects, and two-thirds rent privately with government help). He goes on to say that of the 10.5 million who do not receive help, 5 million who spend at least half their income on shelter are the most desperate. These include the disabled, the elderly and welfare recipients.

De Parle challenges the notion that the government is unable to help, since in the mid-1990s it was spending $66 billion a year on mortgage-interest and property tax deductions for middle- and upper-income families. More than two-thirds of these deductions went to families with incomes above $75,000. Efforts by housing groups such as Habitat for Humanity have scratched the surface of the problem and former President Carter, a great advocate for the group, claimed that Charlotte, North Carolina, would become the first American community to eliminate poverty housing. Though the city is now prospering, this has not been the case.

However, this is not to say that organisations such as Habitat for Humanity are without merit. The formula of self-help, self-build, has indeed been successful, but the national scale is small. Certainly it can be seen as the only housing initiative for poverty-stricken families that addresses urban design issues. Urban and architectural design is generally irrelevant in poverty solutions elsewhere.

By the year 2000, the problem has not diminished. James Fallows, writing in the *New York Times,* says: 'The way a rich nation thinks about its poor will always be convoluted. The richer people become in general, the easier it theoretically becomes for them to share with people who are left out . . . The last time the United States self-consciously thought of itself as rich, in the early 1960s, discussions of how the wealth should be shared were under way even before real prosperity arrived'.[33] When Clinton first ran for president the Dow Jones Average was under 3,500. In a period of just eight years, by 2000 it was 10,500! Investing in stocks is little more than a sophisticated form of gambling, but certainly one with far better odds of winning than the poor have gambling on the weekly state lottery (with odds of approximately 30 million to 1). With this recent prosperity, Fallows asserts, there is far less talk about the poor than when Clinton was first elected.

Accompanied by vivid photographs, Fallows' study ranges from a young single mother from Mexico working as a seamstress in Brooklyn, a makeshift homeless camp in north Las Vegas, a man working as a night auditor in San Jose and living in his car since his divorce, to a couple living in a Dumpster in Santa Monica and a man in Manhattan sheltering near an underpass and making a living by panhandling and burning drug needles in the nearby park.

The computer/financial complex at Silicon Valley, San Francisco, and Seattle, as well as New York, Boston and Austin, provides disproportionate wealth to relatively few Americans. Here Fallows asserts that relatively few people work in 'information technology', which ranges from chips to computers to the Internet, and this last aspect also affects the future shape of cities, as will be discussed below.

THE INTERNET AND ITS RELEVANCE TO CITY PLANNING

If the issue of extreme poverty and homelessness seems to have little connection with some of the conceits of urban design, the emergence of information technology (IT) in the 1980s and 1990s may have a profound impact on the future shape of cities.

In his *City of Bits*, published in 1996, William J. Mitchell described a new vision of urban living.[34] The use of underground fibre-optic systems would reconfigure space and time relationships that would change lives forever. The implication of this work is that people will no longer need the central city – indeed, the edge city condition proposed by Garreau will also be irrelevant. Given the possibilities of computer-literate people working from their homes, there seems to be a return to the cottage industries of the eighteenth century. Mitchell says in his introduction: 'I no longer had to go to work. Not that I suddenly became idle; it was just that the work came to me. I did not have to set out every morning for the mine . . . the fields, the factory, or the office; I simply carried a lightweight laptop computer that gave me access to the materials on which I was working'.[35] Mitchell refers to the RJ-II connections introduced into the back of aeroplane seats.

This celebration of computer-aided design systems, computer-controlled processes and industrial robots may be seen by some as profoundly disturbing. Mitchell goes on to question why this is an architectural and urban design issue. He says that merging civic structures and spatial arrangements of the digital era will shape daily routines. This supposition is probably correct.

The Internet negates geometry though it defines topology of computational nodes and radiating boulevards and, in a contradictory commentary, Mitchell says that these nodes and links can produce Hausemann-like diagrams, yet they are anti-spatial. He includes the terse comment that 'if you are homeless, of course, you are nobody'.[36] This key sentence is profound. If homelessness is of little consequence in the Internet Age, what sort of a future vision of society does this conjure up for those with skills and those without?

John Decker summarises an analysis of William Mitchell's prognosis in an unpublished paper, 'Urban Futures'.[37] A former assistant professor of urban design at Carnegie-Mellon University, Pittsburgh, Decker has specialised in computer applications in his field, and the following is an extract from his hitherto unpublished paper:

Cities are the collective manifestation of our need to build shelter combined with our gregarious nature, the edification of our desire to live in large protected groups.[38] When one begins to consider human action, the engine-city can be viewed as an organic entity, a machine capable of self-regulation. Change is a constant of urban action.[39] A major factor operating in contemporary culture affecting city form is the post-modern perception of the irrelevance of place. Overall, the physical city is a compound machine. It is a device, which consumes fuel, moves and rearranges mass and generates both waste products and heat. In essence, a mechanism operating somewhere between enthalpy and entropy.[40] Many of the major problems of city design and management derive from a lack of formal recognition of the real, visible, extended processes and phenomena that are the city.

This perception can be explained in terms of three phases: anyplace is an(other) place; anyplace is (extended to) every place; and every place is (accessible from) every place. Anyplace refers to the process of homogenisation.[41] Regrettably, many places where one shops, eats and moves are much alike from one North American city to another and, increasingly, everywhere else in the world. Examples are the iconic symbol of McDonald's hamburger franchises or BP gas stations. Most cities of similar size have similar airports, shopping centres, restored historic districts, suburban residential neighbourhoods and office complexes. In an attempt at differentiation they will have new buildings in their skylines and renewal projects such as ballparks (baseball stadiums) or football stadiums (as in Cleveland and Cincinnati, Ohio) or waterfronts (as in Baltimore), yet these are often owned by the same corporations, executed by the same groups of architects and designers and, consequently, are also very similar to one another.

Part of this process is owing to functional convergence. Generating expressways[42] (motorways) by engineering optimisation makes most look and function like any other. This type of homogenised appearance is notable in the design of products such as cars (General Motors, Chrysler and Ford products) or aircraft (Boeing in the US, Airbus in Europe) where stylistic variation increasingly is less important than functional

CityWalk, Univeral Studios, Los Angeles, California, Jerde Partnership International. Architectural Design, vol. 68, no. 1/2, 1998.

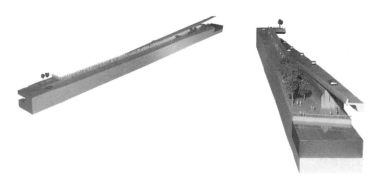

Tunnel Light Portal (a major interstate highway), Boston, Massachusetts, James Carpenter. Architectural Design, vol. 68, no. 7/8, 1997, pp. 40–41.

considerations, economy and mass-production techniques, particularly with the increased use of robotics. This is also evident in the architecture of hospitals, airports, offices and factories where functionalism is applied, though layered with the irrelevant decoration of postmodernism. Shopping malls are consolidations of previously dispersed retail establishments into single large buildings with internal pedestrian streets and characterless exteriors. Yet they, too, may become fossils as Internet shopping replaces that particular buying pattern. The recently completed Kansai Airport in Japan[43] is one of the largest examples of a consolidated city in a singular building complex.

Infrastructure construction has crossed boundaries. Power plants and hydroelectric dams in southern Utah generate electricity for Phoenix, Arizona and Los Angeles, California. There is land set aside in parks and wilderness, though the suggestion by George W. Bush in October 2000, to exploit possible major oil reserves in the huge Arctic wildlife preserve in northern Alaska would negate present conservation policies. Even so, the national park system has an internal infrastructure of lodges, shops and car parks and even in the Rockies, jets linking numerous cities can be observed continuously flying overhead.

Other problems have been induced by hierarchical disjunction between jurisdictions. The expressway is designed to connect nodes at a regional level, which, in turn, disrupts local connections. Market-driven growth seeks less and less regulated territory and therefore becomes piecemeal and disconnected. Each reactively constructed highway over a light rail system opens more territory and exacerbates the problem. According to John Decker, the unfortunate reality of North America has been a luxury of space and this, combined with the fundamental American tradition of favouring individual rights at the expense of the whole, makes the desire for endless extension a fundamental issue of its cities. Regions burdened with absurd levels of political fragmentation, such as post-industrial western Pennsylvania, will continue to decline, losing all capability to compete and attract the opportunities[44] necessary to internally generate sufficient revenue to maintain their crumbling infrastructure. As the city spreads, capital will continuously redistribute to power edges, inducing expanding geographical inequities, with original innerbelt suburbs.[45]

'Everyplace' refers to the alternative phenomena of the current world; the information linkage in infrastructure or the World Wide Web. With sufficient personal resources, anyone, anywhere, can now contact virtually anyone else. This capability radically expands the notion of the irrelevance of place by eliminating spatial and temporal barriers to human interaction. Although communication technology can support interaction with real-time video conferencing, more remote interaction is asynchronous and image-dissociated. Participants are hidden beneath a cloak of anonymity, rendering irrelevant other human barriers such as age, gender and race.

The physical apparatus of the Web is a spatial entity with a hierarchical array, major and minor nodes (hubs and servers), extending every point to every other point. Since every point can connect to any other point, ideally free of any prior configuration, user interaction need not bear any resemblance to the actual space of the Web. User-nets evolve, yet they are antispatial in that they are not arrayed against any real space. All of this complexity of interactions is implied in William Mitchell's pioneering research.[46]

In a type of display environment that immerses a user in a three-dimensional world of sight and sound called virtual

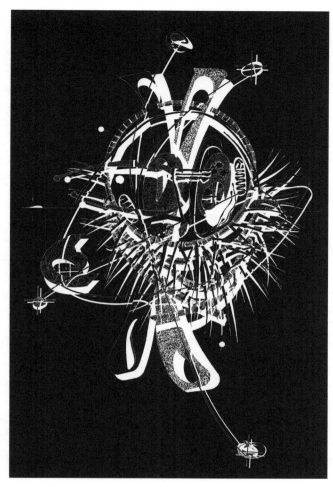

Bioscape Vertigo, an attempt to translate some aspects of the new landscape and the geometries of the new conic 'un' sections of vision, Neil Spiller. Architectural Design, vol. 68, Nol 7/8, 1997, p. 30.

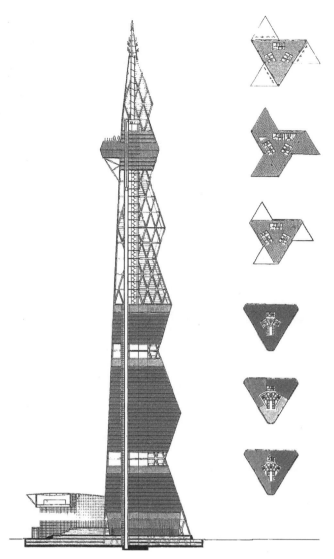

Jakarta Communications Tower, Jakarta, Indonesia (1995). Architectural Design, vol. 65, no. 7/8, 1995, p. 54–55.

reality, the displacement from actual place is even more pronounced. Although in its infancy and using cumbersome electro-mechanical equipment such as helmets/headgear, the illusion of immersion is, nevertheless, compelling, and can create a disorienting kind of interactive reality.[47]

A significant study of virtual reality is that by Howard Rheingold,[48] who has written previous works concerning the cognitive process. According to science fiction writer Arthur C. Clarke: 'In 1955, when I opened *The City and Stars* with a Virtual Reality sequence, I put it a billion years in the future. . . . [Rheingold] shows that the technology already exists all over the world – just as television did in the 1930s . . . Virtual reality won't merely replace television. It will eat it alive'.[49]

Virtual reality was partially derived from flight simulators used by the American Air Force and commercial airlines to train pilots. Such flight simulators teach pilots to understand flying without leaving the ground. The cockpit is part of a motion plat-

form that simulates the motions of an aeroplane. Virtual reality is an extension of this as a simulator. However, it differs in that the two-dimensional screen and joystick of a flight simulator are replaced by a three-dimensional computer-generated representation giving the user the ability to move within a virtual world. However, the equipment thus far is cumbersome, requiring the use of a high-technology helmet with electronic shutter glasses and an electronic glove.

On the other hand, although somewhat limited in its current state of technology, the illusion of immersion is still extremely compelling. Understanding this, users have begun to create interactive configurations called 'cities'. By using what is termed virtual reality markup language (VRML), it is possible to simulate a type of directly accessible three-dimensional world. Users can interact in this world from their personal stations, create their own environments as part of this composite world, and project themselves into it to interact with other remotely projected participants. Anonymity is achieved through the virtual projections being custom-created by the user. Video games employ this technique with role-playing systems with the term 'multi-user dungeons'. Originally only with written interaction, these sites now resemble virtual cities, and this could displace much of the commerce and trade interaction traditionally associated with the physical city.

One such site was termed 'Habitat', in which participants established virtual territories in the form of houses. With its growing number of users, the site's managers may find themselves dealing with issues of city-scale interaction, such as public and private space as well as architectural and behavioural boundaries. The visual representation of the accepted structures of urbanism is utilised, whether civic buildings and blocks, open space or places of assembly.[50] At the lower level or two-dimensional display, there is a surge of Web-based buying, selling and trading.

A recent survey in *Wired* magazine shows that 62 per cent of Americans are 'semi-connected', with 29 per cent 'unconnected' and above this 9 per cent considered 'connected' (individuals using email at least three times a week in addition to computers, fax machines, mobile phones and pagers). Of this 'connected' group, 2 per cent are considered 'super-connected'. The survey defines a majority group and thus a major political force.[51] In *The Net, That's Me. RE: The Digital Future*, author Marcel Bulling advances the notion of a direct Web-supported democracy that will acquire and apply citizen opinion free of government filtration and bias, and has created 'Decision Maker' software to facilitate this process.[52]

Finally, remote interaction, for example using email, means that fairly complex types of work can now be performed at home and 'phoned' in.

IMPLICATIONS FOR THE FUTURE CITY

All of this has serious implications for the morphology of the urban settlements of the future. Although at some point direct human contact is required for most business, many supportive functions, including consultation, can be conducted across great distances, reducing actual travel and the need for physical meetings.

Thus, if skilled individuals work from their homes in distant suburbs via email, teleconferencing and fax, what is the point of the city? What has not yet been addressed here is the psychological cost of such a vision. Human beings are naturally gregarious, a quality also shared in the animal kingdom by wolves, dolphins, whales, elephants, mountain gorillas and so on, all of whom depend for their survival upon positive interaction with each other. Without daily human contact, the vision of the future, from a sociological point of view is bleak indeed. The implications go well beyond the workplace.

If the new urbanism reflects a cycle of a hundred years to return to garden city ideals at the beginning of the twentieth century, in which people will work from their homes, so it may be said in cyclical terms that home shopping may have come full circle. Mail-order shopping, pioneered by the Sears

catalogue more than a century ago, was intended to serve the settlers of the Midwest and then the far west of the US where there were no shops among the new farmsteads. In contrast, the development of Internet shopping, whether for airline tickets, toys or clothing, points to the demise of the shopping mall.

Web-based communication breaks down interaction barriers and opens new areas of cooperation, but also deprives the basic human need for actual physical interaction. Regarding the emergence of cyber cafés, John Decker notes that

> these places of supposed social assembly are where people buy coffee or some other beverage and utilize the provided computers. Yet instead of interacting with other participants in the manner of more traditional cafés (consider the pavement cafés of Paris at the end of the nineteenth century) for the most part they turn their backs on the room as they focus on their computers, possibly interacting in a virtual coffeehouse via the web. This type of behavior has caused some observers to advance nightmare visions of a future where people only interact via virtual means, never leaving their apartments and fearing all actual human contact. Other cyber-prophets suggest that this new way of doing things may render obsolete all previous forms of human organizations and institutions, including the city.

The possible obsolescence of the city may be regarded as heresy in a study of urban design. Yet, in his conclusion to *The City of Bits*, William Mitchell summarises the evolution of the contemporary city through three distinct phases: the pre-industrial city, the post Second World War commuter suburb and the present situation, which he calls 'telepresence'. He describes his own experience of working in a video- and computer-supported Web-work of studios across the world while remaining in his office in Cambridge, Massachusetts, and further suggests that there will be a future where machines and devices disaggregate and miniaturise to the point of becoming as 'intimate' as clothing.[53]

The intentional process of planning and managing cities tends to focus around words such as 'vision', 'design' and 'policy', but it may be argued that the economic engines that build cities are driven by less controllable market forces. Unconsidered physical outcomes of policy are as disruptive to urban fabrics as physical designs applied without considering the desires and behaviour patterns of city dwellers. Ideally, urban design should be visualised policy and policy should be visualised design.[54] The problem is exacerbated in that individual professional tracks charged with building and maintaining these sprawling formations are as separated as the fragmented political fabric.[55]

Urban design is often applied as a reactive intervention, after functional aesthetic or economic failure. Urban design practitioners will include urban design on their calling cards regardless of their parent discipline, whether architecture, city planning, civil engineering, social science, economics, political science, environmental psychology or environmental science.

Lacking visual skills, their capability for effective decision-making is often compromised. If, however, they are presented with believable models that they can see, understand and relate to an overall vision, they will make appropriate decisions, instead of acting from a standpoint of vested interest without that capability.[56]

The separated professional approaches to development, design and the formulation of policy must be unified within the notion of the city, between collective behaviour and physical action. The mythology advocated by many architects that design alone can solve a city's problems is as incorrect as the opposite belief that social ills and inequities must be resolved before any intervention can be attempted. In physics, the discrepancy between light described as a wave and light described as a particle required a new paradigm recognising the circumstances of observation. Quantum physics broke with classical or Newtonian descriptions of reality.[57]

TECHNOLOGY AND TOOLS

The simple act of drawing was a first point of enhancement in our understanding of the world. Drawing involves seeing first, responding to what is seen in the creation of an artefact, and continuing the process through subsequent iterations. Drawing is essential as a technology that facilitates better seeing.[58] However, seeing may be more properly termed 'visualising' – a process of rendering visible a previously abstract concept.[59] The technology of visualisation, by enhancing the depth, point of view and range of our vision, has radically altered our concept of physical reality, an example being the case of complex motion, either very fast, very slow, or reversed in terms of time-altered motion picture photography.

The assemblages of processor chips resemble buildings arrayed against streets and expressways, represented by the printed circuit configuration. Viewed internally, the processor chips themselves begin to approach cellular-organic complexities yet their human-induced tendency towards orthogonal geometry still gives them a city-like appearance.

Computer graphics capability has now expanded into a full palette of options ranging from manipulation of still images to full-motion three-dimensional graphics. There are two basic graphical manipulation environments, raster and vector. Raster environments are those in which a graphical entity or image is broken into discrete points of colour and brightness on the screen – called 'pixels'. Manipulation of the image occurs directly on pixels or groups of pixels and overall resolution of the image is dependent on the number of pixels. In a vector environment, graphical components exist first as geometrically described entities such as points, lines and shapes. They are manipulated directly in geometric terms and memory is dependent on the number and complexity of the components. Unlike image environments, vector programs, even when limited to two dimensions, are capable of essential cinematic access to the virtual space, allowing almost infinite adjustments of points of view and magnification against modelled geometries.

Computer animation is an essential capability in urban simu-lation, allowing reconciliation between objective map-based viewing of the city (as in geographic information systems – GIS) and subjective-sequential ground-based viewing, which is how something as large as a city is actually experienced. This simultaneity between objective and subjective is a constant of urban theory and a useful tool for urban designers when exploring, for example, issues of monumentality or succession of spaces. Viewing the city in accelerated time from a fixed viewpoint is another useful tool. With sufficient data, the recon-figuration of components can be displayed through appropriate periods of time yielding an understanding of spatial behaviour.

When creating views of the city, representation must be considered relative to the scale of the view. Composite or multi-media combinations of the real and the virtual can be used to test proposals in terms of movement.[60] Zooming into a city at successive orders of scale reveals discrete elements and struc-ture in a clear succession of steps. At the lower end of regional or metropolitan scale one can see the extended pattern of contin-uous urbanisation. The configuration that Lynch called 'urban grain'[61] also alludes to the original divisions that David Harvey referred to as economically driven pulverisation of original homogeneous space.[62] Component size and interstitial spaces in the grain reveal a differentiation in land use and division into districts. Also apparent will be topographically induced deformation or separation in the city's layout. At the district scale, the view is close enough that the vertical structure of the city becomes apparent, reaching the limit between two- and three-dimensional representations.[63]

Although the city can be observed photographically at virtu-ally any scale from satellites, graphic reduction in the form of isolations of visual information is useful in revealing relevant structural and spatial relationships and, at the same time, reducing extraneous and confusing visual clutter. Figure-ground, reference to which has been made earlier in this study, is an example of this reduction, and has been referred to by Mario Gandelsonas, Colin Rowe and others as 'delayering'.[64] The process sets up an isolation and recombination of factors, which synthesises sets of spatial relationships within the city.

The real power of design-applied computation is the ability to draw in the third dimension, creating worlds that are acces-sible from any internal or external viewpoint. Multi-screen viewing allows simultaneous views from both subjective and objective standpoints. Referencing allows inclusion of complex non-repetitive entities such as detailed 'models' of the city-scape, yet, depending on the software, updates may not auto-matically take effect in the larger 'model'.[65] Demonstration of view obstruction (visual impact assessment) is an area where spatial simulations have proved useful as decision-making tools.[66]

A shortcoming of present computer simulation is the neglect of 'plantscape'. Tree cover and related vegetation play a significant role in urban visual character, yet highly complex and non-repetitious vegetation is difficult both to model and to maintain in memory. Various software environments can be used mathematically to create realistic computer trees, but memory prohibits their extensive use in an urban model. Symbolically simplified trees can be used for aerial views.

An approach now rapidly developing in two-dimensional re-touching and photocomposing is one that makes the computer-generated image look like a hand-drawn perspective, but the risk here is deviation from the defensible spatial accuracy offered by three-dimensional models.[67] Two-dimensional composites can be powerful tools for demonstrating a proposal to an audience of lay decision-makers, yet a careful method of presentation must be observed so that viewers understand the limits of what they are seeing. A method here is presentation of a photographic view, altered in the computer representation with step-by-step computer-modelled monuments and icons, matched to the real ones visible in the photograph.[68]

Delayering applied in the third dimension yields a powerful way of understanding complex interwoven spatial relationships that could be termed 'volumetric composition'. Combined with topographic or sectional views of city components, these visualisations can reveal internal and external relationships either in isolation or in various combinations. Layers can also be displaced in space to generate an exploded view.[69] Decomposition is an effective way of understanding the structure of a high-rise portion of the city by dividing the buildings vertically from street level up through their tower volumes and, if relevant, below ground. It can also be applied to elevation and street-wall analysis in architectural orders of scale, or the three-dimensional elements of an individual building in terms of visual composition.

Three-dimensional animation is generally thought of as applied to movement or fly-through sequences relative to a proposed or existing urban condition. Environmental phenomena can be viewed from a fixed or moving viewpoint in this animation process. Change in an urban district can be observed through accelerated time, showing the processes of building succession such as the build-up of vertical density.[70]

If driven by mathematical procedures that generate animation of physical processes, if normally invisible and charted by what are termed glyphs, these visualisations can be termed scientific.[71] Computer visualisations are not limited to the real. Imaginary three-dimensional factors can also be made visible. Regulatory envelopes of permissible height and bulk created by zoning codes can be represented as transparent forms over an urban model. The third dimension can also be used to express the magnitude of factors such as traffic flow volumes and resultant congestion. Other relationships such as assessed land value against building height and allowable floor area ratios (plot ratios) can also be applied. Linkage of three-dimensional data to other forms of mathematical data can create a small-scale GIS or facilities management (FM). For example, in a university, a building in the overall model of the campus can link to other files in terms of its individual floor plans with access to furniture, fixtures and other real-time properties, and be transferred to a spreadsheet type of database.

Early examples of the above were the models of various cities constructed by the Chicago office of Skidmore, Owings and Merrill. These models were mostly for internal use and did not become public resources, but the firm's work in this area ultimately yielded a software environment called Architecture and Engineering Series (AES) which is being used at the New

School for Social Research Environmental Simulation Center in New York to develop models of Manhattan and elsewhere.[72] Peter Bosselman's laboratory at Berkeley utilises combinations of both real and computer-based modules to examine climatic factors influenced by building wall locations to establish models for the further development of environmental regulations.[73] Virtual Los Angeles has been constructed by Bill Jepsom at UCLA for application within a range of uses from transportation studies to emergency preparedness. CAD models are combined with satellite images and ground-plane video to generate convincing ground-plane views. The process of data gathering is, however, labour intensive, and the simulations, once created, must run on advanced computers, referred to as 'reality engines', such as Silicon Graphic Onyx 2 line.

COMPREHENSIVE MODELS AND INTELLIGENT SYSTEMS

The ideal of a model management for the city is one that relates concepts to observable reality through simple systems of graphical notation. There is, however, a rift in urban paradigms between the behavioural or sociological approaches to the city and those that are physical and design-derived.

Urban ecological models of the city, such as those advanced by the sociologically driven Chicago School, evolved in various forms in the latter part of the twentieth century. Beginning with the city in terms of concentric rings of distinct social realms extending outward from a dense urban centre, through inner belts of ghettoes towards spacious and wealthy suburbs, the final model became more complex with a distribution of multiple centres creating the polycentric city.[74]

In the late twentieth-century city, layers of growth are deformed around major movement systems, such as freeways that facilitate growth, giving the urban fabric an amoebic-pseudopodal appearance. Los Angeles is a prime example of this type of formation.[75]

The process of observing and generating computer simulations of urban formation analytical studies still follow two basic city structures termed by Kevin Lynch as 'cores' and 'rays'. Lynch's descriptive approach indicated that core and ray configurations related to paths and nodes. Taken in terms of the connective fabric, cores and rays are essentially the same thing, except that cores are more concentrated singularities, for example a downtown district or a university campus, and rays are the connective corridors of roads and buildings. The actual behaviour of a given ray is influenced by surrounding cores, thus rays and cores must be considered together in analysis and design. Growth will propagate along the ray, or drain and disperse depending on the magnitude and action of the cores it connects. Where active rays cross, a new core may be formed, but the efficiency of a ray's movement systems between active large cores may drain smaller intermediary ones.[76]

The descriptive system of core and ray applies to the development of urban computer models whether the starting point is a single city block or a larger model that eliminates much architectural detail. The ideal computer model is one that can be continuously updated to include real change as it occurs as part of the public processes of planning. It is a living master plan free of the limits of fixed publication in terms of time. The graphic conventions it internalises must be simultaneous with the concepts they represent and flexible enough to include a full range of studies from real, current factors to more ephemeral types of conceptualisation. If properly devised, these models become long-term public resources.

Models of this type were created to facilitate development of the Pittsburgh Downtown Plan initiated in 1996. In the preliminary studies, the plan extended the downtown realm beyond the limits of the 'golden triangle' formed by the convergence of the city's two rivers. The computer model had to fully represent this topographic structure, particularly for examination of movement-related views. This was part of a larger initiative called Virtual Pittsburgh, in which all pieces could fit together and retain spatial coordination and edge-plane matching. All modelled components were placed at their real elevation above sea level.

The layer-delayer approach was applied to every level of modelling to build a set of analytical switching capability. The layering structure was initially arrayed into three groups: the environmental-geographic, movement fabric and architectural components.

In terms of the movement fabric on grade, intersections could be isolated and viewed in a way similar to Michael Southworth's analytical methods, and straight street runs, both major and minor, isolated by orientation, yielding a Gandelsonas-derived type of view.

In addition to the analytical layers, additional conceptual derivative models were created to explore the view structure in and around the downtown core. Imaginary view components such as urban rooms and view corridors were represented as several colours of transparent volumes. Major rooms associated with the river spaces were differentiated from smaller internal spaces such as small public squares or surface parking areas.

The next stage was to create a linkage between three-dimensional entities to produce a genuine three-dimensional GIS. Models of this type have been created by Michael Kwartier and Peter Bochek at the Environmental Simulation Center.[77] Kwartier's best-known effort were the models he produced of Lower Manhattan, New York. These explored the conversion of tall buildings, previously offices, to residential canyon-like environments on the lower floors, and included only floors of about 55 metres (180 feet), or 15 storeys.

For remote exploration of cities, a system available from the US Department of Housing and Urban Development, 'Community Connections' allows access to large sets of map-based demographic and economic data.[78] The site, and whatever is proposed on it, exists within a framework of movement infrastructure. If a project cannot be efficiently established due to lack of access or extreme congestion it is doomed to fail. Adding a large amount of floor space into the city raises surrounding demand for access, impacting congestion. Access within the building by elevators and other circulation elements becomes part of the external city's movement system. This has been termed 'the project access tree'.[79] Maximum occupancy of the site vertically is the optimum, but the addition of floor space in the city may have an impact on surrounding vacancy and lease rates, suggesting that these two factors act in opposition. The site, therefore, is part of an active network of environmental, functional and regulatory relationships.[80]

Initial studies to develop a simulation tool termed an Urban Design Decision Support System (UDDSS) have been carried out by Bige Runcer and Michael Shealy under the direction of John Decker at Carnegie-Mellon University. The studies were aimed at exploring possible operational environments and interfaces within two modules: a base model which created sites and buildings into separate floors, building cores allowing modifications to all components; and an economic module allowing the assumption-based analysis of the value of a building against its capacity to generate income.

In the world of artificial intelligence, there has always been a fundamental division between those who approach intelligent behaviour as hyper-compounding reflex actions and others seeking something more essential, in terms of a process that resembles reasoning with the end objective of yielding machine intuition. To achieve what Alan Newell of Carnegie-Mellon University calls 'integrated intelligent systems',[81] many researchers have assembled sets of reflex operations into 'neural' nets named for the brain-like architectures they represent. The goal is that the operational similarities with the brain of these systems will ultimately produce the phenomena of intelligence. These artefacts, as Hugh De Garis calls them, could eventually be extremely large.[82] The vision is that, in combination with robotic components, city systems could be self-constructing, self-maintaining and self-managing – all conducted under an architect-directed city management machine. Such a vision is not impossible (though not necessarily desirable) given the existence, already, of intelligent building skins, robotic car manufacturing, building erection robots and self-painting bridges. However, to many these notions are nightmarish.

Layer-enhanced imaging (LEI) is a relatively low-cost system that allows planners the means to demonstrate step-by-step changes in the environment. It is regarded as an alternative to desktop computer photo simulation, and is the process of adding computerised illustrative information to photographs.[83] Digital layers containing photographic images such as trees or building components are added. The layers are independently created and edited, using programs such as Adobe Photoshop, and used to display sequential changes to the environment.

At the beginning of the 1990s, the Media Laboratory at MIT commenced experiments with holograms using a video image. Holograms are created using laser light on flat surfaces creating apparently three-dimensional images. Thus, buildings can be drawn on a computer screen using the conversion of computerised data into a hologram of a three-dimensional object. Electrical signals with changing voltages are converted on to a piezo-electric crystal. The crystal sends an ultrasonic wave through a tellurium oxide crystal. Laser light passing through the crystal alters to contain holographic information. In the current state of technology, however, this process uses vast and therefore uneconomic computational power.

POPULAR PREDICTIONS FOR THE NEW MILLENNIUM

Throughout the late 1990s, as the new millennium approached, the emerging technology described above was recounted in a plethora of visions for the future. A *New York Times Magazine* special edition[84] discussed such issues as molecular genetic screening to allow parents to shape the destinies of their children, creating equally nightmarish visions of the future, including human cloning. The disappearance of personal privacy with universal and constant visual surveillance is already highly developed, summoning up the Orwellian prophesies of the mid-twentieth century. For example, email can now be decrypted by government agencies, and global positioning system satellites not only allow the car driver to know where he or she is, but can also be monitored outside the vehicle.

An article entitled 'The Next Hundred Years' by James Gleick suggests that 'Privacy will be to the information economy of the next century what consumer protection and environmental concerns have been to the industrial society of the twentieth century'.[85] Yet many users of the Internet hide behind false names in order to avoid verbal harassment and slander. Gleick says that the Internet, ironically, has recreated a small-town world where people mingle and share news. Unlike the intimate small towns of the past where individuals could disappear and re-emerge elsewhere with new identities, the small-town world of the twenty-first century is 'virtually' just one big town.

In the same issue of *New York Times Magazine*, Rem Koolhaas considers the urban landscape,[86] suggesting that the new urban landscape would be a mirage of the Rockefeller Center as 'a forest of skyscrapers, some of them leaning, seemingly felled . . . We promenade on a plaza between two immense floating slabs. Information scrambles across their surfaces of energized crystals: advertisements, jokes, exchange rates'.

George Orwell wrote in 1942 that in an ideal world there would be no demand for canned food, aspirins, record players, machine guns, daily newspapers, telephones and motor cars. Yet the victims of daily life are online addicts who do not know their next-door neighbours, satellite-dish owners who have stopped reading, computer users overwhelmed by email, infuriated by software glitches and baffled by incomprehensible manuals.[87] John Tierney suggests that George Orwell was technophobic.[88] Though envisioning a two-way communication device called the telescreen, Orwell thought that such technology would, in itself, promote tyranny and war. He also predicted the use of paper plates, suggesting a Ministry of Crockery where municipal pick-up trucks would collect dirty dishes in exchange for clean ones.

According to James Gleick, the current television remote control is 'a classic case of technology that worsens the problem it is meant to solve'.[89] The case of changing channels on cable television creates disorienting images, leaving the viewer with a feeling of dissatisfaction, not unlike the feeling after consuming hamburgers at any fast-food chain, creating weight gain without nutrition. As an example, the author of this volume timed the four major networks on early morning news channels in October 2000. In each half-hour segment there were approximately ten to fifteen minutes of advertising, ten minutes of actual news and an unbelievable five to ten minutes of weather forecasts during a month of excellent weather and little rain in the Midwestern states. The noisy commentary of the forecasters was probably more irritating than the advertisements.

However, consider now the everyday use of the telephone or mobile phone. At one time if one had to query payments – for example a bill from a utility company – a real person responded to your call and it took five minutes to resolve the problem. Now it takes twenty minutes. Whether it is an airline office, credit-card company or theatre booking agency, the response is something to the effect of: 'Please select from the following menu' (push buttons 1–5). After this there is another menu (with 1–7 options) followed by the message: 'Hello, your call is very important to us. Currently all our representatives are assisting other customers. Please select from the following options. If at any time you need (!) to repeat the menu, press 4. Hello, your call is very important to us. Please stay on the line. If you are using a rotary phone [of which there are very few in the US today] please stay on the line and a representative will be with you shortly'. Many people even pretend to be using a rotary phone in the hope that a real person will answer their call. The reassurance and options continue *ad nauseam* and after twenty minutes, there is still no human communication. The situation is often further exacerbated by intermittent recorded music, invariably in poor taste.

Similarly, checking in at a major airport used to take five minutes with a paper ticket and a carbon copy. With the new electronic systems it can take up to four times as long. The point is, the quality of life has not improved in the last two decades as a result of our 'modern conveniences'; rather, it has noticeably declined.

Again, the *New York Times Magazine*, in celebrating the new millennium,[90] indicated correctly that the process by which movies are filmed, assembled, distributed and exhibited will eventually be completely digital. This has enormous aesthetic and cultural implications, which will eliminate the 'magical, chemical, poetical process' of the traditional way of filmmaking. Walter March, film editor of *The English Patient* and *The Talented Mr. Ripley,* points out the difference between the brain patterns in people watching television and those watching film. With film, he states, the mind constructs an image of reality out of the alternation of light and dark.

In drawing together a panel of scientific experts to make predictions for the next millennium in constructing a time capsule, there seemed to be no consensus of opinion. One of the points made by Margaret Maclean, former director of documentation at the Getty Conservation Institute, was that digital storage media do not have a long lifespan, suggesting a return to analogue recording. Other members of the panel agreed, noting that digital information is stored in binary code, which requires a computer to read it.

In 1999 *Management Review* indicated that many urban areas across the US have become entertainment destinations with sports complexes and historical districts to create a wider market for retailers.[91] Such an example is San Diego's downtown entertainment district, completed as long ago as 1985, becoming the catalyst for the city's urban renewal. Yet in the same edition there was recognition of the growing worldwide poverty where in 1993, 1.3 billion people worldwide (an increase of 100 million from 1987) earned less than $1 per day.[92]

The predictions of *Time* magazine for the next millennium may appear to some as verging on the absurd.[93] Tom Peters suggests that 90 per cent of white-collar jobs in the US will be destroyed or altered beyond recognition within the next ten to fifteen years. The supposition is that the growing use of enterprise software will be through the development of white-collar robots. Thus, according to Julie Rowe,[94] tissue engineers, gene programmers, artificial intelligence brokers, data researchers, genetic crop and livestock scientists and virtual reality actors will replace, through the Internet, stockbrokers, car dealers, insurance and estate agents and even mail carriers. With distance learning, Rowe claims, teachers will be redundant. Printing will become extinct and the implications are that books will become obsolete. Yet the 'Harry Potter' series of books by British author J. K. Rowling suggests otherwise. Now translated into many languages, their popularity has created a renaissance in reading 'real' books among many millions of children both in the US and elsewhere. Rowe goes on to claim that the position of CEO of large corporations will be filled by global teams of decision-makers and that interstates will have 'smart lanes' enabling computer-driven vehicles to travel bumper-to-bumper at high speeds, eliminating the need for trucking. More ominously, she suggests that with in-vitro fertilisation and cloning, human fathers will also become obsolete.

Daniel Eisenberg in the same issue of *Time* magazine,[95] refers to millions of telecommuters, making the traditional office unnecessary. Yet he acknowledges that though personal computers may be appreciated for solitary pursuits such as PowerPoint presentations and writing, co-workers may need to brainstorm and exchange ideas and even gather round the water cooler or the coffee machine. In this case, face-to-face, he suggests, may be preferable to email and the Web. Privacy will certainly disappear with surveillance cameras everywhere and the opportunity of supervisors to monitor employees' email.

Challenging all of this is the suggestion by Paul Bracken[96] that China will become the superpower of the twenty-first century, replacing the US.

The *New York Times* in its 'Tech 2010' special issue[97] takes, perhaps, a more positive view in examining recent inventions that may foster a better life. A fairly banal example is the genetically engineered ten-inch-tall dwarf tobacco plant developed by scientists at the Salk Institute (a normal plant is five feet tall).[98] This has now introduced the possibility of a dwarf lawn with each blade of grass one-and-a-half inches tall, eliminating the need for mowing lawns in the suburbs and producing everywhere front lawns as lush as those in Beverly Hills, California.[99]

The Adaptive Cruise Control system for motor vehicles, developed by Delphi Automotive Systems, prevents vehicles from rear-ending one another. This is achieved by radar in the front grille, which registers the vehicle in front, calculates its speed relative to the vehicle behind, and sends information to the automatic throttle and braking controls, overriding the driver

and taking precautionary measures. Parallel systems have been developed to prevent rollovers in sports utility vehicles.

A bleaker picture of the future has been illustrated in various films, beginning in the early part of the twentieth century with *Metropolis* (1926). Of the more recent of this genre of film, *Blade Runner* was one of the first, and *The Matrix* one of the most startling. Critics of the latter contradict each other, with some dismissing it as a typical science-fiction view, and others believing it to be a masterpiece even beyond its amazing special effects. Though a counter-view of *The Truman Show* (see page 232), *The Matrix* has its parallels in making people believe they live conventional lives. But unlike *The Truman Show* it takes place in the aftermath of a global nuclear disaster. The focus of the film is on a vastly decayed subway (underground) system, portraying the degradation of the city as a whole. It was co-produced by Joel Silver, who presented such popular films as *Lethal Weapon*. Interestingly, Silver became a passionate follower of Frank Lloyd Wright and later purchased the Storrer House in Los Angeles. His interest in architecture, ironically, is evident in his apocalyptic visions of decaying and destroyed cities in *The Matrix*.

The film's role in contemporary architecture has come a long way since *The Fountainhead* (1949), adapted from the novel by Ayn Rand, portraying an anti-establishment architect, Howard Roark, played by Gary Cooper. With obvious references to the struggles of Frank Lloyd Wright in the 1930s, *The Fountainhead* was the promotion of modernist architecture above anything else, and in the late 1940s had a clearly anti-socialist ideology. Ridley Scott's *Blade Runner* (1982) has exactly the opposite message with its sombre vision of a disintegrating Los Angeles of the future – a precise vision of the Los Angeles of November 2019, with advanced forms of robotic 'replicants' of human beings.

Despite all this, it could be said that George Orwell's predictions in his novel *1984*, first published in 1948, have never really come to pass – at least not yet. The division of the world into three dictatorial superstates constantly at war is belied by the collapse of communism beginning in 1989. Yet in a later film, *Heat* (1995), Michael Mann presented a virtual city of attraction and repulsion – Umberto Eco has referred to Los Angeles as the capital of postmodernity, the hyperspace of a new social ontology.[100] Martin Price states that empirical realities have fused with urban mythologies, blurring the boundaries around the city, investigating its strengths and weaknesses. He rejects the idea that the city is entirely a utopia or a dystopia. Walter Benjamin regards the city in terms of attraction and repulsion in much the same way as Mann.[101] Benjamin and Mann identify the urban structure as a social totality featuring modern and postmodern social and economic structures in terms of time, space and identity.

Paula Massood's 'Mapping the Hood'[102] investigates the utopian/dystopian polarity from a distinctly African-American viewpoint, dealing with the hardships of coming of age. The specific boundaries of films such as *Boyz N the Hood*, *Juice*, *Menace II Society* and *Straight Out of Brooklyn* are Watts in South Central LA, Brooklyn and Harlem. The dystopia reflects economic poverty and segregation within the ghetto.

Likewise, the citizen's frustration with huge metropolitan areas like Los Angeles is eloquently portrayed in Joel Schumacher's film *Falling Down* (1993), in which the central character (Michael Douglas) becomes enraged while he sits in his car in gridlock traffic. Such freeway responses are a catalyst for violence not dissimilar to the Rodney King riots of 1992 in LA, which resulted in the death of 58 people. *Pulp Fiction* offers a similar apocalyptic vision of rage.

The presentation of imagery in film has been transformed recently with the advent of digital technology. Hitherto, spatial representation used analogue technology with collages, animation and additive methods. With digital technology, spaces can be generated synthetically. The computer calculates a transition between incompatible spaces as a hybrid of synthetic and experienced spaces, referred to as 'morphing'. Spaces without scale can be created and what appears to be material space can be in permanent motion.[103] Thus Luc Besson's *The Fifth Element* offers visions for the future of Manhattan, with the island as a high plateau similar to the Acropolis, with canyon-like trenches for the development of new property development.

The Present Reality, Urban Sprawl and Smart Growth

If the above account presents both optimistic and pessimistic views of the immediate urban future, the reality of the present paints another picture. Though there may be jubilation regarding the new urbanism, the reality at the turn of the millennium is very different. Urban sprawl has become, over the last decade, a controversial political issue. As has been previously noted, urban sprawl since the middle of the twentieth century has been facilitated by the large land mass of the US relative to its population, combined with low land values. It has also been enabled by accessibility through the construction of the interstate highway system, creating the expanding suburbs, as well as the freeway systems in metropolitan areas. In addition to these factors is the decline in traditional rural agriculture.

A number of politicians, commenting on the huge quantities of land being developed, have suggested that suburban developments do not create happiness.[104] The 1970s experienced much alarm over the disappearance of farmlands, questioning the ability of the US to feed itself. Ironically, much produce, particularly fruit, is imported from Central America because it is cheaper. The increase in farming efficiency, albeit at the cost of the small family farms that are rapidly disappearing, is through major high-tech agricultural companies. Samuel Staley, an urban economist at the Reason Public Policy Institute of Los Angeles, claims that in 1992, 95.3 per cent of land in the US was undeveloped, and that by 1999 this had reached 95.1 per cent. This seems an unlikely figure unless Canada and Alaska are taken into account, and those statistics for the contiguous US, if that is Staley's claim, seem questionable.[105]

The criticism of suburban life may be seen in American literature, and especially in American cinema in such movies as *The Graduate* (1967). The cartoon show 'The Simpsons' probably shows suburban life at its most cruel, though it contains significant underlying messages.

In the more affluent suburbs, a new phenomenon has occurred in the last few years. Whereas affluent families may have moved out of city neighbourhoods to prestigious addresses in the suburbs, they are no longer content to occupy an existing house in, say, Indian Hill in Cincinnati, instead purchasing it for perhaps two million dollars, demolishing it and building a new five-million-dollar house on the same site. According to the National Association of Home Builders, in 1999 10 per cent of the 1.3 million single-family homes built nationwide were constructed on lots of recently demolished houses, a trend brought about by the shortage of larger houses for sale in fashionable areas. The most tragic example of this is where the owner of one of Frank Lloyd Wright's most beautiful (and the last of his Usonian) houses on the West Coast has applied for demolition, though the reason here is not entirely clear.

The replacement houses mentioned above have a number of specifications. There must be a master bedroom suite with his-and-her jacuzzi bathroom; at least four other bedrooms each with en-suite bathrooms; huge walk-in closets; three- or four-car garages; and an eat-in 'gourmet' kitchen (in contradiction to Frank Lloyd Wright's contention in *The Natural House*[106] that by the end of the twentieth century kitchens would become virtually obsolete: 'people will eat out in restaurants or bring in the caterers'). The 'great room', two-storey for entertaining, is also a prerequisite. New zoning laws restrict not only the floor area ratio to lot size but also the ratio of paved driveways to the garden where grass planting is required.

The phenomenon of the 'guard-gated' community is described by Randall Patterson.[107] Canyon Gate, a suburb in the Houston metropolitan area, is totally controlled. No alterations to these purchased homes are permitted without approval from the Architectural *Control* Committee, and no plant would be allowed in the front yard unless listed on the 'master plant list'. All external painting must be uniform. The gate protects the residents from 'invaders'. Forty kilometres (twenty-five miles) from downtown Houston, the culs-de-sac have signs saying 'No Way Out'.

Martha Stewart remarks upon the changes in the traditional New England small-town of Westport, Connecticut, where she lived in a two-hundred-year-old farmhouse, celebrating the small-town lifestyle of neighbourliness. But chain stores and office complexes were soon to appear, and whereas residents had previously commuted via a reliable rail system to New York City, many non-residents now began commuting to Westport itself. Appropriately, Stewart criticised the visual chaos caused in the small-town setting, with overhead utility lines suspended on 'propped-up' telephone poles, obstructing views of trees and the sky. Again, like the new Canyon Gate development in Texas, over the last decade Westport has experienced the building of high walls with electronic surveillance. Martha Stewart left.[108]

Scottsdale, Arizona, where Frank Lloyd Wright established Taliesin West between 1937 and 1956, was originally located in the heart of the desert wilderness. By 1956 it was still relatively remote, though spoiled by adjacent electricity power-line street pylons. In 1950, fewer than two thousand people lived in Scottsdale, occupying only one square mile. By the turn of the century, Scottsdale covers an area that is three times that of San Francisco, with a population of nearly 170,000. Developers offer one-acre sites in gated communities and the landscape has been cleared of mesquite trees and paloverde. The travel time from downtown Phoenix is over an hour.

The new urban west has the fastest growing metropolitan areas in the country, with job growth in computer technology, telecommunications and, surprisingly, tourism. Pollution is a major problem. Seattle, Washington, and Portland, Oregon, are fortunate to have the lowest pollution count, but Phoenix, New York, and especially Los Angeles and Houston have the highest.[109] Yet Seattle is considered to be among the five worst cities in the US for traffic congestion, with a growth in population from half a million in the 1930s to two-and-a-half million in the 1990s.[110]

Portland, Oregon, is one of the fastest-growing cities in the nation. Set in a beautiful landscape of mountains and forests, unlike Phoenix and Las Vegas it did not allow the uncontrolled growth experienced in Los Angeles and elsewhere. During the late 1970s, the city established the limits of the metropolitan area, bounded by forests and farms. The policy was to control employment, homes and retail within a highly defined area served by light rail and buses as well as motor cars. Suggestions that this would both reduce employment and property values have proven to be unfounded. A policy of dissuading people from using cars, limiting car parking spaces and demolishing a downtown freeway appears to have been successful. Though the population is relatively small at approximately half a million people, high-tech campuses including many research centres have flourished within the tight urban boundaries, and property values for houses have soared rather than declined. Its legislation against urban sprawl is among the strictest in the US. Its attractions are the forests, fruit orchards and winding small rivers adjacent to the urban boundaries. The quality of life it can offer was a key factor in drawing highly skilled professionals to the area. Oregon, with a population of 3.2 million, has drawn half a million new inhabitants within the last fifteen years. Boulder, Colorado, is also a good example in controlling urban growth with the purchase of more than 10,000 hectares (25,000 acres) of land on the edge of the city, near the mountains, to prevent further speculative residential growth and preserve the natural habitat.

Contrary to the above is Edwin Mills' laissez-faire attitude against control: 'In the outdated traditional view, central cities serve as our major population and employment centers, with suburbs playing a minor supporting role . . . There is no question that recent decades in our country have been characterized by higher population and employment growth in the suburbs than in the central cities. The substantive issue is whether this growth has been excessive . . . It is unfortunate, therefore, that today's anti-suburbanization literature is hardly ever written in the context of modern welfare economics'.[111] Mills rails against land-use control and suggests that this decreases property values, yet the experience of Portland, Oregon, and elsewhere would suggest otherwise. Thomas Sowell, in an equally, if not more, vituperative article, suggests that 'urban sprawl is today's contrived crisis',[112] used by politicians as a tool. He suggests

that Al Gore's book *The Earth in the Balance* is 'a classic example of hysterical environmental extremism'.

What both of these reactionary writers fail to mention is the quality of life in the suburbs. William Hamilton[113] outlines how youth is alienated. The Columbine High School massacre in Littleton, Colorado, presented a disturbing image of disaffected teenagers from upper-middle-income families. Hamilton points to the huge areas of disconnected communities that produce psychological disorientation. These communities were intended to be 'safe havens' from the sociological, racial and economic problems of the inner cities. Their lack of character, which Hamilton eloquently describes, results in a lack of identity, diversity and tolerance with no shared civic ideals. The car-based culture leads to dissociation from the reality of contact with other people. Hamilton views the suburbs as ignoring teenagers as the major volatile element of the population. According to William Morrish 'they are basically an unseen population until they pierce their noses . . . they have access to computers and weaponry [and] the sense of alienation that may come from such isolation or neglect will have a much larger impact than it might have before'.

Even new urbanists like Andreas Duany acknowledge that in creating the new towns, seldom were teenagers involved in the public planning process. Teenagers need places to congregate that they can identify as their own. The spheres of home and school are compromised by two-income parents who imagined that moving to the suburbs was going to be beneficial to their children. However, the alienation of suburban teenagers is not a new phenomenon. Half a century ago, the eloquent portrayal by James Dean in *Rebel Without a Cause* displayed the angst of the time. Houses with four bedrooms and four bathrooms provide creature comforts but do not necessarily provide a social environment. Certainly, examples of the new urbanism like Celebration, Florida, provide a physical environment where teenagers can congregate, but the family social environment is lacking.

Architecturally, there has been movement to change the appearances of houses in the suburbs. Timothy Egan[114] refers to traditional suburban homes as 'snout houses', which turn their backs to the street with the front facades composed of two- or three-car garages housing monstrous sport utility vehicles. The front door is obscure. In September 1999, Portland, the icon of good urban design, banned 'snout houses', despite protests from developers that this was a fundamental right in a democracy, and has encouraged designs with porches, bay windows and inviting front doors, though without dictating the designs of the houses themselves, as is the case in many of the new urbanism projects,

In 1995 *Newsweek* magazine[115] produced a formula for new urban living and the promotion of 'smart growth', with Seattle and Portland as obvious examples. The first challenge is to devise an alternative to sprawl, where people can envision children playing in the street. Thus, the idea of suburban houses on half- or one-acre plots was seen as a convenience for the motor car user. Increased density which allows a mixture of housing models would include detached houses, row houses, apartments and 'granny' flats, and the new suburban village would be no more than a quarter-mile to its edge, including the transit stop and a convenience store. Community parks would replace the ornamental lawns on the one-acre plots.

More controversially, there may be mandatory design codes, citing historical examples such as Scarsdale, New York, Mariemont, Ohio, and Lake Forest, Illinois. Sterility in suburban living may be caused by high walls or fences, with guards and gates, isolating residents from the rest of the community, creating a barrier between them and the shops and public squares. The sterility they impose is seen as protecting property values. Changing this is contrary to the ideology of the free-market economy. Oscar Newman attacks this new urbanism as a 'retrogressive sentimentality', where most people remain in these communities for no more than five years.[116]

In the fifteen ways to fix the suburbs, Sandy Felensthal in *Newsweek* suggests the following: Give up lawns because they become an intense preoccupation of residents with all the work they involve only to reflect the owner's vanity. Walkable communities become impossible with large one-acre lots. The ubiquitous corner store that has all but disappeared should be reinstated. Children, the elderly and the handicapped – particularly those without a car – are isolated. The cul-de-sac is controversially seen as counter-productive in the scenario. In terms of sprawl there is still no shortage of land in the US, unlike Japan and Europe. The isolation of the garage from the front facade, already discussed, is seen as a priority, as is the mixture of housing types. Tree planting on street curbsides, particularly flowering trees, creates canopies in neighbourhood streets. Old malls, particularly strip shopping centres are being restored with landscaping and the elimination of peripheral surface car parks with new configurations. Mass transit is seen as essential in the transformation of suburbia together with the creation of new town centres with pedestrian plazas, squares and village greens. The use of high-intensity sodium-vapour streetlights is also alienating. Some innercity areas in cities like Cincinnati have low-intensity lamps, creating 'gaslight' districts. The boundaries of suburban communities should have intensive landscaping to emphasise the dramatic transition between built form and the natural world.

A new role for planners is leading smart-growth audits evaluating jurisdictions in promoting smart-growth principles. David Holden[117] cites the Charlotte-Mecklenburg (North Carolina) Planning Commission's initiative. The population grew from 404,000 in 1980 to 511,000 in 1990 to an estimated 622,000 by 2000. Such growth has produced traffic gridlock, overcrowded schools, loss of open land and expanding development. Typical of many mid-sized metropolitan areas, the construction of a peripheral freeway (the I-485) was begun. Though still incomplete, segments with already built interchanges have stimulated development in the south and northeastern parts of the county.

Definitions of smart growth vary from policies of the American Planning Association, the National Association of Home Builders and the Sierra Club, to the Urban Land Institute. A smart-growth audit would address the following:

1 planning capacity and quality by anticipating for development and growth with a long-term comprehensive plan ensuring an adequate land supply;

2 urban form in terms of compact development, protection of natural resources and public open space;

3 infill development;

4 a variety of housing and mixed uses;

5 walkable neighbourhoods;

6 balanced multi-nodal transportation and the maximisation of existing infrastructure with appropriate and funded new infrastructure;

7 reasonable, predictable, efficient plan review with supporting fiscal policies; and

8 the integration of land use, transportation and infrastructure decisions.

Smart-growth policies encourage land-use and transit plans for development along transit corridors and higher residential densities near transit stations. Community frustration with the impact of growth is increasingly driving a no-growth backlash[118] that would be in opposition to smart-growth policies. No-growth measures are a set of rigid development controls including urban growth boundaries, density limits and residential building permit limits, as well as mandatory voter approval for new housing projects.

Such initiatives were passed in San Diego and Ventura Counties in California in 1998. These were seen as the opposite of the smart-growth philosophy, since they did not include commercial and industrial development that would generate employment and increase the tax base. A smart-growth map was initiated in Austin, Texas, in 1998, in an attempt to balance the economy, the environment and the community. Of the 650 square kilometres (252 square miles), two-thirds were seen as development zones with the remainder encompassing environmentally sensitive areas on the west side of the city.

Palm Beach County, Florida, has a tiered system of future development to protect adjacent agricultural lands.[119] The county has a population of over a million and is expanding at the rate of 20,000 each year. The Managed Growth Tier System, utilising advocacy planning including focus group meetings, public workshops, public hearings and half-day policy development meetings, created a detailed policy framework distinguishing the regions of the county into tiers as urban-suburban, ex-urban, rural, agricultural reserve and the Glades. Urban-suburban would accommodate the population growth, supporting services and employment with residential infill including mixed-use compact development.

Though smart-growth policies may be a step in the right direction in controlling suburban sprawl, more negative signs are evident in the inner city. In 2000, a new planning control was proposed for New York City. The Uniform Bulk Proposal, sponsored by Mayor Giuliani's administration, would permanently alter the Manhattan skyline. The Department of City Planning would set height limits on new skyscrapers, depending on their location, not only in Manhattan but also in Brooklyn and Queens. However, though this may be viewed as a positive measure, the plan abolishes previous zoning laws that actively encouraged developers to create small public parks and squares in exchange for added height. The Lever Building and the Seagram Building on Park Avenue are prime examples.

A design review panel would be created with a system of peer review.

Little appears to have been achieved by this method. The totality of the three-dimensional urban fabric has rarely been considered and a building-by-building assessment has been the preferred methodology. As the critic Herbert Muschamp says: 'The Uniform Bulk Program has stumbled into this context but is in no way part of it. That is what makes its cultural pretensions so ludicrous. Here was an opportunity for city planning to enlarge the conceptual framework of New York. To bring architecture into line with the transformations now overtaking urban life everywhere. That opportunity has been lost'.[120]

A POSTSCRIPT

The last fifty years has seen many initiatives in urban design and development. The pioneering ideas of both Kevin Lynch and Jane Jacobs in the 1950s were indirectly responsible for advocacy planning in the late 1960s, led by professionals such as David Lewis. Yet these visionary ideas, in trying to determine the wishes of citizens and the way citizens – not architects or planners – viewed and understood their urban environment, eventually fell on stony ground.

The development and acceptance of urban design as an identifiable discipline was overtaken by dramatic changes in design ideology. Postmodernism was superseded by deconstructivism, resulting in iconoclastic architecture that often had little to do with the fabric of the city. Indeed, the fabric of the city as opposed to the suburbs and beyond has increasingly been neglected in many areas, though with notable exceptions such as Seattle, Portland, San Francisco, San Diego and Boston.

Though smart growth is now promoted in the ever-increasing expansion of the suburbs and beyond, it does not really address the issues of community living. The bleak view of the future espoused by such experts as William Mitchell is that the traditional city will become redundant. Professionals will remain in their home offices using web sites and the Internet to carry out their tasks. But throughout civilisation humankind has always been gregarious, and therefore interaction is necessary for a healthy society. If the computer encourages people to stay at home, where will that interaction be? Perhaps local health clubs in the suburbs will provide some answers. But shopping malls will not, eventually becoming redundant with the exponential growth in shopping on the Internet. The impending crisis in the diminution or even exhaustion of oil supplies by the middle of the twenty-first century will present further problems unless alternatives like methanol and electric power can replace petroleum. Otherwise, the interstate highway system too is destined for obsolescence.

Certainly, designers over the last fifteen years have re-examined community living. The new urbanist movement is based on the garden city ideal of the beginning of the twentieth century. The results are impressive, particularly in Florida and California. However, these are largely upper-middle-income communities missing the mixture of social groups common in historical cities. The homelessness problem in the US has been largely ignored by the major political parties, and neither has it been addressed by architects, planners or urban designers. Low-income families are predominantly housed in innercity ghettoes – and this in a country regarded as the most powerful and prosperous in the world! However, this is not to be dismissive of the new urbanism, which does at least provide urban environments far better than the public housing projects of the 1960s.

Yet there is this dichotomy between the realised schemes of the new urbanism, which could, perhaps, be extended to mixed-income societies, and the plethora of visionary schemes that may not be realistic.

Maggie Toy's 'Architecture in Cyberspace'[121] offers a completely different view. The term 'cyberspace' was coined by William Gibson in the science fiction novel *Neuromancer* in the 1980s. Maggie Toy suggests the 'cyber' is a residual term from early systems analysis using microprocessors – there is the architecture of topological morphology, cyborgian anthropology and algorithmic complexity – and points out that the most advanced and challenging architecture could not have been conceived without the use of the computer.[122] Marcos Novak of UCLA is an artist and theorist investigating the emerging tectonics of technologically augmented space. Novak sees virtual environments as autonomous architectural spaces, and the Internet as the non-local transurban public domain. Architecture, he says, is the art of elaboration of inhabitable space, beyond accommodation in the direction of excess over need. Space and time are no longer separate, and then there is a vernacular of augmented space-time, body space-time and cyber space-time. 'In the geometry of computer graphics, a lamina is a plane with only one side . . . the lamina is helpful in explaining one of the defining features of virtual space, the delamination of passage. Ordinary passage through an opening involves crossing an invisible pure plane, the plane of the threshold . . . Hyperlink passage replaces this plane with two laminae, a lamina of departure and a lamina of destination.'[123] Karen Franck's work at the New Jersey Institute of Technology produces eerily similar images to those of Novak: 'Visually compelling buildings are only to be seen, where the tactile quality of materials and other sources of sensory stimulation are minimized and where orientation may be confusing. The conditions may be actually inimical to the intended use'.

The Containers of Mind Foundation created by Arakawa and Madeline Gins in New York in 1987, has produced some startling images of the future city. In their project for the Reversible Destiny City for Tokyo Bay they postulate that a radical departure for architecture is the construction of a vast array of contrasting architectural surrounds.[124] The project takes a modular approach and construction was due to start in 1999. A complex housing module was paired with terrain modules composed of three, five or seven planes that rise to form a mound or dip to yield a depression. The module varies considerably, yet remains standard. Some of the modules tilt along either a north–south or an east–west axis. It is not clear whether this is a public or private housing project. If it is a public project, is this eclectic design not imposing a regime on the tenants similar to the new brutalist housing projects in Europe during the 1960s that created disaffection among the residents?

'Hypersurface Architecture'[125] develops these ideas further. Stephen Perrella, in his editorial introduction, says that an analysis of the built environment reveals a systematic deployment of commercial images connected and controlled by the interests of consumer capitalism leading to a system of representation. Perrella, a professor at Columbia University in New York, indicates that the media image is a logic virtually unconnected with architecture and the way architecture thinks about itself. Yet in the current electronic era, the two polarities are beginning to merge in terms of image and form. Perrella says that 'while new technology is taking media into an unbounded zone we know as cyberspace, architectural form is also coming to question its Cartesian foundations'.[126] He illustrates this with mention of the marquee at 1500 Broadway in Times Square, with its curvilinear moving electronic billboard where ABC's early-morning news broadcasts are often displayed. Rebecca Carpenter, a graduate of Columbia University, investigates motion as an ethic within architecture, describing 'blobs', events-space, and 'hypersurfaces'.[127] Using the term 'virtual-actual' she says that this does not mean that the virtual and the actual are inverse images of one another with the present occurring in the middle, but a transformational time structure producing a topological transformation.

The architect-morphologist Haresh Lalvani of the Pratt Institute in New York advances urban design proposals for the Column Museum,[128] which displays a group of morphological encoded columnar structures, while 'fractal high-rise' as a branched fractal column applies to a theoretical design for a glass skyscraper. Underlying this is an investigation of the fundamental behaviour of sheet materials, where materials 'flow' under their own weight according to predetermined morphological laws.

An opposite point of view might be the pursuit of energy conservation across the planet. In *Energy for Planet Earth*, published in 1990[129] and taken from readings from the journal *Scientific American*, an article by Carl Weinberg and Robert Williams titled 'Energy from the Sun' examines various forms of solar energy, including wind and biomass.[130] Among their more controversial findings, the authors maintain that electricity demand in the US could be satisfied by four million 500-kilowatt wind turbines spaced half a kilometre apart over 10 per cent of the US where the wind is favourable. Roughly 90 per cent of the US's potential for wind generation is in twelve states, the majority of which are located in the centrewest. If these predictions are true, then the energy crisis and dependence on oil from the Middle East would be virtually eliminated. In another article, Fulkerson, Judkins and Sanghui address the issue of energy from fossil fuels, pointing out that the combustion of coal, oil and natural gas supplies 88 per cent of the energy purchased in the US but that such gases emitted during burning degrade the environment with the possibility of permanently altering it. Global warming caused by rising levels of carbon dioxide and other greenhouse gases captures heat radiated from the earth. Thus, these contrasting articles set, on the one hand, an optimistic tone proposing the widespread use of wind energy, and on the other the pessimistic view that the use of fossil fuels causes global warming, is finite, and results in increasing damage to the planet.

In optimistic terms, Sir Richard Rogers' 1978 proposal for the autonomous house research project for Aspen, Colorado, showed the way forward not only in solving the energy problem but also producing lyrical architecture and urban design. [131] According to Rogers, the challenge for architects was to develop buildings that incorporated sustainable technologies and so reduce pollution and running costs.

Stephen Perrella summarises the blurring of lines and architecture in hyperspace. A television commercial in 1998 created curious special effects. In thirty seconds the advertisement presented a 'surreal and mutational spatial dynamic: a car zipping through a fragmented cityscape' in a way that had not been seen before. The blurring into one image surface or hypersurface affected meaning and interpretation in the way the surface was manipulated.

If the remarkable advances in media and computer technology have changed lives during the last decade, particularly in the interpretation of the city, the urban problems have not disappeared as a result. Whether in the suburbs or the central city, urban design is the relationship of three-dimensional built form

Modular planes at Reversible Destiny City, Tokyo Bay, Arakawa and Madeline Gins. Architectural Design, vol. 68, no. 11/12, 1998, p. 44.

in real time, relating buildings to each other and to the skeletal forms of urban structure or the public realm. However, this is meaningless if the economic and, particularly, the social needs of the populace are not addressed. They are inextricably bound and failure to recognise this can only portend a dark future.

NOTES

1. Howard, Ebenezer (1898) *Tomorrow: A Peaceful Path to Reform* (London). Howard, Ebenezer (1902) *Garden Cities of Tomorrow* (London). Reprinted in 1946 by Faber & Faber, London. New Revised Edition published by Attic Books, Eastbourne, 1985, with an introduction by Ray Thomas and a bibliography by Stephen Potter.
2. Bellamy, Edward (1988) *Looking Backward*.
3. See Knack, Ruth Eckdish (1998) 'Garden Cities: Past and Future', *Planning*, vol. 64, no. 6 (June), pp. 4–9.
4. Conference 'From Garden Cities to Green Cities and Beyond: Urban Policy for the Twenty-First Century', Cornell University, 17–19 September 1998.
5. Garvin, Alexander, National American Planning Association Conference, Spring 1998.
6. Peter Calthorpe, National American Planning Association Conference, Spring 1998.
7. See Knack, op. cit., p. 7.
8. *Mariemont: A Guide to Citizens and Property Owners*. Also Wright Parks, Warren (1967) *The Mariemont Story: A National Exemplar in Town Planning*. Cincinnati: Creative Writers and Publishers.
9. Nicolin, Pierluigi (ed.) (1986) 'The Form of the American City', *Lotus International*, 2.
10. Ibid., p. 7.
11. Ibid., p. 5.
12. Salicath, Neils (1992) *Homelessness in Industrialized Countries*. The Hague: The International Federation for Housing and Town Planning.
13. Jacobs, Jane (1961) *The Death and Life of Great American Cities*. New York: Modern Library.
14. Sennett, Richard (1971) *The Uses of Disorder: Personal Identity and City Life*. Harmondsworth: Pelican. First published in the US, 1970.
15. Orwell, George (1948) *1984*. London: Penguin Books.
16. Salicath, op. cit.
17. Ibid. See Gosling, David 'Poverty and Homelessness in the United States of America', pp. 185–99.
18. Bender, David and Leone Bruno (eds) (1990) 'The Homeless', in *Opposing Viewpoints*. San Diego: Greenhaven Press.
19. Horowitz, Carl, ibid., pp. 21–27.
20. Rossi, P. H. (1989) *Down and Out in America*. Chicago: University of Chicago Press, pp. 46–62.
21. Ibid., p. 84.
22. Hartman, C. (ed.) (1983) *America's Housing Crisis (Alternative Policies for America)*. Institute for Policy Studies, Boston: Routledge & Kegan Paul.
23. Atlas, John and Peter Drier, ibid., p. 180.
24. Davidoff, Paul, ibid., p. 186.
25. Rossi, Peter (1989) *Without Shelter*. New York: Priority Press.
26. 1990 Annual Report on the Interagency Council on the Homeless. February 1991.
27. Freidrichs, J. (ed.) (1988) 'Affordable Housing and the Homeless', in Elizabeth Huttman, *Homelessness as a Housing Problem in an Inner City in the US*. Berlin: Walter de Gruyter, pp. 157–71.
28. Tucker, William (1990) *The Excluded Americans*. Washington: Regency Gateway, p. 311.
29. Bassuk, Ellen L. (1991) 'Homeless Families', *Scientific American* (December), pp. 66–74.
30. Ibid., p. 72.
31. Ibid., p. 74.
32. De Parle, Jason (1996) 'Slamming the Door', *New York Times*, 20 October, pp. 52–57, 68, 94 and 105.
33. Fallows, James (2000) 'The Invisible Poor', *New York Times*, 19 March, pp. 68–78, 95 and 111.
34. Mitchell, William J. (1996) *City of Bits: Space, Place, and the Infobahn*. Cambridge, MA: MIT Press.
35. Ibid., p. 3.
36. Ibid., p. 10.
37. Decker, John, 'Urban Futures', unpublished paper written specifically for *The Evolution of American Urban Design*.
38. See Branch, Melville C. (1971) 'Comprehensive City Planning', American Planning Association, Chicago. Also McHarg, Ian L. (1971) *Design with Nature*. New York: Doubleday, p. 22, and Mas, William M. (1983) *Landscape and Planning: Environmental Applications*. New York: John Wiley & Sons, pp. 7–8 and 44.
39. Saunders, William (1997) 'Changing Cities', *Harvard Design Magazine*, Winter/Spring, p. 214.
40. Decker, John (1993) 'Simulation Methodologies for Observing Large-Scale Urban Structures', *Landscape and Planning*, no. 26, p. 232.
41. Couch, John S. (1997) 'Culture Incorporated', *Wired*, vol. 5, no. 12, p. 214.
42. Interstate 75 extends from Florida in the south to Detroit in the north. Built in phases over the last four decades, it offers different concepts in highway engineering. For example, I-75 north of Dayton, Ohio, is dead flat and dead boring. South of the Ohio River a later stretch built through northern and central Kentucky is a model of parkway construction where the north and south routes are often separated by significant areas of land, curvilinear in design to help prevent driver boredom and, hence, sleepiness.
43. Tschumi, Bernard (1994) *Event Cities*. Cambridge, MA: MIT Press, p. 105.
44. Taylor, Marcia (1997) 'Examples of Development Costs to the Community', and 'Reshaping the Region: Planning for a Sustainable Future', *American Institute of Architects Journal*, pp. 6–7 and 10.
45. Davies, Mike (1997) 'Ozzie and Harriet in Hell: On the Decline of Inner Suburbs', in Saunders, op. cit., p. 4.
46. Mitchell, op. cit., pp. 8–10.
47. Wodaski, Ron (1996) *Virtual Reality Madness*. Indianapolis: Sams Publishing, p. 6.
48. Rheingold, Howard (1991) *Virtual Reality*. New York: Summit Books.
49. Ibid.
50. Wodaski, op. cit., pp. 118–21.
51. Katz, John (1997) *The Digital Citizen*. Quoted in Couch, op. cit., pp. 68–72.
52. Lehmann-Haupt, Rachel (1997) *Democracy 2.0*. Quoted in Couch, op. cit., p. 59. The implications of Marcel Bulling's proposal for a democratic system of public opinion, free of government interference, could well be extended to television programme ratings. Instead of polls of a thousand or so persons selected at random, the technology is available to major suppliers like Time-Warner Cable to monitor when customers turn off or switch channels, thus giving an accurate reaction of millions of people towards specific cable programmes.
53. Mitchell, op. cit., pp. 8–10.
54. Bachelor, Peter and David Lewis (eds) (1985) 'Urban Design in Action'. North Carolina State University School of Design.
55. In the Midwest, Cincinnati is subject to state controls, an appointed County Planning Commission (whose advice has been regularly disregarded by the three elected County Commissioners), an appointed City Planning Commission, an elected City Council (elected 'at-large' without specific constituencies) and neighbourhood councils, often in the form of town meetings and various 'cities' and 'towns' and 'villages' within the overall framework. Such anarchy is a recipe for planning failure.
56. Bressi, Todd (1995) 'The Real Thing? We're Getting There', *Planning* (July), p. 16.

57. Kafatos, Menas and Robert Nadeau (1990) *The Conscious Universe: Part and Whole in Modern Physical Theory*. New York: Springer Verlag, pp. 36–38.
58. Greenstreet, Robert and James W. Shields (1988) *Architectural Representations*. Englewood Cliffs, NJ: Prentice Hall, pp. 2–3.
59. Cox, D. J. 'The Art of Scientific Visualization', *Academic Computing*, vol. 4, no. 6, p. 20.
60. Decker, John (1992) 'Computers as Tools for Analysis of Urban Spaces: Technological Support for Comprehensive Urban Design Theories', *Cities: the International Journal of Urban Policy and Planning*, vol. 9, no. 3, p. 171.
61. Lynch, Kevin (1960) *The Image of the City*. Cambridge, MA: MIT Press.
62. Harvey, David (1985) *Consciousness and the Urban Experience*. Baltimore, MD: Johns Hopkins University Press.
63. Sagan, Carl, *Cosmos . . . After the Film*, by Eames Powers of Ten.
64. Gandelsonas, Mario (1991) *The Urban Text*. Cambridge, MA: MIT Press, visual portions.
65. Lockhardt, Shawn with Kevin Reagh (1995) *The Autodesk Collection*. New York: Addison-Wesley, p. 377.
66. Ibid., p. 404.
67. Decker, John (1994) 'The Validation of Computer Simulations for Design Guideline Dispute Resolution', *Environment and Behavior*, vol. 26, no. 3, p. 429.
68. Ibid., pp. 435–36.
69. Ibid., p. 420.
70. Such a process was demonstrated in the Fountain Square West study for downtown Cincinnati in 1991/92 by the Center for Urban Design. The computer-generated animation study followed the history of high-rise development over a hundred-year period and was paralleled by a comparative study of public open space of major midwestern cities such as Indianapolis, Columbus, Louisville and Cleveland.
71. Ellson, R. 'Visualization at Work', in Cox, op. cit., pp. 28 and 56.
72. Shanor, Rebecca (1993) 'Visualizing the Future'. The Environmental Simulation Center at the New York School for Social Research Executive Summary, p. 5.
73. Jones, Jennifer (1997) 'Urban Simulation', civic.comww.fcw/civic.com.
74. Kleniewski, Nancy (1997) *Cities, Change and Conflict: A Political Economy of Urban Life*. New York: Wadsworth Publishing, pp. 26–32.
75. Ibid., p. 246.
76. Stern, Michael and William Marsh (eds) (1997) 'The Decentered City: Edge Cities and the Expanding Metropolis', *Landscape and Urban Planning*, vol. 36, no. 4, pp. 243–45.
77. Braine, Bonnie (1997) 'Computers, Cities and Planning', The New School of Environmental Simulation Center. Also, 'Visions of Things to Come', *Metroplanner*, March 1997, pp. 4–6. The Pittsburgh Study is also important in this context as it develops state-of-the-art technology. See 'The Pittsburgh Downtown Plan' (in progress), Michael Stern, lead consultant and John Decker, secondary consultant, City of Pittsburgh, Department of City Planning, Eloise Hirsch, Director.
78. Colomon, Nancy (1996) 'Computers: HUD Maps Communities', *Architecture* (January), pp. 119–20. See also Bedworth, David, Mark Henderson and Philip Wolfe (1991) *Computer-Integrated Design and Manufacturing*. New York: McGraw-Hill, pp. 73–129.
79. Regional Plan Association (1969) *Urban Design Manhattan*. New York: Viking, pp. 29–35.
80. White, Edward (1983) 'Site Analysis', *Architectural Media*, p. 8.
81. See Wallich, Paul (1991) 'Trends in Artificial Intelligence: Silicon Babies', *Scientific American* (December), p. 125.
82. Ibid.
83. See Dubé, Matthew and Russell Smith (1999) 'Don't Dream it, See It: Desktop Simulation Comes to Main Street', *Planning*, Special Issue on Technology (July), pp. 20–22.
84. 'The Next Hundred Years', *New York Times Magazine*, 29 September 1996, pp. 137–91.
85. Ibid., pp. 130–32.
86. Ibid., p. 141.
87. Tierney, John, 'Our Oldest Computer Upgraded', *New York Times Magazine*, 28 September 1997, p. 47.
88. Ibid., p. 49.
89. Ibid., p. 58.
90. 'The Times Capsule', *New York Times Magazine*, 5 December 1999.
91. 'What Are You Doing About the New Global Opportunities?', *Management Review*, March 1999, p. 25.
92. Ibid., p. 19.
93. Peters, Tom (2000) 'What Will We Do For Work?', *Time*, vol. 155, no. 21 (22 May), pp. 68 ff.
94. Ibid., quoting Julie Rowe.
95. Ibid., quoting Daniel Eisenberg.
96. Ibid., quoting Paul Bracken.
97. 'Tech 2010: A Catalog of the New Future', *New York Times Magazine*, 11 June 2000.
98. Ibid., quoting Brian Farnham, p. 55.
99. Ibid., quoting Peter Goodwin, p. 58.
100. Price, Martin (2000) 'Articulating the Cinematic Urban Experience in the City of Make Believe', *Architectural Design*, vol. 170, no. 1 (January), pp. 46–49.
101. See Gilloch, Graeme (1996) *Myth and Metropolis: Walter Benjamin and the City*. Cambridge: Polity Press.
102. Massood, Paula J. (1996) 'Mapping the Hood: the Genealogy of City Space in "Boyz N the Hood" and "Menace II Society"', *Cinema Journal*, vol. 35, no. 2, pp. 85–90.
103. Ibid., p. 61.
104. This latter point may be true. A graduate student of the author said that her life as a child was unhappy. She lived in a distant suburb outside the metropolitan area of Cincinnati. Her affluent parents had built a beautiful home on a 2-hectare (five-acre) site. Until she reached the age of 16, she was totally isolated, though she had friends in high school. To interact socially, she needed to cycle many miles, though once she obtained her driver's license her social life truly commenced. She condemned suburban living.
105. These statistics are drawn from an article in the *New York Times* by John Tierney, 'The Big City: Despite Scare, There Is Plenty of Room for the Suburbs to Keep Sprawling', 22 February 1999, p. 18. This is a reactionary article which states that 'the problem with suburban development isn't a lack of planning. The suburbs were planned all too well . . . now that the resulting suburbs are deemed too diffuse and sterile, today's planners want to impose a different set of rules mandating dense developments . . . to feel like an old New York neighborhood, or a Vermont village, or a small town in Ohio. But all those wonderful old communities had one thing in common: they were built without the interference of state planner'. Tierney omits one essential point, in that twentieth-century society created a mess of wirescape, street signs, advertisements in most suburbs that certainly do not reflect the beauty of an eighteenth-century village in New England.
106. Wright, Frank Lloyd (1954) *The Natural House*. New York: Horizon Press.
107. Patterson, Randall (2000) 'The Serpent in the Garden', *New York Times*, 9 April, p. 58 ff.
108. Ibid., quoting Martha Stewart, p. 62.
109. Environmental Protection Agency statistics, 1996.
110. Source: United States Census Bureau.
111. Mills, Edwin (1999) 'Truly Smart Growth', *Illinois Real Estate Letter*, Summer, pp. 1–7.
112. Ibid., quoting Thomas Sowell, p. 8.
113. Hamilton, William (1999) 'How Suburban Design is Failing American Teenagers', *New York Times*, 6 May. pp. B-1 and B-11.
114. Egan, Timothy (2000) 'In Portland, Houses Are Friendly. Or Else', *New York Times*, 20 April, p. B-1.
115. Felensthal, Sandy (1995) 'Bye-Bye Suburban Dream: 15 Ways to Fix the Suburbs', *Newsweek*, 15 May.
116. Newman, Oscar (1972) *Defensible Space: People and Design in the Violent City*. London: The Architectural Press.

117. Avin, Uri and David Holden (2000) 'Does Your Growth Smart?', in *Planning* (January), pp. 26–31.

118. Ibid., quoting Amelia Lorentz and Kirsten Shaw, pp. 5–9.

119. Meck, Stuart (1998) 'Growing Smart: Initiatives and Applications; Palm Beach County Managed Growth Program', in *Planning*, pp. 4–5.

120. Muschamp, Herbert (2000) 'Reaching for Power Over Streets and Sky', *New York Times*, 14 May, pp. B-1 and B-43.

121. Toy, Maggie (ed.) (1998) 'Architecture in Cyberspace', *Architectural Design*, vol. 68, no. 11/12 (November/December).

122. Ibid., p. 24.

123. This description of the experience of movement through space may seem convoluted to some. The theories of serial vision and navigation, described earlier in this text, may offer a clearer definition.

124. Ibid., p. 43.

125. Toy, Maggie (ed.) (1999) 'Hypersurface Architecture II', *Architectural Design*, vol. 69, pp. 9–10.

126. Ibid., p. 5.

127. Ibid., p. 21.

128. Ibid., pp. 35–36.

129. Piel, Jonathon (ed.) (1991) *Energy for Planet Earth: Readings from Scientific American*. New York: W.H. Freeman.

130. Ibid., pp. 106–18.

131. Rogers, Richard (1997) *Cities for a Small Planet*. Boulder, CO: Westview Press.

BIBLIOGRAPHY

CHAPTER ONE: DEFINITIONS OF URBAN DESIGN

Arnheim, R., *Art and Visual Perception: A Psychology of the Creative Eye* (London: Faber and Faber, Ltd., 1956), p.viii.

Banham, R., *Megastructure: Urban Futures of the Recent Past* (London: Thames and Hudson, 1976), p. 130.

Broadbent, G., R. Bunt and C. Jencks, eds., *Signs, Symbols and Architecture* (New York: John Wiley, Inc., 1980).

Calhoun, J.B., and A.H. Esser, eds., *'Space and the Strategy of Life:' Behavior and Environment* (New York: Plenum Press, 1971).

Cullen, G., *Townscape* (London: Architectural Press, 1961).

Fishman, R., *Urban Utopias of the Twentieth Century* (New York: Basic Books, Inc., 1977).

Gallion, A.B. and S. Eisner, *The Urban Pattern* (New York: Van Nostrand Reinhold, 1950).

Garreau, J., *Edge City: Life on the New Frontier* (Garden City, NY: Doubleday, 1991).

Giedion, S., *Space, Time and Architecture: The Growth of a New Tradition* (Cambridge, MA: Harvard University Press, 1959). First edition, 1941.

Giedion, S., *Walter Gropius* (New York: Reinhold Publishing Co., 1954).

Gosling, D., *Gordon Cullen: Visions of Urban Design* (London: Academy Editions, 1996).

Gosling, D. and B. Maitland, *Concepts of Urban Design* (London: Academy Editions and New York: St. Martin's Press, 1984).

Hinks, R., 'Peep Show and the Roving Eye' (*The Architectural Review*, August 1955).

Howard, Ebenezer, *Garden Cities of Tomorrow* (London: Faber and Faber, 1902). First edition: *Tomorrow: A Peaceful Path to Real Reform* (London, 1898).

Katz, D., and Robert Tyson, trans., *Gestalt Psychology* (London: Methuen & Co., 1951).

Katz, Peter, *The New Urbanism: Toward an Architecture of Community* (New York: McGraw-Hill, 1994).

Keifer, G., *Wahrnehmungs Theorie: Kommunikation und Morphologie* 1971.

Kepes, Gyorgy, *The New Landscape* (Chicago: Paul Theobald and Co., 1956).

Kohlsdorf, M.E., *A Apreensao da Forma da Cidade* (Brasilia, Brazil: Editora Universidade de Brasilia, 1996).

Kohlsdorf, M.E., *Sequencias Espaciais Urbanas*, Monograph. February 1976, Brasilia.

Lawrence, T.E., *The Seven Pillars of Wisdom* (Harmondsworth: Penguin Books, 1964).

Lazzaro, G. di San and S. Hood, trans., *Klee* (London: Thames and Hudson, 1957), p. 107.

Lynch, Kevin, *The Image of the City* (Cambridge, MA: The Technology Press and Harvard University Press, 1960).

Marijuan, J.C., 'Towns in Expansion: Historicist Approach or Perceptual Approach?' MA Dissertation in Urban Design (unpublished). Oxford Polytechnic (now Oxford Brookes University), England, 1978.

Marx, K. (David Fernbach, ed.), *The Revolution of 1848: Political Writings*, vol.1. (Harmondsworth: Penguin Books, 1978).

Moholy-Nagy, L., *Vision in Motion* (Chicago: Paul Theobald, 1956).

Osborne, H., *Oxford Companion of Art* (Oxford: Clarendon Press, 1970).

Piaget, J., and B. Inhelder, *The Child's Conception of Space* (London, 1956).

Venturi, R., D. Scott Brown and S. Izenour, *Learning from Las Vegas* (Cambridge, MA: MIT/Harvard Press, 1972).

Wingler, H., *The Bauhaus: Weimar, Dessau, Berlin, Chicago* (Cambridge, MA: MIT Press, 1978).

Wright, F.L., *The Disappearing City* (New York, 1932).

Wright, F.L., *The Living City* (New York, 1958).

Wulf, F., 'Bei die Veränderung von Verstellungen (Gedachtnis und Gestalt)' 1922, from Ellis, W.D., *A Source of Gestalt Psychology* (London, Routledge & Kegan Paul, 1938).

CHAPTER TWO: 1950–1960

Baldwin, J., *Giovanni's Room* (London: Michael Joseph Ltd., 1957).

Baldwin, J., *Another Country* (New York: Dell Publishing, 1960).

Banerjee, T. and M. Southworth, eds., *City Sense and City Design: Writings and Projects of Kevin Lynch* (Cambridge, MA: MIT Press, 1990).

'Birth of the Cool', Capitol Records T-762, 1949–1950 (Recording notes).

Burroughs, W., *The Naked Lunch* (London: John Calder, Ltd., 1964).

Cage, John D. and Eric Gilder, *The Dictionary of Composers* (London, 1985).

'Charlie Parker Memorial', vol. 2, Savoy Records MG-12009 (Recording notes).

Copeland, Aaron, 'Appalachian Spring', 'The TenderLand Suite', 'Fall River Legend', (CD) RCA Victor 09026–61505–2, Aaron Copland conductor, Boston Symphony Orchestra, rec. 23 April, 1954. Programme notes.

Cutler, L., *Recycling Cities* (Boston: CBI Publishing Inc., 1976).

Eisenstein, S., *The Film Sense* (New York: Meridian Books, 1957).

Fagin, H. and R. Weinberg, eds., *Planning and Community Appearance: American Institute of Architects* (Regional Plan Association Inc., May 1968).

Fortune editors, 'The Exploding Metropolis' (Garden City, NY: Doubleday, 1958).

Gerry Mulligan Quartet, 'Paris Concert' Pacific Jazz PJ-1210, 1954. (Recording notes).

Gibson, J., *The Perception of the Visual World* (Boston: Houghton-Mifflin, 1950).

Gosling, D., *Gordon Cullen: Visions of Urban Design* (London: Academy Editions, 1996).

Gosling, D. and B. Maitland, *The Design and Planning of Retail Systems* (London: Architectural Press, 1976, 1984).

Huyghe, R., ed., *The Larousse Encyclopedia of Modern Art* (Paris: Librairie Larousse, 1961).

Jordy, W.H., 'Mies van der Rohe', *Encyclopedia of Modern Architecture* (London: Thames and Hudson, 1963).

Kerouac, Jack, *On the Road* (New York: Viking Press, 1955).

Meade Lux Lewis, 'Story of Blues' (CD 3506-2, Storyville Records SLP 155; SLP 273 and SL 229, 1939–56). (Recording notes).

'Mulligan Meets Monk', Riverside Records RLP 1106, 1957. (Recording notes).

Mumford, L., *The City in History* (New York: Penguin Books, 1961).

Palazzeti, Sergio, *I Classici del Mobile Moderno* (New York: Palazzeti, 1984. First edition).

'Pyramid', The Modern Jazz Quartet. (Atlantic Records/London Records LTZ-K 15193). (Recording notes).

Saint, A., *The Image of the Architect* (New Haven, Connecticut: Yale University Press, 1983).

Scully, V. Jr., *Louis I. Kahn: Makers of Contemporary Architecture* (New York: George Braziller, 1962).

Selby, Hugh Jr., *Last Exit to Brooklyn* (London: Calder and Boyers, 1966).

Slipe, Walter J., *Selected Urban Design Projects Since World War Two* (Monticello, IL: Council of Planning Librarians, 1958).

Storrer, W.A., *The Frank Lloyd Wright Companion* (Chicago: University of Chicago Press, 1993).

Thiel, Philip, *A Proposed Space Notation* (Berkeley, CA: College of Architecture, University of California, 1959).

Thiel, Philip, *The Urban Spaces at Broadway and Mason: A Visual Survey, Analysis and Representation* (Berkeley, CA: College of Architecture, University of California, 1959).

Thiel, Philip, *People, Paths and Purposes: Notations for a Participatory Envirotecture* (Seattle, WA: University of Washington Press, 1997).

Thomson, D. and Ann Lloyd, eds., 'James Dean, The Grace of Loneliness', *Movies of the Fifties* (London: Orbis Publishing, 1982).

Tunnard, C., *Man-Made America: Chaos or Control?* (New Haven, CT: Yale University Press, 1963).

Tunnard, C., and Henry Hope Read, *American Skyline* (New York: The New American Library, 1956).

Williams, S., *Urban Aesthetics in Planning* (Chicago: American Society of Planning Officials, 1953).

CHAPTER THREE: 1960–1970

Alexander, C., *Notes on the Synthesis of Form* (Cambridge, MA: Harvard University Press, 1964).

Alexander, C., *The City as a Mechanism for Sustaining Human Contact* (Berkeley, CA: Center for Planning and Development, University of California, 1966).

Alexander, C., and S. Chermayeff, *Community and Privacy: Toward a New Architecture of Humanism* (Garden City, NY: Doubleday, 1963).

Appleyard, D., *Selected Bibliography: Environmental/ Behavioral Factors in Urban Design* (Berkeley, CA: Department of Urban and Regional Planning, University of California, 1969).

Appleyard, D., with Kevin Lynch and J.R. Myer, *The View from the Road* (Cambridge, MA: Joint Center for Urban Studies of the Massachusetts Institute of Technology and Harvard University, MIT Press, 1964).

Benevolo, L., *The Origins of Modern Town Planning* (Cambridge, MA: MIT Press, 1967).

Bloomer, K.C., and C.W. Moore, *Body, Memory and Architecture* (New Haven, CT: Yale University Press, 1977).

Broadbent, G., *Emerging Concepts in Urban Space Design* (New York: Van Nostrand Reinhold, 1990).

Broadbent, G., R. Bunt and C. Jencks, eds., *Signs, Symbols and Architecture* (Chichester, England: J. Wiley & Sons Ltd., 1980).

Buckminster Fuller, R., *Utopia as Oblivion: The Prospect for Humanity* (London: Allan Lane, The Penguin Press, 1970).

Calhoun, J.B., and A.H. Esser, eds., *Space and the Strategy of Life: Behavior and Environment* (New York: Plenum Press, 1971).

Cook, David W., *The New Urban Frontier: New Metropolises for America, Design for Dream Cities* (Berkeley, CA: University of California Press, 1964).

Cullen, G., *Townscape* (London: Architectural Press, 1961).

Drew, Kent Irvin, *Urban Aesthetics: Theory and Application of Physical Design Control Within the Urban Renewal Program* (New York, 1965).

Eckbo, Garrett, *Urban Landscape Design* (New York: McGraw-Hill Co., 1964).

Garvin, A., *The American City* (New York: McGraw-Hill, 1995).

Gosling, D., *Rehabilitation Area Design Plan: The Hill District* (New Haven, CT: Official report, City Planning Commission, Aug. 1959).

Gosling, D., *Gordon Cullen: Visions of Urban Design* (London: Academy Editions, 1996).

Groot, J.J. M. de, *Religion in China* (New York: GP Putnam, 1912).

Gruen, Victor, *The Heart of Our Cities* (New York: Simon and Schuster, 1967).

Halprin, L., *Cities* (New York: Reinhold Publishing Corporation, 1963. Revised edition, Cambridge, MA: MIT Press, 1972).

Halprin, L., and Associates, *New York, New York: A Study of the Quality, Character, and Meaning of Open Space in Urban Design* (San Francisco, CA: Chapman Press, 1968)

Hanser, P.M., P.K. Hatt and A.J. Reisg, eds., 'The Changing Population of the Modern City', *Cities and Society: The Revised Reader in Urban Design* (London: Collier Macmillan, 1957).

Harvey, D. and Murray Stewart, 'Social Processes, Spatial Form and the Redistribution of Real Income in an Urban System' in Murray Stewart (ed.) *The City: Problems of Planning* (Harmondsworth, England: Penguin Books, 1972).

Jacobs, Jane, *The Death and Life of Great American Cities* (New York: Modern Library, 1961).

Kepes, Gyorgy, *Sign, Image, Symbol* (New York: G. Braziller, 1966).

Lewis, D., *The Pedestrian in the City* (Princeton, New Jersey: Van Nostrand, 1965, 1966).

Lynch, K., *Introduction to the Postgraduate Study on the Boston Image* (MIT, November, 1957).

Lynch, K., *The Image of the City* (Cambridge, MA: The Technology Press and Harvard University Press, 1960).

Lynch, K., T. Banerjee and M. Southworth, eds., *City Sense and City Design: Writings and Projects* (Cambridge, MA: MIT Press, 1990).

Meier, R.L., *A Communication Theory of Urban Growth* (Cambridge, MA: MIT Press, 1965, 1962).

Meier, R.L., *Megalopolis Formation in the Midwest* (Ann Arbor, Michigan, 1965).

Meier, R.L. and K. Frampton, *Architect* (New York: Oxford University Press, 1976).

Merlin, Pierre, *New Towns* (first published as *Les Villes Nouvelles* by Paris Press Universitaires de France, 1969. English language edition, London: Methuen and Co., Ltd., 1971).

Moore, Lyndon, Turnbull and Whitaker, *The Sea Ranch, California* (Tokyo, Japan: ADA Edition, 1966).

Mumford, Lewis, *The Urban Prospect* (New York: Harcourt, Brace and World, 1968).

Ogilby, J., *Roads through England: Survey of the Roads from Essex* (London: John Bowles and Son, 1757).

Okamota, Rai Y., *Urban Design Manhattan* (New York: Viking Press, 1969).

'Reston, Virginia: A Study in Beginnings' (Washington, D.C.: The Washington Center of Metropolitan Studies, 1964). 'Social Planning and Programs for Reston, Virginia' (The Reston, Virginia, Foundation for Community Programs, Inc., March 1967).

Rudofsky, Bernard, *Streets for People: A Primer for Americans* (Garden City, NY: Doubleday, 1969).

Scott-Brown, Denise, *The Meaningful City* (Berkeley, CA: 1961).

Norberg-Schultz, C., *Intentions in Architecture* (University Press, Allen and Unwin, 1963).

Norberg-Schultz, C., *Existence, Space and Architecture* (London: Studio Vista, 1971).

Sennett, R., *The Uses of Disorder: Personal Identity and City Life* (Harmondsworth, England: Penguin Books, 1970), p. 53.

Thiel, Philip, *A Proposed Space Notation* (Berkeley, CA: College of Architecture, University of California, 1959).

Thiel, Philip, *The Urban Spaces at Broadway and Mason: A Visual Survey, Analysis and Representation* (Berkeley, CA: College of Architecture, University of California, 1959).

Thiel, Philip, *Processional Architecture* (Berkeley, CA: College of Architecture, University of California, 1960).

Thiel, Philip, *An Architectural and Urban Space-Sequence Notation* (Kamakura, Japan, 1960).

Thiel, Philip, *Environmental Design on the Basis of Sequential Experience* (Seattle: University of Washington, 1963).

Thiel, Philip, 'Movement in Japanese Environmental Representation', Urban Planning/Development Series (Seattle: University of Washington, 1964).

Twelfth Urban Design Conference, *New Communities: One Alternative* (Cambridge, MA: Harvard Graduate School of Design, 1968).

Tunnard, C. and Boris Pushkarev, *Man-Made America: Chaos or Control?* (New Haven, CT: Yale University Press, 1963), pp. 13, 72–80, 157–275, 401–440, ix–xii.

University of California at Berkeley, 'Curriculum for CP 258, Urban Design' (Department of Planning, University of California at Berkeley, Spring, 1959).

Venturi, R., *Complexity and Contradiction in Architecture* (New York: Museum of Modern Art, 1968), pp. 16, 17, 23, 117.

Violich, F. 'The Urban General Plan as an Instrument for Guiding Urban Development.' Seminar on Urban Planning at the Inter-American Housing and Planning Center, Bogota, Columbia (Berkeley, 1958).

Wasserman, K., *Merchandising Architecture: The Architecture Implications and Applications of Amusement Parks* (Washington, DC: National Endowment for the Arts, 1978).

Wright, F. Lloyd, *The Living City* (New York, 1958).

CHAPTER FOUR: 1970–1980

Abrams, C., *The City is the Frontier* (New York: Harper Colophon Books, 1965).

Alexander, C., *Notes on the Synthesis of Form* (Cambridge, MA: MIT Press, 1964).

Alexander, C., *The Oregon Experiment* (New York: Oxford University Press, 1975).

Alexander, C., *A Pattern Language: Towns, Buildings, Construction* (New York: Oxford University Press, 1977).

Alexander, C., *A Timeless Way of Building* (New York: Oxford University Press, 1979).

Bacon, E.W., *Design of Cities* (New York: Penguin, 1976).

Banham, R., *Megastructure: Urban Futures of the Recent Past* (London: Thames and Hudson, 1976).

Barnett, J., *Urban Design as Public Policy: Practical Methods for Improving Cities* (New York: Architectural Record Books, 1974).

Barnett, J. and J. Portman, *The Architect as Developer* (New York: McGraw-Hill, 1976).

Berry, Brian and Larry S. Bourne, eds., 'General Features of Urban Commercial Structure' in *International Structure of the City* (New York: Oxford University Press, 1971).

Bloomer, K.C. and C.W. Moore, *Body, Memory and Architecture* (New Haven, CT: Yale University Press, 1977).

Blumenfeld, Hans, *The Modern Metropolis: Its Origins, Growth, Characteristics and Planning* (Cambridge, MA: MIT Press, 1971).

Bourne, L.S. and L.W. Simmons, eds., *Systems of Cities: Readings on Structure, Growth and Policy* (New York: Oxford University Press, 1978).

Broadbent, G., *Emerging Concepts in Urban Space Design* (London: Van Nostrand Reinhold, 1990).

Broadbent, G., R. Bunt and C. Jencks, *Signs, Symbols and Architecture* (Chichester, England: John Wiley and Sons, 1980).

Cutler, L.S., *Recycling Cities for People: The Urban Design Process* (Boston: Cahers Books International, 1976).

Davidoff, Paul and S. Anderson, eds., *Normative Planning: Planning for Diversity and Choice* (Cambridge, MA: MIT Press, 1968).

De Chiara, J., *Urban Planning and Design Criteria* (New York: Van Nostrand Reinhold, 1975).

Dehusses, J., *Delivrez Promethee* (Paris: Flammarion, 1979).

Franzen, Ulrich and P. Rudolph, *The Evolving City: Urban Design Proposals* (New York: Whitney Library of Design for the American Federation of Arts, 1974).

Goodman, R., *After the Planners* (Harmondsworth, England: Pelican Books, 1972).

Gosling, D. and B. Maitland, *Concepts of Urban Design* (London: Academy Editions, 1984).

Habraken, N. and B. Valkenburg, trans., *Supports: An Alternative to Mass Housing* (London: The Architectural Press, 1972).

Habraken, N., J. Boekholt, P. Dinjens, A. Thijseen and Wim Wiewel, trans., *Variations: The Systematic Design of Suppports* (Cambridge, MA: MIT Press, 1976).

Hack, Gary, *Improving City Streets for Use at Night: The Norfolk Experiment* (Cambridge, MA: MIT Press, 1974).

Halpern, K., *Downtown USA: Urban Design in American Cities* (New York: Whitney Library of Design, 1979).

Halprin, L., *Lawrence Halprin Notebooks 1959–1971* (Cambridge, MA: MIT Press, 1972), pp. 33.

Hammerschlag, D., *A Selected Biography on Urban Design* (Monticello, IL: Council of Planning Librarians, 1971).

Jencks, C., *Architecture 2000: Predictions and Methods* (London: Studio Vista, 1971).

Jencks, C., *The Language of Post-Modern Architecture* (London: Academy Editions, 1977).

Jencks, C. and N. Silver, *Adhocism: The Case for Improvisation* (Garden City, NY: Anchor Books, 1973).

Kahn, H. and A.J. Weiner, *Year 2000* (London: Macmillan and Company, 1967).

Kahn, L., ed., *Shelter* (Bolinas, CA: Shelter Publications, 1973).

Kepes, G., ed., *Arts of the Environment* (New York: George Braziller, 1972).

Kriken, J.L., *Developing Urban Designs Mechanisms* (Chicago, IL: American Society of Planning Officials, 1973).

Levi-Strauss, C., *The Savage Mind* (Chicago, 1969).

Lewis, D.N., ed., *The Growth of Cities* (London: Elek Books, 1971).

Lundberg, F., *The Rich and The Super-Rich* (New York: Lyle Stuart, 1968).

Lynch, Kevin, *Site Planning* (Cambridge, MA: MIT Press, 1962).

Lynch, Kevin, *What Time is This Place?* (Cambridge, MA: MIT Press, 1972).

Lynch, Kevin, *Managing the Sense of the Region* (Cambridge, MA: MIT Press, 1976).

Lynch, Kevin, *Wasting Away* (San Francisco, CA: Sierra Club Books, 1990).

Meier, Richard L., *Design of Resource-Conserving Cities* (Berkeley, CA: Institute of Urban and Regional Development, University of California, 1973).

Mumford, Lewis, *The City in History* (Harmondsworth, England: Penguin Books, 1966).

Negroponte, N., *The Architecture Machine* (Cambridge, MA: MIT Press, 1970).

Negroponte, N., *Soft Architecture Machines* (Cambridge, MA: MIT Press, 1970).

Newman, O., *Defensible Space: People and Design in the Violent City* (London: The Architectural Press, 1972).

Norberg-Schultz, C., *Existence, Space and Architecture* (London: Studio Vista, 1971).

Okamoto/Liskmann, Inc., *San Francisco Urban Design Study: External Form and Image Study* (San Francisco, CA: Okamoto/Liskmann, 1970).

Papenek, V., *Design for the Real World* (London: Thames and Hudson, 1972).

Rabbit, Peter, *Drop City* (Paris: Olympia Press, 1971).

Rittel, J., W. Horst, M. Webber, N. Cross, D. Elliot and R. Roy, eds., *Wicked Problems in Man-Made Futures* (London: Hutchinson Educational and Open University Press, 1974).

Rowe, Colin, *Collage City* (Cambridge, MA: MIT Press, 1978).

Rykwert, J., *The Idea of a Town* (London: Faber and Faber, 1976).

Saitowitz, S., *Houston Street Zone Study* (Berkeley, CA: Department of Architecture, University of California, 1976).

Seelig, Peter, *The Architecture of Self-Help Communities (The First International Design Competition for the Urban Environment of Developing Countries)* (New York: Architectural Record Books, 1978).

Sennett, R., *The Uses of Disorder: Personal Identity and City Life* (Harmondsworth, England: Penguin Books, 1970).

Southworth, M. and K. Lynch, *Designing and Managing the Strip* (Cambridge, MA: Joint Center for Urban Studies MIT and Harvard University, 1974).

Southworth, Michael and Susan, *Environmental Quality Analysis and Management for Cities and Regions; A Review of Work in the United States, Town Planning Review* (Liverpool, England: Liverpool University Press, 1973).

Toffler, A., *Future Shock* (London: The Bodley Head, 1970).

Turner, J. and R. Fichter, eds., *Freedom to Build* (New York: Macmillan, 1972).

Venturi, R. and D. Scott-Brown, *Learning from Las Vegas* (Cambridge, MA: MIT Press, 1972).

Vitruvius, M.H.M., trans., *The Ten Books of Architecture* (New York: Dover Publications, 1960).

Waisman, Marina, trans., *Arquitectura Alternativa de Emilio Ambasz* (Editorial Summo, Buenos Aires, Argentina, September, 1977).

Ward, Colin, *Tenants Take Over* (London: Architectural Press Limited, 1974).

Webber, M. and A. Blowers, C. Hamnet and P. Sarre, eds., *Permissive Planning in the Future of Cities* (London: Hutchinson Educational and Open University Press, 1974).

Wolf, M.R. and R.D. Shinn, *Urban Design Within the Comprehensive Planning Process* (Seattle: University of Washington Press, 1970).

Zucker, Paul, *Town and Square* (New York: Columbia University Press, 1959).

CHAPTER FIVE: 1980–1990

Alexander, C., *Rebirth of the Inner City: The North Omaha Plan* (Berkeley, CA: Center for Environmental Structure, 1981).

Alexander, C., *A New Theory of Urban Design* (New York: Oxford University Press, 1987).

Appleyard, D., *Livable Streets* (Berkeley: University of California Press, 1981).

Appleyard, D. and P. Bosselmann, *Urban Design Guidelines for Street Management* (Berkeley: Institute of Urban and Regional Development, University of California, 1982).

Appleyard, D. and A. Jacobs, *Toward an Urban Design Manifesto* (Berkeley: Institute of Urban and Regional Development, University of California, 1982).

Attoe, Wayne, *American Urban Architecture: Catalysts in the Design of Cities* (Berkeley: University of California Press, 1989).

Banerjee, T., *Beyond the Neighborhood Unit: Residential Environments and Public Policy* (New York: Plenum Press, 1984).

Barnett, Jonathan, *An Introduction to Urban Design* (New York: Harper & Row, 1982).

Bender, Richard, *Design Review: A Review of the Processes, Procedures and Potential* (Berkeley, CA: College of Environmental Design, University of California, 1989).

Benevolo, Leonardo, *The History of the City* (Cambridge, MA: MIT Press, 1980).

Blumenfeld, Hans, *Where Did All the Metropolitanites Go?* (Toronto: Department of Urban and Regional Planning, University of Toronto, 1982).

Boyer, Christine M., *Dreaming the Rational City: The Myth of American Planning* (Cambridge, MA: MIT Press, 1983).

Broadbent, G. and C. Jencks, *Signs, Symbols and Architecture* (New York: John Wiley, 1980).

Calthorpe, Peter, *The Pedestrian Pocket Book: A New Suburban Strategy* (New York: Princeton Architectural Press, 1989).

Calthorpe, P. and S. Van Der Ryn, *Sustainable Communities: A New Design Synthesis for Cities, Suburbs and Towns* (San Francisco, CA: Sierra Club Books, 1986).

Christensen, Carol A., *The American Garden City and The New Town Movement* (Ann Arbor, MI: UMI Research Press, 1986).

Cook, Robert S., *Zoning for Downtown Urban Design: How Cities Control Development* (Lexington, MA: Lexington Books, 1980).

Coop Himmelblau, *Architecture is Now: Projects, (Un)buildings, Actions, Statements, Sketches, Commentaries, 1968–1983* (New York: Rizzoli, 1983).

Davis, Howard, *Bibliography on Urban Environmental Design* (Cambridge, MA: School of Architecture and Planning, MIT, 1980).

Descartes, Rene, *Discourse on Method: The Philosophical Writings of Descartes* (Cambridge, England: Cambridge University Press, vol. 1, 1985).

Duany, Andreas, *The Plan of the Village of Deerfield, Merriville, Indiana* (Merriville, IN: A. Duany, 1987).

Eckbo, Garrett & Associates, *Landscape Architecture, Environmental Planning, Urban Design* (Berkeley, CA: Garrett Eckbo & Associates, 1983).

Friedman, John, *American Exceptionalism in Regional Planning, 1933–2000* (Los Angeles, CA: Graduate School of Architecture and Regional Planning, University of California, 1989).

Gasché, R., *The Tain of the Mirror* (Cambridge, MA: Harvard University Press, 1986).

Girouard, Mark, *Big Jim: The Life and Work of James Stirling* (London: Chatto and Windus, 1998).

Gosling, D., *Gordon Cullen: Visions of Urban Design* (London: Academy Editions, 1996).

Greenbie, Barrie B., *Spaces: Dimensions of the Human Landscape* (New Haven, CT: Yale University Press, 1989).

Habraken, N.J. and B. Valkenburg, trans., *Supports: An Alternative to Mass Housing* (London: The Architectural Press, 1972).

Habraken, N.J. et al., *The Grunsfeld Variations: A Report on the Thematic Development of an Urban Tissue* (Cambridge, MA: MIT Department of Architecture, 1981).

Hall, Edward T., *The Handbook of Proximic Research* (Washington, DC: Society for the Anthropology of Visual Communication, 1974).

Hedman, Richard, *Fundamentals of Urban Design* (Washington, DC: Planner's Press, American Planning Association, 1984).

Heidegger, Martin, *The Thing: Poetry, Language, Thought* (New York, 1971).

Holl, Steven, *The Alphabetical City* (New York: Pamphlet Architecture, 1980).

Hoyle, B.S., D.A. Pinder and M.S. Hussein, eds., *Revitalizing the Waterfront: International Dimensions of Docklands Redevelopment* (England: Bellhaven Press, 1988).

Jacobs, Allen B., *Observing and Interpreting the Urban Environment* (Berkeley: Institute of Urban and Regional Development, University of California, 1982).

Jacobs, Allen B., *Looking at Cities* (Cambridge, MA: MIT Press, 1985).

Jacobs, Jane, *Cities and the Wealth of Nations* (New York: Random House, 1984).

Joedieke, Joachim Andreas, and Helmut Jahn, *Design of a New Architecture* (Stuttgart: Karl Kramer, 1986).

Koolhaas, Rem, *Delirious New York* (London: Academy Editions, 1978).

Kostoff, Spiro, *A History of Architecture: Settings and Rituals* (New York: Oxford University Press, 1985).

Krier, Rob and Colin Rowe (foreword) *Urban Space* (London: Academy Editions, 1979).

Lang, John T., *Urban Design: The American Experience* (New York: Van Nostrand Reinhold, 1988).

Le Corbusier, *The City of Tomorrow* (London: The Architectural Press, 1971).

Levi-Strauss, Claude, *The Savage Mind* (Chicago, 1975).

Lewis, Roger, *Shaping the City* (Washington, DC: AIA Press, 1987)

Lynch, Kevin, *A Theory of Good City Form* (Cambridge, MA: MIT Press, 1981).

Lynch, K. and Gary Hack, *Site Planning* (Cambridge, MA: MIT Press, 1984).

Machado, Rodolfo and Jorge Silvetti, *Buildings for Cities* (Cambridge, MA: Harvard University Graduate School of Design; New York: Rizzoli, 1989).

Maxwell, R. and C. Norberg Schultz, *Michael Graves, Buildings and Projects: 1982–1989* (Princeton, NJ: Princeton University Press, 1990).

Meier, Richard L., *Ecological Planning and Design: How to Achieve Sustainable Communities* (University of California Center for Environmental Design Research, 1988).

Moudon, Anne Vernez, ed., *Public Streets for Public Use* (New York: Van Nostrand Reinhold, 1987).

Mumford, Lewis, *The Culture of Cities* (New York, 1938). Republished in expanded form as *The City in History* (Harmondsworth, England: Penguin Books, 1961).

Nietzsche, F., *The Will to Power* (New York, 1967).

Pittas, Michael (Retreat Chairman) and Ann Ferebee (Proceedings Editor), *Education for Urban Design* (New York: Institute for Urban Design, 1982).

Ramati, Raquel, *How To Save Your Own Street*, in collaboration with the Urban Design Group of the Department of City Planning (Garden City, NY: Dolphin Books, 1981).

Ray, Genevieve H., *City Sampler: A Catalogue of Urban Environmental Design Tools and Techniques in Local Government* (Washington, DC: Community Design Exchange, 1984).

Rossi, Aldo, *L'Architettura della Città* (Padova, Italy: Marsilio, 1966).

Rossi, A., G. Conforto, G. de Giorgi, A. Muntoni, M. Pazzaglini, *Il Dibattito Architettonico in Italia, 1945–1975* (Rome: Bulzoni Editore, 1977).

Rubin, Arthur and Jacqueline Elder, *Building for People* (Washington, DC: Environmental Research Division Center for Building Technology, National Engineering Laboratory, U.S. Department of Commerce, 1980).

Saitowitz, Stanley, *Rincon Hill: A Plan for Urban Transformation* (University of California Housing Task Force and San Francisco Department of City Planning, 1981).

Schon, Donald, *The Design Studio* (Architecture and the Higher Learning) (London: RIBA Building Industry Trust, 1985).

Southworth, Michael F., *Learning: Children, Maps and Transit* (Berkeley, CA: University of California, Center for Environmental Design Research, 1988).

Tafuri, Manfredo, *Architecture and Utopia: Design and Capitalist Development* (Cambridge, MA: MIT Press, 1988).

Thiel, Philip, *Visual Awareness and Design: An Introductory Program in Conceptual Awareness, Perceptual Sensitivity and Basic Design Skills* (Seattle, WA: University of Washington Press, 1981).

Trancik, Roger, *Finding Lost Space: Theories of Urban Design* (New York: Van Nostrand Reinhold, 1986).

Tschumi, Bernard, *Manhattan Transcripts: Theoretical Projects* (London: Academy Editions; New York: St. Martin's Press, 1981).

Venturi, R., D. Scott-Brown, and S. Izenour, *Learning from Las Vegas* (Cambridge, MA: MIT Press, 1977)

Vidler, Anthony, *The Third Typology: Rational Architecture* (Brussels: Editions des Archives d'Architecture Moderne, 1978).

Violich, Francis, *Experiencing Places: The Aesthetics of the Participatory Environment* (Berkeley, CA: Center for Environmental Design Research, 1984).

Wines, James, *De-Architecture* (New York: Rizzoli, 1987), p. 37.

Wrenn, Douglas, with J. Casazza and E. Smart, *Urban Waterfront Development* (Washington, DC: Urban Land Institute, 1983).

Wyatt, Mark, *White Knuckle Ride* (London: Salamander Books, 1996), pp. 7–10. See also Throgmorton, Todd, *Rollercoasters of America* (Osceola, WI: Motorbooks International, 1994).

Zevi, Bruno and Pierre Restany, 'The Poetics of the Unfinished' in *SITE: Architecture as Art* (London: Academy Editions, 1980).

CHAPTER SIX: 1990–2000

Abbott, Carl, *Portland: Planning, Politics and Growth in a Twentieth-Century City* (Lincoln, NE: University of Nebraska Press, 1983), pp. 248–266.

Agrest, Diana, *Architecture from Without: Theoretical Framings for a Critical Practice* (Cambridge, MA: MIT Press, 1991).

Agrest, Diana, *Agrest and Gandelsonas: Works* (New York: Princeton Architectural Press, 1995).

Ambasz, Emilio, *Emilio Ambasz 1986–1992* (Tokyo, Japan: atv Publishing, 1993).

Baird, George, *The Space of Appearance* (Cambridge, MA: MIT Press, 1995).

Banerjee, T., *Private Production of Downtown Public Open Space: Experiences of Los Angeles and San Francisco* (Los Angeles, CA: School of Urban and Regional Planning, University of Southern California, 1992).

Banerjee, T. and M. Southworth, *City Sense and City Design: Writings and Projects by Kevin Lynch* (Cambridge, MA: MIT Press, 1990).

Barnett, Jonathan, *The Fractured Metropolis: Improving the New City, Restoring the Old City, Reshaping the Region* (New York: HarperCollins, 1995).

Bedard, Jean Francois, ed., *Cities of Artificial Evacuation: The Work of Peter Eisenman, 1978–1988* (Montreal: Canadian Center for Architecture; New York: Rizzoli, 1994).

Bizios, Georgia, ed., *Architectural Theory & Criticism, Urban Design Theory, Architectural History* (Durham, NC: Eno River Press, 1991).

Bizios, Georgia, ed., *Architectural Design, Architectural Theory & Criticism, Environmental Issues, Human Behavior, Professional Practice, Special Topics, Urban Design Theory and History* (Chapel Hill, NC: Eno River Press, 1994).

Boyer, Christine M., *The City of Collective Memory; Its Historical Imagery and Architectural Entertainments* (Cambridge, MA: MIT Press, 1994).

Boyer, Christine M., *CyberCities: Visual Perception in the Age of Electronic Communication* (New York: Princeton Architectural Press, 1996).

Buchanan, Peter, *Emilio Ambasz, Inventions: The Reality of the Ideal* (New York: Rizzoli International, 1992).

Calthorpe, Peter, *The Next American Metropolis: Ecology, Community and the American Dream* (New York: Princeton Architectural Press, 1993).

Conzen, Michael P., *The Making of the American Landscape* (Boston: Unwin Hyman, 1990).

Coop Himmelblau, *Six Projects for Four Cities* (Darmstadt: Jurgen Hausser, 1990).

Coop Himmelblau, *Architecture in Transition: Between Deconstruction and New Modernism* edited by Peter Noever (Munich: Prestel, 1991).

Davidson, Cynthia, ed., *Eleven Authors in Search of a Building* (New York: Monacelli Press, Inc. 1996).

Duany, Andreas & Elizabeth Plater-Zyberk, *Towns and Town-Making Principles* (Cambridge, MA: Harvard University Graduate School of Design; New York: Rizzoli, 1991)

Eisenman, Peter, *House of Cards* (Oxford: Oxford University Press, 1987).

Eisenman, Peter, *Unfolding Frankfurt* (Berlin: Ernst & Sohn, 1991).

Ellin, Nan, *Postmodern Urbanism* (Cambridge, MA: Blackwell Publishers, 1996).

Flusty, Steven, *Building Paranoia: The Proliferation of Interdictory Space and the Erosion of Spatial Justice* (West Hollywood, CA: Los Angeles Forum for Architecture and Urban Design, 1994).

Gandelsonas, Mario, *The Urban Text* with essays by Joan Copjec, Catherine Ingraham and John Whiteman (Cambridge, MA: MIT Press, 1991).

Garreau, Joel, *Edge Cities: Life on the New Frontier* (New York: Doubleday, 1991).

Garvin, Alexander, *The American City: What Works, What Doesn't* (New York: McGraw-Hill, 1996).

Gehry, Frank, *Frank Gehry: America as Context* (Milan: Electra, 1994).

Gerace, Gloria, ed., *The Getty Design Process* (Los Angeles, CA: The Paul Getty Trust, 1991), p. 19.

Golany, Gideon, *Geo-Space Urban Design* (New York: John Wiley & Sons, 1996).

Gosling, David, *Gordon Cullen: Visions of Urban Design* (London: Academy Editions, 1996).

Gosling, David, 'The Spaces in Between', in *Companion to Contemporary Architectural Thought*, Ben Farmer and Hentie Low, eds. (London: Routledge, 1993).

Gosling, David and B. Maitland, *Concepts of Urban Design* (London: Academy Editions, 1984).

Graves, Michael, *Michael Graves, Buildings and Projects: 1990–1994* (New York: Rizzoli, 1995).

Hays, Michael K. & Carol Burns, eds., *Thinking of the Present: Recent American Architecture* (New York: Princeton Architectural Press, 1990).

Holl, Steven, *Edge of a City* (New York: Princeton Architectural Press, 1991).

Holl, Steven, *Question of Perception: Phenomenology of Architecture* (Tokyo, Japan: E and U, 1994).

Holl, Steven, *Intertwining: Selected Projects 1989–1995*, First edition (New York: Princeton Architectural Press, 1996).

Howard, Ebenezer, *Garden Cities of Tomorrow*, first published as *Tomorrow: A Peaceful Path to Real Reform* (London: Faber & Faber, 1902).

Hudson, Brian J., *Cities on the Shore: The Urban Littoral Frontier* (London/New York: Pinto, 1996).

Jacobs, Allen B., *Great Streets* (Cambridge, MA: MIT Press, 1993).

Jencks, Charles, *Heteropolis: Los Angeles, The Riots and the Strange Beauty of Hetero-Architecture* (London: Academy Editions/Ernst & Sohn, 1993).

Jencks, Charles, *The Architecture of the Jumping Universe* (London: Academy Editions, 1995).

Jencks, Charles, ed., *Frank Gehry, Individual Imagination and Cultural Conservation* (London: Academy Editions; New York: St. Martin's Press, 1995).

Kafka, Franz, *Collected Short Stories* (Prague: Heinrich M. Sohn, 1936).

Katz, Peter, *The New Urbanism: Towards an Architecture of Community* (New York: McGraw-Hill, 1994).

Koolhaas, Rem, *Delirious New York: A Retroactive Manifesto for Manhattan* (New York: Monacelli Press, 1994).

Kostoff, Spiro, *The City Shaped: Urban Patterns and Meaning Through History* (Boston: Little Brown, 1991).

Kostoff, Spiro, *The City Assembled: The Elements of Urban Form Through History* (London: Thames and Hudson, 1998).

Kunstler, James Howard, *Home from Nowhere: Remaking our Everyday World in the Twenty-First Century* (New York: Simon and Schuster, 1996).

Lang, John, *Urban Design: The American Experience* (New York: Van Nostrand Reinhold, 1994).

Lynch, Kevin, *Responding to Social Change* edited by Basil Honkiman (Stroudsburg, PA: Dowden, Hutchinson and Ross, 1975).

Lynch, Kevin, 'Coming Home: The Urban Environment After Nuclear War' in *The Counterfeit Ark: Crisis Relocation for Nuclear War* by J. Leaning and L. Keyes, eds., (Physicians for Social Responsibility, Ballinger Publishing Co., 1984).

Lynch, Kevin, *Wasting Away*, edited by Michael Southworth (San Francisco, CA: Sierra Club Books, 1990).

Machado, Rodolfo and Rodolphe El-Houry, eds., *Monolithic Architecture* (Munich/New York: Prestel, 1995).

Marcus, Clare Cooper and Carolyn Francis, eds., *People Places: Design Guidelines for Urban Open Space* (New York: Van Nostrand Reinhold, 1990).

Mayne, Thom, *Morphosis: Connected Isolation* (London: Academy Editions; New York: St. Martin's Press, 1993).

Mayne, Thom, *Morphosis: Tangents and Outtakes* (Zurich: Artemis, 1993).

Mitchell, William J., *The Logic of Architecture: Design, Computation and Cognition* (Cambridge, MA: MIT Press, 1990).

Mohney, David and Keller Easterling, *Seaside: Making a Town in America* (New York: Princeton Architectural Press, 1991), p. 44.

Morrish, William, *Civilizing Terrains: Mountains, Mounds and Mesas* (San Francisco, CA: William Stout, 1996).

Morrish, William and Catherine Brown, *Planning to Stay* (Minneapolis, MN: Milkweed, 1994), pp. 106–107.

Moss, Eric Owen, *Eric Owen Moss* (London: Academy Editions; Berlin: Ernst & Sohn; New York: St. Martin's Press, 1993).

Moss, Eric Owen, *Eric Owen Moss: Buildings and Projects 2* (New York: Rizzoli, 1996).

Orwell, George, *1984* (Harmondsworth, England: Penguin, 1948).

Post, John, 'The Portland Light Rail Experience' in Wayne Attoe, ed., *Transit, Land Use and Urban Form* (University of Texas, 1988).

Pran, Peter, *Peter Pran of Ellerbe Becket: Recent Works* (London: Academy Editions; New York: St. Martin's Press, 1992).

Rappoport, Amos, *Human Aspects of Urban Form: Towards a Man-Environment Approach to Urban Form and Design* (New York: Van Nostrand Reinhold, 1990).

Scott-Brown, Denise, *Urban Concepts* (London: Academy Editions; New York: St. Martin's Press, 1990).

Scully, Vincent, *American Architecture and Urbanism* (New York: Henry Holt, 1988).

Sennett, Richard, *The Uses of Disorder: Personal Identity and City Life* (Harmondsworth, England: Pelican, 1971). First published in the US in 1970.

Smith, Elizabeth and Russell Ferguson, *Urban Revisions: Current Projects for the Public Realm* (Cambridge, MA: MIT Press, 1994).

Soja, Edward W., *The City: Los Angeles and Urban Theory at the End of the Twentieth Century* (Berkeley, CA: University of California Press, 1996).

Sorkin, Michael, ed., *Variations on a Theme Park* (New York: Noonday Press, 1992).

Southworth, Michael Frank, *Theory and Practice of Contemporary Urban Design: A Look at American Urban Design Plans* (Berkeley, CA: Institute of Urban and Regional Development, 1990).

Southworth, Michael Frank, *Walkable Suburbs: An Evaluation of Neo-Traditional Communities at the Urban Edge* (Berkeley, CA: Institute of Urban and Regional Development, 1995).

Southworth, Michael Frank, *Streets and the Shaping of Towns and Cities* (New York: McGraw-Hill, 1997).

Thiel, Philip, *People, Paths and Purposes: Notations for a Participatory Envirotecture* (Seattle, WA: University of Washington Press, 1997).

Thoreau, Henry David, *Walden* (New York: New American Library, 1960). Originally published in 1854.

Vidler, Anthony, *The Architectural Uncanny: Essays in the Modern Unhomely* (Cambridge, MA: MIT Press, 1992).

Vodidio, Philip, *Contemporary American Architects* (Cologne: Taschen, 1993).

Whyte, William, *City: Rediscovering the Center* (New York: Doubleday, 1988).

Wright, Frank Lloyd, *The Natural House* (New York: Horizon Press, 1954), p. 18.

CHAPTER SEVEN: CONCLUSIONS

Bachelor, Peter, and David Lewis, eds., *Urban Design in Action* (North Carolina State University School of Design, 1985).

Bedworth, David, M. Henderson and P. Wolfe, *Computer Integrated Design and Manufacturing* (New York: McGraw-Hill, 1991).

Bender, David and Leone Bruno, eds., 'The Homeless', in *Opposing Viewpoints* (San Diego: Greenhaven Press, 1990).

Branch, Melville C., *Comprehensive City Planning* (American Planning Association, Chicago).

Gandelsonas, Mario, *The Urban Text* (Cambridge, MA: MIT Press, 1991).

Gilloch, Graeme, *Myth and Metropolis: Walter Benjamin and the City* (New York: Policy Press, 1996).

Greenstreet, Robert and James W. Shields, *Architecture Representations* (Englewood Cliffs, NJ: Prentice Hall, 1988).

Hartman, C., ed., *America's Housing Crisis (Alternative Policies for America)* Institute for Policy Studies. (Boston, MA: Routledge & Kegan Paul, 1983).

Harvey, David, *Consciousness and the Urban Experience* (Baltimore, MD: Johns Hopkins University Press, 1985).

Howard, Ebenezer, *A Peaceful Path to Reform* (London: 1898).

Howard, Ebenezer, *Garden Cities of Tomorrow* (London: 1902). Reprinted in London by Faber & Faber, Ltd., 1946. New Revised Edition by Attic Books, Eastbourne, England, 1985, with an introduction by Ray Thomas and a bibliography by Stephen Potter.

Huttman, Elizabeth, *Homelessness as a Housing Problem in an Inner City in the U.S.* (Berlin: Walter de Gruyter, 1988).

Kafatos, Menas and Robert Nadeau, *The Conscious Universe: Part and Whole in Modern Physical Theory* (New York: Springer Verlag, 1990), pp. 36–38.

Kleniewski, Nancy, *Cities, Change and Conflict: A Political Economy of Urban Life* (New York: Wadsworth Publishing, 1997).

Lynch, Kevin, *The Image of the City* (Cambridge, MA: MIT Press, 1960).

McHarg, Ian L., *Design with Nature* (New York: Doubleday, 1971).

Mas, William M., *Landscape and Planning: Environmental Applications* (New York: John Wiley & Sons, 1983).

Mitchell, William J., *City of Bits: Space, Place and the Infobahn* (Cambridge, MA: MIT Press, 1996).

Parks, Warren Wright, *The Mariemont Story: A National Exemplar in Town Planning* (Cincinnati, OH: Creative Writers and Publishers, 1967).

Piel, Jonathan, ed., *Energy for Planet Earth: Readings from Scientific American* (New York: W.H. Freeman, 1991).

Regional Planning Association, *Urban Design Manhattan* (New York: Viking, 1969).

Rheingold, Howard, *Virtual Reality* (New York: Summit Books, 1991).

Rogers, Richard, *Cities for a Small Planet*, Philip Gumuchdjian, ed. (New York: Westview Press, 1997).

Salicath, Neils, ed., *Homelessness in Industrialized Countries* (The Hague: The International Federation for Housing and Town Planning and The Public Utility Fund of KAB, Copenhagen, Denmark, 1992). See Gosling, David, *Poverty and Homelessness in the United States of America.*

Tschumi, Bernard, *Event Cities* (Cambridge, MA: MIT Press, 1994).

Tucker, William, *The Excluded Americans* (Washington, DC: Regency Gateway, 1990).

Wodaski, Ron, *Virtual Reality Madness* (Indianapolis, IN: Sams Publishing, 1996).

INDEX

Figures in italics indicate captions.

Morrish, William 221, 255
  Civilizing Terrains 222
Morrish, William and Catherine
  Brown: *Planning to Stay*
  222–3
Moscow: New State Museum 18
Moss, Eric Owen 206
Moudon, Anne Vernez 146
Mount Prospect, Illinois:
  Randhurst shopping mall 36,
  80, *81*
Movie Maps project 133
Moynihan, Daniel Patrick 67
MTA line 218
Mumford, Lewis 7, 19, 21, 28, 35,
  99, 108, 115, 184, 191, 195,
  199
  The Culture of Cities 51
  The Urban Prospect 76
Munhall 145
Munich: Institute of Technology
  18
Munsell System 220
Murfreesboro, North Carolina 135
Muschamp, Herbert 204, 210,
  221, 257
Mutual Housing Association of
  New York 143
Myer, John R. *55*, 65, 76, 129

N-geometries 183
Nagger, Avner *83*
Nairn, Ian 46–7
Nash, John 176
Nash, William 66
National Association of Home
  Builders 254, 256
National Community Information
  Exchange Program 243
National Conference on City
  Planning, first (1909) 10
National Endowment for the Arts
  (NEA) 131, 147
  Design Arts Program 147
National Environmental Policy Act
  (1969) 153
National Health Service (NHS)
  241
National Housing Act (1954) 84
  Programme 701 (1955) 84
National Housing Association 10
National Parks System 65
National Register of Historic
  Places 240
Nationale Nederlanden ING Real
  Estate 205
Navajo communities 107, 191
Negroponte, Nicholas 101
  The Architecture Machine 120
  Soft Architecture Machines
  120–1
Nelson, George 28, 29
neo-Constructivism 181
neo-Corbusian philosophy 201
neo-empiricism 194, 199
neo-modernism 194
neo-rationalism 194
neoclassicism 34
Netherlands 223
  pedestrianisation 36
Neughborhood Design Center,
  Baltimore 243
Neuromancer (film) 257
Neutra, Richard *34*, 35, 156, 209
"New Architecture" 17
New Bauhaus 18
'new brutalism' movement 38
new classicism 180
'New Deal' policy 84
New Directions 27

New Harmony, Indiana:
  Athenaeum 209
New Haven, Connecticut 42, 59,
  193
  Dixwell Avenue 63
  Hill District 61, *62*, 64
  New Haven Green 60, *60*
  Prospect Hill District 60–1
  Wooster Square area 61, 193
  Yale Rockefeller Research
    Project 59–64
New Haven City Planning
  Commission 61, 64
New Jersey 11
New Jersey Institute of
  Technology 257
New Orleans, Louisiana 26, 71,
  156, 189
  Piazza d'Italia 134, *134*, 225
  Vieux Carre district 231
New Society 65
New Town Development
  Corporations 169
New Town programme (Britain;
  1950–90) 21, 66
new towns 84–8, 115, 183, 239
new urbanism 22, 103, 115,
  145–7, 201, 207, 218, 230–4,
  240, 255
  precedents of the 239–45
new villages 88
New World Writing 27
New York City 26, 42, 66, 112,
  156, 160, 204, 223, 245
  Actor's Studio 27
  Artists Space 133
  Battery City Park 13–14, 111,
    170, 193, 195, 225
  Bronx 191
  Bronx Developmental Center
    136–7, *137*
  Brooklyn 68, 104, 111, 143,
    191, 245, 253, 256
  Brooklyn Bridge 156
  Central Park 60, 164, 165
  Chinatown 213
  Chrysler Building 168
  Citicorp building 154, *154*, 190
  City College 110, 148, 153, 154
  Clinton, mid-Manhattan 233
  Coney Island 92, 166, *166*
  Corona Park, Flushing 158, 194
  Council on Urban Design 71,
    143
  Downtown Athletic Club 168
  Dreamland 166
  East Island project 122
  Empire State Building 38, 41,
    156, 168
  Fifth Avenue 60, 110, 112, 153
  financial crisis (1991) 243
  Flatiron Building 168
  Future Park, Flushing Meadow
    211
  Grand Central Station 153, 218
  Greenwich Village 28, 67, 68,
    110, 213
  Guggenheim Museum 208
  Harlem 46, 73, 253
  homelessness 243
  Hotel Sphinx 168
  housing 73
  Institute for Architecture and
    Urban Studies 165, 201, 206
  Institute for Urban Design 147
  Landmarks Preservation Law
    153
  Lever Building, Park Avenue 18,
    19, 41, 42, 47, 122, 154, 256
  Lincoln Center 109, 112, 157

Little Italy 213
Lower East Side 199
Lower Manhattan Expressway
  122
Lower Manhattan models 251
Lower Manhattan Urban Design
  Plan 212
Lower Manhattan Waterfront
  134
Luna Park 166
Manhattan 68, 72, 75, 111, 112,
  121, 153, 156, 165, 168,
  169, 170, 178, 189, 191,
  198, 245, 250, 256
  Museum of Modern Art 73, 124,
    163
  'Deconstructivist Architecture'
    (1988) 181
New School for Social Research
  Environmental Simulation
  Center 250
Paraphernalia group of shops
  126
Park Avenue 162, 189
Paz Building, Brooklyn 162
Pennsylvania Station 153
Planning Commission 189
Pocantico Hills 225
port 169
Pratt Institute for Community
  and Environmental
  Development 132
Queens, Brooklyn 191, 256
Radio City Music Hall 165, 168
Rockefeller Center 42, 112, 156,
  165, 168
RCA Building 41
Rockefeller Plaza *41*, 46, 157,
  189
St Peter's Church 153
Seagram Building skyscraper,
  Park Avenue *17*, 18, 41, 47,
  74, 154, 162, 189, 256
Seagram Plaza 190
SoHo 213
South Bronx 143
South Street Seaport Area 147
State Department Corporation
  153
Staten Island 42
Statue of Liberty 156
Steeplechase Park 167
Times Square 75, 112, 153, 157,
  161, 168, 258
transportation proposal 118,
  118
Tribeca 198, 212
UN Building 165
United Nations Secretariat
  Building 41–2
Upper East Side 46
Urban Design Group 110, 111,
  112, 147, 153
  City Planning Department 153
Van Dyke homes 100
Wall Street district 20
Welfare Island (later Roosevelt
  Island) 122, *123*, 165,
  168–9, *169*
Welfare Palace Hotel 169
Westside 73
Woolworth Building 168
Zoning Law 168
New York City Board of Estimate
  143
New York City Plan 243
New York Five 74, 201, 208
New York Foundation 143
New York Landmarks
  Conservancy 212

New York State Housing and
  Regional Planning
  Commission 76
The New York Times 25, 65, 73,
  143, 202, 204, 221, 232,
  233, 234, 244, 253
New York Times Magazine 252
Newark: Columbus homes 100
Newbury Port, Massachusetts 108
Newell, Alan 251
Newman, Morris 224, 225
Newman, Oscar 256
  Defensible Space 99–100, 199
Newsweek 87–8
Newsweek magazine 255
Nicolin, Pierluigi 240
Nicollet island 223
Niemeyer, Oscar 41, 112, 121,
  163, 182, 210
Nietzsche, Friedrich 118, 122,
  180, 181
Nippon Kotsu Bunka Kyokai 220
Noguchi, Isamu 28–9
Nolan, John 10, 84, 231, 240
Nolli, Giambattista 15, *16*, 117,
  150, 155
Norberg-Schulz, Christian 57
Norfolk, Virginia: Ghent
  Neighborhood 112
Norris, Christopher 183
North America 43, 109–10, 240,
  246
Northwest University, Illinois 178
Novak, Marcos 257

Oak Park Community
  Development Plan, Ventura
  County, California 134
Oakland 218
Office dA 213
Office for Metropolitan
  Architecture (OMA) 122,
  165
Office of Downtown Brooklyn
  Development 111
Office of Lower Manhattan
  Development (OLMD) 112
Office of Midtown Development
  (New York) 147
Ogilby, John 37, 65
Oglethorpe, James 10, 84
Ohio 8, 144
Ohio State University: Wexner
  Center for the Visual Arts,
  Columbus 22, 158, 173, 179,
  179, 180, 194, 201, 202,
  203, 206, 225
Okamoto, Rai 75, 133
Old Mauch Chunk Historic
  District 175
Oldenburg, Claes 206
Olmstead, Frederick Law 10, 218
Olwell, Robert 132
Olympia-York 14, 170
Olynthus 9
OMA 178, 180, 181
Opposing Viewpoints 241
Orange County 199
Orange Line 218
Oregon 144, 255
Orlando, Florida 198
orthogonal lines 19
Oruo Preto, Brazil 121, 182
Orwell, George 240, 252
  1984 253
Owen, Robert 209

Page, Clifton 176
Palazzetti, Sergio 29
Palm Beach County, Florida 256